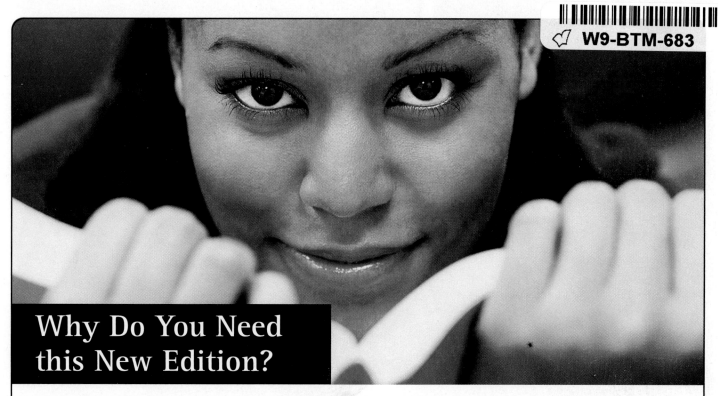

Why Do You Need this New Edition?

1. Every chapter now contains a box called Anthropology Works that provides compelling examples of how knowledge and methods in cultural anthropology can prevent or solve social problems. Examples include: Paul Farmer's work in providing health care in Haiti, Laura Tabac's applied research on men's risky sexual practices in New York City, and Australian Aboriginal women's collaboration with an anthropologist to document and preserve their cultural heritage.

2. Updates throughout the book provide currency and accuracy and strengthen student engagement; for example, the discovery that Neanderthals and modern humans interbred (Chapter 2), how people in the United States and Canada now get most of their health information from the Internet (Chapter 7), a new section on homelessness (Chapter 8), the emergence of Textese (Chapter 11), and discussion of oil-related environmental disasters (Chapter 15).

3. Chapter 10, a revised chapter, Political and Legal Systems, conveys the most critical material from two previously separate chapters to provide a single chapter offering more effective delivery to students of essential material and updates.

4. Several new Key Concepts respond to important current issues: food security, asexuality, social justice, sectarian conflict, corporate social responsibility, and Textese.

5. Many new photographs have been carefully chosen to enliven the textual material and prompt discussion. Photographs arranged in pairs or trios, with linked captions, offer students inspiration for thoughtful mini-essays.

6. MyAnthroLibrary offers a selection of brief, current articles on engaging topics that will enrich each chapter and lead to exciting class discussions.

cultural anthropology

cultural anthropology

SIXTH EDITION

BARBARA MILLER

George Washington University

Prentice Hall

Boston   Columbus   Indianapolis   New York   San Francisco   Upper Saddle River
Amsterdam   Cape Town   Dubai   London   Madrid   Milan   Munich   Paris   Montreal   Toronto
Delhi   Mexico City   Sao Paulo   Sydney   Hong Kong   Seoul   Singapore   Taipei   Tokyo

Editorial Director: *Craig Campanella*
Editor in Chief: *Dickson Musslewhite*
Publisher: *Nancy Roberts*
Editorial Project Manager: *Nicole Conforti*
Editorial Assistant: *Nart Varoqua*
Director of Marketing: *Brandy Dawson*
Senior Marketing Manager: *Laura Lee Manley*
Managing Editor: *Maureen Richardson*
Project Manager: *Marianne Peters-Riordan*
Senior Operations Specialist: *Sherry Lewis*
Senior Art Director: *Nancy Wells*
Text and Cover Designer: *Ilze Lemesis*

Manager, Visual Research: *Beth Brenzel*
Photo Researcher: *Tiffany Turner*
Manager, Rights and Permissions: *Zina Arabia*
Manager, Cover Visual Research & Permissions:
  Karen Sanatar
Cover Art: *Leonid Plotkin/Alamy*
Digital Media Editor: *Rachel Comerford*
Full-Service Project Management: *Nincis Asencio*
Composition: *MPS Limited, a Macmillan Company*
Printer/Binder and Cover Printer: *Lehigh/Phoenix*
Text Font: 10/13 ACaslon-Regular

Credits and acknowledgments borrowed from other sources and reproduced, with permission, in this textbook appear on pages 385–386.

Many of the designations by manufacturers and seller to distinguish their products are claimed as trademarks. Where those designations appear in this book, and the publisher was aware of a trademark claim, the designations have been printed in initial caps or all caps.

Library of Congress Cataloging-in-Publication Data

Miller, Barbara D.
    Cultural anthropology / Barbara Miller. — 6th ed.
       p. cm.
    ISBN-13: 978-0-205-03518-2
    ISBN-10: 0-205-03518-3
    1. Ethnology.   I. Title.
    GN316.M49 2011
    306—dc22

                                        2010036279

10 9 8 7 6 5 4 3 2 1

Prentice Hall
is an imprint of

www.pearsonhighered.com

Student	ISBN-13:	978-0-205-035182
	ISBN-10:	0-205-035183
Exam	ISBN-13:	978-0-205-036042
	ISBN-10:	0-205-03604X
A la carte	ISBN-13:	978-0-205-036097
	ISBN-10:	0-205-036090

brief CONTENTS

CONTENTS

ANTHROPOLOGY works

everyday ANTHROPOLOGY

CRITICAL thinking

CULTURAMA

eye on the ENVIRONMENT

MAPS

"I had no idea all those cultures were out there," said one of my students after taking my introductory cultural anthropology course. Another commented, "I'm a business major, but I am going to keep the books from this course because they will help me in my career. I need to understand people."

Cultural anthropology opens up whole new worlds. Not just "out there," but here, there, and everywhere. The subject matter of cultural anthropology may seem distant, exotic, and "other"—jungle drumbeats and painted faces, for example. This book helps students to encounter those far-away cultures and also to realize that their culture has its own versions of jungle drumbeats and painted faces. "Making the strange familiar" is essential learning in a globalizing world where cultural diversity may equal cultural survival for all of us. "Making the familiar strange" is a priceless revelation because it reduces the divide between "us" and the "other." "We" become "other" through the insights of cultural anthropology.

To achieve this double goal, *Cultural Anthropology*, Sixth Edition, delivers rich and exciting information about the world's cultures and promotes critical thinking and reflective learning. Students will find many points at which they can interact with the material, view their own culture as a culture, and make connections between anthropology and their everyday life in, for example, hairstyles, food symbolism, sleep deprivation, doctor–patient dialogues, racism and sexism, and the meaning of gestures.

The study of the world's cultures involves learning new words and analytical categories, but the effort will pay off in terms of bringing the world's peoples and cultures closer to you. If this book achieves my aspirations, anyone who reads it will live a life that is more culturally aware, enriched, and tolerant.

How This Book Is Organized

The book's organization and pedagogical features are designed to help ensure student engagement and enhanced learning. The 15 chapters are organized in the following way—but professors will find it easy to assign chapters out of order.

The first chapter describes the discipline of anthropology as a whole and provides the foundation for the rest of the book. The second chapter covers the evolution of humanity and culture, providing a bridge that spans our living primate relatives and early human evolution to the emergence of agriculture, cities, and states. The third chapter moves to the subject of how cultural anthropologists define research topics, carry out research, and present their findings.

The next four chapters discuss how people make a living, their patterns of consumption and exchange, how they

reproduce and raise children, and how different cultures deal with illness, suffering, and death. While these four chapters address basic questions of how people feed themselves, reproduce, and stay alive and well, the discussion in each case fans out to include a wide array of cultural interpretations and practices that go far beyond sheer basics.

The next three chapters look at people in groups. One chapter addresses kinship and its changing forms. Another looks at social ties that are not based on kinship. The third considers how people organize themselves politically, how they seek to maintain order, and how they deal with conflict.

While symbolic behavior permeates the entire book, three chapters most directly focus on meaning and symbolism. The chapter on communication pulls much of the book together as it considers the origins and evolution of communication and language, with special attention to contemporary change. The chapter on religion provides cross-cultural categories of religious belief and practice as well as linking "world religions" to specific local transformations. Expressive culture is a wide-ranging subject, and the chapter on it embraces expected topics such as art and music and unexpected topics such as sports, leisure, and travel.

The last two chapters consider two of the most important topics shaping cultural change in our times: migration and international development. These chapters explicitly put culture into motion and show how people are affected by larger structures, such as globalization or violence, and exercise agency in attempting to create meaningful and secure lives.

New to This Edition

Every chapter now contains a box called Anthropology Works that provides compelling examples of how knowledge and methods in cultural anthropology can prevent or solve social problems. Examples include: Paul Farmer's work in providing health care in Haiti, Laura Tabac's applied research on men's risky sexual practices in New York City, and Australian Aboriginal women's collaboration with an anthropologist to document and preserve their cultural heritage.

Updates throughout the book provide currency and accuracy and strengthen student engagement; for example, the discovery that Neanderthals and modern humans interbred (Chapter 2), how people in the United States and Canada now get most of their health information from the Internet (Chapter 7), a new section on homelessness (Chapter 8), the emergence of Textese (Chapter 11), and discussion of oil-related environmental disasters (Chapter 15).

- Chapter 10, a revised chapter, Political and Legal Systems, conveys the most critical material from two previously separate chapters to provide a single chapter offering more effective delivery to students of essential material and updates.

- Several new Key Concepts respond to important current issues: food security, asexuality, social justice, sectarian conflict, corporate social responsibility, and Textese.

- Many new photographs have been carefully chosen to enliven the textual material and prompt discussion. Photographs arranged in pairs or trios, with linked captions, offer students inspiration for thoughtful mini-essays.

- MyAnthroLibrary offers a selection of brief, current articles on engaging topics that will enrich each chapter and lead to exciting class discussions.

Continued Features

Several features continued from the previous edition make this textbook distinctive and effective.

CULTURAMA All chapters include a one-page profile of a cultural group, accompanied by a mini-panorama of two photographs and a map with captions. These brief summaries provide an enticing glimpse into the culture presented.

IN-TEXT GLOSSARY Definitions of the key concepts are provided on the page where the concept is first mentioned and defined. A paginated list of the key concepts appears at the end of each chapter. The glossary at the end of the book contains a complete list of key concepts together with their definitions.

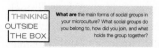

THINKING OUTSIDE THE BOX The Thinking Outside the Box feature provides three or four thought-provoking questions in each chapter, displayed at the bottom of the page. These questions prompt readers to relate an issue to their own cultural experiences or provide an avenue for further research. They can promote class discussion and serve as a basis for a class project.

THE BIG QUESTIONS Three Big Questions are posed at the beginning of each chapter to alert readers to the chapter's overarching themes. They are carried through in the chapter outline as the three major headings. At the end of the chapter, The Big Questions Revisited provides a helpful review of the key points related to each Big Question.

Boxed Features

Everyday Anthropology boxes present cultural examples that connect to everyone's lives and prompt reflective learning. **Critical Thinking** boxes introduce an issue and show how it has been studied or analyzed from different anthropological perspectives. These boxes provide tie-ins to the major theoretical debates in cultural anthropology presented in Chapter 1. Although students may appreciate the interesting material that cultural anthropology offers, they are still likely to ask, "Does this knowledge have any practical applications?" **Anthropology Works** boxes highlight how applied anthropologists work and the relevance of anthropology to preventing and solving social problems.

Eye on the Environment boxes provide material that links culture with some aspect of the environment. These boxes, along with many in-text references to how culture and the environment interact, enable students to make new connections and think critically.

MyAnthroLab is an interactive and instructive multimedia site designed to offer access to a wealth of resources geared to meet the individual teaching and learning needs of every instructor and student. Combining an e-book, video, audio, multimedia simulations, research support, and assessment, MyAnthroLab engages students and gives them the tools they need to enhance their performance in the course.

The Importance of Names

Since the beginning of modern humanity, people have been naming each other, naming their groups and other groups, and naming features of the places they inhabit. People of earlier times often referred to themselves in terms that translate roughly into "The People." As far as they were concerned, they were The People: the only people on earth.

Things are more complicated now. European colonialism, starting in the fifteenth century, launched centuries of rapid contact between Europeans and thousands of indigenous groups around the world. The Europeans named and described these groups in their European languages. The names were not those that the people used for themselves, or if they were, the transliteration into a European language altered local names into something very different from the original.

The Spanish explorers' naming of all the indigenous peoples of North America as Indians is a famous example of a misnomer. Beyond being wrong by thinking they had reached India, the Spanish conquerors who renamed thousands of people and claimed their territory simultaneously erased much of the indigenous people's heritage and identity.

The challenge of using the preferred names for people and places of the world faces us today as people worldwide wrestle with the issue of what they want to be called. Until recently, indigenous peoples of the present-day United States mainland preferred to be called Native Americans, rejecting the pejorative term "Indian." Now, they are claiming and recasting the term "Indian." In Alaska, the preferred term is "Alaska Native," and in Hawai'i it is "Native Hawai'ian." In Canada, preferred terms are "First Nations," "Native Peoples," and "Northern Peoples." From small-scale groups to entire countries, people are attempting to revive precolonial group names and place names. Bombay is now Mumbai, and Calcutta is Kolkata. Group names and place names are frequently contested. Is someone Hispanic or Latino? Is it the Persian Gulf or the Arabian Gulf? Is it Greenland or Kalaallit Nunaat? Does it matter? The answer is yes, resoundingly, yes.

This book strives to provide the most currently accepted names for people, places, objects, activities, and ideas. By the time it is printed, however, some names and their English spellings will have changed. It is an ongoing challenge to keep track of such changes, but doing so is part of our job as citizens of a transforming world.

The Cover Image

Throughout the Amazon region, young girls go through an elaborate ceremony before they are secluded for a period of learning, followed by initiation into adulthood. The special body paint and ornaments of this Peruvian girl are part of the process. Such indigenous Amazonian people are increasingly facing cultural loss and even extinction through pressures from ranchers, miners, industrialists, urban expansion, pollution, and climate change.

In Thanks

The breadth, depth, and quality of this edition are the result of many people's ideas, comments, corrections, and care. For the first edition of Cultural Anthropology, four anthropologists carefully reviewed multiple drafts of the book. I will always be grateful to them for their monumental contribution that helped make this book what it is today: Elliot Fratkin, Smith College; Maxine Margolis, University of Florida; Russell Reid, University of Louisville; and Robert Trotter II, University of Arizona.

The cultural anthropologists who have reviewed various editions of this textbook and offered their critiques and detailed suggestions have shaped this book from start to finish:

Warren D. Anderson, Southeast Missouri State University; Jason Antrosio, Albion College; Diane Baxter, University of Oregon; Monica L. Bellas, Cerritos College; Joyce Bishop, California State University, Sacramento; Ronald Bolender, Mount Vernon Nazarene University; Barbara Bonnekessen, University of Missouri–Kansas City; Peter Brown, University of Wisconsin, Oshkosh; Howard Campbell, University of Texas, El Paso; (the late) Charles R. de Burlo, University of Vermont; Elizabeth de la Portilla, University of Texas at San Antonio; William W. Donner, Kutztown University; Lisa Pope Fischer, Santa Monica College; Pamela J. Ford, Mount San Jacinto College; Monica Frolander-Ulf, University of Pittsburgh, Johnstown; Mary Kay Gilliland, Pima Community College; Nancy Gonlin, Bellevue Community College; Jeanne Humble, Bluegrass Community & Technical College; Ann Kingsolver, University of South Carolina; Courtney Kurlanska, University of New Hampshire; Leslie Lischka, Linfield College; William M. Loker, California State University, Chico; Martin F. Manalansan IV, University of Illinois; Roberta Martine, Fort Hays State University; Corey Pressman, Mt. Hood Community College; Ed Robbins, University of Wisconsin; Jacquelyn Robinson, Albany State University; Harry Sanabria, University of Pittsburgh; Kathleen M. Saunders, Western Washington University; G. Richard Scott, University of Nevada, Reno; Wesley Shumar, Drexel University; David Simmons, University of South Carolina; Kimberly Eison Simmons, University of South Carolina; Lori A. Stanley, Luther College; Margaret Weinberger, Bowling Green State University; Jim Wilce, Northern Arizona University; Peter Wogan, Willamette University; and Katrina Worley, Sierra College.

Many anthropologists and others have provided encouragement, suggestions, feedback, references, and photographs: Lila Abu-Lughod, Abigail Adams, Vincanne Adams, Catherine Allen, Joseph Alter, Matthew Amster, Myrdene Anderson, Donald Attwood, Christopher Baker, Isabel Balseiro, Nancy Benco, Marc Bermann, Alexia Bloch, Elson Boles, Lynne Bolles, John Bowen, Don Brenneis, Alison Brooks, Judith K. Brown, D. Glynn Cochrane, Jeffery Cohen, Carole Counihan, Brian Craik, Liza Dalby, Loring Danforth, Patricia Delaney, Alexander Dent, Linus Digim'rina, Timothy Earle, Daniel Everett, Johannes Fabian, Ilana Feldman, Janina Fenigsen, Elliot Fratkin, Martin Fusi, Maris Boyd Gillette, Richard A. Gould, David Gow, Richard Grinker, Daniel Gross, (the late) Marvin Harris, Tobias Hecht, Cornelia Mayer Herzfeld, Michael Herzfeld, Barry Hewlett, Danny Hoffman, Michael Horowitz, (the late) Robert Humphrey, Lanita Jacobs-Huey, Vicki Jensen, Anstice Justin, Barry D. Kass, Patty Kelly, Laurel Kendall, David Kideckel, Diane E. King, Stuart Kirsch, Dorinne Kondo, Conrad Kottak, Jennifer Kramer, Donald B. Kraybill, Ruth Krulfeld, Joel Kuipers, Takie Lebra, David Lempert, Lamont Lindstrom, Susan

Orpett Long, Luisa Maffi, Beatriz Manz, Debra Martin, Samuel Martínez, Catherine McCoid, Leroy McDermott, Kimber Haddox McKay, Jerry Milanich, Laura Miller, Madhushree Mukerjee, Kirin Narayan, Sarah Nelson, Gananath Obeyesekere, Ellen Oxfeld, Hanna Papanek, Michael G. Peletz, Deborah Pellow, Gregory Possehl, David Price, Joanne Rappaport, Jennifer Robertson, Nicole Sault, Joel Savishinsky, David Z. Scheffel, Nancy Scheper-Hughes, Pankaj Sekhsaria, Bob Shepherd, Richard Shweder, Jennie Smith-Pariola, Chunghee Soh, Kate Spilde Contreras, Anthony Stocks, Patricia Tovar, Sita Venkateswar, Martha Ward, James (Woody) Watson, Rubie Watson, Van Yasek, and Kevin Yelvington.

For this edition, I am grateful to Nancy Roberts, my publisher at Pearson/Prentice Hall, for her support. As always, I have enjoyed working closely on this edition with Monica Ohlinger, my developmental editor, who is the head of Ohlinger Publishing Services in Columbus, Ohio.

I thank the Millers—my parents, siblings, aunts and uncles, and nieces and nephews—for their interest and support. My father's two comments about the book were that it has an awful lot of long words and how do I know so much about sex? "From reading, Dad," was my truthful reply. I am grateful to the Heatons—my former in-laws, including my ex-husband, (late) ex-parents-in-law, brothers- and sisters-in-law, and nieces and nephews—for their enduring friendship.

I thank, especially, my son, Jack Heaton. He was a superb traveling companion on our trip around the world with the Semester at Sea Program in 1996, when I wrote much of the first edition of *Cultural Anthropology*. He continues to be excellent company during our time together in DC. This book is dedicated to him.

Barbara Miller
anthropologyworks@gmail.com
Washington, DC

This book is accompanied by an extensive learning package to enhance the experience of both instructors and students. The author played a major role in developing and updating the material in the Instructor's Resource Manual, MyTest, and the PowerPoint™ slides.

INSTRUCTOR'S RESOURCE MANUAL WITH TESTS (0-205-03627-9)

For each chapter in the text, this valuable resource provides a detailed outline, a list of objectives, discussion questions, and suggested readings and videos. In addition, test questions in multiple-choice, true–false, fill-in-the-blank, and short-answer formats are available for each chapter; the answers are page-referenced to the text. This manual is available within the instructor section of MyAnthroLab for *Cultural Anthropology, Sixth Edition*, or at www.pearsonhighered.com/irc.

MYTEST (0-205-03628-7)

This computerized software allows instructors to create their own personalized exams, to edit any or all of the existing test questions, and to add new questions. Other special features of this program include the random generation of test questions, the creation of alternative versions of the same test, scrambling question sequences, and test previews before printing. This testing program is available within the instructor section of MyAnthroLab for *Cultural Anthropology, Sixth Edition*, or at www.pearsonhighered.com/irc.

POWERPOINT™ PRESENTATION FOR CULTURAL ANTHROPOLOGY (0-205-03629-5)

These PowerPoint slides combine text and graphics for each chapter to help instructors convey anthropological principles and examples in a clear and engaging way. They are available within the instructor section of MyAnthroLab for *Cultural Anthropology, Sixth Edition*, or at www.pearsonhighered.com/irc.

 MyAnthroLab is an interactive and instructive multimedia site designed to help students and instructors improve learning outcomes. It offers access to a wealth of resources geared to meet the individual teaching and learning needs of every instructor and student. Combining an e-book, video, audio, multimedia simulations, research support, and assessment, MyAnthroLab gives students tools they need to enhance their performance in the course. Please see your Pearson sales representative or visit www.myanthrolab.com for more information.

STRATEGIES IN TEACHING ANTHROPOLOGY, SIXTH EDITION (0-205-71123-5)

This book focuses on the "how" of teaching anthropology across all of the discipline's four fields and provides a wide array of associated learning outcomes and student activities. It is a valuable single-source compendium of strategies and teaching "tricks of the trade" from a group of seasoned teaching anthropologists, working in a variety of teaching settings, who share their pedagogical techniques, knowledge, and observations.

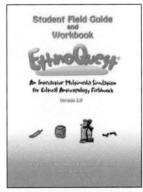

ETHNOQUEST® (0-13-185013-X)

This interactive multimedia simulation includes a series of 10 ethnographic encounters with the culture of a fictional Mexican village set in a computer-based learning environment. It provides students with a realistic problem-solving experience and is designed to help students experience the fieldwork of a cultural anthropologist. Please see your Pearson sales representative for more information about **EthnoQuest®**.

Barbara D. Miller

Barbara Miller is Associate Dean for Faculty Affairs and Professor of Anthropology and International Affairs in the Elliott School of International Affairs of George Washington University. She is Director of the Culture in Global Affairs (CIGA) Program and the Global Gender Initiative in the Elliott School. Before coming to GW in 1994, she taught at Syracuse University, the University of Rochester, SUNY Cortland, Ithaca College, Cornell University, and the University of Pittsburgh. For 30 years, Barbara's research has focused on gender-based inequalities in India, especially the nutritional and medical neglect of daughters in northern regions of the country, and sex-selective abortion. She has also conducted research on culture and rural development in Bangladesh, on low-income household dynamics in Jamaica, and on Hindu adolescents in Pittsburgh. Her current interests include continued research on gender inequalities in health in South Asia and the role of cultural anthropology in informing policy especially as related to women, children, and other disadvantaged groups. She teaches courses on introductory cultural anthropology, medical anthropology, development anthropology, culture and population, health and development in South Asia, and migration and mental health.

Barbara has published many journal articles and book chapters and several books: *The Endangered Sex: Neglect of*

Female Children in Rural North India, Second Edition (Oxford University Press 1997), an edited volume, *Sex and Gender Hierarchies* (Cambridge University Press 1993), and a co-edited volume with Alf Hiltebeitel, *Hair: Its Power and Meaning in Asian Cultures* (SUNY Press 1998). In addition to *Cultural Anthropology*, sixth edition, she is the author of *Cultural Anthropology in a Globalizing World*, second edition (Pearson 2010) and the lead author of *Anthropology*, second edition (Pearson 2008).

She launched a blog in 2009 (anthropologyworks.com) which includes her thoughts about important findings and debates in anthropology, a weekly feature covering anthropologists in the mainstream media, and guests posts. Since its beginning, the blog has had 30,000 visits from people in over 150 countries. You can also follow her, along with 2000 other people worldwide, via Twitter @anthroworks.

"Cultural Anthropology is exciting because it **CONNECTS** with everything, from **FOOD** to **ART**. And it can help prevent or **SOLVE** world problems related to *social inequality* and injustice."

cultural anthropology

◉ What is anthropology?

◉ What is cultural anthropology?

◉ How is cultural anthropology relevant to a career?

ANTHROPOLOGY AND THE STUDY OF CULTURE

1

◀ A Zhuang (zhoo-ANG) girl works in the famously beautiful rice terraces of Long Ji in southern China near its border with Vietnam. The Zhuang, with a population of over 16 million, are the largest of China's many ethnic minorities.

OUTLINE

Introducing Anthropology

Anthropology Works: Delivering Health Care in Rural Haiti

Introducing Cultural Anthropology

Everyday Anthropology: Latina Power in the Kitchen

Culturama: San Peoples of Southern Africa

Cultural Anthropology and Careers

Old bones, *Jurassic Park*, cannibalism, hidden treasure, *Indiana Jones and the Temple of Doom*. The popular impression of anthropology is based mainly on movies and television shows that depict anthropologists as adventurers and heroes. Many anthropologists do have adventures and discover treasures such as ancient pottery, medicinal plants, and jade carvings. But most of their research is not glamorous. Some anthropologists spend years in difficult physical conditions, searching for the earliest fossils of our ancestors. Others live among people in Silicon Valley, California, and study first-hand how they work and organize family life in a setting permeated by modern technology. Some anthropologists conduct laboratory analyses of the contents of tooth enamel to reveal where an individual once lived. Others study designs on prehistoric pottery to learn what the symbols mean, or observe nonhuman primates such as chimpanzees or orangutans in the wild to learn how they live.

Anthropology is the study of humanity, including prehistoric origins and contemporary human diversity. Compared with other disciplines that study humanity (such as history, psychology, economics, political science, and sociology), anthropology is broader in scope. Anthropology covers a much greater span of time than these disciplines, and it encompasses a broader range of topics.

◉ ◉ ◉

Introducing Anthropology

In North America, anthropology is divided into four fields (Figure 1.1) that focus on separate, but connected, subject mater related to humanity:

A member of the Dani people, of Irian Jaya, New Guinea, holding a stone adze, photographed in the 1990s.

Members of a team of anthropologists and students discuss their research project on Silicon Valley culture.

▶ *If you were given a grant to conduct anthropological research, where would you go and what would you study?*

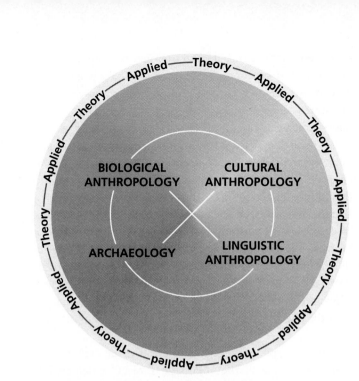

FIGURE 1.1 The Four Fields of Anthropology.

- **Biological anthropology** or *physical anthropology*—the study of humans as biological organisms, including evolution and contemporary variation.
- **Archaeology**—the study of past human cultures through their material remains.
- **Linguistic anthropology**—the study of human communication, including its origins, history, and contemporary variation and change.
- **Cultural anthropology**—the study of living peoples and their cultures, including variation and change. **Culture** refers to people's learned and shared behaviors and beliefs.

Some anthropologists argue that a fifth field, applied anthropology, should be added. **Applied anthropology** (or *practicing anthropology* or *practical anthropology*) is the use of anthropological knowledge to prevent or solve problems or to shape and achieve policy goals.

Biological or Physical Anthropology

Biological anthropology encompasses three subfields. The first, *primatology*, is the study of the nonhuman members of the order of mammals called primates, which includes a wide range of animals from very small, nocturnal creatures to gorillas, the largest members. Primatologists study nonhuman primates in the wild and in captivity. They record and analyze how the animals spend their time, collect and share food, form social groups, rear offspring, develop leadership patterns, and experience and resolve conflicts. Primatologists

are alarmed about the decline in numbers, and even the extinction, of nonhuman primates. Many apply their knowledge to nonhuman primate conservation.

The second subfield is *paleoanthropology*, the study of human evolution on the basis of the fossil record. One important activity is the search for fossils to increase the amount and quality of the evidence related to the way human evolution occurred.

The third subfield is the study of *contemporary human biological variation*. Anthropologists working in this area define, measure, and seek to explain differences in the biological makeup and behavior of contemporary humans. They study such biological factors as DNA within and across populations, body size and shape, human nutrition and disease, and human growth and development.

Archaeology

Archaeology means, literally, the "study of the old," but "the old" is limited to human culture. Therefore, the time depth of archaeology goes back only to the beginnings of *Homo sapiens*, between 300,000 and 160,000 years ago, when they first emerged in Africa. Archaeology encompasses two major areas: *prehistoric archaeology*, which concerns the human past before written records, and *historical archaeology*, which deals with the human past in societies that have written documents. Prehistoric archaeologists often identify themselves with broad geographic regions, studying, for example, Old World archaeology (Africa, Europe, and Asia) or New World archaeology (North, Central, and South America).

Another set of specialties within archaeology is based on the context in which the archaeology takes place. For example, *underwater archaeology* is the study of submerged archaeological

anthropology   the study of humanity, including its prehistoric origins and contemporary human diversity.

biological anthropology   the study of humans as biological organisms, including evolution and contemporary variation.

archaeology   the study of past human cultures through their material remains.

linguistic anthropology   the study of human communication, including its origins, history, and contemporary variation and change.

cultural anthropology   the study of living peoples and their cultures, including variation and change.

culture   people's learned and shared behaviors and beliefs.

applied anthropology   the use of anthropological knowledge to prevent or solve problems or to shape and achieve policy goals.

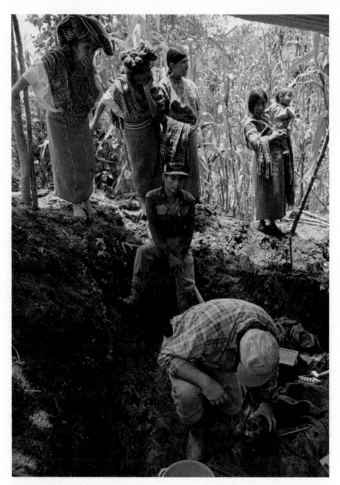

Maya people watch as forensic anthropologist Francisco de León conducts an exhumation of more than 50 bodies in a highland Guatemalan village in 1997.

▶ *Are courses in forensic anthropology offered at your school?*

sites. Underwater archaeological sites may be from either prehistoric or historic times. Some prehistoric sites include early human settlements in parts of Europe, such as household sites discovered in Switzerland that were once near lakes but are now submerged.

The archaeology of the recent past is another important research direction. *Industrial archaeology* focuses on changes in material culture and society during and since the Industrial Revolution. It is especially active in Great Britain, home of the Industrial Revolution. There, industrial archaeologists study such topics as the design of iron bridges, the growth and distribution of china potteries, miners' housing, and cotton mills. An important role of industrial archaeology is the conservation of industrial sites, which are more likely to be neglected or destroyed than are sites that have natural beauty or cultural glamour attached to them.

An example of what could be called the *archaeology of contemporary life* is the "Garbage Project" conducted by archaeologists at the University of Arizona at Tucson (Rathje and Murphy 1992). They have excavated part of the Fresh Kills landfill on Staten Island, near New York City. Its mass is estimated at 100 million tons and its volume at 2.9 billion cubic feet. Thus, it is one of the largest human-made structures in North America. Excavation of pop-top can tabs, disposable diapers, cosmetics containers, and telephone books reveals much about recent consumption patterns and how they affect the environment. One surprising finding is that the kinds of garbage people often blame for filling up landfills, such as fast-food packaging and disposable diapers, cause less serious problems than paper.

Stephen Lubkemann, trained as both a cultural anthropologist and an underwater archaeologist, documents the remains of the hull of DRTO-036, a vessel that wrecked in the Dry Tortugas in the mid-nineteenth century. The vessel lies within Dry Tortugas National Park in the Florida Keys.

▶ *You can access UNESCO's Convention on the Protection of Underwater Heritage on the Internet.*

Iron Bridge, England, is an important site of industrial archaeology. Considered the "birthplace of industry," the site includes the world's first iron bridge and remains of factories, furnaces, and canals.

▶ *Take a virtual tour of the site by going to http://www.ironbridge .org.uk/.*

Newspaper, especially, is a major culprit because of sheer quantity. This information can improve recycling efforts worldwide. The Fresh Kills landfill continues to grow rapidly due to everyday trash accumulation and other less common sources of debris, such as the remains from the World Trade Center in Manhattan following the 9/11 attacks.

Linguistic Anthropology

Linguistic anthropology is devoted to the study of communication, mainly (but not exclusively) among humans. Linguistic anthropology has three subfields: *historical linguistics*, the study of language change over time and how languages are related; *descriptive linguistics*, or structural linguistics, the study of how contemporary languages differ in terms of their formal structure; and *sociolinguistics*, the study of the relationships among social variation, social context, and linguistic variation, including nonverbal communication.

New directions in linguistic anthropology are connected to important current issues. First is a trend to study language in everyday use, or discourse, and how it relates to power structures at local, regional, and international levels (Duranti 1997a). In some contexts, powerful people speak more than less powerful people, whereas sometimes the more powerful people speak less. Power relations may also be expressed through intonation, word choice, and such nonverbal forms of communication as posture and dress. Second is increased attention to the role of information technology in communication, especially the Internet and cell phones. Third is attention to the increasingly rapid extinction of indigenous languages and what can be done about it. These topics are discussed in Chapter 11.

Cultural Anthropology

Cultural anthropology is the study of contemporary people and their cultures. The term *culture* refers to people's learned and shared behaviors and beliefs. Cultural anthropology considers variations and similarities across cultures, and how cultures change over time. Cultural anthropologists learn about culture by spending a long time, typically a year or more, living with the people they study (discussed in Chapter 3).

Prominent areas of specialization in cultural anthropology include economic anthropology, psychological anthropology, medical anthropology, political anthropology, and international development anthropology.

Applied Anthropology: Separate Field or Cross-Cutting Focus?

In the United States, applied anthropology emerged during and after World War II. Its first concern was with improving the lives of contemporary peoples and their needs, so it was more closely associated with cultural anthropology than with the other three fields.

Many anthropologists feel that applied anthropology should be considered a fifth field of anthropology, standing on its own. Many others think that the application of knowledge

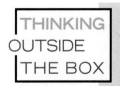

THINKING OUTSIDE THE BOX

What are your impressions of anthropology? How did you acquire them? Make notes of these impressions and review them at the end of the course.

ANTHROPOLOGY works

Delivering Health Care in Rural Haiti

Journalist Tracy Kidder's book, *Mountains Beyond Mountains: The Quest of Paul Farmer, a Man Who Would Cure the World* (2003), is an inspiring story about an inspiring person: Paul Farmer. Farmer earned a Ph.D. in anthropology and a degree in medicine from Harvard University. His training in cultural anthropology and medicine is a powerful prescription for providing health care to the poor.

In his first book, *AIDS and Accusation: Haiti and the Geography of Blame* (1992), he wrote about the coming of HIV/AIDS to Haiti and a rural community's attempt to understand and cope with this devastating new disease. He also describes how the wider world mistakenly blamed Haiti for being the source of the disease. In addition to his scholarly publications, Farmer is an influential health practitioner and activist. As one of the co-founders of Partners in Health, he has helped heal thousands of people. In 2009, Farmer was named U.S. deputy special envoy to Haiti. Since the earthquake in January 2010, he has worked tirelessly to alleviate suffering in Haiti.

Farmer focuses attention on poverty and social justice as primary causes of health problems worldwide. This position has shaken the very foundations of Western medicine.

In my undergraduate cultural anthropology class, when I ask who has

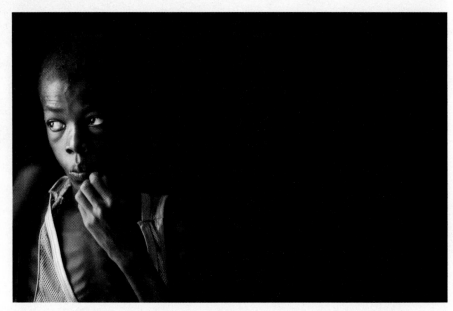

An undernourished Haitian boy at the clinic founded by Dr. Paul Farmer. Partners in Health also offers free medical aid and food to thousands of patients in Haiti's Central Plateau.

heard of Paul Farmer, many hands shoot up. Of these students, most have read *Mountains Beyond Mountains*. A few have heard him speak. This level of awareness of Farmer's contributions to health and anthropology prompted me to create a label that captures Farmer's inspirational role: the Paul Farmer Effect (PFE). This label refers to the Pied Piper role he plays for students: they want to follow his lead; they want to be a Paul Farmer. Students are choosing courses and

selecting majors and minors to help them achieve that goal.

I began to notice the PFE about five years ago, and it is still growing. Because of the PFE, more students each year combine their academic interests in anthropology, global health, and international affairs. These students are beginning to graduate and are going on to pursue humanitarian careers. Thanks to Paul Farmer and the PFE, they are more powerfully informed to make the world a better place.

---

to solve problems, just like theory, should be part of each field (see Figure 1.1). The latter is the author's position, and therefore, many examples of applied anthropology appear throughout this book.

Applied anthropology is an important thread that weaves through all four fields of anthropology:

- Archaeologists are employed in *cultural resource management (CRM)*, assessing the presence of possible archaeological remains before construction projects, such as roads and buildings, can proceed.

- Biological anthropologists are employed as *forensic anthropologists*, participating in criminal investigations

through laboratory work identifying bodily remains. Others work in non-human primate conservation, helping to protect their habitats and survival.

- Linguistic anthropologists consult with educational institutions about how to improve standardized tests for bilingual populations and conduct policy research for governments.

- Cultural anthropologists apply their knowledge to improve policies and programs in every domain of life, including education, health care, business, poverty reduction, and conflict prevention and resolution (see Anthropology Works throughout this book).

Introducing Cultural Anthropology

Cultural anthropology is devoted to studying human cultures worldwide, both their similarities and differences. Cultural anthropology makes "the strange familiar and the familiar strange" (Spiro 1990). Therefore, it teaches us to look at ourselves from the "outside" as a somewhat "strange" culture. A good example of making the familiar strange is the case of the Nacirema (nah-see-RAY-muh), a culture first described in 1956:

> The Nacirema are a North American group living in the territory between the Canadian Cree, the Yaqui and the Tarahumara of Mexico, and the Carib and the Arawak of the Antilles. Little is known of their origin, though tradition states that they came from the east. According to Nacirema mythology, their nation was originated by a culture hero, Notgnihsaw, who is otherwise known for two great feats of strength—the throwing of a piece of wampum across the river Pa-To-Mac and the chopping down of a cherry tree in which the Spirit of Truth resided (Miner 1965 [1956]:415).

The anthropologist goes on to describe the Nacirema's intense focus on the human body. He provides a detailed account of a daily ritual performed within the home in a specially constructed shrine area:

> The focal point of the shrine is a box or chest which is built into the wall. In this chest are kept the many charms and magical potions without which no native believes he could live. These preparations are secured from a variety of specialized practitioners. The most powerful of these are the medicine men, whose assistance must be rewarded with substantial gifts. . . . Beneath the charm box is a small font. Each day every member of the family, in succession, enters the shrine room, bows his head before the charm-box, mingles different sorts of holy water in the font, and proceeds with a brief rite of ablution. (1965:415–416)

If you do not recognize this tribe, try spelling its name backwards. (*Note:* Please forgive Miner for his use of the masculine pronoun in describing Nacirema society in general; his writings are several decades old.)

A Brief History of Cultural Anthropology

The beginning of cultural anthropology goes back to writers such as Herodotus (fifth century BCE; note: BCE stands for "Before the Common Era," a secular transformation of BC, or "Before Christ"), Marco Polo (thirteenth to fourteenth centuries), and Ibn Khaldun (fourteenth century), who traveled extensively and wrote reports about cultures they encountered. More recent conceptual roots are found in writers of the French Enlightenment, such as the philosopher Montesquieu, who wrote in the first half of the eighteenth century. His book *The Spirit of the Laws*, published in 1748 [1949], discussed the temperament, appearance, and government of various people around the world. He explained cultural differences as due to the different climates in which people lived.

In the second half of the nineteenth century, the discovery of the principles of biological evolution by Charles Darwin and others offered for the first time a scientific explanation for human origins. Biological evolution says that early forms evolve into later forms through the process of natural selection, whereby the most biologically fit organisms survive to reproduce while those that are less fit die out. Darwin's model is thus one of continuous progress toward increasing fitness through struggle among competing organisms. The concept of evolution was important in the thinking of early cultural anthropologists.

The most important founding figures of cultural anthropology in the late eighteenth and early nineteenth centuries were Sir Edward Tylor and Sir James Frazer in England and Lewis Henry Morgan in the United States (see Figure 1.2 on page 10). Inspired by the concept of biological evolution, they developed a model of cultural evolution whereby all cultures evolve from lower to higher forms over time. This view placed non-Western peoples at a "primitive" stage and Euro-American culture as "civilization" and assumed that non-Western cultures would either catch up to the level of Western civilization or die out.

Polish-born Bronislaw Malinowski is a major figure in modern cultural anthropology. In the first half of the twentieth century, he established a theoretical approach called **functionalism**: the view that a culture is similar to a biological organism, in which the parts work to support the operation and maintenance of the whole. Religion and family organization, for example, contribute to the functioning of the whole culture. Functionalism is linked to the concept of **holism**, the view that one must study all aspects of a culture in order to understand it.

Franz Boas is considered the founder of North American cultural anthropology (see photo on page 11). Born in Germany and educated in physics and geography, he came to the United States in 1887 (Patterson 2001:46ff). He brought

---

functionalism   the theory that a culture is similar to a biological organism, in which parts work to support the operation and maintenance of the whole.

holism   the perspective in anthropology that cultures are complex systems that cannot be fully understood without paying attention to their different components, including economics, social organization, and ideology.

FIGURE 1.2 Key Contributors to Cultural Anthropology.

Late Nineteenth Century

Sir Edward Tylor	First definition of culture, armchair anthropology
Sir James Frazer	Comparative study of religion, armchair anthropology
Lewis Henry Morgan	Insider's view, cultural evolution, comparative method

Early Twentieth Century

Bronislaw Malinowski	Functionalism, holism, participant observation
Franz Boas	Cultural relativism, historical particularism, advocacy
Margaret Mead	Personality and culture, cultural constructionism, public anthropology
Ruth Benedict	Personality and culture, national character studies
Zora Neale Hurston	Black culture, women's roles, ethnographic novels

Mid- and Late Twentieth Century and Early Twenty-First Century

Claude Lévi-Strauss	Symbolic analysis, French structuralism
Beatrice Medicine	Native American anthropology
Eleanor Leacock	Anthropology of colonialism and indigenous peoples
Marvin Harris	Cultural materialism, comparison, theory building
Mary Douglas	Symbolic anthropology
Michelle Rosaldo	Feminist anthropology
Clifford Geertz	Interpretive anthropology, thick description of local culture
Laura Nader	Legal anthropology, "studying up"
George Marcus	Critique of culture, critique of cultural anthropology
Gilbert Herdt	Gay anthropology
Nancy Scheper-Hughes	Critical medical anthropology
Leith Mullings	Anti-racist anthropology
Sally Engle Merry	Globalization and human rights

with him a skepticism toward Western science gained from a year's study with the Inuit, the indigenous people of Baffin Island (see Map 3.4). He learned from the Inuit that people in different cultures may have different perceptions of even basic physical substances, such as "water." Boas came to recognize the individuality and validity of different cultures. He introduced the now widely known concept of **cultural relativism**, or the view that each culture must be understood in terms of the values and ideas of that culture and not be judged by the standards of another. According to Boas, no culture is more advanced than any other. His position thus contrasted markedly with that of the nineteenth-century cultural evolutionists.

Margaret Mead is Boas's most famous student (see photo on page 11). She contributed to knowledge of South Pacific cultures, gender roles, and the impact of child-rearing practices on personality. Her scholarly works, as well as her columns in popular magazines, had wide influence on U.S. child-care patterns in the 1950s. Mead was thus an early *public anthropologist* who took seriously the importance of bringing cultural anthropology knowledge to the general public in order to create positive social change.

Following World War II, cultural anthropology in the United States expanded substantially in terms of the number of trained anthropologists and departments of anthropology in colleges and universities. Along with this growth came increased theoretical diversity. Several anthropologists developed theories of culture based on environmental factors. They suggested that similar environments (for example, deserts or tropical rainforests or mountains) would predictably lead to the emergence of similar cultures.

cultural relativism the perspective that each culture must be understood in terms of the values and ideas of that culture and not judged by the standards of another culture.

cultural materialism a theory that takes material features of life, such as the environment, natural resources, and mode of livelihood, as the bases for explaining social organization and ideology.

interpretive anthropology the view that cultures are best understood by studying what people think about, their ideas, and the meanings that are important to them.

structurism a theoretical position concerning human behavior and ideas that says large forces such as the economy, social and political organization, and the media shape what people do and think.

agency the ability of humans to make choices and exercise free will even within dominating structures.

Two giants in the history of anthropology. (LEFT) Franz Boas emphasized the four-field approach and the principle of cultural relativism. (RIGHT) Margaret Mead, a student of Boas at Columbia University, moved the Boasian legacy forward by her pioneering research on the cultural construction of personality and gender. She is the woman in the center.

At the same time, French anthropologist Claude Lévi-Strauss was developing a quite different theoretical perspective, known as *French structuralism*. He maintained that the best way to understand a culture is to collect its myths and stories and analyze the underlying themes in them. French structuralism inspired the development of *symbolic anthropology*, or the study of culture as a system of meanings, which was especially prominent in the United States in the latter part of the twentieth century.

In the 1960s, Marxist theory emerged in anthropology, stating the importance of people's access to the means of livelihood. It inspired the emergence of a new theoretical school in the United States called **cultural materialism**. Cultural materialism is an approach to studying culture by emphasizing the material aspects of life, especially the natural environment and how people make a living. Also arising in the 1960s was the theoretical position referred to as **interpretive anthropology**, or *interpretivism*. This perspective developed from both U.S. symbolic anthropology and French structural anthropology. It says that understanding culture should focus on what people think about, their ideas, and the symbols and meanings that are important to them. These two positions are discussed in more detail later in this section.

Since the 1990s, two other theoretical directions have gained prominence. Both are influenced by *postmodernism*, an intellectual pursuit that asks whether modernity is truly progress and questions such aspects of modernism as the scientific method, urbanization, technological change, and mass communication. The first theory is termed **structurism** (I coined this term), the view that powerful structures such as economics, politics, and media shape cultures, influencing how people behave and think, even when they don't realize it. The second theory emphasizes human **agency**, or free will, and the power of individuals to create and change culture by acting against structures. These two positions are revisited at the end of this section.

Cultural anthropology continues to be rethought and refashioned. Over the past few decades, several new theoretical perspectives have transformed and enriched the field. *Feminist anthropology* is a perspective that emphasizes the need to study female roles and gender-based inequality. In the 1970s, early feminist anthropologists realized that anthropology had overlooked women. To address this gap, feminist anthropologists undertook research that explicitly focused on women and girls, half of the world's people. A related area is *gay and lesbian anthropology*, or *queer anthropology*, a perspective that emphasizes the need to study gay people's cultures

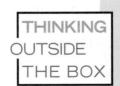

THINKING OUTSIDE THE BOX

This brief history of cultural anthropology describes early contributions by anthropologists, most of whom were white, European or Euro-American, and male. Compare this pattern with the history of some other discipline you have studied. What are some similarities and differences?

Colombian anthropologist Patricia Tovar (center) at an anthropology conference in Colombia. In Central and South America, applied anthropology is an integral part of cultural anthropology.

and discrimination based on sexual identity and preferences. This book presents findings from both these areas.

In North American anthropology, African American, Latino, and Native American anthropologists are increasing in number and visibility. Yet anthropology in North America and Europe remains one of the "whitest" professions (Shanklin 2000). Some steps for moving the discipline toward *antiracist anthropology* include the following (Mullings 2005):

- Examine and recognize anthropology's history of, and implications for, racism.

- Work to increase the diversity of professors, researchers, staff, and students in the discipline.

- Teach about racism in anthropology classes and textbooks.

Worldwide, non-Western anthropologists are increasingly questioning the dominance of Euro-American anthropology and offering new perspectives (Kuwayama 2004). Their work provides useful critiques of anthropology as a largely Western-defined discipline and promises to lead it in new directions in the future.

The Concept of Culture

Although cultural anthropologists are united in the study of *culture*, the question of how to define it has been debated for decades. This section discusses definitions of culture today, characteristics of culture, and bases for cultural identity.

DEFINITIONS OF CULTURE   Culture is the core concept in cultural anthropology, so it might seem likely that cultural anthropologists would agree about what it is. In

the 1950s, an effort to collect definitions of culture produced 164 different ones (Kroeber and Kluckhohn 1952). Since then, no one has tried to count the number of definitions of culture used by anthropologists.

British anthropologist Sir Edward Tylor proposed the first definition in 1871. He stated, "Culture, or civilization . . . is that complex whole which includes knowledge, belief, art, law, morals, custom, and any other capabilities and habits acquired by man as a member of society" (Kroeber and Kluckhohn 1952:81). The phrase "that complex whole" has been the most durable feature of his definition.

In contemporary cultural anthropology, the cultural materialists and the interpretive anthropologists support two different definitions of culture. Cultural materialist Marvin Harris says, "A culture is the total socially acquired life-way or life-style of a group of people. It consists of the patterned repetitive ways of thinking, feeling, and acting that are characteristic of the members of a particular society or segment of society" (1975:144). In contrast, Clifford Geertz, speaking for the interpretivists, believes that culture consists of symbols, motivations, moods, and thoughts and does not include behavior as a part of culture. This book defines culture as learned and shared behavior and beliefs, a definition broader than Geertz's.

Culture exists among all human beings. Some anthropologists refer to this universal concept of culture as *Culture* with a capital *C*. Culture also exists in a more specific way. The term **microculture**, or local culture, refers to distinct patterns of learned and shared behavior and ideas found in local regions and among particular groups. Microcultures are based on ethnicity, gender, age, and more.

Sleep might appear to be one of the most "natural" aspects of human behavior. In fact, culture shapes much about sleep in terms of the amount and quality of sleep, the location of sleep, with whom a person sleeps, infant learning of sleeping at night, personal security during sleep, and the value of dreams. (LEFT) Members of a roving girl gang sleep together on the street in Rio de Janeiro, Brazil. (RIGHT) Employees of wealthy corporation sleep on its private airbus on a flight from London to Delhi.

▶ *Do Internet research on culture, social inequality, and sleep and report on your findings to the class.*

CHARACTERISTICS OF CULTURE   Understanding of the complex concept of culture can be gained by looking at its characteristics.

Culture is Not the Same as Nature   The relationship between nature and culture is of great interest to cultural anthropologists in their quest to understand people's behavior and thinking. This book emphasizes the importance of culture.

A good way to see how culture diverges from, and shapes, nature is to consider basic natural demands of life within different cultural contexts. Universal human functions that everyone must perform to stay alive are eating, drinking, sleeping, and eliminating. Given the primary importance of these four functions in supporting a human being's life, it seems logical that people would fulfill them in similar ways everywhere. But that is not the case.

Eating   Culture shapes what people eat, how they eat, when they eat, and the meanings of food and eating. Culture also defines foods that are acceptable and unacceptable. In China, most people think that cheese is disgusting, but in France, most people love cheese. Throughout China, pork is a widely favored meat. The religions of Judaism and Islam, in contrast, forbid the consumption of pork. In many cultures where gathering wild plant foods, hunting, and fishing are important, people value the freshness of food. They would consider a package of frozen food on a grocery store shelf as way past its time.

Perceptions of taste vary dramatically. Western researchers have defined four supposedly universal taste categories: sweet, sour, bitter, and salty. Cross-cultural research disproves these categories as universals. A prominent East Asian flavor, not on the Western list, is *umami*, or savoriness. To add even more complexity, the Weyéwa (wuh-YAY-wuh) people of the highlands of Sumba, Indonesia (see Map 1.1 on page 14), define seven categories of taste: sour, sweet, salty, bitter, tart, bland, and pungent (Kuipers 1991).

How to eat is also an important aspect of food behavior. The proper way to eat is one of the first things a person needs to learn when living in a foreign culture. Dining rules in India require using only the right hand. The left hand is considered polluted because it is used for personal cleansing after elimination. A person's clean right hand is the preferred eating utensil. Silverware that has been touched by others, even if it has been washed, is considered unclean. In some cultures, it is important to eat only from one's own plate, whereas in others, eating from a shared central platter is considered proper.

Another area of cultural variation involves who is responsible for cooking and serving food. In many cultures, domestic cooking is women's responsibility, but cooking for public feasts is more often something that men do. Power issues may arise about who cooks what for whom (see Everyday Anthropology on page 15).

Drinking   Cross-cultural variations related to drinking are also complex. Every culture defines the appropriate substances to drink, when to drink and with whom, and the meanings of the beverages and drinking occasions. French culture allows for the consumption of relatively large amounts of table wine with family meals, including lunch. In the United States, water is generally served and consumed during family meals. In India, water is served and consumed at the end of the meal. Around the world, different categories of people drink different beverages. In cultures where alcoholic beverages are consumed, men tend to consume more than women.

microculture   a distinct pattern of learned and shared behavior and thinking found within a larger culture.

MAP 1.1 Weyéwa Region in Indonesia.

Sumba, one of Indonesia's many islands, is 75 miles long. The Weyéwa people number about 85,000 and live in small settlements on grassy plateaus in the western part of the island. They grow rice, maize, and millet, and they raise water buffaloes and pigs.

Ethiopian women dining at an Ethiopian restaurant. The main meal consists of several meat and vegetable dishes, cooked with distinctive spices and laid out on injera bread, a soft, flat bread that is torn into small pieces and used to wrap bits of meat and vegetables. The entire meal can be eaten without utensils.

▶ How does this dining scene resemble or differ from a recent meal that you have had in a restaurant?

Culture often defines the meaning of particular drinks and the style of drinking and serving them. Social drinking—whether the beverage is coffee, beer, or vodka—creates and reinforces bonds. Beer-drinking rituals in U.S. college fraternities are a good example. In an ethnographic film entitled *Salamanders*, filmed at a large university in the northeastern United States, the fraternity brothers run to various "stations" in the fraternity house, downing a beer at each (Hornbein and Hornbein 1992). At one point, a brother chugs a beer, turns with a stagger toward the next station, falls flat on his face, and passes out. The movie documents another drinking ritual in which both young men and women at fraternity parties swallow live salamanders, sometimes two or three at a time, with large gulps of beer. (This practice is now forbidden by law.)

Sleeping Common sense might say that sleep is the one natural function that is not shaped by culture because people tend to do it at least once every 24 hours, everyone shuts their eyes to do it, everyone lies down to do it, and most people sleep at night. Going without sleep for an extended period can lead to insanity and even death.

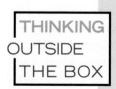

THINKING OUTSIDE THE BOX

Think about your everyday drinking patterns (no matter what the liquid), and then think about your drinking patterns on special occasions, including weekends, holidays, or special events such as weddings. What beverages do you consume, and with whom, and what are the meanings and wider social implications involved?

everyday ANTHROPOLOGY

Latina Power in the Kitchen

Within a family, cooking food for other members can be a sign of love and devotion. It may carry a message that love and devotion are expected in return. Among Tejano (tay-HAH-no) migrant farm workers in the United States, preparing tamales is a symbol of a woman's commitment to her family and thus of the "good wife" (Williams 1984). The Tejanos are people of Mexican descent who live in Texas. Some of them move to Illinois in the summer, where they are employed as migrant workers.

For Tejanos, tamales are a central cultural identity marker. Tamales contain a rich inner mash of pig's head meat wrapped in corn husks. Making tamales is extremely time consuming, and it is women's work. Typically, several women work together over a few days to do the necessary tasks: buying the pigs' heads, stripping the meat, preparing the stuffing, wrapping the stuffing with the corn husks, and baking or boiling the tamale.

Tamales symbolize and emphasize women's nurturance of their husbands. One elderly woman, at home in Texas for Christmas, made 200 tamales with her daughters-in-law, nieces, and god-daughter. They distributed the tamales to friends, relatives, and local taverns. The effort and expense involved were enormous. But for the women, it was worth it. Through their tamale making, they celebrate the holiday, build ties with people whom they may need to call on for support, and maintain communication with tavern owners so that they will watch over male kin who drink at their bars.

Tejano women also use tamale making as a statement of domestic protest. A woman who is dissatisfied with her husband's behavior will refuse to make

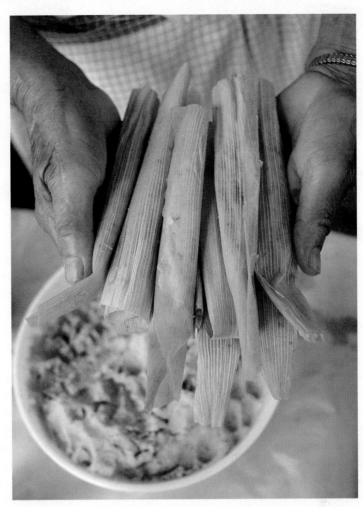

Tamales consist of fried meat and peppers in a cornmeal dough that is encased in cornhusks.

▶ *What is a similarly important food item in your cultural world?*

tamales, a serious statement on her part. The link between being a good wife and making tamales is strong, so a husband can take his wife's unwillingness to make tamales as grounds for divorce. One young Tejano sued his wife for divorce in Illinois on the grounds that she refused to cook tamales for him, in addi-

tion to dancing with other men at fiestas. The judge refused to grant a divorce.

FOOD FOR THOUGHT ▼
Provide an example from your microcultural experience about food being used as a way of expressing social solidarity or social protest.

Sleep, however, is at least as much culturally shaped as it is biologically determined. Cultural influences on sleep include the questions of who sleeps with whom, how much sleep a person should have, and why some people have insomnia or what are called sleep disorders. Across cultures, marked variation exists in rules about where infants and children should sleep: with the mother, with both parents, or by themselves in a separate room. Among indigenous peoples of the

Amazon region of South America, mothers and babies share the same hammock for many months, and breastfeeding occurs whenever the baby is hungry.

Culture shapes the amount of time a person sleeps. In rural India, women sleep fewer hours than men because they have to get up early to start the fire for the morning meal. In fast-track, corporate North America, "type A" males sleep relatively few hours and are proud of that fact—to sleep too

The United Nations seeks to convey a message worldwide that handwashing with soap is an effective way of preventing disease. (LEFT) Women in a village in Bangladesh look out a window beside a poster showing how to wash one's hands properly. (RIGHT) In Lima, Peru, schoolchildren practice handwashing as part of Global Handwashing Day, which is October 12.

▶ *Be prepared to discuss how the UN's promotion of handwashing with soap might need to take into account contexts where people do not have access to soap and clean water?*

much is to be a wimp. A disorder in Japan called *excessive day-time sleepiness* (*EDS*) is common in Tokyo and other large cities (Doi and Minowa 2003). Excessive sleepiness is correlated with more accidents on the job, more absenteeism, decreased productivity, deteriorated personal and professional relationships, and increased rates of illness and death. Women are almost twice as likely as men to experience EDS, and married women are especially vulnerable.

Eliminating   In spite of its basic importance to people everywhere, elimination receives little attention (in print) from anthropologists. Anyone who has traveled internationally knows that there is much to learn about elimination in an unfamiliar context.

The first question is where to eliminate. Differences emerge in the degree to which elimination is a private act or can be done in more or less public areas. In many European cities, public options include street urinals for males but not for females. In most villages in India, houses do not have interior bathrooms. Instead, early in the morning, groups of women and girls leave the house and head for a certain field, where they squat and chat. Men go to a different area. Everyone carries, in his left hand, a small brass pot full of water with which he splashes himself clean. Think about the ecological advantages: This system adds fertilizer to the fields and leaves no paper litter. Westerners may consider the village practice

unclean and unpleasant, but village-dwelling people in India would think that the Western system is unsanitary because using toilet paper does not clean one as well as water does, and they would find the practice of sitting on a toilet less comfortable than squatting.

In many cultures, the products of elimination (urine and feces) are considered polluting and disgusting. Among some groups in Papua New Guinea (Map 1.2), people take great care to bury or otherwise hide their fecal matter for fear that someone will find it and use it for magic against them. A negative assessment of the products of elimination is not universal, however. Among some Native American cultures of the Pacific Northwest region of Canada and the United States, urine, especially women's urine, was believed to have medicinal and cleansing properties and was considered the "water of life" (Furst 1989). In some death rituals, it was sprinkled over the corpse in the hope that it might rejuvenate the deceased. People stored urine in special wooden boxes for ritual use, including for a baby's first bath. (The urine was mixed with water.)

What about hand-washing practices among people in rich countries? One study investigated fecal bacteria on the hands of 404 commuters in five cities in the United Kingdom (Judah et al. 2010). It found that 28 percent of commuters' hands had fecal bacteria on them, and men were more likely to have fecal bacteria on their hands than women. The researchers are now following up to learn more about hand-washing practices with attention to gender differences.

---

symbol   an object, word, or action with culturally defined meaning that stands for something else; most symbols are arbitrary.

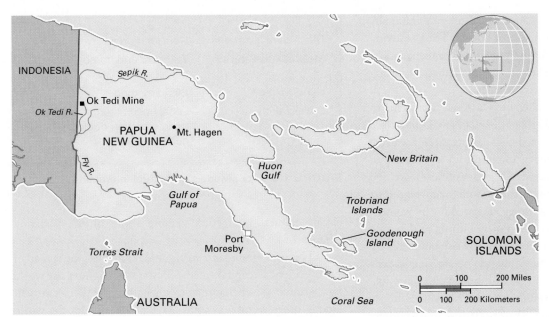

MAP 1.2 Papua New Guinea.

The Independent State of Papua New Guinea (PNG) gained its autonomy from Australia in 1975. Mostly mountainous with coastal lowlands, PNG is richly endowed with gold, copper, silver, natural gas, timber, oil, and fisheries. Its population is around 5,700,000. Port Moresby, the capital, has a high rate of HIV/AIDS infection among the working-age population.

Culture is Based on Symbols Our entire lives—from eating breakfast to greeting our friends, making money, creating art, and practicing religion—are based on and organized through symbols. A **symbol** is an object, word, or action with a culturally defined meaning that stands for something else with which it has no necessary or natural relationship. Symbols are arbitrary (bearing no necessary relationship to that which is symbolized), unpredictable, and diverse. Because symbols are arbitrary, it is impossible to predict how a particular culture will symbolize something. Although one might assume that people who are hungry would have an expression for hunger involving the stomach no one could predict that in Hindi, the language of northern India, a colloquial expression for being hungry is saying that "rats are jumping in my stomach." The linguistic history of Barbara—the name of the author of this book—reveals that originally, in the Greek, it referred to people who were outsiders, "barbarians," and, by extension, uncivilized and savage. On top of that, the Greek term referred to such people as "bearded." The symbolic content of the American name Barbara does not immediately convey a sense of beardedness in its current context because symbolic meaning can change. It is through symbols, arbitrary and amazingly rich in their attributions, that culture is shared, stored, and transmitted over time.

Culture is Learned Because culture is based on symbols that are arbitrary, culture must be learned anew in each context. Cultural learning begins from the moment of birth, if not before. (Some people think that an unborn baby takes in and stores information through sounds heard from the outside world.) A large but unknown amount of people's cultural learning is unconscious, occurring as a normal part of life through observation. Learning in schools, in contrast, is a formal way to acquire culture. Most cultures throughout history have not passed on learning through formal schooling. Instead, children acquire cultural patterns through observation and practice and advice from family members and elder members of the group.

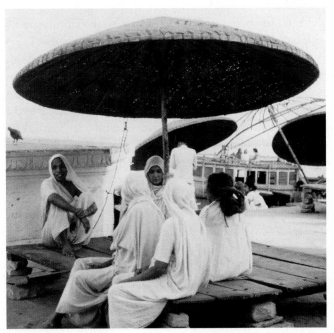

In India, a white sari (women's garment) symbolizes widowhood.

▶ *What might these women think about the Western custom of a bride wearing white?*

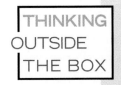

THINKING OUTSIDE THE BOX

Over a week, keep track of how often you wash your hands each day and whether or not you use soap each time. Compare the data from your mini–self-study to those of your classmates. What patterns emerge?

Cultures are Integrated To state that cultures are internally integrated is to assert the principle of holism. Thus, studying only one or two aspects of culture provides an understanding so limited that it is more likely to be misleading or wrong than are more comprehensive approaches.

Consider what would happen if a researcher were to study intertribal warfare in highland Papua New Guinea (see Map 1.2) and focused only on the actual practice of warfare without examining other aspects of culture. A key feature of highland culture is the exchange of pigs at political feasts. To become a political leader, a man must acquire many pigs. Pigs eat yams, which men grow, but pigs are cared for by women. This division of labor means that a man with more than one wife will be able to maintain more pigs and rise politically by giving more feasts. Such feasting enhances an aspiring leader's status and makes his guests indebted to him. With more followers attracted through feasting, a leader can gather forces and wage war on neighboring villages. Success in war brings gains in territory. So far, this example pays attention mainly to economics, politics, and marriage systems. But other aspects of culture are involved, too. Supernatural powers affect the success of warfare. Painting spears and shields with particular designs is believed to increase their power. At feasts and marriages, body decoration (including paint, shell ornaments, and elaborate feather headdresses) is an important expression of identity and status. Looking at warfare without attention to its wider cultural context yields an incomplete picture.

Cultural integration is relevant to applied anthropologists interested in proposing ways to promote positive change. Years of experience show that introducing programs for change in one aspect of culture without considering their effects in other domains is often detrimental to the welfare and survival of a culture. For example, Western missionaries and colonialists in parts of Southeast Asia banned the practice of head-hunting. This practice was connected to many other aspects of the people's culture, including politics, religion, and psychology. A man's sense of identity depended on the taking of a head. While preventing head-hunting might seem like a good thing, its cessation had disastrous consequences for the cultures in which it was practiced because of its central importance.

Cultures Interact and Change Cultures interact with each other and change each other through contact such as trade networks, international development projects, telecommunications, education, migration, and tourism. **Globalization**, the process of intense global interconnectedness and movement of goods, information, and people, is a major force of contemporary cultural change. It has gained momentum through recent technological change, especially the boom in information and communication technologies.

Globalization does not spread evenly, and its interactions with, and effects on, local cultures vary substantially from positive change to cultural destruction and extinction. Four mod-

Clash of civilizations	Conflict model
McDonaldization	Takeover and homogenization model
Hybridization	Blending model
Localization	Local cultural remaking and transformation of global culture

FIGURE 1.3 Four Models of Cultural Interaction.

els of cultural interaction capture some of the variation (Figure 1.3).

The *clash of civilizations* argument says that the spread of Euro-American capitalism and lifeways throughout the world has created disenchantment, alienation, and resentment among other cultural systems. This model divides the world into the "West and the rest."

The *McDonaldization* model says that, under the powerful influence of U.S.-dominated corporate culture, the world is becoming culturally homogeneous. "Fast-food culture," with its principles of mass production, speed, standardization, and impersonal service, is taken to be at the center of this new global culture.

Hybridization, also called *syncretism* and *creolization*, occurs when aspects of two or more cultures combine to form something new—a blend. In Japan, for instance, a grandmother might bow in gratitude to an automated banking machine. In the Amazon region and in the Arctic, indigenous people use satellite imagery to map and protect the boundaries of their ancestral lands.

A fourth pattern is **localization**, the transformation of global culture by local microcultures into something new. Consider the example of McDonald's restaurants. In many Asian settings, people resist the pattern of eating quickly and insist on leisurely family gatherings (Watson 1997). The McDonald's managers accommodate this preference and alter the pace of service to allow for a slower turnover of tables. In Saudi Arabia, McDonald's provides separate areas for families, including women accompanied by a husband or father or brother, and for single men. Single women cannot enter a McDonald's, but the company does offer delivery services. Many other examples of cultural localization exist, throwing into question the notion that a form of Western "mono-culture" is taking over the entire world and erasing cultural diversity.

Multiple Cultural Worlds

Within large cultures, a variety of microcultures exist, as discussed in this section (Figure 1.4). A particular individual in such a complex situation is likely to be a member of several microcultures. Microcultures may overlap or may be related to each other hierarchically in terms of power, status, and rights.

Class	Gender, sexuality
"Race"	Age
Ethnicity, indigeneity	Institution

FIGURE 1.4 Some Bases of Microcultures.

In discussing microcultures, the contrast between *difference* and *hierarchy* is important. People and groups can be considered different from each other in terms of a particular characteristic, but they may or may not be unequal on the basis of it. For example, people with blue or brown eyes might be recognized as different, but this difference does not entail unequal treatment or status. In other instances, such differences do become the basis for inequality.

CLASS **Class** is a category based on people's economic position in society, usually measured in terms of income or wealth and exhibited in terms of lifestyle. Class societies may be divided into upper, middle, and lower classes. Separate classes are, for example, the working class (people who trade their labor for wages) and the landowning class (people who own land on which they or others labor). Classes are related in a hierarchical system, with upper classes dominating lower classes. Class struggle, in the classic Marxist view, is inevitable, as those at the top seek to maintain their position while those at the bottom seek to improve theirs. People at the bottom may attempt to improve their class position by gaining access to resources and by adopting aspects of upper-class symbolic behavior, such as speech, dress, and leisure and recreation activities.

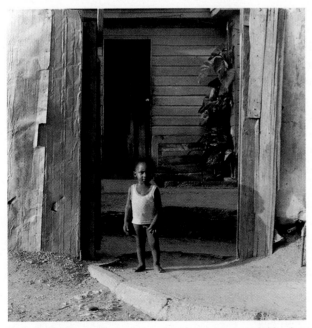

A view into the yard of a house in a low-income neighborhood of Kingston, Jamaica. People in these neighborhoods prefer the term "low-income" to "poor."

Class is a recent social development in human history, extending back in time for only about 10,000 years. It does not exist today in remote local cultures where everyone has equal wealth and sharing food and other resources among the group is expected.

"RACE," ETHNICITY, AND INDIGENOUS PEOPLES
"Race" refers to groups of people with supposedly homogeneous biological traits. The term "race" is extremely complicated, as it is used in diverse ways in different parts of the world and among different groups of people. Therefore, it makes sense to put the word in quotation marks in order to indicate that it has no single meaning. In South Africa, as in the United States, "race" is defined mainly on the basis of skin color. In pre–twentieth-century China, body hair was the key biological basis for racial classification (Dikötter 1998). The "barbarian" races had more body hair than the "civilized" Chinese people.

Chinese writers referred to bearded, male missionaries from Europe as "hairy barbarians." Into the twentieth century, some Chinese anthropologists divided humans into evolutionary stages on the basis of amounts of body hair.

Anthropological and other scientific research demonstrates that biological features alone do not explain or account for a person's behavior or lifestyle. Rather than being a biological category, racial classifications are cultural constructions. They are often associated with discrimination against, and cruelty toward, those "races" considered less worthy by those in power.

Ethnicity refers to a sense of identity among a group based on a sense of a common heritage, language, religion, or other aspect of culture. Examples include African Americans and Italian Americans in the United States, the Croats of Eastern Europe, the Han of China, and the Hutu and Tutsi of Rwanda. This sense of identity may be expressed through political movements to gain or protect group rights and recognition or more quietly stated in how one lives one's daily life. Compared with the term "race," "ethnicity" appears to be a more neutral, less stigmatizing term. But it, too, has been, and still is, a basis for discrimination, segregation, and oppression. The "ethnic cleansing" campaigns conducted in the early

---

globalization increased and intensified international ties related to the spread of Western, especially U.S., capitalism that affects all world cultures.

localization the transformation of global culture by local cultures into something new.

class a way of categorizing people on the basis of their economic position in society, usually measured in terms of income or wealth.

"race" a classification of people into groups on the basis of supposedly homogeneous and largely superficial biological traits such as skin color or hair characteristics.

ethnicity a shared sense of identity among members of a group based on heritage, language, or culture.

1990s by the Serbs against Muslims in the former Yugoslavia are an extreme case of ethnic discrimination. In China, Han ethnic domination over minority ethnic groups has been a reality for centuries. Han political repression of the Tibetan people prompted thousands of Tibetans to flee their homeland. Living in exile, they struggle to keep their ethnic heritage alive.

Indigenous peoples, according to guidelines laid down by the United Nations, are defined as groups that have a long-standing connection with their home territories, a connection predating colonial or other societies that prevail in that territory (Sanders 1999). They are typically a numerical minority and often have lost the rights to their original territory. The United Nations distinguishes between indigenous peoples and *minority ethnic groups* such as the Roma, the Tamils of Sri Lanka, and African Americans. The San peoples of Southern Africa, as well as their several subgroups, are an important example of indigenous peoples whose way of life was dramatically affected first by colonialism and now by globalization (see Culturama).

GENDER   **Gender** refers to culturally constructed and learned behaviors and ideas attributed to males, females, or sometimes a blended, or "third," gender. Gender differs from *sex*, which is based on biological markers, such as genitals and hormones, to define categories of male and female. Cultural anthropology shows that a person's biological makeup does not necessarily correspond to gender. Biology directly determines only a few roles and tasks, such as giving birth and nursing infants.

Cross-culturally, gender differences vary from societies in which male and female roles and worlds are similar or overlapping to those in which gender roles are sharply differentiated. In much of rural Thailand, men and women are about the same size, their clothing is similar, and their agricultural tasks are complementary and often interchangeable (Potter 1977). In contrast, among many groups in highland New Guinea, extreme gender segregation exists in most aspects of life, including the kinds of food men and women eat (Meigs 1984). The men's house physically and symbolically separates the worlds of men and women. Men engage in rituals that purge them of female substances: nose or penis bleeding, vomiting, tongue scraping, sweating, and eye washing. Men possess sacred flutes, which they parade through the village from time to time. If women dare to look at the flutes, men have the right, by tradition, to kill them.

AGE   The human life cycle, from birth to old age, takes people through cultural stages for which appropriate behavior and thinking must be learned anew. In many African herding

Huli men of the Mount Hagen region of highland Papua New Guinea in festive attire for a dance performance.

societies, elaborate age categories for males define their roles and status as they move from being boys with few responsibilities and little status, to young men who are warriors and live apart from the rest of the group, to adult men who are allowed to marry, have children, and become respected elders. "The Hill," or the collective members of the U.S. Senate and the House of Representatives, is a highly age-graded microculture (Weatherford 1981). The Hill is a *gerontocracy* (a group ruled by senior members) in which the older politicians dominate younger politicians in terms of amount of time they speak and how much attention their words receive. It may take a junior member between 10 and 20 years to become as effective and powerful as a senior member.

INSTITUTIONS   *Institutions*, or enduring group settings formed for a particular purpose, have their own characteristic microcultures. Institutions include hospitals, schools and universities, and prisons. Anyone who has entered such an institution has experienced a feeling of strangeness. Until you gain familiarity with the often unwritten cultural rules, you may do things that offend or puzzle people, that fail to get you what you want, and that make you feel marginalized and insecure.

Anthropologists who study educational institutions have shown that schools often replicate and reinforce stereotypes, power relations, and inequalities of the wider society. A study of middle schools in the southwestern Rocky Mountain region of the United States found a situation in which teachers marginalized Mexican immigrant girls (Meador 2005). In this school, Mexican immigrant students are labeled as ESL (English as a second language) students because they are not fluent in English and take special courses designed to improve their English. In addition, the teachers' mental model of a "good student" is a student who is

- motivated to do well in school and gets good grades.
- an athlete.
- popular and has good students as friends.
- comes from a stable family.

indigenous people   groups of people who have a long-standing connection with their home territories that predates colonial or outside societies.

gender   culturally constructed and learned behaviors and ideas attributed to males, females, or blended genders.

colonialists referred to San people as "Bushmen," a derogatory term at the time but one that San people now prefer over what some locals call them. Some San also refer to themselves with the English term "First People."

For many centuries, the San supported themselves through collecting food such as roots and birds' eggs and by hunting eland, giraffe, and other animals. Now, pressure from African governments, farmers, ranchers, game reserves, diamond companies, and international tourism has greatly reduced the San's access to Namibia and Botswana. As described by Richard Lee in the early 1960s, they were highly mobile food collectors and quite healthy (1979). Today, most have been forced from their homeland and live as poor, urban squatters or in government-built resettlement camps. Many work as farm laborers or in the international tourist industry, serving as guides and producing and selling crafts. Others are unemployed. The specific living conditions of the San people depend on government policy toward indigenous people in the particular country where they live.

ceutical company and succeeded in ensuring that the San receive a portion of the profits from the commercial development of hoodia (Hoodia gordonia). Hoodia is extracted from a cactus indigenous to the Kalahari region. An effective appetite suppressant, it is now widely available in North America and on the Internet as diet pills.

Thanks to Alison Brooks, George Washington University, for reviewing this material.

(LEFT) Richard Lee (wearing a shirt) asks Ju/'hoansi men about food plants of the Kalahari desert. This photograph was taken in 1968. Lee and many other researchers affiliated with the Harvard Kalahari research project learned to speak the Ju/'hoansi language.

(CENTER) San people eat part of the hoodia cactus when on long treks in the desert because it suppresses hunger and thirst. Now they cultivate it for commercial production in a diet pill sold in rich countries.

MAP 1.3 Ju/'hoansi Region in Namibia and Botswana. Before country boundaries were drawn, the Ju/'hoansi ranged freely across their traditional territory (shaded area), depending on the seasonal availability of food and water. Now they must show a passport when crossing from one country to another.

Absolute cultural relativism	Whatever goes on within a particular culture cannot be questioned or changed by outsiders as that would be ethnocentric.
Critical cultural relativism	Anyone can pose questions about what goes on in various cultures, including their own culture, in terms of how particular practices or beliefs may harm certain members; follows Lévi-Strauss's comment that no society is perfect and that, therefore, all societies may be able to learn from others and improve.

FIGURE 1.5 Cultural Relativism: Two Views.

It is difficult for many Mexican immigrant children to conform to this image. Mexican girls, or *Mexicanas*, are especially disadvantaged because most are not interested in, or good at, sports. The few Mexicanas who are motivated to try to get good grades are consistently overlooked by the teachers, who instead call on students who are confident, bright, and popular, and who sit in front of the classroom and raise their hands eagerly.

Distinctive Features of Cultural Anthropology

Cultural anthropology has two distinct research goals and two distinct guiding concepts. Researchers and teachers in other disciplines have begun to adopt these goals and concepts in recent decades, so they are now found beyond cultural anthropology. Such cross-disciplinary contributions are something of which cultural anthropology can be proud.

CULTURAL RELATIVISM   Most people grow up thinking that their culture is *the* way of life and that other ways of life are strange and inferior. Cultural anthropologists label this attitude **ethnocentrism**: judging other cultures by the standards of one's own culture rather than by the standards of other cultures. Ethnocentrism has fueled centuries of efforts to change "other" people in the world, sometimes through religious missionary work, sometimes in the form of colonial domination.

The opposite of ethnocentrism is cultural relativism, the idea that each culture must be understood in terms of its own values and beliefs and not by the standards of another culture. Cultural relativism assumes that no culture is better than any other.

One way that some anthropologists have interpreted cultural relativism is *absolute cultural relativism*, which says that whatever goes on in a particular culture must not be questioned

or changed because it would be ethnocentric to question any behavior or idea anywhere (Figure 1.5). The position of absolute cultural relativism, however, can lead in dangerous directions. Consider the example of the Holocaust during World War II, in which millions of Jews, Roma, and other minorities in much of Eastern and Western Europe were killed as part of the German Nazis' Aryan supremacy campaign. The absolute cultural relativist position becomes boxed in, logically, to saying that because the Holocaust was undertaken according to the values of the culture, outsiders have no business questioning it. Can anyone feel comfortable with such a position?

Critical cultural relativism offers an alternative view that poses questions about cultural practices and ideas in terms of who accepts them and why, and whom they might be harming or helping. In terms of the Nazi Holocaust, a critical cultural relativist would ask, "Whose culture supported the values that killed millions of people on the grounds of racial purity?" Not the cultures of the Jews, Roma, and other victims. It was the culture of Aryan supremacists, who were just one group among many. In other words, the situation was far more complex than a simple absolute cultural relativist statement suggests. Rather, it was a case of *cultural imperialism*, in which one dominant group claimed supremacy over minority cultures and took actions in its own interests and at the expense of the subjugated cultures. Critical cultural relativism avoids the trap of adopting a homogenized view. It recognizes internal cultural differences: winners and losers, and oppressors and victims. It pays attention to the interests of various power groups. It can illuminate the causes and consequences of recent and contemporary conflicts, such as those in Rwanda, Iraq, and Afghanistan.

Many cultural anthropologists seek to *critique* (which means "to probe underlying power interests," not "to offer negative comments," as in the general usage of the term "criticism") the behavior and values of groups from the standpoint of a set of generally agreed-on human rights and values. Two issues emerge in this endeavor. First, it is difficult, if not impossible, to generate a universal list of what all cultures would agree to as good and right. Second, as Claude Lévi-Strauss said, "No society is perfect" (1968:385).

VALUING AND SUSTAINING DIVERSITY   Anthropologists value and are committed to maintaining cultural

---

ethnocentrism   judging another culture by the standards of one's own culture rather than by the standards of that particular culture.

biological determinism   a theory that explains human behavior and ideas as shaped mainly by biological features such as genes and hormones.

cultural constructionism   a theory that explains human behavior and ideas as shaped mainly by learning.

American Indian dancers at the 13th annual Chumash Inter-tribal Pow Wow in the Santa Ynez Valley, California.

▶ *Think of examples in your microculture, or another, of attempts to revitalize or maintain the culture across generations. Are such attempts successful or not, and why?*

diversity throughout the world, as part of humanity's rich heritage. Many cultural anthropologists share their expertise and knowledge to support the survival of indigenous peoples and other small-scale groups worldwide.

In the United States, an organization called Cultural Survival helps indigenous peoples and ethnic minorities deal as equals in their interactions with outsiders. Cultural Survival's guiding principle is outlined in the preface of this book. Cultural Survival sponsors programs to help indigenous peoples and ethnic minorities protect and manage their natural environment, claim land rights, and protect their cultural heritage.

Three Theoretical Debates in Cultural Anthropology

Transitioning to theory, this section describes three debates in cultural anthropology that go to the heart of its basic questions about how people behave and think cross-culturally and why people behave and think the way they do. Introduced briefly here, they reappear throughout the book.

BIOLOGICAL DETERMINISM VERSUS CULTURAL CONSTRUCTIONISM **Biological determinism** seeks to explain why people do and think what they do by considering biological factors such as people's genes and hormones. Thus, biological determinists search for the gene or hormone that contributes to behavior such as homicide, alcoholism, or adolescent stress. They also examine cultural practices in terms of how they contribute to the "reproductive success of the species," or how they contribute to the gene pool of subsequent generations by boosting the number of surviving offspring produced in a particular population. In this view, behaviors and ideas that have reproductive advantages are more likely than others to be passed on to future generations. Biological determinists, for example, have provided an explanation for why human males apparently have "better" spatial skills than females. They say that these differences are the result of evolutionary selection because males with "better" spatial skills would have an advantage in securing both food and mates. Males with "better" spatial skills impregnate more females and have more offspring with "better" spatial skills.

Cultural constructionism, in contrast, maintains that human behavior and ideas are best explained as products of culturally shaped learning. In terms of the example of "better" male spatial skills, cultural constructionists would provide evidence that such skills are passed on culturally through learning, not genes. They would say that parents and teachers socialize boys and girls differently in spatial skills and are more likely to promote learning of certain kinds of spatial skills among boys. Though recognizing the role of biological factors such as genes and hormones, anthropologists who favor cultural construction and learning as an explanation for behaviors such as homicide and alcoholism point to childhood experiences and family roles as being perhaps even more important than genes or hormones. Most cultural anthropologists are cultural constructionists, but some connect biology and culture in their work.

INTERPRETIVE ANTHROPOLOGY VERSUS CULTURAL MATERIALISM Interpretive anthropology, or interpretivism, focuses on understanding culture by studying what people think about, their explanations of their lives, and the symbols that are important to them. For example, in understanding the eating habits of Hindus, interpretivists ask why Hindus do not eat beef. Hindus point to their religious beliefs, where cows are sacred and it is a sin to kill and eat them. Interpretivists accept this explanation as sufficient.

Cultural materialism attempts to learn about culture by first examining the material aspects of life: the natural environment and how people make a living within particular environments. Cultural materialists believe that these basic facts of life shape culture, even though people may not realize it. They use a three-level model to explain culture. The bottom level is *infrastructure*, a term that refers to basic material factors such as natural resources, the economy, and population.

(TOP) Traffic in the city of Varanasi (Banaras), northern India. Foreign visitors to India often comment that the presence of so many wandering cows is a sign of wastefulness and inefficiency. (BOTTOM) SUVs, trucks, and buses share the road in Los Angeles. SUVs are still popular in the United States in spite of their poor gas mileage.

▶ *If you were an energy policy maker, what lessons would you draw from this pair of photographs?*

According to this model, infrastructure tends to shape the other two domains of culture: *structure* (social organization, kinship, and political organization) and *superstructure* (ideas, values, and beliefs). This book's chapters are organized roughly in terms of these three categories, but with the recognition that the layers are not neat and tidy but have interconnections.

A cultural materialist explanation for the taboo on killing cows and eating beef involves the fact that cattle in India play a more important role alive than dead or carved into steaks (Harris 1974). The many cattle wandering the streets of Indian cities and villages look useless to Westerners. A closer analysis, however, shows that the seemingly useless population of bovines serves many useful functions. Ambling along, they eat paper trash and other edible refuse. Their excrement is "brown gold," useful as fertilizer or, when mixed with straw and formed into dried patties, as cooking fuel. Most important, farmers use cattle to plow fields. Cultural materialists take into account Hindu beliefs about the sacred meaning of cattle, but they see its relationship to the material value of cattle as symbolic protection, keeping these extremely useful animals out of the meat factory.

Some cultural anthropologists are strong interpretivists, whereas some are strong cultural materialists. Many combine the best of both views.

INDIVIDUAL AGENCY VERSUS STRUCTURISM

This debate concerns the question of how much individual will, or agency, affects the way people behave and think, compared with the power of forces, or *structures*, that are beyond individual control. Western philosophical thought gives much emphasis to the role of agency, the ability of individuals to make choices and exercise free will. In contrast, structurism emphasizes that free choice is an illusion because choices are structured by larger forces such as the economy, social and political organization, and ideological systems.

A prime example is the study of poverty. Those who emphasize agency focus their research on how individuals attempt to act as agents, even in situations of extreme poverty, in order to change their situation as best they can. Structurists, by contrast, would emphasize that the poor are trapped by large and powerful forces. They would describe how the political economy and other forces provide little room for agency for those at the bottom. An increasing number of cultural anthropologists seek to blend a structural perspective with attention to agency.

▣ ▣ ▣

Cultural Anthropology and Careers

Some of you reading this book may take only one anthropology course to satisfy a requirement. Others may become interested in the subject matter and take a few more. Some will decide to major or minor in anthropology. Just one course in anthropology may change your way of thinking about the world and your place in it. More than that, anthropology coursework may enhance your ability to get a job.

Majoring in Anthropology

An anthropology B.A. is a liberal arts degree. It is not, however, a professional degree, such as a business degree or a degree in physical therapy. It provides a solid education relevant to many career directions that are likely to require further study, such as law, criminal justice, medicine and health services, social services, education, humanitarian assistance, international development programs, and business. Students interested in pursuing a B.A. major in anthropology should know that anthropology is at least as useful as other liberal arts majors for either graduate study or a professional career.

Anthropology has several clear advantages over other liberal arts majors, and employers and graduate schools are increasingly recognizing these features. Cultural anthropology provides knowledge about the world's people and diversity. It offers insights about a variety of specialized research methods. Cross-cultural awareness and communication skills are valuable assets sought by business, government, health-care providers, and nongovernmental organizations.

The recurrent question is this: Will it be possible to get a good job related to anthropology with a B.A. in anthropology? The answer is yes, but it takes planning and hard work. Do the following: Gain expertise in at least one foreign language, study abroad, do service learning during your undergraduate years, and conduct an independent research project and write up the results as a professional report or conference paper. Package

these skills on your résumé so that they appear relevant to employers. Do not give up. Good jobs are out there, and coursework and skills in anthropology are increasingly valued.

Anthropology is also an excellent minor. It complements almost any other area of study by adding a cross-cultural perspective. For example, if you are majoring in music, courses about world music will enrich your primary interest. The same applies to subjects such as interior design, psychology, criminal justice, international affairs, economics, political science, and more.

Graduate Study in Anthropology

Some of you may go on to pursue a master's degree (M.A.) or doctoral degree (Ph.D.) in anthropology. If you do, here is some advice: Be passionate about your interest, but also be aware that a full-time job as a professor or as a professional anthropologist is not easy to get.

To expand your possibilities of getting a good job, it is wise to consider combining a professional skill or degree with your degree program in anthropology, such as a law degree, an M.A. degree in project management, a master of public health (M.P.H.), a certificate in disaster relief, or participation in a training program in conflict prevention and resolution.

Living an Anthropological Life

Studying cultural anthropology makes for smart people and people with breadth and flexibility. In North America, college graduates are likely to change careers (not just jobs, but careers) several times in their lives. Because you never know where you are going to end up working, or in what endeavor, it pays to be broadly informed about the world.

Cultural anthropology prompts you to ask original and important questions about the world's people and their relationships with one another, and it helps provide some useful answers.

Beyond career value, cultural anthropology will enrich your daily life by increasing your exposure to the world's cultures. When you pick up a newspaper, you will find several articles that connect with what you have learned in your anthropology classes. You will be able to view your own everyday life as culturally constructed in interesting and meaningful ways. You will be a different person, and you will live a richer life.

What is anthropology?

Anthropology is an academic discipline, like history or economics. It comprises four interrelated fields in its attempt to explore all facets of humanity from its origins through the present. Biological or physical anthropology is the study of humans as biological organisms, including their evolution and contemporary variation. Archaeology is the study of past human cultures through their material remains. Linguistic anthropology is the study of human communication, including its origins, history, and contemporary variation and change. Cultural anthropology is the study of living peoples and their cultures, including variation and change. Culture is people's learned and shared behaviors and beliefs.

Each field makes both theoretical and applied contributions. The perspective of this book is that applied anthropology, just like theoretical anthropology, should be an integrated and important part of all four fields, rather than a separate, fifth field. Examples of applied anthropology in the four fields include forensic anthropology, nonhuman primate conservation, global health programs, literacy programs for refugees, and social marketing.

What is cultural anthropology?

Cultural anthropology is the field within general anthropology that focuses on the study of contemporary humans and their cultures. It has several distinctive features that set it apart from the other fields of general anthropology and from other academic disciplines. The concept of cultural relativism, attributed to Franz Boas, is a guiding principle that other disciplines have widely adopted. Cultural anthropology values and works to sustain cultural diversity.

Culture is the key concept of cultural anthropology, and many definitions for it have been proposed throughout the history of anthropology. Many anthropologists define culture as learned and shared behavior and ideas, whereas others equate culture with ideas alone and exclude behavior as a part of culture. It is easier to understand culture by considering its characteristics: Culture is related to nature but is not the same as nature; it is based on symbols and it is learned; cultures are integrated within themselves; and cultures interact with other cultures and change. Four models of cultural interaction involve varying degrees of conflict, blending, and resistance. People participate in cultures of different levels, including local microcultures shaped by such factors as class, "race," ethnicity, indigeneity, gender, age, and institutions.

Cultural anthropology has a rich history of theoretical approaches and changing topical focuses. Three important theoretical debates are biological determinism versus cultural constructionism, interpretive anthropology versus cultural materialism, and individual agency versus structurism. Each, in its own way, attempts to understand and explain why people behave and think the way they do and to account for differences and similarities across cultures.

How is cultural anthropology relevant to a career?

Coursework in cultural anthropology expands one's awareness of the diversity of the world's cultures and the importance of cross-cultural understanding. Employers in many fields—such as public health, humanitarian aid, law enforcement, business, and education—increasingly value a degree in cultural anthropology. In today's diverse and connected world, being culturally informed and culturally sensitive is essential.

Graduate degrees in cultural anthropology, either at the M.A. or Ph.D. level, are even more likely to lead to professional positions that directly use your anthropological education and skills. Combining graduate coursework in anthropology with a professional degree, such as a master's degree in public health or public administration, or a law degree, is a successful route to a meaningful career outside academia. Cultural anthropology, beyond its career relevance, will enrich your life with its insights.

KEY CONCEPTS

SUGGESTED READINGS

Thomas J. Barfield, ed. *The Dictionary of Anthropology*. Malden, MA: Blackwell Publishing, 1997. This reference work contains hundreds of brief essays on concepts in anthropology, such as evolution, myth, functionalism, and applied anthropology, and on important anthropologists.

Stanley R. Barrett. *Anthropology: A Student's Guide to Theory and Method*. Toronto: University of Toronto Press, 2000. This book organizes the theoretical history of cultural anthropology into three phases and summarizes trends in each. The author discusses how to do research in cultural anthropology.

Mario Blaser, Harvey A. Feit, and Glenn McRae, eds. *In the Way of Development: Indigenous Peoples, Life Projects and Globalization*. New York: Zed Books, in association with the International Development Research Centre, 2004. Twenty chapters contributed by indigenous leaders, social activists, and cultural anthropologists address indigenous peoples' responses to capitalism and indigenous ideas about future change that is positive for them and for the environment.

Ira E. Harrison and Faye V. Harrison, eds. *African-American Pioneers in Anthropology*. Chicago: University of Illinois Press, 1999. This collection of intellectual biographies highlights the contributions of 13 African American anthropologists to the development of cultural anthropology in the United States.

Takami Kuwayama, ed. *Native Anthropology: The Japanese Challenge to Western Academic Hegemony*. Melbourne, Australia: Trans Pacific Press, 2004. The chapters in this book discuss various topics in Japanese anthropology, including "native anthropology," the marginalization of Asian anthropologists, folklore studies, and how U.S. anthropology textbooks present Japan.

James H. McDonald, ed. *The Applied Anthropology Reader*. Boston: Allyn and Bacon, 2002. This collection of over 50 brief essays explores topics in applied cultural anthropology, including ethics, methods, urban settings, health, international development, the environment, education, and business.

R. Bruce Morrison and C. Roderick Wilson, eds. *Native Peoples: The Canadian Experience*, 3rd ed. Toronto, Ontario: Oxford University Press, 2004. This sourcebook on Northern Peoples contains 26 chapters with sections divided by region. Chapters about various cultural groups provide historical context and updates on the current situation.

Thomas C. Patterson. *A Social History of Anthropology in the United States*. New York: Berg, 2001. This history of anthropology in the United States emphasizes the social and political context of the discipline and how that context has shaped theories and methods.

Richard J. Perry. *Five Key Concepts in Anthropological Thinking*. Upper Saddle River, NJ: Prentice-Hall, 2003. The five key concepts are evolution, culture, structure, function, and relativism. The author raises thought-provoking questions about anthropology as Eurocentric.

Pat Shipman. *The Evolution of Racism: Human Differences and the Use and Abuse of Science*. Cambridge, MA: Harvard University Press, 1994. This book offers a history of the "race" concept in Western thought from Darwin to contemporary DNA studies. The author addresses thorny issues such as racism in the United States and Nazi Germany's use of Darwinism.

For further information about topics covered in this chapter, go to MyAnthroLab at **www.myanthrolab.com** and access the following readings in MyAnthroLibrary:

Judah Gaby, Robert Aunger, Wolf-Peter Schmidt, Susan Michie, Stewart Granger, and Val Curtis. 2009. Experimental Pretesting of Hand-Washing Interventions in a Natural Setting. *American Journal of Public Health* 99(S2): 405–411. Val Curtis, medical anthropologist and public health expert, teamed up with five other researchers to measure fecal bacteria on the hands of over 400 people in five cities in the United Kingdom.

Neringa Klumbyte. 2010. The Soviet Sausage Renaissance. *American Anthropologist* 112(1):22–37. Lithuania was the first country to secede from the Soviet Union, and the word *Soviet* is used to refer to the vanished Soviet empire. In the past decade, however, there has been a "Soviet sausage" renaissance in Lithuania. Eating "Soviet sausages" in Lithuania is more complicated than you might think.

Pat Caplan. 2010. "Child Sacrifice" in Uganda? *Anthropology Today* 26(2):4–7. Insights from cultural anthropology suggest that the BBC inappropriately uses the terms "child sacrifice" and "witch doctor" in its *Newsnight* programs about Uganda, thus creating an inaccurate view.

◉ What do living nonhuman primates tell us about human culture?

◉ What role did culture play during hominin evolution?

◉ How has modern human culture changed in the past 12,000 years?

THE EVOLUTION OF HUMANITY AND CULTURE

2

◀ Two of the world's best ultra distance runners. Scott Jurek (left) is U.S. Western States 100 Mile Endurance Run and Badwater 135 Ultra Marathon Champion. Arnulfo Quimare (right), a Tarahumara Indian of Mexico, is the three-time winner of the Ultra Marathon de los Canyons. The running ability of the Tarahumara, who run barefoot or in sandals for long distances over rough terrain, has shaken up the running-shoe industry.

Scientific evidence indicates that modern humans have evolved from a shared lineage with our primate ancestors between 4 and 8 million years ago. But this view is quite recent, dating only from the mid-nineteenth century, when a turning point in European thinking about human origins based on science challenged the biblical narrative of human origins. Two British thinkers, Charles Darwin and Alfred Russel Wallace, independently discovered the principle of **natural selection**, the process by which organisms better adapted to the environment reproduce more effectively compared to less well-adapted forms. This principle, in turn, supported the acceptance of the concept of **evolution**, or inherited and cumulative change in the characteristics of a species, population, or culture.

The scientific view conflicts with some religious perspectives, including Christian *creationism*, based on a literal understanding of biblical writings, that all animal species, including humans, date from the Day of Creation and have always existed in the physical form that they do now. The scientific view of human origins, however, does not conflict with all religious perspectives, including nonliteralist Christians and Buddhists.

Fossils (the preserved remains of a plant or animal of the past), **artifacts** (portable objects made or modified by humans), and new genetic analyses provide strong evidence that modern humans existed before the Christian Day of Creation, estimated to be 4004 BCE. The evidence also shows that human anatomy evolved over time from more ape-like to more human-like, and human cultural capabilities have changed dramatically. Many anthropologists, like other scientists, find ways to reconcile the scientific evidence with their personal religious beliefs.

This chapter accepts the scientific perspective on human evolution. It therefore begins with a discussion of our closest living relatives and how they provide insights into the lives of the earliest human ancestors. It then turns to a description of the main stages in evolution to modern humans. The last section covers the development of settled life, agriculture, and cities and states.

⊡ ⊡ ⊡

Nonhuman Primates and the Roots of Human Culture

According to abundant evidence from genetics, anatomy, physiology, and behavior, humans are *primates*. This section describes primate characteristics in general and then situates humans within the group of primate with whom we are most closely related in order to provide some comparisons.

Primate Characteristics

The **primates** are an order of mammals that includes modern humans. Primates vary in size from several ounces to more than 400 pounds. Some inhabit limited areas, and others range more widely. In defining primate characteristics, *morphology*, or physical form, is a basic consideration because it is related to behavior. Compared to the faces of other mammals such as dogs or cows, primate faces tend to be flat with reduced snouts. Relatedly, primates differ from other mammals in terms of being highly reliant on vision for dealing with their environment and social interactions. Primates have five digits on their hands and feet, opposable thumbs, and they can grasp with both their hands and feet. Primate brains are large in relation to body size. Because of their large brain size, primates take longer to mature than other mammals do. This extended developmental period, combined with the fact that most primate species are highly social, provides a context for the social molding of primate behavior.

In terms of environmental adaptations, most nonhuman primate species live in low-altitude areas of the tropics or subtropics (Map 2.1). A few live in high altitudes in Africa, Nepal, and Japan. Most primate species are *arboreal* (tree-dwelling), *quadrupedal* (moving on all fours), and *diurnal* (active during the day), and most, like humans, have a high degree of **sociality**, or a preference for living in groups and interacting regularly with members of the same species.

MAP 2.1 Where Nonhuman Primates Live Today.

Members of a group of Hanuman langurs in India involved in social behavior. Most primates are highly social and interact with their group-mates in complex ways.

All nonhuman primates in the wild provide for their food needs by **foraging**, or obtaining food available in nature through gathering, hunting, or scavenging. Species vary, however, in terms of the kinds of foods they prefer (Strier 2007). Five major dietary patterns of primates are based on their primary food sources:

- *Frugivores* eat mainly fruit. They have large front teeth, or incisors, to allow them to puncture the flesh of large fruits and transfer pieces into their mouths, like when you bite into an apple. Digestion of fruits occurs in the small intestine, so frugivores have a long small intestine.

- *Folivores* eat primarily leaves. Leaves are difficult to digest because of the chemicals, such as cellulose, in their walls. Folivores' chewing teeth are designed to help them break leaves into small pieces, and bacteria in their digestive systems break down the cell walls of leaves. Some folivores have an expanded large intestine (Milton 1984).

- *Insectivores* eat mainly insects. They have high, sharp cusps on their molar teeth to puncture and break up the insects' hard covering. The contents of insects are quite easy to digest, so insectivores have short and simple guts. Insects are difficult to catch, so the limited food sources mean that insectivores are small-bodied.

- *Gummivores* have a diet that relies on the gums and saps of trees. Some have protruding lower incisors that they use to gouge the outer layer of trees to start the flow of gums and saps. Many have large intestines to help them digest these food sources.

- *Omnivores* are generalists: many kinds of foods make up their diet. Therefore, they lack specialized dental or gut morphology. Humans are omnivores.

Most primates live in a *social group*, or collection of animals that interact regularly. Group life has advantages in terms of information sharing about food sources and protection against threats from other groups. The details of group organization vary. The most common social group among nonhuman primates, by far, is the *multi-male/multi-female (MM/MF) group*. This type of group contains adults of both sexes and the females' offspring. Females make up the core of the group and often have strong alliances with each other. Male membership in these groups is less stable. A rare subvariety is called a *fission-fusion group*, a large group of 50 or more individuals that regularly breaks up into much smaller subgroups for foraging. Although rare among nonhuman primate species overall, the fission-fusion pattern is important because it is found in chimpanzees and bonobos, the nonhuman

natural selection   the process by which organisms better adapted to the environment reproduce more effectively compared with less well-adapted forms.

evolution   inherited and cumulative change in the characteristics of a species, population, or culture.

fossil   the preserved remains of a plant or animal of the past.

artifact   a portable object made or modified by humans.

primates   an order of mammals that includes modern humans.

sociality   the preference for living in groups and interacting regularly with members of the same species.

foraging   obtaining food available in nature through gathering, hunting, or scavenging.

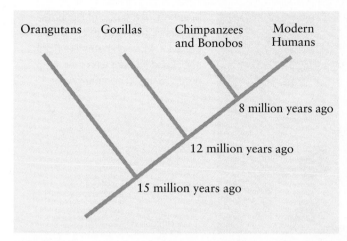

FIGURE 2.1 The Great Apes, Including Modern Humans.

primates most like humans. Thus it is possible that the early human ancestors may have had a fission-fusion form of social organization.

Complex communication and signaling systems are another key feature of nonhuman primate behavior that enables individuals to exist in stable groups. Primates communicate through smell, touch, visual, and vocal channels. The facial muscles of most primates allow for a wider range of expressions compared to other mammals. Primates use facial expressions to communicate threats and fear and to facilitate courtship, play, grooming, and post-conflict reconciliation.

The Great Apes

According to genetic data, modern humans are closely related to the living great apes with whom we shared a *common ancestor* between 4 and 8 million years ago (Figure 2.1). The term **great apes** refers to a category of large, tailless primates that includes the orangutans, gorillas, chimpanzees, bonobos, and humans. All great ape species are considered to be endangered in the wild.

Since our last common ancestor with the other great apes, the human line diverged in two significant ways:

- Human anatomy evolved with an emphasis on habitual locomotion on two legs and much larger brains.

- Humans developed culture, including verbal language, to a more complex degree.

In spite of the many differences between humans and the other great apes, the great apes provide insights into what the lives and behavior of early human ancestors might have been like.

Apes differ from other primates in the absence of a tail, larger brains relative to body size, and the tendency to travel by brachiation. All apes, including humans, are capable of **brachiation**, a form of arboreal travel, using the forelimbs to swing from branch to branch, related to changes in the shoulder anatomy and distinct to apes (Figure 2.2). Apes are typically frugivores, but they eat a variety of other foods, including insects such as termites. Mountain gorillas eat mainly leaves and stalks.

Orangutans are the only Asian great ape. Their habitats are now limited to portions of the islands of Borneo and Sumatra in Southeast Asia (Map 2.2). *Sexual dimorphism* in body size (difference in size between males and females) is marked, with the weight of an adult male (175–200 pounds) roughly double that of an adult female (73–99 pounds). In spite of their large size, however, orangutans are mainly arboreal. Orangutans are frugivorous and spend substantial amounts of time each day locating and consuming food. They are the most solitary of the great apes. When ripe fruit is abundant, however, orangutans congregate temporarily. The only constant social unit is that of a mother and her offspring. A mother and offspring forage together, and mothers often transfer food to immature offspring who solicit food, especially food that is difficult to process (Jaeggi, van Noordwijk, and van Schaik 2008). Orangutans in Sumatra make simple tools from branches that they use for termite and ant fishing. An adult male's territory overlaps the home ranges of several females and is defended from other males. Adult males use large air sacs on their necks to make loud bellowing noises so that they can locate, and usually avoid, each other. The primate line leading to humans split with the orangutans about 15 million years ago.

Gorillas, the largest of the living primates, live in sub-Saharan Africa. Gorillas eat a wide variety of plants, up to 200 species, and supplement their plant diet with termites and ants.

FIGURE 2.2 Brachiation in Action.

Orangutan mother and juvenile in Tanjung Puting National Park on the island of Borneo, Indonesia. DNA evidence suggests that, if the continued loss of their habitat persists, orangutans may be extinct 50 years from now. The most immediate threats include the expansion of palm-oil agriculture, illegal logging, and poaching.

Like orangutans, gorillas have a high degree of sexual dimorphism in body size. In the wild, adult male gorillas weigh between 350 and 400 pounds, whereas adult females weigh between 150 and 200 pounds. Gorillas often live in social groups composed of a single male and multiple females with the females' dependent offspring. Males compete with each other intensely for access to the females. Although they live primarily in dense forests, gorillas are largely terrestrial, adult males especially

---

great apes a category of large and tail-less primates that includes orangutans, gorillas, chimpanzees, bonobos, and humans.

brachiation arboreal travel, using the forelimbs to swing from branch to branch, that is distinct to apes.

knuckle-walking a form of terrestrial travel that involves walking flat-footed while supporting the upper body on the front of fingers bent beyond the knuckle.

MAP 2.2 **Orangutan Regions in Malaysia and Indonesia.** Orangutans are the only great apes living outside Africa. Fossil evidence indicates that their habitats in the past extended throughout Southeast Asia and southern China. They are now limited to pockets of rainforest on the islands of Sumatra and Borneo.

so because of their large body size. They are quadrupedal and travel using a locomotor pattern called **knuckle-walking**. Knuckle-walking is a form of terrestrial travel that involves walking flat-footed while supporting the upper body on the front of fingers bent beyond the knuckle. The human line split with the gorillas about 12 million years ago.

Chimpanzees and bonobos, who live in sub-Saharan Africa, are the great apes most closely related to humans. Chimpanzees are found in several locations in West, Central, and East Africa. Bonobos live only in the Democratic Republic of Congo. Several chimpanzee populations in conservation areas are somewhat protected from human hunting. Because no bonobo population has such protection, they are more heavily hunted and even more endangered.

Compared to orangutans and gorillas, chimpanzees and bonobos are smaller and exhibit less sexual dimorphism in body size. In the wild, adult males weigh between 75 and 150 pounds, adult females between 60 and 100 pounds. Chimpanzees and bonobos are more arboreal than gorillas, but like gorillas, they are knuckle-walkers when on the ground. They are frugivores but occasionally eat other food, including insects, vegetation, and small animals such as monkeys. Chimpanzees in Senegal, for example, consume termites year round and derive substantial calories and nutrients from them (Bogart and Pruetz 2008), a finding that suggests the possibility of termites as an important part of the diet of early human ancestors.

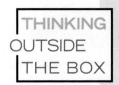

THINKING OUTSIDE THE BOX

What are the main forms of social groups in your microculture? What social groups do you belong to, how did you join, and what holds the group together?

An adult male silverback gorilla knuckle-walking.

▶ *Practice knuckle-walking across a room and consider the role of arm-to-leg length in this form of locomotion.*

Chimpanzees and bonobos spend 25 percent of their time in social interactions, compared with 10 percent for the other great apes, except for humans (Sussman and Garber 2004). Grooming is the major form of social interaction, with most of the interactions occurring between mothers and offspring.

Although chimpanzees and bonobos are alike in many ways, primatologists are also interested in the differences between them and which is the better model for the early human ancestors (Figure 2.3). Bonobos are similar in size to chimpanzees, but they have less sexual dimorphism in body size, so they are more like humans in this respect. Bonobos use two-legged, upright locomotion more than chimpanzees, again appearing more like humans. In terms of diet, both chimpanzees and bonobos hunt and eat small animals, though bonobos hunt less frequently than chimpanzees. Given the diversity in human dietary preferences, which range from veganism to eating meat, it is impossible to speculate on which animal is the better model for early humans on this dimension. Evidence of animal carcass butchery during several stages of hominin evolution suggests that animal protein was an important part of the diet.

Chimpanzees live in large, fluid groups of 50 to 60 individuals, but the entire group is rarely, if ever, together in one area. Subgroups form, dissolve, and reform, sometimes with different members. Adult males often travel together, whereas adult females travel with their offspring. In contrast to many other primate species, chimpanzees are *patrilocal*, a residence pattern in which males stay in their birth group throughout their lives. Females leave their birth group at reproductive age, between 10 and 15 years, to join a new group. Therefore, the core of the large social group is biologically related males, or

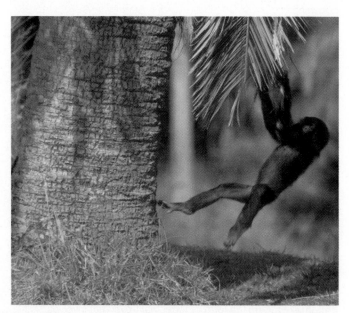

Chimpanzees and bonobos exhibit many examples of cultural behavior including tool use and non-utilitarian activities such as play. (LEFT) A chimpanzee using a stone hammer to crack open a nut. (RIGHT) A bonobo juvenile at play.

Chimpanzees	Bonobos
Terrestrial and arboreal	Terrestrial, more erect posture
Frequent tool users	Little observed tool use
More hunting and meat-eating	Occasional hunting and meat-eating
Hunting by males	Hunting by males and females
Male dominance over females	Female dominance over males
Males share meat	Females share fruit and sometimes meat
Infanticide documented	No infanticide observed
Frequent intergroup aggression	Infrequent intergroup aggression
Less frequent sexual behavior	Frequent sexual behavior
Male–female sexual interactions	Prolific sexual interactions between males and females and same-sex

FIGURE 2.3 Chimpanzee/Bonobo Differences.

Source: Derived from Stanford 1998 and comments by Frans B. M. de Waal, Barbara Fruth, Kano Takayoshi, and William C. McGrew

"gangs," that seek food or defend territory. Sometimes the gangs go outside their home range to seek out and kill members of a neighboring group.

Like chimpanzees, bonobos are patrilocal, but a difference is that migrant bonobo females develop strong alliances with females in their new group, forming *matrifocal* social groups centered on one or more adult female. In contrast to chimpanzees, adult female bonobos dominate the control of food distribution, and males solicit their attention by offering them choice food items. Bonobo social organization is related to the fact that they eat more vegetation, which is common and abundant, than chimpanzees do. Females spend less time foraging and have more time to establish and maintain social ties.

Bonobos have the highest rates of sexual contact of all nonhuman primates. Sexual contact occurs among all possible sex and age combinations, although rarely between close relatives. Bonobo reproductive rates, nonetheless, are similar to those found among chimpanzees. Bonobos thus have high rates of social or recreational sex, and this pattern is related to lower rates of conflict compared to chimpanzees. Bonobos use sexual contact to prevent conflict and to resolve post-conflict situations. Attractive food, or anything of interest to more than one bonobo, sparks sexual interest. The two bonobos will suspend potential competition for the item of interest and briefly mount each other or participate in what primatologists refer to as *G-G rubbing*, or genital–genital rubbing (de Waal and Lanting 1997:109). G-G rubbing is unique to bonobos and may qualify as a cultural innovation. This activity appears to distract the two parties and reframe the relationship as one of alliance and cooperation rather than competition and conflict. In one example of conflict prevention, when one mother struck another mother's infant, the two females participated in intense G-G rubbing rather than hostility, and peace was the outcome.

Current genetic evidence indicates that chimpanzees and bonobos are equally close to modern humans. Behavioral evidence prompts some scholars to argue that chimpanzees are the better model given human patterns of male dominance and high levels of intergroup violence (Wrangham and Peterson 1996). A bonobo model would suggest, in contrast, that humanity's biological heritage includes a propensity for being sexually active, female-centric, and peaceful. Neither model fits all modern human cultures. After all, our lineages split between 4 and 8 million years ago, and much has happened since then in terms of human evolution.

Nonhuman Primate Culture

Culture has long been thought to be unique to humans and their recent ancestors. Increasing evidence, however, indicates that animals other than humans have aspects of culture. In primatology, *culture* is defined as behavior that is learned (not innate) and shared (not individual). Increasing evidence that nonhuman primates have aspects of culture provides increased support for conservation of their environments and their preservation as a species (see Anthropology Works on page 36).

In the 1950s, Japanese primatologists first raised the possibility of nonhuman primate culture (Kawamura 1959). Their findings emerged from a long-term study of macaques, a variety of Old World monkeys, on the island of Koshima, Japan (see Map 3.2, page 64). In order to lure the macaques into areas where they could be observed easily, the researchers provided sweet potatoes on the beach. Soon, an adult female monkey, whom they named Imo, began carrying the potatoes from the beach to a pool of fresh water to wash the sand from the potatoes before eating them. Some of Imo's relatives began to do the same thing, and the behavior spread throughout much of her group.

Later, the primatologists provisioned the monkeys with rice in order to keep them in open areas for longer periods of time. They thought it would take the monkeys a long time to

ANTHROPOLOGY works

Saving Orangutans

Primatologist Biruté Galdikas (pronounced beer-OOH-tay GAL-dee-kas) first went to Indonesia to study orangutans in 1971 (Galdikas 1995). She soon became aware of the threat to the orangutans from local people who capture them for sale to zoos around the world. The poachers separate the young from their mothers, often killing the mothers in the process.

Orangutan juveniles are highly dependent on their mothers, maintaining close bodily contact with them for at least two years and nursing until they are around eight years old. Because of this long period of orangutans' need for maternal contact, Galdikas set up her camp to serve as a way station for orphans. She became the maternal figure. Her first "infant" was an orphaned orangutan, Sugito, who clung to her as though she were its own mother for years.

The survival of orangutans on Borneo and Sumatra (their only habitats worldwide) is critically endangered by massive commercial logging and illegal logging, population resettlement programs, plantations, and other pressures on the rainforests where the orangutans live. A rainforest is an environment, found at mid-latitudes, of tall, broadleaf evergreen trees, with annual rainfall of 400 centimeters (or 60 inches) and no dry season.

Galdikas has devoted her life to orangutan preservation. She says, "I feel like I'm viewing an animal holocaust, and holocaust is not a word I use lightly . . . The destruction of the tropical rainforest is accelerating daily" (Dreifus 2000:D3). During the twentieth century, the orangutan population experienced a huge decrease, from an estimated 315,000 in 1900 to 44,000 in 2000 (IUCN/SSC Conservation Breeding Specialist Group 2004). Aerial surveys (Ancrenaz et al. 2005) and DNA analysis of living orangutans (Goossens et al. 2006) confirm recent and dramatic declines that, if not halted, will lead to extinction of the animal in the next few decades.

Galdikas has studied orangutans longer than anyone else has. She links her knowledge of and love for the orangutans with applied anthropology and advocacy on their behalf. Since the beginning of her fieldwork in Borneo, she has maintained and expanded the Camp Leakey field site and research center (named after her mentor, Lewis Leakey, who inspired her research on orangutans). She cofounded the Orangutan Foundation International, which has several chapters worldwide. She has published many scholarly articles and given public talks around the world on her research. Educating the public about the imminent danger to the orangutans is an important part of her activism. Galdikas and other orangutan experts are lobbying international institutions such as the World Bank to promote forest conservation as part of their loan agreements.

Camp Leakey employs many local people in diverse roles, including antipoaching guards. The OFI sponsors study tours to Borneo for

Primatologist Biruté Galdikas has been studying orangutans in Borneo, Indonesia, for over three decades.

international students and opportunities for them to contribute to conservation efforts.

The success of Galdikas's activism depends on her deep knowledge of orangutans. Over the decades, she has filled thousands of notebooks with her observations of orangutan behavior, along with such details about their habitat as the fruiting times of different species of trees. A donor recently gave software and funding for staff to analyze the raw data (Hawn 2002). The findings will indicate how much territory is needed to support a viable orangutan population and will ultimately facilitate conservation policy and planning.

FOOD FOR THOUGHT ▼
Some people claim that science should not be linked with advocacy because it will create biases in research. Others say that scientists have an obligation to use their knowledge for good causes. Where do you stand in this debate and why?

---

work out how to sort rice grains from beach sand. But Imo promptly started dropping handfuls of sandy rice into the fresh water pools. The sand sank and the rice floated, making it possible for her to collect sand-free rice grains. This practice, too, spread throughout much of the group, especially among younger individuals. The behaviors of Imo and her group, being learned and shared, conform to the definition of nonhuman primate culture.

Comparative studies shed more light on the question of primate culture. Primatologists look for behavioral differences among primates of the same species at different field sites with similar environmental conditions. Comparison of data from seven chimpanzee research sites in East Africa and West Africa revealed 39 differences in tool use, grooming, and other social behaviors that can be explained only as the result of cultural differences and social learning (Whiten et al. 1999). The tools include hammers and anvils for cracking open nuts, probes for antfishing, leaves to sit on, and sticks to fan away flies. Male chimpanzees in some groups in Uganda regularly use leaves to clean their penises after sexual intercourse (O'Hara and Lee 2006).

All great apes build sleeping nests made of twigs and leaves. Comparison of nest-building between chimpanzees in two sites in Senegal (see Map 15.4, page 370), West Africa, reveals that this behavior is an adaptation to threats from predators (Pruetz et al. 2008). The natural environment in both study sites is similar, but the threat level from animal predators differs. In the site where the threat from predators is higher, the chimpanzees build nests in trees at higher levels than in the area where predation is a lesser threat. Building a nest several feet high in a tree requires planning and dealing with problems such as finding materials, transporting them to the nest site, and making sure the nest structure will hold.

Young primates learn cultural behaviors by watching adults. Beyond learning, however, invention also occurs. For three decades, Japanese primatologists have been observing chimpanzees using tools in Bossou, Guinea, West Africa (Yamamoto et al. 2008). But it was only in 2003 that they saw one youthful male, named JJ, transfer his considerable skills at using a stick to retrieve ants on the ground to obtaining them in trees. For the new activity, JJ had to adapt his tools by using a shorter stick. No immigrant chimpanzees had come into the area, so JJ came up with this new approach on his own. Future research is needed to show whether JJ's innovation will spread to others in his group.

Cultural variation in chimpanzee social interaction and communication includes the *grooming hand clasp*, or holding the arm of another individual over his or her head during grooming (McGrew 2004). This greeting occurs in only some groups. Some chimpanzees do a slow bodily display, or "rain-dance," at the start of rain, while others seem able to predict the spread of fires (Pruetz and LaDuke 2008).

A Japanese macaque washing a sweet potato. Sweet potato–washing is an example of nonhuman primate cultural behavior.

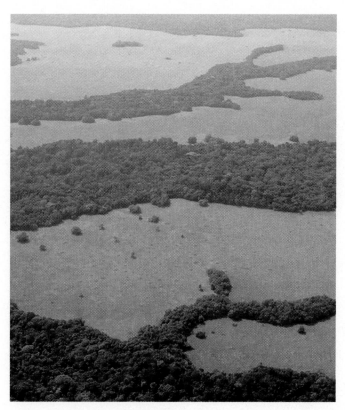

When the early hominins were evolving in Africa, the environment was changing from dense forest to patches of woodland interspersed with grasslands, called savanna.

▶ *How might this type of environment be related to the evolution of bipedalism?*

These intriguing examples suggest how the earliest human ancestors began to develop culture as a key form of adaptation to various environments. In addition to a fruit-based diet, early human ancestors may have regularly eaten insects such as termites. They may have built nests high in trees to protect themselves from predators. They probably lived in flexible social groups and experienced occasional within-group and across-group conflict. They probably had symbolic forms of communication and understanding of their natural environment and its hazards.

▣ ▣ ▣

Hominin Evolution to Modern Humans

This section provides an overview of the several extinct species of early humans with attention to changes in anatomy (physical structure of the body) and culture. **Hominins** is a category of primates that includes modern humans and

hominins a category of primates that includes modern humans and extinct species of early human ancestors that are more closely related to humans than to living chimpanzees and bonobos.

MAP 2.3 Sites of Early Hominins and Archaic *Homo* in Africa.

extinct species of early human ancestors that are more closely related to humans than to living chimpanzees and bonobos. The main hominin evidence includes fossils, artifacts, and new evidence from the growing field of DNA analysis.

The Early Hominins

In the first stage of separation from the other great apes, beginning between 8 to 4 million years ago, all early hominins lived in Africa. These hominins are anatomically distinct from other apes in three ways: changes to the pelvis and lower limbs related to habitual **bipedalism** or upright locomotion on two feet, larger brains, and smaller teeth. These characteristics were probably associated with other important changes including culture, but no direct evidence exists in this area.

TWO EARLIEST SPECIES   The oldest known hominin fossil is *Sahelanthropus tchadensis* (Brunet et al. 2002). Dated to between 7 and 6 million years ago, this fossil was discovered in Toros-Menalla in Chad (Map 2.3). Its discovery is important because it dramatically extends the regional pattern of fossil evidence for the early era beyond eastern and southern Africa into central/western Africa Thus, the early hominins must

This fossil, discovered by a Chad-French team of paleoanthropologists, is nicknamed Toumaï, which means "a much-wanted child born after a long wait." The cranium of Toumaï is a mixture of features. Its dimensions suggest a chimpanzee-sized brain, but it has heavy brow ridges like hominins.

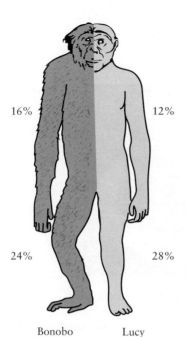

FIGURE 2.4 Lucy's Body Weight Proportions Compared to a Bonobo. Primatologist Adrienne Zihlman found that living bonobos are similar to Lucy in body-weight proportions. Lucy's arms are 12 percent of her body weight and her legs are 28 percent. In bonobos, arms are 16 percent of body weight, and legs 24 percent. This pattern of weight distribution indicates partial bipedal locomotion.

Source: Adapted from an original drawing by Carla Simmons in Sussman 1984:197

have occupied a much wider area of Africa than paleoanthropologists previously thought.

The second oldest primitive hominin species is *Orrorin tugenensis*, named for some fossils found in the Tugen Hills of Kenya that date to 6 million years ago (Senut et al. 2001). While only a few fossils have been found for this species, the collection does include a femur (thighbone). Analysis of its shape and strength indicates bipedalism (Richmond and Jungers 2008).

THE AUSTRALOPITHECINES **Australopithecines** refers to a category of several extinct species of hominins found in East and Central Africa that lived between roughly 4 million and 2 million years ago. Compared to the earliest hominins discussed above, the fossil evidence for this group is relatively rich. "Lucy," the most famous hominin fossil in the world, was found in Hadar, Ethiopia (Johanson 2004). She belongs to the species *Australopithecus afarensis*, which lived from 4.3 million to 3 million years ago. The 1974 discovery of Lucy made headlines because so much of her skeleton was preserved (Figure 2.4).

The australopithecine era is also notable because it provides the first stone tools. The oldest, dated to 2.6 million years ago, are from Gona, Ethiopia (Semaw et al. 2003).

SUMMARY OF THE EARLY HOMININS The anatomy of these early species exhibits evolution away from ape-like characteristics to more human-like characteristics.

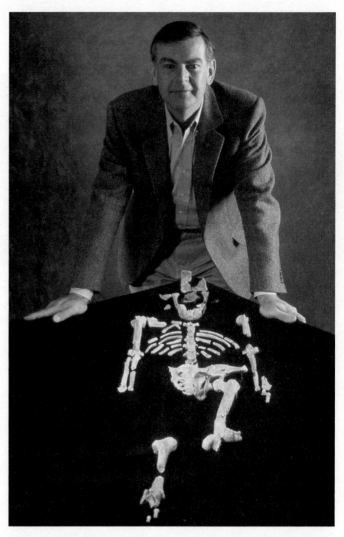

Lucy and Don Johanson, the paleoanthropologist who discovered her. Because they have fossils of about 40 percent of Lucy's skeleton, researchers can make fairly accurate estimates about her stature, body weight, and other characteristics. She was both bipedal and arboreal.

Most would have been around 4 feet tall when standing upright and would have weighed around 100 pounds. Their arms were slightly longer than those of modern humans, and the shortness of their lower limbs would have made them look more like apes than like humans.

Orrorin tugenensis is the earliest fossil evidence for bipedalism, and later fossils such as Lucy confirm the trend, as do the footprints at Laetoli. It is less clear, however, when the early hominins abandoned knuckle-walking or brachiation for complete bipedalism. Although early hominins such as Lucy had a lower body that was fully designed for bipedalism, they retained some aspects of shoulder and upper limb anatomy

---

bipedalism upright locomotion on two feet.

australopithecines a category of several extinct hominin species found in East and Central Africa that lived between 4.5 and 3 million years ago.

CRITICAL thinking

What Is Really in the Toolbox?

It is reasonable to assume that stone tools were not the only tools that archaic *Homo* used, given that other materials were available for tools and a wider variety of uses existed than the probable functions of core tools, flakes, and scrapers.

This exercise asks you to do a mini-experimental study by imagining that you are living in an open woodland environment like that of archaic *Homo*. Imagine your daily life, including how you obtain food and where you sleep at night.

An experimental archaeologist uses a newly made stone tool to cut raw meat.

CRITICAL THINKING QUESTIONS ▼

- Make a list of the activities you would perform over a 24-hour period and what tools you might need for those activities.
- What materials in the savanna would provide useful tools for performing these activities?
- Assume you have 10 tools in your tool kit. Three of them are made from stone: one core tool and two flake tools. What are the other seven tools? What is the likelihood that these other seven tools would be preserved in the archaeological record?

---

suggesting that they were also arboreal, allowing them to seek protection in trees. This combination could have given them a decisive advantage over other animals. Scholars have proposed many theories for the emergence of upright posture and bipedalism (O'Higgins and Elton 2007, Thorpe et al. 2007). One prominent theory holds that upright posture and bipedalism evolved in response to climate change that reduced the areas of dense rainforest and led to increased savannas. A **savanna** environment consists of open plains with tall grasses and patches of trees. Upright posture would have enabled hominins to see other animals and more effectively protect themselves from predators.

Early hominins acquired food through foraging. Their diet was mixed, including a wide variety of fruits, insects, nuts, tubers (fleshy roots of plants), and some animal meat, which was probably scavenged rather than hunted.

Some early hominins made and used simple stone tools. Given that stone tool-making traditions were learned and shared, the early hominins possessed elements of culture.

ARCHAIC *HOMO* **Archaic *Homo*** is a category of extinct hominin species that lived from 2.4 million years to 17,000 years ago, an impressive span of time. Compared to the early hominins, these species have a more modern human-like body shape, larger brains, and smaller jaws and teeth. Stone tools are prominent in the culture of all archaic *Homo* species. They migrated into much of the Old World. Paleoanthropologists argue about whether they are ancestors to modern humans. Some say they all died out, whereas others say they interbred with later species. There is no conclusive proof to support either position at this time.

Homo habilis In Olduvai Gorge, Tanzania, in 1960, Louis and Mary Leakey discovered fossils representing a form they thought was human-like. They argued that the Olduvai evidence should be included in the genus *Homo* because it satisfied the accepted functional criteria of manual dexterity, upright posture, and fully bipedal locomotion. They argued for naming a new species called *Homo habilis* (literally "Handy Human") (Leakey et al. 1964). Associated with *H. habilis* are distinctive stone tools that are named Oldowan because they were first found in Olduvai Gorge.

The **Oldowan tradition** is characterized by *core tools* and *flake tools*. Core tools are made from rounded stones that have had flakes chipped off them, either at one end or along one side. Flake tools are more numerous than core tools. Flake tools are the sharp pieces of stone that break off a core when it is struck. It is unlikely that Oldowan stone tools were the only tools used by their makers. Rather, they were the tools that survived in the archaeological record because they were made of hard stone (see Critical Thinking).

Homo erectus *Homo erectus* ("Upright Human") is the first hominin species that was widely distributed across the Old World. *H. erectus* was a highly successful species in terms of duration, over 2 million years, and in terms of its colonization of much of the Old World.

The average brain size of *H. erectus* was about 1,000 centimeters, or two-thirds the size of the average modern human brain. If you met one of these individuals, you would not mistake him or her for a modern human because of the small head, low forehead, and pronounced brow ridge.

H. erectus is associated with the emergence, around 1.7 million years ago, of a new stone tool tradition called the **Acheulian tradition**, characterized by the prevalence of handaxes (Toth and Schick 1993). A *handaxe* is a two-sided stone tool that is flat, pear-shaped, and flaked on all its edges and on both surfaces. The Acheulian tradition is named after a site in St. Acheul, France, where European archaeologists first discovered handaxes. The oldest Acheulian stone tools are from Ethiopia and Kenya. Acheulian tools, compared to Oldowan tools, were more finely crafted and consistently shaped, indicating more manual dexterity, skill, and planning.

ARCHAIC *HOMO* MOVES OUT OF AFRICA   Around 2 million years ago, archaic *Homo* began to migrate out of Africa. The question of why archaic *Homo* left Africa remains unanswered. Three hypotheses exist:

- Hominins had become meat-eaters, and their preference for meat led them to follow herds of animals as they moved out of Africa to new areas.

MAP 2.4   Dmanisi, Georgia.
The country of Georgia has the distinction of being the site of 1.7 million-year-old hominin fossils found at Dmanisi. Many thousands of years later, during the Neolithic era, modern humans first domesticated grapes and produced wine in this region.

- They were attracted by the cool and arid northern climate, where their ability to adapt to varied conditions gave them an advantage over other species.
- Humans are "natural" migrants—they just have to keep moving.

No matter what the reason for leaving Africa, the general direction of migration was north and east, out of Africa toward the Middle East and then on into Asia. The earliest fossil evidence of hominins outside Africa, dated at 1.8 million years ago, comes from the site of Dmanisi (dih-muh-NEE-see) in the Caucasus region of Georgia (Vekua et al. 2002) (Map 2.4). Dmanisi hominins are small in stature. Their brains are also small, around 600 centimeters, or not much larger than the average brain size of the Australopithecines. Yet their limb proportions are more modern, and they obviously had the capacity for long-distance travel. The stone tools at Dmanisi are core and flake tools, similar to the Oldowan tool kit.

After Dmanisi, a large geographical gap exists as to where *H. erectus* went. Some evidence indicates that *H. erectus*

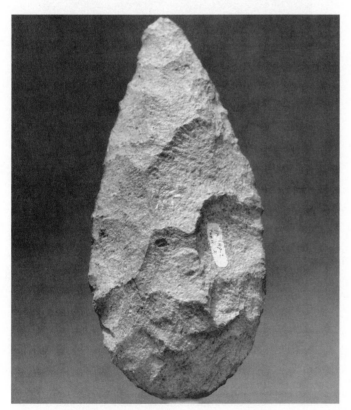

Acheulian handaxe from Tanzania.

▶ *Imagine that you are gripping the widest part in your hand, with the narrow part pointing horizontal or downward, cutting through tree bark or striking at an attacking hyena.*

savanna   an environment that consists of open plains with tall grasses and patches of trees.

archaic *Homo*   a category of several extinct hominin species that lived from 2.4 million years to 19,000 years ago and is characterized by different stone tool traditions, depending on the species.

Oldowan tradition   the oldest hominin tool kit, characterized by core tools and flake tools.

Acheulian tradition   the tool kit of *H. erectus*, used from 1.7 million years ago to 300,000 years ago and characterized by handaxes.

MAP 2.5 Hominin Sites on Islands of Indonesia.
Since the early twentieth century, paleoanthropologists and archaeologists have made important hominin discoveries at several island sites in Indonesia, including Java and Flores. This research demonstrates that early human ancestors were living in this part of the world earlier than anyone had suspected and had sophisticated nautical abilities.

reached Java, in Southeast Asia, as early as 1.8 million years ago (Swisher et al. 1994). How they got to Java is a mystery because there was no land bridge at the time (Map 2.5).

Homo floresiensis Another Asian puzzle is the discovery of a dwarf-sized hominin species, nicknamed the "Hobbit," found on the island of Flores in Indonesia (Map 2.5). The Hobbit's ancestors arrived over one million years ago (Dalton 2010). They survived until around 17,000 years ago. This hominin was just over 3 feet tall, stood upright, and was probably bipedal (Morwood et al. 2004, Brown et al. 2004). Its brain size was small. Stone tools found with the fossils, however, are like those of modern humans who had much larger brains. Scientists have debated whether the Hobbit is a separate species of archaic *Homo* or whether it is a pathologically dwarfed modern human from the recent past. Most current evidence indicates that the Hobbit is a legitimate archaic *Homo* species. Yet, these questions remain: How did a hominin with such a small brain get to Flores? How did it produce modern-style stone tools? How did it survive until recent times?

THE NEANDERTHALS *Homo neanderthalensis*, informally referred to as Neanderthals, was first discovered in a site in Germany called Neanderthal. It is known from more than a hundred sites spread across most of Europe, into what is now Israel and Iraq, and all the way into Siberia (see Map 2.6

Mousterian tradition the tool kit of the Neanderthals, characterized by small, light, and more specialized flake tools, such as points, scrapers, and awls.

Artist's impression, based on fossil remains, of *H. floresiensis*, nicknamed "the Hobbit."

on page 44). The oldest Neanderthal sites are in Western Europe, where Neanderthal remains are found mainly in rock shelters and caves. The Neanderthals survived from 400,000 to 30,000 years ago.

The Neanderthals are highly distinctive in terms of their morphology. Compared to modern humans, they had heavier limb bones, larger brains, and distinctive facial skeletons. Neanderthals were the only hominin species able to tolerate, over thousands of years, the cold temperatures that intermittently affected Europe and northern Asia. Although the distinctive morphology of the Neanderthals may be the result of biological adaptations to a very cold climate, it is likely that they may also have developed cultural adaptations to the cold, including clothing (see Eye on the Environment).

Neanderthals were the first hominins to bury their dead regularly. So their fossil record, in quality and quantity, is better than for other archaic *Homo* species.

eye on the ENVIRONMENT

Clothing as a Thermal Adaptation

During the many thousands of years in which Neanderthals lived in Eurasia, the climate was mainly cold, and winds were likely strong. Neanderthals' biological and cultural adaptations allowed them to survive in latitudes up to 55 degrees N (Gilligan 2007). Their biological adaptations include a short, wide body with short limbs, a body type that allows for conservation of heat. Neanderthal cultural adaptations include cave dwelling and the use of fire to provide heat and light inside the caves. Their Mousterian tool kit, which includes scrapers, points, and awls, indicates that Neanderthals had the ability to make clothing.

Among the many theories about the fate of the Neanderthals, Australian archaeologist Ian Gilligan offers a novel theory. His explanation for Neanderthal extinction involves climate change, Neanderthal morphology, and Neanderthal culture. Gilligan argues that the Neanderthals' biological and cultural adaptations were sufficient under normal and consistent cold regimes but insufficient during severe cold weather spikes that occurred near the end of their time on earth. Most importantly, he differentiates between two types of clothing: simple and complex, and their thermal effectiveness in situations of extreme cold.

- *Simple clothing* is loosely draped around the body and has only one layer.
- *Complex clothing* has multiple layers and the first layer, at least, is fitted to the body.

Simple clothing provides limited protection against cold and wind, whereas complex clothing can protect against severe cold and wind in polar environments.

No surviving remains of clothing from the Neanderthals exist, so archaeologists can only make inferences about the type of clothing they wore from their tools. Given the reasonable assumption that the basic material for Neanderthal clothing was animal hides, these would have required cleaning and scraping in order to make them usable as simple clothing. The Neanderthal Mousterian tool kit was able to perform these tasks, and thus it is likely that they had simple clothing.

Complex clothing, however, requires more careful preparation of the various layers and stitching pieces together to form a fitted layer. More specialized tools such as borers and needles are necessary. The Neanderthals did not possess such tools, but the modern humans who arrived in Eurasia did.

Gilligan's working hypothesis is that the biological adaptation of Neanderthals, along with their cultural ability to produce simple clothing, was effective over many thousands of years. But, in later times, cold temperatures spiked, and the Neanderthals lacked the ability to protect themselves with complex clothing and therefore succumbed to hypothermia. In contrast, the in-coming modern humans lacked biological adaptations to the extreme cold, but they did have the technology to produce complex clothing which allowed them to survive spikes of cold weather better than the Neanderthals could.

Using knowledge of temperature changes during the later Neanderthal era and inferences from the Neanderthal and modern human tool kits, it is possible to generate a reasonable scenario that Neanderthals died out because of their inability to survive extreme cold stress. Although Neanderthals survived for thousands of years in cold conditions, they did not extend their territory from inner Siberia further to Alaska and into the New World, as did their modern human successors. Complex clothing could have made all the difference.

FOOD FOR THOUGHT ▼

What is your experience, in extremely cold weather, with the effectiveness of close-fitting and layered clothing versus loose-fitting and nonlayered clothing?

Given the cold climate, one wonders why burials were performed, as they would have been labor intensive.

Most Neanderthal fossils are found in association with a stone tool kit referred to as the **Mousterian tradition**, named after the site of Le Moustier, France, where such tools were first described. Mousterian tools, compared to Acheulian tools, are smaller and lighter, and more specialized flake tools emerge such as points, scrapers, and awls.

Neanderthals also created material items other than tools that demonstrate their relatively advanced way of thinking and behaving. This book's definition of *expressive culture*, provided in Chapter 13, is behavior and beliefs related to art and leisure. The Neanderthals had elements of expressive culture including portable art, though of a simple sort (see Figure 2.5 on page 44), and flutes. They may have had the capacity for verbal language, though this issue is debated. Another question is whether, and to what extent, Neanderthals interbred with modern humans. The recent sequencing of the Neanderthal genome using ancient DNA indicates that between one and four percent of the genes of living European and Asian populations are traceable to Neanderthal genes (Green et al. 2010). Interbreeding likely occurred in the Middle East around 100,000 years ago.

THINKING OUTSIDE THE BOX

Listen to the interview on the Web with French paleoanthropologist Jean-Jacques Hublin about Neanderthals and their fate: http://www.pbs.org/wgbh/evolution/library/07/3/text_pop/1_073_02.htm. What is Hublin's position?

FIGURE 2.5 Worked Flint Found by the Loire River in Northern France. Dated to 35,000 years ago, this object was made by Neanderthals and is one of the earliest examples of sculpture.

*Labels on figure:*
Flint worked to improve its likeness to a face
Animal bone wedged in hole by flint flakes
10.5 cm

MAP 2.6 Neanderthal Sites and Distribution in the Old World.

The discovery of many Neanderthal sites across the Old World indicates that they occupied an extensive area. During their later period, they overlapped with modern humans in the Middle East and Europe. Whether Neanderthals and modern humans interbred is debated.

*Labels on map:*
Neanderthal
Le Moustier
Shanidar

SUMMARY OF ARCHAIC *HOMO* Compared to the early hominins, the smaller chewing teeth and the smaller and more slender jaws of archaic *Homo* suggest that these species either ate different kinds of food or ate the same food but processed it by drying or cooking. One way to improve dietary quality to support a larger brain was to eat more animal meat, birds, or fish. These foods provide large amounts of energy-rich protein and fat. Eggs, worms, and insects can also provide protein and fat, but in smaller quantities per mouthful. Evidence that these species probably ate meat comes from an unlikely source: tapeworms (Hoberg et al. 2001). The first evidence of tapeworm infection in hominins coincides with the emergence of archaic *Homo* in Africa, a finding that points to the likelihood that they ate substantial amounts of meat. No one knows for sure how such meat was obtained, but most thinking leans toward the view that it was scavenged from animals killed by other predators.

Archaic *Homo* species inhabited a wide variety of habitats including those with temperate climates and those with cold climates. An increasingly complex culture was key to surviving in such varied environments. Evidence that *H. erectus* had reached islands in Southeast Asia more than 1 million years ago means that the species had devised a way to travel by water, presumably using some sort of raft or boat, and could cross substantial distances, at least 15 miles from island to island, on open sea. This achievement marks a major locomotive advance, enabling archaic *Homo* to migrate to and settle in a far wider range of places than are available by foot.

Archaic *Homo* species had aspects of culture including stone tools. Neanderthal artifacts document the beginning of art and music. Neanderthals buried their dead and may have had a sense of supernaturalism or a belief in life after death. They may have had verbal language.

Modern Humans

The term **anatomically modern humans (AMH)** refers to *Homo sapiens*, the species to which modern humans belong; this book uses the term "modern humans." This era is the last period during which any evidence exists of significant morphological change. Compared to the Neanderthals, modern humans have steeper foreheads with smaller brow ridges, smaller faces, smaller incisor teeth, and thinner limb bones. Culture, in contrast, continues to become more elaborate and complex, as people alter how they interact with nature and with each other. In this relatively short period, the number of human species was reduced to one, and modern humans emerged as the only form of human life on the earth.

MODERN HUMAN ORIGINS IN AFRICA No one knows which, if any, of the earlier species may be a direct ancestor to modern humans. At this point, the fossil evidence does not indicate a clear line from any archaic *Homo* species to modern humans. Future fossil evidence may help fill in the gaps. The earliest fossil evidence for modern humans is from a site in Ethiopia and dates to 160,000 years ago. Archaeological evidence also supports the African origins theory of modern humans. Modern tools such as blades that may have been used on the tips of spears and arrows have been found in African sites dated to 300,000 years ago. Given the early date of the archaeological evidence for modernity, it is likely that future fossil discoveries in Africa will be from that time, too. Or, modern behavior may have preceded modern biological evolution.

Blades from Kapthurin, Kenya, dated at 300,000 years ago. Many archaeologists say that these blades, and other early tools, indicate that humans had aspects of modern behavior far in advance of modern anatomy.

Genetic analysis indicates that all modern humans are descended from a common ancestral population that lived in Africa at least 200,000 years ago (Ingman et al. 2000, Quintana-Murci et al. 1999). There are more different versions of genes in contemporary modern human populations in Africa than in all the rest of the world put together (Tishkoff and Verrelli 2003). This finding is consistent with the view that Africa has been the dominant source of the novel genes and gene combinations of modern humans. Many novel versions of genes originated in African populations and then spread into the Middle East, Asia, and Europe (Pääbo 2003).

MODERN HUMANS DURING THE UPPER PALE-OLITHIC IN THE OLD WORLD The **Upper Paleolithic** is the period of modern human occupation in Europe and Eurasia (including the Middle East) 45,000 years ago to 12,000 years ago. During this period, *microliths* and other small, finely made stone and bone tools are the defining elements of technology. Modern humans also made and used tools crafted from organic materials, such as nets and baskets. In many places, they created impressive works of art.

Modern humans, like *Homo erectus* before them, first migrated out of Africa by land to the Middle East, where the oldest modern human fossils outside Africa are found, dated at around 100,000 years ago (Hublin 2000). From there, modern humans probably took a coastal route around the Arabian peninsula, along the coastline of what is now India, and then on to Southeast Asia and the Pacific (Stringer 2000). Modern humans reached Australia around 50,000 years ago. Like the modern humans who later arrived in Europe, modern humans in Australia were prolific artists. Rock paintings in Australia are as old as many of the world-famous Paleolithic cave paintings of Europe.

Other modern humans moved north to Turkey and from there into Eastern and Central Europe. Yet others traveled into Central Asia, Siberia, and eventually the New World.

The arrival of modern humans in Europe marks the beginning of a period of rapidly increasing cultural complexity, often referred to as a cultural revolution or "Golden Age." The first evidence of modern humans in Europe comes from sites in Central Europe, around 40,000 years ago. By around 36,000 years ago, modern humans reached Western Europe. Cultural changes during the European Upper Paleolithic (see Map 2.7 on page 46) include more complex and specialized tool kits. A major leap forward in symbolic thinking is also indicated by many examples of cave art and portable sculpture.

Archaeologists first discovered fossil evidence for modern humans at Cro-Magnon, a rock shelter site in Les Eyzies, France. This site provides the name for the first modern humans in Europe, the **Cro-Magnon** people, who arrived in Europe around 40,000 years ago. Although early Cro-Magnons overlapped in time with Neanderthals, the evidence is unclear as to whether there was interbreeding or cultural exchange.

The Cro-Magnons had a more sophisticated tool kit than the Neanderthals. They also left behind an impressive legacy of art including cave art and portable art. Given their many achievements, some scholars argue that they must have had verbal language. The many cultural accomplishments of the Upper Paleolithic provided the basis for the developments described in the next section of this chapter.

MODERN HUMAN MIGRATIONS INTO THE NEW WORLD By 30,000 years ago, modern humans were migrating from Siberia into present-day Alaska. Two routes are possible: an *ice-free corridor* in Alaska and western Canada, which led them into the rest of North America, and a coastal route. Whichever path they followed—and it may have been both—in just a few thousand years, modern humans had spread throughout most of the unglaciated regions of North America and into Central and South America.

The major body of archaeological evidence about the first modern humans in the New World is that of the **Clovis culture**,

Anatomically Modern Humans (AMH) or *Homo sapiens* or **modern humans**   the species to which modern humans belong and also referred to by that term; first emerged in Africa between 300,000–160,000 years ago and then spread throughout the Old and New Worlds.

Upper Paleolithic   the period of modern human occupation in Europe and Eurasia (including the Middle East) from 45,000–40,000 years ago to 12,000 years ago, characterized by microlithic tools and prolific cave art and portable art.

Cro-Magnons   the first modern humans in Europe, dating from 40,000 years ago.

Clovis culture   New World population characterized by the Clovis point with the earliest site dated to 11,000 years ago in the Southwest United States.

This map shows only a small number of the many sites in Europe from the Upper Paleolithic era. Les Eyzies (lay-zay-zee) is the first site where evidence of Cro-Magnons was discovered. Lascaux (lah-SKOH) and Chauvet (shoh-VAY) are two of the most important cave art sites in Europe. La Magdeleine (la-mahd-LEN) is the site for the fourth and last cultural stage of the Upper Paleolithic. At French Magdalenian sites, the main food source of modern humans was reindeer. At Magdalenian sites in Germany and Russia, evidence exists that people had domesticated dogs, perhaps for hunting.

Upper Paleolithic artifacts. These artifacts were made by the earliest modern humans in Europe.

a population characterized by the *Clovis point* (Haynes 2002). First discovered in New Mexico (see Map 2.8 on page 47), a Clovis point is distinct in that it is bifacial and *fluted*, meaning that it has a long, vertical flake chipped from its base. The oldest Clovis sites are dated to slightly before 11,000 years ago, and shortly thereafter Clovis people spread over most of the unglaciated regions of North America (Waters and Stafford 2001, Haynes 2002). Clovis culture, however, lasted only a short while.

For a long time, archaeologists accepted Clovis sites as the earliest human sites in the New World, a position that left a large gap in time between then and when migrants were likely to have begun arriving and settling in the New World, given archaeological data from Siberia. Recently, several claims for pre-Clovis sites have been made. Monte Verde, in

Chile, is the most definite of the earliest possible pre-Clovis sites in the New World. It suggests a human presence in South America by 12,500 years ago and raises the possibility of coastal migration and settlements (Dillehay 2000). Recovery of genetic data from *coprolites* (fossilized feces) in a site called Paisley Caves in Oregon proves the existence of modern humans in North America around 12,300 years ago (Gilbert et al. 2008). Such discoveries, with their implications for overthrowing the Clovis-first theory, create controversy but also open the way for new models of how the New World was occupied.

It is likely there were several migrant streams of modern humans into the New World. Different groups arrived and settled over different periods, and each made its own contribution to the genetic and cultural diversity of New World populations. No matter when, where, and how modern humans arrived in the New World, they spread rapidly over a diverse range of environments and left their enduring mark in settlement sites, artifacts, and fossils.

SUMMARY OF MODERN HUMANS Starting as early as 300,000 years ago in Africa, modern humans have since then colonized the entire world. Their technological knowledge advanced to include spears and microlithic tools. Plant and animal domestication provided a new degree of control over food sources as well as the ability to follow a more settled life.

Head of the "Woman of Brassempouy". Paleolithic sculpture, mammoth ivory. Musee des Antiquites Nationales, Saint-Germain-en-Laye, France. Reunion des Musees Nationaux. J.G. Berizzi/Art Resource, NY

Examples of Cro-Magnon art. (LEFT) An Upper Paleolithic wall painting at Lascaux, France, depicting a variety of animals. Of the hundreds of figures painted in Lascaux's several galleries, only one depicts a human form, and it has a bird head. (CENTER) A so-called Venus figurine, found at Willendorf, Austria, is carved from fine limestone and is 11 centimeters tall (4 inches). This figurine is 25,000 years old. (RIGHT) A human head carved in mammoth ivory, called the Venus of Brassempouy, is 3.6 centimeters high (an inch and a half). Found in France, it is dated to between 30,000 and 26,000 years ago. Its stratigraphic position was not carefully documented at the time of its discovery. Because of the lack of details about its discovery and its lack of surface corrosion, some archaeologists question its authenticity.

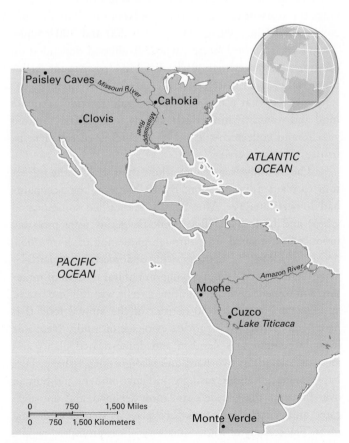

MAP 2.8 New World Sites.

Clovis points are large (11 centimeters long, or about 5 inches), bifacially flaked spear points. So far no evidence of hafting exists, and, given the elegant flaking, some archaeologists think that Clovis points were status items. Because many are found near water sources, another theory is that they were made to be used for sacred offerings.

The Neolithic Revolution and the Emergence of Cities and States

Around 12,000 years ago, people in several places in the Old World started changing their lives in ways that differed fundamentally from previous times. Many began to live in permanent settlements, a residence pattern called **sedentism**. Along with sedentism, people turned to plant and animal domestication instead of relying only on wild foods. Sedentism and plant and animal domestication, along with bipedalism, tool-making, and symbolic communication, are among the most important developments in human evolution (Zeder 2006).

Domestication is the process by which human selection causes changes in the genetic material of plants and animals. Through human selection, new species emerge. The earliest methods of selection could have been as simple as removing undesired plants from around desired plants. Later, more intensive kinds of selection took place, with intentional relocation of desired plants into garden areas. Concerning animal domestication, people may have kept preferred animals and promoted their reproduction while culling less desirable ones. Plant and animal domestication is a major defining feature of humanity's last several thousand years. It supported a new level of food production that promoted the growth of cities and states.

The Neolithic Revolution

The **Neolithic Revolution** refers to a time of rapid transformation in technology related to plant and animal domestication, including tools such as sickle blades and grinding stones. The story of the Neolithic begins in the Old World in Mesopotamia, especially the region called the *Fertile Crescent* between the Tigris and Euphrates Rivers in present day Iraq (Map 2.9). Rye, wheat, and barley were first domesticated here, along with animals such as sheep, goats, cattle, and pigs (Figure 2.6). Later, domestication of other plants and animals occurred in Africa, Asia, and the New World. Some of these events resulted from independent invention, or the creation of a new idea, behavior, or object. In others, diffusion, or the spread of culture through contact, was responsible for the Neolithic transition.

The stages of plant and animal domestication are revealed at several sites in the Middle East. One such site, Abu Hureyra (ah-boo hoo-RYUH-rah) is located near the Euphrates River (Moore et al. 2000). At the time, the region was rich in forest resources and wild grasses, and the climate was warmer and wetter than today. Abu Hureyra, like many Neolithic sites in the region, is a **tell**, a human-made mound resulting from the accumulation of successive generations of

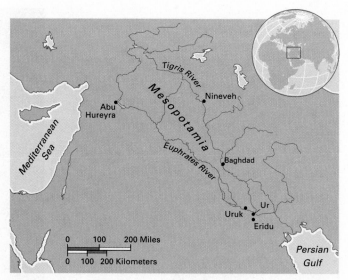

MAP 2.9 Neolithic Sites in the Middle East.
Archaeologists have excavated many important Neolithic sites in the Middle East, including those mentioned in this chapter and shown here. In Iraq, archaeological sites and artifacts are endangered due to the war and looting.

house construction, reconstruction, and trash. Over thousands of years, tells gradually rose above the surrounding plain. The tell at Abu Hureyra is 8 meters high (about 25 feet), and it was occupied from 10,500 to 6000 BCE. The *stratigraphy* (study of the layers over time) of the tell provides the story of change during the Neolithic. The first occupants lived in a village of between 200 and 300 people. They were *sedentary foragers* whose livelihood depended on hunting and gathering but who lived in a permanent settlement rather than in temporary camps. This residence pattern suggests that the environment could provide adequate food and water, within a fairly narrow region. They hunted gazelle and collected wild plants, including cereals, lentils, fruits, nuts, and berries.

The next levels at the site show the stages in the transition to plant domestication. By 10,000 BCE, the occupants had domesticated rye. After 9000 BCE, they had domesticated wheat and barley. The first domestic grains were probably produced on a small scale through gardening or *horticulture*, defined in Chapter 4 as the growing of domesticated plants by using handheld tools and relying on natural sources of moisture and soil enrichment. Hunting gazelle was still important, and gazelle constituted 80 percent of the animal food that people ate. Later levels provide evidence of a fully Neolithic lifestyle combining sedentism and domesticated plants and animals, including two herd animals: goats and sheep. Perhaps because of an increasingly arid environment and human over-hunting, the gazelle population declined, and domesticated animals gradually took their place as sources of animal meat. The scarcity of wild animals may have prompted people to domesticate replacements.

FIGURE 2.6 The Origins
of Selected Plant and Animal
Domesticates.

Source: From *The Human Impact on the
Natural Environments*, 5th Edition, by
Andrew Goudie. Copyright © 2004.
Blackwell Publishers Ltd. Reproduced with
permission of Blackwell Publishers &
Andrew Goudie.

Plants	Region	Approximate Date BCE
Barley, wheat	Middle East	8000–7000
Squash, gourd, maize	Central America	7000–6000
White potato, chile pepper	South America	7000–6000
Rice, millet, water chestnut	East Asia	6000–5000
Pearl millet, sorghum	Africa	3000
African rice	Africa	3000
Animals		
Dog	Russia, Eastern Europe	10,000
Sheep, goat	Middle East	7000
Pig, cattle	Middle East	6000
Chicken	China	6000
Horse	Central Asia	4000
Llama, alpaca	South America	4000
Donkey	Middle East	3500
Bactrian camel	Central Asia	2000
Dromedary camel	Middle East	2000
Turkey	Central America	Unknown

The village grew to 6,000 inhabitants by 7000 BCE, when sedentary life was combined with a more intensive form of domesticated grain production called *agriculture* or *farming*, defined in Chapter 4 as the growing of crops on permanent plots of land by using the plow, irrigation, and fertilizer. The series of sequential transitions at Abu Hureyra is typical of those at other sites in the Middle East.

A different pattern of domesticates emerged in Africa's *Sahel*, the grassland regions south of the Sahara desert. For thousands of years, foragers had occupied this region of rich lakesides and abundant wild grasses. Their economy combined fishing, hunting herd animals, and harvesting wild grasses such as millet, sorghum, and African rice. The domestication of cattle was the first step in the transition to the Neolithic in Africa (Marshall and Hildebrand 2002). The domestication of wild cattle supported the emergence of *pastoralism*, defined in Chapter 4 as an economic strategy in which people depend on domesticated animals for most of their food and which continues to be an important mode of livelihood in the region today.

The transition to the Neolithic in Europe relied on the introduction of plant and animal domesticates from the Middle East. The first plant and animal domesticates appeared in southeastern Europe around 6000 BCE (Richards 2003). By 4000 BCE, the combination of farming and keeping animals had spread across most of Europe. Archaeological evidence for the later Neolithic in Europe documents social status differences, group ceremonies and feasts, and religious sites that drew thousands of pilgrims from wide areas.

British archaeologists discovered the important Neolithic site of Çatalhöyük (shah-tall-hoy-yuck) in 1958. It is located in south-central Turkey (see Map 13.4, page 330) and dates to around 7000 BCE. Only a small portion of the tell has been excavated.

sedentism residence in permanent settlements such as villages, towns, and cities, which began with plant and animal domestication and intensified during the Neolithic era and the emergence of farming.

domestication a process by which human selection causes changes in the genetic material of plants and animals.

Neolithic Revolution a time of rapid transformation in technology, related to plant and animal domestication, which includes tools such as sickle blades and grinding stones.

tell a human-made mound resulting from the accumulation of successive generations of house construction, reconstruction, and trash.

Stonehenge, in southern England, is the most well-known late Neolithic monumental site. Many similar, though smaller, henge monuments exist in the British Isles and elsewhere in Europe and northern Africa. A henge monument is a construction in the shape of a circular enclosure with an opening at one point in the circle. They are generally interpreted as ceremonial sites. The latest evidence about Stonehenge indicates that it was also a burial ground.

PLANT AND ANIMAL DOMESTICATION IN THE NEW WORLD Plant domestication in the New World first began in Middle America (or *Mesoamerica*), the region between North and South America. Later transitions in South America and North America occurred partly through independent invention and partly through the spread of *maize* (corn). Three features distinguish the pattern of plant and animal domestication and sedentism in Middle America:

• The first experiments with domesticated plants took place long before sedentism.

• The first domesticated plants were gourds, squash, beans, and maize, and the first animal domesticates were dogs, turkeys, and honey bees.

• The transition to an entirely agricultural way of life was slower than in the Middle East, extending from 8000 to 2000 BCE.

By 5000 BCE, three domesticated plant species were the most important parts of the diet in Mexico, the so-called *Mesoamerican triad*: maize (corn), squash, and beans. People in the Andes Mountains first domesticated the potato, a member of the tuber family of root crops (Ochoa 1991). Tubers are difficult to find archaeologically because they spread by sending out shoots underground rather than by seeds. Thus the date of 5000 BCE for potato domestication is conjectural, based on the assumption that it occurred around the time of other Andean domesticates, including beans, quinoa (a seed), llamas, alpacas, and guinea pigs. Gourds and squash were domesticated in Ecuador by 10,000 BCE.

By 4000 BCE, people in eastern North America were experimenting with various plants as part of a mixed economic strategy of hunting, collecting wild plants, and cultivating a few domesticated species of seed crops (Smith 1998). The most important indigenous domesticates were seed crops such as goosefoot (similar to spinach, but also grown for its seeds and related to quinoa), sunflowers, and possibly squash. None of these plants, however, could support a sedentary farming population. Between the first and third centuries of the present era, it was the introduction of maize that led to the emergence of farming communities throughout North America.

Cities and States

The word *civilization* literally means "living in cities." A *city* is distinguished from a village or town by having a larger population (more than 10,000 people as a rough guide) and by having more occupational specialization, more elaborate architecture, and central services such as temples, government agencies, and trade organizations. Along with urbanization came the growth of the political institution of the state. A *state*, as defined in Chapter 10, is a centralized political organization encompassing many communities. States are typically bureaucratic; that is, they have specialized units with authority over limited areas

THINKING OUTSIDE THE BOX

Consider the importance of domesticated guinea pigs as food sources in Central and South America and as family pets in North America. What is the likelihood that guinea pigs will become a popular food source in North America and a popular household pet in Central and South America?

(LEFT) The remains of Uruk in southern Mesopotamia. Occupied starting around 5000 BCE, Uruk had the earliest, grandest, and most numerous monumental buildings in Mesopotamia. The Uruk period saw many innovations including the potter's wheel and the development of writing. (RIGHT) An artist's reconstruction of Anu Ziggurat and the White Temple at Uruk, around 3100 BCE. No written documents exist to indicate the amount of labor involved in constructing such monuments, but it was obviously substantial.

of governance, with trained personnel and usually written records. States have the power to levy taxes, keep the peace through use of legitimate force, and wage war.

Cities and states first emerged in the Old World, once again in what is now Iraq. Mesopotamia, which means "the land between two rivers," referring to the Tigris and the Euphrates, is the home of the world's earliest cities, dated to 3500 BCE. Important early cities in Mesopotamia include Uruk, Ur, Eridu, and Nineveh, all of which were preeminent at different times (see Map 2.9 on page 48).

Uruk is a well-studied Mesopotamian city. By 3500 BCE, its population was around 10,000 people, and it grew to a peak of 50,000 (Adams 1981). People lived in houses, made of dried mud-brick, which were packed tightly together and interspersed with narrow, winding streets (Pollock 1999). Surrounding Uruk was a massive brick wall 7 meters (23 feet) high, its numerous gates and guard towers suggesting the need for defense. Monumental architecture included a prominent feature called a *ziggurat*, a massive stepped platform that supported temples and administrative buildings. Government and religion were closely connected, so temples served both sacred and secular purposes, including storage and redistribution of agricultural surpluses, craft production, and economic management and recordkeeping. Commoner laborers and slaves built and maintained the monumental buildings in which state rule and commerce were managed; they wove the fine linen garments that elite men and women wore; and they pressed the high-quality oils consumed at royal feasts.

Early Mesopotamian cities were centers of regional trade, a feature that some archaeologists view as the primary catalyst for the urban revolution (Algaze 2001). Trade is also probably the catalyst for the development of the world's earliest money and writing. Writing was first invented between 3500 and 3000 BCE in Mesopotamia, for financial recordkeeping (Lawler 2001). Mesopotamian writing, or *cuneiform*, used around 1500

signs, many of which referred to specific goods such as bread and oil. Specially trained scribes worked in administrative roles in what was an early sort of *bureaucracy*, a form of administration that is hierarchical and specialized and relies heavily on recordkeeping. The hundreds of thousands of cuneiform tablets that archaeologists have found in early Mesopotamian cities provide a wealth of information about life at the time.

In the New World, cities and states formed later than in the Old World. Another distinct feature is that some New World states, though powerful and extensive, did not have writing. They did, however, have elaborately constructed capital cities, lavish political feasting, competitive sports, and plentiful gold and other wealth.

The Moche (MO-chay) or Mochica civilization emerged around 200 BCE in the deserts of Peru's north coast. Rivers descending from the Andes Mountains fed irrigation works that supported agricultural production to supply dense urban populations (Billman 2002). The Moche civilization is known for distinctive artistic styles and craftwork, especially mold-made portrait vessels and copper, silver, and gold metalwork (Quilter 2002). Warfare was an important component of state formation in the Andes, and Moche ceramics often depict warfare and human sacrifice. Moche civilization reached its height during the first few centuries of the Common Era. At this time, other civilizations were flourishing throughout the Andes, supported by a successful form of agriculture that was well adapted to high altitudes. It relied on a system of raised fields interspersed by canals. This form of agriculture, over time, fell out of practice, but archaeologists discovered evidence of it. Through their efforts, raised field farming is now reviving in the Andes and helping to provide increased food yields (see Anthropology Works, Chapter 4, page 93).

At the time of the Spanish Conquest in 1532, the Inca had formed the largest empire in the world (MacCormack

Moche portrait vessels, considered a brilliant art style, were produced in northern Peru between 100–500 CE. Many of the pieces depict high-status males with elaborate headdresses and face painting. This piece depicts a woman carrying a load.

▶ *Do research to learn whether the vessels are portraits of actual people or represent generic social categories.*

2001). The empire was vast, stretching from Colombia in the north to Chile in the south. The city of Cuzco was the empire's capital, and it was linked to distant provinces by a network of roads and bridges. Llamas and alpacas were important domesticated animals, used for their wool and meat and also as pack animals. Hundreds of varieties of potatoes, the most important food crop, were grown on terraced hillsides. The Inca, although a large and powerful empire, had no writing system. Instead, administrators used a system of knotted cords called *khipu* for recordkeeping (see photo on page 275).

In North America, many complex societies emerged, from the pueblo sites of the southwestern United States to the Iroquois nation of the northeast into Canada. They developed extensive trade networks, engaged in long-distance warfare, and built massive and enduring earthwork monuments. Politically, these societies did not develop state-level institutions but, rather, remained as complex chiefdoms that functioned without urban centers (Earle 1993).

The *Mississippian cultures*, dated to the first century of the Common Era, were located on or near the floodplains of rivers and were based on maize cultivation. Mississippian centers had earthen platform mounds that supported elite residences, ceremonial areas, and burial mounds. Local leaders gained status through the exchange of prestige goods, in which exotic materials and finished goods were traded over large distances (Peregrine 1992). One of the largest Mississippian centers was Cahokia (kuh-HOKE-ee-yuh), in present-day Illinois, which gained regional prominence around the year 1000 (Pauketat 2004). Cahokia is located on a vast floodplain where the Mississippi, Ohio, and Missouri Rivers meet. Fish and waterfowl were plentiful, and maize grew in abundance in the fertile and well-watered soil of the floodplain. Terrestrial game was available in the forested uplands. Control over the intersection of several major exchange routes was a key factor in Cahokia's rise to prominence. Enormous for its time and place, Cahokia covered an area of 13 square kilometers, with a peak population of several thousand people. The site contains a large rectangular plaza surrounded by more than 100 earthwork mounds. The largest, Monk's Mound, was 30 meters (over 98 feet) high and is the largest earthwork in North America. Monk's Mound was built in stages between 900 and 1200 CE. The extent of mound construction at Cahokia is a testament to the organizational capacity of the Cahokian political system to harness labor for construction on a grand scale.

Like other powerful chiefdoms, Cahokia had marked social inequality. This inequality is evident in burials, with

An artist's reconstruction of Cahokia showing thatch-roofed houses and massive earthworks. The site reached prominence around the year 1000 CE and was largely abandoned by 1400 CE.

▶ *Visit the website http://www.cahokiamounds.com/cahokia.html.*

anthropogenic   caused by humans.

abundant prestige goods marking high-status burials. Status and gender differences in diet confirm dietary inequalities (Ambrose et al. 2003). High-status people ate more animal protein and less maize, whereas the diet of low-status people was more dependent on maize. Men ate more protein and less maize than women. The diet of low-status women had the highest proportion of maize, about 60 percent.

The site of Cahokia suffered substantial damage in the late 1800s and early 1900s as a result of urban development, construction of roads and railways, expansion of farmland, and amateur collecting (Young and Fowler 2000). Many mounds were bulldozed, and their contents, including human bones and artifacts such as copper goods and shell beads, were used as landfill. Concern expressed by a few archaeologists raised public awareness and put a halt to the destruction and neglect. Cahokia is now a World Heritage Site, and American Indian groups from across the United States hold regular ceremonies there.

CIVILIZATIONS ARE NOT FOREVER Comparative analysis of many early states shows that all past states have gone through cycles of expansion and decline followed by the rise of new states (Marcus 1998). In fact, periods of decline, rather than the more archaeologically visible episodes of powerful territorial states, are the norm. Why do even the most powerful states always collapse? The answer may lie in the difficulty states have of maintaining territorial integration and extreme social inequality over long periods. Another factor may be the environmental decline that accompanies state building and accumulation.

Some archaeologists think that **anthropogenic** (caused by humans) effects on the environment, such as clearing forests and exhausting the soil, contributed to the collapse of many great and powerful civilizations. Changes during the Neolithic and urban revolutions shed light on humanity's prospects in the future and could provide important cautionary notes about the costs and sustainability of "civilization."

What do living nonhuman primates tell us about human culture?

Humans belong to the category of primates. Primates vary in size from several ounces to more than 400 pounds. All non-human primates in the wild provide for their food needs by foraging. Most primates live in a social group.

According to genetic data, modern humans are closely related to the living great apes with which we share a common ancestor around 8 million years ago. The category of great apes includes the four largest ape species: orangutans, gorillas, chimpanzees, and bonobos. Of these, chimpanzees and bonobos are genetically the most closely related to humans. Although chimpanzees and bonobos are alike in many ways, they also have several differences. Neither the chimpanzee nor bonobo model applies neatly to all modern human cultures.

Many nonhuman primate species have behaviors that are learned and shared and are thus cultural. Examples include tool use for procuring food and symbolic forms of greeting and interaction.

What role did culture play during hominin evolution?

Hominins is a category of primates that includes modern humans and extinct species of early human ancestors that are more closely related to humans than to living chimpanzees and bonobos. Hominin evolution can be divided into three stages: the early hominins, archaic *Homo*, and modern humans.

The early hominins span from 8 million years ago to 2 million years ago. The two oldest species, *Sahelanthropus tchadensis* and *Orrorin tugenensis*, are important, respectively, for showing that early hominins extended from East Africa into West-Central Africa, and they were becoming bipedal. Australopithecine refers to a category of several extinct species of early hominins found in East and southern Africa. The australopithecine era provides the first stone tools.

Archaic *Homo* includes extinct hominin species that lived from 2.4 million years to 17,000 years ago and had a more modern human-like body shape, larger brains, and smaller jaws and teeth. Stone tools are prominent in the cultures of all archaic

Homo species. One species, *Homo erectus*, is the first hominin species to live widely throughout the Old World. The last archaic *Homo* species, the Neanderthals, are known from many sites in Eurasia. They had some aspects of culture, including the beginning of art and music and possibly verbal language.

According to archaeological evidence, modern humans evolved in Africa starting 300,000 years ago, though the earliest fossil evidence is from 160,000 years ago. From Africa, they migrated to the Middle East and Asia, later to Central Asia and Europe, and finally to the New World. The Upper Paleolithic is the period of modern human occupation in Eurasia. The first modern humans in Europe are the Cro-Magnons, who are associated with microlithic tools and cave art.

How has modern human culture changed in the past 12,000 years?

Around 12,000 years ago, some people started changing their lives in ways that differed fundamentally from previous times. The first major change was a trend toward sedentism. With increased sedentism, people turned to plant and animal domestication instead of relying on only wild foods. Plant and animal domestication is a major defining feature of humanity's last several thousand years. It provided new types of foods, such as grains, and an increased level of food production that supported the growth of cities and states.

The Neolithic Revolution was a time of rapid transformation in technology, including tools such as sickle blades and grinding stones. The Neolithic first appeared in Mesopotamia, where plants such as wheat and barley were first domesticated along with animals such as sheep, goats, cattle, and pigs. Domestication of a different array of plants and animals occurred in the Middle East, Africa, China, and the New World.

Following sedentism and domestication, cities developed and then the state as a new form of political organization. Cities and states first emerged in Mesopotamia. In the New World, cities and states formed later than in the Old World. Some New World states operated without writing. In North America, complex societies emerged with extensive trade networks, long-distance warfare, and massive earthwork monuments, but without a state organization.

KEY CONCEPTS

SUGGESTED READINGS

David W. Anthony. *The Horse, the Wheel, and Language.* Princeton, NJ: Princeton University Press, 2007. The author links the domestication of horses around 4800 years ago and the invention of the wheel to the spread of the Proto-Indo-European language, which at the time existed only in spoken form.

Julian Caldecott and Lera Miles. *World Atlas of Great Apes and Their Conservation.* Berkeley: University of California Press, 2005. This overview describes the current distribution and status of the great apes and provides information on their ecology and behavior, habitat requirements and conservation efforts.

Thomas Dillehay. *The Settlement of the Americas: A New Prehistory.* New York: Basic Books, 2000. This book details efforts to determine who were the first modern humans in the Americas.

Frans de Waal and Frans Lanting. *Bonobo: The Forgotten Ape.* Berkeley: University of California Press, 1998. The book describes the behavior and ecology of bonobos. It covers social relationships, leadership, parent–offspring ties, sexuality, and the relevance of bonobos as the best model for humans.

William C. McGrew. *Chimpanzee Material Culture.* Cambridge: Cambridge University Press, 1992. McGrew discusses chimpanzee behavior as observed at several long-term field sites. Topics include chimpanzee culture and similarities and differences between humans and chimpanzees.

Sarah Milledge Nelson, ed. *Worlds of Gender: The Archaeology of Women's Lives around the Globe.* New York: AltaMira Press, 2007. Chapters in this book provide case studies of gender in archaeology.

Sue Savage-Rumbaugh, Stuart G. Shanker, and Talbot J. Taylor. *Apes, Language, and the Human Mind.* Oxford: Oxford University Press, 2001. This book discusses the upbringing of Kanzi, a bonobo who learned to understand spoken English and to communicate using pictorial symbols called lexigrams.

G. J. Sawyer and Viktor Deak, eds. *The Last Human: A Guide to Twenty-Two Species of Extinct Humans.* New York: Yale University Press, 2007. This book provides information on each species: its emergence, habitat, lifestyle, and cultural capabilities.

Eugenie C. Scott. *Evolution vs. Creationism: An Introduction.* Berkeley: University of California Press, 2004. Scott surveys the debate in the United States about teaching evolution in schools. She discusses diverse religious points of view and the scientific evidence for human evolution.

Bruce D. Smith. *The Emergence of Agriculture.* New York: Scientific American Library, 1998. This volume offers an account of the rise of food production in eight world regions, seeking the common processes at work in this transition.

David Whitley, ed. *Handbook of Rock Art Research.* Walnut Creek, CA: AltaMira Press, 2001. An overview of prehistoric rock art worldwide, this book addresses a range of topics from analysis of the meaning of rock art depictions to conservation.

Richard Wrangham. *Catching Fire: How Cooking Made Us Human.* New York: Basic Books, 2009. The author argues that cooked food, starting with *H. erectus,* allowed for more efficient processing of calories to support larger brains and led to pair-bonding between males and females with the latter being the cooks.

PEARSON myanthrolab

For further information about topics covered in this chapter, go to MyAnthroLab at **www.myanthrolab.com** and access the following readings in MyAnthroLibrary:

Brendan M. Buckley et al. 2010. Climate as a Contributing Factor in the Demise of Angkor, Cambodia. *Proceedings of the National Academy of Sciences* 107(15):6748–6752. During the fourteenth and fifteenth centuries, the capital of the vast Khmer Empire experienced decades of drought interspersed with intense monsoons. which led to its decline.

William C. McGrew. 2010. Chimpanzee Technology. *Science* 328(5978):579–580. Fifty years after Jane Goodale first observed a chimpanzee in the Gombe Stream Reserve in Tanzania, McGrew reviews what we now know about chimpanzee technology.

Robin Huw Crompton and Todd C. Pataky. 2009. Stepping Out. *Science* 323(Feb 27):1174–1175. The authors discuss what fossil footprints at Laetoli, Tanzania, and Ilaret, Kenya, reveal about the evolution of bipedalism.

RESEARCHING CULTURE

3

◀ Cultural anthropologist Robert Bailey and biological anthropologist Nadine Peacock, members of a Harvard University fieldwork team, conversing with some Ituri people who live in the rainforests of the eastern part of the Democratic Republic of Congo.

This chapter is about how cultural anthropologists do research to learn about people's shared and learned behavior and beliefs. The first section discusses how methods in cultural anthropology have evolved since the late nineteenth century. The second section covers the steps involved in a research project. The chapter concludes by addressing two urgent topics in cultural anthropology research.

◉ ◉ ◉

Changing Research Methods

Methods in cultural anthropology today are different in several ways from those used during the nineteenth century. Most cultural anthropologists now gather data by doing **fieldwork**, going to the *field*, which is wherever people and cultures are, to learn about culture through direct observation. They also use a variety of specialized research techniques depending on their particular goals.

From the Armchair to the Field

The term *armchair anthropology* refers to how early cultural anthropologists conducted research by sitting at home in their library and reading reports about other cultures written by travelers, missionaries, and explorers. These early thinkers never visited the places they wrote about and had no direct experience with the people whose customs they discussed.

In the late nineteenth and early twentieth centuries, anthropologists hired by European colonial governments moved a step closer to learning directly about people of other cultures. They traveled to their home country's colonies in Africa and Asia, where they lived near, but not with, the people they were studying. This approach is called *verandah anthropology* because, typically, the anthropologist would send out for "natives" to come to his verandah (verandah anthropologists, like armchair anthropologists, were men) for interviewing. Although verandah anthropology was an improvement on armchair anthropology, it still involved distance between the anthropologist and people's everyday experiences, and it meant that the anthropologist was learning about an entire culture from just a few select "informants" (who were also typically men).

In the United States during the mid-nineteenth century, Lewis Henry Morgan took steps toward learning about people and their culture through direct observation and interactions with more than just a few individuals out of context. A lawyer, Morgan lived in Rochester, New York, near the Iroquois territory. He became well acquainted with many of the Iroquois

Bronislaw Malinowski during his fieldwork in the Trobriand Islands, 1915–1918.

and gained insights into their everyday lives (Tooker 1992). Morgan showed that Iroquois behavior and beliefs make sense if an outsider spends time learning about them, in context and through direct interactions and experience. His writings changed the prevailing Euro-American perception of the Iroquois and other Native American tribes as "dangerous savages."

Participant Observation

Another major turning point occurred in the early twentieth century, during World War I, laying the foundation for the cornerstone method in cultural anthropology: fieldwork combined with participant observation. **Participant observation** is a research method for learning about culture that involves living in a culture for an extended period while gathering data.

The "father" of participant observation is Bronislaw Malinowski. He is credited with inventing a new approach to learning about culture while he was in the Trobriand Islands in the South Pacific during World War I (see Culturama).

Ethnographic research in the early twentieth century often involved photography. This Andaman girl wears the skull of her deceased sister. Indigenous people of the Andaman Islands revere the bones of their dead relatives and would not want them to be taken away, studied, or displayed in a museum.

---

fieldwork research in the field, which is any place where people and culture are found.

participant observation basic fieldwork method in cultural anthropology that involves living in a culture for a long time while gathering data.

CULTURAMA

The Trobriand Islanders of Papua New Guinea

The Trobriand Islands are named after eighteenth-century French explorer Denis de Trobriand. They include 22 flat coral atolls east of the island of New Guinea. The indigenous Trobriand population lives on four main islands. Kiriwina is by far the most populated, with about 28,000 people (digim'Rina, personal communication 2006). The Papua New Guinea (PNG) district office and an airstrip are located on Kiriwina at Losuia.

The islands were first colonized by Great Britain and then ceded to Australia in 1904 (Weiner 1988). The British attempted to stop local warfare and to change many other aspects of Trobriand culture. Christian missionaries introduced the game of cricket as a substitute for warfare (see Chapter 13 for further discussion). In 1943, Allied troops landed as part of their Pacific operations. In 1975, the islands became part of the state of Papua New Guinea (PNG).

Island-to-island cultural differences exist. Even within one island, people may speak different dialects, although everyone speaks a version of the language called Kilivila (Weiner 1988). The Trobrianders grow much of their own food, including root crops such as yams, sweet potatoes, and taro; beans and squash; and bananas, breadfruit, coconuts, and betel nuts. Pigs are the main animal raised for food and as prestige items. In the latter part of the twentieth century, Trobrianders were increasingly dependent on money sent to them by relatives working elsewhere in PNG. Current development projects are encouraging people to plant more fruit trees, such as mango (digim'Rina 2005).

Kinship emphasizes the female line, and mothers and daughters form the core of household groups along with males related by blood. A woman's husband, and her child's father, lives with his female relatives

by blood, and not with his wife and children. Fathers, even though just visitors, spend as much time caring for their children as mothers do (Weiner 1988). Fathers of political status give their children, both boys and girls, highly valued shell earrings and necklaces to wear. Mothers give daughters prized red skirts.

Trobriand children attend Western-style schools on the islands, and many go to mainland PNG and beyond for further studies. Today, elders worry that young people do nothing but dream about "money" and fail to care for the heritage of their ancestors. Another concern is that commercial over-fishing is endangering the coral reefs.

Thanks to Linus S. digim'Rina, University of Papua New Guinea, and Robert Foster, University of Rochester, for reviewing this material.

TROBRIAND ISLANDS

Kaileuna Losuia

Lagoon Kitava

Kiriwina

0   20   40 Miles

0   20   40 Kilometers

Vakuta

(LEFT) Trobriand men's coveted trade goods include this shell necklace and armlet.

(CENTER) A Trobriand girl wears a valued skirt at a dance in honor of the ancestors on Kiriwina Island. She and other female participants coat their skin with coconut oil and herbs and wear decorative flowers.

MAP 3.1 Trobriand Islands of Papua New Guinea. Also known as the Kiriwina Islands, these islands are an archipelago of coral atolls lying off the eastern coast of the island of New Guinea.

See more at   **PEARSON myanthrolab**

- Living with the people for an extended period of time
- Participating in and observing people's everyday life
- Learning the local language

FIGURE 3.1 Three Elements of Field Methods in Cultural Anthropology.

For two years, he resided in a tent alongside the local people, participating in their activities and living, as much as possible, as one of them. He also learned to understand and speak their language.

With these innovative approaches, which are now standard features of field research in cultural anthropology (Figure 3.1), Malinowski was able to learn about Trobriand culture in context, rather than through secondhand reports. By learning the local language, he could talk with the people without the use of interpreters and thus gain a much more accurate understanding of their culture.

Through the mid-twentieth century, a primary goal of cultural anthropologists was to record as much as possible of a people's language, songs, rituals, and social life because many cultures were disappearing. At this time, most cultural anthropologists did fieldwork in small, relatively isolated cultures, and they thought they could study everything about such cultures, following the principle of holism (defined in Chapter 1). Typically, the anthropologist (a White man) would go off with his notebooks to collect data on a standardized list of topics, including economics, family life, politics, religion, language, art and crafts, and more. If he was married, his wife might help out by providing information on women's lives.

Today, few if any such seemingly isolated cultures remain due to globalization and mass communication including the Internet. Cultural anthropologists have devised new research methods so that they can study larger-scale cultures, global– local connections, and rapid cultural change. One methodological innovation of the late twentieth century helps to address these new issues: **multisited research**, which is fieldwork conducted on a topic in more than one location (Marcus 1995). Although especially helpful in studying migrant populations in both their place of origin and their new location, multisited research is useful for studying many topics.

Lanita Jacobs-Huey conducted multisited fieldwork in order to learn about the language and culture of hair styles among African American women (2002). She chose a range of sites throughout the United States and in London,

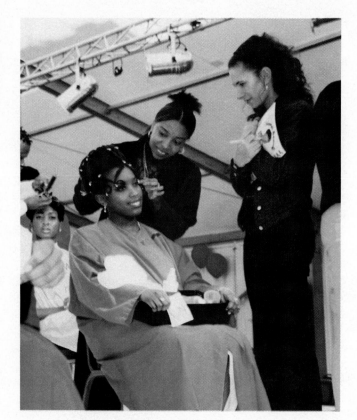

Lanita Jacobs-Huey's field sites include hairstyling competitions throughout the United States and in London, England. Here, a judge evaluates the work of a student stylist at the Afro Hair & Beauty Show in London.

England, in order to explore the many facets of the far-from-simple topic of hair: beauty salons, regional and international hair expos and training seminars, Bible study meetings of a nonprofit group of Christian cosmetologists, stand-up comedy clubs, a computer-mediated discussion about the politics of Black hair, and a cosmetology school in Charleston, South Carolina.

Another advance in methods is related to the need for applied research to produce knowledge with usable results for governments, nongovernmental organizations (NGOs) and businesses (see Anthropology Works). Rather than spending a year or more in the field, they rely on expert knowledge of the culture, a teamwork approach, and short-cut methods, or *rapid-research methods*, to provide information within a few weeks. Although such research lacks the depth and nuance of traditional extended fieldwork, but it has the advantage of providing "good enough" insights for practical applications.

---

multisited research   fieldwork conducted in more than one location in order to understand the culture of dispersed members of the culture or relationships among different levels of culture.

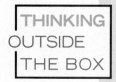

THINKING OUTSIDE THE BOX

As you read this chapter, consider the similarities and differences between research methods in cultural anthropology and research in other disciplines.

ANTHROPOLOGY works

What's for Breakfast in California?

Cultural anthropologist Susan Squires is one of the brains behind the General Mills breakfast food Go-Gurt®. During its first year of production in 1991, Go-Gurt generated sales of $37 million.

Squires, who earned a Ph.D. in cultural anthropology from Boston University, is a pioneer in *consumer anthropology*, or the use of anthropological research methods to identify what people do and say in their everyday lives in order to inform product development and design.

In contrast to traditional anthropological methods that involve long-term participant observation, consumer research relies on short-term, drop-in visits, often of a small sample of people who are representative of a larger population. Typically, an anthropologist and a designer work as a team in the field.

Research into the development of Go-Gurt took Squires and an industrial designer into the homes of middle-class families in suburban California to observe their breakfast behavior and food choices. On their first day of research, they arrived at a residence at 6:30 a.m. laden with video cameras and other equipment, prepared to have breakfast with a family they had never met. They repeated this process with more families at breakfast time and were able to build up a picture of habits and preferences.

Squires found that a major factor shaping breakfast food choice was the need to leave home early for work or school. Breakfast time is often a rushed

A middle-class family breakfast in California. Recent studies claim that multitasking involving telephone conversations and being on the Internet detracts from the quality of social relationships and the ability to concentrate. Whether or not such claims are true, a media-saturated lifestyle does affect eating in terms of the kind of food consumed and social interaction at mealtime.

affair, cut short by the need to get in the car or meet the bus. At the same time, she learned that parents want their children to eat healthy food for breakfast, while children are frequently uninterested in eating anything so early in the morning.

Squires realized that the ideal breakfast food for such busy families should be portable, healthy, fun, and come in a disposable container. The answer: yogurt packaged so that it can be eaten by squeezing it out of the package, bypassing the need for a spoon. One

mother said that her daughter thinks she is eating a popsicle when she has Go-Gurt for breakfast.

The work of Susan Squires demonstrates how cultural anthropology can benefit business and the everyday lives of consumers. Two assets of consumer anthropology are its attention to people's behavior and preferences in everyday life and its ability to describe cultural variation and similarities that can translate to effective product design.

⬚ ⬚ ⬚

Doing Fieldwork in Cultural Anthropology

Fieldwork in cultural anthropology can be exciting, frustrating, scary, boring, and sometimes dangerous. One thing is true: It transforms the lives of everyone involved. This section explores the stages of a fieldwork research project, starting with the initial planning and ending with the analysis and presentation of the findings.

Beginning the Fieldwork Process

Before going to the field, the prospective researcher must select a research topic and prepare for the fieldwork itself. These steps are critical to the success of the project.

PROJECT SELECTION Finding a topic for a research project is a basic first step. The topic should be important and feasible. Cultural anthropologists often find a topic to research by carrying out a *literature review*, which is the formal term for reading what others have already written about the subject and assessing its strengths and gaps.

For example, cultural anthropologists realized during the 1970s that anthropological research to date had ignored women and girls, and this is how feminist anthropology began (Miller 1993).

Important events and trends often inspire a research project. The HIV/AIDS epidemic and its rapid spread continue to prompt much research as do other new health threats. The plight of many international migrants and refugees provides a pressing topic for study. Conflicts in Afghanistan, Iraq, Sudan, and other places spur cultural anthropologists to ask what causes such conflicts and how post-conflict reconstruction can be most effectively accomplished (Lubkemann 2005). Climate change and environmental issues have gained a prominent place in recent years as cultural anthropologists document how local groups are being affected by rapid alterations in their way of life due to drought, declining animal and fish populations, and rising temperatures.

Rather than focusing on a region or cultural group, some cultural anthropologists choose to examine a particular item or commodity within its cultural context, such as sugar (Mintz 1985), cars (D. Miller 2001), beef (Caplan 2000), money (R. Foster 2002), shea butter (Chalfin 2004), wedding dresses (Foster and Johnson 2003), coca (Allen 2002), or cocaine (Taussig 2004). The item provides a window for understanding the social relations surrounding its production, use, and trade, and what it means in terms of people's identities.

Another idea for a research project is a *restudy*, or fieldwork conducted in a previously researched community. Many previous studies offer a foundation on which later studies can build, providing insights into changes that have occurred or offering a new angle. One of Bronislaw Malinowski's major contributions to anthropology is his classic study, *Argonauts of the Western Pacific* (1961 [1922]) and its detailed examination of the Trobriand Island **kula**, a trading network linking many islands through which men maintain long-standing partnerships involving the exchange of everyday goods, such as food, as well as highly valued necklaces and armlets (see Culturama). More than half a century later, Annette Weiner traveled to the Trobriand Islands to study wood carving. She settled in a village near the place Malinowski had done his research and immediately began making startling observations: "On my first day in the village, I saw women performing a mortuary [death] ceremony in which they distributed thousands of bundles of strips of dried banana leaves and hundreds of beautifully decorated fibrous skirts" (1976:xvii). Weiner was intrigued and decided to change her research project to investigate women's exchange patterns. Power and prestige derive from both men's and women's exchange networks. Reading Malinowski alone informs us about the former, but in isolation from half of the islands' population:

In focusing on a single commodity, cultural anthropologists reveal much about local and global cultures. (TOP) Children working on a sugarcane plantation in the Philippines. (CENTER) A model dressed as "Miss Chiquita" stands in front of the Brandenburg Gate in Berlin during Germany's International Green Week and agricultural fair. (BOTTOM) Villagers chewing coca leaves in highland Peru.

women. Weiner's book *Women of Value, Men of Renown* (1976) provides an account of women's trading and prestige activities as well as how they are linked to those of men. Building on the work of her predecessor, Weiner shows how a full understanding of one domain requires knowledge of the other.

PREPARING FOR THE FIELD After defining the research topic, it is important to secure funding to carry out the research. Academic anthropologists can apply for grants from a variety of sources, governmental and nongovernmental. Several sources of funding are also available for advanced graduate students. Undergraduate students have a more difficult time finding grants to support fieldwork, but some succeed.

Related to the funding question is whether it is appropriate for an anthropologist to conduct research while employed in the research setting. Employment provides financial support for the research, but it raises some problems. A basic dilemma, discussed later in the chapter, is the ethical principle that anthropologists cannot do "undercover" research. If you are working in a factory, for example, while studying what goes on in the factory, you must get people's permission for your study, something that is not always easy. More positively, a work role can help gain people's trust and respect. A British graduate student worked as a bartender in a tourist town in Ireland (Kaul 2004). This position placed him at the center of the village, and people respected him as a hard-working person, thus greatly adding to his ability to learn about the local culture, at least as revealed from a bartender's perspective.

If the project involves international travel, the host government may require a visa and an application for permission to conduct research. These formalities may take a long time and may even be impossible to obtain. The government of India, for example, restricts research by foreigners, especially research related to "sensitive" topics such as tribal people, border areas, and family planning. China's restrictions against foreign anthropologists doing fieldwork have been eased since the 1980s, but it is still not easy to get permission to do fieldwork and participant observation.

Many countries require that researchers follow official guidelines for the *protection of human subjects*. In the United States, universities and other institutions that support or conduct research with living people must establish *institutional review boards* (*IRBs*) to monitor research to make sure that it conforms to ethical principles. IRB guidelines follow a medical model related to the need to protect people who participate as "subjects" in medical research. Normally, IRBs require informed consent, in writing, from the research participants. **Informed consent** is an aspect of research ethics requiring that the researcher inform the research participants of the intent, scope, and possible effects of the study and seek their agreement to be in the study. Obtaining written consent from research participants is reasonable and feasible in many anthropological research projects. Written consent, however, is often not reasonable or feasible, especially in oral-based cultures where most people are not literate. Fortunately, IRBs are gaining more experience with the contexts in which cultural anthropologists do

research. Some universities' IRBs will waive the requirement for written informed consent, allowing oral informed consent instead. IRB guidelines do change, so check your institution's website for the latest policy.

Depending on the project's location, preparation for the field may involve buying specialized equipment, such as a tent, warm clothing, waterproof clothing, and sturdy boots. Health preparations may require immunization against contagious diseases such as yellow fever. For research in a remote area, a well-stocked medical kit and basic first-aid training are essential. Research equipment and supplies are another important aspect of preparation. Cameras, video recorders, tape recorders, and laptop computers are now basic field equipment.

If a researcher is unfamiliar with the local language, intensive language training before going to the field is critical. Even with language training in advance, cultural anthropologists often find that they cannot communicate in the local version of the language they studied in a classroom. Therefore, many fieldworkers rely on help from a local interpreter throughout their study or, at least, in its early stages.

Working in the Field

A basic first step in establishing a fieldwork project is to decide on the particular location or locations for the research. The second is to find a place to live.

SITE SELECTION A research *site* is the place where the research takes place. The researcher often has a basic idea of the area where the fieldwork will occur, for example, a *favela* (shantytown) in Brazil, a village in Scotland, or a factory in Malaysia. But it is often impossible to know in advance exactly where the project will be located. Selecting a research site depends on many factors. It may be necessary to find a large village if the project involves class differences in work patterns, or a clinic if the study concerns health-care behavior. It may be difficult to find a village, neighborhood, or institution in which the people welcome the researcher and the project. Often, housing shortages mean that even the most welcoming community cannot provide space for an anthropologist.

Here is an example in which a combination of factors came together in a positive way. Jennifer Robertson was seeking a research site in Japan for a study of urban population

---

kula a trading network, linking many of the Trobriand Islands, in which men have long-standing partnerships for the exchange of everyday goods, such as food, as well as highly valued necklaces and armlets.

informed consent an aspect of fieldwork ethics requiring that the researcher inform the research participants of the intent, scope, and possible effects of the proposed study and seek their consent to be in the study.

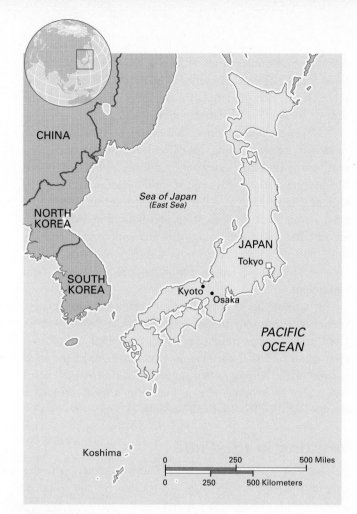

MAP 3.2 Japan.

The State of Japan, or Nihon-koku or Nippon-koku, encompasses more than 3000 islands, most of which are mountainous. Its population is nearly 129 million. Greater Tokyo, with 30 million residents, is the largest metropolitan area in the world. Japan has the world's second largest economy.

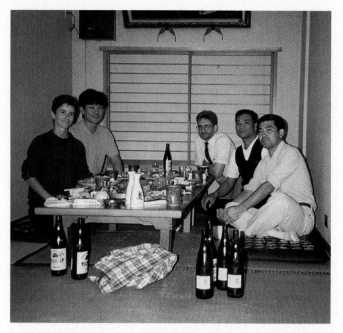

Jennifer Robertson (FAR LEFT) celebrates the publication of her book, *Native and Newcomer* (1991), with several administrators from Kodaira City Hall. This informal gathering at a local restaurant followed a formal ceremony at the City Hall, where Robertson presented her book to the mayor of Kodaira, an event covered by city and regional newspapers.

▶ *What cultural features are noteworthy about this gathering?*

change. She selected Kodaira, a suburb of Tokyo (Map 3.2), because of advice from a Japanese colleague. It had available housing and offered a good fit with her research interests. By happy coincidence, she was also familiar with the area:

> I spent my childhood and early teens in Kodaira [but] my personal past did not directly influence my selection of Kodaira as a fieldsite and home. . . . That I wound up living in my old neighborhood in Kodaira was determined more by the availability of a suitable apartment than by a nostalgic curiosity about my childhood haunts. As it turned out, I could not have landed at a better place at a better time. (1991:6)

rapport   a trusting relationship between the researcher and the study population.

GAINING RAPPORT **Rapport** is a trusting relationship between the researcher and the study population. In the early stages of research, the primary goal is to establish rapport with key leaders or decision makers in the community who may serve as *gatekeepers* (people who formally or informally control access to the group or community). Gaining rapport involves trust on the part of the study population, and that trust depends on how the researcher presents herself or himself. In many cultures, people have difficulty understanding why a person would come to study them because they do not know about universities and research and cultural anthropology. They may provide their own explanations based on previous experience with outsiders whose goals differed from those of cultural anthropologists, such as tax collectors, family planning promoters, and law-enforcement officials.

Stories about *false role assignments* can be humorous. During his 1970s fieldwork in northwest Pakistan, Richard Kurin reports that, in the first stage of his research, the villagers thought he was an international spy from America, Russia, India, or China (1980). Over time, he convinced them that he was not a spy. So what was he? The villagers came up with several roles for Kurin. First, they speculated that he was a teacher of English because he was tutoring one of the village boys. Second, they guessed that he must

MAP 3.3 Syria.

The Syrian Arabic Republic historically included the present-day territories of Lebanon, Israel, the Palestinian Territories, and parts of Jordan. The population of Syria is 19 million people. The capital city, Damascus, with a population of 3 million people, is one of the oldest continually occupied cities in the world.

be a doctor because he gave people aspirin. Third, they thought he might be a lawyer who could help them in local disputes because he could read court orders. Last, they decided that he was a descendant of a local clan because of the similarity of his last name and that of an ancestral king. For Richard Kurin, the last of these—being a true "Karan"—was best of all.

Being labeled a spy continues to be a problem for anthropologists. Christa Salamandra, a Western-trained doctoral student in anthropology, went to Damascus, Syria (Map 3.3), to do research for her dissertation in anthropology (2004). Although Damascus has an ancient history, it is increasingly cosmopolitan. Damascenes, however, have little exposure to anthropology. Syria has no university with a department of anthropology, and there are no Syrian anthropologists. Salamandra's research interests in popular culture (movies, cafés, and fashion) perplexed the local people, who decided she must be a foreign spy. One person said to her, "Your question is CIA, not academic" (2004:5). Nevertheless, she managed to carry out her study and write a book about popular culture in Damascus.

Another situation of an assumed spying role arose in North Carolina, even though the anthropologist, Mary Anglin, shared citizenship with the people (2002). During her fieldwork in a mica-processing factory in the western part of the state, some people thought she was an industrial spy. Anglin came from the northeastern United States, so she was not a "southerner." Moreover, she had no kin connections in the region and no "family" (she was single). The Irish-Scottish residents of the area did not quickly welcome her, but she managed to get the factory owner to let her spend time in the factory as a participant-observer. Several of the women factory workers befriended her, but many of the local people continued to be suspicious. At one point, a rumor circulated that Anglin was learning about mica processing in order to sell the information to competitors. The rumor died down, but the factory owner later banned her from entering the factory.

GIFT-GIVING AND EXCHANGE Giving gifts to people involved in the research can help the project proceed, but gifts should be culturally and ethically appropriate. Learning the local rules of exchange is important (Figure 3.2).

Matthews Hamabata, a Japanese American who did fieldwork in Japan, learned about the complexities of gift-giving among Japanese business families (1990). He developed a close relationship with one family, the Itoos, and helped their daughter apply for admission to universities in the United States. When the applications were completed, Mrs. Itoo invited him to an expensive restaurant to celebrate. After the dinner, she handed him a small, carefully wrapped package, expressing her embarrassment at the inadequacy of her gift in relation to all that he had done for her daughter. When he returned home, he opened the gift. It was a box of chocolates. Upon opening the box, he discovered 50,000 yen (about US$250). Hamabata felt insulted: "Who do the Itoos think they are? They can't buy me or my services!" (1990:21–22). He asked some Japanese friends what he should do. They told him that the gift signaled the Itoos' wish to have a long-standing relationship and that returning the money to the Itoos would be an insult. They advised him to give a return gift later on, in order to maintain the relationship. His gift should leave him ahead by about 25,000 yen, given his status as an anthropologist in relation to the Itoos' status as a rich business family. This strategy worked, and the relationship between Hamabata and the Itoos remained intact.

- What an appropriate gift is
- How to deliver a gift
- How to behave as a gift-giver
- How to behave when receiving a gift
- If and how to give a follow-up gift

FIGURE 3.2 Culture and Gift-Giving in the Field.

MICROCULTURES AND FIELDWORK Class, race, gender, and age all affect how the local people will perceive and welcome an anthropologist. Some examples illustrate how microcultures influence rapport and affect the research in other ways.

Class In most fieldwork situations, the anthropologist is more wealthy and powerful than the people studied. This difference is obvious to the people. They know that the anthropologist must have spent hundreds or thousands of dollars to travel to the research site. They see the anthropologist's expensive equipment (camera, tape recorder, video recorder, even a vehicle) and valuable material goods (stainless steel knives, cigarettes, flashlights, canned food, and medicines).

Many years ago, Laura Nader urged that anthropologists should also *study up* by doing research among powerful people such as members of the business elite, political leaders, and government officials (1972). As one example of this approach, research on the high-fashion industry of Japan placed the anthropologist in touch with members of the Japanese elite—influential people capable of taking her to court if they felt she wrote something defamatory about them (Kondo 1997). Studying up has prompted greater attention to accountability to the people being studied, whether or not they are able to read what the anthropologist has written about them or are wealthy enough to hire a lawyer if they do not like how they and their culture have been presented.

"Race"/Ethnicity For most of its history, cultural anthropology has been dominated by Euro-American White researchers who study "other" cultures that are mainly non-White and non-Euro-American. The effects of "Whiteness" on role assignments range from the anthropologist being considered a god or ancestral spirit to being reviled as a representative of a colonialist past or neocolonialist present. While doing research in a village in Jamaica called Haversham, Tony Whitehead learned how "race" and status interact (1986). Whitehead is an African American from a low-income family. Being of a similar "race" and class as the rural Jamaicans with whom he was doing research, he assumed that he would quickly build rapport because of a shared heritage. The people of Haversham, however, have a complex status system that relegated Whitehead to a position that he did not predict, as he explains:

> I was shocked when the people of Haversham began talking to me and referring to me as a "big," "brown," "pretty-talking" man. "Big" was not a reference to my weight but to my higher social status as they perceived it, and "brown" referred not only to my skin color but also to my higher social status. . . . More embarrassing than

bothersome were the references to how "pretty" I talked, a comment on my Standard English speech pattern. . . . Frequently mothers told me that their children were going to school so that they could learn to talk as pretty as I did. (1986:214–215)

This experience prompted Whitehead to ponder the complexities of "race" and status cross-culturally.

Gender If a female researcher is young and unmarried, she is likely to face more difficulties than a young unmarried man or an older woman, married or single, because people in most cultures consider a young unmarried female on her own as extremely unusual. Rules of gender segregation may dictate that a young unmarried woman should not move about freely without a male escort, attend certain events, or be in certain places. A woman researcher who studied a community of gay men in the United States says:

> I was able to do fieldwork in those parts of the setting dedicated to sociability and leisure—bars, parties, family gatherings. I was not, however, able to observe in those parts of the setting dedicated to sexuality—even quasi-public settings such as homosexual bath houses. . . . Thus my

American anthropologist Liza Dalby in formal geisha dress during her fieldwork on geisha culture in Kyoto, Japan.

▶ *Besides learning to dress correctly, what other cultural skills did Liza Dalby probably have to learn?*

Tobias Hecht plays a game with some of the street children in his study in Rio de Janeiro, Brazil.

portrait of the gay community is only a partial one, bounded by the social roles assigned to females within the male homosexual world. (Warren 1988:18)

Gender segregation may also prevent male researchers from gaining access to a full range of activities. Liza Dalby, a White American, lived with the geishas of Kyoto, Japan, and trained to be a geisha (1998). This research would have been impossible for a man to do.

Age Typically, anthropologists are adults, and this fact tends to make it easier for them to gain rapport with people their age than with children or the aged. Although some children and adolescents welcome the participation of a friendly adult in their daily lives and respond to questions openly, others are more reserved.

Other Factors A researcher's role is affected by even more factors than those just discussed, including religion, dress, and personality. Being the same religion as the residents of a Jewish home for the aged in California helped a Jewish anthropologist establish rapport (Myerhoff 1978). This positive engagement is evident in a conversation between the anthropologist (A) and a woman named Basha (B):

B: "So, what brings you here?"

A: "I'm from the University of Southern California. I'm looking for a place to study how older Jews live in the city." At the word university, Basha moved closer and nodded approvingly. "Are you Jewish?" she asked.

A: "Yes, I am."

B: "Are you married?" she persisted.

A: "Yes."

B: "You got children?"

A: "Yes, two boys, 4 and 8," I answered.

B: "Are you teaching them to be Jews?" (1978:14)

The anthropologist was warmly accepted, and her plan for one year of research grew into a long-standing relationship. In contrast, being Jewish posed a potential problem in another context (Freedman 1986). Diane Freedman conducted research in rural Romania in the 1980s. Given the pervasiveness of anti-Semitism there, she was reluctant to tell the villagers that she was Jewish and also reluctant to lie. Early in her stay, she attended the village church. The priest asked what her religion was. She opted for honesty and found, to her relief, that being Jewish had no negative effects on her research.

CULTURE SHOCK **Culture shock** is the feeling of uneasiness, loneliness, and anxiety that occurs when a person shifts from one culture to a different one. The more different the two cultures are, the more severe the shock is likely to be. Culture shock happens to many cultural anthropologists, no matter how much they have tried to prepare themselves for fieldwork. It also happens to students who study abroad, Peace Corps volunteers, and others who spend a long time living in another culture.

Culture shock can range from problems with food to language barriers and loneliness. Food differences were a major problem in adjustment for a Chinese anthropologist who came to the United States (Huang 1993). American food never gave him a "full" feeling. An American anthropologist who went to Pohnpei, an island in the Federated States of Micronesia (see Map 12.7), found that her lack of skills in the local language caused her the most serious adjustment problems (Ward 1989). She says, "Even dogs understood more than I did. . . . [I will never] forget the agony of stepping on a woman's toes. Instead of asking for forgiveness, I blurted out, 'His canoe is blue'" (1989:14).

A frequent psychological aspect of culture shock is the feeling of reduced competence as a cultural actor. At home, the anthropologist is highly competent, carrying out everyday tasks, such as shopping, talking with people, and mailing a package, without thinking. In a new culture, the simplest tasks are difficult and one's sense of self-efficacy is undermined.

THINKING OUTSIDE THE BOX

Think of a situation in which you experienced culture shock, even as the result of just a brief cross-cultural encounter. How did you feel? How did you cope? What did you learn from the experience?

---

culture shock persistent feelings of uneasiness, loneliness, and anxiety that often occur when a person has shifted from one culture to a different one.

FIGURE 3.3 Two Research
Approaches in Cultural Anthropology.

Research Approach	Process	Data
Deductive (Etic)	Hypothesis followed by data collection	Quantitative data for hypothesis testing
Inductive (Emic)	No hypothesis, data collection follows from participants' lead	Qualitative data for descriptive insights

Reverse culture shock may occur after coming home. An American anthropologist describes his feelings on returning to San Francisco after a year of fieldwork in a village in India:

> We could not understand why people were so distant and hard to reach, or why they talked and moved so quickly. We were a little frightened at the sight of so many white faces and we could not understand why no one stared at us, brushed against us, or admired our baby. (Beals 1980:119)

Fieldwork Techniques

The goal of fieldwork is to collect information, or *data*, about the research topic. In cultural anthropology, variations exist about what kinds of data to emphasize and the best ways to collect data.

DEDUCTIVE AND INDUCTIVE RESEARCH A **deductive approach** is a form of research that starts from a research question or *hypothesis*, and then involves collecting relevant data through observation, interviews, and other

---

deductive approach (to research) a research method that involves posing a research question or hypothesis, gathering data related to the question, and then assessing the findings in relation to the original hypothesis.

inductive approach (to research) a research approach that avoids hypothesis formation in advance of the research and instead takes its lead from the culture being studied.

quantitative data numeric information.

qualitative data non-numeric information.

etic an analytical framework used by outside analysts in studying culture.

emic insiders' perceptions and categories, and their explanations for why they do what they do.

interview a research technique that involves gathering verbal data through questions or guided conversation between at least two people.

questionnaire a formal research instrument containing a preset series of questions that the anthropologist asks in a face-to-face setting, by mail, or by e-mail.

---

methods. An **inductive approach** is a form of research that proceeds without a hypothesis and involves gathering data through unstructured, informal observation, conversation, and other methods. Deductive methods are more likely to collect **quantitative data**, or numeric information, such as the amount of land in relation to the population or the numbers of people with particular health problems. The inductive approach in cultural anthropology emphasizes **qualitative data**, or nonnumeric information, such as recordings of myths and conversations and filming of events. Most anthropologists, to varying degrees, combine deductive and inductive approaches and quantitative and qualitative data.

Cultural anthropologists have labels for data collected in each approach. **Etic** (pronounced like the last two syllables of "phonetic," or eh-tik) refers to data collected according to the researcher's questions and categories, with the goal of being able to test a hypothesis (Figure 3.3). In contrast, **emic** (pronounced like the last two syllables of "phonemic," or ee-mik) refers to data collected that reflect what insiders say and understand about their culture, and insiders' categories of thinking. Cultural materialists (review Chapter 1) are more likely to collect etic data, whereas interpretivists are more likely to collect emic data. Again, however, most cultural anthropologists collect both types of data.

PARTICIPANT OBSERVATION The phrase *participant observation* includes two processes: participating, or being part of the people's lives, and, at the same time, carefully observing. These two activities may sound simple, but they are actually quite complex.

Being a participant means that the researcher adopts the lifestyle of the people being studied, living in the same kind of housing, eating similar food, wearing similar clothing, learning the language, and participating in the daily round of activities and in special events. The rationale is that participation over a long period improves the quality of the data. The more time the researcher spends living among the people, the more likely it is that the people will live their "normal" lives. In this way, the researcher is able to overcome the *Hawthorne effect*, a research bias that occurs when participants change their behavior to conform to the perceived expectations of the researcher. The Hawthorne effect was discovered in the 1930s in a study of an industrial plant in the United States. During the study, research participants altered their behavior in ways they thought would please the researcher.

An anthropologist cannot be everywhere, participate in everything, or observe everyone, so choices are involved in where to be and what to observe. As mentioned earlier, gender, age, and other microcultural factors may limit the anthropologist's participation in certain domains or activities. The sheer need for sleep may mean that the anthropologist misses something important that happens at night, such as a ritual or a moonlight hunting expedition.

Although participant observation is often equated with the casual term "hanging out," in fact, it means constant choices about where to be on a particular day at a particular time, what one observes, with whom, and what, by default, one misses. Depending on the research topic, participant observation may focus on who lives with whom, who interacts with whom in public, who are leaders and who are followers, what work people do, how people organize themselves for different activities, rituals, arguments, festivals, funerals, and far more.

TALKING WITH PEOPLE   Common sense tells you that participating and observing are important, but what about talking to people and asking questions such as "What is going on here?" "What does that mean?" and "Why are you doing that?" The process of talking to people and asking them questions is such an important component of participant observation that the method should actually be called *participant observation and talking*. Cultural anthropologists use a variety of data-collection techniques that rely on talking with people, from informal, casual, and unplanned conversations to more formal methods.

An **interview** is a technique for gathering verbal data through questions or guided conversation. It is more purposeful than a casual conversation. An interview may involve only two people, the interviewer and the interviewee, or several people in what are called *group interviews* or *focus groups*. Cultural anthropologists use different interview styles and formats, depending on the kinds of information they seek, the amount of time they have, and their language skills. The least structured type of interview is an *open-ended interview*, in which the respondent (interviewee) takes the lead in setting the direction of the conversation, determining the topics to be covered, and choosing how much time to devote to a particular topic. The interviewer does not interrupt or provide prompting questions. In this way, the researcher discovers what themes are important to the person.

A **questionnaire** is a formal research instrument containing a preset series of questions that the anthropologist asks in a face-to-face setting or by mail or e-mail. Cultural anthropologists who use questionnaires favor a face-to-face setting. Like interviews, questionnaires vary in the degree to which the questions are *structured* (close ended) or *unstructured* (open ended). Structured questions limit the range of possible responses—for example, by asking research participants to rate their positions on a particular issue as "very positive," "positive," "negative," "very negative," or "no opinion." Unstructured interviews generate more emic responses.

When designing a questionnaire, the researcher should have enough familiarity with the study population to be able to develop questions that make cultural sense. Researchers who take a ready-made questionnaire to the field with them should ask another researcher who knows the culture to review the questionnaire in advance to see whether it makes sense. Further revisions may be required in the field to make the questionnaire fit local conditions. A *pilot study* using the questionnaire among a small number of people in the research area can expose areas that need further revision.

COMBINING OBSERVATION AND TALKING   A combination of observation of what people actually do with verbal data about what people *say* they do and think is essential for a well-rounded view of a culture (Sanjek 2000). People may say that they do something or believe something, but their behavior may differ from what they say. For example, people may say that sons and daughters inherit equal shares of family property when the parents die. Research into what really happens may reveal that daughters do not, in fact, inherit equal shares. Similarly, an anthropologist might learn from people and their laws that discrimination on the basis of skin color is illegal. Research on people's behavior might reveal clear examples of discrimination. It is important for an anthropologist to learn about both what people say and what happens. Both are "true" aspects of culture.

SPECIALIZED METHODS   Cultural anthropologists also use several kinds of specific research methods. The choice depends on the anthropologist's research goals.

Life History   A *life history* is a qualitative, in-depth description of an individual's life as narrated to the researcher. Anthropologists differ in their views about the value of the life history as a method in cultural anthropology. Early in the twentieth century, Franz Boas rejected this method as unscientific because research participants might lie or exaggerate (Peacock and Holland 1993). Others disagree, saying that a life history

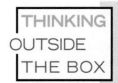

THINKING OUTSIDE THE BOX

Given the emphasis on observation in fieldwork, is it possible for a blind person to become a cultural anthropologist?

Life histories are a longstanding method of data collection in cultural anthropology. (TOP) Marjorie Shostak interviewing Nisa during fieldwork among the Ju/'hoansi in 1975. (BOTTOM) This Sri Lankan woman, whose life story Gananath Obeyesekere analyzed, is a priestess to a deity. She stands in the shrine room of her house, holding her matted, snaky hair.

▶ *What would you tell an anthropologist about your life?*

reveals rich information on individuals and how they think, no matter how "distorted" their reports are. For example, some anthropologists have questioned the accuracy of parts of *Nisa: The*

Life and Times of a !Kung Woman (Shostak 1981), probably the most widely read life history in anthropology. It is a book-length story of a Ju/'hoansi woman of the Kalahari desert of southern Africa (review Culturama, Chapter 1, page 21). Presented in Nisa's voice, the book offers details about her childhood and several marriages. The value of the narrative is not so much whether it is "true" or not; rather, the value is that we learn from Nisa what she wants to tell us, her view of her experiences. That counts as "data" in cultural anthropology, for it is "truly" what she reported to Marjorie Shostak.

In the early days of life history research, anthropologists tried to choose an individual who was somehow typical, average, or representative. It is not possible, however, to find one person who is representative of an entire culture in the scientific sense. Instead, anthropologists seek individuals who occupy particularly interesting social niches. For example, Gananath Obeyesekere (oh-bay-yuh-sek-eruh) analyzed the life histories of four Sri Lankan people, three women and one man (1981). Each became a Hindu religious devotee and ascetic, distinguished by their hair, which is permanently matted into long, twisted coils that look like snakes. If they try to comb out the tangles, they cannot succeed because, according to the devotees, a deity is present in their matted hair. Obeyesekere suggests that all four people had suffered deep psychological afflictions during their lives, including sexual anxieties. Their matted hair symbolizes their suffering and provides them with a special status as holy, thus placing them beyond the rules of married life, including conjugal sexual relations.

Time Allocation Study A *time allocation study* is a quantitative method that collects data on how people spend their time each day on particular activities. This method relies on standard time units and then labeling or coding the activities that occur within certain time segments (Gross 1984). Activity codes must be adapted to fit local contexts. For example, activity codes for various kinds of work would not be useful in a time allocation study in a retirement home. Data can be collected through observation that may be continuous, at fixed intervals (for instance, every 48 hours), or on a random basis. Continuous observation is extremely time-consuming and means that the number of people observed is limited. Spot observations help increase the number of observations but may inadvertently miss important activities. Another option for data collection is to ask people to keep daily time logs or diaries.

Texts Many cultural anthropologists collect and analyze *textual material*, a category that includes written or oral stories, myths, plays, sayings, speeches, jokes, transcriptions of people's everyday conversations, and material on the Internet and social media outlets.

In the early twentieth century, Franz Boas recorded thousands of pages of texts from American Indians of the Northwest

Coast of Canada, including myths, songs, speeches, and accounts of how to perform rituals. These collections provide valuable records of cultures that have changed since the time of his fieldwork. Surviving tribal members have consulted them in order to recover forgotten aspects of their culture.

Boas would be interested to know about new studies in cultural anthropology that analyze Internet websites for their social meaning. The Internet has been labeled a modern-day Pandora's box because it makes available to the viewing public any and all knowledge and opinions, right or wrong, evidence-based or not. Anna Kata, a graduate student in anthropology at McMaster University in Canada, examined several Internet sites for the *social discourse*, or shared themes, about the dangers of vaccination (2010). As background, she consulted published data showing that around 74 percent of Americans and 72 percent of Canadians are online. Of them, between 75 and 80 percent of users search for health information, and of them, 70 percent say that the information they access influences their medical treatment decisions, so the Internet plays a large role in people's medical decision-making. Using Google as her search engine, Kata applied several criteria to label a particular website as "anti-vaccination." In all, she examined eight America and Canadian sites for content analysis. The prominent themes that emerged are: safety (vaccines are poisons); effectiveness (vaccines are not effective); alternative medicine favored over vaccines ("back to nature"); civil liberties (parental rights); conspiracy theories (accusations of cover-up); religion (go with God-given immune system); misinformation about vaccine studies; and emotional appeals (personal testimonies). Combating anti-vaccination views with education is necessary but not sufficient, Kata concludes. Analysis of the social discourse on the Internet can help pinpoint areas that need specific attention.

Archival and Historical Sources   Many cultural anthropologists who work in cultures with a written history gain important insights into the present from records of the past preserved in archives maintained in institutions such as libraries, churches, and museums. Ann Stoler pioneered the use of archival resources in understanding the present in her study of Dutch colonialism in Java (1985) (see Map 1.1, page 14). Her archival research exposed details about colonial policies, the culture of the colonizers, and relationships with indigenous Javanese people.

National archives in London, Paris, and Amsterdam, to name just a few places, contain records of colonial contact and relations. Regional and local archives contain information about land ownership, agricultural production, religious practices, and political activities. Parish churches throughout Europe keep detailed family histories extending back hundreds of years.

Important information about the past can also come from fieldwork among living people through an approach called the

In Sudan, a multidisciplinary team comprising anthropologists, engineers, and agricultural experts from the United States and Sudan meet to discuss a resettlement project.

anthropology of memory. Anthropologists collect information about what people remember as well as gaps in their memory, revealing how culture shapes memories and how memories shape their culture. Jennifer Robertson's (1991) research about neighborhood people's memories of life in Kodaira, Japan before the influx of immigrants is an example of this kind of research. She used both interview data and archival data.

Multiple Research Methods and Team Projects   Most cultural anthropologists use a mix of several different methods for their research because just one would not provide all the varieties of data necessary to understand a given topic. For example, consider what interviews with people in 100 households would provide in breadth of coverage, and then add what you could learn from life histories collected from a subset of five men and five women to provide depth, as well as what long-term participant observation with these people would contribute.

Anthropologists, with their in-depth insights about real people and real people's lives, are increasingly taking part in multidisciplinary research projects, especially projects with an applied focus. Such teamwork strengthens the research by adding more perspectives and methods. For example, a team project uses mixed methods such as data from group interviews, one-on-one interviews, participant observation, and mapping to provide detailed information on Inuit place names and environmental knowledge (see Eye on the Environment on page 72).

Recording Culture

How does an anthropologist keep track of all the information collected in the field and record it for future analysis? As with everything else about fieldwork, things have changed since the early times when a notebook and pencil were the major recording tools. Taking detailed notes, nonetheless, is still a cultural anthropologist's trademark method of recording data.

eye on the ENVIRONMENT

Inuit Place Names and Landscape Knowledge

The South Baffin Island Place Name Project is dedicated to collecting and recording Inuit place names and landscape knowledge as a means to preserving climatically important information (Henshaw 2006).

Inuit is a cluster name for many indigenous peoples who live in the Arctic region of Canada, Alaska, and Greenland. Before contact with Europeans, Inuit life was one of constant mobility. Now, most Inuit are settled in villages and towns. As a result, their detailed knowledge of migration routes, locations along these routes, and how to adapt to changing conditions when on the move are being lost.

One project looks at **toponymy** (to-PAH-nuh-mee), or the naming of places. Inuit toponymy is one aspect of a rich set of **indigenous knowledge**, or local understanding of the environment, climate, plants, and animals.

The South Baffin Island Place Names Project used several methods for collecting data. The first step was community-wide workshops, with 10 to 15 people gathered together in a community hall. The researchers laid out large maps, and the Inuit added place names to the map and explained their importance.

The second step was conducting one-on-one interviews with Inuit elders. These elders have lived in particular areas and can provide specialized knowledge about their use (for shelter, fishing and hunting, and storage), routes to and from the site, and likely weather conditions.

The third step was participant observation. The anthropologists, with Inuit collaborators, went to many of the sites. They gained firsthand experience about travel conditions to and from the sites

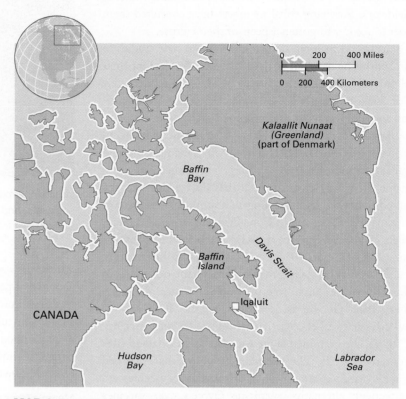

MAP 3.4 **Baffin Island in Northeast Canada.**
Baffin Island is the largest island in the Canadian Arctic and has a population of around 11,000. The Inuit name for the island is Qikiqtaaluk. It is part of the territory of Nunavut of which Iqaluit, a town of about 3,000 people, is the capital.

and conditions at the sites. They made video recordings and took photographs.

The fourth step was analytical and archival. The researchers created a computer database, linking the ethnographic data to maps.

This research project has many uses. It will provide a data baseline, starting with elders' memories and narratives of important sites and migration routes. It will show, over time, environmental changes that have occurred and how people are adapting to them. It will create an archive of indigenous

knowledge that can be used by future generations of Inuit in protecting their cultural heritage.

FOOD FOR THOUGHT ▼
Choose an ordinary day in your week, create a map of where you go, and take notes about how key locations are named (such as your dorm room, dining hall, classrooms, and other locations). What names do you use for key sites, and what do the place names mean to you? How would you change your daily route depending on differences in the weather or season?

FIELD NOTES *Field notes* consist of daily logs, personal journals, descriptions of events, and notes about those notes. Ideally, researchers should write up their field notes each day. Trying to capture, in the fullest way possible, the events of even a single day is a monumental task and can result in dozens of pages of handwritten or typed field notes. Laptop computers now enable anthropologists to enter their daily observations directly into the computer.

TAPE RECORDINGS, PHOTOGRAPHS, AND VIDEOS
Tape recorders are a major aid to fieldwork. Their use may raise problems, however, such as research participants' suspicions

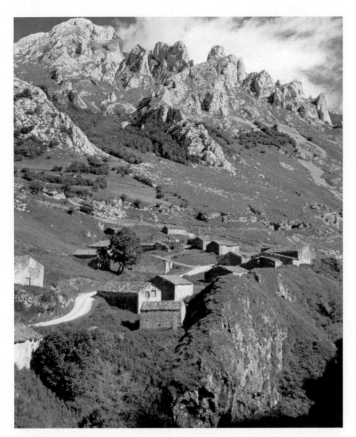

Asturias is located in the far north of Spain. It has extensive coastal beaches but the inland is mainly mountainous. The traditional economy was based in fishing and agriculture. Coal mining and steel production were important in the mid-twentieth century but have declined.

about a machine that can capture their voices, and the ethical issue of protecting the identities of people whose voices are preserved on tape. María Cátedra reports on her use of tape recording during her research in the Asturias region of rural Spain (Map 3.5):

> At first the existence of the "apparatus," as they called it, was part wonder and part suspect. Many had never seen one before and were fascinated to hear their own voice, but all were worried about what I would do with the tapes. . . . I tried to solve the problem by explaining what I would do with the tapes: I would use them to record correctly what people told me, since my memory was not good enough and I could not take notes quickly enough. . . . One event helped people to accept my integrity in regard to the "apparatus." In the second *braña* [small settlement] I visited, people asked me to play back what the people of the first *braña* had told me, especially some songs sung by a group of men. At first I was going to do it, but then I instinctively refused because I did not have the first people's permission. . . . My stand was quickly known in the first *braña* and commented on with approval. (1992:21–22)

To be useful for analysis, tape recordings have to be transcribed (typed up), either partially or completely.

MAP 3.5 Spain.

The Kingdom of Spain is the largest of the three countries occupying the Iberian Peninsula. The geography is dominated by high plateaus and mountain ranges. Spain's population exceeds 40 million. Spain's administrative structure is complex, including autonomous communities, such as Andalucia and Catalonia, and provinces. The central government is granting more autonomy to some localities, including the Basque area.

Each hour of recorded talk takes between 5 and 8 hours to transcribe.

Like tape recordings, photographs or videos capture more detail than scratch notes. Any researcher who has watched people performing a ritual, taken scratch notes, and then tried to reconstruct the details of the ritual later on will know how much of the sequencing and related activity is lost to memory within just a few hours. Reviewing photographs or a video recording of the ritual provides a surprising amount of forgotten or missed material. The trade-off, however, is that if you are using a camera or video recorder, you cannot take notes at the same time.

Kirsten Hastrup describes her use of photography in recording the annual ram exhibition in Iceland (see photo and Map 3.6 on page 74) that celebrates the successful herding in of the sheep from mountain pastures. This event is exclusively for men, but they allowed her to attend:

> The smell was intense, the light somewhat dim and the room full of indiscernible sounds from some 120 rams and about 40 men. A committee went from one ram to the next noting their impressions of the animal, in terms of its general beauty, the size of the horns and so forth. Measurements were made all over but the decisive measure (made by hand) was the size and weight of the ram's testicles. The air was

toponymy   the naming of places.

indigenous knowledge   local understanding of the environment, climate, plants, animals, and making a living.

MAP 3.6 Iceland.
The Republic of Iceland has a population of 300,000. A volcanic island, Iceland is the fifth-richest country in the world, according to GDP (gross domestic product) per capita. It has a high quality of life and ranked second in the 2005 United Nations Human Development Index. Iceland's economy is based in exporting fish and fish products, technology, and tourism.

A scene at the National Icelandic Ram Festival in Iceland.

loaded with sex and I realized that the exhibition was literally and metaphorically a competition of sexual potence . . . . I heard endless sexual jokes and very private remarks. The bursts of laughter followed by side-glances at me conveyed an implicit question of whether I understood what was going on. I did. (1992:9)

Hastrup took many photographs. After they were developed, she was disappointed by how little of the totality of the event they conveyed.

Data Analysis

During the research process, an anthropologist collects a vast amount of data in many forms. How does he or she put the data into a meaningful form? In data analysis, as with data collection, two basic varieties of data exist: *qualitative* (prose-based description) and *quantitative* (numeric presentation).

ANALYZING QUALITATIVE DATA Qualitative data include descriptive field notes, narratives, myths and stories, songs and sagas, and more. Few guidelines exist for undertaking a qualitative analysis of qualitative data. One procedure is to search for themes or patterns. This approach involves exploring the data, or "playing" with the data, either "by hand" or with the use of a computer. Jennifer Robertson's analysis of her Kodaira data was inspired by writer Gertrude Stein's (1948) approach to writing "portraits" of individuals, such as Picasso. Robertson says that Stein was a superb ethnographer who was able to illuminate the "bottom nature" of her subjects and their worlds through a process that Stein referred to as "condensation." To do this, "she scrutinized her subjects until, over time, there emerged for her a repeating pattern of their words and actions. Her literary portraits . . . were condensations of her subjects' repeatings" (Robertson 1991:1). Like Stein, Robertson reflected on all that she had experienced and learned in Kodaira, beginning with the years when she lived there as a child. Emerging from all this was the dominant theme, *furusato*, which literally means "old village." References to *furusato* appear frequently in people's accounts of the past, conveying a sense of nostalgia for a more "real" past.

Many qualitative anthropologists use computers to help sort the data for *tropes* (key themes). Computer scanning offers the ability to search vast quantities of data more quickly and perhaps more accurately than with the human eye. The range of software available for such data management is expanding. The quality of the results, though, still depends on careful and complete inputting of the data, as well as an intelligent coding scheme that will tell the computer what it should be scanning for in the data.

The presentation of qualitative data relies on people's own words—their stories, explanations, and conversations. Lila Abu-Lughod followed this approach in conveying Egyptian Bedu (bed-oo) women's narratives in her book *Writing Women's Worlds* (1993). Abu-Lughod offers a light authorial framework that organizes the women's stories into thematic clusters such as marriage, production, and honor. Although she provides an introduction to the narratives, she offers no conclusion, thereby prompting readers to think for themselves about the meanings of the stories and what they say about Egyptian Bedu women's lives.

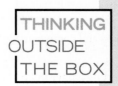

THINKING OUTSIDE THE BOX

Have you ever had the experience of taking photographs of a place, event, or people and then being terribly disappointed because the results did not capture the essence of your experience? What was missing from the photographs?

Item	Urban				Rural			
	Group 1	Group 2	Group 3	Total	Group 1	Group 2	Group 3	Total
Number of Households	26	25	16	67	32	30	16	78
Food	60.5	51.6	50.1	54.7	74.1	62.3	55.7	65.8
Alcohol	0.2	0.4	1.5	0.6	0.5	1.1	1.0	0.8
Tobacco	0.8	0.9	0.9	0.9	1.1	1.7	1.2	1.4
Dry Goods	9.7	8.1	8.3	8.7	8.8	10.2	14.3	10.5
Housing	7.3	11.7	10.3	9.7	3.4	5.7	3.9	4.4
Fuel	5.4	6.0	5.0	5.6	3.7	3.9	4.1	3.9
Transportation	7.4	8.2	12.4	8.9	3.0	5.3	7.6	4.9
Health	0.3	0.6	0.7	0.5	1.5	1.4	1.7	1.5
Education	3.5	2.8	3.1	3.2	1.2	2.1	3.0	1.9
Entertainment	0.1	0.9	1.1	0.6	0.0	0.1	0.3	0.2
Other	5.2	8.3	6.9	6.8	2.1	6.0	6.9	4.6
Total*	100.4	99.5	100.3	100.2	99.4	99.8	99.7	99.9

*Totals may not add up to 100 due to rounding.

Source: From "Social Patterns of Food Expenditure Among Low-Income Jamaicans" by Barbara D. Miller in *Papers and Recommendations of the Workshop on Food and Nutrition Security in Jamaica in the 1980s and Beyond*, ed. by Kenneth A. Leslie and Lloyd B. Rankine, 1987.

FIGURE 3.4 Mean Weekly Expenditure Shares (Percentage) in 11 Categories by Urban and Rural Expenditure Groups, Jamaica, 1983–1984.

Some anthropologists question the value of such artistic, interpretive approaches because they lack scientific verifiability. Too much depends, they say, on the individual selection process of the anthropologist, and interpretation often depends on a small number of cases. Interpretive anthropologists respond that verifiability, in the scientific sense, is not their goal and, in fact, is not a worthwhile goal for cultural anthropology. Instead, they seek to provide a plausible interpretation or a fresh understanding of people's lives that offers detail and richness.

ANALYZING QUANTITATIVE DATA Analysis of quantitative, or numeric, data can proceed in several directions. Some of the more sophisticated methods require knowledge of statistics, and many require the use of a computer and a software package that can perform statistical computations. The author's research on low-income household budgets in Jamaica involved the use of computer analysis, first to divide the sample households into three income groups (lower, medium, and higher) and second to calculate percentages of expenditures in three categories of goods and groups of goods: food, housing, and transportation (Figure 3.4). Because the number of households was quite small (120), the analysis could have been done "by hand," but using the computer made the analysis proceed more quickly and more accurately.

REPRESENTING CULTURE Ethnography, or a detailed description of a living culture based on personal observation and study, is the main way that cultural anthropologists present their findings about culture. In the early phase of cultural anthropology, in the first half of the twentieth century, ethnographers wrote about "exotic" cultures located far from their homes in Europe and North America. The early ethnographers tended to treat a particular local group or village as a unit unto itself with clear boundaries. Since the 1980s, ethnographies have changed in several ways:

- Ethnographers now treat local cultures as connected with larger regional and global structures and forces. Edward Fischer's book *Cultural Logics and Global Economics: Maya Identity in Thought and Practice* (2001) takes the topic of Maya political activism in Guatemala as its focus and sets it within the context of changing economic systems more widely.

- Ethnographers tend to focus on one topic of interest and avoid a more holistic approach. Laura Miller studied ideas and practices about the body and beauty in Japan. In her book *Body Up: Exploring Contemporary Japanese Body Aesthetics* (2006), she explores beauty salons, beauty products, changing ideas of female and male beauty, and ideas about diet.

- Ethnographers study Western, industrialized cultures as well as other cultures. Philippe Bourgois's research in East Harlem in New York City for his book *In Search of Respect: Selling Crack in El Barrio* (1995) explores how people in one neighborhood cope with poverty and dangerous living conditions. Although this topic sounds like it fits more in sociology than anthropology, a cultural anthropologist will provide contextual details about the everyday experiences and perspectives of the people based on participant observation.

ethnography a firsthand, detailed description of a living culture, based on personal observation.

Urgent Issues in Cultural Anthropology Research

This section considers two urgent issues in cultural anthropology research: fieldwork ethics and safety during fieldwork.

Ethics and Collaborative Research

Anthropology was one of the first disciplines to create and adopt a code of ethics. Two events in the 1950s and 1960s prompted cultural anthropologists to reconsider their role in research in relation to the sponsors of their research and to the people with whom they were studying. The first was *Project Camelot* of the 1950s; it was a plan of the U.S. government to influence political leadership in South America in order to strengthen U.S. interests (Horowitz 1967). The U.S. government employed several anthropologists to collect information on political leaders and events, without revealing their purpose.

The second major event was the Vietnam War (or the American War, as people in Vietnam refer to it). It brought to the forefront of anthropology questions about government interests in ethnographic information, the role of anthropologists during wartime, and the protection of the people with whom anthropologists conduct research. Two bitterly opposed positions emerged within anthropology. On one side was the view that all Americans, as citizens, should support the U.S. military effort in Vietnam. People on this side said that any anthropologist who had information that could help subvert communism should provide it to the U.S. government. The other position stated that an anthropologist's responsibility is, first and always, to protect the people being studied, a responsibility that takes priority over politics. Anthropologists taking this position opposed the war and saw the people of South Vietnam as victims of Western imperialism. They uncovered cases in which some anthropologists submitted information about people's political affiliations to the U.S. government, with the result being military actions and death of the people exposed by the research.

This period was the most divisive in the history of U.S. anthropology. It led, in 1971, to the adoption by the American Anthropological Association (AAA) of a code of ethics. The AAA code of ethics states that an anthropologist's primary responsibility is to ensure the safety of the people participating in the research. A related principle is that cultural anthropology does not condone covert, or "undercover," research.

Both of these central principles now create controversy among anthropologists in terms of whether or not cultural anthropologists should participate in the U.S. Human Terrain System (HTS). The HTS seeks to reduce wartime casualties of the U.S. military and civilians by employing cultural anthropologists and others knowledgeable about the local culture in on-the-ground operations. The rationale is reasonable: culturally informed and sensitive militaries will avoid offending local people and will be more effective in bringing closure to war or counter-insurgency operations (González 2009). While that sounds good, a major problem arises because joining the HTS is likely to place the anthropologist in a position of providing information about local people to the military whose war interests may, in fact, end up harming people. The principle of "do no harm" is impossible, some argue, to reconcile with military action.

COLLABORATIVE RESEARCH A new direction in methods explicitly seeks to involve members of the study population in collaborative research—from data collection to analysis and presentation. **Collaborative research** is an approach to learning about culture that involves the anthropologist working with members of the study population as partners and teammates rather than as "subjects". This strategy, from the start, forces a reconsideration of how anthropologists refer to the people being studied, especially the long-standing term "informant." The term sounds related to espionage or war and implies a passive role on handing over information to someone else. As noted earlier in this chapter, IRBs use the term "human subject," which cultural anthropologists reject for similar reasons. Cultural anthropologists favor the term *research participant*.

Luke Eric Lassiter is a pioneer in collaborative methods. In a recent project, Lassiter involved his undergraduate anthropology students in a collaboration with members of the African American community of Muncie, Indiana. This project resulted in a book with shared authorship among Lassiter, the students, and the community members (2004). The project collected information about African American life that is now housed in a library archive.

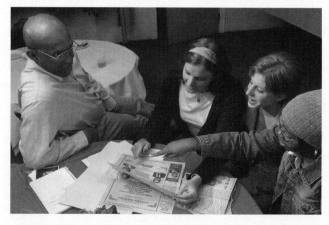

The collaborative research team led by Luke Eric Lassiter includes Muncie community members (far left and far right) and students and faculty from Ball State University.

---

collaborative research an approach to learning about culture that involves anthropologists working with members of the study population as partners and participants rather than as "subjects."

Cultural anthropologists are working to find better ways to share the benefits of research with the people and places they study. Research methods in cultural anthropology have come a long way from the armchair, to new strategies for nonhierarchical research. More progress lies ahead, however, in democratizing anthropology and making everyone a "barefoot anthropologist."

Safety in the Field

Fieldwork can involve serious physical and psychological risks to the researcher and to members of his or her family. The image of "the anthropologist as hero" has muffled, to a large degree, both the physical dangers and the psychological risks of fieldwork. Dangers from the physical environment are often serious and can be fatal. In the 1980s, the slippery paths of the highland Philippines claimed the life of Michelle Zimbalist Rosaldo, a major figure in late twentieth-century cultural anthropology (review Figure 1.2, page 10). Disease is a frequent problem. Many anthropologists have contracted infectious diseases that have chronic effects or that may be fatal.

Violence figures prominently in some, but not most, fieldwork experiences. During the five years that Philippe Bourgois conducted fieldwork in East Harlem, New York, he witnessed the following: a shooting outside his window, a bombing and machine-gunning of a numbers joint, a shoot-out and police car chase in front of the pizza parlor where he was eating, the aftermath of a fire-bombing of a heroin house, a dozen serious fights, and "almost daily exposure to broken-down human beings, some of them in fits of crack-induced paranoia, some suffering from delirium tremens, and others in unidentifiable pathological fits of screaming and shouting insults to all around

The food-ration queue at an emergency clinic in Sierra Leone, 2001. While conducting research in this war-torn country, Danny Hoffman used traditional fieldwork techniques, such as participant observation and interviews. But he had to be alert to risks specific to research during war. Hoffman believes that anthropologists must be willing to take such risks in order to provide knowledge about the complex causes and consequences of war that are overlooked by most journalists.

them" (1995:32). He was rough-handled by the police several times because they did not believe that he was a professor and not a drug-dealer. He was once mugged for the sum of $8. Although his research placed him in danger, it also enabled him to gain an understanding, from the inside, of everyday violence in the lives of desperately poor and addicted people.

Anthropological research may involve danger from political violence or even war. *War zone anthropology*, or research conducted within zones of violent conflict, can provide important insights into topics such as the militarization of civilian lives, civilian protection, the cultural dynamics of military personnel, and postconflict reconstruction (Hoffman and Lubkemann 2005). This kind of research requires skills and judgment that anthropology classes or books on research methods do not typically address (Nordstrom 1997, Kovats-Bernat 2002). Previous experience in conflict zones as a worker in international aid organizations or the military is helpful.

What about fieldwork danger in supposedly normal situations? After more than 20 years of fieldwork in the Kalahari desert, Nancy Howell (1990) suddenly had to confront the issue of danger in the field when one of her teenage sons was killed and another injured in a truck accident in Botswana, while with their father, Richard Lee, who was doing fieldwork there. In the months following the accident, she heard from many anthropologist friends who shared stories about other fieldwork accidents.

Howell contacted the American Anthropological Association (AAA) to see what advice it provides about fieldwork safety. The answer, she learned, was "not much." The AAA responded with financial support for her to undertake a detailed inquiry into fieldwork hazards in anthropology. Howell drew a sample of 311 anthropologists listed as employed in the AAA's *Guide to Departments*. She sent them a questionnaire asking for information on gender, age, work status, health status, and work habits in the field; she also asked about health problems and other hazards they had experienced. She received 236 completed questionnaires, a high response rate indicating strong interest in the study.

Her analysis revealed regional variation in risk and danger. The highest rates were in Africa, followed by India, the Asia/Pacific region, and Latin America. Howell offers recommendations about how anthropologists can prepare themselves more effectively for preventing and dealing with fieldwork risks. They include increasing risk awareness, training in basic medical care, and learning about fieldwork safety in anthropology classes.

Research methods in cultural anthropology have come a long way from the time of the armchair anthropologists. Topics have changed, as have techniques of data gathering and data analysis. New concerns about ethical research, including for the military, and fieldworkers' safety continue to arise and reshape research practices.

How do cultural anthropologists conduct research?

Cultural anthropologists conduct research by doing fieldwork and using participant observation. In the nineteenth century, early cultural anthropologists did armchair anthropology, meaning that they learned about other cultures by reading reports written by explorers and other untrained observers. The next stage was verandah anthropology, in which an anthropologist went to the field but did not live with the people. Instead, the anthropologist would interview a few members of the study population where he (there were no women cultural anthropologists at this time) lived, typically on his verandah.

Fieldwork and participant observation became the cornerstones of cultural anthropology research only after Malinowski's innovations in the Trobriand Islands during World War I. His approach emphasized the value of living for an extended period in the field, participating in the daily activities of the people, and learning the local language. These features are the hallmarks of fieldwork in cultural anthropology today.

New techniques continue to develop in response to changing times. They include multisited research, in which the anthropologist studies a topic at more than one location, and consumer research which relies on rapid research techniques to deliver information for product design and development that responds to users' needs and preferences.

What does fieldwork involve?

Fieldwork in cultural anthropology involves several stages. The first is to choose a research topic. A good topic is timely, important, and feasible. Ideas for topics can come from a literature review, restudies, current events and pressing issues, and sheer luck. Once in the field, the first steps include site selection, gaining rapport, and dealing with culture shock. Microcultures affect how anthropologists gain rapport and shape their access to particular cultural domains. Participating appropriately in the culture involves learning local forms of giftgiving and other types of exchange to express gratitude for people's hospitality, time, and trust.

Research techniques vary between being more deductive or more inductive and accordingly will emphasize gathering quantitative or qualitative data. Cultural materialists tend to focus on quantitative data, whereas interpretivists gather qualitative data. When in the field, anthropologists take daily notes, often by hand but now also using computers. Several other methods of documenting culture include photography, audio recording, and video recording.

Anthropologists' theoretical orientation, research goals, and the types of data collected affect their approach to data analysis and presentation. Quantitative data may involve statistical analysis and presentation in graphs or tables. The presentation of qualitative data is more likely to be descriptive.

What are some urgent issues in cultural anthropology research today?

Questions of ethics have been paramount to anthropologists since the 1950s. In 1971, U.S. anthropologists adopted a set of ethical guidelines for research to address their concern about what role, if any, anthropologists should play in research that might harm the people being studied. The AAA code of ethics states that an anthropologist's primary responsibility is to avoid doing harm to the people involved. Further, cultural anthropologists should never engage in covert research and should always explain their purpose to the people in the study and preserve the anonymity of the location and of individuals.

Collaborative research is a recent development that responds to ethical concerns by pursuing research that involves the participants as partners rather than as subjects.

Safety during fieldwork is another important issue. Danger to anthropologists can come from physical sources such as infectious diseases and from social sources such as political violence. A survey of anthropologists in the 1980s produced recommendations about increasing safety during fieldwork.

KEY CONCEPTS

collaborative research, p. 76
culture shock, p. 67
deductive approach (to research), p. 68
emic, p. 68

ethnography, p. 75
etic, p. 68
fieldwork, p. 58
inductive approach (to research), p. 68

indigenous knowledge, p. 73
informed consent, p. 63
interview, p. 68
kula, p. 63
multisited research, p. 60
participant observation, p. 58

qualitative data, p. 68
quantitative data, p. 68
questionnaire, p. 68
rapport, p. 64
toponymy, p. 73

SUGGESTED READINGS

Michael V. Angrosino. *Projects in Ethnographic Research*. Long Grove, IL: Waveland Press, 2005. This brief manual provides students with ideas about what conducting research in anthropology is like. It discusses the fundamental stages of three projects, with insights into how students can conduct their own research.

H. Russell Bernard. *Research Methods in Cultural Anthropology: Qualitative and Quantitative Approaches*, 3rd ed. Newbury Park, CA: Sage Publications, 2002. This is a sourcebook of anthropological research methods providing information about how to design a research project, methods of data collection, and data analysis and presentation.

Kathleen M. DeWalt and Billie R. DeWalt. *Participant Observation: A Guide for Fieldworkers*. New York: AltaMira Press, 2002. This book is a comprehensive guide to doing participant observation.

Alexander Ervin. *Applied Anthropology: Tools and Perspectives for Contemporary Practice*. Boston: Allyn and Bacon, 2005. Chapters discuss links between anthropology and policy, the history of applied anthropology, ethics, and specialized methods.

Carolyn Fluehr-Lobban. *Ethics and the Profession of Anthropology: A Dialogue for Ethically Conscious Practice*, 2nd ed. Philadelphia: University of Pennsylvania Press, 2003. The chapters in this volume address topics such as covert research, indigenous people's cultural rights, informed consent, and ethics in researching culture in cyberspace.

Peggy Golde, ed. *Women in the Field: Anthropological Experiences*. 2nd ed. Berkeley: University of California Press, 1986. Chapters in this classic collection discuss Margaret Mead's fieldwork in the Pacific, Laura Nader's fieldwork in Mexico and Lebanon, Ernestine Friedl's fieldwork in Greece, and Jean Briggs's fieldwork among the Inuit of the Canadian Arctic.

Joy Hendry. *An Anthropologist in Japan: Glimpses of Life in the Field*. London: Routledge, 1999. This book describes the author's original research design, how her focus changed, and how she reached unanticipated conclusions.

Choong Soon Kim. *One Anthropologist, Two Worlds: Three Decades of Reflexive Fieldwork in North America and Asia*. Knoxville: University of Tennessee Press, 2002. The author reflects on his fieldwork, conducted over 30 years, on Japanese industry in the American South and on Korean families displaced by the Korean war and partition.

Luke Eric Lassiter. *The Chicago Guide to Collaborative Ethnography*. Chicago: University of Chicago Press, 2005. This handbook for doing collaborative anthropology includes historical and theoretical perspectives on collaborative anthropology, exposing its roots in feminist, humanist, and critical anthropology.

Carolyn Nordstrom and Antonius C. G. M. Robben, eds. *Fieldwork under Fire: Contemporary Studies of Violence and Survival*. Berkeley: University of California Press, 1995. The chapters of this book discuss fieldwork experiences in Palestine, China, Sri Lanka, the United States, Croatia, Guatemala, and Ireland.

Tom Ric with Mette Louise Berg, eds. *Future Fields*, special issue of the online journal *Anthropology Matters*, Vol. 6, No. 2, 2004. This issue includes 11 articles that address a range of methodological issues cultural anthropologists face today, including emotional, financial, and ethical challenges as well as how to cope in situations of physical danger. The journal is open access at http://www.anthropologymatters.com.

PEARSON myanthrolab

For further information about topics covered in this chapter, go to MyAnthroLab at **www.myanthrolab.com** and access the following readings in MyAnthroLibrary:

Anna Kata. 2010. A Postmodern Pandora's Box: Anti-Vaccination Information on the Internet. *Vaccine* 28:1709–1716. A graduate student in cultural anthropology mines the Internet for data.

Ann E. Kingsolver. 2010. "Like Frogs in a Well": Young People's Views of the Future Expressed in Two Collaborative Research Projects in Sri Lanka. *Human Organization* 69:1–9. This article discusses collaborative research conducted with youth in Sri Lanka about their perceived needs and views of the future.

Susan Squires. 2002. Doing the Work: Customer Research in the Product Development and Design Industry. In Susan Squires and Bryan Byrne, eds. *Creating Breakthrough Ideas: The Collaboration of Anthropologists and Designers in the Product Development Industry*. Pp. 102–124. Westport, CT: Bergin and Garvey. A leading consumer anthropologist describes the fieldwork she did that led to a new breakfast food product for suburban American families.

◉ How do cultural anthropologists study economic systems?

◉ What are the five modes of livelihood?

◉ How are the five modes of livelihood changing?

MAKING A LIVING

◀ Dharavi is a low-income neighborhood of Mumbai (formerly Bombay), India, and perhaps the largest "slum" in Asia. Most residents are poor and, if employed, work in low-paying and insecure jobs. Dharavi has been depicted in many Indian films, including the award winning movie, *Slumdog Millionaire*.

4

During the many thousands of years of human prehistory, people made their living by collecting food and other necessities from nature. All group members had equal access to life-sustaining resources. Most people throughout the world now live in economies much different from this description.

◉ ◉ ◉

Culture and Economic Systems

In anthropology, the term **economic system** includes three components:

- *Livelihood* or production—making goods or money
- *Consumption*—using up goods or money
- *Exchange*—the transfer of goods or money between people or institutions

Economic anthropology is the subfield of cultural anthropology that focuses on economic systems cross-culturally. It differs from the discipline of economics in several ways. First, the subject matter of economic anthropology is much wider. It covers all economics systems, not just modern capitalism. Second, economic anthropologists' methods are different; they collect data, both qualitative and quantitative, mainly through fieldwork and participant observation rather than analyzing statistics from "canned" datasets or census information. Third, economic anthropologists believe that it is important to gather emic data in order to understand people's own concepts and categories related to making a living, rather than applying Western concepts and categories.

In spite of these differences, however, some shared territory exists. Some economists do learn a foreign language, and some try to learn about people's actual economic behavior and thought by conducting fieldwork. In turn, some economic anthropologists analyze large, quantitative datasets. Most fruitfully, some economists and some economic anthropologists work together on important issues such as the effects of globalization on local economies, how climate change is affecting food production, and **food security**, the ability of an individual, household, group or country, to obtain an adequate diet over time in order to sustain health.

---

economic system   the linked processes of livelihood, consumption, and exchange.

food security   the ability of an individual, household, group, or country to obtain an adequate diet over time in order to sustain health.

mode of livelihood   the dominant way of making a living in a culture.

Categorizing Livelihoods

Many years of research on economic systems has produced a rich body of knowledge about livelihoods in diverse settings, the topic of this chapter. Anthropologists organize this information by sorting it into categories, called *modes*. The next section describes five modes of livelihood. A **mode of livelihood** is the dominant way of making a living in a culture.

Categorizing a certain society as having a particular mode of livelihood implies an emphasis on a particular type of livelihood, but it does not mean that only one kind of economic activity exists. In a given society, some people will be involved in the prevailing productive activity, and others will not. A particular individual may be involved in more than one way of making a living. For example, a person could be a farmer and a herder. Another point to keep in mind is that the five modes of livelihood, in reality, blend with and overlap each other. Therefore, some cultures do not fit well within any one mode. Real life is always more complicated than the categories researchers create.

Figure 4.1 presents the five modes of livelihood in order of their historical appearance in the human record. This diagram does not mean that a particular mode evolves into the one following it—for example, foragers do not necessarily transform into horticulturalists, and so on. Nor does this

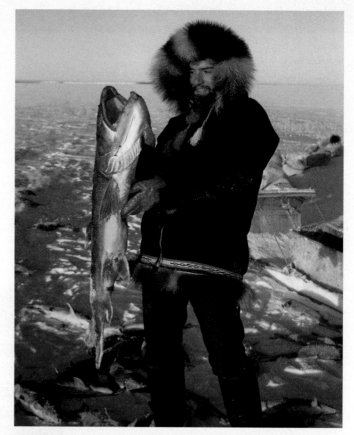

During his fieldwork among the Hare Indians in Northwest Canada, anthropologist Joel Savishinsky holds a 25-pound trout. His dog team is resting behind him.

Foraging	Horticulture	Pastoralism	Agriculture	Industrialism/Informatics
Reason for Production				**Reason for Production**
Production for use				Production for profit
Division of Labor				**Division of Labor**
Family-based				Class-based
Overlapping gender roles				High degree of occupational specialization
Property Relations				**Property Relations**
Egalitarian and collective				Stratified and private
Resource Use				**Resource Use**
Extensive and temporary				Intensive and expanding
Sustainability				**Sustainability**
High degree				Low degree

FIGURE 4.1 Modes of Livelihood.

ordering imply a judgment about the sophistication or superiority of more recent modes of livelihood. Figure 4.1 is not a model of "progress" from left to right. The oldest system involves complex and detailed knowledge about the environment that a contemporary city dweller would find difficult to learn quickly enough to ensure survival.

Modes of Livelihood and Globalization

Economic anthropologists provide unique insights into local economic systems. Now, more than ever, they are studying how local and global economic systems, and the people involved, are linked. Most important, the spread of Western industrial capitalism since the early twentieth century has had, and continues to have, marked effects on all other livelihood patterns that it meets. This process has created a *world economy*, in which countries compete for a share of the wealth (Wallerstein 1979). The competing countries enter the arena with unequal shares of power, a situation that tends to perpetuate global inequalities in wealth. In this view, the modern world economy is stratified into three major areas: the core, the periphery, and the semiperiphery.

Core areas monopolize the most profitable activities, such as high-tech service, manufacturing, and financial activities. They have the strongest governments, which play a dominating role in the affairs of other countries. *Peripheral areas* are relegated to the least profitable activities, including livelihood of raw materials, foodstuffs, and labor-intensive goods, and they must import high-tech goods and services from the core. They tend to have weak governments and are dominated, either directly or indirectly, by core states. *Semiperipheral areas* stand in the middle.

In this model, economic benefits are highly unequal across regions, with core areas profiting most. Core countries have about 20 percent of the world's population and control 80 percent of the world's wealth (and they create 80 percent of the world's pollution). Politically, the core continues to increase its economic power and political influence through international organizations such as the World Trade Organization (WTO) and regional arrangements such as the North American Free Trade Agreement (NAFTA). Countries in the peripheral and semiperipheral areas continue to be at a disadvantage and find it difficult to move up to becoming part of the core. The last section of this chapter returns to the topic of globalization and livelihood change.

◉ ◉ ◉
Making a Living: Five Modes of Livelihood

While reading this section, please bear in mind that anthropologists are uneasy about such large categories as those described here because they do not reflect the complexity of life in any particular situation. Rough as they are, however, the five categories will help you organize the cross-cultural examples presented in this book.

Foraging

Foraging, as defined in Chapter 2, is a mode of livelihood based on obtaining food that is available in nature through methods such as gathering, hunting, fishing, or scavenging. The oldest way of making a living, foraging, is a livelihood

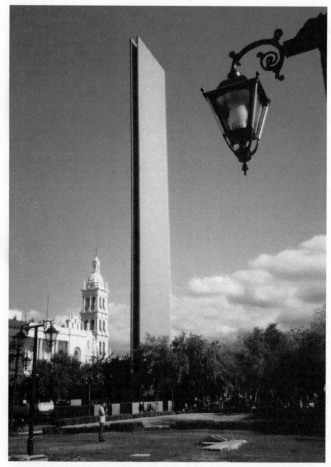

Monterrey, Mexico, is the second most important city in Mexico after the capital. Because of its strong steel industry, it is called "the Pittsburgh of Mexico." It has several major beer breweries and is home to the Mexican Baseball Hall of Fame. The city center has monuments of both Spanish colonialism and cosmopolitan modernity.

strategy that humans share with our nonhuman primate relatives.

Foraging supported humanity since our beginnings many millions of years ago. But now it is in danger of extinction. Today, only 250,000 people worldwide provide for their livelihood predominantly from foraging. Most contemporary foragers live in what are considered marginal areas, such as deserts, tropical rainforests, and the circumpolar region. These areas, however, often contain material resources that are in high demand in core areas, such as oil, diamonds, gold, and expensive tourist destinations. Thus, the basis of their survival is threatened by what is called the *resource curse*: People in rich countries desire the natural resources in their areas, which leads to conversion of foraging land to mines, plantations, or tourist destinations, in turn leading to the displacement of foragers from their homeland.

---

extensive strategy   a form of livelihood involving temporary use of large areas of land and a high degree of spatial mobility.

Depending on the environmental context, foragers' food sources include nuts, berries and other fruits, surface-growing vegetables such as melons, roots, honey, insects, and eggs. Foragers trap and hunt a wide variety of birds, fish, and animals. Successful foraging requires sophisticated knowledge of the natural environment and seasonal changes in it. Most critical is knowledge about the location of water sources and of various foods, how to follow animal tracks, how to judge the weather, and how to avoid predators. This unwritten knowledge is passed down over the generations (review Eye on the Environment, Chapter 3, page 72).

Foragers rely on a diverse set of tools used for gathering, transporting, and processing wild foods. Tools include digging sticks for removing roots from the ground and for penetrating the holes dug by animals in order to get the animals out, bows and arrows, spears, nets, and knives. Baskets are important for carrying food. For processing raw materials into edible food, foragers use stones to mash, grind, and pound. Meat can be dried in the sun or over fire, and fire is used for cooking either by boiling or by roasting. These activities involve few nonrenewable fuel sources beyond wood or other combustible substances for cooking. Foraging is an **extensive strategy**, a mode of livelihood requiring access to large areas of land and unrestricted population movement. Cultural anthropologists distinguish two major varieties of foraging that are related to different environmental contexts: *temperate-climate foraging* and *circumpolar foraging* (Figure 4.2).

The Ju/'hoansi people of southern Africa, as studied in the 1960s, moved several times during a year, depending on

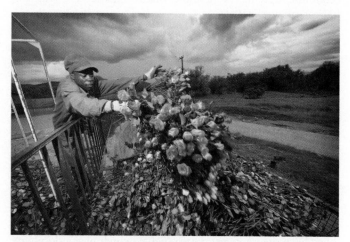

The promise and perils of economic globalization are evident in the cut flower industry. In Kenya, many farmers now grow flowers for export instead of food for their own consumption. The cash income allows them many benefits of a "modern" life. When things go wrong, as in 2010 when volcanic ash from Iceland closed European airports, Kenyan farmers had to dump flowers and many workers were laid off.

	Temperate-Region Foragers	Circumpolar-Region Foragers
Diet	Wide variety of nuts, tubers, fruits, small animals, and occasional large game	Large marine and terrestrial animals, small seasonal plants
Gender division of labor in food procurement	Men and women forage; men hunt large game	Men hunt and fish
Shelter	Casual construction, nonpermanent, little maintenance	Time-intensive construction and maintenance, some permanent

FIGURE 4.2 Temperate and Circumpolar Foraging Systems Compared.

the seasonal availability of water sources (review Culturama, Chapter 1, page 21). Each cluster of families regularly returned to "their" territory, reconstructing or completely rebuilding their shelters with sticks for frames, and leaf or thatch coverings. Shelters are sometimes attached to two or three small trees or bushes for support. The amount of time involved in gathering and processing food and constructing shelters is modest.

In contrast to foragers of temperate climates, those living in the circumpolar regions of North America, Europe, and Asia devote more time and energy to obtaining food and providing shelter. The specialized technology of circumpolar peoples includes spears, nets, and knives, as well as sleds and the use of domesticated animals to pull them. Dogs or other animals used to pull sleds are an important aspect of circumpolar peoples' technology and social identity (see Everyday Anthropology on page 86). Considerable amounts of labor are needed to construct and maintain igloos or log houses.

Protective clothing, including coats, gloves, and boots, is another feature of circumpolar foraging that is time intensive in terms of making and maintaining.

DIVISION OF LABOR Among foraging peoples, the *division of labor*, or occupational specialization (assigning particular tasks to particular individuals), is based on gender and age. Among temperate foraging cultures, a minimal gender-based division of labor exists. Temperate foragers get most of their everyday food by gathering roots, berries, grubs, small birds and animals, and fish, and both men and women collect these basic foods. Hunting large animals, however, tends to involve only men, who go off together in small groups on long-range expeditions. Large game provides a small and irregular part of the diets of temperate-climate foragers. In circumpolar groups, a significant part of people's diet comes from large animals (such as seals, whales, and bears) and fish. Hunting and fishing tend to involve only men. Among

A Ju/'hoansi traditional shelter.

everyday ANTHROPOLOGY

The Importance of Dogs

Dogs were the first domesticated animal, with archaeological evidence of their domestication from sites in Eastern Europe and Russia dating to around 18,000 years ago. In spite of dogs' long-standing importance to humans around the world, few cultural anthropologists have focused attention on humans and their dogs. One of the rare ethnographies to do so provides insights about the economic, social, and psychological importance of dogs among a group of circum-polar foragers.

Fewer than 100 Hare Indians constitute the community of Colville Lake in Canada's Northwest Territories (Savishinsky 1974). They live by hunting, trapping, and fishing in one of the harshest environments in the world. Joel Savishinsky went to Colville Lake to study how people there cope with environmental stress. Environmental stress factors include extremely cold temperatures, long and severe winters, extended periods of isolation, hazardous travel conditions along with the constant need for mobility during the harshest periods of the year, and sometimes food scarcity. Social and psychological stress factors also exist, including contact with outsiders.

Savishinsky discovered the importance of dogs to the Hare people early in his research:

> Later in the year when I obtained my own dogteam, I enjoyed much greater freedom of movement, and was able to camp with many people whom I had previously not been able to keep up with. Altogether I travelled close to 600 miles by dogsled between mid-October and early June. This constant contact with dogs, and the necessity of learning how to drive, train and handle them, led to my recognition of the social and psychological, as well as the ecological, significance of these animals in the lives of the people. (1974:xx)

Among the 14 households, there are a total of 224 dogs. Some households have as many as four teams, with an average of six dogs per team, corresponding to people's estimation that six dogs are required for travel.

More than being economically useful, dogs play a significant role in people's emotional lives. They are a frequent topic of conversation:

> Members of the community constantly compare and comment on the care, condition, and growth of one another's animals, noting special qualities of size, strength, color, speed, and alertness (1974:169).

Emotional displays, uncommon among the Hare, are significant between people and their dogs:

> The affectionate and concerned treatment of young animals is participated in by people of all ages, and the nature of the relationship bears a striking resemblance to the way in which people treat young children. Pups and infants are, in essence, the only recipients of unreserved positive affect in the band's social life. . . . (1974:169–170)

---

circumpolar foragers, therefore, the division of labor is strongly gender-divided.

Age is a basis for task allocation in all modes of livelihood, including foraging. Young boys and girls help collect food. Elderly people tend to stay at the camp area where they are responsible for caring for young children.

PROPERTY RELATIONS The concept of *private property,* in the sense of owning something that can be sold to someone else, does not exist in foraging societies. Instead, the term **use rights** is more appropriate. It means that a person or group has socially recognized priority in access to particular resources such as gathering areas, hunting and fishing areas, and water holes. This access is willingly shared with others by permission. Among the Ju/'hoansi, family groups control

---

use rights   a system of property relations in which a person or group has socially recognized priority in access to particular resources such as gathering, hunting, and fishing areas and water holes.

---

access to particular water holes and the territory surrounding them (Lee 1979:58–60). Visiting groups are welcome and will be given food and water. In turn, the host group, at another time, will visit other camps and be offered hospitality there. In India's Andaman Islands (see Culturama on page 88), each family group controls a known offshore area for fishing. Sharing access to these resources is expected but only if permission has been requested and granted. Encroaching on someone else's area without permission is a serious misdemeanor and is likely to result in violence.

FORAGING AS A SUSTAINABLE SYSTEM When untouched by outside influences and with abundant land available, foraging systems are *sustainable,* which means that crucial resources are regenerated over time in balance with the demand that the population makes on them. North Sentinel Island, one island in the Andaman Islands, provides a clear case because its inhabitants have long lived in a "closed" system. So far, the few hundred indigenous people live in almost complete isolation from the rest of the

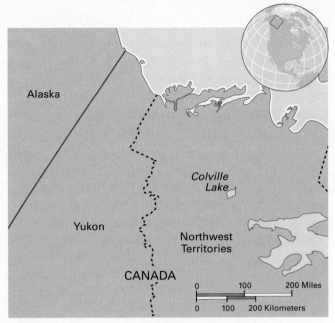

MAP 4.1 Hare Region near Colville Lake in Northwest Canada.

Early European colonialists named the local people Hare because of their reliance on snowshoe hares for food and clothing. The Hare people became involved in the wage-labor economy and were afflicted by alcoholism, tuberculosis, and other diseases. Efforts to reestablish claims to ancestral lands began in the 1960s.

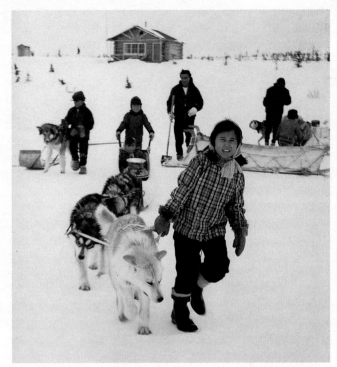

Hare Indian children use their family's sled to haul drinking water to their village.

FOOD FOR THOUGHT ▼
Think of a culture (perhaps yours) in which dogs or some other domesticated animals are a focus of intense human interest. How do people and the animals in question interact? Are there age and gender differences in human relationships with domesticated animals?

world, other than the occasional helicopter flying overhead and the occasional attempt by outsiders to land on their territory.

One reason for the sustainability of foraging is that foragers' needs are modest. Anthropologists have typified the foraging lifestyle as the *original affluent society* because needs are satisfied with minimal labor efforts. This term is used metaphorically to remind people living in contemporary consumer cultures that foraging is not a miserable, inadequate way to make a living, contrary to most ethnocentric thinking. In the 1960s, when the Ju/'hoansi people were still foragers, their major food source was mongongo nuts. At that time, these nuts were so abundant that there was never a shortage (Howell 1986). In addition, hundreds of species of edible plants and animals were available, with seasonal variations. The Ju/'hoansi were slender and often complained of hunger throughout the year. Their thinness may be an adaptation to seasonal fluctuations in food supply. Rather than maximizing food intake during times of plenty, they minimize it. Mealtime is not an occasion for stuffing oneself. Ju/'hoansi culture taught that it is good to have a hungry stomach, even when food is plentiful.

Because foragers' needs for goods are limited, minimal labor efforts are required to satisfy them. Foragers typically work fewer hours a week than the average employed North American. In traditional (undisturbed) foraging societies, the people spend as few as five hours a week collecting food and making and repairing tools. They have much time for storytelling, playing games, and resting. Foragers also traditionally enjoyed good health. During the early 1960s, the age structure and health status of the Ju/'hoansi compared well with people in the United States of around 1900 (Lee 1979). They had few infectious diseases or health problems related to aging, such as arthritis.

Horticulture

Both horticulture and pastoralism are recent modes of livelihood, having emerged only as recently as 12,000 years ago in the Middle East and then later in Africa, Asia, Europe, and

CULTURAMA

The Andaman Islanders of India

The Andaman Islands are a string of islands in the Bay of Bengal that belong to India. For an unknown number of centuries, many of the islands were inhabited by people who fished, gathered, and hunted for their livelihood. During the eighteenth century, when European countries were expanding trade routes to the Far East, the Andaman Islands were of major strategic importance as a stopping place.

At the time of the first, small settlements of the British in the late eighteenth century, the total indigenous population was estimated at between 6000 and 8000 (B. Miller 1997). Today, more than 400,000 people live on the islands, mostly migrants from the Indian mainland. The total number of indigenous people is about 400. British colonialism brought contagious diseases and increased death from violence among disrupted Andaman groups and between the Andaman people and the British.

Only four surviving clusters of indigenous Andamanese now exist. The smallest group, just a few dozen people, consists of the remnants of the so-called Great Andamanese people. They live on a small island near Port Blair, the capital, in what is essentially a reservation area. Several groups of Great Andamanese people formerly lived throughout North and Middle Andaman Islands, but no indigenous people inhabit these islands now. The so-called Jarawa, numbering perhaps two hundred, live in a reserved area on the southwest portion of South Andaman. Currently, no outsider knows their language or what name they use for themselves. Jarawa is a term that the Great Andamanese people use for them. The Onge, around a hundred in number, live in one corner of Little Andaman Island. Another hundred people or so live on North Sentinel Island. Outsiders call them the "Sentinelese." No one has established communication with them, and almost no one from the outside has gotten closer than arrow-range of their shore.

The 2005 tsunami disrupted much of the Andaman Island landscape, particularly areas that had been cleared of mangroves and other trees. As far as anyone knows, none of the indigenous people died as a direct result of the tsunami, though many immigrant settlers did (Mukerjee 2005). The future of the indigenous people is more endangered by external culture, in the form of immigration and development, than from nature.

Thanks to Madhusree Mukerjee, independent scholar and activist, and Sita Venkateswar, Massey University, for reviewing this material.

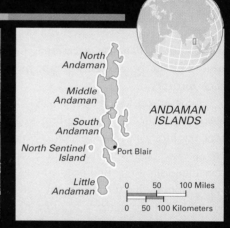

(LEFT) A Jarawa woman receives a handout from a passenger bus driver on the Andaman Trunk Road (ATR). Part of the ATR passes through the Jarawa reservation on South Andaman Island.

(CENTER) Government officials from Pt. Blair make periodic visits by boat to the Jarawa area to attempt to build Jarawa trust. This landmark incident, of getting some Jarawa to board a government boat, occurred in 1998. The Jarawa occupy land that is rich in resources such as ancient hardwood trees. Rumors are that the administration wants to remove the Jarawa from their territory and exploit it for logging, tourism, and other commercial interests.

MAP 4.2 **Andaman Islands of India.** The 576 islands are geologically part of Myanmar and Southeast Asia. The British Empire controlled them until India's independence in 1947.

See more PEARSON myanthrolab

the Western Hemisphere. Both depend on the domestication of plants and animals—that is, the process by which human selection causes genetic changes in plants and animals and leads to their greater control by humans in terms of their location and their reproduction.

Horticulture is a mode of livelihood based on cultivating domesticated plants in gardens using hand tools. Garden crops are often supplemented by foraging and by trading with pastoralists for animal products. Horticulture is still practiced by many thousands of people throughout the world. Prominent horticultural regions are found in sub-Saharan Africa, South Asia, Southeast Asia and the Pacific, Central America, South America, and the Caribbean islands. Major horticultural crops include yams, corn, beans, grains such as millet and sorghum, and several types of roots, all of which are rich in protein, minerals, and vitamins.

Horticulture involves the use of handheld tools, such as digging sticks, hoes, and carrying baskets. Rain is the sole source of moisture. Horticulture requires rotation of garden plots in order for them to regenerate. Thus, another term for horticulture is *shifting cultivation*. Average plot sizes are less than 1 acre, and 2.5 acres can support a family of five to eight members for a year. Yields can support semipermanent villages of 200 to 250 people. Overall population density per square mile is low because horticulture, like foraging, is an extensive strategy. Horticulture is more labor intensive than foraging because of the energy required for plot preparation and food processing. Anthropologists distinguish five phases in the horticultural cycle (Figure 4.3).

Surpluses in food supply are possible in horticulture. These surpluses enable trade relationships and can lead to greater wealth for some people. Horticulture was the

Clearing: A section of the forest is cleared, partially or completely, by cutting down trees and brush and then setting the area on fire to burn off other growth. The fire creates a layer of ash that is rich fertilizer. The term *slash-and-burn cultivation* refers to this stage of clearing.

Planting: People use digging sticks to loosen the soil. They plant seeds by scattering them (called broadcasting) or they insert cuttings of plants in the loose soil.

Weeding: Horticulture involves little weeding because the ash cover and shady growing conditions keep weed growth down.

Harvesting: This phase requires substantial labor to cut or dig crops and carry them to the residential area.

Fallowing: Depending on the soil and the crop grown, the land must be left unused for a specified number of years so that it regains its fertility.

FIGURE 4.3 Five Stages in Horticulture.

foundation for complex and rich civilizations, such as the Maya civilization of Mexico and Central America, which flourished between 200 and 900 CE.

DIVISION OF LABOR Gender and age are the key factors structuring the division of labor, with men's and women's work roles often being clearly differentiated. Typically, men clear the garden area while both men and women plant and tend the staple food crops. This pattern exists in New Guinea, much of Southeast Asia, and parts of West and East Africa. Food processing involves women often working in small groups, whereas men more typically form small groups for hunting and fishing for supplementary food. Among many horticultural groups, women grow the staple food crops while men grow the "prestige foods" used in ritual feasts. In such contexts, men have higher public status than women.

Two unusual horticultural cases involve extremes in terms of gender roles and status. The first is the precontact Iroquois of central New York State (Brown 1975) (see Map 4.3 on page 90). Iroquois women cultivated maize, the most important food crop, and they controlled its distribution. This control meant that they were able to decide whether the men would go to war, because a war effort depended on the supply of maize to support it. A contrasting example is that of the Yanomami of the Venezuelan Amazon (see Map 4.4 on page 91) (Chagnon 1992). Yanomami men clear the fields and tend and harvest the crops. They also do much of the cooking for ritual feasts. Yanomami women, though, are not idle. They play an important role in providing

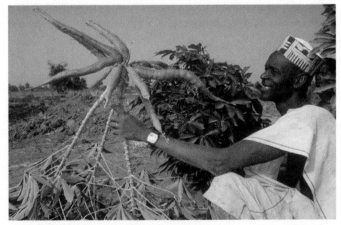

Cassava, also called manioc, is a root crop grown extensively in western Africa. This man displays a cassava plant grown in Niger. Cassava and millet, a grain, are the staple foods for many West Africans.

▶ Do research to find some West African recipes that include cassava or millet.

horticulture a mode of livelihood based on growing domesticated crops in gardens, using simple hand tools.

MAP 4.3 Precolonial Iroquois Region.
At the time of the arrival of the European colonialists, the six nations of the Iroquois extended over a wide area. The Mohawk stood guard over the eastern door of the confederacy's symbolic long house, and the Seneca guarded the western door. The six nations worked out a peace treaty among themselves and established a democracy. A great orator named Hiawatha promoted the treaty throughout the tribes, and a Mohawk woman was the first to approve it.

This reconstruction of a pre-colonial Iroquois scene depicts long-houses in which many families lived and shows women in important productive roles.

the staple food that comes from manioc, a starchy root crop that requires substantial processing work—it has to be soaked for a long time to remove toxins and then scraped into a mealy consistency. Among the Yanomami, however, men are the dominant decision makers and have more social power than Yanomami women do.

Although anthropologists cannot explain the origins of the different divisions of labor in horticulture, they do know that the differences are related to men's and women's status (Sanday 1973). Analysis of many horticultural societies shows that women's contribution to food production is a necessary but not sufficient basis for women's high status. In other words, if women do not contribute to producing food, their status will be low. If they do contribute, their status may, or may not, be high. The critical factor appears to be control over the distribution of what is produced, especially public distribution beyond the family. Slavery is a clear example of how a major role in production does not bring high status because slaves have no control over the product and its distribution.

Children do more productive work in horticultural societies than in any other mode of livelihood (Whiting and Whiting 1975). The *Six Cultures Study* is a research project that examined children's behavior in horticultural, farming, and industrial settings. Children among a horticultural group, the Gusii (goo-see-eye) of western Kenya, performed the most tasks at the youngest ages. Gusii boys and girls care for

siblings, collect fuel, and carry water. Among the Gusii and in other horticultural societies, children do so many tasks because adults, especially women, are busy working in the fields and markets. Children's work in the domestic domain fulfills what are adult roles in other economic systems.

PROPERTY RELATIONS Private property, as something that an individual can own and sell, is not characteristic of horticultural societies. Use rights are typically important, although they are more clearly defined and formalized than among foragers. By clearing and planting an area of land, a family puts a claim on it and its crops. The production of surplus goods allows the possibility of social inequality in access to goods and resources. Rules about sharing within the larger group decline in importance as some people gain higher status.

HORTICULTURE AS A SUSTAINABLE SYSTEM Fallowing is crucial in maintaining the viability of horticulture. Fallowing allows the plot to recover lost nutrients and improves soil quality by allowing the growth of weeds whose root systems keep the soil loose. The benefits of a well-managed system of shifting cultivation are clear, as are the two major constraints involved: the time required for fallowing and the need for access to large amounts of land so that some land is in use while other land is fallowed. Using a given plot for too many seasons or reducing fallowing time quickly results in depletion of soil nutrients, decreased crop production, and soil erosion.

Pastoralism

Pastoralism, or herding, is a mode of livelihood based on domesticated animal herds and the use of their products, such as meat and milk, for 50 percent or more of the diet. Pastoralism has long existed in the Middle East, Africa, Europe, and Central Asia, especially where rainfall is limited and unpredictable. In the Western Hemisphere, the only indigenous pastoralist system in existence before the arrival of the Spanish in the fifteenth century was in the Andean region of the New World; it was based on domesticated llamas (Barfield 2001). Sheep, goats, horses, and cattle became prominent after the Spanish conquest. Some Native American groups in the southwestern United States still rely on herding animals.

Worldwide, the six major species in pastoralist systems are sheep, goats, cattle, horses, donkeys, and camels. Three others have more restricted distribution: yaks at high altitudes in Asia, reindeer in northern sub-Arctic regions, and llamas in highland South America. Many pastoralists keep dogs for protection and for help with herding. Pastoralism can succeed in a variety of environments, depending on the animal involved. For example, reindeer herding is done in the circumpolar regions of Europe and Asia, and cattle and goat herding is common in India and Africa.

In terms of food, pastoralism provides primarily milk and milk products, with occasional slaughtering of animals for meat. Thus, pastoralists typically form trade links with foragers, horticulturalists, or farmers in order to obtain food and other goods that they cannot produce themselves. Prominent trade items are food grains and manufactured items, such as cooking pots, for which they offer milk, animals, hides, and other animal products.

Like foraging and horticulture, pastoralism is an extensive strategy. A common problem for all pastoralists is the continued need for fresh pasture and water for their animals. Herds must move or else the grazing area will become depleted. A distinction within the pastoralist category is based on whether the herds move over short or long distances (Fratkin, Galvin, and Roth 1994). The Qashqa'i

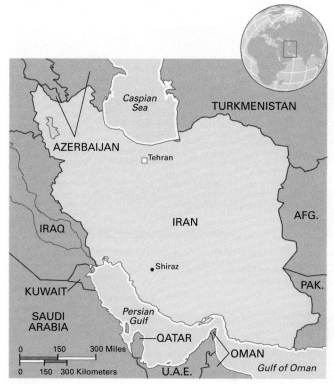

MAP 4.5 Iran.

The Islamic Republic of Iran is one of the world's most mountainous countries. Its economy is based on oil, family farming, and small-scale trading. Iran is OPEC's second-largest oil producer and has the second-largest natural gas reserves in the world after Russia. The population of Iran is over 68 million. The official language is Persian (Farsi) and Shi'a Islam is the official state religion.

(kash-kie) of Iran are long-distance herders of sheep and camels (Beck 1986). Iran offers a varied and rich natural resource base that supports pastoralism, agriculture, and large urban centers, including the capital city of Shiraz (Map 4.5). The pastoralism of the Qashqa'i involves seasonal migration to remote pastures separated by about 300 miles. The vast distances make the Qashqa'i vulnerable to raids and create the need for negotiation with village leaders along the route for permission to cross their land. To deal with this vulnerability, the Qashqa'i developed linkages across several tribes that can be mobilized, temporarily, to create a large political unit under one leader. The Qashqa'i are an example of a pastoralist system in which political organization is highly developed.

DIVISION OF LABOR Families and clusters of related families are the basic production unit. Gender and age are, again, key factors in the allocation of work. In many pastoralist cultures, gender roles are clearly divided. Men are in charge

MAP 4.4 Yanomami Region in Brazil and Venezuela.

The Yanomami region is supposedly protected from outsiders. But miners, ranchers, loggers, and other commercial developers have encroached on the reserve, extracting natural resources and sexually exploiting women and children.

pastoralism   a mode of livelihood based on keeping domesticated animals and using their products, such as meat and milk, for most of the diet.

The gender division of labor often seems quite arbitrary, as in these two examples. (LEFT) Girls are in charge of herding water buffaloes to the Ganges River, at Varanasi, India, for watering. (RIGHT) Among the Ariaal, herders of northern Kenya, men are in charge of herding camels.

of herding—moving the animals from place to place. Women are responsible for processing the herd's products, especially the milk. A cultural emphasis on masculinity characterizes many herding populations. Reindeer herding among the Saami of Finland is closely connected to male identity to the extent that the definition of being a man is to be a reindeer herder (see Anthropology Works, Chapter 15, page 362). In contrast, women are the herders among the Navajo of the American Southwest. Navajo men's major work role is crafting silver jewelry.

The size of the animal involved is sometimes, but not always, related to the gender division of herding. Girls and women are often herders of smaller animals, perhaps because smaller animals need to graze less widely and can be kept penned near the house. Boys and men tend the animals that are pastured farther away. Children play important roles in tending herds. Among the cattle-herding groups of Eastern Africa, for example, parents want to have many children to help out with the herds.

PROPERTY RELATIONS The most important forms of property among pastoralists are, by far, animals, followed by housing (such as tents or yurts) and domestic goods (cooking ware). Depending on the group, ownership of animals is inherited through males, most commonly, or, less frequently, through females, as among the Navajo. A concept of private property exists for animals, which the family head may trade for other goods. A family's housing materials are also their own. Use rights, however, regulate pasture land and migratory

routes, and these rights tend to be informally regulated through an oral tradition.

PASTORALISM AS A SUSTAINABLE SYSTEM Pastoralists have developed sustainable cultures in extremely varied environments, from the relative lushness of Iran to the more depleted situation of Mongolia. Pastoralism is a highly successful and sustainable economic system that functions in coexistence with other economic systems. As with foraging and horticulture, however, when outside forces squeeze the space available for migration, overexploitation of the environment soon results. A major cause of decline in pastoralism is loss and fragmentation of territory (Galvin 2009). Many governments contribute to this situation because they want the land used by pastoralists for commercial agriculture, mining, and tourism. Furthermore governments disapprove of pastoralists crossing country borders at will, as they did for centuries before colonial powers drew modern political boundaries. Furthermore, pastoralists' movements make it difficult for governments to tax them and to provide services for them. Therefore, governments attempt to *sedentarize* (settle down) them and turn them into farmers or laborers. Many pastoralists, however, such as the Dinka cattle herders of southern Sudan, look with disdain upon a settled life and consider working with their hands disgusting (*The Economist* 2010).

Agriculture

Agriculture is a mode of livelihood that involves growing crops on permanent plots with the use of plowing, irrigation, and fertilizer; it is also called *farming*. In contrast to foraging, horticulture, and pastoralism, agriculture is an **intensive strategy**. Intensification involves the use of techniques that allow the same plot of land to be used repeatedly without losing its fertility. Crucial inputs include substantial amounts of

---

agriculture a mode of livelihood that involves growing crops with the use of plowing, irrigation, and fertilizer.

intensive strategy a form of livelihood that involves continuous use of the same land and resources.

ANTHROPOLOGY works

Something Old, Something New in Bolivian Farming

An archaeological research project near the shores of Lake Titicaca in highland Bolivia uncovered prehistoric remains of raised fields separated by an intricate system of canals (Straughan and Schuler 1991). When the Spanish colonialists arrived, they abandoned the raised-field system and replaced it with their type of cultivation.

By the twentieth century, Bolivian farmers struggled to produce adequate crops of potatoes from the boggy soil. Frosts also took their toll on the plants before they matured.

Two archaeologists who had been doing research in the region for several years convinced a local farmer to experiment with the indigenous raised-field system, suggesting that what worked a thousand years ago might succeed again. The other villagers were skeptical but watched with interest as the potato plants on the raised field grew taller than they had ever seen. Then, right before the harvest, 90 percent of the village crop was lost due to a heavy frost. Most of the potatoes in the experimental raised field, however, were fine. They had been protected by a thick mist that had formed over the field. The sun's warmth during the day heats up the canal water, which, in turn, warms the fields at night when the temperature drops.

Raised beds in Bolivia. This ancient strategy, now revived, helps prevent erosion, improves the organic content of the soil, captures moisture, and protects crops from frost damage. It is called *waru waru* in Quechua, meaning a network of canals and embankments.

The community eventually adopted the new–old system, and crop yields rose significantly. Moreover, algae and aquatic plants began to grow in the canals along with nitrogen-fixing bacteria. When the canals are cleaned annually, they yield a rich residue of organic material that can be used to fertilize the fields. The Bolivian government has started a training program to promote the raised-field technique as a way to increase the nation's food supply. Local people now welcome the archaeologists with enthusiasm when they visit.

The Lake Titicaca region, once the center of a rich civilization, was reduced to poverty by the effects of European colonialism. Now, through archaeological findings about the past, the agricultural economy is reviving and thriving.

Major international aid organizations such as Oxfam are getting involved and promoting the old-new system. For a photo essay about an Oxfam project in one part of Bolivia, go to the Oxfam website and explore, searching for their success stories about farming.

---

labor for weeding, use of natural and chemical fertilizers, and control of water supply. The earliest agricultural systems are documented from the Neolithic period, beginning around 12,000 years ago in the Middle East (review Chapter 2). Agricultural systems now exist worldwide, on all continents except Antarctica.

Agriculture relies on the use of domesticated animals for plowing, transportation, and organic fertilizer either in the form of manure or composted materials. It is highly dependent on artificial water sources such as irrigation channels or terracing the land. Like the modes of livelihood already discussed, agriculture involves complex knowledge about the environment, plants, and animals, including soil types, precipitation patterns, plant varieties, and pest management. Long-standing agricultural traditions are now being increasingly displaced by methods introduced from the outside, and so the world's stock of indigenous knowledge about agriculture is declining rapidly along with the cultures and languages associated with it. Realizing the seriousness of this loss, anthropologists and others seek to document such knowledge before it is lost. Positive examples of reviving old ways of farming include the raised-field farming in pre-Hispanic Bolivia (see Anthropology Works).

FIGURE 4.4 Three Hypotheses to Explain Male Dominance in the Gender Division of Labor in Family Farming.

In agricultural societies, occupational specialization is greater than in the previously discussed modes of livelihood. Instead of people repairing their own tools, some people take on this work as a full-time job and trade their labor for food with farmers. Other specializations that emerge as full-time occupations are political leaders, religious leaders or priests, healers, artisans, potters, musicians, and traders. Two types of agriculture are discussed next.

FAMILY FARMING **Family farming** (formerly termed *peasant farming*) is a form of agriculture in which production is geared to support the family and to produce goods for sale. Today, more than 1 billion people, or about one-sixth of the world's population, make their living from family farming. Found throughout the world, family farming is more common in countries such as Mexico, India, Poland, and Italy than in more industrialized countries. Family farmers exhibit much cross-cultural variety. They may be full-time or part-time farmers; they may be more or less closely linked to urban markets; and they may be poor and indebted or well-off and powerful. Major activities in family farming include plowing, planting seeds and cuttings, weeding, caring for irrigation systems and terracing, harvesting crops, and processing and storing crops.

Division of Labor The family is the basic labor unit, and gender and age are important in organizing work. Most family-farming societies have a marked gender-based division of labor. Cross-cultural analysis of gender roles reveals that men perform most of the labor in over three-fourths of the societies (Michaelson and Goldschmidt 1971). Anthropologists have proposed various theories to explain why productive work on so many family farms is male dominated (Figure 4.4). The remaining one-fourth of the sample includes cultures in which men's and women's roles are balanced and cultures in which women play the dominant role.

In farming systems where men play the major role in agriculture, women are likely to work in or near the home, processing food, maintaining the household, and caring for children (Ember 1983). This division of labor results in the *public/private dichotomy* in family farm societies, in which men are more involved with the outside, public world and women are more involved in the domestic domain. In this variety of family farming, men work more hours per week than in foraging, horticultural, and pastoralist systems. Women's work hours, in contrast, are as high as they are in horticultural and pastoralist systems.

In family farms in the United States and Canada, men typically have the main responsibility for daily farm operations; women's participation ranges from equal to minimal (Barlett 1989). Women do run farms in the United States and Canada, but generally only when they are divorced or widowed. Women are usually responsible for managing the domestic domain. On average, women's daily work hours are 25 percent more than those of men. A trend is for family farm women to take salaried jobs off the farm to help support the farm.

Balanced work roles between men and women in family farming frequently involve a pattern in which men do the agricultural work and women do marketing. This gender division of labor is common among highland indigenous groups of Central and South America. For example, among the Zapotec Indians of Mexico's southern state of Oaxaca (wuh-HAK-uh), men grow maize, the staple crop, and cash crops

---

family farming   a form of agriculture in which farmers produce mainly to support themselves but also produce goods for sale in the market system.

industrial capital agriculture   a form of agriculture that is capital-intensive, substituting machinery and purchased inputs for human and animal labor.

such as bananas, mangoes, coconuts, and sesame (Chiñas 1992) (see Map 6.3, page 140). Women sell produce in the town markets, and they make tortillas, which they sell from their houses. The family thus derives its income from the labor of both men and women working interdependently. Male status and female status are quite equal in such contexts.

Female farming systems, in which women and girls play the major role in livelihood, are found mainly in southern India and Southeast Asia where wet rice agriculture is practiced. This is a highly labor-intensive way of growing rice that involves starting the seedlings in nurseries and transplanting them to flooded fields. Men are responsible for plowing the fields using teams of water buffaloes. Women own land and make decisions about planting and harvesting. Women's labor is the backbone of this type of farming. Standing calf-deep in muddy water, they transplant rice seedlings, weed, and harvest the rice. Why women predominate in wet rice agriculture is an intriguing question but impossible to answer. Its consequences for women's status, however, are clear. In female farming systems, women have relatively high status. They own land, play a central role in household decision making, and have substantial personal autonomy (Stivens et al. 1994).

Children's roles in agricultural societies range from prominent to minor, depending on the context (Whiting and Whiting 1975). *The Six Cultures Study*, mentioned earlier in this chapter, found low rates of child labor in agricultural villages in North India and Mexico compared to high rates among the horticultural Gusii in Kenya. In many agricultural contexts, however, children's labor participation is high. In villages in Java, Indonesia, and in Nepal, children spend more time caring for farm animals than adults do (Nag, White, and Peet 1978). Girls between 6 and 8 years old spend more time

than adults in child care, and girls work more hours each day than boys. Children in the United States are not formally employed in farm work, but many family farms rely on children's contributions on weekends and during summer vacations. Amish farm families in the United States and Canada rely to a large extent on children's labor.

Property Relations   Family farmers make substantial investments in land, such as clearing, terracing, and fencing, and these investments are linked to the development of firmly defined and protected property rights. Rights to land can be acquired and sold. Formalized, often written, guidelines exist about inheritance of land and transfer of rights to land through marriage. Social institutions such as law and police exist to protect private property rights.

In family farming systems where male labor and decision making predominate, women and girls are excluded from land rights. Conversely, in female farming systems, inheritance rules regulate the transmission of property rights more often through females.

INDUSTRIAL AGRICULTURE   **Industrial capital agriculture** produces crops through capital-intensive means, using machinery and inputs such as processed fertilizers instead of human and animal labor (Barlett 1989). It is commonly practiced in the United States, Canada, Germany, Russia, and Japan and is increasingly being adopted in emerging countries such as India, Brazil, Mexico, and China.

Industrial agriculture has brought with it the *corporate farm*, a huge agricultural enterprise that produces goods solely for sale and are owned and operated by companies entirely reliant on hired labor. Industrial agriculture has major social effects (see Figure 4.5 on page 96).

Family farmers typically know their land, inch by inch, and their animals. Commercial farming separates owners from the vast amount of land and the many animals involved. (LEFT) Family farming in highland Ecuador. A man plows while women in the family follow, planting seed potatoes. (RIGHT) Commercial dairy farming is not exactly hands-on.

- Increased use of complex technology including machinery, chemicals, and genetic research on new plant and animal varieties.

  Social effects: This feature results in displacement of small landholders and field laborers. For example, replacing mules and horses with tractors for plowing in the U.S. South during the 1930s led to the eviction of small-scale sharecroppers from the land because the landowners could cultivate larger units.

- Increased use of capital (wealth used in the production of more wealth) in the form of money or property.

  Social effects: The high ratio of capital to labor enables farmers to increase production but reduces flexibility. If a farmer invests in an expensive machine to harvest soybeans and then the price of soybeans drops, the farmer cannot simply switch from soybeans to a more profitable crop. Capitalization is most risky for smaller farms, which cannot absorb losses easily.

- Increased use of energy (primarily gasoline to run the machinery and nitrates for fertilizer) to grow crops. This input of energy often exceeds the calories of food energy yielded in the harvest. Calculations of how many calories of energy are used to produce a calorie of food in industrial agricultural systems reveal that some 2.5 calories of fossil fuel are invested to harvest 1 calorie of food—and more than 6 calories are invested when processing, packaging, and transport are taken into account.

  Social effects: This energy-heavy mode of production creates farmers' dependence on the global market of energy supplies.

Source: Adapted from "Industrial Agriculture" by Peggy F. Barlett in *Economic Anthropology,* ed. by Stuart Plattner. Copyright © 1989. Published by Stanford University Press.

FIGURE 4.5 Three Features of Industrial Agriculture and Their Social Effects.

Much of the labor demand in industrial agriculture is seasonal, creating an ebb and flow of workers, depending on the task and time of year. Large ranches hire seasonal cowboys for roundups and fence mending. Crop harvesting is another high-demand point. Leo Chavez studied the lives of undocumented (illegal) migrant laborers from Central America who work in the huge tomato, strawberry, and avocado fields owned by corporate farms in southern California (1992). Many of the migrants are Maya people from Oaxaca, Mexico (see Map 6.3, page 140). They cross the border illegally in order to find work to support their families. In the San Diego area of southern California, they live temporarily in shantytowns, or camps. Here is what a men's camp is like on Sunday when they do not go to work in the fields:

> On Sundays, the campsites take on a community-like appearance. Men bathe, and wash their clothes, hanging them on trees and bushes, or on lines strung between the trees. Some men play soccer and basketball, using a hoop someone has rigged up. Others sit on old crates or tree-stumps as they relax, talk, and drink beer. Sometimes the men talk about fights from the night before. With little else to do, nowhere to go, and few outsiders to talk to, the men often drink beer to pass the time on Saturday nights and Sundays. Loneliness and boredom plague them during nonworking hours. (1992:65)

THE SUSTAINABILITY OF AGRICULTURE Agriculture requires much more in the way of labor inputs, technology, and the use of nonrenewable natural resources than the economic systems discussed earlier. The ever-increasing spread of corporate agriculture worldwide is now displacing other long-standing practices and resulting in the destruction of important habitats and cultural heritage sites in its search for land, water, and energy sources. Intensive agriculture is not a sustainable system. Furthermore, it is undermining the sustainability of foraging, horticulture, and pastoralism. Anthropologists have pointed to the high costs of agriculture to the environment and even referred to it as the "worst mistake" in human history, a catastrophe from which we have never recovered (Diamond 1994 [1987]). With agriculture, life did improve for many people, but not for all. Elites emerged with greater access to wealth and health than the landless poor and laboring classes. Diets changed to include more starchy food and more processed food. With the vast surpluses of food created by agricultural production, elaborate state systems developed with lethal and potentially abusive power. Other downsides of agriculture include the toll it takes on the environment: soil exhaustion from repeated use, soil and water pollution from fertilizers and pesticides, and air pollution from tractors, transportation, and processing plants.

Industrialism and the Information Age

Industrialism/informatics is the mode of livelihood in which goods and services are produced through mass employment in business and commercial operations and through the creation, manipulation, management, and transfer of information via electronic media. In industrial capitalism, the form of capitalism found in most industrialized nations, most goods are produced not to meet basic needs but to satisfy consumer demands for nonessential goods. Employment in agriculture decreases while jobs in manufacturing and the service sector increase. In some industrialized countries, the number of manufacturing jobs is declining, with more people being employed in service occupations and in the growing area of information processing such as computer programming, data processing, and communications.

An important distinction exists between the **formal sector**, which is salaried or wage-based work registered in official statistics, and the **informal sector**, which includes work that is outside the formal sector, not officially registered, and sometimes illegal. If you have done babysitting and were paid cash that was not formally recorded by your employer (for tax-deduction purposes) or by you (for income tax purposes), then you have participated in the informal sector. Informal sector activities that are illegal are referred to as being part of the *underground economy*, a huge and uncounted part of global and local economies worldwide.

THE FORMAL SECTOR: FACTORY STUDIES The formal sector includes a wide variety of occupations, ranging from stable and lucrative jobs to unstable or part-time and less lucrative jobs. Cultural anthropologists have done studies of small-scale workplaces, especially factories.

In one factory study, a team of cultural anthropologists and university graduate students studied the role of ethnicity in social relationships in a Miami clothing factory (Grenier et al. 1992). The clothing plant, a subsidiary of the largest U.S. clothing manufacturer, employs about 250 operators, mainly women. The majority of employees are Cuban women who, fleeing from the Castro regime, immigrated to Miami many years ago. As these employees have begun to retire, they are being replaced by new immigrants from Central America as well as by Haitians and African Americans.

The workers are organized into a union, but members of the different ethnic groups have more solidarity with each other than with people in the union. Interethnic rivalry exists around the issue of management's treatment of members of different groups. Many non-Cuban workers claim that management favors Cuban employees. Some supervisors and managers expressed ethnic stereotypes, but not always consistent ones: "Depending on whom one listens to, Haitians are either too slow or too fast; Cubans may talk too much or be extraordinarily dedicated workers" (Grenier 1992:75). Managers see ethnic-based competition and lack of cooperation as a key problem that they attempt to deal with in various ways.

A street vendor in Kingston, Jamaica. In many modernizing countries, city planners are taking steps to make street vending illegal on the grounds that such informal stands are unsightly.

▶ *If you were the mayor of Kingston, what position would you take on the street vending issue?*

For example, management banned workers from playing personal radios and installed a system of piped-in music by a radio station that supposedly alternates between "American" and "Latino" songs.

THE INFORMAL SECTOR: STREET VENDORS, DRUGS, AND SEX WORK Uncounted millions of people work in the informal sector. Many are involved in small-scale vending on the street, selling fruits and vegetables, beverages, cigarettes, snacks, books and magazines, ice cream, and souvenirs. Depending on the context, they may or may not have to pay for the location of their stand. Their rights to sell from a particular location are less secure than for someone who owns a shop. Some countries are seeking to remove street vendors in order to create a more modern city look.

Informal economies also operate at the global level, including the illegal trafficking of people and goods. The illegal drug industry links informal economies at the global level to the local level. Neither international drug dealers nor street sellers pay income tax on their profits, and their earnings are

industrialism/informatics a mode of livelihood in which goods are produced through mass employment in business and commercial operations and through the creation and movement of information through electronic media.

formal sector salaried or wage-based work registered in official statistics.

informal sector work that is not officially registered and sometimes illegal.

not part of the official gross national product (GNP) of any country. Currently, the drug traffic from Central and South America into North America is a multibillion-dollar business. Most of the supply moves through Mexico (see Map 6.3, page 140).

Fieldwork in a small, rural town in Mexico's central highlands shows how the legal and illegal economies related to drug trafficking are intertwined (McDonald 2005). This ethnography of the local *narcoeconomy*, or an economy based on the production and sale of addictive drugs, reports, "None of this could happen without deep interconnections between drug traffickers, and networks of well-placed politicians, civil servants, and security forces of various kinds" (p. 115). How does the narcoeconomy affect local life in central Mexico? This ordinary town became a site of extraordinary inequalities: new, opulent houses for some, high-end clothing stores, a cybercafé, and a day spa. New farmers, willing to participate in the narcoeconomy, are moving in and gaining legitimacy in the community. These farmers are typically young men who come from local farm families and have worked in U.S. drug trafficking networks. They are hardworking and interested in promoting local economic development. Through their experiences in the United States, they gained business skills and they understand the importance of networking. The positive features of this situation, however, are part of an economic system that is illegal.

In many parts of the world, sex work is illegal. In the United States, it is legal only in the state of Nevada, where income from sex work is taxable. In neighboring Mexico, options for legalized, state-controlled female sex work exist (Kelly 2008). Patty Kelly did fieldwork in a legal brothel in Chiapas, Mexico (see Map 6.3, page 140), called the Zona Galactica. She uses the term *prostitution* to refer to the exchange of sexual intercourse for money, and it is therefore one form of *sex work*, which is a broader category that includes services such as erotic dancing, phone sex, and participation in erotic films and other media formats (2008:26). Although the women prostitutes' situation in the legal brothel in Chiapas is not ideal by any means, it has advantages compared to contexts in which prostitution is illegal and prostitutes have absolutely no security or protection.

In Thailand (see Map 6.6, page 151), laws about sex work are complicated (Jeffrey 2002). It is illegal to sell sex, but not to buy it. Recent legal reforms, however, pertain to the age of the sex seller and involve a prison sentence for anyone having sex with someone 15 years of age or younger. Nevertheless, child sex work in Thailand is an increasingly important part of the economy. The growing fear of HIV/AIDS among men who seek commercial sex leads to the demand for ever-

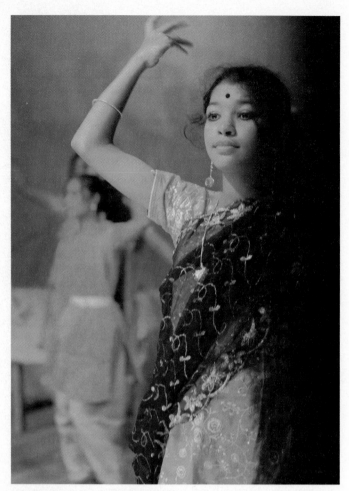

Theater class in rural Bangladesh. Children of commercial sex workers attend boarding school, through support from a Dutch non-governmental organization.

younger sex workers, who clients assume are less likely to be carriers of the virus. Recruitment of children as young as 6 years old began in the 1990s.

How do children become involved in commercial sex work? Family poverty is a major part of the answer in Thailand. Low and declining incomes in rural northern Thailand continue to prompt parents to send children into sex work. Within the context of severe and increasing poverty in northern Thailand, however, a village-based study provides further details about how culture shapes family decisions to send daughters into sex work (Rende Taylor 2005). In northern Thailand generally, and in the

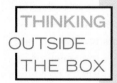

THINKING OUTSIDE THE BOX

Some people think that child sex workers should be unionized to protect them. Others argue that unionization signals acceptance of this role for children. Where do you stand on this issue and why?

study village, daughters are valued members of the family. Along with their value come obligations to the family. From an early age, the eldest daughter is expected to assume major household responsibilities, including care of her younger siblings. The youngest daughter will inherit the house and, with it, the obligation to care for her aging parents. Middle daughters are the ones most likely to be sent outside to earn an income, often in commercial sex work. Parents are more concerned about the welfare of the family than about a daughter's involvement in commercial sex work. They say, "The problem here isn't that our daughter sells her body . . . it's that we have no food to eat" (Rende Taylor 2005:416).

Research in a small slum community on the edge of a tourist town, frequented mainly by Europeans, reveals that the children reject the view of child prostitutes as mere victims (Montgomery 2001). They believe the work they do is moral because it is done in support of their family. The child sex workers and their pimps, also children, exercise some choice in deciding which clients to accept and which to reject. These insights do not deny the fact that the child sex workers are exploited and sometimes seriously harmed. They do, however, provide a fuller picture by showing how the children define their work as related to family obligations and how they seek to protect themselves within a context of limited options.

Certainly, the voices of the children should be heard. But scholars and activists must look beyond the children's emic worlds to the global, macroeconomic structures that generate and support the people who pay for sex with children and the poverty in the communities that send children into sex work. So far, the author of this textbook has not seen a study of the people who seek commercial sex.

◉ ◉ ◉

Changing Livelihoods

This section looks at recent changes in the five modes of livelihood. Contemporary economic globalization is the latest of many outside forces exerted on local economies. Most notably, European colonialism, starting in the fifteenth century, had dramatic effects on indigenous people's livelihood, mainly through the introduction of cash crops such as tea, coffee, and cotton; co-optation and control of local labor through slavery, indentureship, and hire; and taking over land for colonial plantations and other enterprises.

As noted at the beginning of this chapter, the spread of Western capitalism continues to have far-reaching effects on the local economies with which it comes in contact. In the later part of the twentieth century, surging economic growth in Asia, the demise of socialism in the former Soviet Union, and the increasing economic power of the United States throughout the world combined to spur the growth of a global economy. Social scientists vigorously debate the effects of economic globalization on poverty and inequality. Economists, relying on country-level figures about changing income levels and distribution, often take the view that economic globalization is beneficial, overall, because it increases economic growth. Cultural anthropologists, who work with local-level data and a more "on the ground" view tend to emphasize the negative effects of capitalist expansion into noncapitalist settings (Blim 2000). They point to three major transformations:

- Dispossession of local people of their land and other resource bases and substantial growth in the numbers of unemployed, displaced people. Global capitalism has displaced millions of people from their land and contributed to the growth of the unemployed urban poor.

- Recruitment of former foragers, horticulturalists, pastoralists, and family farmers to work in low levels of the industrialism/informatics sector and their exploitation in that setting. Such people become dependent wage workers as opposed to independent providers.

- Increases in export commodity production in periphery regions in response to the demands of a global market and decreases in food production for family use. This trend may provide higher incomes for people but it also reduces their independent ability to feed themselves and increases their risk of food insecurity. It also promotes *mono-cropping* (planting a single crop variety) and leads to the decline of biodiversity.

Examples exist of some foraging-horticultural groups choosing to become involved in the global economy on their own terms (Godoy et al. 2005). Far more often, however, these cultures have been destroyed by the intrusion of Western economic interests, their local knowledge has been lost, and the people have become demoralized, distressed, ill, and suicidal. The following cases illustrate how small-scale cultures react to and deal with Western capitalism and globalization.

Foragers: The Tiwi of Northern Australia

The Tiwi (tee-wee) live on two islands off the north coast of Australia (Map 4.6) (Hart, Pilling, and Goodale 1988).

MAP 4.6 **Tiwi Region in Northern Australia.**
The Tiwi Islands consist of Bathurst and Melville Islands. The total number of Tiwi is about 2500 people. Most Tiwi live on Bathurst Island. In 2001, the Tiwi Islands Local Government Area was established, launching a new era of local government with statutory authority.

(TOP) The altar of the Australia Nguiu Aboriginal Catholic Church, Bathurst Island, integrates Tiwi art. (BOTTOM) Artist Alan Kerinaiua from Tiwi Design works on a painting of a sting ray.

As foragers, the Tiwi gathered food, especially root vegetables such as yams, nuts, grubs, small lizards, and fish. Women provided the bulk of the daily diet with their gathered root vegetables and nuts that they ground and cooked into porridge. Men sometimes hunted kangaroos, wild fowl, and other game such as goanna (large lizards). Vegetables, nuts, and fish were abundant year round. The Tiwi lived a more comfortable life than Aboriginal groups of the mainland, where the environment was less hospitable.

The Tiwi have long been in contact with foreign influences, beginning in the 1600s with the arrival of the Portuguese, who were attracted to the islands as a source of iron. Later, in 1897, an Australian named Joe Cooper came to the islands and kidnapped two native women to train as mainland guides. Cooper and his group greatly changed the Tiwi by introducing a desire for Western goods, especially tobacco. Later, Japanese traders arrived and offered Tiwi men manufactured goods in return for Tiwi women. In the early 1900s, the French established a Catholic mission on one island. The missionaries promoted reading of the Bible and criticized local marriage customs, which allowed a man to have multiple wives. The year 1942 brought World War II to the Tiwi as the Japanese bombed and strafed a U.S. airstrip. Military bases were prominent on the islands, and Tiwi dependency on Western manufactured goods increased. In just a few decades, the Tiwi had experienced major culture shock from contact with outsiders.

In the second half of the twentieth century, Tiwi lifestyle changed substantially. Instead of being regularly on the move in the bush, the Tiwi became settled villagers living in houses built of corrugated iron sheets. Tiwi men now play football (soccer) and water polo and engage in competitive javelin throwing. Tiwi produce art, especially carving and painting, for sale in Australia and internationally. Tiwi are active in public affairs and politics, including the aboriginal rights movement.

Another major factor of change is international tourism, a force that the Tiwi are managing with dignity and awareness. One Tiwi commented that tourism may mean that "white people too will learn to live with and survive in the country" (Hart, Pilling, and Goodale 1988:144–145).

Horticulturalists: The Mundurucu of the Brazilian Amazon

Outside economic and political factors have had major effects on horticultural societies throughout the world. In the Amazon, one force of change is the rubber industry. Its impact on indigenous peoples ranges from their being able to maintain many aspects of traditional life, to the complete loss of traditional lifeways. Like the Tiwi, the Mundurucu have experienced neither cultural preservation nor complete loss (Murphy and Murphy 1985).

After the arrival of Brazilians who were commercial rubber producers in the Amazon in the late nineteenth century, many Indians began to work for the Brazilians as latex tappers. For over a century, Mundurucu men combined their horticultural tasks with seasonal work collecting latex in the rubber area. Marked cultural change occurred when many Mundurucu people opted to leave their traditional villages, migrating to live in the rubber area year-round.

In the traditional villages, men live in a separate structure at one side of the village. Husbands visit wives and children in their houses. In the rubber settlement, husbands and wives live together in their own houses, and there is no separate men's house. In the traditional villages, women's communal work groups share water-carrying tasks. Such groups do not exist in the rubber settlement villages. Husbands in the new villages have taken on the task of carrying the water, so men work harder than they did in the traditional village. Although women in the settlement area work more hours per day than men, they believe that life is better because they like living in the same house with their husbands.

Pastoralists: The Herders of Mongolia

In the early 1990s, cultural anthropologist Melvyn Goldstein and biological anthropologist Cynthia Beall (1994)

gained permission to do fieldwork among herders in Mongolia, a landlocked and mountainous country located between Russia and China (Map 4.7). The Mongolian rural economy has long been, and still is, heavily dependent on animal herds. The "big five" animals are sheep, goats, yaks, horses, and camels. Sheep and goats provide meat and clothing and some milk; yaks are most important for dairy products because they give milk all year; and horses and camels provide transportation.

MAP 4.7 Mongolia.

Mongolia, with its population of 2.9 million and its vast territory, is the most sparsely populated country of the world. After Kazakhstan, it is the world's second-largest landlocked country. Mountains lie to the north and west and the vast Gobi Desert to the south. The environment is well suited to pastoralism but not to farming. One-third of the population makes a living primarily from pastoralism. Ulan Bator is the capital and largest city, with nearly 40 percent of the population living in and around the city. Many residents are squatters who have migrated to the city in hope of employment and live in a circle of encampments surrounding the capital. Tibetan Buddhism is Mongolia's primary religion.

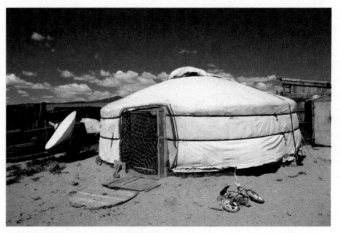

Even the most remote areas of Mongolia are now connected to the wider world through satellite dishes.

Goldstein and Beall wanted to study the effects of the transformation from a socialist, collectivized economy to a capitalist, market system. Starting in the 1950s, the (then) Soviet Union ruled Mongolia and sought to transform it into an agricultural and industrial state. The government established urban centers, and the urban population began to grow while the rural population declined. The state provided all social services such as health and education. There was no homelessness or unemployment. Official policy regarding pastoralism banned private ownership and collectivized all herds. The transition was difficult. Collectivization resulted in a 30 percent reduction of livestock, as owners chose to slaughter animals rather than collectivize them (Barfield 1993). Subsequently, state policy was altered to allow herders to control some animals as their own.

By the early 1990s, the government's main policy was privatization, a process of transferring collective ownership and provision of goods and services to a system of private ownership. Collective ownership of herds was abandoned, and family-organized livelihood was reinstated.

Goldstein and Beall selected a remote region for their research: the Moost district in the Altai Mountain area in the southeastern part of the country, which is 99.9 percent pasture. At the time, the area contained about 4000 people and 115,000 head of livestock. Goldstein and Beall set up their tent and were immediately welcomed by an invitation to have milk-tea, a hot drink made of tea, water, milk, butter, and salt. During their stay, they spoke with many of the herders, participated in their festivals, and learned about people's perceptions of economic change. First, the people had to adjust to the dramatic restructuring of their economy from private family herding to collectivized herding. Then, in just a few decades, they had to adjust back to private herding.

The transition to privatization created serious problems for the herders. Their standard of living declined markedly in the 1990s. Goods such as flour, sugar, candy, and cooking oil were no longer available. Prices for meat fluctuated widely, making it difficult for them to know how to manage their herd size efficiently. Social services such as health care and schools were less available and of lower quality.

Family Farmers: The Maya of Chiapas, Mexico

Frank Cancian, in 1960, did fieldwork among the Maya of Zinacantán, located in the Chiapas region of Mexico (see Map 6.3, page 140). He returned in 1983 to conduct a restudy and thus learned of changes that had taken place in the intervening twenty years (1989). At the time of his first research, most Zinacantecos were family farmers, making a living by growing corn and selling some of their crops in a nearby city. They were largely independent of outside forces in terms of their own food supply. The community was closely knit, its social boundaries defined by people's commitment to community roles and ceremonies. Twenty years later, both the local economy and the social system had changed dramatically.

The main cause of change was a large increase in public spending by the government in the 1970s. This spending supported the construction of roads, dams, schools, and housing throughout the Chiapas region. The government also sponsored outreach programs to promote agricultural change, mainly crop diversification and ways to increase production. Another important factor was the oil boom in northern Chiapas and Tabasco province, which brought unprecedented amounts of cash into the local economy.

By the early 1980s, 40 percent of the households had no land at all and planted no corn. Most people had become involved in wage work, and unemployment, rather than a bad farming season, was the major threat to food security. Wage work included the new opportunities in road construction, government jobs, transportation (of people, food goods, and flowers), and full-time trading in urban markets reachable by the new roads.

This story, in its general outlines, is similar to that of many family farmers throughout the world, especially in developing countries. It involves transformation from production mainly for own use to production mainly for sale within a cash economy geared toward making a profit. Overall, the area became more prosperous, more monetized, and more dependent on the outside economy. A second characteristic is the dislocation of farm owners from their land and their recruitment in the wage labor force. Many self-employed farmers sold their land and entered the wage economy. A third trend is increasing social inequality. Although many Zinacantecos raised their incomes substantially during this period, many others did not. Those who had the ability to buy a truck and take advantage of the new opportunities for urban trade created by the roads were the ones who became rich. Households with the least access to cash were left behind, and these households were characteristically headed by single women.

Global Capitalism: Taiwanese Industrialists in South Africa

In South Africa during the 1990s, after the dismantling of apartheid, political leaders adopted a Western-style, capitalist economic policy (Hart 2002). One step toward expanding production and trade was to forge links with Taiwanese businesses in hopes of transferring to South Africa the Asian economic "miracle." Several Taiwanese industries were established outside major urban areas. Although there is no simple explanation for the so-called Asian economic miracle, one component was family-based production in which power hierarchies based on age and gender ensure compliance among workers.

Taiwanese managers tried to use such a hierarchical family system in South Africa in order to ensure a smoothly functioning labor force. Research in Taiwanese knitwear factories in KwaZulu-Natal province, western South Africa (see Map 9.5, page 222), reveals substantial worker resentment against the Taiwanese managers. Women workers were especially vocal. Taiwanese patterns of communicating with women workers by using an idiom of family did not work with the South Africans. The women said they felt as though they were being treated like animals. The Taiwanese industrialists were separated from the workers by a wide racial, economic, and social divide. Imposing hierarchical family metaphors failed to create a cooperative workforce in South Africa. Many of the Taiwanese industrialists found themselves a focal point of local political conflict. In one town, a Chinese welcome monument was removed.

Karl Marx predicted that capitalism would wither away, but it has not yet done so. Through contemporary globalization, its effects are ever more powerfully felt in localities worldwide. Marx would be interested to observe how the Tiwi are developing international tourism, how the Maya people in Chiapas took up road construction for cash, and how Taiwanese knitwear manufacturers in KwaZulu-Natal encounter problems in cross-cultural labor management. He would perhaps also be amused to see how, at the same time, cultural anthropologists are trying to document and understand these changes.

How do cultural anthropologists study economic systems?

Cultural anthropologists define economic systems as including three interrelated processes: livelihood (or production), consumption, and exchange. They study economic systems cross-culturally including systems other than modern capitalism. They divide cross-cultural patterns of making a living into five modes: foraging, horticulture, pastoralism, agriculture, and industrialism/informatics.

The current world system economy is increasingly competitive and unequal, placing some countries in the core, where their strong governments protect and expand their economic interests. Some countries are in the semiperiphery, and many are in the periphery. Anthropologists study local economic systems as well as regional and global economic factors that affect local economies.

What are the five modes of livelihood?

Foraging relies on collecting food that is available in nature. In foraging societies, the division of labor is based on gender and age, with temperate foragers having more gender overlap in tasks than circumpolar foragers. All group members have equal rights to resources. Foraging has long-term sustainability when not affected by outside pressure.

Horticulture and pastoralism are extensive strategies that depend on domesticated plants (horticulture) and animals (pastoralism). Horticulture requires fallowing, and pastoralism requires the constant movement of animals to fresh pastures. The division of labor varies, including situations in which men do more productive work, those where women do more work, and those in which workloads are shared between men and women. Use rights are the prominent form of property relations. Both have long-term sustainability when not affected by encroachments.

Family farming systems produce crops for their own use and for sale in the market. Most family farming systems involve more male labor in the fields and more female labor in the domestic domain. Agriculture's sustainability is limited by the need to replenish the land.

In industrialism/informatics, the division of labor is highly differentiated by class, gender, and age. Widespread unemployment is found in many industrial economies. In capitalist societies, private property is the dominant pattern. Industrialism/informatics lacks sustainability, given its high demand for nonrenewable energy.

How are the five modes of livelihood changing?

Foragers are being incorporated into settled economies as their access to land is constricted by outside forces and as governments force them to sedentarize. Many former foraging people now work as farm laborers and in other jobs of low status in the mainstream cash economy. Others are advocating for the revitalization of their culture in the new global economy, producing art for sale on the world market, developing cultural tourism opportunities for outsiders, or gaining a share in profits related to commercialization of their indigenous knowledge.

Horticulture and pastoralism are under great pressure from the competing economic forms of agriculture and industrialism. Many former horticulturalists have migrated to plantations or urban areas and become part of the cash economy. States have pressured pastoralists to settle down. Family farms are declining worldwide in number as corporate farms increase. The labor supply has changed from being family based to including a high proportion of migrant laborers.

The Information Age has only recently emerged, with its emphasis on economic processes that involve virtual workplaces and the movement of information, creating the new, combined mode of livelihood called industrialism/informatics. Capitalism increasingly involves international investments and location of production sites in countries where wages are low. Such situations implicate culture in complex ways, including managerial issues and cross-cultural communication.

KEY CONCEPTS

agriculture, p. 92
economic system, p. 82
extensive strategy, p. 84
family farming, p. 94
food security, p. 82

formal sector, p. 97
horticulture, p. 89
industrial capital agriculture, p. 94
industrialism/informatics, p. 97
informal sector, p. 97

intensive strategy, p. 92
mode of livelihood, p. 82
pastoralism, p. 91
use rights, p. 86

SUGGESTED READINGS

Anne Allison. *Nightwork: Sexuality, Pleasure and Corporate Masculinity in a Tokyo Hostess Club*. Chicago: University of Chicago Press, 1994. Based on the author's participant observation, this book explores what it is like to work as a hostess in a club that caters to corporate male employees and discusses men's corporate work culture.

Michael Blim. *Equality and Economy: The Global Challenge*. New York: AltaMira Press, 2005. The author examines the relationships between global capitalism and social inequality at three levels: households, states, and international.

Jans Dahl Saqqaq: *An Inuit Hunting Community in the Modern World*. Toronto: University of Toronto Press, 2000. This ethnography of the Saqqaq, people of eastern Greenland, is based on fieldwork carried out at several times since 1980.

S. Ann Dunham. *Surviving against the Odds: Village Industry in Indonesia*. Durham, NC: Duke University Press, 2009. The author, an economic anthropologist and mother of President Barack Obama, spent 14 years study metal-workers in Java, Indonesia. This book documents their way of life and her commitment to helping ensure its survival.

Hallie Eakin. *Weathering Risk in Rural Mexico: Climatic, Institutional, and Economic Change*. Tucson: University of Arizona Press. 2007. Eakin documents the local effects of globalization and climate change through ethnographic studies of three agricultural communities in central Mexico.

J. A. English-Lueck. *Cultures@SiliconValley*. Stanford: Stanford University Press, 2002. A team of professors and anthropology students at San Jose State University conducted research for over a decade in Silicon Valley to learn about people's lives in a "technology-saturated" environment.

Nandini Gunewardena and Ann Kingsolver, eds. *The Gender of Globalization: Women Navigating Culture and Economic Marginalization*. Albuquerque, NM: School of American Research Press, 2007. Contributing authors use feminist ethnographic methods to examine how neoliberal capitalist policies affect women in Argentina, Sri Lanka, Mexico, Ghana, the United States, India, Jamaica, and elsewhere.

Patty Kelly. *Lydia's Open Door: Inside Mexico's Most Modern Brothel*. Berkeley: University of California Press, 2008. This ethnography focuses on the personal histories and experiences of women who work in a state-run brothel in the capital city of Chiapas, Mexico's poorest state.

Stephen A. Marglin. *The Dismal Science: How Thinking Like an Economist Undermines Community*. Cambridge, MA: Harvard University Press, 2008. Marglin provides an anthropological critique of economics, with attention to how economists' views of autonomous, self-interested individuals and market relationships erode a sense of community.

Heather Montgomery. *Modern Babylon? Prostituting Children in Thailand*. New York: Bergahn Books, 2001. The author conducted fieldwork in a tourist community in Thailand where many parents commit their children to prostitution. She gained a view of this system from the perspective of the children and their parents.

Katherine S. Newman. *Falling from Grace: The Experience of Downward Mobility in the American Middle Class*. New York: The Free Press, 1988. This book provides ethnographic research on downwardly mobile people of New Jersey as a "special tribe," with attention to the effects of downward mobility on middle-class family life.

Deborah Sick. *Farmers of the Golden Bean: Costa Rican Households and the Global Coffee Economy*. Dekalb, IL: Northern Illinois University Press, 1999. This book is about coffee-producing households in Costa Rica and the difficulties that coffee farmers face as a consequence of unpredictable global forces.

Michael K. Steinberg, Joseph J. Hobbs, and Kent Mathewson, eds. *Dangerous Harvest: Drug Plants and the Transformation of Indigenous Landscapes*. New York: Oxford University Press, 2004. The chapters in this book address opium and the people of Laos, opium production in Afghanistan and Pakistan, struggles over coca in Bolivia, marijuana growing by the Maya, use of kava in the Pacific, and policy questions.

PEARSON
myanthrolab

For further information about topics covered in this chapter, go to MyAnthroLab at **www.myanthrolab.com** and access the following readings in MyAnthroLibrary:

Pat Caplan, 2010. Death on the Farm: Culling Badgers in North Pembrokeshire. *Anthropology Today* 26(2):14–18. Farming is becoming an increasingly risky way of making a living throughout Great Britain. In Wales, badgers are implicated in high rates of bovine tuberculosis (bTB). Heated discussions are underway as to whether or not the badger population should be reduced.

Bruce C. Forbes, Florian Stammler, Timo Kumpula, Nina Meschtyb, Anu Pajunen, and Elina Kaarlejärvi. 2009. High Resilience in the Yamal-Nenets Social–Ecological System, West Siberian Arctic, Russia. *Proceedings of the National Academy of Sciences* 106(52):22041–22048. Some groups of west Siberian herders have been able to maintain their livelihood in spite of the incursion of a large mining operation.

Olga F. Linares, From Past to Future Agricultural Expertise in Africa: Jola Women of Senegal Expand Market-Gardening. 2009. *Proceedings of the National Academy of Sciences* 106(50):21074–21079. Forty years of fieldwork show how Senegalese women are adapting to economic change and using their traditional farming knowledge to feed their families.

- What is consumption in cross-cultural perspective?

- What is exchange in cross-cultural perspective?

- How are consumption and exchange changing?

CONSUMPTION AND EXCHANGE

◀ The annual yam harvest festival in the Trobriand Islands of Papua New Guinea is a time when a man demonstrates his status and seeks to gain political followers.

5

Imagine that it is the late eighteenth century and you are a member of the Kwakwaka'wakw (KWA-kwuh-kayuh-wah-kwah) of British Columbia in Canada's Pacific Northwest region (see Culturama at the end of this chapter, page 128). You and your tribal group are invited to a **potlatch**, a feast in which the host lavishes the guests with abundant quantities of the best food and many gifts (Suttles 1991). The most honorable foods are fish oil, high-bush cranberries, and seal meat, and they will be served in ceremonial wooden bowls. Gifts include embroidered blankets, household articles such as carved wooden boxes and woven mats, canoes, and items of food. The more the chief gives, the higher his status rises and the more his guests are indebted to him. Later, when it is the guests' turn to hold a potlatch, they will give away as much as, or more than, their host did.

The Pacific Northwest region is rich in fish, game, berries, and nuts, among other foods. Nonetheless, given regional climatic variation, food supplies were often uneven, with some groups each year having surpluses while others faced scarcity. The potlatch system helped to smooth out these variations: Groups with a surplus would sponsor a potlatch and those experiencing a leaner year were guests. In this way, potlatching established a social safety net across a wide area of the Northwest. This brief sketch of potlatching shows the linkages among the three economic processes of making a livelihood, consumption, and exchange. Potlatches are related to food supply, they are opportunities for consumption, and they involve exchange.

Chapter 4 began the discussion of economic systems with the subject of making a living or production. This chapter provides cross-cultural examples of the modes of the other two components of economic systems:

- **Mode of consumption**: the dominant way, in a culture, of using up goods and services.

---

potlatch   a grand feast in which guests are invited to eat and to receive gifts from the hosts.

mode of consumption   the dominant pattern, in a culture, of using things up or spending resources in order to satisfy demands.

mode of exchange   the dominant pattern, in a culture, of transferring goods, services, and other items between and among people and groups.

minimalism   a mode of consumption that emphasizes simplicity, is characterized by few and finite consumer demands, and involves an adequate and sustainable means to achieve them.

consumerism   a mode of consumption in which people's demands are many and infinite and the means of satisfying them are insufficient and become depleted in the effort to satisfy these demands.

leveling mechanism   an unwritten, culturally embedded rule that prevents an individual from becoming wealthier or more powerful than anyone else.

- **Mode of exchange**: the dominant way, in a culture, of transferring goods, services, and other items between and among people and groups.

The chapter's last section provides examples of contemporary change in consumption and exchange.

◉ ◉ ◉
Culture and Consumption

This section examines the concept of consumption, cross-cultural patterns of consumption budgets, and consumption inequalities. It also presents two theoretical positions on food *taboos*, or rules about forbidden food.

What Is Consumption?

Consumption has two meanings: First, it is a person's "intake" in terms of eating or other ways of using things; second, it is "output" in terms of spending or using resources to obtain those things. Thus, for example, "intake" is eating a sandwich; "output" is spending money at the store to buy a sandwich. Both activities fit within the term "consumption."

People consume many things. Food, beverages, clothing, and shelter are the most basic consumption needs in most cultures. People also may acquire tools, weapons, means of transportation, computers, books and other items of communication, art and other luxury goods, and energy for heating and cooling their residence. In noncash economies, such as that of foragers, people "spend" time or labor in order to provide for their needs. In money-based economies, such as industrialized contexts today, most consumption depends on having cash or some virtual form of money.

Modes of Consumption

In categorizing varieties of consumption, it makes sense to consider two contrasting modes, with mixed modes in the middle (Figure 5.1). They are based on the relationship between demand (what people want) and supply (the resources available to satisfy demand):

- **Minimalism**: a mode of consumption characterized by few and finite consumer demands and an adequate and sustainable means to achieve them. It is most characteristic of free-ranging foragers but is also found to some degree among horticulturalists and pastoralists.

- **Consumerism**: a mode of consumption in which people's demands are many and infinite, and the means of satisfying them are never sufficient, thus driving colonialism, globalization, and other forms of expansionism. Consumerism is the distinguishing feature of industrial/informatic cultures. Globalization is spreading consumerism throughout the world.

Foraging	Horticulture	Pastoralism	Agriculture	Industrialism/Informatics
Mode of Consumption				**Mode of Consumption**
Minimalism				Consumerism
Finite needs				Infinite needs
Social Organization of Consumption				**Social Organization of Consumption**
Equality/sharing				Class-based inequality
Personalized products are consumed				Depersonalized products are consumed
Primary Budgetary Fund				**Primary Budgetary Fund**
Basic needs				Rent/taxes, luxuries
Mode of Exchange				**Mode of Exchange**
Balanced exchange				Market exchange
Social Organization of Exchange				**Social Organization of Exchange**
Small groups, face-to-face				Anonymous market transactions
Primary Category of Exchange				**Primary Category of Exchange**
The gift				The sale

FIGURE 5.1 Modes of Livelihood, Consumption, and Exchange.

The social organization and meaning of consumption varies cross-culturally. As noted in Chapter 4, foragers are generally egalitarian, whereas social inequality characterizes most agricultural and industrialism/informatics societies. In foraging peoples, sharing within the group is the norm, and everyone has equal access to all resources. Among the Ju/'hoansi (review Culturama in Chapter 1, page 21), "Even though only a fraction of the able-bodied foragers go out each day, the day's return of meat and gathered foods are divided in such a way that every member of the camp receives an equitable share" (Lee 1979:118).

The distribution of personal goods such as clothing, beads, musical instruments, or smoking pipes is also equal. An important process that operates among small-scale societies and works to keep people equal with each other is called a leveling mechanism. **Leveling mechanisms** are unwritten, culturally embedded rules that prevent an individual from becoming wealthier or more powerful than anyone else. They are maintained through social pressure and gossip. An important leveling mechanism among the Ju/'hoansi requires that any large game animal killed be shared with the group, and its killer must be modest, insisting that the meat is meager (Lee 1969). Ju/'hoansi hunters gain no social status or power through their provision of meat. The same applies to other foragers. Leveling mechanisms are important in horticultural and pastoralist societies, too. For example, when someone's herd grows "too large," that person will be subject to social

pressure to sponsor a large feast in which many of the herd animals are eaten.

Sharing is also a key value among many contemporary Indian tribes such as the Cheyenne of the Great Plains region of the United States (Moore 1999). Within the family, exchange goes on continuously and includes not just food but also tools, jewelry, and even vehicles. Sharing extends to people beyond the family who are considered part of the group. A Cheyenne woman told anthropologist John Moore about her observations at a child-care center where Anglo people also took their children: "'White people are funny,' she said. 'They spend half their time telling kids which toys are theirs, and the other half trying to get them to share'" (1999:179).

At the other end of the consumption continuum is consumerism, with the United States as the primary example, being the major consumerist country of the world. Since the 1970s, consumption levels in the United States have been the highest of any society in human history, and they show no sign of decline. The mass media send out seductive messages promoting consumerism as the way to happiness. Since China began to adopt aspects of capitalism, it has quickly become a consumerist giant. In the world's poorest countries, too, rising numbers of middle- and upper-class people pursue consumerism.

Minimalism was sustainable over hundreds of thousands of years, for most of humanity's time on earth. The amount of goods that the world's population consumed in the past

Well-stocked and brightly lit candy shops are a prominent part of urban nightlife in Valencia, Spain. Sugarcane was introduced into Spain by the Arabs. Later, the Spanish established the first sugarcane plantations on Madeira and the Canary Islands using enslaved laborers from Africa.

▶ *Log your food and drink consumption every day for a week and assess the role that sugar plays in the results.*

50 years equals what was consumed by all previous generations in human history. The growth of consumerism worldwide has major costs:

- To the *environment and biological species diversity*: at risk of survival are natural features such as rivers and lakes, forests, mountains, and beaches; and nonhuman primates and hundreds of other species.

- To the world's *cultural diversity*: at risk of survival are people who currently occupy tropical rainforests, circumpolar regions, deserts, and mountain areas where sought-after resources exist such as pristine tourist destination sites, minerals, and energy sources.

- To the *poor* everywhere: people whose real and relative incomes place them in poverty and who experience an ever-widening gap between themselves and the well-off and the super-rich.

In the United States, concern about the negative effects of consumerism tends to focus on the natural environment (especially unspoiled and remote places for vacations such as national parks and beaches) and endangered nonhuman species rather than on the endangerment and possible extinction of indigenous peoples and other nonindustrialized people—minimalists who "tread lightly on the land." The tragic irony is that more people in North America probably know about an endangered bird species, the spotted owl, than about any single endangered human group.

consumption fund   a category of a personal or household budget used to provide for consumption needs and desires.

Some countries have policies that seek to control consumerism and its negative effects. The government of Sweden has invested in public transportation and bicycle paths in cities in order to reduce the use of cars. London recently placed a tax on cars entering the city. San Francisco is working on a plan to recycle dog waste and use it to create energy.

As consumerism spreads throughout the world, changes in the social relations involved in consumption also occur. In small-scale societies—such as those of foragers, horticulturalists, and pastoralists—consumption items are typically produced by the consumers themselves for their own use. If not, they are likely to be produced by people with whom the consumer has a personal, face-to-face relationship—in other words, *personalized consumption*. Everyone knows where products came from and who produced them. This pattern contrasts markedly with consumption in our contemporary globalized world, which is termed *depersonalized consumption*. Multinational corporations manage the production of most of the goods that people in industrialized countries consume. These products often are multisourced, with parts assembled in diverse parts of the world by hundreds of unknown workers. Depersonalized consumption, by distancing consumers from workers who actually produce goods, makes it more possible for workers to be exploited.

Even in the most industrialized/informatics contexts, though, depersonalized consumption has not completely replaced personalized consumption. The popularity of farmers' markets in urban centers is an example of personalized consumption in which the consumer buys produce from the person who grew it and with whom the consumer may have a friendly conversation, perhaps while sampling one of the farmer's apples.

(LEFT) Sydney, Australia. The demand for electricity in urban centers worldwide has prompted construction of many large dams to provide hydro-electric power as well as other environmentally risky projects such as coal mining. Cities have substantially higher energy demands than rural areas. (RIGHT) In the United Kingdom, as elsewhere in Europe, mini-cars are popular due to their fuel efficiency and ease of parking.

▶ *Do research to discover the gas mileage of an average new car in the United States or Canada and compare it to that of a mini-car.*

Consumption Funds

Anthropologists define a **consumption fund** as a category within a person's or household's budget used to provide for his or her needs and desires. Cross-cultural analysis reveals five categories that appear to be relevant universally:

- *Basic needs fund*: for food, beverages, shelter, clothing, fuel, and the tools involved in producing or providing for them
- *Recurrent costs fund:* for maintenance and repair of tools, animals, machinery, and shelter
- *Entertainment fund:* for leisure activities
- *Ceremonial fund:* for social events such as rituals
- *Rent and tax fund:* for payments to landowners or governments for use of land, housing, or services

The categories apply universally, but the proportion of the budget allocated to each category varies widely and in relation to the mode of consumption. Remember: The "spending" involved may be in time, labor, or money, depending on the cultural context.

In the budget of free-ranging foragers, the largest share of expenditures goes into the basic needs fund. Foragers in temperate climates, however, spend far fewer hours per week collecting food than those in circumpolar climates. The next most important consumption fund among foragers is the recurrent costs fund, which supports repair and maintenance of tools and baskets, weapons, and shelter. Smaller shares are devoted to the entertainment fund and the ceremonial fund. Nothing goes into the rent and tax fund, because access to all land and other resources is free.

Consumption budgets in consumerist cultures differ in several ways from those in foraging, minimalist cultures. First, the absolute size of the budget is larger. People in agricultural and industrial/informatic societies work longer hours (unless they are unemployed), so they "spend" more of their time and labor providing for their consumption than foragers. Depending on their class position, they may have weekly cash budgets that are worth far more than their earnings due to stored wealth. Second, the relative size of the consumption funds varies in household budgets cross-culturally. Take as an example an imagined middle-class person in the United States. His or her consumption funds, compared to those of a forager, might look like this: The basic needs fund is a small portion of the total budget, given the increased overall size of the budget. This finding is in line with the economic principle that budgetary shares for food and housing (basic needs) decline as income rises. For example, someone who earns a total of $1000 a month and spends $800 on food and housing spends 80 percent of his budget in that category. Someone who makes $10,000 a month and spends $2000 a month on food and housing spends only 20 percent of her budget in this category, even though she spends more than twice as much as the first person, in an absolute sense. The largest share of the budget is the rent and tax fund. In some agricultural contexts, tenant farmers have to pay one-third to one-half of their crops to the landlord as rent. Income taxes

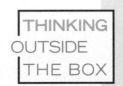

THINKING OUTSIDE THE BOX

Estimate your monthly expenditures in terms of the five funds. What proportion of your total expenditures goes to each fund? Do your expenditures fit well within the five categories or are different categories needed?

Around the world, millions of children live in poverty, either begging or laboring to get food for themselves and their families. (TOP) Homeless children rest by a storefront grate in Ho Chi Minh City, Vietnam. (BOTTOM) A girl picks coffee beans in Guatemala.

▶ *Should a child have the right to work, or should more international pressure be brought to bear against child labor?*

claim well over 50 percent of personal income in countries such as Japan, Sweden, the Netherlands, and Italy. The entertainment fund receives a larger share than the ceremonial fund.

---

entitlement   a culturally defined right to life-sustaining resources.

cash crop   a plant grown primarily for sale rather than for one's own use.

Theorizing Consumption Inequalities

Amartya Sen, an economist and a philosopher, proposed the theory of entitlements in order to explain why some groups suffer more than others during a famine (1981). An **entitlement** is a culturally defined right to provide for one's life needs. According to Sen, everyone has a set, or "bundle," of entitlements. For example, a person might own land, earn cash from a job, be on welfare, or live off an inheritance. Some entitlements are more secure and lucrative than others. *Direct entitlements* are the most secure form. In an agricultural society, for example, owning land that produces food is a direct entitlement. *Indirect entitlements* depend on exchanging something in order to obtain consumer needs: labor, animal hides, money, or food stamps. Because indirect entitlements involve dependency on other people or institutions, they are riskier bases of support than direct entitlements are. When a factory shuts down, animal hides drop in value, or a food-stamp program ends, a person depending on those entitlements is in trouble. During times of economic decline, scarcity, or disaster, people with indirect entitlements are the most vulnerable to impoverishment, hunger, and forced displacement.

ENTITLEMENTS CROSS-CULTURALLY   Entitlements vary depending on the type of economic system. In foraging societies, everyone has the same entitlement bundle. Entitlements are mainly direct, with the exception of infants and very old people who depend on sharing from group members for food and shelter. In industrial capitalist societies, entitlements are mainly indirect. People who grow all their own food are a small proportion of the total population, and even they depend on indirect entitlements for electricity and inputs required for maintaining their lifestyles. In highly monetized economies, the most powerful entitlements are those that provide a large and steady cash income, such as a good job. Other strong entitlements include home ownership, savings, stocks and bonds, and a retirement fund.

Internationally, entitlement theory exposes contrasts between countries that have secure and direct access to life-supporting resources and those that do not. Countries that produce food surpluses have a more secure entitlement to food than countries that are dependent on imports, for example. Replacing food crops with **cash crops**—plants grown primarily for sale, such as coffee or tobacco, rather than for own use—shifts a country from having mainly direct food entitlements to having mainly indirect entitlements. The same applies to access to energy sources that may be important for transportation to work or for heating homes. Direct access to energy resources is preferable to indirect access. This formula, however, leaves out the important factor of political power as exercised by the core countries of today's global economy. Many core countries lack direct access to critical resources, notably oil, yet they use political force to maintain access to such resources.

Skiers and snowboarders line up to ride the lift to the top of the Middle East's first indoor ski resort, Ski Dubai, at the Mall of the Emirates in Dubai. It is housed in one of the world's largest malls and features a ski slope with five runs.

▶ *Plan a fantasy two-week trip to Dubai: How will you get there, where will you stay, where will you eat, what will you do, and how much will the trip cost?*

At the country level, governments affect people's entitlements through policies related to employment, welfare programs, health care, and tax structures, among others. Political leaders and powerful policy makers decide how many people will live in poverty and how many will be allowed to become rich, or even super-rich. They decide on whether to fund programs that transfer wealth from the rich to the poor or to enact regressive tax structures that tax lower-income people at higher rates than the rich.

The entitlement concept can also be applied to *intra-household* entitlements, or shares of important resources that are allocated to particular household members. Households do not always provide equal entitlements for all members. A household member who is employed and earns wages, for example, may have a more secure position in terms of resources such as preferred food than someone who does not. Commonly, men have more secure intra-household entitlements than women. For example, inheritance practices may ensure that sons receive assets such as land or the family business, whereas daughters are excluded. Intra-household entitlements may also affect expenditures on health care depending on the status and value of particular members.

During crises, entitlement structures often become glaringly clear. Famines are a good example. Famine is defined as massive levels of death resulting from food deprivation in a geographically widespread area. Most people think that famines are caused by overpopulation or by natural disasters such as droughts and floods. Comparative analyses of many famine situations prove, however, that neither overpopulation nor natural disasters are sufficient explanations for famine (Sen 1981). Calculations of world food supply in relation to population prove that there is enough food produced every year to feed the world's population. Furthermore, although natural factors are often catalysts of famine, they do not always cause famine.

In Louisiana and Mississippi, the hurricanes of 2005 caused many deaths, massive loss of private and commercial property, and displacement of thousands of people. But they did not cause a famine. Anthony Oliver-Smith, an anthropologist who specializes in disasters, has said that there is no such thing as a purely *natural* disaster (2002). His point is that culture always shapes the patterns of human suffering and loss following a "natural" disaster. The social pattern of population displacement as a result of the 2005 hurricanes is testimony to the cultural shaping of disasters.

Entitlement analysis can help improve the effectiveness of humanitarian aid during famines and other crises (Harragin 2004). During the famine in southern Sudan in 1988 (see Map 15.6, page 374), relief workers failed to understand the local cultural pattern of sharing, which extends to the last cup of rice. As food supplies decreased, local people continued to share whatever food was available. As a result, many people were surviving, but barely. When the food supply declined even more, the social safety net was unable to stretch further. Suddenly hundreds of people were dying. If relief workers had known about the culture of sharing unto death, they might have been able to forecast the breaking point before it happened and to bring in food aid sooner.

THREE CONSUMPTION MICROCULTURES This section provides examples of three consumption microcultures: class, gender, and "race." Microcultures have distinct

THINKING OUTSIDE THE BOX

What is in your personal entitlement bundle? Conduct a self-analysis of your daily consumption needs (food, shelter, entertainment, and other things) and how you provide for them. Then, imagine how you would provide for these needs if your usual entitlements are of no value.

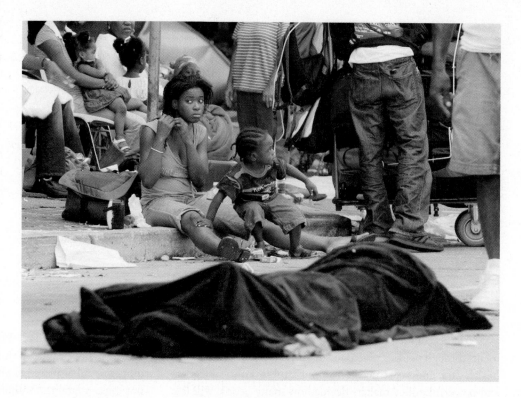

In the aftermath of Hurricane Katrina in 2005, a corpse lies covered as evacuees line the streets outside the convention center in New Orleans, Louisiana. After acknowledging that the initial federal effort to aid victims had failed, President George W. Bush deployed additional U.S. troops to the area.

▶ Using the Internet, learn what roles cultural anthropologists played in the post-hurricane situation in the Gulf Coast area.

entitlement patterns, related levels of health and welfare, and identity associated with consumption. Depending on the cultural context, social inequality may play an important role and have major effects on human welfare.

Class and the Game of Distinction in Israeli Birthday Parties Class differences, defined in terms of levels of income, are reflected in distinctive consumption patterns. Although class differences in consumption may seem too obvious to be worth studying, they constitute an important and growing area in anthropology.

A landmark study about consumer preferences, or "tastes," was conducted by a team of French researchers led by French anthropologist/sociologist Pierre Bourdieu (1984). They sent questionnaires to several thousand people, based on a national sample, and received 1000 responses. Statistical analysis of the responses revealed clear class patterns in, for example, choice of favorite painters or pieces of music. Preferences corresponded with educational level and father's occupation. An overall pattern of *distance from necessity* in tastes and preferences characterized members of the educated upper classes, who were more likely to prefer abstract art. Their goal was to keep "necessity" at a distance. In comparison, the working classes were closer to "necessity," and they preferred realist art. Bourdieu provides the concept of the *game of distinction* in which people of the upper classes continually adjust their preferences to distance themselves from the lower classes, whereas members of the lower classes tend to adopt aspects of upper-class preferences in order to gain status.

Cross-culturally, events such as weddings, funerals, and children's birthday parties are often occasions requiring large expenditures that send messages about the status (real or aspired) of the hosts. Children's birthday parties are a less studied topic but one with much potential, especially because such parties are becoming increasingly popular in cultures around the world. In Israel, children's birthday parties have recently become expensive events among middle-class and upper-class urbanites (Goldstein-Gidoni 2003). Parents hire birthday party professionals to create special themes. "Around the World" themes are popular, especially those drawing on Japanese, Spanish, South American, and Middle Eastern motifs. A current craze for Japanese culture, such as gardens and food, means that the Japanese theme is one of the most popular. "Around the World" birthday party themes are ostensibly to help the children learn about other places and people. At the same time, they make a statement about how cosmopolitan, well-off, and stylish the hosts are.

Not everyone, everywhere, buys into the game of distinction. Many individuals and wider social movements actively resist the spread of upper-class consumption patterns and promote alternative cultural practices.

Women's Deadly Diet in Papua New Guinea Consumption patterns are often marked by gender and related to discrimination and inequality. Specific foods may be considered "men's food" or "women's food." An example of lethal gender inequalities in food consumption comes from highland Papua New Guinea (Map 5.1).

The story begins with the eruption of a mysterious disease, with the local name of *kuru*, among the Fore (for-ay), a horticultural people of the highlands (Lindenbaum 1979). Between 1957 and 1977, about 2500 people died of kuru. Most victims, however, were women. The first signs of kuru

MAP 5.1 Location of the Kuru Epidemic in Papua New Guinea.

are shivering tremors, followed by a progressive loss of motor ability along with pain in the head and limbs. Kuru victims could walk unsteadily at first but would later be unable to get up. Death occurred about a year after the first symptoms appeared.

American medical researchers revealed that kuru was a neurological disease. Australian cultural anthropologist Shirley Lindenbaum pinpointed the cultural cause of kuru: cannibalism. Kuru victims had eaten the flesh of deceased people who had died of kuru.

Why were most of the kuru victims women? Lindenbaum learned that among the Fore, it was considered acceptable to cook and eat the meat of a deceased person, although it was not a preferred food. The preferred source of animal protein is meat from pigs, and men receive preferential access to the best food. Fore women had begun to eat human flesh more often because of increased scarcity of pigs. Population density in the region had risen, more land was being cultivated, and forest areas had decreased. Pigs live in forest areas, so as their habitat became more restricted, their numbers declined. The Fore could not move to more pig-abundant areas because they were bounded on the east, west, and north sides by other groups. The south was a harsh and forbidding region. These factors, combined with the Fore's male-biased system of protein consumption, forced women to turn to the less preferred protein source of human flesh. By eating the flesh, including brains, of kuru victims, they contracted the disease.

"Race" and Children's Shopping in New Haven Throughout the world, in countries with "race"-based social categories, inequalities in consumption and quality of life exist, often in spite of anti-discrimination legislation. In the United States, racism and racial discrimination affect many areas of life from access to housing, neighborhood security and services, schooling,

health, and whether a person is likely to be ignored by a taxi or stopped by a police officer for speeding. Racial inequality between Black and White Americans has risen steadily since the 1970s in terms of income, wealth, and property ownership, especially house-ownership (Shapiro 2004). Those at the top of the income distribution have increased their share of the wealth most. The share of total income that goes to the top 1 percent of families is nearly the same size as the total income share of the bottom 40 percent.

How is this happening in a country dedicated to equality of opportunity? A large part of the answer lies in the simple fact that, in a capitalist system, inequality leads to more inequality through the transfer of wealth and property across generations. Those who have wealth and property are able to establish their children's wealth through college tuition payments, house down payments, and other financial gifts. The children of poor parents have to provide for their education and housing costs from their wages alone, a fact that makes it far less likely that they will be able to pursue higher education or buy a home.

As a graduate student in anthropology at Yale University, Elizabeth Chin decided to do her dissertation research on consumption patterns among schoolchildren in a poor, African American neighborhood in New Haven, Connecticut (2001) (Map 5.2). In terms of per capita income, Connecticut is the wealthiest state in the United States. It also harbors some of the

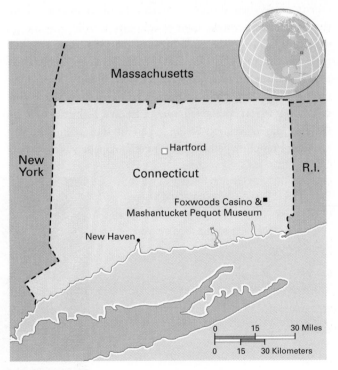

MAP 5.2 Connecticut, United States.

In terms of per capita income, Connecticut is the wealthiest state in the United States. Its population of about 3.5 million includes a majority of Whites (76 percent), predominantly of Italian, Irish, and English descent. Blacks and Latinos constitute about 10 percent of the population each. Indian tribal peoples are 0.3 percent.

most severe poverty and racial inequality in its major cities. Chin describes New Haven as a "patchwork of clearly delineated neighborhoods that can veer quite suddenly from the abjectly poor to the fabulously wealthy" (2001:vii). These zones are largely divided into White and Black groups who are fearful and suspicious of each other. During her research in "Newhallville," Chin found that the Black and White cultural worlds are clearly separate and deeply unequal. In the Black neighborhood, 50 percent of children age five and under were living in poverty.

Chin formed a relationship with one fifth-grade class of 22 students. She spent time in the classroom. She explored the neighborhood with some of the children, visited with them and their families in their homes, and accompanied them on shopping trips to the mall. The children are bombarded with media messages about consumption, but they have little money to spend. Some receive an allowance for doing household chores; some receive small amounts of pocket money on an ad hoc basis; and some earn money from small-scale ventures such as a cucumber stand. They learn about the basics of household finances and the costs of daily life early on. Seeing their families strain every day to put meals on the table teaches them about the negative effects of overindulgence: "From divvying up the milk to figuring out where to sleep, there is an emphasis on sharing and mutual obligation" (2001:5).

These practical lessons shape how the children spend their money when they go to the mall. Practicality and generosity guide their shopping choices. In order to learn about the children's decisions, Chin would give a child $20 and go with him or her to the mall. Most of the girls spent over half their money on gifts for family members, especially their mothers and grandmothers (2001:139). The girls knew their mothers' shoe sizes and clothing sizes. One boy, just before school was to start in the fall, spent $10 on a T-shirt to wear on the first day of school, $6 on a pair of shorts, and the rest on school supplies: pencils, pens, notebook paper, and a binder

(2001:135). In her two years of research, Chin never heard a Newhallville child nag a caretaker about buying him or her something or whine about personal consumption desires.

Birthday parties are rare events in Newhallville. The one birthday party Chin observed involved an $18 ice-cream cake. Birthday gifts are few. One girl received three gifts on her tenth birthday: a jump rope and a bingo game from her mother, wrapped in brown paper made from a grocery bag, and an inexpensive plastic toy from her grandmother (2001:72). There was no party, but her mother baked a chocolate cake for her.

Forbidden Consumption: Food Taboos

Cultural anthropologists have a long-standing interest in trying to explain culturally specific food taboos, or rules about prohibited foods. Cultural materialists and symbolic anthropologists disagree about why food taboos exist.

WHAT CULTURAL MATERIALISM SAYS Cultural materialist Marvin Harris (review Chapter 1) asks why there are Jewish and Muslim taboos on eating pig when pig meat is so enthusiastically consumed in many other parts of the world (1974). He says, "Why should gods so exalted as Jahweh and Allah have bothered to condemn a harmless and even laughable beast whose flesh is relished by the greater part of mankind?" (1974:36). Harris proposes that we consider the role of environmental factors during early Hebrew times and the function of this prohibition in terms of its fit to the local ecology.

Within the overall pattern of this mixed farming and pastoralist complex, the divine prohibition of pork constituted a sound ecological strategy. The pig is thermodynamically ill-adapted to the hot, dry climate of the Negev, the Jordan Valley, and the other lands of the Bible and the Koran. Compared to cattle, goats, and sheep, the pig has an inefficient

Preparation for a feast in the highlands of Papua New Guinea, where people place much value on consuming roasted pig meat.

▶ *What are the high-status foods in your cultural world(s)?*

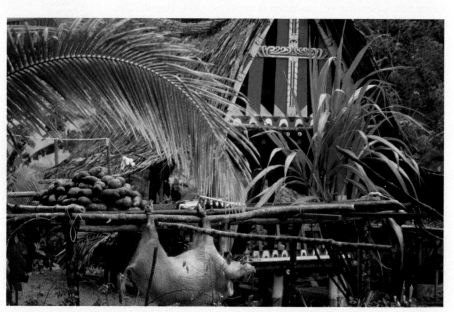

system for regulating its body temperature. Despite the expression "to sweat like a pig," it has been proved that pigs can't sweat at all (1974:41–42).

Raising pigs in this context would be a luxury. On the other hand, in "pig-loving" cultures of Southeast Asia and the Pacific, climatic factors, including temperature, humidity, and the presence of forest cover (good for pigs) promote raising pigs. There, pigs offer an important protein source that complements the major root crops: yams, sweet potatoes, and taro. Harris acknowledges that not all religiously sanctioned food practices can be explained ecologically and that food practices often serve to communicate and promote social identity. But analysis of food consumption should always consider ecological and material factors of production as basic.

What Symbolic Anthropologists Say   Symbolic anthropologist Mary Douglas argues, in contrast to Harris, that what people eat has less to do with the material conditions of life (the environment or hunger) than with what food means and how food communicates meaning and identity (1966). For Douglas, people's emic categories about food provide a mental map of the world and people's place in it. *Anomalies*, or things that do not fit into culturally defined categories, become reminders to people of moral problems or things to avoid.

Douglas uses a symbolic approach in examining food categories and anomalies as laid out in the Old Testament book of Leviticus. One rule says that people may eat animals with cloven hoofs and that chew a cud. On the basis of this rule, animals that do not satisfy both criteria are anomalies, and such animals are considered unclean and are taboo as food. These anomalies include camels, pigs, and hares. A pig, for example, has cloven hoofs, but it does not chew a cud. In the interpretation of Douglas, the food rules in Leviticus are a symbolic system defining completeness and purity (the animals one can eat) in contrast to incompleteness and impurity (the animals one cannot eat). By extension, she argues, people who know these rules and follow them are constantly reminded of God's perfection, completeness, and purity. When people follow these rules, they communicate their identity as pure and godly to other people. Thus, according to Douglas, food choices are not about the nutritional content of the food; rather, they have to do with symbols and meaning. She downplays studying the "practical" aspects of food because, she says, that distracts analysts from studying the meaning of food.

Anthropologists, no matter which theoretical perspective they favor about food taboos, recognize that there is more to food than just eating. Douglas emphasizes the importance of food rules as codes, ways of communicating meaning, and this interpretation is clearly valid. Harris says that economic and political aspects of food choices must be considered for a full understanding, and this point is valid, too.

⊚ ⊚ ⊚
Culture and Exchange

Exchange is the transfer of something that may be material or immaterial between at least two persons, groups, or institutions. Cultural anthropologists have done much research on gifts and other forms of exchange, starting with Malinowski's work on the kula in the South Pacific (review Culturama, Chapter 3, page 59) and Boas's research on potlatching among Northwest Coast Indians. In all economic systems, individuals and groups exchange goods and services with others. But variation exists in what is exchanged, how goods are exchanged, when exchange takes place, and the meaning of exchange.

What Is Exchanged?

The items that people exchange range from seashells to stocks and bonds and may be purely utilitarian (Figure 5.2). Items of exchange may carry meanings and have a history, or "social life," of their own, as prized kula items do (Appadurai 1986).

In contemporary industrialized societies, money is the major item of exchange, and such economies are referred to as *monetized*. In nonmarket economies, money plays a less important role, and time, labor, and goods are prominent exchange items. As nonmarket economies are connected, through globalization, they are confronted with the (to them) peculiar and mysterious meaning of Western money. Often, they localize the meanings of money, by treating particular bills as more special than others. In many cultures, money has completely replaced other valued items of exchange, such as shell wealth in Papua New Guinea.

Nonmonetary exchange exists in contemporary industrial societies, too. Hosting dinner parties, exchanging gifts at holiday times, and sharing a bag of potato chips with a friend are examples of common forms of nonmonetary exchange. Some scholars also include kisses, glances, and loyalty (Blau 1964).

MATERIAL GOODS   Cross-culturally, food is one of the most common exchange goods both in everyday life and on ritual occasions. Daily meals involve some form of exchange,

Category	Examples
Material goods	Food to family and group members Gifts for special occasions such as weddings Money
Nonmaterial goods	Myths, stories, rituals Time, labor
People	Offspring in marriage Slavery

FIGURE 5.2   Items of Exchange.

everyday ANTHROPOLOGY

The Rules of Hospitality

In much of the Middle East, where women spend most of their time in the domestic domain, social visits among women are eagerly anticipated and carefully planned events with complex rules about what foods and drinks should be served (Wikan 1982). In Oman, when women go outside the home, they wear head veils, face masks, and full-length gowns. Their main social activity consists of visits to other women in their homes. A typical visit involves sitting, chatting, and eating snacks.

Social etiquette dictates what should be served and how. Coffee and dates are the traditional entertainment foods offered to close neighbors. Biscuits (cookies), caramel candies, and popcorn are favored snacks. Beyond the particular snack item, the number of dishes offered is important. For neighbors who interact on a daily basis, a single dish is typical. All other visitors should be offered at least two plates with different contents, or else the hostess will be considered stingy. In the case of many guests, the number of plates must be increased, with a minimum of four plates, and the variety of snacks must be greater. Another rule of visitor etiquette requires that guests should leave approximately half of the food served to them; it will be consumed by members of the hostess' household (1982:130–132).

Cooked food, such as meat and sweets, is served when entertaining guests at weddings, seasonal feasts, and burials. In such situations, when cooked food is served, the hosts may never eat with their guests: "Even if the consequence is that the guest must eat all alone, in a separate room, it would be disrespectful to arrange it otherwise" (1982:133).

FOOD FOR THOUGHT ▼
How do these Omani rules of hospitality resemble or contrast with your rules of hospitality? Think about your choices of items served, numbers of items, and other choices you make about what to serve and how to serve it when entertaining guests.

A Bedu (Bedouin) woman of Muscat, Oman.

▶ *Assume you are going to Oman for a semester abroad. What should you know about the culture before you go?*

---

as do most ceremonies and rituals. In many cultures, arranging a marriage involves many stages of food gifts and countergifts exchanged between the families of the couple.

Wedding exchanges among the Nias of northern Sumatra, Indonesia (see Map 8.3, page 190), provide an illustration of a complex set of exchanges. From the betrothal to the actual marriage, a scheduled sequence of events occurs at which culturally stipulated food and other gifts are exchanged between the families of the bride and groom (Beatty 1992). At the first meeting between the families, when the prospective groom expresses his interest in a betrothal, he and his party visit the bride's house and are fed. The guests receive the lower jaw of a pig (the portion of honor), and they take away with them raw and cooked portions of the pig for the father of the groom-to-be (1992:121). Within the next week or two, the prospective groom brings a gift of 3 to 12 pigs to confirm the engagement. He returns the container used for the pig meat given to him on the previous visit, filled with a certain kind of nut. The groom gives more pigs and gold as the major gift to seal the marriage. For many years following the wedding, the two families continue to exchange gifts.

On an everyday level, exchanges of food and beverages are important in friendships. Among friends, food exchanges involve their own, largely unconscious rules of etiquette (see Everyday Anthropology).

Exchanging alcoholic beverages is an important feature of many community ritual events in Latin America. In a highland village in Ecuador, the San Juan fiesta is the high point of the year (Barlett 1980). The fiesta consists of four or five days during which small groups of celebrants move from house to house, dancing and drinking. The anthropologist reports on the event:

> I joined the groups consisting of the president of the community and the elected *alcaldes* (councilmen and police), who were accompanied by their wives, a few friends, and

THINKING
OUTSIDE
THE BOX

You have invited Jesus, the Buddha, Muhammad, and Moses to dinner. What are you serving?

Omani biotech scientist, Ms. Wahida al-Amri, at work in her lab in the Omani Marine Science and Fisheries Center.

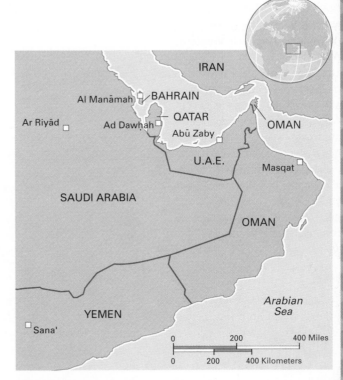

MAP 5.3 Oman.

The Sultanate of Oman is mainly a vast desert plain with a hot, dry climate. The population of nearly 3 million includes over 500,000 immigrant laborers. The economy is based mainly on crude oil. The major religion is Ibādī Islam, a more liberal version of Islam than Sunni or Shi'a Islam. Arabic is the official language, with English a widely spoken second language. Several dialects of Arabic are spoken.

some children. We met each morning for a hearty breakfast at one house, began drinking there, and then continued eating and drinking in other homes throughout the day and into the evening. . . . Some people drink for only one or two days, others prefer to make visits mainly at night, some people drink day and night for four days. (1980:118–119)

Guests who drink at someone's house will later serve their former hosts alcohol in return.

SYMBOLIC GOODS Intangible valuables such as myths (sacred stories) and rituals (sacred practices) may be exchanged in ways similar to material goods. In the Balgo Hills region of Australia (see Map 5.4 on page 120), long-standing exchange networks transfer myths and rituals among regionally dispersed groups of women (Poirier 1992). The women may keep important narratives and rituals for a limited time and then must pass them on to other groups. One is the *Tjarada*, a love-magic ritual with an accompanying narrative. The Tjarada came to the women of Balgo Hills from the north. They kept it for about 15 years and then passed it on to

another group in a ceremony that lasted for three days. During the time that the Balgo Hills women were custodians of the Tjarada, they incorporated some new elements into it. These elements are retained even after its transfer to the next group. Thus, the Tjarada contains bits of local identity of each group that has had it. A sense of community and responsibility thereby develops and is sustained among the groups that have held the Tjarada.

LABOR In labor-sharing groups, people contribute labor to other people on a regular basis (for seasonal agricultural work such as harvesting) or on an irregular basis (in the event of a crisis such as the need to rebuild a barn damaged by fire). Labor-sharing groups are part of what is called the *moral economy* because no one keeps formal records on how much any family puts in or takes out. Instead, accounting is based on trust and socially regulated. In Amish communities of North America (see Culturama, Chapter 6, page 136), sharing labor is a central part of life. When a family needs a new barn that requires group labor, a barn-raising party is called. Many families join in to help. Men provide manual labor, and women provide food.

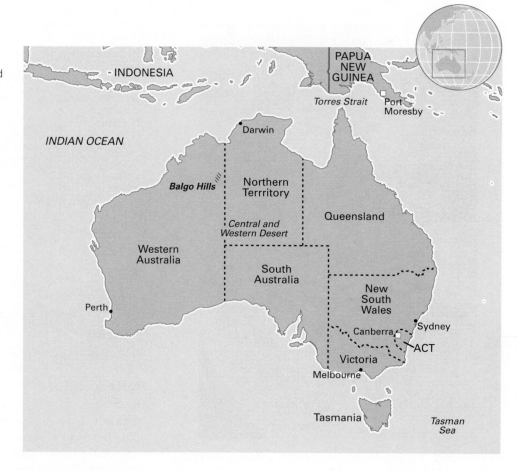

MAP 5.4 The Balgo Hills (Wirrimanu) Region in Western Australia.

The Balgo Hills community is located on the northern edge of the Tanami and Great Sandy Deserts. One of Australia's most isolated indigenous desert settlements, it nevertheless has a flourishing art center. Balgo paintings and glass are highly sought after by collectors. To learn about Balgo art and artists, visit http://www.aboriginalartonline.com/regions/balgo.php.

MONEY For most of humanity's existence, people did not purchase things. They collected or made things they needed themselves, shared, or exchanged items for other things. The invention of money is recent, only a few thousand years ago. **Money** is a medium of exchange that can be used for a variety of goods (Godelier 1971). Money exists cross-culturally in such diverse forms as shells, salt, cattle, furs, cocoa beans, and iron hoes.

Modern money, in the form of coins and paper bills, has the advantages of being portable, divisible, uniform, and recognizable (Shipton 2001). On the other hand, modern money is vulnerable to economic changes such as inflation, which reduces its value. The use of modern money is spreading throughout the world. Nonmonetary cultures, however, often adopt modern money in limited ways. They may prohibit its use in religious exchanges or in life-cycle rituals such as marriages. All forms of money, even modern money, are symbolic. They have meaning to the user, and they are associated with the user's identity and sense of self. The color and design of a

---

money a medium of exchange that can be used for a variety of goods.

balanced exchange a system of transfers in which the goal is either immediate or eventual equality in value.

unbalanced exchange a system of transfers in which one party seeks to make a profit.

generalized reciprocity exchange involving the least conscious sense of interest in material gain or thought of what might be received in return.

pure gift something given with no expectation or thought of a return.

This raffia cloth, from the Democratic Republic of Congo, is woven from palm fibers. Throughout central Africa, raffia cloth functions as limited-purpose money, or money that can be used only for specific purposes, such as marriage or compensation for wrongdoing. It cannot be used for commercial transactions such as buying food, a house, or a car.

	Balanced Exchange			Unbalanced Exchange	
	Generalized Reciprocity	**Expected Reciprocity**	**Redistribution**	**Market Exchange**	**Theft, Exploitation**
Actors	Kin, friends	Trading partners	Leader and pooling group	Buyers/sellers	Nonkin, nonfriends, unknown
Return	Not calculated or expected	Expected at some time	Feast and give-away	Immediate payment	No return
Example	Buying coffee for a friend	Kula	Moka	Internet shopping	Shoplifting

FIGURE 5.3 Keeping Track of Exchange.

credit card, for example, may signify status, such as "platinum" for the biggest spenders. As the European Union was forming, lengthy discussion was devoted to what the new currency would look like. As e-money becomes increasingly used, it will be interesting to see what kinds of meaning are attached to it.

PEOPLE Exchange in human beings relegates humans to objects. Throughout history, some people have been able to gain control of other people and treat them as items of exchange, as in slavery and human trafficking. The enslavement of people from many regions of Africa during European colonialism from the fifteenth to nineteenth centuries stands as one of the most heinous processes of treating humans as commodities in the full light of day, with no legal sanctions involved for slave traders or owners. This process cruelly transformed thousands of people into property that could be bought and sold, used and abused, and even murdered.

A long-standing debate in anthropology concerns women as objects of exchange in marriage. Lévi-Strauss proposed many years ago that the exchange of women between men is one of the most basic forms of exchange among humans (1969 [1949]). He based his assertion on the universality of some sort of *incest taboo*, which he defined as a rule preventing a man from marrying or cohabiting with his mother or sister (Chapter 8 provides the current definition). Such a rule, he says, is the logic driving the exchange of women among men: "The fact that I can obtain a wife is, in the final analysis, the consequence of the fact that a brother or father has given her up" (1969:62). Thus, the avoidance of incest forces men to develop exchange networks with other men and, by extension, leads to the emergence of social solidarity more widely. For Lévi-Strauss, the incest taboo provides the foundation for human social organization.

Feminist anthropologists say that this theory overlooks much ethnographic evidence to the contrary. Men do not have rights over women in foraging societies; instead, women

make their own choices about partners (Rubin 1975). In many horticultural and agricultural societies of Southeast Asia, men do not exchange women (Peletz 1987). Instead, women select grooms for their daughters. This pattern turns Lévi-Strauss's theory on its head because it involves women organizing the exchange of men.

Modes of Exchange

Parallel to the two contrasting modes of consumption described earlier (minimalism and consumerism), two distinct modes of exchange can be delineated (Figure 5.3):

- **Balanced exchange**: a system of transfers in which the goal is either immediate or eventual balance in value.
- **Unbalanced exchange**: a system of transfers in which one party attempts to make a profit.

BALANCED EXCHANGE The category of balanced exchange contains two subcategories based on the social relationship of the two parties involved in the exchange and the degree to which a "return" is expected. **Generalized reciprocity** is a transaction that involves the least conscious sense of interest in material gain or thought of what might be received in return, and when. Such exchanges often involve goods and services of an everyday nature, such as a cup of coffee. Generalized reciprocity is the main form of exchange between people who know each other well and trust each other. Therefore, it is the main form of exchange in foraging societies. It is also found among close kin and friends cross-culturally.

A **pure gift** is something given with no expectation or thought of a return. The pure gift is an extreme form of generalized reciprocity. Examples of a pure gift include donating money for a food drive, or making donations to famine relief, blood banks, and religious organizations. Some people say that a truly pure gift does not exist because one always gains something, no matter how difficult to measure, in giving—even if it is just the good feeling of generosity. Parental care of children is said to be a pure gift by some, but others do not agree. Those who say that parental care is a pure gift argue that most parents do not consciously calculate how much they have spent on their children with the intention of "getting it back" later on. Those who do not consider parental care a pure gift say that even if the "costs" are not consciously calculated, parents have unconscious expectations about what their children will "return" to them, whether the return is material (care in old age) or immaterial (making the parent feel proud).

Expected reciprocity is the exchange of approximately equally valued goods or services, usually between people of roughly equal social status. The exchange may occur simultaneously between both parties, or it may involve an understanding about the time period within which the exchange will be completed. This aspect of timing contrasts with generalized reciprocity, in which there is no fixed time limit for the return. In expected reciprocity, if the second party fails to complete the exchange, the relationship will break down. Balanced reciprocity is less personal than generalized reciprocity and, according to Western definitions, more "economic."

The kula is an example of a system of expected reciprocity (review Culturama, Chapter 3, page 59). Men exchange necklaces and armlets, giving them to their exchange partners after keeping them for a while. Partners include neighbors as well as people on faraway islands who are visited via long canoe voyages on high seas. Trobriand men are distinguished by the particular armlets and necklaces that they exchange, and certain armlets and necklaces are more prestigious than others. One cannot keep one's trade items for long because the kula code dictates that "to possess is great, but to possess is to give." Generosity is the essence of goodness, and stinginess is the most despised vice. Kula exchanges should involve items of equivalent value. If a man trades a very valuable necklace with his partner, he expects to receive in return a very valuable armlet as an equivalent gift). At the time, if one's partner does not possess an equivalent item, he may have to give an intermediary gift, which stands as a token of good faith until a proper return gift can be given. The clinching gift comes later and balances the original gift. The equality of exchange ensures a strong bond between the trading partners and is a

statement of trust. When a man arrives in an area where it may be dangerous because of previous raids or warfare, he can count on having a friend to give him hospitality.

Redistribution is a form of exchange in which one person collects goods or money from many members of a group and provides a social "return" at a later time. At a public event, even several years later, the organizer returns the pooled goods to everyone who contributed by sponsoring a generous feast. Compared to the two-way pattern of exchange involved in reciprocity, redistribution involves some centricity. It contains the possibility of inequality because what is returned may not always equal, in a material sense, what each individual contributed. The pooling group may continue to exist, however, because it benefits from the leadership skills of the person who mobilizes contributions. If a neighboring group threatens a raid, people turn to their redistributive leader for political leadership (discussed further in Chapter 10).

UNBALANCED EXCHANGE **Market exchange**, a prominent form of unbalanced exchange, is the buying and selling of commodities under competitive conditions in which the forces of supply and demand determine value and the seller seeks to make a profit (Dannhaeuser 1989:222). In market transactions, the seller and buyer may or may not have a personal relationship. They may or may not be social equals. Their exchange is not likely to generate social bonding. Many market transactions take place in a marketplace, a physical location in which buying and selling occur. The market system evolved from other, less formal contexts of **trade**, formalized exchange of one thing for another according to set standards of value.

The market system is associated with regional specialization in producing particular goods and trade between regions. Certain products are identified with a particular town or region. In Morocco, the city of Fez (see Map 6.2, page 139) is famous for its blue-glazed pottery, whereas the Berber people of the Atlas Mountains are known for their fine wool blankets and rugs. In Oaxaca, Mexico (see Map 6.3, page 140), some villages are known for their blankets, pottery, stone grinders, rope, and chili peppers (Plattner 1989). Specialization develops with illegal commodities too. For example, Jamaican marijuana is well known for its high quality, and many tourists travel to Jamaica, especially the Negril area in the west, in order to buy this product in its many forms. Increasingly, producers of regionally distinct products, such as champagne, are copyrighting the regional name to prevent its use by producers of similar products from outside the region.

Marketplaces range from informal, small stands that appear in the morning and disappear at night, to huge multi-storied shopping centers. One variety found in many parts of the world is a *periodic market*, a site for buying and selling that takes place on a regular basis (for example, monthly) in a particular location but without a permanent physical structure.

---

expected reciprocity an exchange of approximately equally valued goods or services, usually between people roughly equal in social status.

redistribution a form of exchange that involves one person collecting goods or money from many members of a group, who then, at a later time and at a public event, "returns" the pooled goods to everyone who contributed.

market exchange the buying and selling of commodities under competitive conditions, in which the forces of supply and demand determine value.

trade the formalized exchange of one thing for another according to set standards of value.

Scenes at two permanent markets. (LEFT) In China, many marketers are women. These two women display their wares in a permanent food market in a city about an hour's drive from Shanghai. (RIGHT) Workers at Tsukiji, the world's largest fish market in Tokyo, transport frozen tuna on hand carts for the upcoming auction.

▶ *For a research project, learn more about Ted Bestor's research on Tsukiji.*

Sellers appear with their goods and set up a table with perhaps an awning. In contrast, permanent markets are built structures situated in fixed locations. Marketplaces, however, are more than just places for buying and selling. They involve social interactions and even performances. Sellers solicit customers, shoppers meet and chat, government officials drop by, religious organizations may hold services, and traditional healers may treat toothaches. The particularities of how markets are structured, spatially and socially, and how culture shapes market transactions are rich topics for ethnographic research.

Ted Bestor conducted research over many years in Tsukiji (tsee-kee-jee), the world's largest fish market, located in Tokyo (2004). Tsukiji connects large-scale corporations that supply most of the seafood with small-scale family-run firms that continue to dominate Tokyo's retail food trade. Bestor describes the layout of the huge market, with inner and outer sections as a basic division. The outer market attracts younger, hipper shoppers looking for unusual, trendy gourmet items and a more authentic-seeming shopping experience. It contains sushi bars, noodle stalls, knife shops, and chopstick dealers, as well as temples and graveyards. The inner market contains 11 fresh produce market subdivisions. The seafood section by far overshadows the "veggie" markets in size and transaction level. It is subdivided into several main buildings where auctions occur, activities such as deliveries and dispatches take place, and rows of retail stalls serve 14,000 customers each morning. Bestor gained insight into the verbally coded conversations between experienced buyers and sellers in the stalls that are more likely to yield a better price than what an inexperienced first-time buyer will get. Stalls do not typically post prices, so buyers and sellers have to negotiate them. The verbal codes involve phrases such as "morning mist on a white beach," which, depending on the number of syllables in the phrase, conveys a price offer.

OTHER FORMS OF UNBALANCED EXCHANGE

Several forms of unbalanced exchange other than market transactions exist. In extreme instances, no social relationship is involved; in others, sustained unequal relationships are maintained over time between people. These forms include taking something with no expectation of giving any return. They can occur in any mode of production, but are most likely to be found in large-scale societies where more options (other than face-to-face) for balanced exchange exist.

Gambling *Gambling*, or gaming, is the attempt to make a profit by playing a game of chance in which a certain item of value is staked in hopes of acquiring the much larger return that one receives if one wins the game. If one loses, that which was staked is lost. Gambling is an ancient practice and is common cross-culturally. Ancient forms of gambling include dice throwing and card playing. Investing in the stock market can be considered a form of gambling, as can gambling of many sorts through the Internet. Although gambling may seem an odd category within unbalanced exchange, its goal of making a profit seems to justify its placement here. The fact that gambling within "high" capitalism is on the rise justifies anthropological attention to it. In fact, some scholars have referred to the present stage of Western capitalism as casino capitalism, given the propensity of investors to play risky games in the stock market (Klima 2002).

ANTHROPOLOGY works

Evaluating Indian Gaming

In 2006, the Center for California Native Nations (CCNN) at the University of California at Riverside released an evaluation of the effects of Indian gaming in California (Spilde Contreras 2006). *Note:* According to current preferences of the people involved, the terms Indian or Indian tribe are used instead of Native American.

Kate Spilde Contreras, applied cultural anthropologist, directed the multidisciplinary team of anthropologists, political scientists, economists, and historians. The research objective was to evaluate the social and economic effects of Indian gaming operations on tribal and local governments in California. The study relies mainly on public data, especially the 1990 and 2000 U.S. Censuses, to supply a "before" and "after" picture during the initial growth phase of Indian gaming in the state. To learn about more recent changes, the research team conducted surveys of tribal and local government officials and in-depth case studies of individual tribal governments.

Findings indicate two important factors that shape the effects of Indian gaming in California: gaming establishments are owned by tribal governments, and gaming establishments are located on existing tribal trust lands. Therefore, gaming revenues support community and government activities of the tribal communities, and employment generation is localized within the tribal communities.

Indian reservations in California are more economically heterogeneous than elsewhere in the United States. Since the development of gaming, California

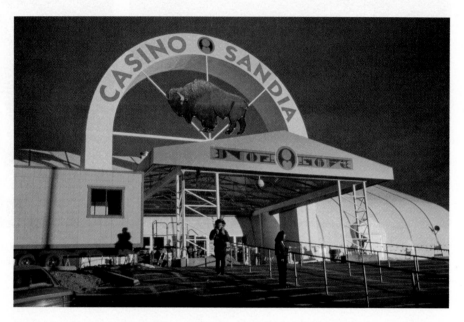

Casino Sandia, located in the Sandia Pueblo in northern New Mexico, is one of many casinos in the state established in the hope of raising funds to improve the lives of Indian people.

also has greater economic inequality between gaming and nongaming reservations than is found in other states. By 2000, the fastest average income growth on California reservations occurred on gaming reservations. A policy response to this situation is a tribal-state gaming contract, the Revenue Sharing Trust Fund (RSTF) that provides for sharing of gaming revenue with nongaming communities.

Spilde Contreras's team considered the effects on gaming beyond the reservation. They found that areas within 10 miles of gaming reservations experienced significant employment increases, greater income growth, and more educational expansion than those farther away. Given the fact

that reservations in California are located in the poorest regions, this location effect is progressive; that is, it helps poorer communities in favor of helping better-off communities.

Although the income and other effects of gaming in California are clearly substantial for Indians and their neighbors, Spilde Contreras points to the large gaps that still exist between conditions on Indian reservations and those for most Americans.

FOOD FOR THOUGHT ▼
How does the recent development of Indian casinos connect with the theoretical perspective of structure versus agency? (Review the discussion of these perspectives in Chapter 1.)

Indian tribal gambling establishments in the United States have mushroomed in recent years. Throughout the United States, Indian casinos are so financially successful that they are perceived as an economic threat to many state lotteries. The Pequot Indians of Connecticut (see Map 5.2, page 115), a small tribe of around 200 people, now operate the most lucrative gaming establishment in the world, Foxwoods Resort and Casino, established in 1992. Through gaming, many Indian

tribal groups have become successful capitalists. An important question is what impact casinos will have on Indian tribal people, and anthropologists are involved in trying to answer this question (see Anthropology Works).

Theft *Theft* is taking something with no expectation or thought of returning anything to the original owner for it. It is the logical opposite of a pure gift. Anthropologists have neglected the study of theft, no doubt a reasonable response because theft is an illegal activity that is difficult to study and might involve danger.

A rare study of theft focused on food stealing by children in West Africa (Bledsoe 1983). During fieldwork among the Mende people of Sierra Leone (see Map 6.5, page 149), Caroline Bledsoe learned that children in town stole fruits such as mangoes, guavas, and oranges from neighborhood trees. Bledsoe at first dismissed cases of food stealing as rare exceptions, but then she realized that she "rarely walked through town without hearing shouts of anger from an adult and cries of pain from a child being whipped for stealing food" (1983:2). Deciding to look into children's food stealing more closely, she asked several children to keep diaries. Their writings were dominated by themes of *tiefing*, the local term for stealing. Fostered children, who are temporarily placed in the care of friends or relatives, do more food tiefing than children living with their birth families do. Such food stealing can be seen as children's attempts to compensate for the inadequate food they receive in their foster homes.

Although much theft worldwide is motivated by skewed entitlements and need, much is also driven by greed. Cultural anthropologists, for obvious reasons, have not done research on high-level theft involving expensive commodities such as drugs, gems, and art, nor have they examined corporate financial malpractice as a form of theft. Given the ethical requirement of informed consent (review Chapter 3), it is unlikely that any anthropologist would be given permission to study such criminal activity.

Exploitation *Exploitation*, or getting something of greater value for less in return, is a form of extreme and persistent unbalanced exchange. Slavery is a form of exploitation in which people's labor power is appropriated without their consent and with no recompense for its value. As discussed in Chapter 2, slavery as a practice emerged with states.

Social relationships that involve sustained unequal exchange do exist between members of different social groups that, unlike pure slavery, involve no overt coercion and entail a certain degree of return by the dominant member to the subdominant member. Some degree of covert compulsion or dependence is likely to be present, however, in order for relationships of unequal exchange to endure.

Relationships between the Efe (eff-ay), who are "pygmy" foragers, and the Lese (less-ay), who are farmers, in the Ituri Forest region of the Democratic Republic of Congo exemplify sustained unequal exchange (Grinker 1994) (Map 5.5). The Lese live in small villages. The Efe are seminomadic and live in temporary camps near Lese villages. Men of each group maintain long-term, hereditary exchange partnerships with each other. The Lese give cultivated foods and iron to the Efe, and the Efe give meat, honey, and other forest goods to the Lese.

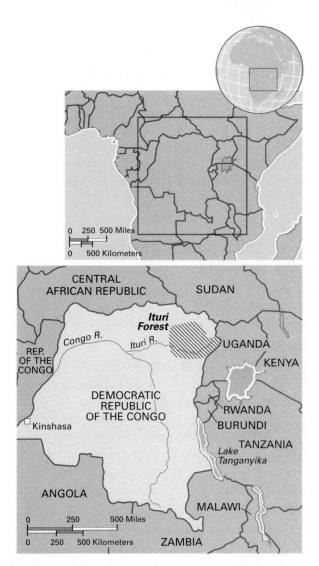

MAP 5.5   Lese and Efe Region in the Democratic Republic of Congo.

The Lese and Efe live in the Ituri Forest, a dense tropical rainforest in the northern part of the Congo River Basin. Cultural Survival supports the Ituri Forest Peoples Fund, which promotes the health and education of Efe foragers and Lese farmers. Go to the Internet to learn about the projects of the Ituri Forest Peoples Fund.

Each Efe partner is considered a member of the "house" of his Lese partner, although he lives separately. Their main link is the exchange of food items, a system conceptualized by the Lese not as trade but as sharing of co-produced goods by partners living in a single unit. Evidence of inequality exists, however, in these relationships, with the Lese having the advantage. The Efe provide much-wanted meat to the Lese, but this role gives them no status. Rather, it is the giving of cultivated foods by the Lese to the Efe that conveys status. Another area of inequality is marital and sexual relationships. Lese men may marry Efe women, and their children are considered Lese. Efe men, however, cannot marry Lese women.

Changing Patterns of Consumption and Exchange

Powerful market forces controlled by the core countries are the main factors affecting changing patterns of consumption and exchange. Local cultures, though, variously adopt and adapt globalizing products and their meanings. Sometimes they resist them outright.

Sugar, Salt, and Steel Tools in the Amazon

Katherine Milton, a biological anthropologist, has studied the nutritional effects of Western contact on the consumption patterns and health of indigenous foragers in the Brazilian Amazon. She comments:

> Despite the way their culture traditionally eschews possessions, forest-living people embrace manufactured goods with amazing enthusiasm. They seem to appreciate instantly the efficacy of a steel machete, ax, or cooking pot. It is love at first sight. . . . There are accounts of Indian groups or individuals who have turned their backs on manufactured goods, but such people are the exception. (1992:40)

The attraction to Western goods has its roots in the early decades of the twentieth century, when the Brazilian government sought to "pacify" Amazonian groups by placing cooking pots, machetes, axes, and steel knives along trails. This technique proved so successful that it is still used to "contact" remote groups. According to Milton:

> Once a group has been drawn into the pacification area, all its members are presented with various trade goods—standard gifts include metal cooking pots, salt, matches, machetes, knives, axes, cloth hammocks, T-shirts, and shorts. . . . Once the Indians have grown accustomed to these new items, the next step is to teach them that these gifts will not be repeated. The Indians are now told that they must work to earn money or must manufacture goods for trade so that they can purchase new items.
>
> Unable to contemplate returning to life without steel axes, the Indians begin to produce extra arrows or blowguns or hunt additional game or weave baskets beyond what they normally need so that this new surplus can be traded. Time that might, in the past, have been used for other tasks—subsistence activities, ceremonial events, or whatever—is now devoted to production of barter goods. (1992:40)

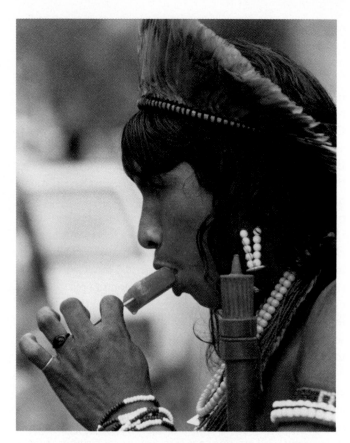

A member of the Kayapo tribe of Brazil eats a popsicle during a break in a meeting of indigenous peoples to protest a dam-building project. Tooth decay, diabetes, and obesity are rising among indigenous peoples worldwide as a result of changing consumption patterns.

Adoption of Western foods has negatively affected the nutrition and health of indigenous Amazonian peoples. They have begun to use table salt and refined sugar. Previously, they consumed small quantities of salt made by burning certain leaves and collecting the ash, and sugar came from wild fruits, in the form of fructose. Sucrose, in contrast, tastes exceptionally sweet, and the Indians get hooked on it. Tooth decay, obesity, and diabetes are new and growing health risks. Milton comments, "The moment manufactured foods begin to intrude on the indigenous diet, health takes a downward turn" (1992:41).

Social Inequality in Russia and Eastern Europe

As the countries of the former Soviet Union entered the global market economy, income inequality within those countries grew dramatically. The rich now own mansions and Mercedes-Benz cars. The influx of Western goods, including sugared soft drinks and junk food, was nicknamed *pepsistroika* by an anthropologist who did fieldwork in Moscow around the time of the transition to capitalism (Lempert 1996). Advertising messages encourage people to adopt new diets that include unhealthy amounts of rich food.

From 1961 to 1988, the consumption of calories, proteins, and fats in what are now Russia and Eastern Europe were above the level recommended by the World Health Organization and exceeded those of most middle-income countries worldwide (Cornia 1994). These countries had full employment and little income inequality, so the high consumption levels were widely shared. This is not to say that diets were perfect. Especially in urban areas and among lower-income groups, people's diets contained less good-quality meat, fruits, vegetables, and vegetable oils. People tended to overconsume cholesterol-heavy products such as eggs and animal fats, as well as sugar, salt, bread, and alcohol.

Income levels and consumption quality have fallen among the newly created poor. Now, there are two categories of poor people: the ultra-poor (those whose incomes are below the subsistence minimum, or between 25 and 35 percent of the average wage) and the poor (those whose incomes are above the subsistence minimum, but below the social minimum, or between 35 and 50 percent of the average wage). The largest increases in the number of ultra-poor occurred in Bulgaria, Poland, Romania, and Russia, where between 20 and 30 percent of the population are ultra-poor and another 20 to 40 percent are poor. Overall calorie and protein intake fell significantly. People in the ultra-poor category substitute less expensive sources of nutrients. They now consume more animal fats and starch, and less milk, animal proteins, vegetable oils, minerals, and vitamins. Rates of low-birthweight babies rose in Bulgaria and Romania, reflecting the deterioration in maternal diets, and the rate of childhood anemia rose dramatically in Russia.

Global Networks and Ecstasy in the United States

In the late 1990s, a sharp increase in the use of ecstasy occurred in the United States (Agar and Reisinger 2003). Ecstasy, or MDMA (an abbreviation for its chemical name), is an illicit drug that produces a high without, apparently, leading to clinical dependence. Fieldwork and interviews in Baltimore, Maryland, revealed that ecstasy use "took off" in the late 1990s as the "up and coming" drug of choice among youth. As one research participant commented, "A lot of people I know like rolling, taking a pill of ecstasy and going to, like, a club or going to a school dance. I mean, alcohol is up and coming among teenagers, like it's always been, but I think ecstasy's making a pretty powerful fight" (2003:2).

Official statistics confirmed this rise: In 1998, 10 percent of Baltimore County high school seniors reported that they had tried ecstasy; in 2001, the number had increased to nearly 20 percent. Nationwide statistics on reported use, arrests of distributors, and numbers of MDMA-related seizures reveal a similar pattern of increased use during this period. What accounts for this change? Two anthropologists conducted research to assess their hypothesis that there was a major change in the systems that produced and delivered the drug, leading to increased availability.

The standard story of the supply chain goes like this: Ecstasy is produced in the Netherlands and Belgium, distributed to the United States by Israelis, with a fuzzy role for Russian organized crime along the way. Two anthropologists studied websites and media reports in 2000 and discovered a much more complicated story. They found a network of multiple and shifting production sites all over the world, including the largest illicit drug lab ever reported in Canadian history. Distribution channels are also highly diffuse. Although the simpler story may have been true in 1998, it was no longer true two years later. Perhaps as demand rose in the United States and elsewhere, this rise prompted the development of a wider network of production and distribution.

Alternative Food Movements in Europe and North America

Starting in Europe in the 1980s, several alternative food movements have grown in Europe and North America (Pratt 2007). *Alternative food movements* seek to reestablish direct links between food producers, consumers, and marketers by promoting consumption of locally grown food and food that is not mass produced. Such movements exist in direct opposition to the agro-industrial food system, which:

- leads to economic ruin of small-scale producers who promote biodiversity.
- shifts diet to fast foods, convenience food, take-away food, and microwave preparation.
- transforms meals into eating on the run.
- promotes a depersonalized, global market and supply chain, with Walmart as the prime example.
- has little regard for the environmental consequences of mass production and global marketing.

Many alternative food movements exist. One of the first, Italy's Slow Food Movement, started in the late 1980s and has spread around the world. Naming itself in opposition to Western "fast food," the Slow Food Movement celebrates local agricultural traditions, seeks to protect consumers in terms of food quality, and advocates for social cooking, dining, and conviviality.

CULTURAMA

The Kwakwaka'wakw of Canada

Several Northern First Nations recently adopted the name *Kwakwaka'wakw* to refer to a cluster of 20 linguistically related groups of Canada's Pacific Northwest region (Macnair 1995). Kwakwaka'wakw means "the people who speak Kwak'wala." It replaces the earlier term "Kwakiutl," which refers to only one of the several groups, and is therefore insulting to members of the other groups.

Their territory includes many islands as well as the waterways and deep inlets penetrating the Coast Mountains, a region of dense forests and sandy beaches. In earlier times, travel was mainly by canoe. Families moved seasonally with all their belongings packed in the canoe (Macnair 1995).

The Kwakwaka'wakw are famous for aspects of their material culture, including tall, carved wooden totem poles, canoes, masks, and serving bowls, as well as richly decorated capes, skirts, and blankets.

Cedar is vital to the Kwakwaka'wakw. They use its wood for the objects just mentioned and the inner bark for garments. Women pounded the bark strips with a whalebone beater until the fibers separated and became soft. They wove the strips on a loom or handwove them into mats used for sleeping on.

The first contact with Whites occurred in 1792, when explorer Captain George Vancouver arrived (Macnair 1995). At that time, the Kwakwaka'wakw numbered around 8000 people. Franz Boas arrived in 1886 and carried out research with the help of George Hunt, born of an English father and a high-ranking Tlingit (Northwest Coast) mother.

In the late nineteenth century, colonial authorities and missionaries disapproved of matters such as marriage arrangements and the potlatch, and enacted legislation to promote change, including a ban on potlatching from 1884 to 1951. The people continued, however, to potlatch in secret.

The Royal British Columbia Museum (RBCM) in Victoria, British Columbia, Canada, worked closely with Kwakwaka'wakw communities to document their potlatches and promote cultural revitalization (Kramer, personal communication 2006). The first legal potlatch of recent times, hosted by Mungo Martin in 1953, was held outside the RBCM.

Thanks to Jennifer Kramer, University of British Columbia, for reviewing this material.

(LEFT) Canoes and their crews from other Kwakwaka'wakw villages gather at Alert Bay in 1999 to help celebrate the opening of the newly built Big House.

(CENTER) Kwakwaka'wakw students practice the hamat'sa dance at a school in Alert Bay, under the tutelage of K'odi Nelson.

MAP 5.6   The Kwakwaka'wakw Region in Canada. The total number of Kwakwaka'wakw is more than 5000 people.

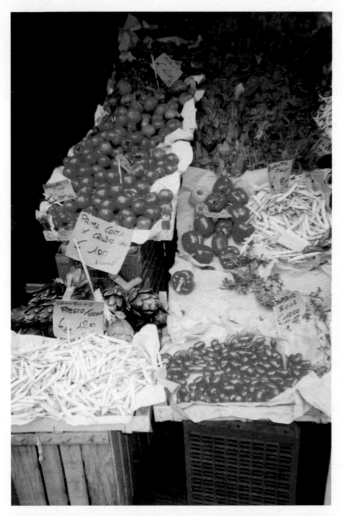

The weekly market in Pistoia, a small town near Firenze (Florence), Italy, is set up each Saturday next to the main church. According to government regulations, all food items are supposed to have labels that identify where they were grown.

Continuities and Resistance: The Enduring Potlatch

Potlatching among native peoples of the northwest coast of the United States and Canada was subjected to decades of opposition from Europeans and Euro-Americans (Cole 1991). The missionaries opposed potlatching as an unChristian practice. The government thought it was wasteful and excessive, out of line with their goals for the "economic progress" of the Indians. In 1885, the Canadian government outlawed the potlatch. Of all the Northwest Coast tribes, the Kwakwaka'wakw (see Culturama) resisted this prohibition most strongly and for the longest time. In Canada, potlatches are no longer illegal. But it took a long battle to remove restrictions.

Reasons for giving a potlatch today are similar to those in the past: naming children, mourning the dead, transferring rights and privileges, celebrating marriages, and raising totem poles (Webster 1991). The length of time devoted to planning a potlatch, however, has changed. In the past, several years were involved compared to about a year now. Still, it takes much organization and work to accumulate enough goods to ensure that no guest goes away empty-handed, and the guest list may include between 500 and 1000 people. Another change is in the kinds of goods exchanged. Typical potlatch goods now include crocheted items (such as cushion covers, blankets, and potholders), glassware, plastic goods, manufactured blankets, pillows, towels, articles of clothing, and sacks of flour and sugar. The potlatch endures but changes.

What is consumption in cross-cultural perspective?

Consumption includes a person's "intake" in terms of eating or other ways of using things and "output" in terms of spending or using resources to obtain those items. Anthropologists delineate two major modes of consumption. The first is minimalism, which is characterized by finite needs, the means of satisfying them, and sustainability. The second is consumerism, the mode of consumption with infinite needs, the inability to satisfy all needs, and lack of sustainability. Foraging societies typify the minimalist mode of consumption. The consumerist mode of consumption is most clearly associated with industrialism/informatics.

In nonmarket economies, most consumers either produce the goods they use themselves or know who produced them. This is called personalized consumption. In market economies, consumption is largely depersonalized through globalized mass production.

Anthropologists define five consumption funds, the proportions of which vary in different economic systems. Microcultures such as "race"/ethnicity, class, and gender are linked to specific consumption patterns which may affect human welfare.

A long-standing area of interest in cultural anthropology is cross-cultural patterns of food taboos and why such taboos exist. Cultural materialists provide interpretations that consider the ecological and environmental contexts of such food taboos and how taboos make sense to people's material lives. Symbolic/interpretive anthropologists interpret food taboos as systems of meaning and identity.

What is exchange in cross-cultural perspective?

Exchange refers to the transfer of goods, both material and intangible, or services between people, groups, or institutions. Cross-culturally, people and groups exchange a wide variety of goods and services. Nonmarket exchange long existed without the use of money. Modern money is now found throughout most of the world.

Anthropologists define two modes of exchange. In balanced exchange, items of roughly equal value are exchanged over time between people who have a social relationship. In unbalanced exchange, the value of items transferred is unequal and there may or may not be a social relationship between the seller and buyer.

Market exchange, the main form of unbalanced exchange, is a transaction in which the seller's goal of making a profit overrides social relationships. Markets exist in many forms. Some are impermanent and irregular; some are impermanent and regular, as in a weekly farmer's market; and others are permanent. Recent technological developments have led to the creation of virtual marketplaces.

How are consumption and exchange changing?

Globalizing capitalism is leading to many changes in consumption and exchange around the world. Globalization appears to provide benefits to securely entitled people in core countries. In other areas, it affects production, consumption and exchange in complex ways.

Many indigenous people are attracted by Western goods, such as steel axes and processed food. The nutritional and health status of many such groups has declined with the adoption of Western-style foods, especially large amounts of sugar and salt in food.

Other examples of change include the decline in consumption of nutritious food and increase in alcohol consumption in countries of the former Soviet Union, the rising popularity of the drug ecstasy among youth in the United States, and the rise of new food movements promoting small farm food production and local food consumption.

In spite of the powerful effects of globalization, some local cultures are reclaiming rights to their traditional forms of production, consumption, and exchange. The revitalization of the potlatch in the Pacific Northwest is an example.

KEY CONCEPTS

SUGGESTED READINGS

Theodore C. Bestor. *Tsukiji: The Fish Market at the Center of the World.* Berkeley: University of California Press, 2004. This ethnography of Tsukiji, the huge fish market in Tokyo, describes how it is a workplace for thousands of people, a central node in the Japanese fishing industry, and part of the global economy.

Denise Brennan. *What's Love Got to Do with It? Transnational Desires and Sex Tourism in the Dominican Republic.* Durham, NC: Duke University Press, 2004. This is an account of global sex tourism in the town of Sosúa, Dominican Republic, where Afro-Dominican and Afro-Haitian women sell sex to foreign, White tourists.

Michael F. Brown. *Who Owns Native Culture?* Cambridge, MA: Harvard University Press, 2003. This book documents the efforts of indigenous peoples to redefine heritage as a resource over which they claim proprietorship. It considers specific cases and proposes strategies for defending the rights of indigenous people within a market system.

Elizabeth Chin. *Purchasing Power: Black Kids and American Consumer Culture.* Minneapolis: University of Minnesota Press, 2001. The author did research with a fifth-grade class in a low-income, African American neighborhood in New Haven, Connecticut. These 10-year-olds, motivated by a strong sense of family responsibility, spend their money mainly on practical items and gifts for family members rather than status symbols.

Dwight B. Heath. *Drinking Occasions: Comparative Perspectives on Alcohol and Culture.* New York: Taylor & Francis, 2000. This book provides an ethnological review of alcohol consumption and looks at questions such as when people drink alcohol, where people drink, who drinks and who does not, what people drink, and why people drink.

Ann Kingsolver. *NAFTA Stories: Fears and Hopes in Mexico and the United States.* Boulder, CO: Lynne Reiner Publishers, 2001. The author collected and followed stories about NAFTA (North American Free Trade Agreement) during the early 1990s as told by everyday people in Mexico City and two cities in Morelos, Mexico.

Catherine Lutz and Anne Lutz Fernandez. *Carjacked: The Culture of the Automobile and Its Effects on Our Lives.* New York: Palgrave Macmillan, 2010. This book inquires into the importance of cars in the lives of Americans, especially those living in the suburbs, and the contradiction that cars make us free. They argue for a rebalanced transportation system.

Bill Maurer. *Mutual Life, Limited: Islamic Banking, Alternative Currencies, Lateral Reason.* Princeton, NJ: Princeton University Press, 2005. This comparison of Islamic bankers who seek to avoid interest with local currency proponents who seek to provide an alternative to capitalist financial mechanisms shows how both resist and sometimes replicate Western capitalism.

Lisa Rofel. *Desiring China: Experiments in Neoliberalism, Sexuality, and Public Culture.* Durham, NC: Duke University Press, 2007. Fieldwork in Beijing and Hangzhou informs this study of new material and sexual desires in contemporary China.

For further information about topics covered in this chapter, go to MyAnthroLab at **www.myanthrolab.com** and access the following readings in MyAnthroLibrary:

Rebecca Cassidy. 2009. "Casino Capitalism" and the Financial Crisis. *Anthropology Today* 25(4):10–13. The author critiques the concept of "casino capitalism," finding it of no help in understanding the financial crisis that began in 2008. She did research with casino gamblers in London.

Ana Eliza Port Laurenco et al. 2008. Nutrition Transition in Amazonia: Obesity and Socioeconomic Change in the Suruí Indians form Brazil. *American Journal of Human Biology* 20(50):564–571. The authors document dietary changes among an Amazonian group and show how they relate to the emergence of obesity in the population.

Tristam Riley-Smith, The Temple of Trade: On Consumerism, 2010. Chapter 2 in *The Cracked Bell: America and the Afflictions of Liberty.* New York: Skyhorse Publishing. Pp. 45–76. Riley-Smith is a British anthropologist who spent several years in the United States while working for the British Embassy. In this chapter he offers a cultural view of American consumerism.

◉ How are modes of reproduction related to modes of livelihood?

◉ How does culture shape fertility in different contexts?

◉ How does culture shape personality over the life cycle?

REPRODUCTION AND HUMAN DEVELOPMENT

◀ In Havana, Cuba, a girl celebrates her fifteenth birthday known as a *fiesta de quince*. In Hispanic culture globally, a girl's fifteenth birthday is a coming-of-age ceremony marked by lavish expenditures on an elegant gown and a party including a fancy cake.

OUTLINE

Modes of Reproduction
  Culturama: The Old Order Amish of the United States and Canada
Culture and Fertility
  Anthropology Works: Studying Sexual Behavior among MSM in New York City
Personality and the Life Cycle
  Critical Thinking: Cultural Relativism and Female Genital Cutting

This chapter covers cross-cultural patterns of sexuality and having children and the formation of personality and identity over the life cycle. The first section provides an overview of reproduction in relation to modes of livelihood. The second section traces the connections between culture and **fertility**, or the rate of births. The third section provides insights into how culture shapes personality and identity throughout the life cycle.

◉ ◉ ◉

Modes of Reproduction

A **mode of reproduction** is the dominant pattern, in a culture, of population change through the combined effect of fertility (birth rate) and mortality (death rate). Cultural anthropologists have enough cross-cultural data to provide the general characteristics of only three modes of reproduction (Figure 6.1) that correspond to three of the five modes of livelihood discussed in Chapter 4.

The Foraging Mode of Reproduction

Evidence about the foraging mode of reproduction comes from a classic study based on fieldwork conducted with the Ju/'hoansi in the 1970s (Howell 1979) (review Culturama in Chapter 1, page 21). The study shows that *birth intervals* (the

time between a birth and the next birth) among the Ju/'hoansi are often several years in duration. What accounts for these long birth intervals? Two factors are most important: breastfeeding and women's low level of body fat. Frequent and long periods of breastfeeding inhibit progesterone production and suppress ovulation. Also, a certain level of body fat is required for ovulation. Ju/'hoansi women's diets contain little fat, and their regular physical exercise as foragers keeps their body fat level low, further suppressing ovulation. Thus, diet and work are key factors underlying Ju/'hoansi population dynamics.

Ju/'hoansi women, during the time of the study, typically had between two and three live births, of which two children survived into adulthood. This mode of reproduction is adaptive to the Ju/'hoansi environment and sustainable over time. Among the Ju/'hoansi who have become farmers or laborers, the number of births per woman are higher. This change is related to the facts that their diet contains more grains and dairy products and women are less physically active.

The Agricultural Mode of Reproduction

The agriculture mode of reproduction is associated with the highest birth rates of the three modes discussed here. **Pronatalism**, an attitude or policy that encourages childbearing,

Foraging	Agriculture	Industrialism/Informatics
Population Growth	**Population Growth**	**Population Growth**
Moderate birth rates	High birth rates	Industrialized nations—negative
Moderate death rates	Declining death rates	population growth
		Developing nations—high
Value of Children	**Value of Children**	**Value of Children**
Moderate	High	Mixed
Fertility Control	**Fertility Control**	**Fertility Control**
Indirect means	Increased reliance on direct means	Direct methods grounded in science
Low-fat diet of women	Induced abortion	and medicine
Women's work and exercise	Infanticide	Chemical forms of contraception
Prolonged breastfeeding	Pronatalist techniques	In vitro fertilization
Spontaneous abortion	Herbs	Abortion
Direct means		
Induced abortion		
Infanticide		
Social Aspects	**Social Aspects**	**Social Aspects**
Homogeneous fertility	Emerging class differences	Stratified fertility
Few specialists	Increasing specialization	Globally, nationally, and locally
	Midwifery	Highly developed specialization
	Herbalists	

FIGURE 6.1 Modes of Livelihood and Reproduction.

is prevalent among farm families cross-culturally. It is prompted by the need for a large labor force to work the land, care for animals, process food, and do marketing. In this context, having many children is a rational reproductive strategy related to the mode of livelihood. Thus, farming people who live in family farming systems have their own "family planning," but one that promotes rather than prevents the birth of many children.

High birth rates of seven or more children per woman exist in several low-income agricultural countries of Africa, such as Niger (7.4 births per woman), Somalia, (6.7 births per woman), Uganda (6.7 births per woman), and Angola (6.5 births per woman) (Population Reference Bureau 2009). Cross-country variation in birth rates in farming populations does exist, however, partly because of recent declines due to reduced demands for family labor. Lower rates, of two or three children per woman, are found in many agricultural countries in South America, such as Venezuela, Chile, and Argentina.

Within countries, the cultural groups with the highest birth rates in the world are the Mennonites and Hutterites. They are Christians of European descent living mainly in the United States and Canada. Women in these groups typically have between 8 and 10 children who survive into adulthood. High birth rates also characterize the Amish, a closely related group (see Culturama on page 136).

In another pronatalist context, rural North India, having many children—especially sons—is important in farming families. Young boys learn to do farm work with their father. As adults, they are responsible for plowing the farm and for protecting the family land from take-overs by neighboring farmers. When Western family planning experts visited villages in North India in the late 1950s to promote the idea of small families, the farmers expressed dismay (Mamdani 1972). To them, a large family, especially one with many sons, is a sign of wealth and success, not poverty and failure.

The Industrial/Informatic Mode of Reproduction

In industrial societies, either capitalist or socialist, reproduction declines to the point of either *replacement-level fertility*, in which the number of births equals the number of deaths, leading to maintenance of the current population size, or *below-replacement-level fertility*, in which the number of births is less than the number of deaths, leading to population decline. Children in these contexts are less useful in production because of the reduced labor demands of industrialism. Furthermore, children in most industrialized countries must attend school and therefore cannot work for their families much during the school year. Parents respond by having fewer children and by investing more resources in them.

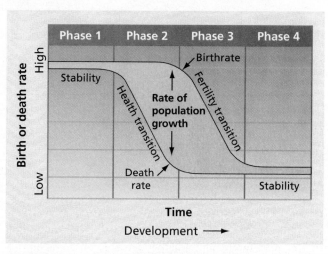

FIGURE 6.2 Model of the Demographic Transition.

Source: Nebel, Bernard J.; Wright, Richard T, *Environmental Science: The Way The World Works*, 7th edition. Copyright © 2000. Electronically reproduced by permission of Pearson Education, Inc. Upper Saddle River, New Jersey.

Population changes that take place during the transition to the industrial/informatic mode of reproduction correspond to what is called the **demographic transition**, a process during which the agricultural pattern of high fertility and high mortality becomes the industrial pattern of low fertility and low mortality. There are two phases in the demographic transition model (Figure 6.2). In the first phase, mortality declines because of improved nutrition and health, so population growth rates increase. The second phase occurs when fertility also declines. At this point, low rates of population growth occur to the extent that many industrial/informatic countries have below-replacement fertility including Japan, Canada, the United States, and countries in Europe.

While such low rates of population growth are welcomed by many thinkers as reducing the burden on the environment, leaders of some countries worry about labor shortages and a declining tax base. A new study may provide hope for the latter because it shows that in some of the most highly developed countries, the fertility rate began to rise to replacement levels starting around 2005 (Myrskylä, Kohler, and Billari 2009). These countries include the United States, several European countries, Israel, and New Zealand. But several highly developed countries did not follow the trend, including Canada, Japan, South Korea, and Australia. In

fertility the rate of births in a population or the rate of population increase in general.

mode of reproduction the predominant pattern, in a culture, of population change through the combined effect of fertility (birth rate) and mortality (death rate).

pronatalism an attitude or policy that encourages childbearing.

demographic transition the change from the agricultural pattern of high fertility and high mortality to the industrial pattern of low fertility and low mortality.

The Old Order Amish of the United States and Canada

The Amish are Christians who live in rural areas of the United States and Canada. At the time of this writing, in the early twenty-first century, their total population is about 200,000. Their ancestry traces to German-speaking Swiss Anabaptists in the sixteenth century. To escape religious persecution, they migrated to North America, starting in the early eighteenth century and continuing into the mid-nineteenth century. There are no Amish in Europe today.

The term *Old Order Amish* refers to the main body of the Amish people. A small minority, known as *New Order Amish*, broke off from the Old Order in the late 1960s. Both groups use horse-drawn transportation, but the New Order Amish accept more technology.

The Amish speak a German-derived dialect. They wear modest clothing and dress similarly to each other. They avoid using electricity from power grids, but solar-generated electricity and 12-volt batteries are allowed. Education beyond the eighth grade is seen as unnecessary. A basic theme in Amish life is the need to guard against "worldly" (non-Amish, mainstream U.S.) values, dependencies, and hurriedness, and to maintain the family as a unit that lives and works together. Working with one's own hands is valued, as are humility and modesty. Farming is the traditional means of livelihood among the Amish.

The Amish have many children, typically six or seven per woman. Even though some children leave and join "the English" (non-Amish), their population is doubling every 20 years. In Lancaster County, Pennsylvania, the heartland of the Old Order Amish, a steep rise in population growth starting in the 1970s has exceeded the availability of farmland (Kraybill and Nolt 2004). Now, several hundred Amish businesses exist. Many are small scale and operate from the home, but many others are large scale and earn millions of dollars per year. Amish who enter business try to retain Amish values of family solidarity by working at home and selling products from their homes. Many, though, increasingly work in businesses outside their homes, together with the English.

Amish youth have the opportunity of deciding whether to be baptized into the faith when they are 16 years old. At this time, called *rumspringa* in Pennsylvania Dutch, or "running around," the young people are allowed to explore the customs of the English world, including television. Most stay at home during rumspringa, spending time with Amish friends on the weekends. In rare cases, some experiment with alcohol, drugs, and sex (Shachtman 2006). Around 90 percent of Amish teenagers decide to accept Amish ways and be baptized, choosing a lifestyle that emphasizes humility and community solidarity rather than the "worldly" lifestyle of individualism and competition.

Thanks to Donald B. Kraybill, Elizabethtown College, for reviewing this material.

MAP 6.1 **Old Order Amish Population of North America.** The states of Ohio, Pennsylvania, and Indiana have the largest number of Old Order Amish.

(LEFT) Members of an Amish household sit around their kitchen table.

(CENTER) A farmer mows alfalfa with a team of mules and a gasoline engine to power the mower. This mechanism enhances his farm work but does not break the Old Order Amish rule against using tractors in the field.

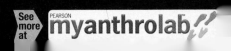

order to explain the pattern and the cases that do not fit the pattern, local-level research is required to get beneath aggregated country-level statistics and to examine more closely the assumption that hyper-development allows for more women to have babies.

The industrial/informatic mode of reproduction has three distinguishing features. First, social inequality is reflected in population patterns, referred to as *stratified reproduction*. Typically, middle-class and upper-class people tend to have few children, but these children have high survival rates. Among the poor, however, both fertility and mortality rates are high. Brazil, a newly industrializing state, has the world's most extreme income inequality. Parallel to its economic inequality is extremely stratified reproduction.

A second characteristic of industrial/informatic contexts is population aging, when the proportion of older people increases relative to younger people. In Japan, the national fertility rate declined to replacement level in the 1950s and later reached the below-replacement level (Hodge and Ogawa 1991). Japan is currently experiencing a decline in population growth of about 15 percent per generation and, simultaneously, rapid aging of the population. As many people enter the senior category, they create a population bulge that is not balanced by the number of younger people (Figure 6.3). A population projection for the year 2050 suggests that the bulge will increase.

A third distinguishing feature of industrial/informatic demographics is the high level of involvement of scientific (especially medical) technology in all aspects of pregnancy: becoming pregnant, preventing pregnancy, and terminating pregnancy (Browner and Press 1996). This trend is accompanied by increasing levels of specialization in providing the new services.

Culture and Fertility

Culture shapes human fertility from its very start, if conception is considered to be the fertilization of an ovum. The following discussion begins with sexual intercourse, the normal way that fertilization occurs, and continues through pregnancy and birth with attention to how culture shapes these biological processes.

Sexual Intercourse

Sexual intercourse usually involves private, sometimes secret, beliefs and behaviors. Anthropological research on sexual practices is thus particularly challenging. The ethics of participant observation prohibit intimate observation or participation, so data can be obtained only indirectly. Biases in people's verbal reports about sexual beliefs and behavior are likely for several reasons. People may be too shy or otherwise unwilling to discuss sex or, conversely, boastful and inflating the truth. Many people may simply be unable to answers questions such as "How many times did you have sexual intercourse last year?" If people do provide detailed information, it might be inappropriate for an anthropologist to publish it because of the need to protect confidentiality.

Bronislaw Malinowski wrote the first anthropological study of sexuality (1929), based on his fieldwork in the Trobriand Islands (review Culturama in Chapter 3, page 59). His writings describe the sexual lives of children, sexual techniques, love magic, erotic dreams, husband–wife jealousy, and other topics. Since the late 1980s, it has become increasingly important to study how culture affects sexuality because of the spread of sexually transmitted diseases (STDs), including HIV/AIDS. Without understanding variations in sexual values and practices, it is impossible to design effective programs for preventing and controlling STDs (see Anthropology Works on page 138).

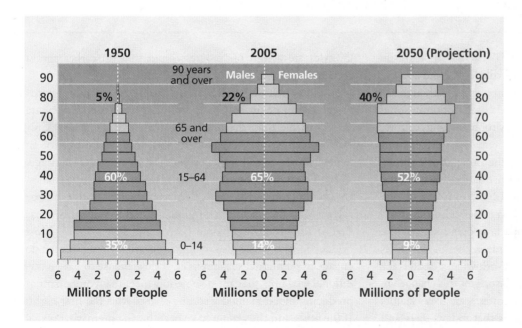

FIGURE 6.3 Changes in the Population Pyramid of Japan.

Source: Statistics Bureau, MIC, Ministry of Health, Labor and Welfare. Reproduced with permission.

ANTHROPOLOGY works

Studying Sexual Behavior among MSM in New York City

Lara Tabac, medical anthropologist, works at the New York City Department of Health and Mental Hygiene (DOHMH), along with another cultural anthropologist and 6000 other employees (2003). Her unit is the DOHMH's Epidemiology Services. *Epidemiology* is the study of the factors that cause health and disease in different populations, and it provides information to public health-care providers so they can improve their programs.

Tabac is hired to collect qualitative information from New Yorkers about their behavior and how it relates to their health, specifically MSM (men who have sex with men).

Tabac describes her job as an "unusual joint venture of words and numbers (2003)." She explains that the department is highly quantitative. It uses statistics to determine health-action agendas. The numbers "tell how many, but they do not tell why. In order to be responsive to the health needs of New Yorkers, the DOHMH needs to know why. This is where I come in."

Anthropological training reinforced and shaped Tabac's natural tendency to observe and ask questions. She puts her skills and interests to work: "I do a lot of listening on a wide range of topics, and I need only a MetroCard to reach far-flung and eclectic neighborhoods

Two gay men in New York City.

peopled with individuals who share their health dilemmas and life struggles with me, as well as their suggestions for improving the services and programs that will ultimately affect them (2003)."

Tabac wants to learn about condom use among the MSM population: who uses or does not use condoms, and why they do or do not do so. To gather qualitative information, Tabac has spent many hours conducting interviews. She says, "As a technique, interviewing is crucial for gaining a deep understanding of sensitive issues. . . . People tend to be more honest when they don't feel as

though they are going to be judged by their peers" (2003). Tabac comments that every interview for the project has been valuable.

Tabac finds her job with the DOHMH challenging and socially relevant. She took the job because she wanted to help improve people's lives. She has not been disappointed.

FOOD FOR THOUGHT ▼
Are you inspired by this story to want to follow in Lara Tabac's footsteps? If yes, why? If not, why not?

WHEN TO BEGIN HAVING INTERCOURSE? Biologically speaking, sexual intercourse between a fertile female and a fertile male is normally required for human reproduction, although artificial insemination is becoming a widely used option in some contexts. Biology, interacting with environment and culture, defines the time span within which a female is fertile: from **menarche** (pronounced men-ar-kee), the onset of menstruation, to **menopause**, the cessation of menstruation. Globally, the beginning of menarche varies from 12 to 14 years of age (Thomas et al. 2001). Generally, girls in richer countries reach menarche a few years earlier than girls in poorer countries do. For example, the estimated age at menarche in Japan is 12.5 years, but in Haiti it is 15.5 years. Worldwide, a trend is for the age at menarche to be earlier. The reasons for this change are not completely clear. Diet and activity patterns are likely factors involved. The underlying assumption is that today's diets and

lifestyles are a sign of "progress," and thus an earlier age at menarche is an indicator of societal well-being.

Cultures, however, socialize children regarding the appropriate age to begin sexual intercourse, and cultural rules are more variable than the biological marker of menarche. Cultural guidelines vary by gender, class, race, and ethnicity. In many cultures, sexual activity should begin only with marriage. This rule often applies more strictly to females than to males. In Zawiya (zuh-WEE-yuh), a Muslim town of northern Morocco (Map 6.2), a bride's virginity is highly valued, whereas that of the groom is ignored (Davis and Davis 1987). Most brides conform to the ideal. Some unmarried young women do engage in premarital sex, however. If they choose to have a traditional wedding, they must somehow meet the requirement of producing blood-stained wedding sheets after the first night. If the bride and the groom have been having premarital sexual

A bride wearing traditional wedding clothing in the city of Meknès, Morocco.

relations, the groom may assist in the deception by nicking a finger with a knife and bloodying the sheets himself. Another option is to buy fake blood sold in drugstores.

INTERCOURSE FREQUENCY AND FERTILITY Cross-culturally, the frequency of sexual intercourse varies widely. The relationship between frequency of sexual intercourse and fertility, though, is not simple. A common assumption is that people in cultures with high fertility rates have sexual intercourse frequently. Without modern birth control, such as condoms, birth control pills, and intrauterine devices (IUDs), intercourse frequency would seem, logically, to produce high rates of fertility.

A classic study of reported intercourse frequency among Euro-Americans in the United States and Hindus in India, however, throws this assumption into question (Nag 1972). The Indians had intercourse less frequently (less than twice a week) than the Euro-Americans did (two to three times a week) in all age groups. Several features of Indian culture limit the frequency of sexual intercourse. First, the Hindu religion teaches the value of sexual abstinence, thus providing ideological support for limiting sexual intercourse. Hinduism also suggests that one should abstain from intercourse on many sacred days: the first night of the new moon, the first night of the full moon, the eighth day of each half of the month (the light half and the dark half), and sometimes on Fridays. As many as 100 days each year could be observed as days of abstinence. Another factor is Hindu men's belief in what anthropologists term the *lost semen complex*, which links men's health and strength to the retention of semen. An anthropologist learned about this complex during his fieldwork in North India:

> Everyone knew that semen was not easily formed; it takes forty days and forty drops of blood to make one drop of semen. . . . Semen of good quality is rich and viscous, like the cream of unadulterated milk. . . . Celibacy was the first requirement of true fitness, because every sexual orgasm meant the loss of a quantity of semen, laboriously formed. (Carstairs 1967:83–86, quoted in Nag 1972:235)

MAP 6.2 Morocco.
The Kingdom of Morocco is the westernmost country of the Arab world. A border dispute continues with the Western Sahara, which Morocco has administered since 1975. Morocco's population is 30 million. The terrain ranges from coastal lowlands to rugged interior mountains. Morocco's economy is based on mining phosphates, remittances, and tourism. It is one of the world's largest producers and exporters of cannabis and the world's largest per capita consumer of sugar. Most Moroccans are Sunni Muslims. The official language is classical Arabic, but Moroccan Arabic is widely spoken. More than 40 percent of the people speak a variety of Berber.

The fact remains, however, that fertility is higher in India than in many other parts of the world where such religiously based restrictions on sexual intercourse do not exist. Obviously, sheer frequency of intercourse is not the explanation because it takes only one act of sexual intercourse at the right time of the month to create a pregnancy. The point of this discussion is to show that *reverse reasoning* (assuming

---

menarche the onset of menstruation.

menopause the cessation of menstruation.

that high fertility means people have nothing better to do than have sex) is wrong. The cultural dynamics of sexuality in India function to restrain sexual activities and thus keep fertility lower than it otherwise would be.

Fertility Decision Making

Within the context of the family unit, decision makers weigh factors influencing why and when to have a child. At the state level, governments plan their overall population target on the basis of fertility goals that are sometimes pronatalist and sometimes *antinatalist* (opposed to many births). At the global level, powerful economic and political interests influence the reproductive policies of countries and, in turn, of families and individuals.

AT THE FAMILY LEVEL Within the family, parents and other family members consider, consciously or unconsciously, the value and costs of children (Nag 1983). Cross-cultural research indicates that four factors are most important in affecting the desire for children:

- Children's labor value
- Children's value as old-age support for parents
- Infant and child mortality rates
- Economic costs of children

The first three factors have a positive effect on fertility: When children's value is high in terms of labor or old-age support, fertility is likely to be higher; when infant and child mortality rates are high, fertility rates tend to be high in order to "replace" offspring who do die. In the case of child costs—including direct costs (for food, education, and clothing, for example) and indirect costs (employment opportunities that the mother gives up)—the relationship is negative. Higher costs reduce the desire for children. In industrial/informatic contexts, child costs are high and child labor value declines dramatically. Mandatory school attendance also pulls children out of the workforce and may involve direct costs for fees, uniforms, and supplies. States that provide old-age security and pension plans also reduce the need for children.

Husbands and wives may not always have the same preferences about the number of children they desire. In a highland village in the Oaxaca region of Mexico (Map 6.3), men want more children than women do (Browner 1986). Of women with only one child, 80 percent were content with a family of that size. Most men (60 percent) who were satisfied with their present family size had four or more children. One woman said, "My husband sleeps peacefully through the night, but I have to get up when the children need something. I'm the one the baby urinates on; sometimes I have to get out of bed in the cold and change both our clothes" (1986:714).

Depending on the gender division of labor and on other social features, families may prefer sons, daughters, or a balance of each. Preference for sons is widespread, especially in South Asia (including India and Pakistan) and East Asia (China and Korea), but it is not universal. Throughout much of Southeast Asia, for example, people prefer a balanced number of sons and daughters. A preference for daughters exists in some parts of Africa south of the Sahara and in some Caribbean populations.

MAP 6.3 Mexico.
The United Mexican States is the most populous Spanish-speaking country in the world. It was subjected to Spanish rule for three centuries before gaining independence. Its population is 107 million, and the capital, Mexico City, has a population of 20 million people. Mexico has a mixed economy of industry, agriculture, and trade, and is the fourth-largest oil producer in the world. Ethnically, the population consists of Mestizos (60 percent), Indians (30 percent), and Whites (9 percent). Southern states have the highest proportion of Indians.

A family planning clinic in Egypt. Throughout much of the world, Western-style family planning advice is controversial because it may conflict with local beliefs and values.

▶ *In your cultural experience, what is the prevailing attitude about family planning?*

AT THE STATE LEVEL State governments formulate policies that affect rates of population growth within their boundaries. These policies vary from being antinatalist to pronatalist, and they vary in terms of the methods of fertility management promoted. Factors that affect government policies include economic factors, such as projected jobs and employment levels, public services, and maintaining the tax base, as well as other factors, such as filling the ranks of the military, maintaining ethnic and regional proportions, and dealing with population aging.

AT THE GLOBAL LEVEL The most far-reaching layer that affects fertility decision making occurs at the international level, where global power structures such as pharmaceutical companies and religious leaders influence country- and individual-level decision making. In the 1950s, there was a wave of enthusiasm among Western nations for promoting family planning programs of many types in developing countries. In the 1990s, the United States adopted a more restrictive policy toward family planning, withdrew support for such options as abortion, and began to promote abstinence as the foundation of population control.

Fertility Control

People in all cultures since prehistory have had ways of influencing fertility, including ways to increase it, reduce it, and regulate birth spacing. Some ways are direct, such as using herbs or medicines that induce abortion. Others are indirect, such as long periods of breastfeeding, which reduce the chances of conception.

INDIGENOUS METHODS Hundreds of direct indigenous fertility control methods are available cross-culturally (Newman 1972, 1985).

Research in Afghanistan during the 1980s found over 500 fertility-regulating techniques in just one region (Hunte 1985). In Afghanistan, as in most nonindustrial cultures, it

is women who possess this information. Specialists, such as midwives or herbalists, provide further expertise. Of the total number of methods in the Afghanistan study, 72 percent were for increasing fertility, 22 percent were contraceptives, and 6 percent were used to induce abortion. Most methods involve plant and animal substances. Herbs are made into tea and taken orally. Some substances are formed into pills, some steamed and inhaled as vapors, some vaginally inserted, and others rubbed on the woman's stomach.

INDUCED ABORTION A review of 400 societies found that induced abortion was practiced in virtually all of them (Devereaux 1976). Cross-culturally, attitudes toward induced abortion range from absolute acceptability to conditional approval (abortion is acceptable but only under specified conditions), tolerance (abortion is regarded with neither approval nor disapproval), and opposition and punishment for offenders. Methods of inducing abortion include hitting the abdomen, starving oneself, taking drugs, jumping from high places, jumping up and down, lifting heavy objects, and doing hard work. Some methods clearly are dangerous to the pregnant woman. In Afghanistan, a midwife inserts an object such as a wooden spoon or stick treated with copper sulfate into the pregnant woman to cause vaginal bleeding and eventual abortion of the fetus (Hunte 1985).

The reasons women seek to induce abortion are usually related to economic and social factors (Devereaux 1976).

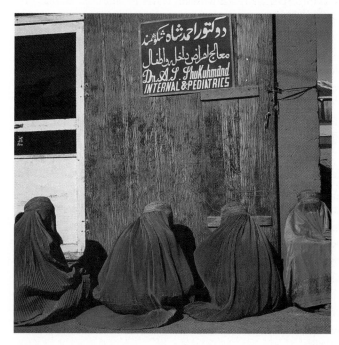

Women waiting their turn at a clinic in Afghanistan. The geographical terrain and distance make it difficult to get to a clinic in cases of emergency. Rates of maternal mortality in remote areas of Afghanistan are probably the highest in the world.

▶ *What is the maternal mortality rate in your home country and how does it vary by region, class, or ethnicity?*

Pastoralist women, for example, frequently carry heavy loads, sometimes for long distances. This lifestyle does not allow women to care for many small children at one time. Poverty is another frequent motivation. A woman who is faced with a pregnancy in the context of limited resources may find abortion preferable to bearing a child that cannot be fed. Culturally defined "legitimacy" of a pregnancy and social penalties for bearing an illegitimate child provide long-standing motivations for abortion, especially in Western societies.

Some governments regulate access to abortion, either promoting it or forbidding it. Since the late 1980s, China has pursued a rigorous campaign to limit population growth (Greenhalgh 2008). Its One-Child-per-Couple Policy, announced in 1978, restricted most families to having only one child. The policy involved strict surveillance of pregnancies, strong group disapproval directed toward women pregnant for the second time or more, and forced abortions and sterilizations. Inadvertently, this policy simultaneously led to an increase in the killing and abandoning of girl babies by parents who were driven by a preference for sons.

Religion and abortion are often related, but there is no simple relationship between what a particular religion teaches about abortion and what people actually do. Catholicism forbids abortion, but thousands of Catholic women have sought abortions throughout the world. Predominantly Catholic countries have laws making induced abortion illegal. This is the case in Brazil where, in spite of Catholic beliefs and the law, many women, especially poor women, resort to abortion. In one impoverished shantytown in the city of Recife in the northeast, one-third of the women said that they had aborted at least once (Gregg 2003:71–72). Illegal abortions are more likely to have detrimental effects on women's health than safe, legal abortion services. Several local studies conducted in the northeastern part of Brazil, the country's poorest region, report high percentages, up to one-fourth, of maternal deaths due to complications from illegal abortion (McCallum 2005:222).

Islamic teachings forbid abortion. Abortion of female fetuses is nonetheless practiced covertly in Pakistan and by Muslims in India. Hinduism teaches *ahimsa*, or nonviolence toward other living beings, including a fetus whose movements have been felt by the mother. Thousands of Hindus, however, seek abortions every year. In contrast, Buddhism provides no overt rulings against abortion. Japanese Buddhism teaches that all life is fluid and that an aborted fetus is simply "returned" to a watery world of unshaped life and may later come back (LaFleur 1992). This belief is compatible with people's frequent use of induced abortion as a form of birth control in Japan.

THE NEW REPRODUCTIVE TECHNOLOGIES
Since the early 1980s, new forms of *reproductive technology*, or methods that seek to bypass biology to offer options for childbearing to infertile couples, have emerged and are now available in many places around the world.

In Japan, people regularly visit and decorate *mizuko,* small statues in memory of their "returned" fetuses.

▶ *In your cultural world, what is the definition and status of a fetus? Does a fetus have rights? Should it?*

In vitro fertilization (*IVF*), in which eggs cells are fertilized outside the womb, is highly sought after by many couples in Western countries, especially middle- and upper-class couples, among whom infertility is inexplicably high. It is also available in many cities worldwide (Inhorn 2003). As IVF spreads globally, people interpret it within their own cultural frameworks. A study of male infertility in two Middle Eastern cities—Cairo in Egypt and Beirut in Lebanon—reveals the close connection between masculine identity and fertility (Inhorn 2004). While married couples want to have children, if the husband is infertile, IVF is not a clear option. In these cities, infertile men face social stigma and feelings of deep inadequacy. In addition, third-party donation of sperm is not acceptable according to Islam. These couples are trying to balance their desire for children with Muslim values.

Infanticide

Infanticide, or the deliberate killing of offspring, is widely practiced cross-culturally, although it is rarely a frequent or common practice. Infanticide takes two major forms: direct infanticide and indirect infanticide (Harris 1977). *Direct infanticide* is the death of an infant or child resulting from actions such as beating, smothering, poisoning, and drowning. *Indirect infanticide*, a more subtle process, may involve prolonged practices such as food deprivation, failure to take a sick infant to a clinic, and failure to provide warm clothing in winter.

The most frequent motive for direct infanticide reported cross-culturally is that the infant was "deformed" or very ill

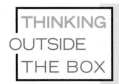

THINKING OUTSIDE THE BOX

In your microculture, is there a preference about the desired number of sons and daughters? Is there a preference for their birth order?

(Scrimshaw 1984:490–491). Other motives for infanticide include the infant's sex, an adulterous conception, an unwed mother, the birth of twins, and too many children in the family. A study of 148 cases of infanticide in contemporary Canada found that the mothers convicted of killing their offspring were relatively young and lacked financial and family resources to help them (Daly and Wilson 1984).

Among the poor of northeastern Brazil, indirect infanticide is also related to harsh conditions and poverty (Scheper-Hughes 1992). In a shantytown called Bom Jesus, in the state of Pernambuco, Brazil, life expectancy is low. Available data on infant and child mortality in Bom Jesus since the 1960s led anthropologist Nancy Scheper-Hughes to coin the painfully ironic phrase *the modernization of mortality*. The modernization of mortality in Brazil is class based, mirroring a deep division in entitlements between the rich and the poor. Economic growth in Brazil has brought rising standards of living for many. The

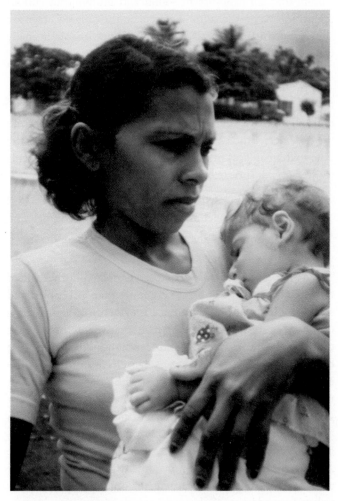

In Bom Jesus, a shantytown in northeastern Brazil, a doctor at the local clinic told this mother that her son was dying of anemia and that she needed to feed him red meat. The mother said, "Now, where am I going to find the money to feed my hopeless son rich food like that?"

▶ *What is your perspective on Western bonding theory, and how did you come to have this view?*

infant mortality rate (deaths of children under the age of 1 year per 1,000 births) declined dramatically in recent decades. This decline, however, is unevenly distributed. High infant death rates are concentrated among the poorest classes of society. Poverty forces mothers to selectively (and unconsciously) neglect babies that seem sickly or weak, sending them to heaven as "angel babies" rather than struggling to keep them alive. People's religious beliefs, a form of Catholicism, provide psychological support for indirect infanticide by allowing mothers to believe that their dead babies are safe in heaven. (This ethnographic case is discussed further in the next section.)

◉ ◉ ◉

Personality and the Life Cycle

Personality is an individual's patterned and characteristic way of behaving, thinking, and feeling. Cultural anthropologists think that personality is formed largely through *enculturation* (also called socialization), or the learning of culture through both informal and formal processes. They study how various cultures enculturate their members into having different personalities and identities. Cultural anthropologists also investigate how personalities vary according to cultural context, and some ask why such variations exist. Others study how changing cultural contexts affect personality, identity, and well-being over the life cycle.

Birth, Infancy, and Childhood

This section first considers the cultural context of birth itself. It then discusses cultural variations in infant care and how they may shape personality and identity. Last, it deals with the topic of gender identity formation in infancy.

THE BIRTH CONTEXT The cultural context of birth affects an infant's psychological development. Brigitte Jordan (1983), a pioneer in the cross-cultural study of birth, conducted comparative research on birth practices in Mexico, Sweden, the Netherlands, and the United States. She studied the birth setting, including its location and who is present, the types of attendants and their roles, the birth event, and the postpartum period. Among Maya women in Mexico, the midwife is called in during the early stages of labor. One of her tasks is to give a massage to the mother-to-be. She also provides psychological support by telling stories, often about other women's birthing experiences. The husband is expected to be present during the labor so that he can see "how a woman suffers." The woman's mother should be present, too,

---

infanticide   the killing of an infant or child.

personality   an individual's patterned and characteristic way of behaving, thinking, and feeling.

along with other female kin, such as her mother-in-law, godmother, sisters, and friends. Thus, a Maya mother is surrounded by a large group of supportive people.

In the United States, hospital births are the norm. The newborn infant is generally taken to the nursery, where it is wrapped in cloth and placed in a plastic crate under bright lights, rather than being cared for by a family member. Some critics argue that the hospital-based system of highly regulated birth is extremely technocratic and too managed, alienating the mother—as well as other members of the family and the wider community—from the birthing process and the infant (Davis-Floyd 1992). This critique has prompted a consideration of how to improve the way birth is conducted in the United States.

The Western medical model of birth contrasts sharply with non-Western practices. Sometimes they come into direct conflict. In such situations, anthropological expertise can mediate the conflict by providing what medical specialists now refer to as *cultural sensitivity*, or cultural awareness and respect.

BONDING Many contemporary Western psychological theorists say that parent–infant contact and bonding at the time of birth is crucial for setting in motion parental attachment to the infant. Western specialists say that if bonding is not established at the time of the infant's birth, it will not develop later. Explanations for juvenile delinquency or other unfavorable child development problems often include references to a lack of proper infant bonding at birth.

Nancy Scheper-Hughes (1992) questions Western bonding theory. She argues that bonding does not necessarily have to occur at birth to be successful. Her observations in Brazil show that many low-income mothers do not exhibit bonding with their infants at birth. Bonding occurs later, if the child survives infancy, when it is several years old. She proposes that this pattern of later bonding is related to the high rate of infant mortality among poor people of northeast Brazil. If women were to develop strong bonds with their newborn infants, they would suffer untold amounts of grief. Western bonding is adaptive in low-mortality, low-fertility societies in which strong maternal attachment is reasonable because infants are likely to survive.

GENDER IN INFANCY Anthropologists distinguish between *sex* and *gender* (see Chapter 1). Sex is something that everyone is born with. In the view of Western science, it has three biological markers: genitals, hormones, and chromosomes. A male has a penis, more androgens than estrogens, and the XY chromosome. A female has a vagina, more estro-

gens than androgens, and the XX chromosome. Increasingly, scientists are finding that these two categories are not airtight. In all populations, up to 10 percent of people are born with indeterminate genitals, similar proportions of androgens and estrogens, and chromosomes with more complex distributions than simply XX and XY.

Gender, in contrast, is a cultural construction and is highly variable across cultures (B. Miller 1993). In the view of most cultural anthropologists, a high degree of human "plasticity" (or personality flexibility) allows for substantial variation in personality and behavior. More biologically inclined anthropologists, however, continue to insist that many sex-linked personality characteristics are inborn.

Proving the existence of innate (inborn) gender characteristics is made difficult by two factors. First, it is impossible to collect data on infants before they are subject to cultural treatment. Culture may begin to shape infants even in the womb, through exposure to sound and motion, but current scientific data on the cultural effects on the prenatal stage are slim. Once birth takes place, culture shapes infants in many ways, including how people handle and interact with them. There is thus no such thing as a "natural" infant.

Second, it is difficult, if not impossible, to study and interpret the behavior of infants to try to ascertain what is "natural" and what is "cultural" without introducing biases from the observers. Studies of infants have focused on assessing the potential innateness of three major Euro-American personality stereotypes (Frieze et al. 1978:73–78):

- That infant males are more aggressive than infant females
- That infant females are more social than infant males
- That infant males are more independent than infant females

What is the evidence? Studies conducted in the United States indicate that boy babies cry more than girl babies, and some people accept this difference as evidence of higher levels of inborn aggression in males. An alternative interpretation is that baby boys, on average, tend to weigh more than girls at birth. They therefore are more likely to have a difficult delivery from which it takes time to recover. So they cry more, but not because of aggressiveness. In terms of sociability, baby girls smile more often than boys, and some researchers claim that this difference confirms innate personality characteristics. But culture, not nature, may be the explanation because American caretakers smile more at baby girls than they smile at baby boys. Thus, the more frequent smiling of girls is likely to be a learned behavior. In terms of independence or dependence, studies thus far reveal no clear differences in how upset baby boys and girls are when separated from their caretakers. Taken as a whole, studies seeking to document innate differences between girls and boys are not convincing.

Cultural anthropologists who take a constructionist view make two further points. They note that, if gender differences

---

puberty a time in the human life cycle that occurs universally and involves a set of biological markers and sexual maturation.

adolescence a culturally defined period of maturation from the time of puberty until adulthood that is recognized in some, but not all, cultures.

are innate, it is odd that cultures go to so much trouble to enculturate offspring into a particular gender. Also, if gender differences are innate, then they should be the same throughout history and across all cultures, which they clearly are not. The following material explores cross-cultural cases of how culture constructs gender, beginning with childhood.

Socialization During Childhood

The *Six Cultures Study* (mentioned in Chapter 4) is a classic cross-cultural research project designed to provide comparative data on how children's activities and tasks shape their personalities (Whiting and Whiting 1975). Researchers used similar methods at six sites (Figure 6.4), observing children between the ages of 3 and 11 years. They recorded the children's behavior, such as caring for and being supportive of other children; hitting other children; and performing tasks such as child care, cooking, and errands. The data collected were analyzed in terms of two major personality types: nurturant-responsible and dependent-dominant. A *nurturant-responsible personality* is characterized by caring and sharing acts toward other children. The *dependent-dominant personality* involves fewer acts of caregiving, more acts that assert dominance over other children, and more need for care by adults.

Of the six cultures, the Gusii children of southwestern Kenya had the highest frequency of a nurturant-responsible personality type. They were responsible for the widest range of tasks and at earlier ages than children in any other culture in the study, often performing tasks that an Orchard Town, United States, mother does. Although some children in all six cultures took care of other children, Gusii children (both boys and girls) spent the most time doing so. They began taking on this responsibility at a very young age, between five and eight years old.

In contrast, Orchard Town children had the highest frequency of the dependent-dominant personality type. The differences correlate with the mode of livelihood. In the research sites in Kenya, Mexico, and the Philippines, all reliant on horticulture, children were more nurturant-responsible.

Horticultural Groups

Gusii people, Kenya

Maya people, Oaxaca, Mexico

Tarong people, Philippines

Intensive Agriculture or Industrial Groups

Taira village, Okinawa, Japan

Rajput people, village in North India

Middle-class Euro-Americans, Orchard Town,
New England, United States

Source: Whiting and Whiting (1975).

FIGURE 6.4 Groups in the Six Cultures Study.

Livelihood in the sites in Japan, India, and the United States were based on either intensive agriculture or industry.

How do these different modes of livelihood influence child personality? The key underlying factor is women's work roles. In the horticultural societies, women are an important part of the labor force and spend much time working outside the home. Their children take on many family-supportive tasks and thereby develop personalities that are nurturant-responsible. When women are mainly occupied in the home, as in the second group of cultures, children have fewer tasks and less responsibility. They develop personalities that are more dependent-dominant.

This study has many implications for Western child-development experts. For one thing, what happens when the dependent-dominant personality develops to an extreme level—into a *narcissistic personality*? A narcissist is someone who constantly seeks self-attention and self-affirmation, with no concern for other people's needs. Consumerism supports the development of narcissism via its emphasis on identity formation through ownership of self-defining goods (clothing, electronics, cars) and access to self-defining services (vacations, therapists, fitness salons). The *Six Cultures Study* suggests that involving children more in household responsibilities might result in less self-focused personality formation and more nurturant-responsible people.

Adolescence and Identity

The transition from "childhood" to "adulthood" involves certain biological events, as well as cultural events, that shape the transition to adulthood.

Is Adolescence a Universal Life-Cycle Stage?

Puberty is a time in the human life cycle that occurs universally and involves a set of biological markers. In males, the voice deepens and facial and body hair appear; in females, menarche and breast development occur; in both males and females, pubic and underarm hair appear and sexual maturation is achieved. **Adolescence**, in contrast, is a culturally defined period of maturation from around the time of puberty until the attainment of adulthood, usually marked by becoming a parent, getting married, or becoming economically self-sufficient.

Some scholars say that all cultures define a period of adolescence. A comparative study using data on 186 societies argues for the universal existence of a culturally defined phase of adolescence (Schlegel 1995). The researchers point to

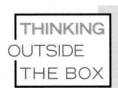

THINKING OUTSIDE THE BOX

Try to recall your daily activities when you were 5 years old, 10 years old, and 15 years old. What tasks did you do? In terms of the Six Cultures Study categories, which type of personality do you have?

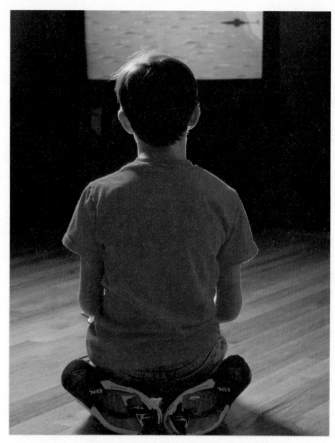

(LEFT) A Yanomami boy acquiring skills necessary for hunting and warfare through play. (RIGHT) An American boy playing a video game.

▶ *Consider examples of children's games that may provide learning and skills related to adult roles in your culture.*

supportive evidence in the fact that people in cultures as diverse as the Navajo and the Trobriand Islanders have special terms comparable to the American term "adolescent" to refer to a person between puberty and marriage. Following a biological determinist, Darwinian model, they interpret the supposedly universal phases of adolescence as being adaptive in an evolutionary sense. The logic is that adolescence provides training for parenthood and thus contributes to enhanced reproductive success and survival of parents' genes.

Other anthropologists view adolescence as culturally constructed, highly variable, and thus impossible to explain on only biological grounds. These researchers point out that people in many cultures recognize no period of adolescence. In some others, identification of an adolescent phase is recent. Moroccan anthropologist Fatima Mernissi (1987), for example, states that adolescence became a recognized life-cycle phase for females in Morocco only in the late twentieth century:

> The idea of an adolescent unmarried woman is a completely new idea in the Muslim world, where previously you had only a female child and a menstruating woman who had to be married off immediately so as to prevent dishonorable engagement in premarital sex. (1987:xxiv)

Another line of evidence supporting a cultural constructionist view is that, in different cultures, the length and elabo-

ration of adolescence varies for males and females. In many horticultural and pastoralist societies in which men are valued as warriors, a long period between boyhood and adulthood is devoted to training in warfare and developing solidarity among males of similar ages. This pattern occurs, for example, among the Maasai (sometimes spelled Masai). The Maasai are pastoralists, numbering over 500,000, who live in a large area crossing Kenya and Tanzania (Map 6.4). The extended adolescent period for males has nothing to do with training for parenthood. Maasai females, by contrast, move directly from being girls to being wives with no adolescent period in between. They learn adult roles when they are children.

Among some highland groups in New Guinea, long periods of male initiation that involve institutionalized homosexual relationships also do not fit within the Darwinian interpretation. Gilbert Herdt conducted research with the Sambia, highland horticulturalists of Papua New Guinea, and learned about their secret male initiation practices (1987). The Sambia believe that, in order for a young boy to mature into a healthy adult, he must join a secret, all-male initiation group. A boy becomes a partner of a senior male who regularly transfers his semen to the youth orally. The Sambia believe that the youth is nourished by ingesting semen. After a certain length of time in the initiation group, the "grown" youth rejoins society as a man. At that time he will marry a woman and raise children.

A Maasai warrior's mother shaves her son's head during part of his initiation ceremony into adulthood. This ritual validates her status as a mother, as well as her son's adulthood.

In some cultures, females have long adolescent phases during which they live separated from the wider group and gain special knowledge and skills (Brown 1978). After this period of seclusion, they reemerge as full-fledged women and marry.

A cultural explanation exists for why gender affects whether a young person has an adolescent phase of life. Cultural materialism (Chapter 1) explains this variation by saying that a long and marked period of adolescence is preparation for any of several culturally valued adult roles: worker, warrior, or parent. Confirmation of this hypothesis comes from the finding that an extended adolescence for females in nonindustrial societies occurs in cultures where adult females are important as food producers (Brown 1978).

COMING OF AGE AND GENDER IDENTITY
Margaret Mead made famous the phrase "coming of age" in her book *Coming of Age in Samoa* (1961 [1928]). The phrase can refer generally to the period of adolescence or specifically to a ceremony or set of ceremonies that marks the boundaries of adolescence. What are the psychological aspects of such special events for the children who go through them? Some ceremonies have a sacrificial element, with symbolic death and rebirth. Most coming-of-age ceremonies are gender specific, highlighting the importance of adult roles of men and women. These ceremonies often involve marking the body of the initiate in some way. Such marking may include scarification, tattooing, and genital surgery.

In many societies, adolescent males undergo genital surgery that involves the removal of part of the skin around the tip of the penis; without this operation, the boy would not become a full-fledged male. Among many African pastoralist groups, such as the Maasai, adolescent males go through a circumcision ceremony that marks the end of adolescence and the beginning of manhood and full membership in the group. A young Maasai male, in a first-person account of his initiation into manhood, describes the "intolerable pain" he experi-

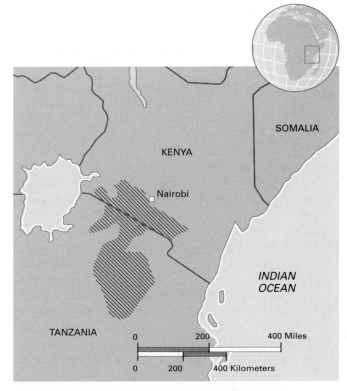

MAP 6.4 Maasai Region of Kenya and Tanzania.
An estimated 350,000 Maasai live in Kenya and 150,000 in Tanzania. The climate is semiarid and arid.

enced following the circumcision, as well as his feeling of accomplishment two weeks later when his head was shaved and he became a warrior: "As long as I live, I will never forget the day my head was shaved and I emerged a man, a Maasai warrior. I felt a sense of control over my destiny so great that no words can accurately describe it" (Saitoti 1986:71).

Less common worldwide is **female genital cutting (FGC)**, or *female circumcision*, a term that refers to a range of practices involving partial or total removal of the clitoris and labia. In some contexts, FGC is practiced along with *infibulation*, the stitching together of the vaginal entry, leaving a small aperture for drainage of menstrual blood. These procedures are usually performed when a girl is between 7 and 15 years of age. In the Sahelian countries, extending from Africa's west to east coast (see Map 14.6, page 353), many people practice some form of female genital cutting. FGC is also found in Egypt, in some groups of the Middle East (particularly among Bedu tribes), and among some Muslim groups in South and Southeast Asia. In terms of religion, FGC is often, but not always, associated with people who are Muslim. In Ethiopia, some Christian groups practice it. Genital cutting occurs in many groups in which female labor participation is high, but also in others where it is not.

Scholars have no good explanation for the regional and social distribution of FGC. Anthropologists who study this

---

female genital cutting (FGC) a range of practices involving partial or total removal of the clitoris and labia.

CRITICAL thinking

Cultural Relativism and Female Genital Cutting

In cultures that practice female genital cutting (FGC), it is a necessary step toward full womanhood. Fathers say that an uncircumcised daughter is unmarriageable. Others say that removing the labia makes a woman beautiful by removing "male" parts. The prevailing Western view, increasingly being shared by many people who have long practiced female genital cutting, is that FGC is both a sign of low female status and an unnecessary cause of women's suffering.

Female genital cutting is linked with several health risks, including those related to the surgery itself (shock, infection) and future genito-urinary complications (Gruenbaum 2001). Infibulation scars the vaginal canal and may lead to problems during childbirth, sometimes causing the death of the infant and mother.

Having an infibulated bride's husband "open" her, using a stick or knife to loosen the aperture, is both painful and an opportunity for infection. After giving birth, a woman is usually reinfibulated, and the process begins again. Health experts say that repeated trauma to the woman's vaginal area increases the risk of contracting HIV/AIDS.

The Western view argues that the effects of both clitoridectomy and infibulation on a woman's sexual enjoyment are negative—for one thing, clitoral orgasm is no longer possible. Some experts say that FGC is related to the high level of infertility in many African countries, although a comparative study of fertility data from the Central African Republic, Côte d'Ivoire, and Tanzania found no clear relationship between FGC and infertility (Larsen and Yan 2000).

Outsiders often view these practices in oversimplified terms and in the most extreme forms. What are the views of insiders? Is there any evidence for female agency? Or is it all structure and should anthropologists support FGC liberation movements? One voice that transcends insider–outsider divisions is that of Fuambai Ahmadu, who was born and raised in Washington, DC, and is descended from a prominent Kono lineage in Sierra Leone (2000).

In 1991, Ahmadu traveled to Sierra Leone with her mother and other family members for what she refers to as her "circumcision." Upon her return, she wrote about her initiation experience and what it meant to her. Although the physical pain was excruciating (in spite of the use of anesthetics), "the positive aspects have been much more profound" (2000:306). Through the initiation, she became part of a powerful female world. Her analysis addresses the effects of genital cutting on health and sexuality. Ahmadu argues that Westerners exaggerate these issues by focusing on infibulation rather than

---

practice ask the people involved for their views. Many young girls say they look forward to the ceremony so that they will be free from childhood tasks and can take on the more respected role of an adult woman. In other cases, anthropologists have reported hearing statements of resistance (Fratkin 1998:60). Fewer issues force the questioning of cultural relativism more clearly than female genital cutting (see Critical Thinking).

Initiation rites often involve themes of death and rebirth as the initiate loses his or her former identity and emerges with a new one. During the early 1990s, Abigail Adams conducted research on initiation rituals at what was then a men's military school, the Virginia Military Institute (VMI) (2002). Freshmen students, called "Rats," are each assigned to an upperclassman, called a "Dyke." The freshman year involves continuous humiliation and other forms of abuse for the Rats. Dykes treat their Rats like infants, telling them how to eat, bathe, and talk and yelling at them in baby talk. The culminating initiation ritual for the Rats takes place during March. The town's fire truck sprays the outskirts of the campus to create a large area of mud. The Rats have to crawl through the mud while sophomores and juniors attack them, shout at them, push them down, sit on them, and fill their eyes, ears, faces, and clothes with mud. The Rats can barely see as they grope their way along, and many lose their pants. The ordeal continues over two banks of earth and a ditch, with continuous harassment from the sophomores and juniors. When the Rats finally reach the top of the second bank, the Dykes rush to greet them, tenderly wash the mud off them, and wrap them in blankets. The moment when the mud is washed away is the transition of the Rat into a cadet.

Breaking Out, a rite of passage at a military academy in Virginia when it was an all-men's school.

▶ *What rite of passage have you been through, and how would you analyze it anthropologically?*

MAP 6.5 Sierra Leone.

The Republic of Sierra Leone was an important center of the transatlantic slave trade. Its capital, Freetown, was established in 1792 as a home for African slaves who fought with the British during the American Revolution. Sierra Leone's coast is covered with mangrove swamps, while the interior is plateau, forests, and mountains. The population is 6 million. Sierra Leone suffered a terrible civil war from 1991 to 2002, causing thousands of deaths and the displacement of 2 million people. It has the lowest per capita income in the world. English is the official language, but most people speak local, tribal languages.

on the less extreme forms. She adds, however, that if global pressures against the practice continue, she will go along with that movement and support "ritual without cutting" (2000:308).

CRITICAL THINKING QUESTIONS ▼
- Why do you think FGC is a prominent issue in human rights debates in the West, whereas male circumcision and other forms of initiation (such as fraternity and sorority hazing) are not?
- Where do you stand on FGC and why?
- What kinds of cultural remodeling of the female body are practiced in your culture?

Adams interprets this ritual as a birthing event, with the newborn emerging blinded by and covered with fluids, then cleaned and blanketed. One senior said that being a Dyke "is like having my own child" (2002:39). Many aspects of this ritual, however, are ambiguous, not least of which is the term "Dyke" for male "mothers" (or "fathers"?). The Breaking Out initiation ritual is no longer practiced at VMI. In the mid-1990s, VMI, as the recipient of public funds, was under pressure to admit women in order to be compliant with the law. After a drawn-out legal battle that ended up in the Supreme Court, VMI admitted its first women students in 1997. Breaking Out has been replaced with a long weekend series of events involving physical and field challenges.

SEXUAL IDENTITY AND GENDER PLURALISM

Scholars have long debated whether sexual preferences and gender identity are biologically determined (ruled by genetic or hormonal factors) or culturally constructed and learned. Biological anthropologist Melvin Konner (1989) takes a middle position, saying that both factors play a part, but simultaneously warning that no one has a simple answer to the question of why an individual is gay.

The cultural constructionist position emphasizes socialization and childhood experiences as more powerful than biology in shaping sexual orientation. These anthropologists find support for their position in the cross-cultural record and its cases in which people change their sexual orientation once, or sometimes more than once, during their lifetimes. The Sambia of Papua New Guinea are one example. In the Gulf state of Oman, the *xanith* (hah-neeth) is another example (Wikan 1977) (Map 5.3, page 119). A xanith is a man who, for a time, becomes more like a woman, wears female clothing, and has sex with other men. Later, the xanith returns to a standard male role, marries a woman, and has children. Thus, given the same biological material, some people assume different sexual identities over their lives.

No matter what one's theoretical perspective is, it is clear that homosexuals are discriminated against in many contexts in which heterosexuality is the norm. In the United States, homosexuals are disproportionately victims of hate crimes, housing discrimination, and problems in the workplace, including wage and benefits discrimination. They often suffer from being stigmatized by their parents, peers, and the wider society. The psychological damage to their self-esteem by social stigma and discrimination is related to the fact that homosexual youth in the United States have substantially higher suicide rates than heterosexual youth.

Some cultures allow for a third gender, which is neither purely "male" nor purely "female," according to a particular culture's definition of those terms. As with the xanith of Oman, these gender categories offer ways for "males" to cross gender lines and assume more "female" behaviors, personality characteristics, and dress. Among some American Indians, a **berdache** (ber-DASH) is a male, in terms of genitals, who opts to wear female clothing, engages in sexual intercourse with a man or a woman, and does female tasks such as basket weaving and pottery making (Williams 1992). A person may become a berdache in a variety of ways. Sometimes parents, especially if they have several sons, choose one to become a berdache. Sometimes a boy who shows interest in typically female activities or who likes to wear female clothing is allowed to become a berdache. Such a child is a focus of pride for the family, never a source of disappointment or stigma.

During decades of contact with Euro-American colonizers, including Christian missionaries, the outsiders viewed the berdache role with disapproval and ridicule (Roscoe 1991). American Indian cultures began to suppress their berdache tradition. Starting in the 1980s, as American Indians' cultural pride began to grow, the open presence of the berdache and the **amazon**, a woman who takes on male roles and behaviors, has returned. Contemporary American Indian cultures, compared with mainstream White culture, are more accepting of gender role fluidity and the contemporary concept of being gay.

In India, the counterpart of the berdache is a **hijra** (hij-ruh). Hijras dress and act like women but are neither truly male nor truly female (Nanda 1990). Many hijras were born with male genitals or with genitals that were not clearly male or female. Hijras have the traditional right to visit the home of a newborn, inspect its genitals, and claim it for their group if the genitals are neither clearly male nor clearly female. Hijras born with male genitals may opt to go through an initiation ceremony that involves cutting off their penis and testicles. Hijras roam large cities of India, earning a living by

A Zuni berdache wearing a traditional woman's ceremonial dress and holding a pottery bowl with sacred corn meal.

begging from store to store and threatening to lift their skirts if not given money. Because women do not sing or dance in public, hijras play an important role as performers in public events, especially as dancers or musicians. Mainstream Indians do not admire or respect hijras, and no family would be delighted to hear that their son has decided to become a hijra.

In mainland and island Southeast Asia (Map 6.6), the situation is more open, with a wide range of gender options, or **gender pluralism**. Gender pluralism is the existence in a culture of multiple categories of femininity, masculinity, and blurred genders that are tolerated and legitimate (Peletz 2006:310). In Thailand, three gender categories have long existed: *phuuchai* (male), *phuuyung* (female), and *kathoey* (transvestite/transsexual/hermaphrodite) (Morris 1994). A kathoey is "originally" a male who crosses into the body, personality, and dress defined as female. The sexual orientation of kathoeys is flexible, including either male or female partners. In contemporary Thailand, explicit discussion and recognition of homosexuality exists, usually couched in English terms, conveying a sense of its foreignness. The words for lesbian are *thom* (from the word "tomboy") and *thut* (an ironic usage from the U.S. movie *Tootsie*, about a heterosexual man playing the part of a woman).

Yet another category exists in the area of sexuality: **asexuality**. An asexual person is someone who does not

berdache   a blurred gender category, usually referring to a person who is biologically male but who takes on a female gender role.

amazon   a person who is biologically female but takes on a male gender role.

hijra   in India, a blurred gender role in which a person, usually biologically male, takes on female dress and behavior.

gender pluralism   the existence within a culture of multiple categories of femininity, masculinity, and blurred genders that are tolerated and legitimate.

asexuality   lack of sexual attraction or interest in sexual activity.

matrescence   motherhood, or the cultural process of becoming a mother.

patrescence   fatherhood, or the cultural process of becoming a father.

couvade   customs applying to the behavior of fathers during and shortly after the birth of their children.

The South Korean transgender musical group "Lady" includes four transsexuals.

experience sexual attraction. Asexuals exist around the world and are beginning to come out and identify themselves through websites and in public arenas, such as gay rights parades, even though asexuals are not gay (Scherrer 2008).

Adulthood

For most people, adulthood means entering into some form of marriage or long-term domestic relationship and having children. The following discussion considers the psychological aspects of parenthood and the "senior years."

BECOMING A PARENT   In Euro-American culture, a woman becomes a mother when she gives birth. **Matrescence** is the cultural process of becoming a mother (Raphael 1975). Like adolescence, matrescence varies cross-culturally in terms of duration and meaning. In some cultures, a woman is transformed into a mother as soon as she thinks she is pregnant. In others, she becomes a mother and is granted full maternal status only when she delivers an infant of the "right" sex, as in much of northern India, where son preference is strong.

In many nonindustrial cultures, matrescence occurs in the context of supportive family members. Some cultures promote prenatal practices, abiding by particular food taboos, which can be regarded as part of matrescence. Such rules make the

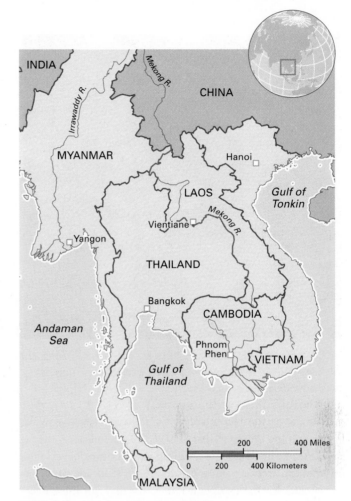

MAP 6.6   Mainland Southeast Asia.
Mainland Southeast Asia comprises Myanmar, Thailand, Laos, Vietnam, Cambodia, and Malaysia. Although each country has a distinct history, the region shares a tropical monsoon climate, emphasis on wet-rice agriculture, and ethnic contrasts between highlanders and lowlanders. Many national and ethnic languages exist. Languages in the Mon-Khmer language family have the most speakers. Theravada Buddhism, Islam, and Christianity are the major religions. Growth in industry and informatics has created an economic upsurge in many parts of the region.

pregnant woman feel that she has a role in ensuring that the pregnancy turns out well. In the West, medical experts increasingly define the prenatal period as an important phase of matrescence, and they have issued many scientific and medical rules for potential parents, especially mothers (Browner and Press 1996). Pregnant women are urged to seek prenatal examinations, be under the regular supervision of a doctor who monitors the growth and development of the fetus, follow particular dietary and exercise guidelines, and undergo a range of tests such as ultrasound scanning. Some anthropologists think that such medical control of pregnancy leads to the greater likelihood of postpartum depression, as a result of the mother's lack of agency in the process of matrescence.

Patrescence, or the cultural process of becoming a father, is less marked cross-culturally than matrescence. One exception to this generalization is **couvade** (coo-VAHD),

An Aka father and his son. Aka fathers are affectionate caretakers of infants and small children. Compared with mothers, they are more likely to kiss and hug children.

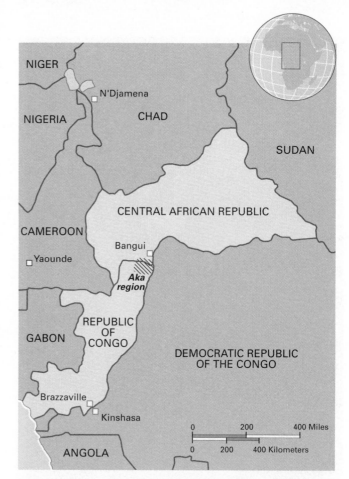

MAP 6.7 Aka Region of the Central African Republic and the Democratic Republic of Congo.

The 30,000 Aka are tropical forest foragers who know hundreds of plants and animals. They eat roots, leaves, nuts, fruits, mushrooms, honey, grubs, caterpillars, and meat from monkeys, rats, mongooses, and porcupines. They trade meat to farmers for manioc and other cultivated foods. They are socially egalitarian, and their religious beliefs are indigenous. Diaka, their main language, is tonal. The Aka territory is critically endangered by commercial loggers.

beliefs and customs applying to a father during his wife's pregnancy and delivery (Broude 1988). In some cases, the father takes to his bed before, during, or after the delivery, and he may experience pain and exhaustion. Couvade often involves rules for the expectant father: He may not hunt a certain animal, eat certain foods, or cut objects. Early theories of why couvade exists relied on Freudian interpretations that men were identifying with the female role in contexts where the father role was weak. Cross-cultural data indicate the opposite, because couvade occurs in societies where fathers have prominent roles in child care. In these contexts, couvade is a phase of patrescence: The father's proper behavior helps ensure a safe delivery and a healthy baby. Another interpretation of couvade is that it offers indirect support for the mother.

Once the baby is born, who takes care of it? The widespread pattern of women being the major caretakers of infants and children has led many people to think that something biologically innate about females makes them especially suited to caretaking roles. Most cultural anthropologists agree that child care is predominantly the responsibility of females worldwide—but not universally. They seek to provide a cultural construction explanation rather than a genetic or hormonal one. As evidence, they point to the cross-cultural variation in child-care roles. For example, throughout the South Pacific, child care is shared across families, and women breastfeed other women's babies. Paternal involvement varies cross-culturally as well. Among Aka foragers of the Central African Republic (Map 6.7), paternal child care is prominent (Hewlett 1991). Aka fathers are intimate, affectionate, and helpful, spending half their time each day holding or within close reach of their infants. Fathers are more likely to hug and kiss their infants

than mothers are. The definition of good fatherhood among the Aka means being affectionate toward children and assisting the mother when her workload is heavy. Among the Aka, gender equality prevails and violence against women is unknown. This high level of paternal involvement is related to all these patterns and supports a constructionist view of parenting and gender roles rather than a biological determinist view.

MIDDLE AGE In many industrial/informatic societies, a major turning point for men is the fortieth birthday. According to a study of men turning 40 in the United States, the *40 syndrome* involves feelings of restlessness, rebelliousness, and unhappiness that often lead to family breakups (Brandes 1985). A possible reason behind the emphasis on the age 40 as a turning point for males is that it is the current midpoint of a typical life span for a middle-class American man. In cultures with shorter life spans, a so-called midlife crisis would necessarily occur at some point other than the age of 40 years. The midlife crisis in America seems strongly embedded in contemporary culture and its fear and denial of death (Shore 1998).

Menopause, or the cessation of menstruation, is a significant aspect of middle age for women in many, but not all, cultures. A comparative study examined differences in the perception and experience of menopause among Maya women of Mexico and rural Greek women (Beyene 1989). Among the Maya women, menopause is not a time of stress or crisis. They consider menstruation an illness and look forward to its end. Menopause among these women is not associated with physical or emotional symptoms. None of the women reported hot flashes or cold sweats. No role changes were associated with menopause. In contrast, the rural Greek women recognized menopause, or *exapi* (eh-SHAP-ee), as a natural phenomenon that all women experience, which is a phase of hot flashes, especially at night, that may last about a year. The women did not think exapi was serious and did not regard it as worthy of medical attention. Postmenopausal women emphasized the relief and freedom they felt. Postmenopausal women can go into cafes by themselves, something they would never do otherwise, and they can participate more fully in church ceremonies. In Japan, likewise, menopause is minimally stressful and women rarely consider it something that warrants medical attention (Lock 1993).

THE SENIOR YEARS   The senior life-cycle stage may be a development of contemporary human society, because, like most other mammals, our early ancestors rarely lived beyond their reproductive years. Cross-culturally, the category of the aged is variably recognized, defined, and valued. In many cultures, elders are highly revered as having great wisdom based on their life experiences. In others, aged people become burdens to their families and to society.

Cross-cultural comparisons reveal that the status of elderly people is higher and their welfare more secure in contexts where they continue to live with their families (Lee and Kezis 1979). This pattern is, however, more likely to be found in nonindustrial societies than in industrialized ones, where the elderly live with younger kin less frequently. Instead, they are increasingly experiencing a shift to living in age-segregated residences such as "retirement homes," where they have to create new social roles and ties and find new ways of gaining self-esteem and personal satisfaction. Research conducted in a retirement home in a small town in central New York state shows that having a pet promotes a person's sense of well-being (Savishinsky 1991).

THE FINAL PASSAGE: DEATH AND DYING   It may be that no one in any culture welcomes death, unless he or she is in very poor health and suffering greatly. The contemporary United States, with its dependence on medical technology, appears to play a leading role in resistance to death, often at high financial and psychological costs. In many other cultures, a greater degree of acceptance prevails.

A study of attitudes toward death and dying among Alaskan Inuits revealed a pervasive feeling that people are active participants in their death rather than passive victims (Trelease 1975). The person near death calls friends and neighbors together, is given a Christian sacrament, and then, within a few hours, dies. The author comments, "I do not suggest that everyone waited for the priest to come and then died right away. But the majority who did not die suddenly did some degree of planning, had some kind of formal service or celebration of prayers and hymns and farewells" (1975:35).

Terminally ill people, especially in industrial/informatic societies with a high level of medical technology, are likely to be faced with choices about how and where they should die, at home or in a hospital, and whether they should prolong their lives with "unusual means" or opt for "physician-assisted suicide." Depending on the cultural context, the options are affected not only by the degree of medical technology and health-care services available but also by matters of kinship and gender role ideals (Long 2005). In urban Japan, terminally ill people have clear ideas of what is a "good death" and two major "scripts" for a "good death." A modern script of dying in a hospital is widely accepted, because it reduces burdens on family members. But a value on dying surrounded by one's family members still prevails; this practice reassures the dying person that he or she will be remembered.

In many cultures, the inability to perform a proper burial and funeral for a deceased person is a cause of serious social suffering. Among refugees from Mozambique living in neighboring Malawi, the greatest cause of stress was being forced to leave behind deceased family members without providing a proper burial for them (Englund 1998). Such improperly treated deaths mean that the unhappy spirit of the deceased will haunt the living. This belief is related to the high rate of mental-health problems among the refugees. A culturally informed recommendation for reducing their anxiety is to provide them with money to travel home and to perform a proper funeral for their deceased relatives. In that way, the living may carry on in greater peace.

Anthropologists know little about people's grief at the death of a loved one or a close community member. It might seem that sadness and grief, as well as a period of mourning, are only natural. But the outward expression of grief varies from extended, dramatic, public grieving that is overtly emotional to no visible sign of grief at all. The latter pattern is the norm in Bali, Indonesia (see Map 2.2, page 33), where people's faces remain impassive at funerals and no vocal lamenting occurs (Rosenblatt et al. 1976). Do impassive faces and silence mean that the Balinese feel no sadness? Such different modes of expression of loss may be related to the healing process for the survivors by providing socially accepted rules of behavior—in other words, a script for loss. Either highly expressive public mourning or repressed grief may be equally effective, depending on the context.

6 the BIG questions REVISITED

⊙ How are modes of reproduction related to modes of livelihood?

Cultural anthropologists define three modes of reproduction that are related to foraging, agriculture, and industrialism/informatics. They differ in terms of desired and actual fertility.

For thousands of years, foragers maintained a balanced level of population through direct and indirect means of fertility regulation. A classic study of the Ju/'hoansi shows how foragers' lifestyles, including a low-fat diet and women's physical activity, suppress fertility.

As sedentary lifestyles increased and food surpluses became more available and storable with agriculture, population growth increased. The highest rates of population growth in human prehistory and history are found among settled agriculturalists. Contemporary examples of high-fertility agriculturalists are the Amish and Mennonite people of North America.

⊙ How does culture shape fertility in different contexts?

Cross-culturally, many techniques exist for increasing fertility, reducing it, and regulating its timing. From culture to culture, values differ about the right age for people to start having sexual relations and how often they do so. In terms of cultural practices that directly affect fertility, hundreds of different traditional methods exist, including the use of herbs and other natural substances for either preventing or promoting fertilization and for inducing abortion if an undesired pregnancy occurs.

In nonindustrialized societies, knowledge about fertility regulation, as well as its practice, is largely unspecialized and available to all women. In the industrial/informatic mode of reproduction, scientific and medical specialization increases, and most knowledge and expertise are in the hands of professionals rather than of women. Class-stratified access to fertility-regulating methods now exists both globally and within nations.

Population growth is also shaped through the practice of infanticide, which, though of ancient origin, still exists today. It is sometimes performed in response to limited family resources, perceptions of inadequate "fitness" of the child, or preferences regarding the gender of offspring.

⊙ How does culture shape personality over the life cycle?

Cultural anthropologists emphasize the effects of infant care practices on personality formation, including gender identity. Other cross-cultural studies show that variations in the gender division of labor and children's work roles in the family correspond to varying personality patterns. Adolescence, a culturally defined time beginning around puberty and running until adulthood, varies cross-culturally from being nonexistent to involving detailed training and elaborate ceremonies.

In contrast to the sharp distinction between "male" and "female" in Euro-American culture, many cultures have traditions of third or blurred gender identities. Gender pluralism is found in many cultures, especially in some American Indian and Asian cultures. Asexuality, when a person has no sexual attraction, is a newly recognized category of personal identity.

Cross-culturally, adult roles usually involve parenthood. In nonindustrial societies, learning about motherhood is embedded in other aspects of life and knowledge about birthing and child care is shared among women. In industrialized/informatic cultures, science and medicine play a large part in defining the maternal role.

The senior years are generally shorter in nonindustrialized societies than in industrialized/informatic societies, in which life spans tend to be longer. Elderly men and women in nonindustrial cultures are treated with respect, are assumed to know the most, and retain a strong sense of their place in the culture. Increasingly in industrialized/informatic societies, elderly people live apart from their families and spend many years in age-segregated institutions such as retirement homes or alone.

KEY CONCEPTS

adolescence, p. 144
amazon, p. 150
asexuality, p. 150
berdache, p. 150
couvade, p. 150

demographic transition, p. 135
female genital cutting (FGC), p. 147
fertility, p. 135
gender pluralism, p. 150

hijra, p. 150
infanticide, p. 143
matrescence, p. 150
menarche, p. 139
menopause, p. 139

mode of reproduction, p. 135
patrescence, p. 150
personality, p. 143
pronatalism, p. 135
puberty, p. 144

SUGGESTED READINGS

Robbie E. Davis-Floyd. *Birth as an American Rite of Passage,* 2nd ed. Berkeley: University of California Press, 2003. This book provides a cultural critique of the dominant U.S. model of birth as "technocratic" and patriarchal.

Jessica L. Gregg. *Virtually Virgins: Sexual Strategies and Cervical Cancer in Recife, Brazil.* Stanford, CA: Stanford University Press, 2003. Research with women residents of a poor urban area in northeast Brazil and with women cancer victims in a neighborhood maternity clinic shows how the women attempt to deal with racism, sexism, poverty, and violence.

Ellen Gruenbaum. *The Female Circumcision Controversy: An Anthropological Perspective.* Philadelphia: University of Pennsylvania Press, 2001. The author draws on her more than five years of fieldwork in Sudan and discusses how change is occurring through economic development, the role of Islamic activists, health educators, and educated African women.

Shahram Khosravi. *Young and Defiant in Tehran.* Philadelphia: University of Pennsylvania Press, 2008. This ethnographic study documents how youths in the Iranian capital contest official culture and parental domination.

Robert A. LeVine and Rebecca S. New, ed. *Anthropology and Child Development: A Cross-Cultural Reader.* Malden, MA: Blackwell Publishing, 2008. Twenty-four chapters discuss childhood around the world. The collection includes classic essays by Boas, Mead, and Malinowski, as well as recent studies. Some chapters present case studies and some are comparative. Topics range from child care in the Kalahari desert to children's play in Italy.

Michael Moffatt. *Coming of Age in New Jersey: College and American Culture.* New Brunswick, NJ: Rutgers University Press, 1991. Based on a year's participant observation in a college dormitory in a university in the eastern United States, this study discusses sexuality, race relations, and individualism.

Leith Mullings and Alaka Wali. *Stress and Resilience: The Social Context of Reproduction in Central Harlem.* New York: Kluwer Academic, 2001. Documenting the daily efforts of African Americans to contend with oppressive conditions, this ethnography focuses on the experiences of women during pregnancy.

Frances Norwood. *The Maintenance of Life: Preventing Social Death through Euthanasia Talk and End-of-Life Care, Lessons from The Netherlands.* Durham, NC: Carolina Academic Press, 2009. Norwood conducted participant observation on end-of-life discourse, home death, and euthanasia in the Netherlands.

Michael G. Peletz. *Gender Pluralism: Southeast Asia since Early Modern Times.* New York: Routledge, 2008. This book provides an understanding of the historical cultural traditions of cross-dressing and the current political climate toward transvestites and homosexuals in Southeast Asia.

Sarah Pinto. *Where There Is No Midwife: Birth and Loss in Rural India.* New York: Bergahn Books, 2008. Pinto examines women's experiences with childbirth and infant death in a poor region in rural northern India with high rates of infant mortality.

Nancy Scheper-Hughes. *Death without Weeping: The Violence of Everyday Life in Brazil.* Berkeley: University of California Press, 1993. This book is a landmark "ethnography of death," based on fieldwork in a shantytown in northeastern Brazil. The author argues that extreme social inequality in Brazil creates a stratified demography.

John W. Traphagan. *Taming Oblivion: Aging Bodies and the Fear of Senility in Japan.* Albany: State University of New York Press, 2000. The author conducted fieldwork in a small town north of Tokyo to investigate people's attitudes and practices related to old age, especially as aging people attempt to prevent the onset of the *boke* condition, or what Westerners call senility.

Andrea S. Wiley. *An Ecology of High-Altitude Infancy: A Biocultural Perspective.* New York: Cambridge University Press, 2004. Ladakh is a district in India's far north, high in the Himalayas. Wiley focuses on the links between biology and culture in birth, in infant health and survival, and in women's reproductive health.

PEARSON
myanthrolab

For further information about topics covered in this chapter, go to MyAnthroLab at **www.myanthrolab.com** and access the following readings in MyAnthroLibrary:

Ahmadu, Fuambai. 2009. Disputing the Myth of the Sexual Dysfunction of Circumcised Women: An Interview with Fuambai Ahmadu. *Anthropology Today* 25:14–17. Richard Shweder, a strong cultural relativist, interviews a woman of Sierra Leone descent who grew up in the United States and chose to return to Sierra Leone for initiation into her lineage.

Sabine, Gabrysch et al. 2009. Cultural Adaptation of Birthing Services in Rural Ayacucho Peru. *Bulletin of the World Health Organization* 87:724-729. A team of public health researchers learns from the local women what a birthing clinic should provide so that the services are compatible with their culture.

Uehara, Ray T. 2009. Development the Agta Database: A Computer Scientist's Adventure into the World of Anthropology. *Practicing Anthropology* 31:38–42. Cultural anthropologist Thomas Headland requested help from Uehara in developing a database for all his population data on the Agta, foragers of the Philippines. This article chronicles the project and the challenges of working across disciplines.

DISEASE, ILLNESS, AND HEALING

◀ Shaman Gray Squirrel of the
Navajo of New Mexico prepares
a sand painting as part of a four-
day ritual to bring rain. Sand
paintings are now also produced
on paper or canvas for sale in the
commercial art market. They have
nothing to do with rain making.

Primatologist Jane Goodall witnessed the consequences of a polio epidemic among the chimpanzees she was studying in Tanzania (Foster and Anderson 1978:33–34). A group of healthy animals watched a stricken member try to reach the feeding area but did not help him. Another badly paralyzed chimpanzee was simply left behind when the group moved on. Humans also sometimes resort to isolation and abandonment of those who are ill and dying. But compared to our nonhuman primate relatives, humans have created more complex ways of interpreting health problems and highly creative methods of preventing and curing them.

Medical anthropology is one of the most rapidly growing areas of research in anthropology. This chapter first describes how people in different cultures think and behave regarding health, illness, and healing. The second section considers three theoretical approaches in medical anthropology. The chapter concludes by discussing how globalization is affecting health.

◉ ◉ ◉

Ethnomedicine

Since the early days of anthropology, the topic of **ethnomedicine**, or the study of cross-cultural health systems, has been a focus of research. A *health system* encompasses many areas: perceptions and classifications of health problems, prevention measures, diagnosis, healing (magical, religious, scientific, healing substances), and healers. Ethnomedicine has expanded its focus to include topics such as perceptions of the body, culture and disability, and change in indigenous or "traditional" healing systems, especially as resulting from globalization.

In the 1960s, when the term *ethnomedicine* first came into use, it referred only to non-Western health systems and was synonymous with the now abandoned term *primitive medicine*. The early use of the term was ethnocentric. Contemporary **Western biomedicine (WBM)**, a healing approach based on modern Western science that emphasizes technology in diagnosing and treating health problems related to the human body, is an ethnomedical system, too. Medical anthropologists now study WBM as a cultural system intimately bound to Western values. Thus, the current meaning of the term *ethnomedicine* encompasses health systems everywhere.

---

ethnomedicine   the study of cross-cultural health systems.

Western biomedicine (WBM)   a healing approach based on modern Western science that emphasizes technology for diagnosing and treating health problems related to the human body.

disease   in the disease–illness dichotomy, a biological health problem that is objective and universal.

illness   in the disease–illness dichotomy, culturally shaped perceptions and experiences of a health problem.

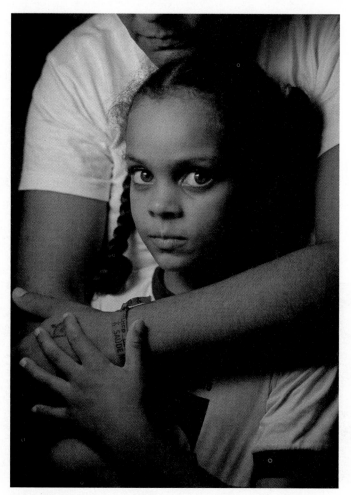

This Brazilian girl, age nine years, is HIV positive. Her mother contracted HIV from her husband and transmitted it to her child at birth.

Perceptions of the Body

In Japan, the concept of *gotai* refers to the ideal of maintaining bodily intactness in life and death, to the extent of not piercing one's ears (Ohnuki-Tierney 1994:235). When Crown Prince Naruhitao was considering whom to marry, one criterion for the bride was that she not have pierced ears. Underlying the value on intactness is the belief that an intact body ensures rebirth. Historically, a warrior's practice of beheading a victim was the ultimate form of killing because it violated the integrity of the body and prevented the enemy's rebirth. *Gotai* is an important reason for the low rates of surgery in Japan—compared to the United States—and the widespread popular resistance to organ transplantation.

Ideals about the female body are implicated in the high rate of caesarian births in Brazil (McCallum 2005). Ethnographic research in Salvador, a major city of the state of Bahia (bah-EE-yuh) in northeastern Brazil (Map 7.1), reveals that vaginal childbirth is considered more "primitive," painful, and destructive of a woman's sexuality than caesarian delivery. One doctor said that "more and more, the vulva and the vagina are becoming the organs of sexuality and not parturition"

MAP 7.1 Federative Republic of Brazil.

Brazil, a federation of 26 states, is the largest and most populous country in Latin America and the fifth largest worldwide. Its total population is about 188 million, and São Paulo, its largest city, has a population of 11 million. The economy is based on manufacturing, mining, agriculture, and technology. Ethnically, it comprises Europeans, Africans, Indians, and Asians. The official language is Portuguese. Roman Catholicism is the predominant religion, and Brazil has the largest Roman Catholic population in the world. Brazil has the world's most extreme economic and social inequality with many people, especially in the south and east, living in wealth and comfort while others in the urban favelas (slums) and in the rural northeast experience extreme poverty, deprivation, and violence.

(2005:226). Doctors recommend a caesarian delivery as safe, practical, and causing no "esthetic damage."

Euro-American popular and scientific thinking emphasizes a separation of the mind from the body. Thus, Western medicine has a special category called "mental illness," which treats certain health problems as though they were located only in the mind. In contrast, in the many cultures in which a mind–body distinction does not exist, there is no category of "mental illness" and treatment is more holistic.

Cultures also vary in terms of whether people consider the body to be a bounded physical unit, with healing focused on the body alone, or connected to a wider social context, in which case healing addresses the body within the social sphere. Variations in the definition of a living body versus a dead body are also prominent worldwide. Different organs may be seen as critical. In the United States, a person may be declared dead while the heart is still beating, so long as the brain is judged to be "dead." In many other cultures, people do not accept a brain-based definition of life and death (Ohnuki-Tierney 1994).

Defining and Classifying Health Problems

Emic diversity in labeling health problems presents a challenge for medical anthropologists and health-care specialists. Western labels, which biomedically trained experts accept as true, accurate, and universal, often do not correspond to the labels in other cultures. One set of concepts that medical anthropologists use to sort out the many cross-cultural labels and perceptions is the *disease–illness dichotomy*. In this model, **disease** refers to a biological health problem that is objective and universal, such as a bacterial or viral infection or a broken arm. **Illness** refers to culturally specific perceptions and experiences of a health problem. Medical anthropologists study both disease and illness, and they show how both must be understood within their cultural contexts.

A first step in ethnomedical research is to learn how people label, categorize, and classify health problems. Depending on the culture, the following may be bases for labeling and classifying health problems: cause, *vector* (the means of transmission, such as mosquitoes), affected body part, symptoms, or combinations of these.

Often, knowledgeable elders are the keepers of ethnomedical knowledge, and they pass it down through oral traditions. Among American Indians of the Washington–Oregon region, many popular stories refer to health (Thompson and Sloat 2004). The stories convey messages about how to prevent health problems, avoid bodily harm, relieve afflictions, and deal with old age. For example, here is the story of Boil, a story for young children:

> Boil was getting bigger.
> Her husband told her to bathe.
> She got into the water.
> She disappeared. (2004:5)

THINKING OUTSIDE THE BOX

IN YOUR MICROCULTURE, what are some prevailing perceptions about the body and how are they related to medical treatment?

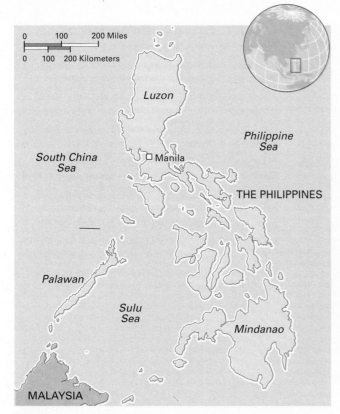

MAP 7.2 The Philippines.

The Republic of the Philippines comprises over 7000 islands, of which around 700 are populated. The population is 85 million, with two-thirds living on Luzon. The economy is based on agriculture, light industry, and a growing business-processing outsourcing (BPO) industry. Over 8 million Filipinos work overseas and remit more than $12 billion a year, a large part of the country's GDP. Although Filipino and English are the official languages, more than 170 languages are spoken. The Philippines has the world's third-largest Christian population, with Roman Catholicism predominant.

Other, longer stories about Boil add complexities about the location of the boil and how to deal with particular boils, revealing indigenous patterns of classification.

A classic study among the Subanun (soo-BAH-nun) people focused on their categories of health problems (Frake 1961). In the 1950s, the Subanun were horticulturalists living in the highlands of Mindanao, in the Philippines (Map 7.2). An egalitarian people, all Subanun, even young children, had substantial knowledge about health problems. Of their 186 labels for health problems, some are a single term, such

---

culture-specific syndrome   a collection of signs and symptoms that is restricted to a particular culture or a limited number of cultures.

somatization   the process through which the body absorbs social stress and manifests symptoms of suffering.

susto   fright/shock disease, a culture-specific illness found in Spain and Portugal and among Latino people wherever they live; symptoms include back pain, fatigue, weakness, and lack of appetite.

- Rash
- Eruption
- Inflammation
  — Eruption
  — Inflamed/Quasi-Bite
  — Ulcerated
- Sore
  — Distal Ulcer
       Shallow
       Deep
  — Proximal Ulcer
       Shallow
       Deep
  — Simple Sore
  — Spreading Sore
- Ringworm
  — Exposed
  — Hidden
  — Spreading Itch
- Wound

Source: Adapted from Frake 1961:118, Figure 1.

FIGURE 7.1   Subanun Categories of *Nuka*, Skin-Related Health Problems.

as "itch," which can be expanded on by using two words, such as "splotchy itch." Skin diseases are common afflictions among the Subanun and have several degrees of specificity (Figure 7.1).

In Western biomedicine, panels of medical experts have to agree about how to label and classify health problems according to scientific criteria. Classifications and descriptions of thousands of afflictions are published in thick manuals that physicians consult before they give a diagnosis. In countries where medical care is privatized, the code selected may determine whether the patient's costs are covered by insurance or not. The *International Classification of Diseases (ICD)*, now in its tenth edition (1993), is a major source for coding health problems according to Western biomedical standards. Even though it contains abundant details on many health problems and is carefully arranged according to a complex coding system, its categories often prove to be inadequate. For example, following the attacks of September 11, 2001, on the United States, medical personnel who had to classify the cause of death of those who perished at the four sites and the health problems of survivors found the *ICD-10* codes of little help.

Further, the *ICD-10* is biased toward diseases that Western biomedicine recognizes and ignores health problems of many other cultures. Anthropologists have discovered many health problems around the world, often referred to as culture-specific syndromes. A **culture-specific syndrome** is a health problem with a set of symptoms associated with a particular

Name of Syndrome	Distribution	Attributed Causes	Description and Symptoms
Anorexia nervosa	Middle- and upper-class Euro-American girls; globalizing	Unknown	Body wasting due to food avoidance; feeling of being too fat; in extreme cases, death
Hikikomori	Japan, males from adolescence through adulthood	Social pressure to succeed in school and pursue a position as a salaryman	Acute social withdrawal; refusal to attend school, or leave their room for months, sometimes years
Koro	China and Southeast Asia, men	Unknown	Belief that the penis has retracted into the body
Peito aberto (open chest)	Northeastern Brazil, especially women, perhaps elsewhere among Latino populations	Excessive worry about others	Enlarges the heart and "bursts" through it causing "openings in the heart"
Retired Husband Syndrome (RHS)	Japan, older women whose husbands are retired	Stress	Ulcers, slurred speech, rashes around the eyes, throat polyps
Sufriendo del agua (suffering from water)	Valley of Mexico, low-income people, especially women	Lack of access to secure and clean water	Anxiety
Susto	Spain, Portugal, Central and South America, Latino immigrants in the U.S. and Canada	Shock or fright	Lethargy, poor appetite, problems sleeping, anxiety

Sources: Chowdhury 1996; Ennis-McMillan 2001; Faiola 2005; Gremillion 1992; Kawanishi 2004; Rehbun 1994; Rubel, O'Nell, and Collado-Ardón 1984.

FIGURE 7.2 Selected Culture-Specific Syndromes.

culture (Figure 7.2). Social factors such as stress, fear, or shock often are the underlying causes of culture-specific syndromes. Biophysical symptoms may be involved, and culture-specific syndromes can be fatal. **Somatization**, or embodiment, refers to the process through which the body absorbs social stress and manifests symptoms of suffering.

For example, **susto**, or "fright/shock disease," is found in Spain and Portugal and among Latino people wherever they live. People afflicted with susto attribute it to events such as losing a loved one or having a terrible accident (Rubel, O'Nell, and Collado-Ardón 1984). In Oaxaca, southern Mexico (see Map 6.3, page 140), a woman said her susto was brought on by an accident in which pottery she had made was broken on its way to market, whereas a man said that his came on after he saw a dangerous snake. Susto symptoms include loss of appetite, lack of motivation, breathing problems, generalized pain, and nightmares. The researchers analyzed many cases of susto in three villages. They found that the people most likely to be afflicted were those who were socially marginal or experiencing a sense of role failure. For example, the woman with the broken pots had also suffered two spontaneous abortions and was worried that she would never have children. In Oaxaca, people with susto have higher mortality rates than other people. Thus, social marginality, or a deep

sense of social failure, can place a person at a higher risk of dying. It is important to look at the deeper causes of susto.

Medical anthropologists first studied culture-specific syndromes in non-Western cultures. This focus created a bias in thinking that they exist only in "other" cultures. Now anthropologists recognize that Western cultures also have culture-specific syndromes. Anorexia nervosa and a related condition, bulimia, are culture-bound syndromes found mainly among White middle-class adolescent girls of the United States, although some cases have been documented among African American girls in the United States and among young males (Fabrega and Miller 1995). Since the 1990s, and perhaps as a result of Western globalization, cases have been documented in Hong Kong and in cities in Japan and India. Anorexia nervosa's cluster of symptoms includes self-perception of fatness, aversion to food, hyperactivity, and, as the condition progresses, continued wasting of the body and often death.

No one has found a clear biological cause for anorexia nervosa, although some researchers claim that it has a genetic basis. Cultural anthropologists say that much evidence suggests a strong role for cultural construction. One logical result of the role of culture is that medical and psychiatric treatments are notably unsuccessful in curing anorexia nervosa (Gremillion 1992). Extreme food deprivation can become addictive and entrapping, and the affliction becomes intertwined with the body's biological functions. Extended fasting makes the body unable to deal with ingested food. Thus, medical treatment may involve intravenous feeding to override the biological block. Sometimes nothing works, and the affliction is fatal.

Pinpointing the cultural causes of anorexia nervosa, however, is difficult. Some experts cite societal pressures on girls that lead to excessive concern with looks, especially body weight. Others feel that anorexia is related to girls' unconscious resistance to controlling parents. For such girls, food intake may be one thing over which they have power.

Ethno-Etiologies

People in all cultures, everywhere, attempt to make sense of health problems and try to understand their cause, or *etiology*. The term **ethno-etiology** refers to a cross-culturally specific causal explanation for health problems and suffering.

Among the urban poor of northeastern Brazil, people consider several causal possibilities when they are sick (Ngokwey 1988). In Feira de Santana, the second-largest city in the state of Bahia in the northeast (see Map 7.1 on page 159), ethno-etiologies can be natural, socioeconomic, psychological, or supernatural. Natural causes include exposure to the environment. For example, people say that humidity and rain cause rheumatism, excessive heat causes dehydration, and some types of winds cause migraines. Other natural explanations for illness take into account the effects of aging, heredity, personality, and gender. Contagion is another natural explanation, as are the effects of certain foods and eating habits. In the psychosocial domain, emotions such as anger and hostility cause certain health problems. In the supernatural domain, spirits and magic can cause health problems. The African–Brazilian religions of the Bahia region encompass many spirits who can inflict illness. They include spirits of the unhappy dead and devil-like spirits. Some spirits cause specific illnesses; others bring general misfortune. In addition, envious people with the evil eye cast spells on people and cause much illness. People also recognize the lack of economic resources, proper sanitation, and health services as structural causes of health problems. In the words of one person, "There are many illnesses because there are many poor" (1988:796).

The people of Feira de Santana also recognize several levels of causality. In the case of stomachache, they might blame a quarrel (*underlying cause*), which prompted the aggrieved party to seek the intervention of a sorcerer (*intermediate cause*), who cast a spell (*immediate cause*), which led to the resulting illness. The multilayered causal understanding opens the way for many possible avenues of treatment.

The multiple understandings of etiology in Bahia contrast with the scientific understandings of causality in Western biomedicine. The most striking difference is the tendency for biomedical etiologies to exclude structural issues and social inequality as causal factors of illness. Medical anthropologists use the term **structural suffering**, or social suffering, to refer to health problems caused by powerful forces such as poverty, war, famine, and forced migration. Such structural factors affect health in many ways, with effects ranging from anxiety and depression to death.

An example of a culture-specific syndrome that clearly implicates structural factors as causal is *sufriendo del agua*, or "suffering from water" (Ennis-McMillan 2001). Research in a poor community in the Valley of Mexico, located in the central part of the country (see Map 6.3 on page 140), reveals that sufriendo del agua is a common health problem, especially among women. The immediate cause is the lack of water for drinking, cooking, and washing. Women, who are responsible for cooking and doing the washing, cannot count on water coming from their taps on a regular basis. This insecurity makes the women feel anxious and constantly in a state of nervous tension. The lack of access to water also means that the people are at higher risk of cholera, skin and eye infections, and other biophysical problems. A deeper structural cause of sufriendo del agua is unequal development. The construction of piped water systems in the Valley of Mexico bypassed low-income communities in favor of servicing wealthier urban neighborhoods and supplying water for irrigation projects and the industrial sector. In Mexico, as a whole, nearly one-third of the population has inadequate access to clean drinking water and to a dependable supply of water for bathing, laundry, and cooking.

Prevention

Many practices, based in either religious or secular beliefs, exist cross-culturally for preventing misfortune, suffering, and illness. Among the Maya of Guatemala (Map 7.3), *awas* is a common childhood illness (Wilson 1995). Children born with awas have lumps under the skin, marks on the skin, or

---

ethno-etiology   a culturally specific causal explanation for health problems and suffering.

structural suffering   human health problems caused by such economic and political factors as war, famine, terrorism, forced migration, and poverty.

community healing   healing that emphasizes the social context as a key component and that is carried out within the public domain.

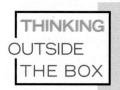

THINKING OUTSIDE THE BOX

Discuss some examples of culture-specific syndromes in your microculture or on your campus.

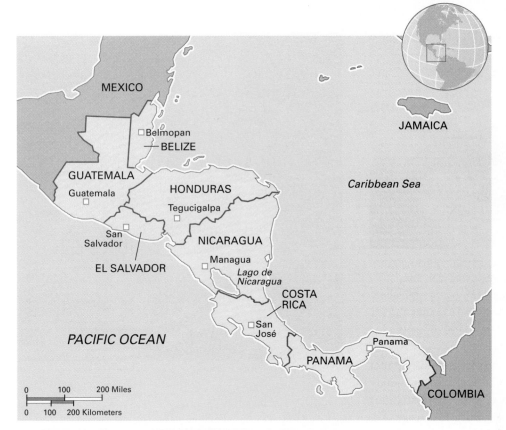

MAP 7.3 Central America.
The countries of Central America share a similar geography as part of a long isthmus with a mountainous spine, active volcanoes, and rich soil. A federation that linked much of the region into the United Provinces of Central America existed from 1824 to 1838. The population of the region, around 40 million people, includes indigenous peoples and people of mixed indigenous and European ancestry. European colonialism has left a strong mark on the region, which is now heavily influenced by the United States and its interests in hemispheric hegemony. Bananas are the leading export crop of the region.

albinism. People say that events that happen to the mother during her pregnancy cause awas: She may have been denied food she desired or have been pressured to eat food she did not want, or she may have encountered a rude, drunk, or angry person (usually a man). Therefore, to prevent awas in babies, the Maya are extremely considerate of pregnant women. A pregnant woman, like land before planting, is sacred. People make sure to give her the food she wants, and they behave with respect in her presence. The ideal is that a pregnant woman should be content.

Examples of ritual health protection worldwide include charms, spells, and sacred strings tied around parts of the body. An anthropologist working in rural northern Thailand (see Map 6.6 on page 151) learned about a health protection practice that involved the display of carved wooden phalluses throughout a village (Mills 1995). In 1990, fear of an attack by a widow ghost spread throughout the area. It was based on several radio reports of unexplained deaths of Thai migrant men working in Singapore. People interpreted the sudden deaths of men as caused by widow ghosts. People believe that widow ghosts roam about, searching for men whom they take as their "husbands" and with whom they have sexual intercourse. Mary Beth Mills was conducting research in Baan Naa Sakae village at the time of the fear. After being away for a few days, she returned to the village to find all 200 households decorated with wooden phalluses in all shapes and sizes:

Ranging from the crudest wooden shafts to carefully carved images complete with coconut shell testicles and fishnet

pubic hair, they adorned virtually every house and residential compound. The phalluses, I was told, were to protect residents, especially boys and men, from the "nightmare deaths" (*lai tai*) at the hands of malevolent "widow ghosts" (*phii mae maai*) (1995:249).

In the study area, spirits (*phii*) are a recognized source of illness, death, and other misfortunes. One variety of phii, a widow ghost is the sexually voracious spirit of a woman who had an untimely and perhaps violent death. When a seemingly healthy man dies in his sleep, the people blame a widow ghost who arrives in the night and has extreme sex with a sleeping man to the extent that he dies. The wooden phalluses were protection against a possible widow ghost attack. The people said the giant penises are decoys: The sex-starved spirits take their pleasure with the wooden penises and, satisfied, leave the men unharmed. As the radio reports ceased, villagers' concerns about the widow ghosts faded and they removed the phalluses.

Healing Ways

The material that follows describes two approaches to healing, one in southern Africa and the other in Malaysia, Southeast Asia. It also discusses healers and healing substances.

COMMUNITY HEALING   A general distinction can be drawn between private healing and **community healing**. The former addresses bodily ailments in social isolation, whereas the latter encompasses the social context as crucial to healing.

Two forms of illness prevention. (LEFT) Throughout northern India, people believe that tying on strings provides protection from malevolent spirits and forces. This Muslim baby has five protective strings. (RIGHT) A carved phallus displayed in a northern Thai village is intended to protect men from widow ghost attacks.

Compared with Western biomedicine, many non-Western systems use community healing. An example of community healing comes from the Ju/'hoansi foragers of the Kalahari desert in southern Africa (review Culturama, Chapter 1, page 21). Ju/'hoansi healing emphasizes the mobilization of community "energy" as a key element in the cure:

> The central event in this tradition is the all-night healing dance. Four times a month on the average, night signals the start of a healing dance. The women sit around the fire, singing and rhythmically clapping. The men, sometimes joined by the women, dance around the singers. As the dance intensifies, *num* or spiritual energy is activated by the healers, both men and women, but mostly among the dancing men. As num is activated in them, they begin to *kia* or experience an enhancement of their consciousness. While experiencing kia, they heal all those at the dance. (Katz 1982:34)

The dance is a community event in which the entire camp participates. The people's belief in the healing power of num brings meaning and efficacy to the dance through *kia*.

Does community healing "work"? In both ethnic and Western terms, the answer is yes. It "works" on several levels. People's solidarity and group sessions may support mental and physical health, acting as a health protection system. When people fall ill, the drama and energy of the all-night dances may act to strengthen the afflicted in ways that Western science would have difficulty measuring. In a small, close-knit group, the dances support members who may be ill or grieving.

---

humoral healing   healing that emphasizes balance among natural elements within the body.

shaman or **shamanka**   a male and female healer, respectively.

A Ju/'hoansi healer in a trance, in the Kalahari desert, southern Africa. Most Ju/'hoansi healers are men, but some are women.

▶ *In your microculture, what are the patterns of gender, ethnicity, and class among various kinds of healers?*

Umbanda is a popular religion in Brazil and, increasingly, world-wide. Its ceremonies are often devoted to healing through spiritual means. In this session, tourists at the back of the room watch as Umbanda followers perform a dance related to a particular deity.

▶ *What is your opinion on the role of spirituality in health and healing, and on what do you base your view?*

An important aspect of the Ju/'hoansi healing system is its openness. Everyone has access to it. The role of healer is also open. There is no special class of healers with special privileges. More than half of all adult men and about 10 percent of adult women are healers.

HUMORAL HEALING **Humoral healing** is based on a philosophy of balance among certain elements within the body and within the person's environment (McElroy and Townsend 1996). In this system, food and drugs have different effects on the body and are classified as either "heating" or "cooling"—the quotation marks indicate that these properties are not the same as thermal measurements. Diseases are the result of bodily imbalances—too much heat or coolness—that must be counteracted through dietary and behavioral changes or medicines that will restore balance.

Humoral healing systems have been practiced for thousands of years in the Middle East, the Mediterranean, and much of Asia. In the New World, indigenous humoral systems exist and sometimes blend with those which Spanish colonialists brought with them. Humoralism has shown substantial resilience in the face of Western biomedicine as a source of healing for many people. Local people also reframe Western biomedicine in classifying biomedical treatments as either heating or cooling.

In Malaysia (see Map 2.2 on page 33), several different humoral traditions coexist, reflecting the region's history of contact with outside cultures. Malaysia has been influenced by trade and contact between its indigenous culture and that of India, China, and the Arab-Islamic world for around 2000 years. Indian, Chinese, and Arabic health systems all define health as the balance of opposing elements within the body, although each has its own variations (Laderman 1988:272). Indigenous belief systems may have been compatible with these imported models because they also were based on concepts of heat and coolness.

Insights into these indigenous systems before outsiders arrived come from accounts about the Orang Asli, indigenous peoples of the interior of the Malaysian peninsula who are relatively unaffected by contact. A conceptual system of hot–cold opposition dominates Orang Asli cosmological, medical, and social theories. The properties and meanings of heat and coolness differ from their counterparts in Islamic, Indian, and Chinese humoralism in several ways. In the Islamic, Indian, and Chinese systems, for example, death is the result of too much coolness. Among the Orang Asli, excessive heat is the primary cause of mortality. In their view, heat emanates from the sun and is associated with excrement, blood, misfortune, disease, and death. Humanity's hot blood makes people mortal, and their consumption of meat speeds the process. Heat causes menstruation, violent emotions, aggression, and drunkenness.

Coolness, in contrast, is vital for health among the Orang Asli. Staying in the forest protects against the harmful effects of the sun. Following this logic, the treatment of illness aims to reduce or remove heat. If someone were to fall ill in a clearing, the entire group would relocate to the coolness of the forest. The forest is also a source of cooling leaves and herbs. Healers are cool and retain their coolness by bathing in cold water and sleeping far from the fire. Extreme cold, however, can be harmful. Dangerous levels of coolness are associated with the time right after birth, because the mother is believed to have lost substantial heat. The new mother should not drink cold water or bathe in cold water. She increases her body heat by tying sashes around her waist that contain warmed leaves or ashes, and she lies near a fire.

HEALERS In an informal sense, everyone is a "healer," because self-diagnosis and treatment are likely the first steps when anyone feels ill. Yet, in all cultures, some people become recognized as having special abilities to diagnose and treat health problems. Cross-cultural evidence indicates some common features of healers (Figure 7.3 on page 166).

In different cultures, specialists include midwives, bone-setters (those who reset broken bones), **shamans** or **shamankas** (male or female healers, respectively, who mediate between humans and the spirit world), herbalists, general practitioners, psychiatrists, nurses, acupuncturists, chiropractors, dentists, and hospice care providers. Some healing roles may have higher status and more power and may receive higher pay than others.

THINKING OUTSIDE THE BOX

What steps do you take to treat yourself when you have a cold or headache? If you take medicine, do you know what materials are in the medicine?

- *Selection:* Certain individuals may show more ability for entry into healing roles. In Western medical schools, selection for entry rests on apparently objective standards, such as pre-entry exams and college grades. Among the indigenous Ainu of northern Japan, healers were men who had a special ability to go into a sort of seizure called *imu* (Ohnuki-Tierney 1980).

- *Training:* The period of training may involve years of observation and practice and may be arduous and even dangerous. In some non-Western traditions, a shaman must make dangerous journeys, through trance or use of drugs, to the spirit world. In Western biomedicine, medical school involves immense amounts of memorization, separation from family and normal social life, and sleep deprivation.

- *Certification:* Healers earn some form of ritual or legal certification, such as a shaman going through a formal initiation ritual that attests to his or her competence.

- *Professional image:* The healer role is demarcated from that of ordinary people through behavior, dress, and other markers, such as the white coat in the West and the Siberian shaman's tambourine for calling the spirits.

- *Expectation of payment:* Compensation in some form, whether in kind or in cash, is expected for formal healers. Payment level may vary, depending on the status of the healer and other factors. In rural northern India, strong preference for sons is reflected in payments to the midwife that are twice as high for the birth of a son as for a daughter. In the United States, medical professionals in different specializations receive markedly different salaries.

FIGURE 7.3 Criteria for Becoming a Healer.

Midwifery is an example of a healing role that is endangered in many parts of the world because birth has become increasingly medicalized and brought into the institutional realm of the hospital rather than the home. In Costa Rica, a government campaign to promote hospital births with a biomedical doctor in attendance achieved a rate of 98 percent of all births taking place in hospitals by the end of the twentieth century (Jenkins 2003). This achievement means that midwives, especially in rural areas, can no longer support themselves, and they are abandoning their profession. The promotion of hospital births has destroyed the positive elements of community-based midwifery and its provision of social support and techniques such as massage for the mother-to-be.

phytotherapy   healing through the use of plants.

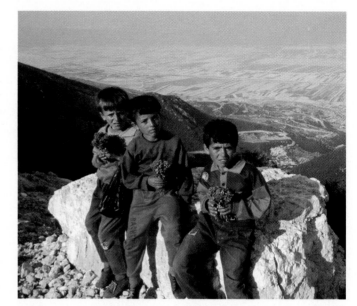

These boys are selling hyssop, a medicinal herb, in Syria. In Unani (Islamic) traditional medicine, hyssop is used to alleviate health problems such as asthma.

▶ *Do research to learn more about hyssop and its medicinal uses.*

HEALING SUBSTANCES   Around the world, thousands of different natural or manufactured substances are used as medicines for preventing or curing health problems. Anthropologists have spent more time studying the use of medicines in non-Western cultures than in the West, although a more fully cross-cultural approach is emerging that also examines the use and meaning of Western pharmaceuticals (Petryna, Lakoff, and Kleinman 2007).

Phytotherapy is healing through the use of plants. Cross-culturally, people know about and use many different plants for a wide range of health problems, including gastrointestinal disorders, skin problems, wounds and sores, pain relief, infertility, fatigue, altitude sickness, and more (see Eye on the Environment). Increasing awareness of the range of potentially useful plants worldwide provides a strong incentive for protecting the world's cultural diversity, because it is people, especially indigenous people, who know about botanical resources (Posey 1990).

Leaves of the coca plant have for centuries been a key part of the health system of the Andean region of South America (Allen 2002). Coca is important in rituals, in masking hunger pains, and in combating the cold. In terms of health, Andean people use coca to treat gastrointestinal problems, sprains, swellings, and colds. The leaf may be chewed or combined with herbs or roots and water to make a *maté (mah–tay)*, a medicinal beverage. Trained herbalists have specialized knowledge about preparing matés. One maté, for example, is for treating asthma. The patient drinks the beverage, made of a ground root and coca leaves, three to four times a day until cured.

Minerals are also widely used for prevention and healing. For example, many people worldwide believe that bathing in

Local Botanical Knowledge and Child Health in the Bolivian Amazon

The Tsimané (see-mah-nay) are a foraging–horticultural society of Bolivia's northeastern Amazon region, numbering about 8000 (McDade et al. 2007). Although most Tsimané make a living from horticulture, complemented by some gathering and hunting, new opportunities for wage work are becoming increasingly available in logging camps or on cattle ranches, or by selling products from the rainforest. At the time of the study described here, in 2002–2003, the Tsimané were not much affected by outside forces and still relied heavily on local resources for their livelihood.

The study focused on mothers' botanical knowledge and the health of their children. The word *botany* refers to knowledge about plants. Household visits and interviews with mothers provided data on mothers' knowledge of plants. Children's health was assessed with three measures: concentrations of C-reactive protein (or CRP, a measure of both immunity and "infectious burden"), skinfold thickness (which measures body fat), and stature, or height (which indicates overall progress in growth and development).

The results of the study showed a strong relationship between mothers' knowledge of plants and the health of their children. Botanical knowledge promotes healthier children through nutritional inputs; that is, more knowledgeable mothers tend to provide healthier plant foods to their children. It also improves children's health by providing herbal ways of treating their illnesses. The overall conclusion is that a mother's knowledge of local plant resources contributes directly to the benefit of her children. In contrast, levels of formal schooling of mothers and household wealth had little, if anything, to do with child health.

Given the positive effects of mothers' botanical knowledge and use of local plants to promote their children's health, it is critical that access to plant resources by indigenous people be protected and sustained and that local botanical knowledge be respected and preserved.

FOOD FOR THOUGHT ▼

What do you know about the effects on your health of particular plants that you eat? When you eat herbs such as oregano or parsley, for example, do you think about their health effects?

MAP 7.4   The Republic of Bolivia.
Situated in the Andes Mountains, Bolivia is the poorest country in South America, although it is rich in natural resources, including the second largest oil field in South America after Venezuela. The population of 10 million includes a majority of indigenous people of nearly 40 different groups. The largest are the Aymara (2 million) and the Quechua-speaking groups (1.5 million). Thirty percent of the population is *mestizo* and 15 percent are of European descent. Two-thirds of the people are low-income farmers. The official religion is Roman Catholicism, but Protestantism is growing. Religious syncretism is prominent. Most people speak Spanish as their first language, although Aymara and Quechua are also common. Bolivia's popular fiesta known as *El carnival de Oruro* is on UNESCO's list of Intangible Cultural Heritage.

water that contains high levels of sulfur or other minerals promotes health and cures ailments such as arthritis and rheumatism. Thousands of people every year go to the Dead Sea, which lies beneath sea level between Israel and Jordan, for treating skin diseases. Bathing in the sulfur springs near the Dead Sea and plastering oneself with mud from the shore provide relief from skin ailments such as psoriasis. Throughout East Asia, including Japan, bathing in mineral waters is popular as a health-promotion practice.

In a more unusual practice, thousands of people worldwide visit "radon spas" every year, seeking the therapeutic effects of low doses of radon gas to alleviate the symptoms of

Guests are undergoing radon treatment at the Kyongsong Sand Spa in Haonpho-ri, North Korea. The spa, and its hot spring, has a 500-year history as a healing center. The treatment shown here is a "sand bath" used for chronic diseases such as arthritis, postoperative problems, and some female problems.

arthritis and other afflictions. In the United States, many radon spas are located in mines in the mountains of Montana (Erickson 2007). At one such spa, the Free Enterprise Mine, the recommended treatment is to go into the mine for one-hour sessions, two or three times daily, for up to a total of about 30 sessions. The mine contains benches and chairs, and clients read, play cards, chat, or take a nap. Some "regulars" come back every year and make plans to meet up with friends from previous visits.

Pharmaceutical medicines are becoming increasingly popular worldwide. Although these medicines have many benefits, some negative effects include over-prescription and frequent use without a prescription. The sale of patent medicines is often unregulated, and self-treating individuals can buy them in a local pharmacy. The popularity and overuse of capsules and injections has led to a growing health crisis related to the emergence of drug-resistant disease strains.

◎ ◎ ◎

Three Theoretical Approaches

The first major theoretical approach to understanding health systems emphasizes the importance of the environment in shaping health problems and how they spread. The second highlights symbols and meaning in people's expression of suffering and healing practices. The third points to the need to look at structural factors as the underlying causes of health problems and examines Western biomedicine as a cultural institution.

The Ecological/Epidemiological Approach

The **ecological/epidemiological approach** examines how aspects of the natural environment interact with culture to cause health problems and to influence their spread throughout the population. According to this approach, research should focus on gathering information about the environmental context and social patterns that affect health, such as food distribution within the family, sexual practices, hygiene, and degree of contact with outsiders. Research methods and data tend to be quantitative and etic, although a growing tendency is to include qualitative and emic data in order to provide a context for understanding the quantitative data (review Chapter 3).

The ecological/epidemiological approach seeks to yield findings relevant to public health programs. It can provide information about groups that are at risk of specific problems. For example, although hookworm is common throughout rural China, epidemiological researchers learned that rice cultivators have the highest rates. The reason is that hookworm spreads through *night soil* (human excrement used as a fertilizer) that is applied to the rice fields in which the cultivators work.

Another significant environmental factor that has important effects on health is urbanization. As archaeologists have documented about the past, settled populations living in dense clusters are more likely than mobile populations to experience a range of health problems, including infectious

---

ecological/epidemiological approach   an approach within medical anthropology that considers how aspects of the natural environment and social environment interact to cause illness.

Agricultural work done in standing water increases the risk of hookworm infection. Hookworm is endemic throughout China.

▶ *Is hookworm a threat where you live? What is the major infectious disease in your home region?*

diseases and malnutrition (Cohen 1989). Such problems are apparent among many recently settled pastoralist groups in East and West Africa. One study compared the health status of two groups of Turkana men in northwest Kenya (see Map 6.4, page 147): those who were mobile pastoralists and those who lived in a town (Barkey, Campbell, and Leslie 2001). The two groups differ strikingly in diet, physical activities, and health. Pastoralist Turkana eat mainly animal foods (milk, meat, and blood), spend much time in rigorous physical activity, and live in large family groups. Settled Turkana men eat mainly maize and beans. Their sedentary (settled) life means less physical activity and exercise. In terms of health, the settled men had more eye infections, chest infections, backache, and cough/colds. Pastoralist Turkana men were not, however, free of health problems. A fourth of the pastoralist men had eye infections, but among the settled men, a half had eye infections. In terms of nutrition, the settled Turkana were shorter and had greater body mass than the taller and slimmer pastoralists.

Cities present many stressors to human health as well as opportunities for improved health through greater access to health care. Typically, cities comprise diverse social categories, varying by class and ethnicity. These groups have different experiences of health risks. In the United States, the incidence of tuberculosis (TB) has increased in recent years, mainly in urban areas (DeFerdinando 1999). Tuberculosis is spread by infected humans, and its rate of spread is increased by crowding, poverty, poor housing, and lack of access to health care. In the United States, rates of tuberculosis are generally higher in southern than in northern states, with the exceptions of New York and Illinois, given their large urban populations. Beginning in the 1990s, outbreaks of *multidrug-resistant tuberculosis* (*MDRTB*), a

new strain of TB that is resistant to conventional drugs, led to its being recognized by public health authorities as a major "new" infectious disease. Even more recently, the new threat of *extra–multidrug-resistant tuberculosis* (*XMDRTB*) has emerged. New forms of the disease mutate more rapidly than scientists are able to develop drugs to combat them.

Anthropologists have applied the ecological/epidemiological approach to the study of the impaired health and survival of indigenous peoples resulting from colonial contact. They show that the effects of colonial contact are devastatingly detrimental, ranging from the quick and outright extermination of indigenous peoples, to resilient adjustment among other groups, to drastically changed conditions.

In the Western Hemisphere, European colonialism brought a dramatic decline in the indigenous populations, although disagreement exists about the numbers involved (Joralemon 1982). Research indicates that the precontact New World was largely free of the major European infectious diseases, such as smallpox, measles, and typhus, and perhaps also of syphilis, leprosy, and malaria. Therefore, the exposure of indigenous peoples to these infectious diseases likely had a massive impact, given those people's complete lack of resistance. One analyst compared colonial contact to a "biological war":

> Smallpox was the captain of the men of death in that war, typhus fever the first lieutenant, and measles the second lieutenant. More terrible than the conquistadores on horseback, more deadly than sword and gunpowder, they made the conquest by the whites a walkover as compared to what it would have been without their aid. (Ashburn 1947:98, quoted in Joralemon 1982:112)

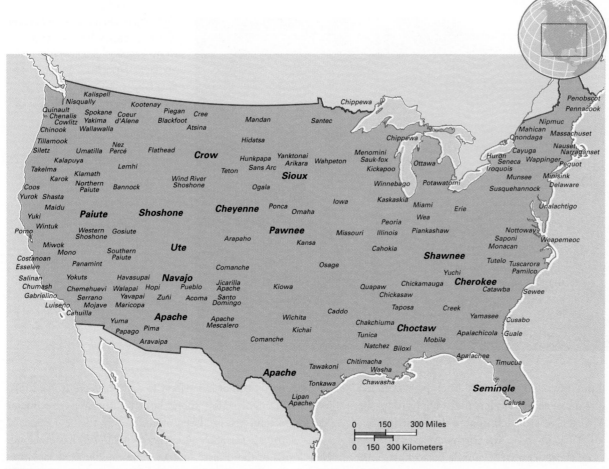

MAP 7.5 Precolonial Distribution of Indian Tribes in the 48 United States.

Before the arrival of European colonialists, Indians were the sole occupants of the area. The first English settlers were impressed by their height and robust physical health.

This quotation emphasizes the importance of the three major diseases in New World colonial history: smallpox, measles, and malaria. A later arrival, cholera, also had severe effects because its transmission through contaminated water and food is enhanced in areas of poor sanitation.

Besides being ravaged by infectious diseases, indigenous populations were decimated by outright killing, enslavement and harsh labor practices, and the psychological damage produced by losing one's livelihood, social ties and support, and access to ancestral burial grounds (Map 7.5 and Map 7.6).

Enduring effects of European colonialism among indigenous peoples worldwide include high rates of depression and suicide, low self-esteem, high rates of child and adolescent drug use, and high rates of alcoholism, obesity, and hypertension. **Historical trauma** refers to the intergenerational transfer of the emotional and psychological effects of colonialism from parents to children (Brave Heart 2004). It is closely associated with substance abuse as a way of attempting to cover the continued pain it induces. Troubled parents create a difficult family situation for children, who tend to replicate their parents' negative coping mechanisms. The concept of historical trauma helps to expand the scope of traditional

epidemiological studies by drawing on factors from the past to explain the social and spatial distribution of contemporary health problems. Such an approach may prove more effective than a biomedical one in devising culturally appropriate ways to alleviate health problems.

The Interpretivist Approach

Some medical anthropologists examine health systems as systems of meaning. They study how people in different cultures label, describe, and experience illness and how healing systems offer meaningful responses to individual and communal distress. Interpretivist anthropologists have examined aspects of healing, such as ritual trance, as symbolic performances. The French anthropologist Claude Lévi-Strauss established this approach in a classic essay called "The Effectiveness of Symbols" (1967). He examined how a song sung by a shaman during childbirth among the Kuna Indians of Panama (see Map 9.4, page 218) helps women through a difficult delivery. The main point is that healing systems provide meaning to people who are experiencing seemingly meaningless forms of suffering. The provision of meaning offers psychological support to

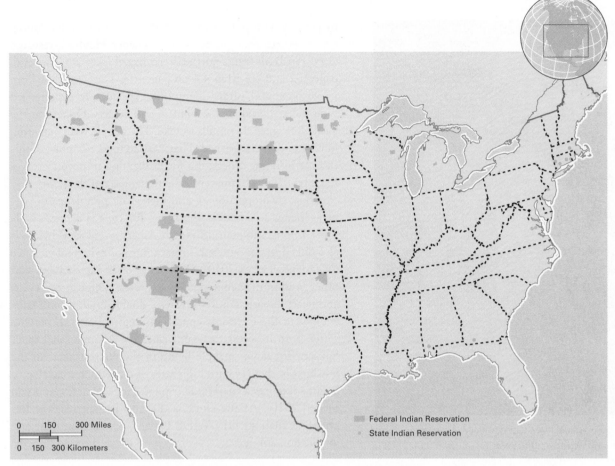

MAP 7.6 Designated Reservations in the 48 United States.
Federal Indian reservations today make up a small percentage of the U.S. landmass. Reservations are allocated to "recognized tribes." Several states recognize no tribes. Many Indians live off of the reservations, often as poorly employed or unemployed urban residents.

the afflicted and may enhance healing through what Western science calls the **placebo effect,** or *meaning effect*, a positive result from a healing method due to a symbolic or otherwise nonmaterial factor (Moerman 2002). In the United States, depending on the health problem, between 10 and 90 percent of the efficacy of medical prescriptions lies in the placebo effect. Several explanatory factors may be involved in the meaning effect: the confidence of the specialist prescribing a treatment; the act of prescription itself; and concrete details about the prescription, such as the color and shape of a pill.

Critical Medical Anthropology

Critical medical anthropology focuses on analyzing how structural factors—such as the global political economy, global media, and social inequality—affect the prevailing health system, including types of afflictions, people's health status, and their access to health care. Critical medical anthropologists show how Western biomedicine itself often serves to bolster the institution of medicine to the detriment of helping the poor and powerless. They point to the process of **medicalization**, or labeling a particular issue or problem as medical and requiring

medical treatment when, in fact, its cause is structural. In this way, people are prescribed pills and injections for poverty, pills and injections for forced displacement from one's home, and pills and injections for being unable to provide for one's family.

SOCIAL INEQUALITY AND POVERTY An important topic to launch this discussion is social inequality and poverty. No matter how you measure these factors, they always have something to say about health. Substantial evidence indicates that poverty is the primary cause of morbidity

---

historical trauma the intergenerational transfer of the detrimental effects of colonialism from parents to children.

placebo effect a positive result from a healing method due to a symbolic or otherwise nonmaterial factor.

critical medical anthropology an approach within medical anthropology involving the analysis of how economic and political structures shape people's health status, their access to health care, and the prevailing medical systems that exist in relation to them.

medicalization the labeling of a particular issue or problem as medical and requiring medical treatment when, in fact, that issue or problem is economic or political.

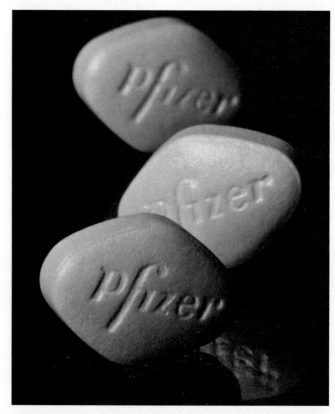

Pharmaceutical companies invest substantially in the design and color of new pills and advertising to promote sales. The tablets of Pfizer's erectile dysfunction drug Viagra are shaped to suggest energy and perkiness, and their arrangement in the photo also conveys activity and motion.

▶ *What about the choice of the color blue?*

(sickness) and mortality (death) in both industrialized and developing countries (Farmer 2005). It may be manifested in different ways—for example, in child malnutrition in Chad or Nepal or through street violence among the urban poor of wealthy countries.

At the broadest level comparing richer countries with poorer countries, distinctions exist between the most common health problems of rich, industrial countries and those of poor, less industrial countries. In the former, major causes of death are circulatory diseases, malignant cancers, HIV/AIDS, excess alcohol consumption, and the smoking of tobacco. In poor countries, tuberculosis, malaria, and HIV/AIDS are the three leading causes of death.

Within the developing world, rates of childhood malnutrition are inversely related to income. In other words, as income increases, so does calorie intake as a percentage of recommended daily allowances (Zaidi 1988). Thus, increasing the income of the poor is the most direct way to improve child nutrition and health. Yet, in contrast to this seemingly logical approach, most health and nutrition programs around the world focus on treating the health results of poverty rather than its causes.

Critical medical anthropologists describe the widespread practice of medicalization, or treating health problems caused by poverty with pills or other medical options, in developing countries. An example is Nancy Scheper-Hughes's research (1992) in Bom Jesus, northeastern Brazil (review Chapter 6, page 132 and see Map 4.4 on page 91). The people of Bom Jesus, poor and often unemployed, frequently experienced symptoms of weakness, insomnia, and anxiety. Doctors at the local clinic gave them pills to take. The people were, however, hungry and malnourished. They needed food, not pills. In this case, as in many others, the medicalization of poverty serves the interests of pharmaceutical companies, not the poor.

The disproportionate and increasing prevalence of diabetes (being used here as shorthand for Type II diabetes mellitus) among the poor, in North America and worldwide, is also linked to poverty and is thus a form of structural violence (Mendenhall et al. 2010). Diabetes is often intertwined with other conditions such as obesity, depression, high stress levels, and heart disease. Poverty creates a double bind: it both contributes to these chronic conditions, and it limits those who suffer from it access to health care. For example, in Dar es Salaam, Tanzania , people living in the poorest areas in the outskirts of the city have high rates of diabetes, but getting to a clinic requires a major bus trip (Kolling, Winkley, and von Deden 2010). At the clinic, a diabetes patient receives less attention than an HIV/AIDS patient, whose treatment and medication are free.

CULTURAL CRITIQUE OF WESTERN BIOMEDICAL TRAINING Since the 1980s, critical medical anthropologists have studied Western biomedicine as a cultural system. Though recognizing many of its benefits, they point to ways in which WBM could be improved—for example, by reducing reliance on technology, broadening an understanding of health problems as they relate to structural conditions and not just biological conditions, and diversifying healing through alternative methods such as massage, acupuncture, and chiropracty.

Some critical medical anthropologists have conducted research on Western medical school training. One study of obstetric training in the United States involved interviews with 12 obstetricians, 10 male and 2 female (Davis-Floyd 1987). As students, they absorbed the technological model of birth as a core value of Western obstetrics. This model treats the body as a machine. The physician uses the assembly-line approach to birth in order to promote efficient production and quality control. One of the residents in the study explained, "We shave 'em, we prep 'em, we hook 'em up to the IV and administer sedation. We deliver the baby, it goes to the nursery and the mother goes to her room. There's no room for niceties around here. We just move 'em right on through. It's not hard to see it like an assembly line" (1987:292). The goal is the "production" of a healthy baby. The doctor is a technical expert in charge of achieving this goal, and the mother takes second place. One obstetrician

Medical students in training in a Western biomedical setting. These students are observing brain surgery.

▶ *What does this scene convey about values and beliefs of Western medicine?*

said, "It is what we all were trained to always go after—the perfect baby. That's what we were trained to produce. The quality of the mother's experience— we rarely thought about that. Everything we did was to get that perfect baby" (1987:292).

This goal involves the use of sophisticated monitoring machines. One obstetrician said, "I'm totally dependent on fetal monitors, 'cause they're great! They free you to do a lot of other things. . . . I couldn't sit over there with a woman in labor with my hand on her belly, and be in here seeing 20 to 30 patients a day" (1987:291). The use of technology also conveys status to the physician. One commented, "Anybody in obstetrics who shows a human interest in patients is not respected. What is respected is interest in machines" (1987:291).

How do medical students learn to accept the technological model? Davis-Floyd's research points to three key processes. One way is through physical *hazing*, a harsh rite of passage involving, in this case, stress caused by sleep deprivation. Hazing extends throughout medical school and the residency period.

Second, medical school training in the United States involves a process of *cognitive retrogression*, in which students relinquish critical thinking and thoughtful ways of learning. During the first two years of medical school, most courses are basic sciences and students must memorize vast quantities of material. The sheer bulk of memorization forces students to adopt an uncritical approach. This mental overload socializes students into a uniform pattern, giving them tunnel vision in which the knowledge of medicine assumes supreme importance. As one obstetrician said,

Medical school is not difficult in terms of what you have to learn—there's just so much of it. You go through, in a six-week course, a thousand-page book. The sheer bulk of information is phenomenal. You have pop quizzes in two or three courses every day the first year. We'd get up around 6, attend classes till 5, go home and eat, then head back to school and be in anatomy lab working with a cadaver, or something, until 1 or 2 in the morning, and then go home and get a couple of hours of sleep and then go out again. And you did that virtually day in and day out for four years, except for vacations. (1987:298–299)

Third, in a process termed *dehumanization*, medical school training works to erase humanitarian ideals through an emphasis on technology and objectification of the patient. One obstetrical student explained, "Most of us went into medical school with pretty humanitarian ideals. I know I did. But the whole process of medical education makes you inhuman . . . by the time you get to residency, you end up not caring about anything beyond the latest techniques you can master and how sophisticated the tests are that you can perform" (1987:299).

◉ ◉ ◉

Globalization and Change

With globalization, health problems move around the world and into remote locations and cultures more rapidly than ever before. The HIV/AIDS epidemic is one tragic example. Other new epidemics include severe acute respiratory syndrome (SARS) and H1N1 flu. At the same time, Western culture, including biomedicine, is on the move. Perhaps no other aspect of Western culture, except for the capitalist market system and the English language, has so permeated the rest of the world as Western biomedicine. But the cultural flow is not one-way: Many people in North America and

Fighting AIDS in South Africa. (LEFT) Activist Noxolo Bunu demonstrates how to use a female condom. It is not clear if they will gain popularity and help reduce sexually transmitted diseases. (RIGHT) Social stigma often adds to the suffering of HIV/AIDS victims. The billboards, near Soweto in South Africa, promote condom use and seek to reduce social rejection and stigma.

Europe are turning to forms of non-Western and nonbiomedical healing, such as acupuncture and massage therapy. This section considers new and emerging health challenges, changes in healing, and examples of how applied medical anthropology has gained increasing relevance.

New Infectious Diseases

In the mid-twentieth century, scientific advances such as antibiotic drugs, vaccines against childhood diseases, and improved technology for sanitation dramatically reduced the threat from infectious disease. The 1980s, however, were the beginning of an era of shaken confidence, with the onset and rapid spread of the HIV/AIDS epidemic.

New contexts for exposure and contagion are created through increased international travel and migration, deforestation, and development projects, among others. Increased travel and migration have contributed to the spread of HIV/AIDS and SARS. Deforestation is related to higher rates of malaria, which is spread by mosquitoes; mosquitoes thrive in pools of water in open, sunlit areas, as opposed to forests. Development projects such as constructing dams and clearing forests often create unintended health problems for local people.

Diseases of Development

A **disease of development** is a health problem caused or increased by economic development projects. For example, the construction of dams and irrigation systems throughout the tropical world has brought dramatically increased rates of *schistosomiasis* (shish-to-suh-my-a-sis), a disease caused by the presence of a parasitic worm in the blood system. Over 200 million people suffer from this debilitating disease, with prevalence rates the highest in sub-Saharan countries in

Africa (Michaud, Gordon, and Reich 2005). The larvae hatch from eggs and mature in slow-moving water such as lakes and rivers. When mature, they can penetrate human (or other animal) skin with which they come into contact. Once inside the human body, the adult schistosomes breed in the veins around the human bladder and bowel. They send fertilized eggs into the environment through urine and feces. These eggs then contaminate water, in which they hatch into larvae.

Anthropological research has documented steep increases in the rates of schistosomiasis at large dam sites in developing countries (Scudder 1973). The increased risk is caused by the dams slowing the rate of water flow. Stagnant water systems offer an ideal environment for development of the larvae. Opponents of the construction of large dams have used this information in support of their position.

Increased obesity in many countries can also be viewed as a disease of development, somewhat ironically. In developed countries around the world, rising rates of childhood obesity have generated concern about the children's health and the toll they will take on public health systems as they age. The so-called "child obesity epidemic" surely has health implications, but its causes are not first and foremost medical and the most effective steps to its prevention are also outside the medical domain (Moffat 2010). In general, prevention has to do with changing the child's diet and activity patterns, and these changes can help reduce weight as well.

Medical Pluralism

Contact between cultures may lead to a situation in which aspects of both cultures coexist: two (or more) different languages, religions, systems of law, or health systems, for example. The term **medical pluralism** refers to the presence of multiple health systems within a society. The coexistence of many forms of healing provides clients a range of choices and

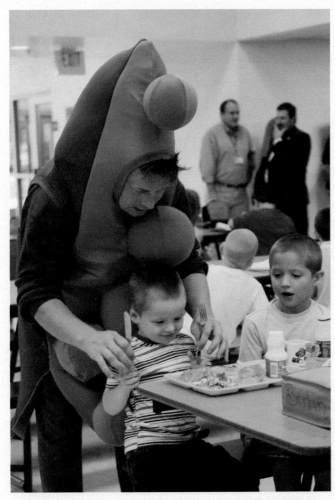

Award-winning English chef Jamie Oliver is also a food activist. He has worked to improve school lunches in England, and in March 2010, he came to Huntington, West Virginia, to do the same. Huntington has been called the least healthy city in the least healthy state of the United States. His efforts to convince the school cook at Central City Elementary School to improve the quality of school meals, however, met with strong resistance from the school cook, the students, and city administrators. The students even rejected his healthy chicken nuggets.

▶ *Is Jamie Oliver just an elitist food snob trying to change West Virginia food culture?*

enhances the quality of health. In other cases, people are confronted by conflicting models of illness and healing, a situation that can result in misunderstandings between healers and clients and in unhappy outcomes.

SELECTIVE PLURALISM: THE CASE OF THE SHERPA The Sherpa of Nepal (see Culturama on page 176) are an unusual example of a culture in which the preference for traditional healing systems remains strong and is combined with the selective use of Western biomedicine (Adams 1988). Healing therapists available in the Upper Khumbu (khoom-boo) region in northeastern Nepal fit into three categories:

- Orthodox Buddhist practitioners, including *lamas*, whom Khumbu people consult for prevention and cure through their blessings, and *amchis*, who practice Tibetan medicine, a humoral healing system.

- Unorthodox religious or shamanic practitioners, who perform divination ceremonies for diagnosis.

- Biomedical practitioners who work in a clinic that was first established to serve tourists. The clinic was established as a permanent medical facility in 1967, and many Sherpa selectively use it.

Thus, three varieties of health care exist in the region. Traditional healers are thriving, unthreatened by changes brought by the tourist trade, the influx of new wealth, and notions of modernity. The question of why Western biomedicine has not completely taken over other healing practices requires a complicated answer. One part of the answer is that high-mountain tourism does not deeply affect local production and social relations. Although it brings in new wealth, it does not require large-scale capital investment from outside as, for example, mega-hotel tourist developments have elsewhere. So far, the Sherpa maintain control of their productive resources, including trekking knowledge and skills.

CONFLICTING EXPLANATORY MODELS In many other contexts, however, anthropologists have documented conflicts and misunderstandings between Western biomedicine and local health systems. Miscommunication often occurs between biomedical doctors and patients in matters seemingly as simple as a prescription that should be taken with every meal. The Western biomedically trained doctor assumes that this means three times a day. But some people do not eat three meals a day and thus unwittingly fail to follow the doctor's instructions.

One anthropological study of a case in which death resulted from cross-cultural differences shows how complex the issue of communication across medical cultures is. The "F family" are immigrants from American Samoa (Map 7.8 on page 177) living in Honolulu, Hawai'i (Krantzler 1987). Neither parent speaks English. Their children are "moderately literate" in English but speak a mixture of English and Samoan at home. Mr. F was trained as a traditional Samoan healer. Mary, a daughter, was first stricken with diabetes at age 16. She was taken to the hospital by ambulance after collapsing, half-conscious, on the sidewalk near her home in a Honolulu

---

disease of development   a health problem caused or increased by economic development activities that have detrimental effects on the environment and people's relationship with it.

medical pluralism   the existence of more than one health system in a culture; also, a government policy to promote the integration of local healing systems into biomedical practice.

CULTURAMA

The Sherpa of Nepal

The word *Sherpa* means "person." About 150,000 Sherpa live in Nepal, mainly in the northeastern region. Several thousand live in Bhutan and Sikkim, and in cities of Europe and North America.

In Nepal, the Sherpa are most closely associated with the Khumbu region. Khumbu is a valley set high in the Himalayas, completely encircled by mountains and with a clear view of Mount Everest (Karan and Mather 1985). The Sherpa have a mixed economy involving animal herding, trade between Tibet and India, small businesses, and farming, with the main crop being potatoes. Since the 1920s and the coming of Western mountaineers, Sherpa men have become increasingly employed as guides and porters for trekkers and climbers. Many Sherpa men and women now run guest houses or work in guest houses as cooks, food servers, and cleaners.

The Sherpa are organized into 18 separate lineages, or *ru* ("bones"), with marriage taking place outside one's birth lineage. Recently, they have begun marrying into other ethnic groups, thus expanding the definition and meaning of what it is to be Sherpa. Because of increased intermarriage, the number of people who can be considered Sherpa to some degree is 130,000. Status distinctions include "big people," "middle people," and "small people," with the middle group being the largest by far (Ortner 1999:65). The main privilege of those in the top level is not to carry loads. Those in the poorest level are landless and work for others.

The Sherpa practice a localized version of Tibetan Buddhism that contains non-Buddhist elements having to do with nature spiritualism that connects all beings. The place name Khumbu, for example, refers to the guardian deity of the region.

Tourism has been, and still is, a major change factor for the Sherpa. In Khumbu, the number of international tourists per year exceeds the Sherpa population.

Global warming is also having significant effects. Glaciers are melting, lakes are rising, and massive flooding is frequent. Some of the swollen lakes are in danger of breaking their banks (United Nations Environment Programme 2002). Many community development projects are aimed at reforestation, planting fruit orchards, and protecting and expanding local knowledge of medicinal herbs.

Thanks to Vincanne Adams, University of California at San Francisco, for reviewing this material.

(LEFT) A Sherpa porter carries a load up a steep mountain path in the Himalayas. Porters earn relatively good wages, especially when they work for international tourists.

(CENTER) Nepali children learn writing in a school supported by the Himalayan Trust, an organization founded by Sir Edmund Hillary in 1961, after he climbed Mount Everest and asked the local people he met how he could help them.

MAP 7.7 Nepal. The Kingdom of Nepal has a population of almost 30 million. Most of its territory is in the Himalayas, and Nepal has 8 of the world's 10 highest mountains.

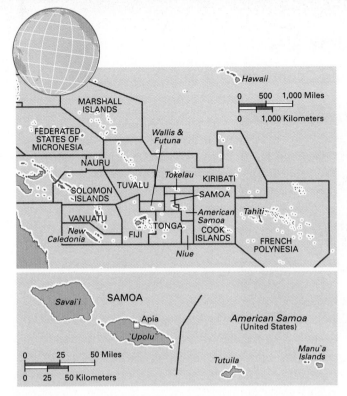

MAP 7.8 Samoa and American Samoa.

Samoa, or the Independent State of Samoa, was known as German Samoa (1900–1919) and Western Samoa (1914–1997) until recognized by the United Nations as a sovereign country. Its population is around 177,000. American Samoa, or Amerika Samoa in Samoan English, is a territory of the United States with a population of about 57,000. During World War II, U.S. Marines in American Samoa outnumbered the local population and had a strong cultural influence. Unemployment rates are now high and the U.S. military is the largest employer.

housing project. After several months of irregular contact with medical staff, she was again brought to the hospital in an ambulance, unconscious, and she died there. Her father was charged with causing Mary's death through medical neglect.

In the biomedical view, her parents failed to give Mary adequate care, even though the hospital staff took pains to instruct her family about how to give insulin injections, and Mary was shown how to test her urine for glucose and acetone and counseled about her diet. She was to be followed up with visits to the outpatient clinic, and, according to the clinic's unofficial policy of linking patients with physicians from their own ethnic group, she was assigned to see the sole Samoan pediatric resident. Over the next few months, Mary was seen once in the clinic by a different resident, missed her next three appointments, came in once without an appointment, and was readmitted to the hospital on the basis of test results from that visit. At that time, she, her parents, and her older sister were once again advised about the importance of compliance with the medical advice they were receiving. Four months later, she returned to the clinic with blindness in one eye and diminished vision in the other. She was diagnosed with cataracts, and the Samoan physician again advised Mary about the seriousness of her illness and the

need for compliance. The medical experts increasingly judged that "cultural differences" were the basic problem and that, in spite of all their attempts to communicate with the F family, they were basically incapable of caring for Mary.

The family's perspective, in contrast, was grounded in *fa'a Samoa*, the Samoan way. Their experiences in the hospital were not positive from the start. When Mr. F arrived at the hospital with Mary the first time, he spoke with several different hospital staff, through a daughter as translator. It was a teaching hospital, so various residents and attending physicians had examined Mary. Mr. F was concerned that there was no single physician caring for Mary, and he was concerned that her care was inconsistent. The family observed a child die while Mary was in the intensive care unit, reinforcing the perception of inadequate care and instilling fear over Mary's chance of surviving in this hospital.

Language differences between Mary's family and the hospital staff added to the problem:

> When they asked what was wrong with her, their perception was that "everyone said 'sugar.'" What this meant was not clear to the family; they were confused about whether she was getting too much sugar or too little. Mary's mother interpreted the explanations to mean she was not getting enough sugar, so she tried to give her more when she was returned home. Over time, confusion gave way to anger, and a basic lack of trust of the hospital and the physicians there developed. The family began to draw on their own resources for explaining and caring for Mary's illness, relying heavily on the father's skills as a healer. (1987:330)

From the Samoan perspective, the F family behaved logically and appropriately. The father, as household head and healer in his own right, felt he had authority. Dr. A, though Samoan, had been resocialized by the Western medical system and alienated from his Samoan background. He did not offer the personal touch that the F family expected. Samoans believe that children above the age of 12 are no longer children and can be expected to behave responsibly, so the family's assigning of Mary's 12-year-old sister to assist with her insulin injections and in recording results made sense to them. Also, the hospital in American Samoa does not require appointments. Cultural misunderstanding was the ultimate cause of Mary's death.

Applied Medical Anthropology

Applied medical anthropology is the application of anthropological knowledge to further the goals of health-care providers. It may involve improving doctor–patient communication in multicultural settings, making recommendations about culturally

---

applied medical anthropology the application of anthropological knowledge to furthering the goals of health-care providers.

ANTHROPOLOGY works

Promoting Vaccination Programs in Developing Countries

Vaccination programs in developing countries, especially as promoted by UNICEF, are introduced with much fanfare. But they are sometimes met with little enthusiasm by the target population. In India, many people are suspicious that vaccination programs are clandestine family planning programs (Nichter 1996). In other instances, fear of foreign vaccines prompts people to reject inoculations. Overall, acceptance rates of vaccination are lower than Western public health planners expected.

To understand why people reject inoculations, medical anthropologists conducted surveys in several countries. The results revealed that many parents have a partial or inaccurate understanding of what the vaccines protect against. Some people did not understand the importance of multiple vaccinations. Public health promoters incorporated findings from the survey in two ways:

- Educational campaigns for the public that addressed its concerns

- Education for the public health specialists about the importance of understanding and paying attention to local cultural practices and beliefs

A young girl in Bangladesh, photographed in 1975, has the raised bumps of smallpox. In 1977, the World Health Organization announced that smallpox had been eradicated in Bangladesh.

▶ *Has smallpox been eradicated worldwide?*

FOOD FOR THOUGHT ▼
If your job was to promote wider acceptance of vaccinations in your home country, what would you want to know before you began an education campaign?

---

appropriate health intervention programs, or providing insights about factors related to disease that medical practitioners do not usually take into account. Applied medical anthropologists draw on ethnomedical knowledge and on any of the three theoretical approaches or a combination of them.

REDUCING LEAD POISONING AMONG MEXICAN AMERICAN CHILDREN

An example of the positive impact of applied medical anthropology is in the work of Robert Trotter on lead poisoning among Mexican American children (1987). The three most common sources of lead poisoning of children in the United States are the following:

- Eating lead-based paint chips
- Living near a smelter where the dust has high lead content
- Eating or drinking from pottery made with an improperly treated lead glaze

The discovery of an unusual case of lead poisoning by health professionals in Los Angeles in the 1980s prompted investigations that produced understanding of a fourth cause: the use by many Mexican Americans of a traditional healing remedy, *azarcón*, which contains lead, to treat a culture-specific syndrome called *empacho*. Empacho is a combination of indigestion and constipation believed to be caused by food sticking to the abdominal wall.

The U.S. Public Health Service asked Trotter to investigate the availability and use of azarcón. He went to Mexico and surveyed the contents of herbal shops. He talked with *curanderos* (traditional healers). His findings convinced the U.S. government to place restrictions on azarcón and a related remedy called *greta*. Trotter also made recommendations about the need to provide a substitute remedy for the treatment of empacho that would not have harmful side effects. He offered ideas about how to advertise the substitute in a culturally effective way. Throughout his involvement, Trotter played several roles—researcher, consultant, and program developer—all of which brought anthropological knowledge to the solution of a public health problem.

---

cultural broker   someone who is familiar with two cultures and can promote communication and understanding across them.

PUBLIC HEALTH COMMUNICATION   Much work in applied medical anthropology involves health communication (Nichter 1996). Anthropologists can help health educators in the development of more meaningful messages through these methods:

- Addressing local health beliefs and health concerns
- Taking seriously all local illness terms and conventions
- Adopting local styles of communication
- Identifying subgroups within the population that may be responsive to different types of messages and incentives
- Monitoring the response of communities to health messages over time and facilitating corrections in communication when needed
- Exposing and removing possible "blaming the victim" in health messages

These principles helped health-care officials understand local responses to public vaccination programs in several countries of Asia and Africa (see Anthropology Works). In this, and so many other ways, an anthropologist can serve as a **cultural broker**, someone who is familiar with two cultures and can promote communication and understanding across them.

WORKING TOGETHER: WESTERN BIOMEDICINE AND NONBIOMEDICAL SYSTEMS   Since 1978, the World Health Organization has endorsed the incorporation of traditional healing practices into national health systems. This policy emerged in response to several factors. First is the increasing appreciation of the value of many non-Western healing traditions. Another is the shortage of trained biomedical personnel. Third is the growing awareness of the deficiencies of Western biomedicine in addressing a person's psychosocial context.

Debates continue about the efficacy of many traditional medical practices compared with biomedicine. For instance, opponents of the promotion of traditional medicine claim that it has no effect on such infectious diseases as cholera, malaria, tuberculosis, schistosomiasis, leprosy, and others. They insist that it makes no sense to allow for or encourage ritual practices against cholera, for example, when a child has not been inoculated against it. Supporters of traditional medicine as one component of a pluralistic health system point out that biomedicine neglects a person's mind, soul, and social setting. Traditional healing practices fill that gap.

What is ethnomedicine?

Ethnomedicine is the study of the health systems of specific cultures. Health systems include categories and perceptions of illness and approaches to prevention and healing. Research in ethnomedicine shows how perceptions of the body differ cross-culturally and reveals both differences and similarities across health systems in perceptions of illness and symptoms. Culture-specific syndromes are found in all cultures, not just non-Western societies, and many are now becoming global.

Ethnomedical studies of healing, healing substances, and healers reveal a wide range of approaches. Community healing is more characteristic of small-scale nonindustrial societies. Community healing emphasizes group interaction and treating the individual within the social context. Humoral healing seeks to maintain balance in bodily fluids and substances through diet, activity, and behavior. In industrial/informatic societies, biomedicine emphasizes the body as a discrete unit, and treatment addresses the individual body or mind and frames out the wider social context. Biomedicine is increasingly reliant on technology and is increasingly specialized.

What are three major theoretical approaches in medical anthropology?

Ecological/epidemiological medical anthropology emphasizes links between the environment and health. It reveals how certain categories of people are at risk of contracting particular diseases within various contexts in historical times and the present.

The interpretivist approach focuses on studying illness and healing as a set of symbols and meanings. Cross-culturally, definitions of health problems and healing systems for these problems are embedded in meaning.

Critical medical anthropologists focus on health problems and healing within a structurist framework. They ask what power relations are involved and who benefits from particular forms of healing. They analyze the role of inequality and poverty in health problems. Some critical medical anthropologists have critiqued Western biomedicine as being a system of social control.

How are health, illness, and healing changing during globalization?

Health systems everywhere are facing accelerated change in the face of globalization, which includes the spread of Western capitalism as well as new diseases and new medical technologies. The "new infectious diseases" are a challenge to health-care systems in terms of prevention and treatment. Diseases of development are health problems caused by development projects that change physical and social environments, such as dams and mines, and by the changing diets and activity patterns of people who live in developed settings which can lead to chronic conditions such as diabetes and obesity.

The spread of Western biomedicine to many non-Western contexts is a major direction of change. As a consequence, medical pluralism exists in all countries. The availability of Western patent medicines has had substantial positive effects, but widespread overuse and self-medication can result in negative health consequences for individuals and the emergence of drug-resistant disease strains.

Applied medical anthropologists play several roles in improving health systems. They may inform medical care providers of more appropriate forms of treatment, guide local people about their increasingly complex medical choices, help prevent health problems by changing detrimental practices, or improve public health communication by making it more culturally informed and effective.

KEY CONCEPTS

SUGGESTED READINGS

Eric J. Bailey. *Medical Anthropology and African American Health*. New York: Greenwood Publishing Group, 2000. This book explores the relationship between cultural anthropology and African American health-care issues. One chapter discusses how to do applied research in medical anthropology.

Bernhard M. Bierlich. *The Problem of Money: African Agency and Western Biomedicine in Northern Ghana*. New York: Bergahn Books, 2008. Fieldwork among the Dagomba people provides the basis for this description of ambivalent attitudes toward Western biomedicine and other aspects of modernity.

Nancy N. Chen. *Breathing Spaces: Qigong, Psychiatry, and Healing in China*. New York: Columbia University Press, 2003. This ethnography explores *qigong* (chee-gung), a charismatic form of healing popular in China that involves meditative breathing exercises.

Paul Farmer. *Pathologies of Power: Health, Human Rights, and the New War on the Poor*. Berkeley: University of California Press, 2005. Farmer blends interpretive medical anthropology with critical medical anthropology in his study of how poverty kills through diseases such as tuberculosis and HIV/AIDS.

Bonnie Glass-Coffin. *The Gift of Life: Female Spirituality and Healing in Northern Peru*. Albuquerque: University of New Mexico Press, 1998. The author examines women traditional healers in northern Peru. She provides a descriptive account of their practices and an account of how two healers worked to cure her of a spiritual illness.

Richard Katz, Megan Biesele, and Verna St. Davis. *Healing Makes Our Hearts Happy: Spirituality and Cultural Transformation among the Kalahari Ju/'hoansi*. Rochester, VT: Inner Traditions, 1997. This book presents the story of how traditional healing dances help the Ju/'hoansi cope with recent and contemporary social upheaval.

Carol Shepherd McClain, ed. *Women as Healers: A Cross-Cultural Perspective*. New Brunswick, NJ: Rutgers University Press, 1989. Case studies discuss women healers in Ecuador, Sri Lanka, Mexico, Jamaica, the United States, Serbia, Korea, Southern Africa, and Benin.

David McKnight. *From Hunting to Drinking: The Devastating Effects of Alcohol on an Australian Aboriginal Community*. New York: Routledge, 2002. McKnight documents the history of drinking in Australia, causes of excessive alcohol consumption, and vested interests of authorities in the sale of alcohol to Aboriginal people.

Ethan Nebelkopf and Mary Phillips, eds. *Healing and Mental Health for Native Americans: Speaking in Red*. New York. AltaMira Press, 2004. Chapters address mental health and substance abuse among Native North Americans and provide cases of healing that involve Native American culture.

Merrill Singer. *Something Dangerous: Emergent and Changing Illicit Drug Use and Community Health*. Long Grove, IL: Waveland Press, 2005. This ethnography combines theory with research and applied anthropology about drug use and public health responses in the United States.

Paul Stoller. *Stranger in the Village of the Sick: A Memoir of Cancer, Sorcery, and Healing*. Boston: Beacon Press, 2004. After being diagnosed with lymphoma, the author enters the "village of the sick" as he goes through diagnostic testing, chemotherapy, and eventual remission. He describes being a cancer patient in the United States and how he found strength through his earlier association with a West African healer.

Johan Wedel. *Santería Healing*. Gainesville: University of Florida Press, 2004. This book discusses Santería healing in Cuba. The author conducted interviews with priests and others knowledgeable about Santería and observed many Santería consultations.

PEARSON

myanthrolab

For further information about topics covered in this chapter, go to MyAnthroLab at **www.myanthrolab.com** and access the following readings in MyAnthroLibrary:

Linda M. Hunt and Isabel Montemayor. 2010. Health Care Needs in Crisis: An Exploratory Study of Latinos in the Midwest. *Practicing Anthropology* 32:9–14. The authors draw on what they learned from focus groups and interviews carried out in a mid-sized city in the midwestern region of the United States. They offer recommendations to help Latinos and other marginalized groups gain access to health services.

Vinay Ramnath Kamat and Daniel J. Nyato. 2010. Soft Targets or Partners in Health? Retail Pharmacies and their Role in Tanzania's Malaria Control Program. *Social Science and Medicine* 71: 626–633. What happens when a new treatment for malaria is supposed to be adopted in a developing country? Research with owners and managers of retail pharmacies and informal drug shops in Dar es Salaam provides an answer.

Brian McKenna. 2010. Take Back Medical Education: The "Primary Care" Shuffle. *Medical Anthropology* 29:6–14. This editorial reports on an ethnographic study of a $6 million dollar project at Michigan State University and three surrounding communities to make medical education more community-oriented. Did it work?

the **BIG** questions

- How do cultures create kinship?

- What are cross-cultural patterns of households and domestic life?

- How are kinship and households changing?

KINSHIP AND DOMESTIC LIFE

◀ A Minangkabau bride in Sumatra, Indonesia, wears an elaborate gold headdress. The Minangkabau are the largest matrilineal culture in the world.

OUTLINE

How Cultures Create Kinship

Everyday Anthropology: What's in a Name?

Culturama: The Minangkabau of Indonesia

Households and Domestic Life

Anthropology Works: Preventing Wife Abuse in Rural Kentucky

Changing Kinship and Household Dynamics

Learning how another culture's kinship system works is as challenging as learning another language. Robin Fox became aware of this challenge during his research among the Tory Islanders of Ireland (Map 8.1) (1995 [1978]). Some Tory Island kinship terms are similar to American English terms; for example, the word *muintir* means "people" in its widest sense, as in English. It can also refer to people of a particular social category, as in "my people," and to close relatives. Another similarity is in *gaolta*, the word for "relatives" or "those of my blood." Its adjectival form refers to kindness, like the English word *kin*, which is related to "kindness." Tory Islanders have a phrase meaning "children and grandchildren," also like the English term *descendants*. One major difference is that the Tory Island word for "friend" is the same as the word for "kin." This usage reflects the cultural context of Tory Island with its small population, all related through kinship. So, logically, a friend is also kin.

All cultures have ways of defining *kinship*, or a sense of being related to another person or persons. Cultures also provide guidelines about who are kin and the expected behavior of kin. Starting in infancy, people learn about their particular culture's **kinship system**, the predominant form of kin relationships in a culture and the kinds of behavior involved. Like language, one's kinship system is so ingrained that it is taken for granted as something natural rather than cultural.

This chapter first considers cultural variations in three features of kinship systems. It then focuses on a key unit of domestic life: the household. The last section provides examples of contemporary change in kinship and household organization.

⊚ ⊚ ⊚

How Cultures Create Kinship

In all cultures, kinship is linked with modes of livelihood and reproduction (Figure 8.1). Nineteenth-century anthropologists found that kinship was the most important organizing principle in nonindustrial, nonstate cultures. The kinship group performs the functions of ensuring the continuity of the group by arranging marriages; maintaining social order by setting moral rules and punishing offenders; and providing for the basic needs of members by regulating production, consumption, and distribution. In large-scale industrial/informatic societies, kinship ties exist, but many other kinds of social ties draw people together as well.

Nineteenth-century anthropologists also discovered that definitions of who counts as kin in the cultures they studied differed widely from those of Europe and the United States. Western cultures emphasize as primary "blood" relations, or relations through birth from a biological mother and biological father (Sault 1994). "Blood" is not a universal basis for

---

kinship system   the predominant form of kin relationships in a culture and the kinds of behavior involved.

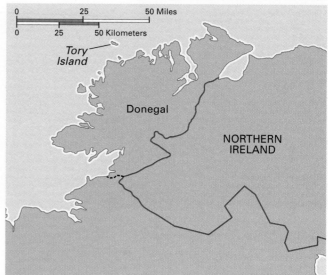

MAP 8.1   Ireland.

Ireland's population is about 4 million. The geography is low central plains surrounded by a ring of mountains. Membership in the European Union (EU) and the rising standard of living earned Ireland the nickname of the Celtic Tiger. Its economic opportunities attracted immigrants from places as diverse as Romania, China, and Nigeria. Most people are Roman Catholics, followed by the Anglican Church of Ireland.

kinship, however. Even in some cultures with a "blood"-based understanding of kinship, variations exist in defining who is a "blood" relative and who is not. For example, in some cultures, male offspring are considered of one "blood," whereas female offspring are not.

Among the Inuit of northern Alaska, behavior is a nonblood basis for determining kinship (Bodenhorn 2000). In this context, people who act like kin are kin. If a person stops acting like kin, then he or she is no longer a kinsperson. So, among the Inuit, someone might say that a certain person "used to be" his or her cousin.

Foraging	Horticulture	Pastoralism	Agriculture	Industrialism/Informatics
Descent and Inheritance				**Descent and Inheritance**
Bilineal		Unilineal (matrilineal or patrilineal)		Bilineal
Marital Residence				**Marital Residence**
Neolocal or bilocal		Matrilocal or patrilocal		Neolocal
Household Type				**Household Type**
Nuclear		Extended		Nuclear or single-parent or single-person

FIGURE 8.1 Modes of Livelihood, Kinship, and Household Structure.

Studying Kinship: From Formal Analysis to Kinship in Action

Anthropologists in the first half of the twentieth century focused on finding out who, in a particular culture, is related to whom and in what way. Typically, the anthropologist would conduct an interview with a few people, asking questions such as "What do you call your brother's daughter?" "Can you (as a man) marry your father's brother's daughter?" and "What is the term you use to refer to your mother's sister?" The anthropologist would ask an individual to name all of his or her relatives, explain how they are related to the interviewee, and provide the terms by which he or she refers to them.

From this information, the anthropologist would construct a *kinship diagram*, a schematic way of presenting the kinship relationships of an individual, called *ego*, using a set of symbols to depict all the kin relations of ego (Figure 8.2). A kinship diagram depicts ego's relatives, as remembered by ego. In cultures in which kinship plays a major role in social relations, ego may be able to provide information on dozens of relatives. When I took a research methods course as an undergraduate, one assignment was to interview someone who was not an American and construct a kinship chart based on the information collected. I interviewed a student from an urban, middle-class business family in India. He recalled over 60 relatives on both his father's and mother's sides. My kinship diagram of his relatives required several sheets of paper taped together.

In contrast to a kinship diagram, a *genealogy* is a schematic way of presenting a family tree, constructed by beginning with the earliest ancestors that can be traced, then working down to the present. A genealogy, thus, does not begin with ego. When Robin Fox attempted to construct kinship diagrams beginning with ego, the Tory Islanders were uncomfortable with the approach. They preferred to proceed genealogically, so he followed their preference. Tracing a family's complete genealogy may involve archival research in the attempt to construct as complete a history as possible. In Europe and the United States, Christians have long followed

Characters	Relationships	Kin Abbreviations
⬤ female	= is married to	**Mo** mother
△ male	≈ is cohabiting with	**Fa** father
⌀ deceased female	≁ is divorced from	**Br** brother
⧖ deceased male	≉ is separated from	**Z** sister
● female "ego" of the diagram	⊙ adopted-in female	**H** husband
▲ male "ego" of the diagram	◬ adopted-in male	**W** wife
	│ is descended from	**Da** daughter
	⊓ is the sibling of	**S** son
		Co cousin

FIGURE 8.2 Symbols Used in Kinship Diagrams.

Eskimo Kinship Terms	Iroquois Kinship Terms

Eskimo kinship terms:
Uncle — Aunt — Mo — Fa — Uncle — Aunt
Co Co — Co Co — Z — Br — Co Co — Co Co

Iroquois kinship terms:
MoBr — Mo — Mo — Fa — Fa — FaZ
Co Co — Z Br — Z — Br — Z Br — Co Co

Eskimo kinship terminology, like that of most Euro-Americans, has unique terms for kin within the nuclear household that are not used for any other relatives: mother, father, sister, brother. This fact is related to the importance of the nuclear household. Another feature is that the same terms are used for relatives on both the mother's side and the father's side, a property that is related to bilineal descent.

Iroquois kinship terminology operates in unilineal systems. One result is that there are different terms for relatives on the mother's and father's sides and distinctions between cross and parallel cousins. Another feature is the "merging" of one's mother with one's mother's sister (both are referred to as "mother") and of one's father with one's father's brother (both are referred to as "father").

FIGURE 8.3 Two Kinship Naming Systems.

a practice of recording their genealogy in the front of the family Bible. Many African Americans and other people are consulting DNA analysts to learn about their ancestry and cultural heritage.

Decades of anthropological research have produced a mass of information on *kinship terminology*, or the words people use to refer to kin. For example, in Euro-American kinship, a child of one's father's sister or brother or one's mother's sister or brother is referred to by the kinship term "cousin." Likewise, one's father's sister and one's mother's sister are both referred to as "aunt," and one's father's brother and one's mother's brother are both referred to as "uncle." "Grandmother" and "grandfather" refer to the ascending generation on either one's father's or one's mother's side. This merging pattern is not universal. In some cultures, different terms apply to kin on one's mother's and father's sides, so a mother's sister has a kinship term different from that referring to a father's sister. Another type of kinship system emphasizes solidarity along lines of siblings of the same gender. For example, among the Navajo of the American southwest, one's mother

and one's mother's sisters have the same term, which translates into English as "mother."

Early anthropologists classified the cross-cultural variety in kinship terminology into six basic types, named after groups first discovered to have those systems. Two of the six types, for purposes of illustration, are the Iroquois type and the Eskimo type (Figure 8.3). Anthropologists place various cultures with similar kinship terminology, no matter where they lived, into one of the six categories. Thus, the Yanomami people of the Amazon are classified as having an Iroquois naming system. Contemporary anthropologists who study kinship have moved beyond these categories because they feel that the six kinship types do not shed light on actual kinship dynamics. This book, therefore, presents only the two examples and avoids going into detail on the six classic types.

Current interest in the study of kinship shows how it is related to other topics, such as globalization, ethnic identity, and even terrorism. Anthropologists have come a long way, from classifying kinship to showing how it matters. They focus on three key factors that, cross-culturally, construct kinship relations: descent, sharing, and marriage.

Descent

Descent is the tracing of kinship relationships through parentage. It is based on the fact that everybody is born from someone else. Descent creates a line of people from whom someone is descended, stretching through history. But not all cultures reckon descent in the same way. Some cultures have a **bilineal descent** system, in which a child is recognized as being related by descent to both parents. Others have a **unilineal descent** system, which recognizes descent through only one parent, either the father or the mother. The distribution of bilineal and unilineal systems is roughly correlated

descent   the tracing of kinship relationships through parentage.

bilineal descent   the tracing of descent through both parents.

unilineal descent   the tracing of descent through only one parent.

patrilineal descent   a descent system that highlights the importance of men in tracing descent, determining marital residence with or near the groom's family, and providing for inheritance of property through the male line.

matrilineal descent   a descent system that highlights the importance of women by tracing descent through the female line, favoring marital residence with or near the bride's family, and providing for property to be inherited through the female line.

In Yemen, descent is strongly patrilineal. (LEFT) Some members of a Bedu household in Yemen. The Bedu are a small proportion of the Yemeni population. (RIGHT) Boys playing in Hababa, Yemen. In this patrilineal culture, public space is segregated by gender.

with different modes of livelihood (see Figure 8.1, page 185). This correspondence makes sense because economic systems—production, consumption, and exchange—are closely tied to the way people are socially organized.

UNILINEAL DESCENT   Unilineal descent is the basis of kinship in about 60 percent of the world's cultures, making it the most common form of descent. This system tends to be found in societies with a fixed resource base. Thus, unilineal descent is most common among pastoralists, horticulturalists, and farmers. Inheritance rules that regulate the transmission of property through only one line help maintain cohesiveness of the resource base.

Unilineal descent has two major forms. One is **patrilineal descent**, in which kinship is traced through the male line. The other is **matrilineal descent**, in which kinship is traced through the female line. In a patrilineal system, only male children are considered members of the kinship lineage. Female children "marry out" and become members of the husband's lineage. In matrilineal descent systems, only daughters are considered to carry on the family line and sons "marry out."

Patrilineal descent is found among about 45 percent of all cultures. It occurs throughout much of South Asia, East Asia, the Middle East, New Guinea, northern Africa, and among some horticultural groups of sub-Saharan Africa. The world's most strongly patrilineal systems are found in East Asia, South Asia, and the Middle East (see Everyday Anthropology on page 188).

Matrilineal descent exists in about 15 percent of all cultures. It traces kinship through the female line exclusively, and the lineage consists of mothers and daughters and their daughters. Matrilineal descent is found among many Native North American groups; across a large band of central Africa; among many groups of Southeast Asia and the Pacific, and

Australia; in parts of eastern and southern India; in a small pocket of northern Bangladesh; and in parts of the Mediterranean coast of Spain and Portugal. Matrilineal societies are found among foragers and in agricultural societies. Most matrilineal cultures, however, are horticulturalist economies in which women dominate the production and distribution of food and other goods. Often, but not always, matrilineal kinship is associated with recognized public leadership positions for women, as among the Iroquois and Hopi. The Minangkabau (*muhnan-ka-bow*, with the last syllable rhyming with "now") of Indonesia are the largest matrilineal group in the world (see Culturama on page 190).

BILINEAL DESCENT   Bilineal descent traces kinship from both parents equally to the child. Bilineal descent is found in about one-third of the world's cultures (Murdock 1965 [1949]:57). The highest frequency of bilineal descent is found at opposite ends of the modes-of-livelihood diagram. For example, Ju/'hoansi foragers have bilineal descent, as do most urban professionals in North America. Both foraging and industrialism/informatics cultures rely on a flexible gender division of labor in which both males and females contribute, more or less equally, to making a living. Bilineal descent makes sense for foraging and industrial/informatic groups because it allows for small family units and spatial mobility.

Marital residence tends to follow the prevailing direction of descent rules. *Patrilocality*, or marital residence with or near the husband's family, occurs in patrilineal societies, whereas *matrilocality*, or marital residence with or near the wife's family, occurs in matrilineal societies. *Neolocality*, or marital residence in a place different from either the bride's or groom's family, is common in Western industrialized society. Residence patterns have political, economic, and social implications. Patrilineal descent and patrilocal residence,

everyday ANTHROPOLOGY

What's in a Name?

Naming children is always significant. Parents may follow cultural rules that a first-born son receives the name of his father's father or a first-born daughter receives the name of her mother's mother. Some parents believe that a newborn should not be formally named for a year or two, and the child is instead referred to by a nickname. Others think that a name must convey some special hoped-for attribute for the child or that a name should be unique.

The village of Ha Tsuen is located in the northwest corner of a rural area of Hong Kong (Watson 1986). About 2500 people live in the village. All the males belong to the same patrilineage and all have the same surname of Teng. They are descended from a common male ancestor who settled in the region in the twelfth century. Daughters marry into families outside the village, and marital residence is patrilocal.

Women do not own property, and they have no control over the household economy. Few married women are employed in wage labor. They depend on their husbands for financial support.

Local politics is male dominated, as is all public decision making. A woman's status as a new bride is low, and the transition from daughter to bride can be difficult psychologically. Women's primary role is in reproduction, especially of sons. As a woman bears children, especially sons, her status in the household rises.

The local naming system reflects the power, importance, and autonomy of males. All children are first given a name, referred to as their *ming*, when they are a few days old. If the baby is a boy, the 30-day ceremony is as elaborate as the family can afford. It may include a banquet for many neighbors and the village elders and the presentation of red eggs to everyone in the community. For a girl, the 30-day ceremony may involve only a special meal for close family members. Paralleling this expenditure bias toward sons is the thinking that goes into selecting the *ming*. A boy's ming is distinctive and flattering. It may have a classical literary connection. A girl's ming often has negative connotations, such as "Last Child,"

"Too Many," or "Little Mistake." One common ming for a daughter is "Joined to a Brother," which implies the hope that she will be a lucky charm, bringing the birth of a son to her mother next. Sometimes, though, people give an uncomplimentary name to a boy, such as "Little Slave Girl." The reason behind this naming practice is protection—to trick the spirits into thinking the baby is only a worthless girl so that the spirits will do no harm.

Marriage is the next formal naming occasion. When a male marries, he is given or chooses for himself a *tzu*, or marriage name. Gaining a tzu is a key marker of male adulthood. The tzu is not used in everyday address, but appears mainly on formal documents. A man also has a *wai hao*, "outside name," which is his public nickname. As he enters middle age, he may take a *hao*, or courtesy name, which he chooses and which reflects his aspirations and self-perceptions.

In the case of a woman, her ming ceases to exist when she marries. She

for example, facilitate the formation of strongly bonded groups of men who can be mobilized for warfare.

Sharing

Many cultures emphasize kinship ties based on acts of sharing and support. These relationships may be either informal or ritually formalized. Godparenthood and blood brotherhood are examples of sharing-based kinship ties that are ritually formalized.

KINSHIP THROUGH FOOD SHARING Sharing-based kinship is common in mainland Southeast Asia, Australia, and Pacific island cultures (Carsten 1995). Among inhabitants of one of Malaysia's many small islands, sharing-based kinship starts in the womb when the mother's blood feeds the fetus. After birth, the mother's breast milk nourishes the infant. This tie is crucial. A child who is not breastfed will not "recognize" its mother. Breastfeeding is also the basis of the incest rule. People who have been fed from the same breast are kin and may not marry. After the baby is weaned, its

most important food is cooked rice. Sharing cooked rice, like breast milk, becomes another way that kinship ties are created and maintained, especially between women and children. Men are often away on fishing trips, in coffee shops, or at the mosque and so are not likely to have rice-sharing kinship bonds with children.

ADOPTION AND FOSTERING Another form of sharing-based kinship is the transfer of a child or children from the birth parent(s) to the care of someone else. *Adoption* is a formal and permanent form of child transfer. Common motivations for adoption include infertility and the desire to obtain a particular kind of child (often a son). Motivations for the birth parent to transfer a child to someone else include a premarital pregnancy in a disapproving context, having "too many" children, and having "too many" of a particular gender. Among the Maasai pastoralists of East Africa, a woman with several children might give one to a friend, neighbor, or aged person who has no child to care for her or him.

MAP 8.2 Hong Kong.
The formal name of Hong Kong is the Hong Kong Special Administrative Region of the People's Republic of China. A world center of finance and trade, it lacks natural resources and agricultural land, so it imports most of its food and raw materials. With 7 million residents, Hong Kong's population density is high. Most of the population is ethnic Chinese, and many practice ancestor worship. Ten percent of the population is Christian. Religious freedom is protected through Hong Kong's constitution.

no longer has a name. Instead, her husband refers to her as *nei jen*, "inner person," because now her life is restricted to the domestic world of the household, her husband's family, and the neighborhood. People may also refer to her by *teknonyms*, or names for someone based on their relationship to someone else, such as "Wife of So and So" or "Mother of So and So." In old age, she becomes *ah po*, "Old Woman."

Throughout their lives, men accumulate more and better names than women. They choose many of the names themselves. Over the courses of their lives, women have fewer names than men have. Women's names are standardized, not personalized, and women never get to choose any of their names.

FOOD FOR THOUGHT ▼
Do Internet research on baby naming practices. Do you like your first name? If you would prefer a different first name, what would it be and why?

Since the mid-1800s, adoption has been a legalized form of child transfer in the United States. Judith Modell, cultural anthropologist and adoptive parent, studied people's experiences of adoptees, birth parents, and adoptive parents in the United States (1994). She found that the legal process of adoption constructs the adoptive relationship to be as much like a biological one as possible. In *closed adoption*, the adopted child receives a new birth certificate and the birth parent ceases to have any relationship to the child. A recent trend is toward *open adoption*, in which adoptees and birth parents have information about each other's identity and are free to interact with one another. Of the 28 adoptees Modell interviewed, most were interested in searching for their birth parents. The search for birth parents involves an attempt to discover "who I really am." For others, such a search is backward looking instead of being a path toward identity formation. Thus, in the United States, adoption legalizes sharing-based kinship but does not always replace a sense of descent-based kinship for everyone involved.

Fostering a child is sometimes similar to a formal adoption in terms of permanence and a sense of kinship. Or it may be temporary placement of a child with someone else for a specific purpose, with little or no sense of kinship. Child fostering is common throughout sub-Saharan Africa. Parents foster out children to enhance the child's chances for formal education or so that the child will learn a skill, such as marketing. Most foster children go from rural to urban areas and from poorer to better-off households. Fieldwork conducted in a neighborhood in Accra, Ghana (Map 8.4 on page 191), sheds light on the lives of foster children (Sanjek 1990). Child fostering in the neighborhood is common: About one-fourth of the children were foster children. Twice as many of the foster children were girls as boys. School attendance is biased toward boys. All of the boys were attending school, but only 4 of the 31 girls were. An important factor affecting the treatment of the child is whether the fostered child is related to his or her sponsor. Although 80 percent of the foster children as a whole were kin of their sponsors, only 50 percent of the girls

CULTURAMA

The Minangkabau of Indonesia

The Minangkabau are the world's largest matrilineal culture, numbering between 4 and 5 million (Sanday 2002). Most live in West Sumatra, Indonesia, and about 500,000 live in Malaysia. The Minangkabau are primarily farmers, producing substantial amounts of surplus rice. Many Minangkabau, both women and men, take up employment in Indonesian cities for a time and then return home.

In this strongly matrilineal kinship system, Minangkabau women hold power through their control of land passed down through the lineage, the products of that land, and agricultural employment on their land (Sanday 2002). Many have prominent positions in business, especially having to do with rice. Men are more likely to become scholars, merchants, and politicians. Inheritance of property, including farmland and the family house, passes from mothers to daughters.

Members of each submatrilineage, constituting several generations, live together in one house or several nearby houses. Often, men and older boys live in a separate structure, such as the village mosque. In the household, the senior woman controls the power, and she makes decisions in all economic and ceremonial matters. The senior male of the sublineage has the role of representing its interests to other groups, but he is only a representative, not a powerful person in his own right.

Water buffaloes are important in both the Minangkabau rice economy and symbolically. The roofline of a traditional house has upward curves that echo the shape of water buffalo horns. Minangkabau women's festive headdresses have the same shape. The Minangkabau are mostly Muslims, but they mix their Muslim faith with elements of earlier traditions and Hinduism. They have long-standing traditions of music, martial arts, weaving, wood carving, and making fine filigree jewelry of silver and gold.

Many of the traditional wooden houses and palaces in Western Sumatra are falling into a state of disrepair (Vellinga 2004). The matrilineal pattern of only women living in the house is changing, and today men and women are more likely to live together in nuclear households.

Thanks to Michael G. Peletz, Emory University, for reviewing this material.

(LEFT) A traditional wooden Minangkabau longhouse with its distinctive upward-pointing roof. The house interiors are divided into separate "bays" for submatrilineal groups. Many are no longer places of residence but are used as meeting halls or are falling into ruin.

(CENTER) The symbolic importance of water buffaloes, apparent in the shape of traditional rooftops, is reiterated in the shape of girls' and women's ceremonial headdress. The headdress represents women's responsibilities for the growth and strength of Minangkabau culture.

MAP 8.3 Minangkabau Region in Indonesia. The shaded area shows the traditional heartland of Minangkabau culture in western Sumatra. Many Minangkabau people live elsewhere in Sumatra and in neighboring Malaysia.

See more at PEARSON **myanthrolab**

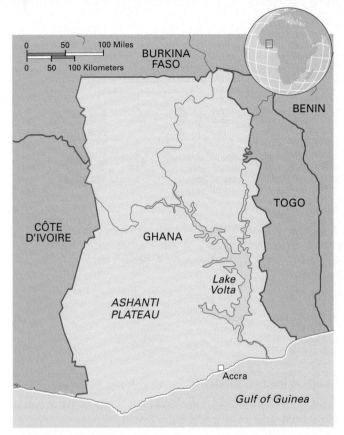

MAP 8.4 Ghana.

The Republic of Ghana has over 20 million people. Ghana has rich natural resources and exports gold, timber, and cocoa. Agriculture is the basis of the domestic economy. Several ethnic groups exist, with the Akan people constituting over 40 percent of the population. English is the official language, but another 80 or so languages are also spoken. Over 60 percent of the people are Christian, 20 percent follow traditional religions, and 16 percent are Muslim.

were kin. People who sponsor nonkin girls make a cash payment to the girl's parents. These girls cook, do housecleaning, and assist in market work by carrying goods or watching the trading area. Fostered boys, most of whom are kin of their sponsors, do not perform such tasks because they attend school.

RITUALLY ESTABLISHED KINSHIP   Ritually defined ties between adults and children born to other people are common among Christians, especially Catholics, worldwide. Relationships between godparents and godchildren often involve strong emotional ties and financial flows from the former to the latter.

Among the Maya of Oaxaca, Mexico (see Map 6.3, page 140), godparenthood is both a sign of the sponsor's status and the means to increased status for the sponsor (Sault 1985). A parent's request that a particular person sponsor his or her child is a public acknowledgment of the sponsor's standing. The godparent gains influence over the godchild and can call on the godchild for labor. Being a godparent of many children means that the godparent can amass a large

labor force when needed and gain further status. Most godparents in Oaxaca are husband–wife couples, but many are women alone, a pattern that reflects the high status of Maya women.

Marriage

The third major basis for forming close interpersonal relationships is through marriage or other forms of "marriage-like" relationships, such as long-term cohabitation. The following material focuses on marriage.

TOWARD A DEFINITION   Anthropologists recognize that some concept of *marriage* exists in all cultures, though it may take different forms and serve different functions. What constitutes a cross-culturally valid definition of marriage is, however, open to debate. A standard definition from 1951 is now discredited: "Marriage is a union between a man and a woman such that children born to the woman are the recognized legitimate offspring of both parents" (Barnard and Good 1984:89). This definition says that the partners must be of different genders, and it implies that a child born outside a marriage is not socially recognized as legitimate. Exceptions exist to both these features cross-culturally. Regarding the gender of partners, same-gender marriages are legal in Denmark, Norway, and Holland. Their legal status is a subject of ongoing debate in the United States and Canada.

Regarding the second, many cultures do not define the legitimacy of children on the basis of whether they were born within a marriage. Women in the Caribbean region, for example, typically do not marry until later in life. Before that, a woman has sequential male partners with whom she bears children. None of her children is considered more or less "legitimate" than any other.

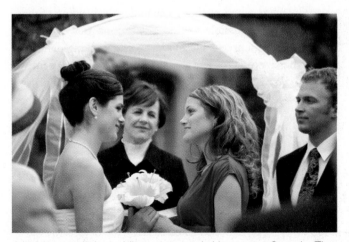

A lesbian couple's wedding ceremony in Vancouver, Canada. The rights of LGBT (lesbian, gay, bisexual, and transgender people) are contested around the world. Canada was the first country in the western hemisphere to legalize same-sex marriage. In 2010, Argentina, a largely Catholic country, legalized same-sex marriage, making it the tenth country in the world to do so.

Cross-Cousin Marriage

FaZ Fa Mo MoBr

FaZDa FaZS S Da MoBrS MoBrDa

A daughter marries either her father's sister's son or her mother's brother's son. A son marries either his father's sister's daughter or his mother's brother's daughter.

Parallel-Cousin Marriage

FaBr Fa Mo MoZ

FaBrS FaBrDa Da S MoZS MoZDa

A daughter marries either her father's brother's son or her mother's sister's son. A son marries either his father's brother's daughter or his mother's sister's daughter.

FIGURE 8.4 Two Types of Cousin Marriage.

Other definitions of marriage focus on rights over the spouse's sexuality. But not all forms of marriage involve sexual relations; for example, the practice of *woman–woman marriage* exists among the Nuer of southern Sudan (see Map 15.6, page 374) and some other African groups (Evans-Pritchard 1951:108–109). In this type of marriage, a woman with economic means gives gifts to obtain a "wife," goes through the marriage rituals with her, and brings her into the residential compound just as a man would who married a woman. This wife contributes her productive labor to the household. The two women do not have a sexual relationship. Instead, the woman who marries into the household will have sexual relations with a man. Her children, though, will belong to the compound into which she married.

The many practices that come under the heading of marriage make it impossible to find a definition that will fit all cases. One might accept the following as a working definition of **marriage**: a more or less stable union, usually between two people, who may be, but are not necessarily, co-residential, sexually involved with each other, and procreative with each other.

---

marriage a union, usually between two people who are likely to be, but are not necessarily, coresident, sexually involved with each other, and procreative.

incest taboo a strongly held prohibition against marrying or having sex with particular kin.

endogamy marriage within a particular group or locality.

parallel cousin offspring of either one's father's brother or one's mother's sister.

cross-cousin offspring of either one's father's sister or one's mother's brother.

exogamy marriage outside a particular group or locality.

SELECTING A SPOUSE All cultures have preferences about whom one should and should not marry or with whom one should and should not have sexual intercourse. Sometimes these preferences are informal and implicit, and other times they are formal and explicit. They include both *rules of exclusion* (specifying whom one should not marry) and *rules of inclusion* (specifying who is a preferred marriage partner).

An **incest taboo**, or rule prohibiting marriage or sexual intercourse between certain kinship relations, is one of the most basic and universal rules of exclusion. In his writings of the 1940s, Claude Lévi-Strauss proposes a reason for the universality of incest taboos by saying that, in premodern societies, incest avoidance motivated men to exchange women between families. In his view, this exchange is the foundation for all social networks and social solidarity beyond the immediate group. Such networks promote trade between areas with different resources and peace through ties established by bride exchange. So, for him, the incest taboo has important social and economic functions: It impels people to create social organization beyond the family.

Contemporary genetic research suggests an alternate theory for universal incest taboos. It says that larger breeding pools reduce the frequency of genetically transmitted conditions. Like the theory of Lévi-Strauss, the genetic theory is functional. Each theory attributes the universal existence of incest taboos to their adaptive contribution to human survival

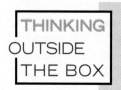

THINKING
OUTSIDE
THE BOX

Do some research on Match.com or Chemistry.com to learn what cultural preferences people mention in their profiles.

and success, though in two different ways. Anthropological data support both theories, but ethnographic data provide some puzzles to consider.

The most basic and universal form of incest taboo is against marriage or sexual intercourse between fathers and their children and between mothers and their children. Although most cultures forbid brother–sister marriage, a few exceptions exist. The most well-known example of brother–sister marriage as an accepted practice comes from Egypt at the time of the Roman Empire (Barnard and Good 1984:92). Brother–sister marriage was the norm among royalty, and it was common among the general population, with between 15 and 20 percent of marriages between full brothers and sisters.

Further variations in close-relation marriage arise with regard to cousins. Incest taboos do not universally rule out marriage with cousins. In fact, some kinship systems promote cousin marriage, as discussed next.

Many preference rules exist cross-culturally concerning whom one should marry. Rules of **endogamy**, or marriage within a particular group, stipulate that the spouse must be from a defined social category. In kin endogamy, certain relatives are preferred, often cousins. Two major forms of cousin marriage exist. One is marriage between **parallel cousins**, either between children of one's father and one's father's brother or between children of one's mother and one's mother's sister—the term *parallel* indicates that the linking siblings are of the same gender (see Figure 8.4). Parallel-cousin marriage is favored by many Muslim groups in the Middle East and northern Africa. The second form of cousin marriage is between **cross-cousins**, either between children of one's father and one's father's sister or between children of one's mother and one's mother's brother—the term *cross* indicates the different genders of the linking siblings. Hindus of southern India favor *cross-cousin marriage*. Although cousin marriage is preferred, it nonetheless is a minority of all marriages in the region. A survey of several thousand couples in the city of Chennai (formerly called Madras) (Map 8.5) in southern India showed that three-fourths of all marriages involved unrelated people, whereas one-fourth were between first cross-cousins or between uncle and niece, which is considered to be the same relationship as that of cross-cousins (Ramesh, Srikumari, and Sukumar 1989).

Readers who are unfamiliar with cousin marriage may find it objectionable on the basis of the potential genetic disabilities from close inbreeding. A study of thousands of such marriages in southern India, however, revealed only a small difference in rates of congenital problems compared to cultures in which cousin marriage is not practiced (Sundar Rao 1983). Marriage networks are diffuse, extending over a wide area and offering many options for "cousins." This situation contrasts to the much more closed situation of a single village or town. In cases where cousin marriage exists among

MAP 8.5 South India.
The states of southern India, compared to the northern states, have lower population density, lower fertility rates, higher literacy rates, and less severe gender inequality. Agriculture is the mainstay of the region's economy, and the population is predominantly rural. Industry, information technology, and business process outsourcing (BPO) are of increasing importance in cities.

a small and circumscribed population, then the possibility of negative genetic effects is high.

Endogamy may also be based on location. Village endogamy is preferred in the eastern Mediterranean among both Christians and Muslims. It is also the preferred pattern among Muslims throughout India and among Hindus of southern India. Hindus of northern India, in contrast, forbid village endogamy and consider it a form of incest. Instead, they practice village **exogamy**, or marriage outside a defined social group. For them, a spouse should live in a far-off village or town. In India, marriage distance is greater in the north than in the south, and northern brides are thus far less likely to be able to maintain regular contact with their birth family. Many songs and stories of northern Indian women convey sadness about being separated from their birth families.

Hypergyny	The groom may be wealthier, more educated, older, or taller.
Hypogyny	The bride may be wealthier, more educated, older, or taller.
Isogamy	The bride and groom have similar wealth, education, age, or height.

FIGURE 8.5 Status Considerations in Partner Selection (Heterosexual Pairing).

Status considerations often shape spouse selection (Figure 8.5). (The following discussion pertains to heterosexual marriage.) *Hypergyny*, or "marrying up," refers to a marriage in which the bride's status is lower than the groom's. Hypergyny is widely practiced in northern India, especially among upper-status groups. It is also prominent among many middle- and upper-class people in the United States. Because of hypergyny, women in top professions such as medicine and law—especially women medical students in North America—are having a difficult time finding appropriate partners, since there are few, if any, options for them to "marry up." The opposite pattern is *hypogyny*, or "marrying down," a marriage in which the bride has higher status than the groom. Hypogyny is rare cross-culturally. *Isogamy*, marriage between partners who are status equals, occurs in cultures where male and female roles and status are equal.

Subtypes of status-based hypergyny and hypogyny occur on the basis of factors such as age and even height. Age hypergyny refers to a marriage in which the bride is younger than the groom, a common practice worldwide. In contrast, age hypogyny is a marriage in which the bride is older than the groom. Age hypogyny is rare cross-culturally but has been increasing in the United States due to the marriage squeeze on women who would otherwise prefer a husband of equal age or somewhat older.

Physical features, such as ability, looks, and appearance, are factors that may be explicitly or implicitly involved in spouse selection. Facial beauty, skin color, hair texture and length, height, and weight are variously defined as important. Height hypergyny (in which the groom is taller than the bride) is more common in male-dominated contexts. Height-isogamous marriages are common in cultures where gender roles are relatively equal and where *sexual dimorphism* (differences

in shape and size of the female body compared with the male body) is not marked, as in much of Southeast Asia.

The role of romantic love in spouse selection is debated by biological determinists and cultural constructionists. Biological determinists argue that feelings of romantic love are universal among humans because they play an adaptive role in uniting males and females in offspring care. Cultural constructionists, in contrast, argue that cross-culturally romantic love is an unusual factor influencing spouse selection (Barnard and Good 1984:94). The cultural constructionists point to variations in male and female economic roles to explain cross-cultural differences in the emphasis on romantic love. Romantic love is more likely to be an important factor in relationships in cultures where men contribute more to subsistence and where women are therefore economically dependent on men. Whatever the cause of romantic love, biological or cultural or both, it is an increasingly common basis for marriage in many cultures (Levine et al. 1995).

Within the United States, microcultural variations exist in the degree to which women value romantic love as a basis for marriage (Holland and Eisenhart 1990). One study interviewed young American women entering college from 1979 to 1981 and again in 1987 after they had graduated and begun their adult lives. The research sites were two southern

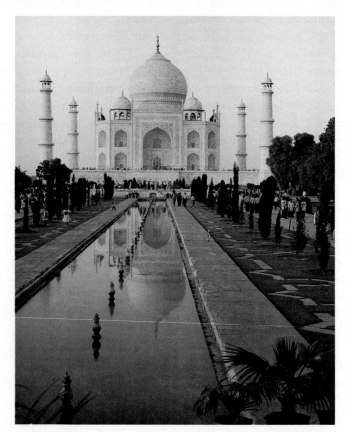

The Taj Mahal, located in Agra, northern India, is a seventeenth-century monument to love. It was built by the Mughal emperor Shah Jahan as a tomb for his wife, Mumtaz Mahal, who died in childbirth in 1631.

dowry the transfer of cash and goods from the bride's family to the newly married couple.

brideprice the transfer of cash and goods from the groom's family to the bride's family and to the bride.

brideservice a form of marriage exchange in which the groom works for his father-in-law for a certain length of time before returning home with the bride.

Type		Where Practiced
Dowry	Goods and money given by the bride's family to the married couple	Europe and Asia; agriculturalists and industrialists
Groomprice	A form of dowry: goods and money given by the bride's family to the married couple and to the parents of the groom	South Asia, especially northern India
Brideprice (or bride-wealth)	Goods and money given by the groom's family to the parents of the bride	Asia, Africa, and Central and South America; horticulturalists and pastoralists
Brideservice	Labor given by the groom to the parents of the bride	Southeast Asia, the Pacific, and Amazonia; horticulturalists

FIGURE 8.6 Types of Marriage Exchanges.

colleges in the United States, one attended mainly by White Euro-Americans and the other by African Americans. A contrast between the groups of women emerged. The White women were much more influenced by notions of romantic love than the Black women were. The White women were also less likely to have strong career goals and more likely to expect to be economically dependent on their spouse. The Black women expressed independence and strong career goals. The theme of romantic love supplies young White women with a model of the heroic male provider as the ideal, with her role being one of attracting him and providing the domestic context for their married life. The Black women were brought up to be more economically independent. This pattern is related both to African traditions in which women earn and manage their own earnings and to the racially discriminatory job market in the United States that places African American men at a severe disadvantage.

Arranged marriages are formed on the basis of parents' considerations of what constitutes a "good match" between the families of the bride and groom. Arranged marriages are common in many Middle Eastern, African, and Asian countries. Some theorists claim that arranged marriages are "traditional" and love marriages are "modern." They believe that arranged marriages will disappear with modernity. Japan presents a case of an industrial/informatic economy with a highly educated population in which arranged unions still constitute a substantial proportion of all marriages, about 25 to 30 percent (Applbaum 1995). The most important criteria for a spouse are the family's reputation and social standing; the absence of undesirable traits, such as a case of divorce or mental illness in the family; education; occupation; and income.

MARRIAGE GIFTS   Most marriages are accompanied by exchanges of goods or services between the families of the bride and groom (Figure 8.6). The two major forms of marital exchanges cross-culturally are dowry and brideprice. **Dowry** is

the transfer of goods, and sometimes money, from the bride's side to the new married couple for their use. The dowry includes household goods such as furniture, cooking utensils, and, sometimes, rights to a house. Dowry is the main form of marriage transfer in farming societies throughout Eurasia, from Western Europe through the northern Mediterranean and into China and India. In much of India, dowry is more accurately termed *groomprice*, because much of the goods and money pass not to the new couple but rather to the groom's family (Billig 1992). In China during the Mao era, the government considered dowry a sign of women's oppression and made it illegal. The practice of giving dowry in China has returned with increased personal wealth and consumerism, especially among the newly rich urban populations (Whyte 1993).

Brideprice, or *bridewealth*, is the transfer of goods or money from the groom's side to the bride's parents. It is common in horticultural and pastoralist cultures. **Brideservice**, a subtype of brideprice, is the transfer of labor from the groom to his parents-in-law for a designated period. It is practiced in some horticultural societies, especially in the Amazon.

Many marriages involve balanced gifts from both bride's and the groom's side. A long-standing pattern in the United States placed the major burden of the costs of the wedding and honeymoon on the bride's side, with the groom's side responsible for paying for the rehearsal dinner the night before the wedding. A trend toward shared costs by the bride and groom may indicate more equal relations in the marriage as well.

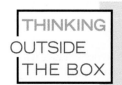

THINKING OUTSIDE THE BOX

What is your opinion about the relative merits of love marriages versus arranged marriages, and on what do you base your opinion?

FORMS OF MARRIAGE   Cultural anthropologists distinguish two forms of marriage on the basis of the number of partners involved. **Monogamy** is marriage between two people—a male or female if the pair is heterosexual, or two people of the same gender in the case of a homosexual pair. Heterosexual monogamy is the most common form of marriage cross-culturally, and in many countries it is the only legal form of marriage.

Polygamy is marriage involving multiple spouses, a pattern allowed in many cultures. Two forms of polygamous marriage exist. The more common of the two is **polygyny**, marriage of one man with more than one woman. **Polyandry**, or marriage between one woman and more than one man, is rare. The only place where polyandry is commonly found is in the Himalayan region that includes parts of Tibet, India, and Nepal. Nonpolyandrous people in the area look down on the people who practice polyandrous marriage as backward (Haddix McCay 2001).

◉ ◉ ◉

Households and Domestic Life

In casual conversation, North Americans might use the words *family* and *household* interchangeably to refer to people who live together. Social scientists, however, propose a distinction between the two terms. A **family** is a group of people who consider themselves related through kinship. In North American English, the term may include both "close" and "distant" relatives. All members of a family do not necessarily live together or have strong bonds with one another. But they are still "family."

A related term is the **household**, either a person living alone or one or more persons who occupy a shared living

The Hausa are an important ethnic group of Ghana. This photograph shows a display of Hausa dowry goods in Accra, the capital city. The most valuable part of a Hausa bride's dowry is the *kayan dak'i* ("things of the room"), consisting of bowls, pots, ornamental glass, and cookware, which are conspicuously displayed in the bride's marital house so that the local women can get a sense of her worth. The bride's parents pay for these status items and for utilitarian items such as everyday cooking utensils.

space and who may or may not be related by kinship. Most households consist of members who are related through kinship, but an increasing number do not. An example of a nonkin household is a group of friends who live in the same apartment. This section of the chapter looks at household forms and organization cross-culturally and at relationships between and among household members.

The Household: Variations on a Theme

This section considers three forms of households and the concept of household headship. The topic of female-headed households receives detailed attention because this pattern of headship is widely misunderstood.

HOUSEHOLD FORMS   Household organization is divided into types according to how many married adults are involved. The **nuclear household** (which many people call

---

monogamy   marriage between two people.

polygamy   marriage involving multiple spouses.

polygyny   marriage of one husband with more than one wife.

polyandry   marriage of one wife with more than one husband.

family   a group of people who consider themselves related through a form of kinship, such as descent, marriage, or sharing.

household   either one person living alone or a group of people who may or may not be related by kinship and who share living space.

nuclear household   a domestic unit containing one adult couple (married or partners) with or without children.

extended household   a coresidential group that comprises more than one parent–child unit.

stem household   a coresidential group that comprises only two married couples related through males, commonly found in East Asian cultures.

The woman on the lower right is part of a polyandrous marriage, which is still practiced among some Tibetan peoples. She is married to several brothers, two of whom stand behind her. The older man with the sash in the front row is her father-in-law.

the nuclear family) is a domestic group that contains one adult couple (married or "partners"), with or without children. An **extended household** is a domestic group that contains more than one adult married couple. The couples may be related through the father–son line (making a *patrilineal extended household*), through the mother–daughter line (a *matrilineal extended household*), or through sisters or brothers (a *collateral extended household*). Polygynous (multiple wives) and polyandrous (multiple husbands) households are *complex households,* domestic units in which one spouse lives with or near multiple partners and their children.

The precise cross-cultural distribution of these various types of households is not known, but some broad generalizations can be offered. First, nuclear households are found in all cultures but are the exclusive household type in only about one-fourth of the world's cultures (Murdock 1965 [1949]:2). Extended households are the most important form in about half of all cultures. The distribution of these two household forms corresponds roughly with the modes of livelihood (see Figure 8.1, page 185). The nuclear form is most characteristic of economies at the two extremes of the continuum: foraging groups and industrialized/informatic societies. This pattern reflects the need for spatial mobility and flexibility in both modes of production. Extended households constitute a substantial proportion of households in horticultural, pastoralist, and farming economies.

In Japan and other parts of East Asia, a subtype of the extended household structure has endured within the context of an industrial/postindustrial and urban economy. The *ie*, or **stem household**, is a variation of an extended household containing two (and only two) married couples related through the male line. Only one son remains in the household, bringing in his wife, who is expected to perform the important role of caretaker for the husband's parents as they age. Although people throughout East Asia still prefer the ie, it is increasingly difficult to achieve due to changing economic aspirations of children, who do not want to dedicate their lives to caring for their aging parents. Aging parents who find that none of their children is willing to live with them and take responsibility for their care exert considerable pressure on an adult child to come and live with them (Traphagan 2000). A compromise is for an adult child and his or her spouse to live near the parents but not with them.

HOUSEHOLD HEADSHIP The question of who heads a household is often difficult to answer. This section reviews some approaches to this question and provides insights into how cross-cultural perceptions about household headship differ.

The *household head* is the primary person, or persons, responsible for supporting the household financially and making major decisions. This concept of household head is based on a Euro-American view that emphasizes the income contribution of the head, traditionally a man. European colonialism spread the concept of the male, income-earning head of household around the world, along with laws that placed household authority in male headship.

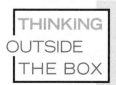

THINKING OUTSIDE THE BOX

In your microculture, what are the prevailing ideas about wedding expenses and who should pay for them?

The stem household is still common in rural areas of China and Taiwan, but the nuclear household is on the rise. Sons still try to be responsible for their parents by hosting them for visits, providing meals, and making sure they are cared for in their old age.

The model of a male household head influences the way official statistics are gathered worldwide. If a household has a coresident man and woman, there is a tendency to report the household as male headed. In Brazil, for example, the official definition of household head considers only a husband to be head of the household, regardless of whether he contributes to the household budget. Single, separated, or widowed women who are responsible for household support are deprived of the title of household head. If they happen to have a man visiting them on the day the census official arrives, he is considered to be the household head (de Athayde Figueiredo and Prado 1989:41). Similarly, according to official reports, 90 percent of households in the Philippines are headed by males (Illo 1985). Filipino women, however, play a prominent role in income generation and budgetary control, and both partners share major decision making. Thus coheadship would be a more appropriate label for many households in the Philippines and elsewhere.

Matrifocality refers to a household pattern in which a woman (or women) is the central, stable domestic figure around whom other members cluster (González 1970). In a matrifocal household, the mother is likely to be the primary or only income provider. The concept of matrifocality does not exclude the possibility that men may be part of the household, but they are not the central income providers or decision makers. The number of woman-headed households is increasing worldwide, and these households tend to be poorer than other households. In general, a woman-headed household can come about if a partner never existed, if a partner existed at one time, but for some reason—such as separation, divorce, or death—is no longer part of the

household, or if a partner exists but is not a coresident because of migration, imprisonment, or some other form of separation.

In terms of the healthy functioning of households, it is not simply the gender of the household head that is critical. What matters are the resources to which the head has access, both material and social, such as property ownership, a decent job, kinship and other supportive social ties, and living in a safe neighborhood.

Intrahousehold Dynamics

How do household members interact with each other? What are their emotional attachments, rights, and responsibilities?

This matrifocal household in rural Jamaica includes two sisters and their children.

What are the power relationships between and among members of various categories, such as spouses, siblings, and those of different generations? Kinship systems define what the content of these relationships should be. In everyday life, people may conform more or less to the ideal.

SPOUSE–PARTNER RELATIONSHIPS This section discusses three areas of spousal relationships: marital satisfaction and sexual activity over the life course.

A landmark study of marriages in Tokyo in 1959 compared marital satisfaction of husbands and wives in love marriages and in arranged marriages (Blood 1967). In all marriages, marital satisfaction declined over time, but differences between the two types emerged. The decline was greatest for wives in arranged marriages and least for husbands in arranged marriages. In love-match marriages, both partners' satisfaction dropped dramatically (a bit earlier for wives and a bit later for husbands), but both husbands and wives reported nearly equal levels of satisfaction after they had been married nine years or more.

Sexual activity of couples can be both an indication and a cause of marital satisfaction. Analysis of reports of marital sex from a 1988 survey in the United States shows that frequency per month declines steadily with the duration of marriage, from an average of 12 times per month for people ages 19 to 24 years to less than once a month for people 75 years of age and older (Call, Sprecher, and Schwartz 1995). Older married people have sex less frequently. Less happy people have sex less frequently. Within each age category, sex is more frequent among three categories of people:

- Those who are cohabiting but not married
- Those who cohabited before marriage
- Those who are in their second or later marriage

In seeking to learn whether such decline is more widespread, an anthropologist and a statistician joined forces to analyze data from a survey conducted with over 90,000 women in 19 developing countries (Brewis and Meyer 2004). One of the survey questions was "When was the last time you had sexual intercourse [with a spouse]?" The *honeymoon effect* (having more frequent sex in the first year of marriage) is significant in only five countries: Brazil, Benin, Ethiopia, Mali, and Kazakhstan. Significant reductions in frequency after the first year of marriage occur in all countries but one: Burkina Faso in West Africa. What is going on here? One factor is that Burkina Faso couples have a significantly lower frequency of reported marital sex during the first year of marriage; in other words, couples do not go through a honeymoon phase of frequent sexual intercourse, and so activity in following years is not that much lower. These intriguing results at the country level need to be followed up by research on local cultural practices and patterns.

Japanese salarymen singing karaoke in a bar.

Cultures everywhere also define the proper role of a wife or husband. In Japan, a "good wife" should care for her husband's needs and make sure that any problems in the household do not erupt into the public domain (Borovoy 2005). Many Japanese salarymen (corporate workers) consume substantial amounts of alcohol after work. They return home late and drunk. It is the duty of the "good wife" to provide dinner for her husband and get him to go to bed, so he can make it to work the next day. The wives face a profound cultural dilemma: If they continue to perform well the role of the "good wife," they are "codependent" in the husband's alcohol abuse, and contribute to the continuance of the problem. Many middle-class Japanese wives are joining support groups to help them deal with their situation by building new roles for themselves beyond that of the "good wife."

SIBLING RELATIONSHIPS Sibling relationships are an understudied aspect of intrahousehold dynamics. One example comes from research in a working-class neighborhood of Beirut, Lebanon (Joseph 1994). The anthropologist became friendly with several families and was especially close to Hanna, the oldest son in one of them. Hanna was an attractive young man, considered a good marriage choice, with friends across religious and ethnic groups. Therefore, the author reports her shock when she once heard Hanna shouting at his 12-year-old sister Flaur and slapping her across the face. Further observation of the relationship between the two suggested that Hanna was playing a fatherly role to Flaur. He was especially irritated with her if she lingered on the street near their apartment building, gossiping with other girls: "He would forcibly escort her upstairs to their apartment, slap her, and demand that she behave with dignity" (1994:51). Adults in the household thought nothing was wrong. They said that Flaur enjoyed her brother's aggressive attention. Flaur herself

---

matrifocality a household pattern in which a female (or females) is the central figure around whom other members cluster.

commented, "It doesn't even hurt when Hanna hits me." She said that she hoped to have a husband like Hanna.

An interpretation of this kind of brother–sister relationship, common in Arab culture, is that it is part of a socialization process that maintains and perpetuates male domination in the household: "Hanna was teaching Flaur to accept male power in the name of love . . . loving his sister meant taking charge of her and that he could discipline her if his action was understood to be in her interest. Flaur was reinforced in learning that the love of a man could include that male's violent control and that to receive his love involved submission to control" (1994:52).

DOMESTIC VIOLENCE BETWEEN PARTNERS   Violence between domestic partners, with males dominating as perpetrators and women as victims, is found in nearly all cultures, although in varying forms and frequencies (Brown 1999). Wife beating is more common and more severe in contexts where men control the wealth. It is less common and less severe where women's work groups and social networks exist (Levinson 1989). The presence of women's work groups is related to a greater importance of women in production and matrifocal residence. These factors provide women with the means to leave an abusive relationship. For example, among the Garifuna (guh-REE-fuh-nuh), an African–Indian people of Belize, Central America, incidents of spouse abuse occur, but they are infrequent and not extended (Kerns 1999). Women's solidarity in this matrifocal society limits male violence against women.

Increased domestic violence worldwide throws into question the notion of the house as a refuge or place of security. In the United States, evidence exists of high and increasing rates of intrahousehold abuse of children (including sexual abuse), violence between spouses or partners, and abuse of aged family members. Anthropological research helps policy makers and social workers better understand the factors affecting the safety of individuals within households so that they are able to design more effective programs to promote personal safety (see Anthropology Works).

HOUSEHOLDS WITHOUT A HOME   The definition of a household includes "sharing a living space." In most cultures, that means a "home" of some sort—a structure in which people prepare and share meals, sleep, and spend time with each other in a secure environment. The ideal of a household living in a home is increasingly out of reach of millions of people around the world. The major reasons for homelessness, of families and individuals, are: poverty, warfare and conflict, natural disasters, mental illness and other disabilities, substance abuse, and domestic violence.

Addressing these causes, to prevent homelessness, is of critical importance. At the same time, providing services for those who are homeless is essential and must be based on knowledge about particular people's situation, potentials, and needs. Cultural anthropologist Philippe Bourgois and photographer Jeff Schonberg collaborated, in an effort they call *photo-ethnography*, to produce a book about homeless people in San Francisco who are addicted to heroin (2009). They followed 12 people to learn about how they became homeless, how they cope with social marginality and addiction, and the social bonds they create with other homeless people. It's impossible to reduce the many lessons of their book into a few sentences here, but one takeaway is that, in the immediate term, social policies are needed to promote *harm reduction* through providing safe injection places and clean needle programs for addicts. Providing such care for homeless

A shared bedroom in a battered-women's shelter, Tel Aviv, Israel. Many people wonder why abused women do not leave their abusers. Part of the answer lies in the unavailability and low quality of shelters throughout much of the world.

ANTHROPOLOGY works

Preventing Wife Abuse in Rural Kentucky

Domestic violence in the United States is reportedly highest in the state of Kentucky. Ethnographic study of domestic violence in Kentucky reveals several cultural factors related to the high rate of wife abuse (Websdale 1995). The study included interviews with 50 abused wives in eastern Kentucky, police officers, shelter employees, and social workers.

Three categories of isolation exist in rural Kentucky that make domestic violence particularly difficult to prevent:

1. *Physical isolation*: The women reported a feeling of physical isolation in their lives. Abusers' tactics were more effective because of geographical isolation. Tactics include disabling motor vehicles so the wife cannot leave the residence, destroying motor vehicles, monitoring odometer readings on motor vehicles, driving recklessly to intimidate the wife, and discharging firearms at, for example, a pet.

It is difficult or impossible for an abused woman to leave a home located many miles from the nearest paved road, especially if the woman has children. In rural Kentucky, no public transportation serves even the paved road. Nearly one-third of households at the time of the study had no phones. Getting to a phone to report abuse

results in delay, gives police the impression that the call is less serious, and increases a woman's sense of hopelessness. Sheriffs have a reputation for not attending to domestic calls.

2. *Social isolation*: Gender roles promote a system of "passive policing." Men are seen as providers, and women are tied to domestic work and child rearing. When women do work outside the home, their wages are about 50 percent of men's wages. Marital residence is often in the vicinity of the husband's family. Thus, a woman is separated from the potential support of her natal family and is limited in seeking help in the immediate vicinity because the husband's family is likely to be nonsupportive of her. Local police officers view the family as a private unit, so they are not inclined to intervene in family problems. Because the home is the man's world and men are supposed to be dominant in the family, police are unwilling to arrest husbands accused of abuse. In some instances, the police take the batterer's side because they share the belief in a husband's right to control his wife.

3. *Institutional isolation*: Social services for battered women in Kentucky are scarce, especially in rural areas. The fact that abused women often

know the people who run the services ironically inhibits the women from approaching them, given the value of family privacy. Other institutional constraints include low levels of schooling, lack of child-care centers to allow mothers the option to work outside the home, inadequate health services, and religious teaching of fundamentalist Christianity which supports values such as the idea that it is a woman's duty to stay in a marriage and "weather the storm."

These findings suggest some recommendations. First, rural women need more and better employment opportunities to reduce their economic dependency on abusive partners. To address this need, rural outreach programs should be strengthened. Expanded telephone subscriptions would decrease rural women's institutional isolation. Because of the complexity of the social situation in Kentucky, however, no single solution will be sufficient.

FOOD FOR THOUGHT ▼
Since the study was conducted, cell phone use has expanded worldwide. Will cell phones be likely to reduce women's isolation in rural Kentucky?

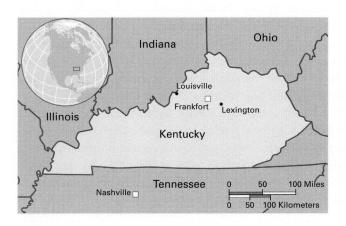

MAP 8.6 **Kentucky, United States.**

Located in the southeastern United States, in the Appalachian region, Kentucky's population is over 4 million. It has more farmers per square mile than any other state. Per capita income is 43rd in the 50 states. Before being occupied by British settlers in the late eighteenth century, Kentucky was the hunting grounds of the Shawnees and Cherokees. The current population is about 91 percent White, 7 percent Black, 0.6 percent American Indian, and 0.9 percent Asian. Kentucky is known for thoroughbred horse breeding and racing, bourbon and whiskey distilling, barbeque, and bluegrass music.

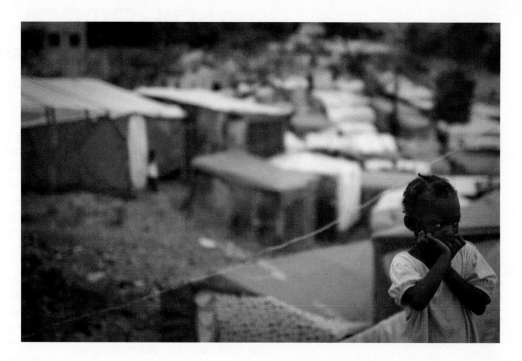

Life in tents. A girl looks over an expanse of a vast array of tents three months after the January 2010 earthquake in Haiti which killed hundreds of thousands of people and displaced between one and two million people. The devastation left many widows, widowers, and orphans, thus destroying households as well as homes.

addicts is something that many countries are doing. Perhaps making it more possible for more people to live in homes would help, too.

<hr />

⊙ ⊙ ⊙
Changing Kinship and Household Dynamics

This section provides examples of how marriage and household patterns are changing. Many of these changes have roots in colonialism, whereas others are the result of recent changes caused by globalization.

Change in Descent

Matrilineal descent is declining worldwide as a result of both European colonialism and contemporary Western globalization. European colonial rule in Africa and Asia contributed to the decline in matrilineal kinship by registering land and other property in the names of assumed male heads of household, even where females were the heads (Boserup 1970). This process eroded women's previous rights and powers. Western missionaries contributed further to transforming matrilineal cultures into patrilineal systems (Etienne and Leacock 1980). For example, European colonial influences led to the decline of matrilineal kinship among Native North Americans. Before European colonialism, North America had one of the largest distributions of matrilineal descent worldwide. A comparative study of kinship among three reservation-based Navajo groups in Arizona shows that matrilineality is stronger where conditions most resemble the pre-reservation era (Levy, Henderson, and Andrews 1989).

Among the Minangkabau of Indonesia (review Culturama, this chapter), three factors explain the decline of matrilineal kinship (Blackwood 1995):

- Dutch colonialism promoted the image of male-headed nuclear families as an ideal.
- Islamic teachings idealize women as wives and men as household heads.
- The modernizing Indonesian state has a policy of naming males as household heads.

Change in Marriage

Although the institution of marriage in general remains prominent, many of its details, including courtship, the marriage ceremony, and marital relationships, are changing. New forms of communication are profoundly affecting courtship. In a village in western Nepal (see Map 7.7, page 176) people's stories of their marriages reveal that arranged marriages have decreased and elopement has increased since the 1990s.

Nearly everywhere, the age at first marriage is rising. The later age at marriage is related to increased emphasis on completing a certain number of years of education before marriage and to higher material aspirations, such as being able to own a house. Marriages between people of different nations and ethnicities are increasing, partly because of growing rates of international migration. Migrants take with them many of their marriage and family practices. They also adapt to rules and practices in their area of destination. Pluralistic practices evolve, such as conducting two marriage ceremonies—one conforming to the "original" culture and the other to the culture in the place of destination.

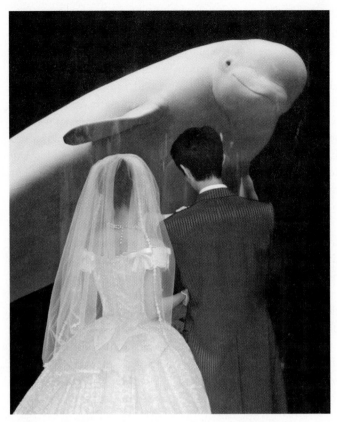

A beluga whale watches while a Japanese couple holds a wedding ceremony at an aquarium in Yokohama, Japan. The ceremony, called "Dolphin Wedding," costs nearly $3,000 for 15 minutes and a maximum of 60 attendees.

▶ *What is your fantasy for a special wedding setting? How much would you be willing to pay for it? Consider how your culture may be shaping your answers to these questions.*

A *marriage crisis* is a cultural situation in which many people who want to marry cannot do so for one reason or another. Marriage crises are more frequent now than in the past, at least as perceived and reported by young people in the so-called marriage market. Throughout much of sub-Saharan Africa, many young men are unable to raise enough money for the brideprice and other marriage expenses. The reason these days often has to do with high rates of unemployment. A case study in a town of about 38,000 people in Niger, West Africa illustrates these points (Masquelier 2005). Among the Mawri, who are Muslim, marriage is the crucial ritual that changes a boy into a man. The economy has been declining for some time, and typical farm or other wages are worth less than they were in earlier times. Marriage costs for the groom, however, have risen. While wealthy young men can afford to give a car to the bride's parents, most young Mawri men cannot afford even a standard brideprice. They remain sitting at home in their parents' house, something that, ordinarily, only females do. The many young, marriage-age women who remain single gain a reputation of being immoral, occupying a new and suspect social space between girl and wife. In China, a different kind of marriage crisis exists and is growing. Population experts project that, by 2020, about 2 million men in China will not be able to find a woman to marry. This situation is due to the one-child policy (review Chapter 6), the preference for sons, and the resulting unbalanced sex ratio (Global Times 2010).

On a more positive note, let's consider weddings. Weddings are important, culture-revealing events. Style changes in weddings worldwide abound, and they all mean something in terms of the choices people make to mark the event. Factors to consider in examining changes in wedding styles are the ceremony, costs, appropriate clothing, and the possibility of a honeymoon. The Western-style *white wedding*, so-named because the bride wears a white dress, is spreading around the world, though with fascinating local adaptations in terms of its features, including what the bride and groom wear, the design of the wedding cake, floral displays, and more. Throughout Asia, advertisements and upscale stores display the Western-style white wedding gown, but not in India, where white clothing for women signifies widowhood and is inauspicious. A resurgence of local, folksy styles is occurring in some contexts. In Morocco, for example, an urban bride may wear a Western style white gown for one part of the wedding ceremony and an "exotic" Berber costume (long robes and ornate silver jewelry characteristic of the mountain pastoralists) at another stage of the ceremony. The blending of Western and non-Western elements signals a family's complex identity in a globalizing world.

Changing Households

Globalization is creating rapid change in household structure and intrahousehold dynamics. One assumption is that the frequency of extended households will decline with industrialization and urbanization and the frequency of nuclear households will rise. Given what this chapter mentioned earlier about the relationship between nuclear households and industrialism/informatics, it is highly possible that the spread of this mode of livelihood will cause an increase in the number of nuclear households, too.

This projection finds strong confirmation in the changes that have occurred in household structure among the Kelabit (kell-uh-bit) people of highland Borneo since the early 1990s (Amster 2000) (see Map 8.7 on page 204). One Kelabit settlement was founded in 1963 near the Indonesian border. At the time, everyone lived in one longhouse with over 20 family units. It was a "modern" longhouse, thanks to roofing provided by the British army and the innovation of private sleeping areas. Like more traditional longhouses, though, it was an essentially egalitarian living space within which individuals could freely move. Today, that longhouse is no more. Most of the young people have migrated to coastal towns and work in jobs related to the offshore oil industry. Most houses are now single-unit homes with an emphasis on privacy. The elders complain of a "bad silence" in

MAP 8.7 Kelabit Region in Malaysia.

The Kelabit people's homeland is the Kelabit Highlands in Sarawak, a plateau ringed by mountain peaks that are forest covered. One of Malaysia's smallest indigenous tribes, they number around 6000 people, or 0.4 percent of Sarawak's population of 1.5 million, and 0.03 percent of Malaysia's total population of 22 million. Less than one-third of the Kelabit people now live in the highlands.

the village. No one looks after visitors with the old style of hospitality. There is no longer one common longhouse for communal feasts and rituals.

International migration is another major cause of change in household formation and internal relationships (discussed further in Chapter 15). A dramatic decline in fertility can occur in one generation when members of a farming household in, for example, Taiwan or Egypt migrate to England, France, Canada, or the United States. Having many children makes economic sense in their homeland, but not in the new destination. Many such migrants decide to have only one or two children. They tend to live in small, isolated nuclear households. International migration creates new challenges for relationships between parents and children. The children often become strongly identified with the new culture and have little connection with their ancestral culture. This rupture creates anxiety for the parents and conflict between children and parents over issues such as dating, dress, and career goals.

In 1997, the people of Norway were confronted with the case of the kidnapping of an 18-year-old Norwegian citizen named "Nadia" (Wikan 2000). Her parents took her to Morocco and held her captive there. The full story is

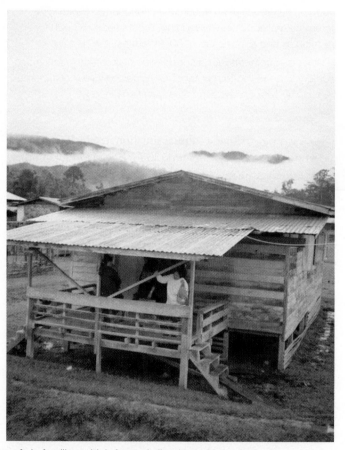

(LEFT) A modern-style Kelabit longhouse built in the 1990s. It is the home of six families which formerly lived in a 20-family longhouse, seen in the background, that is being dismantled. (RIGHT) Since the 1990s, houses built for a nuclear unit have proliferated in the highlands. These houses stand on the site of a former multiunit longhouse.

complicated, but the core issues revolve around conflict between Moroccan and Norwegian family values. Nadia's parents felt that she should be under their control and that they had the right to arrange her marriage in Morocco. Nadia had a Norwegian concept of personal autonomy. In the end, Nadia and her parents returned to Norway, where the courts ruled that, for the sake of the family, the parents would not be jailed for kidnapping their daughter. The case brought stigma to Nadia among the Muslim community of Norway, who viewed her as a traitor to her culture. She now lives at a secret address and avoids publicity. An anthropologist close to this case who served as an expert witness during the trial of the parents reports that, in spite of her seclusion, Nadia offers help to other young women.

The shape of households is also changing. In the United States, at the beginning of the twenty-first century, three kinds of households are most common: households composed of couples living in their first marriage, single-parent households, and households formed through remarriage. A rising fourth category is the *multigenerational household*, a form of extended household, in which an *adult child* lives with his or her parent or parents. In the United States, the economic downturn appears to be related to the fact that the number of Americans living in multigenerational households rose by 5 percent from 2007 to 2008 (Pew Center 2010). The increase in multigenerational households began in the 1980s with the influx of immigrants, but it clearly accelerated during the economic crisis. Now 16 percent of the population lives in homes with multiple generations. Marriage age for young adults has risen as well, and these unmarried young people are most likely to live with their parent or parents.

Another, even more tragic trend, is the number of households without homes. Modern homelessness is the result of many causes. The consequences are also complex, but never positive. Being without a secure place to live puts every family value in jeopardy.

Kinship, households and domestic life are certainly not dull or static topics. Just trying to keep up with changing patterns in North America is a daunting task, to say nothing of tracking changes worldwide.

How do cultures create kinship?

Key differences exist between unilineal and bilineal descent systems. Within unilineal systems, further important variations exist between patrilineal and matrilineal systems in terms of property inheritance, residence rules for married couples, and the relative status of males and females. Worldwide, unilineal systems are more common than bilineal systems. Within unilineal kinship systems, patrilineal kinship is more common than matrilineal kinship.

A second important basis for kinship is sharing. Sharing one's child with someone else through either informal or formal processes is probably a cultural universal. Sharing-based kinship is created through food transfers, including breastfeeding (in some cultures, children breastfed by the same woman are considered kin and cannot marry). Ritualized sharing creates kinship, as in the case of godparenthood.

The third basis for kinship is marriage, another universal factor, even though definitions of marriage may differ substantially. All cultures have rules of exclusion and preference rules for spouses. These rules affect factors such as kinship relationships of potential spouses, region, class, wealth, education, perceptions of "looks," and more.

What are cross-cultural patterns of households and domestic life?

A household may consist of a single person living alone or may be a group comprising more than one person, each of whom may or may not be related by kinship; these individuals share a living space and, often, financial responsibilities for the household.

Nuclear households consist of a mother and father and their children, but they also can be just a husband and wife without children. Nuclear households are found in all cultures but are most common in foraging and industrial/informatic societies. Extended households include more than one nuclear household. They are most commonly found in cultures with a unilineal kinship system.

Household headship can be shared between two partners or can be borne by a single person, as in a woman-headed household. Studies of intrahousehold dynamics between parents and children and among siblings reveal complex power relationships as well as sharing and, sometimes, violence.

How are kinship and households changing?

Recent forces of change, starting with European colonialism and now globalization, have had, and continue to have, marked effects on kinship formation and household patterns and dynamics. Matrilineal systems have been declining in distribution since European colonialist expansion began in the 1500s.

Many aspects of marriage are changing, including a trend toward later age at marriage in many developing countries. Although marriage continues to be an important basis for the formation of nuclear and extended households, other options (such as cohabitation) are increasing in importance in many contexts, including urban areas in developed countries. Wedding ceremonies provide a window into cultures and how they are changing. The globalizing white wedding is simultaneously being localized to fit with existing cultural values and practices.

Multigenerational households in the United States have been increasing since the 1980s but jumped substantially starting in 2007 with the economic crisis. At the same time, more people worldwide are homeless, many of them striving to maintain family ties while many others are alone and lack kin relationships and support.

KEY CONCEPTS

SUGGESTED READINGS

Irwin Altman and Joseph Ginat, eds. *Polygamous Families in Contemporary Society*. New York: Cambridge University Press, 1996. This book provides a detailed account of polygyny as practiced in two fundamentalist Mormon communities of Utah.

Dorothy Ayers Counts, Judith K. Brown, and Jacquelyn C. Campbell, eds. *To Have and to Hit: Cultural Perspectives on Wife Beating*. Champaign–Urbana: University of Illinois Press, 1999. Chapters include an introductory overview and cases from Australia, southern Africa, Papua New Guinea, India, Central America, the Middle East, and the Pacific.

Amy Borovoy. *The Too-Good Wife: Alcohol, Codependency, and the Politics of Nurturance in Postwar Japan*. Berkeley: University of California Press, 2005. This book explores the experiences of middle-class women in Tokyo who participated in a weekly support meeting for families of substance abusers. The women attempt to cope with their husbands' alcoholism while facing the dilemma that being a good wife may be part of the problem.

Deborah R. Connolly. *Homeless Mothers: Face to Face with Women and Poverty*. Minneapolis: University of Minnesota Press, 2000. Poor, White women on the margin of mainstream society in Portland, Oregon, describe how they attempt to be good mothers with no money, no home, and no help.

Charles N. Durran, James M. Freeman, and J.A. English-Lueck. *Busier Than Ever! Why American Families Can't Slow Down*. Stanford, CA: Stanford University Press, 2007. The authors followed the daily activities of 14 American families in California. Their findings show how people try to balance the demands of work and family in a cultural context in which "busyness," or always being busy, is an indication of success and the good life.

Helen Bradley Foster and Donald Clay Johnson, eds. *Wedding Dress across Cultures*. New York: Berg, 2003. Chapters examine the evolution and ritual functions of wedding attire in cultures such as those of urban Japan, Alaskan Indians, Swaziland, Morocco, Greece, and the Andes.

Jennifer Hirsch. *A Courtship after Marriage: Sexuality and Love in Mexican Transnational Marriages*. Berkeley: University of California Press, 2003. This study uses an innovative method of pairing 13 migrant women living in Atlanta, Georgia, with 13 nonmigrant counterparts in two rural towns in Mexico to learn about marriage and married life.

Höjdestrand, Tove. 2009. *Needed by Nobody: Homelessness and Humanness in Post-Socialist Russia*. Ithaca, NY: Cornell University Press. A permanent address is Russia is the precondition for all civil rights and social benefits. This ethnography describes the lives of the homeless in St. Petersburg.

Suad Joseph, ed. *Intimate Selving in Arab Families: Gender, Self, and Identity*. Syracuse, NY: Syracuse University Press, 1999. Chapters discuss family life and relationships in Arab culture, with attention to connectivity, gender inequality, and the self. Case studies are from Lebanon and Egypt.

Laurel Kendall. *Getting Married in Korea: Of Gender, Morality, and Modernity*. Berkeley: University of California, 1996. This book examines preferences about desirable spouses, matchmaking, marriage ceremonies and their financing, and the effect of Korean women's changing work roles on their marital aspirations.

Kanchana Ruwanpura. *Matrilineal Communities, Patriarchal Realities: A Feminist Nirvana Uncovered*. Ann Arbor: University of Michigan Press, 2007. This book describes Muslim, Sinhala, and Tamil households headed by women in Sri Lanka.

Toby Alice Volkman, ed. *Cultures of Transnational Adoption*. Durham, NC: Duke University Press, 2005. Chapters discuss Korean adoptees as a global family, transnational adoption in North America, shared parenthood among low-income people in Brazil, and representations of "waiting children."

PEARSON
myanthrolab

For further information about topics covered in this chapter, go to MyAnthroLab at **www.myanthrolab.com** and access the following readings in MyAnthroLibrary:

Amster, Matthew H. 2000. It Takes a Village to Dismantle a Longhouse. *Thresholds* 20:65–71. The author's fieldwork among the Kelabit people informs this discussion of the decline of longhouse living in favor of nuclear households.

Marcus, Anthony. 2005. Whose Tangle Is It Anyway? The African-American Family, Poverty and United States Kinship. *The Australian Journal of Anthropology* 16:47–61. The author carried out participant observation among homeless African-American and Latino men and their families in New York City. His findings show that all families in the United States share the same values about marriage and reproduction, poor African Americans face more stress in achieving these values.

Chassidy Puchala, Sarah Paul, Carla Kennedy, Lewis Mehi-Madrona. Using Traditional Spirituality to Reduce Domestic Violence within Aboriginal Communities. *Journal of Alternative and Complementary Medicine* 16:89–96. Canadian aboriginal victims of domestic abuse who were referred to a Traditional Healing Elder were helped, perhaps through hearing stories of nonviolent relationships.

SOCIAL GROUPS AND SOCIAL STRATIFICATION

9

◀ Uyghurs (WEE-gers) are a Turkic ethnic population. Most live in China's Xinjiang Uyghur Autonomous Region (XUAR) and are Muslim. The Chinese state puts pressure on Uyghurs, particularly young women, to leave the XUAR to work in factories in Han regions of the south where they encounter language and other cultural barriers.

In the early 1800s, when French political philosopher Alexis de Tocqueville visited the United States and characterized it as a "nation of joiners," he implied that people in some cultures are more likely to join groups than are people in other cultures. The questions of what motivates people to join groups, what holds people together in groups, and how groups deal with leadership and participation have intrigued scholars in many fields for centuries.

This chapter focuses on nonkin groups and microculture formation. Chapter 1 defined several factors related to microcultures: class, "race," ethnicity, indigeneity, gender, age, and institutions such as prisons and retirement homes. This chapter looks at how microcultures shape group identity and organization and the relationships among different groups in terms of hierarchy and power. It first examines a variety of social groups ranging from small scale to large scale and then considers inequalities among social groups. The last section looks at the concept of civil society and provides examples of it.

◉ ◼ ◉

Social Groups

A **social group** is a cluster of people beyond the domestic unit who are usually related on a basis other than kinship, although kinship relationships may exist between people in the group. Two basic categories exist: the **primary group**, consisting of people who interact with each other and know each other personally, and the **secondary group**, consisting of people who identify with one another on some common ground but who may never meet with one another or interact with each other personally.

Members of all social groups have a sense of rights and responsibilities in relation to the group. Membership in a primary group, because of the face-to-face interaction, involves more direct accountability about rights and responsibilities than does membership in a secondary group.

Modes of livelihood affect the formation of social groups, with the greatest variety of groups found in agricultural and industrial–informatic societies (Figure 9.1). One theory explaining this pattern is that mobile populations, such as foragers and pastoralists, are less likely to develop enduring social groups beyond kin relationships simply because they

have less social density and less continuous interaction than more settled populations have. Although foragers and pastoralists have fewer types of social groups, they do not completely lack social groupings. A prominent form of social group among foragers and pastoralists is an **age set**, a group of people close in age who go through certain rituals, such as circumcision, at the same time.

Although it is generally true that settled populations have more social groups, as a way to organize society, some important exceptions exist. In accordance with this generalization, many informal and formal groups are active throughout Africa, Latin America, and Southeast Asia, but such groups are less prominent in South Asia, a region that includes Pakistan, India, Nepal, Bhutan, Bangladesh, and Sri Lanka. In Bangladesh (Map 9.1), for example, a densely populated and agrarian country of South Asia, indigenous social groups are rare. The most prominent ties beyond the immediate household are kinship based (Miller and Khan 1986). In spite of the lack of indigenous social groups, Bangladesh has gained world renown since the later twentieth century for its success in forming local groups through an organization called the Grameen Bank, which offers *microcredit* (small loans) to poor people to help them start small businesses. Likewise, throughout the rest of South Asia, the modern era has seen the rise of many active social groups, including those dedicated to preserving traditional environmental knowledge, promoting women and children's health and survival, and advocating for lesbian and gay rights.

MAP 9.1 Bangladesh.
The People's Republic of Bangladesh is located on a deltaic floodplain with rich soil and risk of flooding. One of the world's most densely populated countries, Bangladesh has nearly 150 million people living in an area about the size of the state of Wisconsin. Bangladesh is the world's third-largest Muslim-majority country.

---

social group   a cluster of people beyond the domestic unit who are usually related on grounds other than kinship.

primary group   a social group in which members meet on a face-to-face basis.

secondary group   a group of people who identify with one another on some basis but may never meet with one another personally.

age set   a group of people close in age who go through certain rituals, such as circumcision, at the same time.

Foraging	Horticulture	Pastoralism	Agriculture	Industrialism/Informatics
Characteristics				**Characteristics**
Informal and primary			Formal and secondary	
Egalitarian structure			Recognized leadership	
Ties based on balanced exchange		Ritual ties	Dues and fees	
Functions				**Functions**
Companionship		Special purposes		
		Work, war, lobbying government		
Types				**Types**
Friendship	Friendship			Friendship
	Age-based work groups			Urban youth gangs
	Gender-based work groups			Clubs, associations
			Status Groups:	
			Class, "race," ethnicity, caste, age, gender	
			Institutional Groups:	
			Prisons, retirement homes	
			Quasi-Political Groups:	
			Human rights, environmental groups	

FIGURE 9.1 Modes of Livelihood and Social Groups.

This section describes a variety of social groups, starting with the most face-to-face, primary groups of two or three people based on friendship. It then moves to larger and more formal groups, such as countercultural groups and activist groups.

Friendship

Friendship refers to close social ties between at least two people in which the ties are informal, are voluntary, and involve personal, face-to-face interaction. Generally, friendship involves people who are nonkin, but in some cases kin are also friends. (Recall the Tory Islanders discussed in Chapter 8.) Friendship fits into the category of a primary social group.

One question that cultural anthropologists ask is whether friendship is a cultural universal. Two factors make it difficult to answer this question. First, insufficient cross-cultural research exists to answer the question definitively. Second, defining friendship cross-culturally is problematic. It is likely, however, that something like "friendship" is a cultural universal but shaped in different degrees from culture to culture (see Everyday Anthropology on page 212).

SOCIAL CHARACTERISTICS OF FRIENDSHIP People choose their friends, and friends remain so on a voluntary basis. Even so, the criteria for who qualifies as a friend may be culturally structured. For instance, gender segregation may prevent cross-gender friendships and promote same-gender friendships, and racial segregation limits cross-"race" friendships. Another characteristic of friendship is that friends are supportive of each other, psychologically and sometimes materially. Support is mutual, shared back and forth in an expectable way (as in balanced exchange; see Chapter 5). Friendship generally occurs between social equals, although there are exceptions, such as friendships between older and younger people, between a supervisor and a staff worker, or between a teacher and a student.

Sharing stories is often a basis of friendship groups. According to a study that focused on interactions among men's friendship groups in rumshops in Guyana (gy-AH-nuh) (see Map 9.2 on page 213), Indo-Guyanese men who have known each other since childhood spend time every day at the rumshop, eating, drinking, and regaling each other with stories (Sidnell 2000). Through shared storytelling about village history and other aspects of local knowledge, men display their equality with each other. The pattern of storytelling, referred to as "turn-at-talk," in which efforts are made to include everyone as a storyteller in turn, also serves to maintain equality and solidarity. These friendship groups are tightly knit, and the members can call on one another for economic, social, and political help.

Participant observation and interviews with a sample of rural and urban, low-income Jamaicans reveals that cell phone use is frequent (Horst and Miller 2005). Jamaicans are keenly aware of their call lists and how often they have kept in touch with the many individuals on their lists. Cell phones allow for "linking up," or creating extensive networks that include close friends, possible future sexual partners, and members of one's church. Phone numbers of kin are also prominent on people's cell-phone-number lists. By linking up periodically with people on their lists, low-income Jamaicans maintain friendship and other ties with people on whom they can call when they

Making Friends

People's daily activities are often the basis of friendship ties. In Andalucia, southern Spain (see Map 3.5, on page 73), men and women pursue separate kinds of work and, relatedly, have different friendship patterns (Uhl 1991). Men's work takes place outside the house and neighborhood, either in the fields or in manufacturing jobs. Women devote most of their time to unpaid household work within the domestic domain. This dichotomy is somewhat fluid, however, as women's domestic roles sometimes take them to the market or the town hall.

For men, an important category of friend is an *amigo*, a friend with whom one casually interacts. This kind of friendship is acted out and maintained in bars where men drink together nightly. Bars are a man's world. Amigos share common experiences of school, sports and hobbies, and working together. In contrast, women refer to their friends using kin terms or as *vecina*, "neighbor," reflecting women's primary orientation to family and neighborhood.

Differences also emerge in the category of *amigos(as) de verdad*, or "true

A shepherd in Andalucia, southern Spain. In rural areas of Andalucia, as in much of the Mediterranean region, the division of labor is distinct and according to gender, with men working outside the home and women working inside or near the home. Friendship formation follows this pattern. Men form ties with men in cafes and bars after work, and women establish ties with other women in the neighborhood.

friends." True friends are those with whom one shares secrets without fear of betrayal. Men have more true friends than women do, a pattern that reflects their wider social networks.

FOOD FOR THOUGHT ▼
What categories of friends do you have? Are friends in some categories "closer" or "truer" than others? What is the basis of close friendship?

---

need support. Cell phones allow a more extensive network of friends and other contacts than was previously possible.

FRIENDSHIP AMONG THE URBAN POOR Carol Stack wrote a landmark book in the early 1970s showing how friendship networks promote economic survival among low-income, urban African Americans (1974). She conducted fieldwork in "The Flats," the poorest section of a Black community in a large midwestern city. She found extensive networks of friends "supporting, reinforcing each other— devising schemes for self help, strategies for survival in a community of severe economic deprivation" (1974:28).

People in the Flats, especially women, maintain a set of friends through exchange: "swapping" goods (food, clothing) needed by someone at a particular time, sharing "child keeping," and giving or lending food stamps and money. Such exchanges are part of a clearly understood pattern—gifts and favors go back and forth over time. Friends thus bound together are obligated to each another and can call on each other in time

of need. In opposition to theories that suggest the breakdown of social relationships among the very poor, this research documents how poor people strategize and cope through social ties.

In the intervening decades, many other studies have documented the positive aspects of friendship among people of all social classes. Friendship, like all other social groups, has its downside, however, since one is never friends with everyone. More vividly, bullying, or behavior that serves to belittle and often viciously exclude individuals, can be considered the harsh opposite of befriending someone. To date, almost no anthropological research has been conducted on bullying.

Clubs and Fraternities/Sororities

Clubs and *fraternities/sororities* are social groups that define membership in terms of a sense of shared identity and objectives. They may comprise people of the same ethnic heritage, occupation or business, religion, or gender. Although many clubs appear to exist primarily to serve functions of sociability

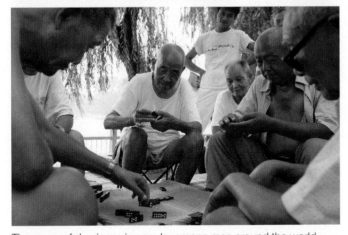

The game of dominoes is popular among men around the world. Men often play dominoes in public spaces, cheered on by male friends as here (TOP) in a low-income neighborhood in Rio de Janeiro, Brazil, in Baghdad, Iraq (CENTER), and in Beijing, China (BOTTOM).

▶ *Twenty years from now, do you think men in these same contexts will be playing dominoes? If not, what might they be playing?*

America, clubs raise funds to sponsor special events and support individual celebrations, meet personal financial needs, and send cards and flowers for funerals. Members attend each other's birthday parties and death rites as a group. The clubs thus offer the women psychological support, entertainment, and financial help. A political aspect exists, too. Club members often belong to the same political party and attend political rallies and events together. The clubs therefore constitute political interest groups that can influence political outcomes. Politicians and party workers confirmed that real pressure is exerted on them by women individually and in groups.

College fraternities and sororities are highly selective groups that serve a variety of explicit functions, such as entertainment and social service. They also form bonds between members that may help in securing jobs after graduation. Few anthropologists have studied the "Greek system" on U.S. campuses. An exception is Peggy Sanday, who was inspired to study college fraternities after the gang rape of a woman student by several fraternity brothers at the campus where she teaches. Her book *Fraternity Gang Rape: Sex, Brotherhood, and Privilege on Campus* (1990) explores initiation rituals and how they are related to male bonding solidified by victimization and ridicule of women. Gang rape, or a "train," is a prevalent practice in some,

MAP 9.2 **Caribbean Countries of South America.**

The ethnically and linguistically diverse countries of the Caribbean region of South America include Guyana, Suriname, and French Guiana. Guyana, or the Co-operative Republic of Guyana, is the only South American country whose official language is English. Other languages are Hindi, Wai Wai, and Arawak. Its population is 800,000. The Republiek Suriname, or Suriname, was formerly a colony of the Netherlands and is the smallest independent state in South America. Its population is 440,000. Dutch is the official language, but most Surinamese also speak Sranang Tongo, or Surinaams, a mixture of Dutch, English, Portuguese, French, and local languages. French Guiana is an overseas department of France and is thus part of the European Union. The smallest political unit in South America, its population is 200,000. Its official language is French, but several other languages are spoken, including indigenous Arawak and Carib.

and psychological support, deeper analysis often shows that these groups have economic and political roles as well.

Women's clubs in a lower class neighborhood in Paramaribo, Suriname (see Map 9.2), have multiple functions (Brana-Shute 1976). Here, as is common elsewhere in Latin

Fraternities and sororities, or "Greek" organizations on college campuses, serve a wide variety of functions, from hedonistic partying as at this weekend gathering (LEFT) at the University of San Francisco to performing public service. They may also create and promote new cultural forms of expression. Step dancing grew out of African American school-yard dancing and was picked up and developed by college fraternities and sororities. At Howard University, a historically Black university in the United States, the Delta Sigma Theta Sorority step team members (RIGHT) are national winners in this performance genre.

not all, fraternities. Fraternity party invitations may hint at the possibility of a "train." Typically, the brothers seek out a "party girl"—a somewhat vulnerable young woman who may be especially needy of acceptance or especially high on alcohol or other substances (her drinks may have been "spiked"). They take her to one of the brothers' rooms, where she may or may not agree to have sex with one of the brothers, and she often passes out. Then a "train" of men have sex with her. Rarely prosecuted, the male participants reinforce their sense of privilege, power, and unity with one another through a group ritual involving abuse of a female outsider.

In many indigenous Amazonian groups, the men's house is fiercely guarded from being entered by women. If a woman trespasses on male territory, men punish her by gang rape. One interpretation of this cultural practice is that men have a high degree of anxiety about their identity as fierce warriors and as sexually potent males (Gregor 1982). Maintaining their identity as fierce and forbidding toward outsiders involves taking an aggressive position in relation to women of their own group.

Cross-culturally, women do not tend to form *androphobic* ("man-hating" or otherwise anti-male) clubs, the logical parallel of *gynophobic* ("woman-hating" or otherwise anti-female) men's clubs. College sororities, for example, are not mirror images of college fraternities. Although some sororities' initiation rituals are psychologically brutal to the pledges, bonding among the members does not involve abusive behavior toward men.

COUNTERCULTURAL GROUPS Several kinds of groups comprise people who, for one reason or another, are

outside the mainstream of society and resist conforming to the dominant cultural pattern. The so-called *hippies* of the 1960s were one such group. One similarity among these groups, as with clubs and fraternities, is the importance of bonding through shared initiation and other rituals.

YOUTH GANGS The term **youth gang** refers to a group of young people, found mainly in urban areas, who are often considered a social problem by adults and law enforcement officials (Sanders 1994).

Youth gangs vary in terms of how formally they are organized. Like clubs and fraternities, gangs often have a recognized leader, formalized rituals of initiation for new members, and symbolic markers of identity, such as tattoos or special clothing. An example of an informal youth gang with no formal leadership hierarchy or initiation rituals is that of the "Masta Liu" in Honiara, the capital city of the Solomon Islands in the South Pacific (Jourdan 1995) (Map 9.3). Unemployment is the primary unifying feature of the male youths who become Masta Liu. Most have migrated to the city from the countryside to escape what they consider an undesirable lifestyle there: working in the fields under control of their elders. Some Liu live with extended kin in the city; others organize Liu-only households. They spend their time wandering around town, referred to locally as going *wakabaot*, in groups of up to 10:

> They stop at every shop on their way, eager to look at the merchandise but afraid to be kicked out by the security guards; they check out all the cinemas only to dream in front of the preview posters . . . not even having the $2 bill that will allow them to get in; they gaze for hours on end, and without moving, at the electronic equipment displayed

youth gang a group of young people, found mainly in urban areas, who are often considered a social problem by adults and law enforcement officials.

MAP 9.3 The Solomon Islands.

This country consists of nearly 1000 islands. Its capital, Honiara, is located on the island of Guadalcanal. The population is 540,000. Most of the people earn a living through small-scale farming and fishing. Commercial exploitation of local timber has led to severe deforestation. Over 70 languages are spoken, and an additional 4 have recently gone extinct. The majority of the people are Christian, mainly Anglican. The Solomons were the site of some of the bitterest fighting during World War II.

in the Chinese shops, without saying a word: One can read in their gaze the silent dreams they create. (1995:210)

Street gangs are a more formal variety of youth gang. They generally have leaders and a hierarchy of membership roles and responsibilities. They are named, and their members mark their identity with tattoos or "colors." Much popular thinking associates street gangs with violence, but not all are involved in violence. An anthropologist who did research among nearly 40 street gangs in New York, Los Angeles, and Boston learned much about why individuals join gangs, providing insights that also contradict popular thinking (Jankowski 1991). One common perception is that young boys join gangs because they are from homes with no male authority figure with whom they identify. In the gangs studied, about half of the gang members were from intact nuclear

households. Another common perception is that the gang replaces a missing feeling of family. This study showed that the same number of gang members reported having close family ties as those who did not.

Why, then, did young men join an urban gang? The research revealed that many gang members had a particular personality type called a *defiant individualist*. The defiant individualist type has five characteristics:

- Intense competitiveness
- Mistrust of others
- Self-reliance
- Social isolation
- A strong survival instinct

A structurist view suggests that poverty, especially urban poverty, leads to the development of this kind of personality, which is a reasonable response to the prevailing economic obstacles and uncertainty. To explain the global spread of urban youth gangs, structurists point to widespread economic changes in urban employment opportunities. In many countries, a declining urban industrial base has created persistent poverty in inner-city communities. At the same time, schooling and the popular media promote aspirations for a better life. Urban gang members, in this view, are the victims of large structural forces beyond their control that both inspire them to want aspects of a successful lifestyle and prevent them from achieving the legal means to obtain their aspirations. Many of these youths want to be economically successful, but social conditions channel their interests and skills into illegal pursuits rather than into legal pathways to achievement.

BODY MODIFICATION GROUPS One of the many countercultural movements in the United States includes people who have a sense of community strengthened through forms of body alteration. James Myers (1992) did research in California among people who feel that they are a special group because of their interest in permanent body modification, especially genital piercing, branding, and cutting. Fieldwork involved participant observation and interviews: Myers was involved in workshops organized for the San Francisco sadomasochist (SM) community; he attended the Fifth Annual Living in Leather Convention held in Portland, Oregon, in 1990; he spent time in tattoo and piercing studios; and he talked with students and others in his hometown who were involved in these forms of body modification. The study population included males and females,

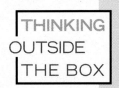

THINKING OUTSIDE THE BOX

Think of some examples in which socially excluded groups have contributed to changing styles of music, dress, and other forms of expressive culture of so-called *mainstream groups*.

A Cambodian boy dances to hip hop music in Phnom Penh, the capital city. Established by a former U.S. gang member who was deported after being convicted of armed robbery, the Tiny Toones center also teaches disc-jockey skills and rapping to nearly 400 children. Tiny Toones and its founder Tuy Sobil, better known as Kay Kay, have won praise for helping drug addicts and poor street kids transform their lives.

heterosexuals, gays, lesbians, bisexuals, and SMers. The single largest group was SM homosexuals and bisexuals. The study population was mainly White, and most had either attended or graduated from college.

Myers witnessed many modification sessions at workshops: Those seeking modification go up on stage and have their chosen procedure done by a well-known expert. Whatever the procedure, the volunteers exhibit little pain—usually just a sharp intake of breath at the moment the needle passes through or the brand touches skin. After that critical moment, the audience breathes an audible sigh of relief. The volunteer stands up and adjusts his or her clothing, and members of the audience applaud. This public event is a kind of initiation ritual that binds the expert, the volunteer, and the group together. Pain is an important part of many rites of passage. In this case, the audience witnesses and validates the experience and becomes joined to the initiate through witnessing.

The study revealed that a prominent motivation for seeking permanent body modification was a desire to identify with a specific group of people. As one participant said,

> It's not that we're sheep, getting pierced or cut just because everyone else is. I like to think it's because we're a very special group and we like doing something that sets us off from others. . . . Happiness is standing in line at a cafeteria and detecting that the straight-looking babe in front of you has her nipples pierced. I don't really care what her sexual orientation is, I can relate to her. (1992:292)

Cooperatives

Cooperatives are a form of economic group in which surpluses are shared among the members and decision making follows the democratic principle of each individual member having one vote (Estrin 1996). Agricultural and credit cooperatives are the most common forms of cooperatives worldwide, followed by consumer cooperatives.

In Panama's eastern coastal region, indigenous Kuna (koo-nuh) women long have sewn beautiful *molas*, or cloth with appliquéd designs (Map 9.4 on page 218). Kuna make this cloth for their own use as clothing, but since the 1960s, molas have been important items for sale both on the world market and to tourists who come to Panama (Tice 1995). Revenue from selling molas to tourists, as well as internationally, is now an important part of the household income of the Kuna. Some women continue to operate independently, buying their own cloth and thread and selling their molas either to an intermediary who exports them or in the local tourist market. But many women have joined cooperatives that offer them greater economic security. The cooperative buys cloth and thread in bulk and distributes it to the women. The women are paid almost the entire sale price for each mola, with only a small amount of the eventual sale prices being taken out for cooperative dues and administrative costs. Their earnings are steadier than what the fluctuating tourist season offers. Other benefits from being a member of the cooperative include its use as a consumer's cooperative (buying rice and sugar in bulk for members), a source of mutual strength and support, and a place for women to develop greater leadership skills and to take advantage of opportunities for political participation in the wider society.

Self-Help Groups

Recent years have seen a worldwide proliferation of *self-help groups*, or groups formed to achieve specific personal

(LEFT) A Tahitian chief wears tattoos that indicate his high status. (RIGHT) A woman with tattooed arms in the United States.

▶ *In your microcultural experience, what do tattoos mean to you when you see someone with them?*

goals, such as coping with illness or bereavement, or lifestyle changes such as trying to exercise more or lose weight. Self-help groups also increasingly are using the Internet to form virtual support communities. Anthropologists who study these groups focus on why members join, on rituals of solidarity, and on leadership and organization patterns.

An ethnography of Alcoholics Anonymous (AA) groups in Mexico City (see Map 6.3, page 140) reports that most members are low-income, working-class males (Brandes 2002). They migrated to Mexico City from rural areas several decades earlier to find work and improve their standard of living. Their drinking problems are related both to their poverty and to the close links between alcohol consumption and male gender identity in Mexico: A "real man" consumes a lot of alcohol. Through a dynamic of shared stories and regular meetings, AA members in Mexico City achieve a high rate of sobriety.

The success of AA in Mexico is leading to a rapid proliferation of AA groups around the world. Membership globally is growing at about 10 percent a year, a remarkably high rate

of growth for a self-help organization. At the end of the twentieth century, Latin America accounted for almost one-third of total AA membership worldwide. Thus, a model of a middle-class self-help organization that originated in the United States has been adopted and culturally localized by low-income men throughout Latin America.

◼ ◼ ◼

Social Stratification

Social stratification consists of hierarchical relationships among different groups, as though they were arranged in layers, or *strata*. Stratified groups may be unequal on a variety of measures, including material resources, power, human welfare, education, and symbolic attributes. People in groups in higher positions have privileges not experienced by those in lower echelon groups, and they are likely to be interested in

---

social stratification   a set of hierarchical relationships among different groups as though they were arranged in layers, or "strata."

Kuna Indian woman selling *molas*, San Blas Islands, Panama.

▶ *Learn more about molas from the Web.*

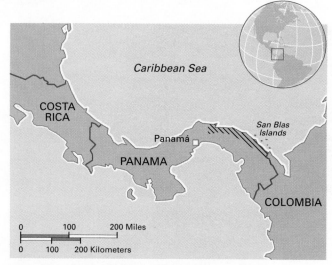

MAP 9.4 Kuna Region in Panama.

The Kuna are an indigenous people who live mainly in the eastern coastal region of Panama, including its offshore islands. Some live in cities, and a few live in villages in neighboring Colombia. The Kuna population is around 150,000. Farming, fishing, and tourism are important parts of the economy. Each community has its own political organization, and the Kuna as a whole are organized into the Kuna General Congress. Most speak Kuna, or Dulegaya ("People's Language"), and Spanish. They follow traditional religious practices, often with a mixture of Christian elements.

maintaining their privileged positions. Social stratification appeared late in human history, most clearly with the emergence of agriculture. Now some form of social stratification is nearly universal.

Analysis of the categories—such as class, "race," gender, age, and indigeneity—within stratification systems reveals a crucial difference among them in the degree to which membership in a given category is an **ascribed position**, based on qualities of a person gained through birth, or an **achieved position**, based on qualities of a person gained through action. Ascribed positions may be based on one's "race," ethnicity, gender, age, or physical ability. These factors are generally out of the control of the individual, although some flexibility exists for gender (through surgery and hormonal treatments) and for certain kinds of physical conditions. Also, one can sometimes "pass" as a member of another "race" or ethnic group. Age is

---

ascribed position   a person's standing in society based on qualities that the person has gained through birth.

achieved position   a person's standing in society based on qualities that the person has gained through action.

status   a person's position, or standing, in society.

mestizaje   literally, a racial mixture; in Central and South America, indigenous people who are cut off from their Indian roots, or literate and successful indigenous people who retain some traditional cultural practices.

an interesting ascribed category because an individual goes through several different status levels associated with age. Achievement as a basis for group membership means that a person's membership in the group is based on some valued attainment. Ascribed systems are thus more "closed," and achievement-based systems more "open," in terms of mobility, either upward or downward, within the system. Some scholars of social status believe that modernization during the twentieth century and increased social complexity led to a rise in achievement-based positions and a decline in ascription-based positions. The material that follows explores how social categories define group membership and relations of inequality among groups.

Societies place people into categories—student, husband, child, retired person, political leader, or member of Phi Beta Kappa—referred to as a person's **status**, or position or standing in society (Wolf 1996). Each status has an accompanying role, which is expected behavior for someone of a particular status, and a "script" for how to behave, look, and talk. Some statuses have more prestige attached to them than others. Within societies that have marked status positions, different status groups are marked by a particular lifestyle, including the goods they own, their leisure activities, and their linguistic styles. The maintenance of group position by the higher status categories is sometimes accomplished by exclusionary practices in relation to lower-status groups through a tendency toward group in-marriage and socializing only

(TOP) Salvatore Ferragamo headquarters in Firenze (Florence), Italy. Top brand names such as Ferragamo are highly sought after by consumers internationally who can afford to buy these luxury goods. (BOTTOM) Warren Buffett, the world's third richest man in 2010. American businessman, investor, and philanthropist, Buffett is worth around US $62 billion. He is, however, known for his frugal life style.

▶ *For a class project, do research for a report on Buffett's biography with attention to cultural context.*

within the group. Groups, like individuals, have status, or standing, in society.

Achieved Status: Class

Social class (defined in Chapter 1) refers to a person's or group's position in society and is defined primarily in economic terms. In many cultures, class is a key factor in determining a person's status, whereas in others, it is less important than, for example, birth into a certain family. Class and status, however, do not always match. A rich person may have become wealthy in disreputable ways and never gain high status. Both status and class groups are secondary groups, because a person is unlikely to know every other member of the group, especially in large-scale societies.

In capitalist societies, the prevailing ideology is that the system allows for upward mobility and that every individual has the option of moving up. Some anthropologists refer to this ideology as *meritocratic individualism*, the belief that rewards go to those who deserve them (Durrenberger 2001). In contrast, a structurist perspective points to the power of economic class position in shaping a person's lifestyle and his or her ability to choose a different one. Obviously, a person who was born rich can, through individual agency, become poor, and a poor person can become rich. In spite of exceptions to the rule, a person born rich is more likely to lead a lifestyle typical of that class, just as a person born poor is more likely lead a lifestyle typical of that class.

The concept of class is central to the theories of Karl Marx. Situated within the context of Europe's Industrial Revolution and the growth of capitalism, Marx wrote that class differences, exploitation of the working class by the owners of capital, class consciousness among workers, and class conflict were forces of change that would eventually spell the downfall of capitalism.

Ascribed Status: "Race," Ethnicity, Gender, and Caste

Four major ascribed systems of social stratification are based on divisions of people into unequally ranked groups on the basis of, respectively, "race," ethnicity (defined in Chapter 1), gender, and caste, the last a ranked group determined by birth and often linked to a particular occupation and to South Asian cultures. Like status and class groups, these four categories are secondary social groups, because no one can have a personal relationship with all other members of the entire group. Each system takes on local specificities, depending on the context. For example, "race" and ethnicity are interrelated and overlap with conceptions of culture in much of Latin America, although what they mean in terms of identity and status differs in different countries in the region (de la Cadena 2001). For some, the concept of **mestizaje** (mes-tee-SAH-hay),

A mural greets visitors on the exterior of Oakland's Ella Baker Center For Human Rights, a non profit social-justice organization that lobbies for green jobs programs for inner-city youth. The concept of green jobs programs was invented by Van Jones, the White House's Special Advisor for Green Jobs during 2009. Oakland is one of the most violent cities in the United States, with high levels of pollution, poverty, and unemployment. The green jobs program's goal is to prepare inner-city inhabitants to compete for the green jobs that will be created in the next 10 years.

from the word *mestizo*, literally means "racial" mixture. In Central and South America, it refers either to people who are cut off from their Indian roots or to literate and successful people who retain some indigenous cultural practices. One has to know the local system of categories and meanings attached to them to understand the dynamics of inequality that go with them.

Systems based on differences defined in terms of "race," ethnicity, gender, and caste share some important features with each other and with class-based systems. First, they relegate large numbers of people to particular levels of entitlement to livelihood, power, security, esteem, and freedom (Berreman 1979 [1975]:213). This simple fact should not be overlooked. Second, those with greater entitlements dominate those with lesser entitlements. Third, members of the dominant groups tend to seek to maintain their position, consciously or unconsciously. They do this through institutions that control ideology among the dominated and through institutions that physically suppress potential rebellion or subversion by the dominated (Harris 1971, quoted in Mencher 1974:469). Fourth, in spite of efforts to maintain systems of dominance, instances of subversion and rebellion do occur, indicating the potential for agency among the oppressed.

"RACE" Racial stratification is a relatively recent form of social inequality. It results from the unequal meeting of two formerly separate groups through colonization, slavery, and other large-group movements (Sanjek 1994). Europe's "age of discovery," beginning in the 1500s, ushered in a new era of global contact. In contrast, in relatively homogeneous cultures, ethnicity is a more important distinction than "race." In contemporary Nigeria, for example, the population is

largely homogeneous, and *ethnicity* is the more salient term (Jinadu 1994). A similar situation prevails in other African states as well as in the Middle East, Central Europe and Eurasia, and China.

A key feature of racial thinking is its insistence that behavioral differences among peoples are "natural," inborn, or biologically caused. Throughout the history of racial categorizations in the West, such features as head size, head shape, and brain size have been accepted as reasons for behavioral differences. Writing early in the twentieth century, Franz Boas contributed to de-linking supposed inborn, racial attributes from behavior (review Chapter 1). He showed that people with the same head size but from different cultures behaved differently and that people with various head sizes within the same cultures behaved similarly. For Boas and his followers, culture, not biology, is the key explanation for behavior. Thus, "race" is not a biological reality; there is no way to divide the human population into "races" based on certain biological features. Yet social race and racism exist. In other words, in many contexts the concept of "race" has a social reality in terms of people's entitlements, status, and treatment. In spite of some progress in reducing racism in the United States in the twentieth century, racial discrimination persists.

Racial classifications in the Caribbean and in Latin America involve complicated systems of status classification. The complexity results from the variety of contact over the centuries between peoples from Europe, Africa, Asia, and indigenous populations. Skin tone is one basis of racial classification, but it is mixed with other physical features and economic status as well. In Haiti, for example, racial categories take into account physical factors such as skin texture,

Seven-year-old samba queen Julia Lira performs ahead of the musicians during the first night of Rio de Janeiro's famed carnival parades, in Brazil, in 2010. The Brazilian population exhibits a range of skin tones.

depth of skin tone, hair color and appearance, and facial features (Trouillot 1994). Racial categories also include a person's income, social origin, level of formal education, personality or behavior, and kinship ties. Depending on how these variables are combined, a person occupies one category or another—and may even move between categories. Thus, a person with certain physical features who is poor will be considered to be a different "color" than a person with the same physical features who is well off.

An extreme example of racial stratification was the South African policy of apartheid, the legally sanctioned segregation of dominant Whites from non-Whites. White dominance in South Africa (Map 9.5 on page 222) began in the early 1800s with White migration and settlement. In the 1830s, slavery was abolished. At the same time, increasingly racist thinking developed among Whites (Johnson 1994:25). Racist images, including images of Africans as lazy and politically disorganized, served as part of the rationale for colonialist domination. In spite of years of African resistance to White domination, the Whites succeeded in maintaining and increasing their control for nearly two centuries. In South Africa, Blacks constitute 90 percent of the population, a numerical majority that was long dominated, through strict apartheid, by the White minority until 1994. During apartheid, every measure of the quality of life—infant mortal-

ity, longevity, education—showed great disparity between the Whites and the Africans. In addition to suffering from physical deprivation, Black South Africans experienced psychological suffering through constant personal insecurity caused by the threat and actuality of police raids and other forms of violence directed against them. Now, Black South Africans continue to face the scourge of continuing poverty and disentitlement as well as excess death and suffering from HIV/AIDS.

In contrast to the explicitly racist discrimination of South African apartheid, racism exists even where it is against the law to discriminate against people on the basis of race. In such contexts, structural violence as played out through racism is often denied by those in power, a fact that makes it especially difficult to fight.

ETHNICITY Ethnicity is group membership based on a shared sense of identity that may be based on history,

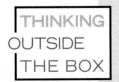

THINKING OUTSIDE THE BOX

With which ethnic or other kind of social group do you identify? What are the bases of this identification? Is your social group relatively high or low in terms of social status?

In 2003, the Treatment Action Campaign (TAC) began a program of civil disobedience to prompt the government of South Africa to sign and implement a National Prevention and Treatment Plan for HIV/AIDS. The TAC uses images of Hector Peterson, the first youth killed in the Soweto uprising against apartheid, and slogans such as "The Struggle Continues: Support HIV/AIDS Treatment Now."

▶ *Take a position, and be prepared to defend it, on whether or not a country's government should take responsibility for preventing and treating HIV/AIDS.*

MAP 9.5 South Africa.

The Republic of South Africa experienced the highest level of colonial immigration of any African country. Its rich mineral wealth attracted interest from global powers through the Cold War era. Of its population of over 46 million, 80 percent are Black South Africans. The rest are of mixed ethnic backgrounds (referred to as "Coloureds"), Indian (from India), or White descendants of colonial immigrants. South Africa has 11 official languages, and it recognizes 8 nonofficial languages. Afrikaans and English are the major languages of the administration. Nonofficial languages include those of the San and other indigenous peoples.

territory, language, or religion, or a combination of these (Comaroff 1987). Ethnicity can be a basis for claiming entitlements to resources (such as land, buildings, or artifacts) and for defending or regaining those resources.

States are interested in managing ethnicity to the extent that it does not threaten security. China has one of the most formalized systems for monitoring its many ethnic groups, and it has an official policy on ethnic minorities, meaning the non-Han groups (Wu 1990). The government lists 54 groups other than the Han majority, which constitutes about 94 percent of the total population. The other 6 percent of the population is made up of these 54 groups, about 67 million people. The non-Han minorities occupy about 60 percent of China's land mass and are located in border or "frontier" areas such as Tibet, Yunnan, Xinjiang, and Inner Mongolia. Basic criteria for defining an ethnic group include language, territory, economy, and "psychological disposition." The Chinese government establishes strict definitions of group membership and group characteristics; it even sets standards for ethnic costumes and dances. The Chinese treatment of the Tibetan people is especially severe and can be considered ethnocide, or annihilation of the culture of an ethnic group by a dominant group.

The Chinese government's treatment of Tibetan traditional medicine over the past several decades illustrates how the Han majority exploits aspects of minority cultures. In

1951, China forcibly incorporated Tibet, and the Chinese government undertook measures to bring about the social and economic transformation of what was formerly a de-centralized, Buddhist feudal regime. This transformation has caused increasing ethnic conflict between Tibetans and Han Chinese, including demonstrations by Tibetans and crackdowns from the Chinese. Traditional Tibetan medicine has become part of the Chinese–Tibetan conflicts because of its cultural significance and importance to religion in Tibetan society (Janes 1995:7). Previously based on a model of apprenticeship training, it is now westernized and involves several years of classroom-based, lecture-oriented learning followed by an internship. At Tibet University, only half of all formal lecture-based instruction is concerned with traditional Tibetan medicine. Curriculum changes have reduced the integrity of Tibetan medicine: It has been separated from its Buddhist content, and parts of it have been merged with a biomedical approach. Some might say that, overall, traditional Tibetan medicine has been "revived" in China, but stronger evidence supports the argument that the state has co-opted it and transformed it for its own purposes.

People of one ethnic group who move from one niche to another are at risk of exclusionary treatment by the local residents. Roma (often called Gypsies by outsiders, a term that Roma consider to be derogatory), are a **diaspora population**, a dispersed group living outside their original homeland. Roma are scattered throughout Europe and the United States (see Culturama). Their status within mainstream

---

diaspora population a dispersed group of people living outside their original homeland.

CULTURAMA

The Roma of Eastern Europe

The Roma are Europe's largest minority population. They live in nearly all the countries of Europe and Central Asia. In Europe, their total is between 7 and 9 million people (World Bank 2003). They are concentrated in Eastern Europe, where they constitute around 10 percent of the population.

The Roma have a long history of mobility and marginality ever since several waves of migrants left their original homeland in northern India between the ninth and fourteenth centuries CE (Crowe 1996). The lifestyle of many Roma in Europe continues to involve movement, with temporary camps of their wagons appearing overnight on the outskirts of a town. Most settled Roma live in marginalized areas that lack decent housing, clean water, and good schools. Members of mainstream society look down on, and even despise, the Roma.

In Budapest, Hungary, the Roma minority is the most disadvantaged ethnic group (Ladányi 1993). Not all Roma in Budapest, however, are poor.

About 1 percent have gained wealth. The other 99 percent live in substandard housing in the slums of inner Pest. Since the fall of state socialism in Hungary, social discrimination against the Roma has increased. Some Roma communities are mobilizing to improve their living conditions. The government instituted a policy allowing the Roma a degree of self-government (Schaft and Brown 2000).

In Slovakia, one-third of the Roma live in ghetto-like enclaves called *osada* (Scheffel 2004). These settlements lack clean water, sewage treatment, reliable electricity, access to decent housing, good schools, and passable roads. Osada exist in close proximity to affluent neighborhoods of ethnic Slovaks, or "Whites." In one village, Svinia (SVEEH-nee-yuh), roughly 700 Roma are crowded together on 1 hectare of swampy land while their 670 ethnic Slovak neighbors own over 1400 hectares of land (2004:8).

As more Eastern European countries seek to enter the European Union, they are initiating programs to improve Roma living conditions and enacting laws to prevent discrimination. After Hungary joined the European Union in 2004, it elected two Roma to the EU Parliament. In Bulgaria, the Roma won a court case in 2005 declaring that segregated schools were unconstitutional. Fieldwork in Slovakia, however, indicates that the government there is doing little to improve the lives of the Roma.

The global economic crisis that began in 2008 led to increased ethnic violence against Roma throughout Eastern Europe. The economic downturn hit European countries with large Roma populations particularly hard, including Hungary, Romania, Slovakia, and Serbia. Some politicians and extremist groups in these countries blame the Roma for taking away jobs from non-Roma people.

Thanks to David Z. Scheffel, Thompson Rivers University, for reviewing this material.

0 100 200 Miles
0 100 200 Kilometers

POLAND

CZECH REPUBLIC

SLOVAKIA

UKRAINE

SLOVENIA

HUNGARY

ROMANIA

BOSNIA & HERZEGOVINA

SERBIA

BULGARIA

MACEDONIA

(LEFT) The Roma settlement of Svinia in 1993. The standard of living has not improved since the 1990s, but the population has increased by nearly 50 percent, resulting in overcrowding and high levels of stress.

(CENTER) Roma children's access to school facilities is severely restricted. A few Romani schoolchildren participate in the school lunch program, but in a separate room next to the cafeteria.

MAP 9.6 **Roma Population in Eastern Europe.** Romania has the highest number of Roma of any country in the world, between 1 and 2 million. Macedonia has the highest percentage of Roma in its population.

See more at PEARSON **myanthrolab**

society is always marginal in terms of economic, political, and social measures.

Examples of marginality and stigma experienced by minority ethnic groups are plentiful. Incoming migrants are often at risk of discrimination, as is the case of Indo-Canadians, immigrants from India to Canada. Research undertaken with nearly 300 Indo-Canadians in Vancouver, British Columbia, revealed that half of the respondents reported experiencing some form of discrimination in the recent past (Nodwell and Guppy 1992). The percentage was higher among men (54 percent) than among women (45 percent). The higher percentage for men was consistent across the four categories of discrimination listed: verbal abuse, property damage, workplace discrimination, and physical harm. Overall, verbal abuse was the most frequent form of discrimination reported by both men and women. Indo-Canadians of the Sikh faith who were born in India say that they experience the highest levels of discrimination in Canada. Apparently, however, their actual experience of discrimination is not greater than that for other Indo-Canadians. The difference is that Sikhs who were born in India are more sensitive to discrimination than others. Sikhism, as taught and practiced in India, supports a strong sense of honor, which should be protected and, if wronged, avenged. The study discussed here helps explain differences in perception of discrimination among ethnic migrants. It does not, however, explain why such high levels of discriminatory treatment exist in a country committed to ethnic tolerance.

GENDER AND SEXISM   Like other forms of social inequality, gender inequalities, based on perceived differences between people born male or female or somewhere in between, vary from one culture to another. This book has already presented many examples of gender inequality, and more will appear in later chapters. The discussion that follows highlights some features of male dominance cross-culturally.

Patriarchy, or male dominance in economic, political, social, and ideological domains, is common but not universal. It also varies in severity and results. In its most severe forms, women and girls are completely under the power of men and can be killed by men, with no societal response. So-called

honor killings, for example, of girls and women who defy rules of virginity or arranged marriage and are murdered by male kin, are examples of extreme patriarchy (Kurkiala 2003). Less violent, but also serious, is the effect of patriarchy on girls' education. In many countries, girls are not sent to school at all, or if they are, they attend for fewer years or attend schools of lower quality than their brothers.

The logical opposite of patriarchy is **matriarchy**, or female dominance in economic, political, social, and ideological domains. Matriarchy is so rare in contemporary cultures that anthropologists are not certain that it even exists—or has ever existed. Among the Iroquois at the time the European colonialists arrived, women controlled public finances, in the form of maize, and they determined whether or not war would be waged. They also chose the leaders, although the leaders were male. It is not clear whether the Iroquois were in fact matriarchal or might more accurately be considered gender egalitarian with a mixed and balanced gender system. A stronger case for a truly matriarchal society is found in the Minangkabau people of Malaysia and Indonesia (see Culturama, page 190).

CASTE AND CASTEISM   The **caste system** is a social stratification system linked with Hinduism and based on a person's birth into a particular group. It exists in its clearest form in India, among its Hindu population, and in other regions with large Hindu populations such as Nepal, Sri Lanka, and Fiji. The caste system is particularly associated with Hindu peoples because ancient Hindu scriptures are taken as the foundational sources for defining the major social categories called *varnas*, a Sanskrit word meaning "color" (Figure 9.2). The four varnas are the *Brahmans*, priests; the *Kshatriyas*, warriors; the *Vaishyas*, merchants; and the *Shudras*, laborers. Adolescent males of the first three varnas go through a ritual ceremony of initiation and "rebirth,"

---

patriarchy   the dominance of men in economic, political, social, and ideological domains.

matriarchy   the dominance of women in economic, political, social, and ideological domains.

caste system   a form of social stratification linked with Hinduism and based on a person's birth into a particular group.

dalit   the preferred name for the socially defined lowest groups in the Indian caste system; the name means "oppressed" or "ground down."

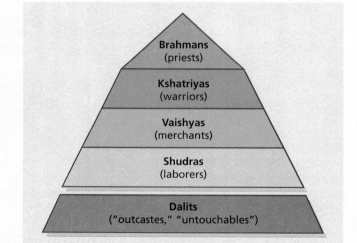

FIGURE 9.2   Model of India's Varna Categories.

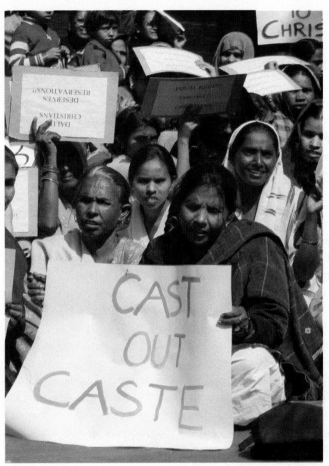

Three views of caste in India. (TOP LEFT) Only a special category of Brahman priests can officiate at the Chidambaram temple in Tamil Nadu, southern India. Here, members of a mixed-age group sit for a moment's relaxation. (BOTTOM LEFT) A village carpenter in front of his house in a north Indian village. The status of carpenters is mid-level, between the elites and those who deal with polluting materials such as animal hides or refuse. (TOP RIGHT) In New Delhi, India, Dalit Christians and Dalit Muslims mobilize to assert their rights within the larger Dalit movement that is dominated by Hindus.

after which they may wear a sacred thread across their chest, indicating their purity and high status as "twice born." Beneath the four varna groups are people ranked so low that they are outside the caste system itself—hence the English term "outcast." Another English term for them is "untouchables," because people of the upper varnas avoided any kind of contact with them in order to maintain their own purity. Mahatma Gandhi, himself a member of an upper caste, renamed them *harijans* ("children of god") in his attempt to raise their status into that of the Shudras. Currently, members of this category have adopted the term **dalit** (dah-lit), which means "oppressed" or "ground down."

The four traditional varnas and the dalit category contain many hundreds of locally named groups called castes, or, more appropriately, *jatis* (jah-tees, or birth groups). The term *caste* comes from the Portuguese word *casta*, meaning "breed" or "type." Portuguese colonialists first used it in the fifteenth century to refer to the closed social groups they encountered. Jati, an emic term, conveys the meaning that a

Hindu is born into his or her group. Jatis are ascribed status groups. Just as the four varnas are ranked relative to each other, so are all the jatis within them. For example, the jati of Brahmans is divided into priestly and nonpriestly subgroups; the priestly Brahmans are separated into household priests, temple priests, and funeral priests; the household priests are broken down into two or more categories; and each of those are divided into subgroups based on lineage ties (Parry 1996:77). Within all these categories exist well-defined status hierarchies.

Status levels also exist among dalits. In western Nepal, which, like India, has a caste system, dalit artisans such as basket weavers and ironsmiths are the highest tier (Cameron 1995). They do not touch any of the people beneath them. The second tier includes leatherworkers and tailors. The bottom tier comprises people who are "untouchable" to all groups, including other dalits, because their work is extremely polluting according to Hindu rules. This category includes musicians (because some of their instruments are made of leather and they perform in public) and sex workers.

Indian anthropologist M. N. Srinivas (1959) contributed the concept of the *dominant caste* to refer to the tendency for one caste in any particular village to control most of the land and, often, to be numerically preponderant as well. Brahmans are at the top of the social hierarchy in terms of ritual purity, and they are often, but not always, the dominant caste. Throughout northern India, it is common for jatis of the Kshatriya varna to be the dominant village group. This is the case in Pahansu village, where a group called the Gujars is dominant (Raheja 1988). The Gujars constitute the numerical majority, and they control most of the land. Moreover, they dominate in the *jajmani system*, a patron-provider system in which landholding patrons (*jajmans*) are linked, through exchanges of food for services, with Brahman priests, artisans (blacksmiths, potters), agricultural laborers, and other workers such as sweepers. In Pahansu, Gujars have power and status as the major patrons, supporting many different service providers who are beholden to them.

Some anthropologists have described the jajmani service system as one of mutual interdependence that provides security for the less well-off. Others argue that the system benefits those at the top to the detriment of those at the bottom. This perspective, from "the bottom up," views the patron-service system and the entire caste system as one of exploitation by those at the top (Mencher 1974). The benign interpretation is based on research conducted among the upper castes who present this view. From low-caste people's perspective, it is the

patrons who have the power. Dissatisfied patrons can dismiss service providers, refuse them loans, or not pay them. Service providers who are dissatisfied with the treatment they receive from their patrons have little recourse. In addition, male patrons often demand sexual access to females of service-providing households.

Throughout South Asia, the growth of industrial manufacturing has reduced the need for some service providers, especially tailors, potters, and weavers. Many of these people have left their villages to work in urban areas. The tie that remains the strongest is between patrons and their Brahman priests, whose ritual services cannot be replaced by machines.

The caste system involves several mechanisms that maintain it: marriage rules, spatial segregation, and ritual. Marriage rules strictly enforce jati endogamy (in-group marriage, review Chapter 8). Marriage outside one's jati, especially in rural areas and particularly between a higher caste female and lower caste male, is cause for punishment, often lethal, by caste elders and other local power holders. Nonetheless, a trend toward inter-jati marriages is emerging among educated people in urban areas.

Spatial segregation functions to maintain the privileged preserve of the upper castes and to remind the lower castes continually of their marginal status. In many rural villages, dalits live in a completely separate neighborhood into which no upper-caste person will venture. Ritual rules and practices also serve to maintain dominance. The rich upper-caste leaders sponsor important annual festivals, thereby regularly restating their claim to public prominence (Mines 1994).

Social mobility within the caste system has traditionally been limited, but instances have been documented of group "up-casting." Several strategies exist, including gaining wealth, affiliation or merger with a somewhat higher jati, education, migration, and political activism (Kolenda 1978). A group that attempts to gain higher jati status takes on the behavior and dress of twice-born jatis. These include men wearing the sacred thread, vegetarianism, non-remarriage of widows, seclusion of women from the public domain, and the giving of larger dowries for the marriage of a daughter. Some dalits have opted out of the caste system by converting to Christianity or Buddhism. Others are becoming politically organized through the Dalit Panthers, a social movement seeking greater power and improved economic status for dalits.

The Indian constitution of 1949 declared that discrimination on the basis of caste is illegal. Constitutional decree, however, did not bring an end to these deeply structured inequalities. In the late twentieth century, the government of India instituted policies to promote the social and economic advancement of dalits, such as reserving for them places in medical schools, seats in the government, and

---

civil society   the collection of interest groups that function outside the government to organize economic and other aspects of life.

public-sector jobs. This affirmative action plan infuriates many of the upper castes, especially Brahmans, who feel most threatened.

Is the caste system on the decline? Surely, aspects of it are changing. Especially in large cities, people of different jatis can "pass" and participate on a more nearly equal basis in public life—if they have the economic means to do so.

◉ ◉ ◉

Civil Society

Civil society consists of the social domain of diverse interest groups that function outside the government to organize economic, political, and other aspects of life. According to the German philosopher G. W. F. Hegel, civil society encompasses social groups and institutions that exist between the individual and the state. The Italian social theorist Antonio Gramsci defined two types of civic institutions: those that support the state, such as the church and schools, and those that oppose state power, such as trade unions, social protest groups, and citizens' rights groups.

Civil Society for the State: The Chinese Women's Movement

In some instances, governments seek to build civil society to further their own goals. The women's movement in China is an example of such a state-created organization. Canadian anthropologist Ellen Judd (2002) conducted a study of the women's movement in China, within the constraints that the government imposes on anthropological fieldwork by foreigners. Under the Mao leadership, foreign anthropologists were not allowed to do research of any sort in China. The situation began to change in the 1980s when some field research, within strict limitations, became possible.

Judd developed a long-term relationship with China over several decades, having lived there as a student from 1974 to 1977, undertaking long-term fieldwork there in 1986, and returning almost every year since for research or some other activity, such as being involved in a development project for women or attending the Beijing Fourth World Conference on Women. According to Judd, "These various ways of being in China all allowed me some interaction with Chinese women and some knowledge of their lives" (2002:14). In her latest project to study the Chinese women's movement, she wanted to conduct research as a cultural anthropologist would normally do, through intensive participant observation over a long time.

Even now, the Chinese government limits such research, keeping foreigners at a distance from everyday life. Judd was not allowed to join the local women's organization or to speak privately with any of the women. Officials accompanied her on all household visits and interviews. She was allowed to attend meetings, however, and she had access to all the public information about the goals of the women's movement, which is called the Women's Federations. A policy goal of the Chinese government is to improve the quality of women's lives, and the Women's Federations were formed to address that goal. The government oversees the operation at all levels, from the national level to the township and village. The primary objective is to mobilize women, especially rural women, to participate in literacy training and market activities.

Judd's fieldwork, constrained as it was by government regulations, nevertheless yielded insights. She learned, through interviews with women members, about some women who have benefited from the programs, and she discovered how important education for women is in terms of their ability to enter into market activities. The book she wrote is largely descriptive, focusing on the public face of the Women's Federations in one locale. Such a descriptive account is the most that can emerge from research in China at this time. Given that the women's organizations are formed by and for the government, this example stretches the concept of civil society.

Activist Groups: CO-MADRES

Activist groups are groups formed with the goal of changing certain conditions, such as political repression, violence, and human rights violations. In studying activist groups, cultural anthropologists are interested in learning what motivates the formation of such groups, what their goals and strategies are, and what leadership patterns they exhibit. Many anthropologists work for or with activist groups to support social justice (see Anthropology Works on page 228).

CO-MADRES of El Salvador (see Map 14.5, page 349) is a women-led social movement in Latin America (Stephen 1995). CO-MADRES is a Spanish abbreviation for an organization called, in English, the Committee of Mothers and Relatives of Political Prisoners, Disappeared and Assassinated of El Salvador. It was founded in 1977 by a group of mothers protesting the atrocities committed by the U.S.-backed Salvadoran government and military against a coalition of progressive groups including many indigenous people. During the civil war that lasted from 1979 until 1992, a total of 80,000 people died and 7000 more disappeared, or 1 in every 100 Salvadorans.

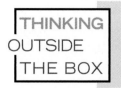

THINKING OUTSIDE THE BOX

Do Internet research to learn about CO-MADRES now: Does it still exist? If so, what are its objectives, activities, and achievements?

ANTHROPOLOGY works

Forensic Anthropology for the Maya of Guatemala

Fredy Peccerelli, a forensic anthropologist, risks his personal safety working for victims of political violence in Guatemala, his homeland. Peccerelli is founder and executive director of the Guatemalan Forensic Anthropology Foundation (FAFG). FAFG is dedicated to the recovery and identification of the remains of thousands of indigenous Maya whom Guatemalan military forces "disappeared" or outright killed during the brutal civil war that raged from the mid-1960s to the mid-1990s.

Peccerelli was born in Guatemala. His family immigrated to the United States when his father, a lawyer, was threatened by death squads. He grew up in New York City and attended Brooklyn College in the 1990s. But he felt a need to reconnect with his heritage and began to study anthropology as a vehicle that would allow him to serve his country.

The FAFG scientists excavate clandestine mass graves, exhume the bodies, and identify them through several means, such as matching dental and/or medical records. In studying skeletons, they try to determine the person's age, gender, ancestry, and lifestyle. DNA studies are few because of the expense. The scientists also collect information from relatives of the victims and from eyewitnesses of the massacres. Since 1992, the FAFG team has discovered and exhumed approximately 200 mass grave sites.

Peccerelli sees the foundation's purpose as applying scientific principles to basic human concerns. Bodies of identified victims are returned to their families to allow them some

In Guatemala City, a woman, with her daughter, observes the pictures of people who lost their lives during the civil war. Some experts argue that the war against the indigenous Maya is not over.

sense of closure about what happened to their loved ones. Families can honor their dead with appropriate burial ceremonies.

The scientists also give the Guatemalan government clear evidence on the basis of which to prosecute the perpetrators of these atrocities. Members of the long-standing military rulers still hold powerful positions within the government.

Peccerelli, his family, and his colleagues have been harassed and threatened. Bullets have been fired into Peccerelli's home, and it has been burglarized. Eleven FAFG scientists have received written death threats.

Nevertheless, the United Nations and other human rights organizations have made it clear to the government that they support FAFG's investigations, and exhumations continue with heightened security measures.

The American Association for the Advancement of Science honored Peccerelli and his colleagues in 2004 for their work in promoting human rights at great personal risk. In 1999, *Time* magazine and CNN chose Peccerelli as one of 50 "Latin American Leaders for the New Millennium." During the same year, the Guatemalan Youth Commission named him an "icon" for the youth of the country.

The initial CO-MADRES group comprised nine mothers. A year later, it had grown to nearly 30 members, including some men. During the 1980s, the growing organization gained support from other Latin American countries, as well as from Australia, the United States, Canada, and European countries. Unfortunately, the group's increased visibility also attracted repression from the Salvadoran government. Its

office was bombed several times during the 1980s, 48 members of CO-MADRES have been detained, and five have been assassinated. Harassment and disappearances continued even after the signing of the Peace Accords in January 1992: "In February 1993, the son and the nephew of one of the founders of CO-MADRES were assassinated in Usulutan. This woman had already lived through the experience of her own detention, the detention and gang rape of her daughter, and the disappearance and assassination of other family members" (1995:814).

In the 1990s, CO-MADRES focused on holding the state accountable for human rights violations during the civil war, providing protection for political prisoners, seeking assurances of human rights protection in the future, working against domestic violence, educating women about political participation, and initiating economic projects for women. The work of CO-MADRES, throughout its history, has incorporated elements of both the "personal" and the "political," concerns of mothers and other family members for lost kin and for exposing and halting human rights abuses of the state and the military. One lesson from the CO-MADRES is that activist groups formed by women that are based on kinship and domestic concerns, but their impact can reach the top of the public political hierarchy.

New Social Movements and the New Social Media

Social scientists have begun to use the term *new social movements* to refer to the many social activist groups that emerged in the late twentieth century around the world. (Chapter 15 presents some examples in the context of international development.) These groups are often formed by oppressed minorities such as indigenous peoples, ethnic groups, women, and the poor.

New social movements are taking advantage of new forms of communication through the Internet to broaden their membership, exchange ideas, and raise funds (Escobar 2002). Internet-enhanced social movements now often play important political roles. In a positive way, the Internet allows new social movements to build a following and potentially transform society. The campaign for the election of U.S. President Barack Obama in 2008 successfully mobilized support through the Internet, for example. Formal political leaders around the world are paying increased attention to enhancing their personal websites and those of their parties and communicating through Facebook, Twitter, and many more channels.

9 the BIG questions REVISITED

What are social groups and how do they vary cross-culturally?

Social groups can be classified in terms of whether all members have face-to-face interaction with one another, whether membership is based on ascription or achievement, and how formal the group's organization and leadership structure are. They extend from the most informal, face-to-face groups, such as those based on friendship, to groups that have formal membership requirements and whose members are widely dispersed and never meet each other. All groups have criteria for membership, often based on a perceived notion of similarity in terms of gender or class identity, work roles, opposition to mainstream culture, economic goals, or self-improvement.

Many groups require a formal ritual of initiation of new members. In some cases, initiation into the group involves dangerous or frightening activities that serve to bond members to one another through a shared experience of helplessness.

What is social stratification?

Social stratification consists of hierarchical relationships between and among different groups, usually on the basis of some culturally defined concept of status. The degree of social inequality among groups of different status is highly marked in agricultural and industrial–informatics societies. Marked status inequalities are not characteristic of most foraging societies. Status inequalities are variable in pastoralist and horticultural societies, with leveling mechanisms typically at play to prevent the formation of severe inequalities.

Depending on the context, categories such as class, "race," ethnicity, gender, and rank may determine group and individual status. India's caste-based system is an important example of a rigid structure of severe social inequality based on a person's birth group. According to ancient Hindu scriptures, the population is divided into mutually exclusive groups with different rights and privileges. Discrimination on the basis of caste is banned by the Indian constitution, yet it still exists, as does racism in other contexts, even though formally illegal.

What is civil society?

Civil society consists of the diverse interest groups that function outside the government to organize economic, political, and other aspects of life. It encompasses voluntary social groups and institutions.

Civil society groups can be divided into those that support government policies and initiatives, and thus further the interests of government, and those that oppose government policies and actions. The Chinese Women's Movement is an example of the former, and CO-MADRES in El Salvador is an example of the latter.

Starting at the end of the twentieth century, many new social movements have emerged around the world. Their activity is enhanced through cyberpower: the availability of new forms of information and communication technology. E-mail, the Internet, and cell phones help civil society groups gain visibility and stay in touch with their supporters.

KEY CONCEPTS

SUGGESTED READINGS

Mark Anderson. *Black and Indigenous: Garifuna Activism and Consumer Culture in Honduras*. 2010. Minneapolis: University of Minnesota Press. Based on fieldwork, this book charts contemporary change among the Garifuna people, who are descended from a mix of African, Carib, European, and other populations. They are now organizing to achieve their goals.

Sandra Bell and Simon Coleman, eds. *The Anthropology of Friendship*. New York: Berg, 1999. Following an introductory chapter by the editors on the anthropology of friendship, case studies discuss friendship in contemporary Melanesia, friendship as portrayed in Icelandic sagas, friendship in the context of a game of dominoes in a London pub, how friendship creates support networks in northern Europe, and the globalization of friendship ties in East Africa.

Rosabelle Boswell. *Le malaise créole: Ethnic Identity in Mauritius*. New York: Bergahn Books, 2007. This book examines the marginalization of the Creole population in Mauritius. Most Creoles are descendants of slaves brought to the island from mainland Africa between the seventeenth and nineteenth centuries.

Stanley Brandes. *Staying Sober in Mexico City*. Austin: University of Texas Press, 2002. This ethnography of Alcoholics Anonymous groups in Mexico City focuses on how these groups help low-income men remain sober through social support. Although emphasizing the role of human agency, the author argues that the high rate of alcoholism among poor Mexican men must be viewed in the context of structural conditions.

Kia Lilly Caldwell. *Negras in Brazil: Re-Envisioning Black Women, Citizenship, and the Politics of Identity*. New Brunswick, NJ: Rutgers University Press, 2007. Fieldwork over more than a decade in several cities of Brazil informs this study of how Afro-Brazilian women see themselves as women, as Black, and as Brazilian. Narratives of 35 women show the connections between "race," gender, and social activism.

Liliana Goldin, ed. *Identities on the Move: Transnational Processes in North America and the Caribbean Basin*. Austin: University of Texas Press, 2000. This collection offers chapters on identity formation and change in the process of voluntary migration or displacement and on how states label and exclude transnationals, often in racialized ways.

Thomas A. Gregor and Donald Tuzin, eds. *Gender in Amazonia and Melanesia: An Exploration of the Comparative Method*. Berkeley: University of California Press, 2001. Two anthropologists, one a specialist on indigenous peoples of Amazonia and the other on New Guinea, edited this volume, which includes a theoretical overview chapter and several chapters addressing similarities and differences between the two regions.

Steven Gregory and Roger Sanjek, eds. *Race*. New Brunswick: Rutgers University Press, 1994. Chapters discuss racism in the United States and the Caribbean, how "race" articulates with other inequalities, and racism in higher education and anthropology.

Jake Kosek. *Understories: The Political Life of Forests in Northern New Mexico*. Durham, NC: Duke University Press, 2007. This book is based on fieldwork in New Mexico and archival research. It exposes the racial, class, and other factors that shape the political disputes over forest resources in the Española Valley.

Anupama Rao. *The Caste Question: Dalits and the Politics of Modern India*. Berkeley: University of California Press, 2009. Combining anthropology and history, this book shows how Dalits work to overcome stigmatization and gain recognition.

Cris Shore and Stephen Nugent, eds. *Elite Cultures: Anthropological Perspectives*. New York: Routledge, 2002. This volume contains ethnographic cases from around the world addressing how elites maintain their positions, how elites represent themselves to others, and how anthropologists study elites.

Karin Tice. *Kuna Crafts, Gender and the Global Economy*. Austin: University of Texas Press, 1995. This ethnography looks at how the tourist market has affected women's production of molas in Panama and how women have organized into cooperatives to improve their situation.

Kevin A. Yelvington. *Producing Power: Ethnicity, Gender, and Class in a Caribbean Workplace*. Philadelphia: Temple University Press, 1995. This ethnography examines class, "race," and gender inequalities as linked processes of social stratification within the context of a factory in Trinidad and in the wider social sites of households, neighborhoods, and global interconnections.

For further information about topics covered in this chapter, go to MyAnthroLab at **www.myanthrolab.com** and access the following readings in MyAnthroLibrary:

Isar P. Godreau and Hilda Llórens. 2010. "Pulling Up Myths by the Root:" Designing and Implementing an Anti-Racist Curriculum about the African Heritage for Third Graders in Puerto Rico. *Practicing Anthropology* 32:26–31. In Puerto Rico, African heritage and blackness are at the bottom of the social hierarchy. Research with third-graders, teachers, and parents yields ideas about an anti-racist intervention.

Craig Jeffery, Roger Jeffery and Patricia Jeffery. 2004. Degrees without Freedom: The Impact of Formal Education on Dalit Young Men in North India. *Development and Change* 35:963–986. How can formal education undermine longstanding social hierarchies? Young dalit men with education find it difficult to convert education into secure employment.

Laura R. Murray, Sheri A. Lippman, Angela A. Donini, and Deanna Kerrigan. 2010. "She's a Professional Like Anyone Else:" Social Identity among Brazilian Sex Workers. *Culture, Health, and Sexuality* 12:293–306. In some instances, female sex workers who join organizations are able to reduce their vulnerability and risk of contracting HIV/AIDS. Race, class, and gender inequalities, however, often prevent organizing, which is the situation in an area of southern Brazil near the Bolivian border.

◉ How do politics vary cross-culturally?

◉ How do cultures maintain social order and deal with conflict?

◉ How are political and legal systems changing?

POLITICAL AND LEGAL SYSTEMS

10

◀ A political leader of the Ashanti people of Ghana, West Africa. British colonialists referred to such leaders with the English term "chief." Perhaps the English word "king" might have been more appropriate.

This chapter covers topics in political and legal anthropology, two subfields of cultural anthropology. *Political anthropology*, discussed in the first section, addresses the area of human behavior and thought related to public power—who has it and who does not, degrees of power, bases of power, abuses of power, relationships between political and religious power, political organization and government, social conflict and social control, and morality and law. *Legal anthropology*, the subject of the second section, is the study of socially accepted ways of maintaining social order and resolving conflict. The chapter's third section provides examples of change in the areas of politics and social order.

◉ ◉ ◉

Politics, Political Organization, and Leadership

Compared with political scientists, cultural anthropologists take a broader view of *politics* that includes many kinds of behavior and thought beyond formal party politics and government as most readers of this book have experienced. Cultural anthropologists offer examples of political systems and behavior that do not look "political" to people who have grown up in modern states.

This book uses the term *politics* to refer to the organized use of public power, not the more private micropolitics of family and domestic groups. **Power** is the ability to bring about results with the potential or actual use of force. Closely related to power are authority and influence. **Authority** is the ability to bring about results based on a person's status, respect, and reputation in the community. Authority differs from power in two ways: power is backed up by the potential use of force, and power can be wielded by an individual who lacks authority. **Influence** is the ability to bring about results by exerting social or moral pressure. Unlike authority, influence may be exerted from a low-status, marginal position.

All three terms are relational. A person's power, authority, or influence exists in relation to other people. Power implies the greatest likelihood of a coercive and hierarchical relationship, and authority and influence offer the most scope for consensual, cooperative decision making. Power, authority, and influence are all related to politics, power being the strongest basis for action and decision making—and potentially the least moral.

Political anthropologists define **political organization** as the groups within a culture that are responsible for public decision making and leadership, maintaining social cohesion and order, protecting group rights, and ensuring safety from external threats. Cultural anthropologists cluster the many forms of political organization that occur cross-culturally into four types that are loosely related to the modes of livelihood (Figure 10.1).

Power, authority, and influence are variations on how a person can achieve desired outcomes. (TOP) Police in China practice how to protect schoolchildren from a possible attack. Police have power. (CENTER) Matilda House, an elder of the Ngambri-Ngunnawal People of Australia joins hands with former prime minister, Kevin Rudd, and Brendan Nelson, leader of the Liberal Party, during a ceremony in 2008, marking the first time that Australia's new parliament received a traditional indigenous welcome. She has authority. (BOTTOM) Irish singer Bono at a press conference in 2008 where he hammered G8 countries for falling far behind in aid pledges to Africa. He has influence.

Foraging	Horticulture		Pastoralism	Agriculture	Industrialism/Informatics
Political Organization					**Political Organization**
Band	Tribe	Chiefdom		Confederacy	State
Leadership					**Leadership**
Band leader	Headman/Headwoman Big-man Big-woman	Chief	Paramount chief		King/queen/president prime minister/emperor
Social Conflict					**Social Conflict**
Face-to-face Small-scale Rarely lethal	Armed conflict Revenge killing			War	International war Technological weapons Massively lethal Ethnic conflict Standing armies
Social Control					**Social Control**
Norms Social pressure Ostracism					Laws Formal judiciary Permanent police Imprisonment
Trends					

Increased population density and residential centralization ————————▶

More surpluses of resources and wealth ————————▶

More social inequality/ranking ————————▶

Less reliance on kinship relations as the basis of political structures ————————▶

Increased internal and external social conflict ————————▶

Increased power and responsibility of leaders ————————▶

Increased burdens on the population to support political organization ————————▶

FIGURE 10.1 Modes of Political Organization, Conflict, and Social Control.

Bands

A **band**, the form of political organization associated with foraging groups, involves flexible membership and no formal leaders. Just as foraging has been the predominant mode of livelihood for almost all of human existence, the band is humanity's oldest form of political organization. And just as foraging is in danger of extinction as a way of life, so is band political organization.

A band typically comprises between 20 and a few hundred people at most, all related through kinship. These units come together at certain times of the year, depending on their foraging patterns and ritual schedule.

Band membership is flexible: If a person has a serious disagreement with another person or a spouse, one option is to leave that band and join another. Leadership is informal, with no one person named as a permanent leader. Depending on events, such as organizing the group to relocate or to send people out to hunt, a particular person may be a leader for that event, someone whose advice and knowledge are especially respected.

All members of the group are social equals, and a band leader has no special status. He has a certain degree of authority or influence, perhaps as a respected hunter or storyteller, but he does not have power and cannot force others to accept his views. Social leveling mechanisms prevent anyone from accumulating much authority or influence. Political activity in

power the ability to take action in the face of resistance, through force if necessary.

authority the ability to take action based on a person's achieved or ascribed status or moral reputation.

influence the ability to achieve a desired end by exerting social or moral pressure on someone or some group.

political organization groups within a culture that are responsible for public decision making and leadership, maintaining social cohesion and order, protecting group rights, and ensuring safety from external threats.

band the form of political organization of foraging groups, with flexible membership and minimal leadership.

San hunters examining animal tracks near Kalahari Gemsbok National Park, a transnational park spanning Botswana and Namibia that is advertised as a natural area free from human influence. The San, like many indigenous peoples worldwide, are excluded from living and foraging in their traditional territories that are protected by law for the use of tourists as "natural" places.

bands involves mainly decision making about migration, food distribution, and the resolution of interpersonal conflicts. External conflict between groups is rare because territories of different bands are widely separated and the population density is low.

The band level of organization barely qualifies as a form of political organization, because groups are flexible, leadership is ephemeral, and there are no signs or emblems of political affiliation. Some anthropologists argue, therefore, that true politics did not exist in undisturbed band societies.

Tribes

A **tribe** is a more formal type of political organization than the band. Typically associated with horticulture and pastoralism, tribal organization arose between 10,000 and 12,000 years ago with the emergence of these modes of livelihood. A tribe is a political group that comprises several bands or lineage groups, each with a similar language and lifestyle and each occupying a distinct territory. Tribal groups may be connected through a clan structure, in which most people claim descent from a common ancestor although they may be unable to trace the exact relationship. Kinship is the primary basis of membership. Tribal groupings contain from a hundred to several thousand people. Tribes are found in the Middle East, South Asia, Southeast Asia, the Pacific, and Africa, as well as among Native Americans.

A tribal headman (most tribal leaders are male) is a more formal leader than a band leader. A headman must be hardworking and generous and must possess good personal skills. A headman is a political leader on a part-time basis only. This role is more demanding than that of a band leader.

MAP 10.1 Kayapo Region in Brazil.
The Kayapo live in several rainforest villages in the Matto Grosso plains region. Their population is around 7000. The Kayapo use their traditional political organizing skills to help them deal with outsiders who seek to pursue commercial logging, mining, and hydroelectric development in the area.

Chief Paul Payakan, leader of the Kayapo (Map 10.1). Payakan was instrumental in mobilizing widespread resistance among the Kayapo and several other Amazonian tribes to the construction of a large hydroelectric dam at Altamira on the Xingu River.

▶ *Find updated information on the Kayapo and the proposed Altamira dam project on the Web.*

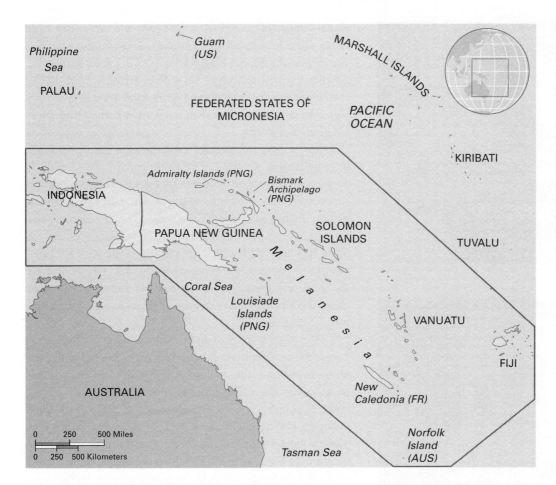

MAP 10.2 Melanesia. Melanesia is a region in the South Pacific that includes the independent states of Papua New Guinea, the Republic of Vanuatu, the Solomon Islands, and Fiji, as well as many islands that are controlled by other countries. It also encompasses the western part of the island of New Guinea, which is controlled by Indonesia, and islands to the west of it, though the people there do not self-identify as Melanesians.

Depending on the mode of livelihood, a headman will be in charge of determining the times for moving herds, planting, and harvesting and for setting the time for seasonal feasts and celebrations. Internal and external conflict resolution is also his responsibility. A headman relies mainly on authority and persuasion, rather than on power. These strategies are effective because tribal members are all kin and are loyal to each other.

BIG-MAN AND BIG-WOMAN LEADERSHIP In between tribal and chiefdom organizations is the **big-man system** or **big-woman system**, a form of political organization in which individuals build a political base and gain prestige, influence, and authority through a system of *redistribution* based on personal ties and grand feasts (review Chapter 5). Anthropological research in Melanesia (Map 10.2), a large region in the South Pacific extending from New Guinea to Fiji, established the existence of big-man politics (Sahlins 1963). Similar favor-based political systems are found elsewhere, including in contemporary states.

Political ties of a successful big-man or big-woman include people in several villages. A big-man tends to have marginally greater wealth than his followers, although people continue to expect him to be generous. The core supporters of a big-man tend to be kin, with extended networks that include nonkin. A big-man has heavy responsibilities. He is responsible for regulating internal affairs, such as the timing of crop planting, and external affairs, such as intergroup feasts, trade, and war. In some instances, a big-man is assisted in carrying out his responsibilities by a group of other respected men. These councils include people from the big-man's different constituencies.

In several tribes in the Mount Hagen (HAH-gen) area of the Papua New Guinea highlands (see Map 1.2, page 17), an aspiring big-man develops a leadership position through a process called **moka** (Strathern 1971). Moka is a strategy for developing political leadership in Melanesia that involves

---

tribe a form of political organization that comprises several bands or lineage groups, each with a similar language and lifestyle and occupying a distinct territory.

big-man system or **big-woman system** a form of political organization midway between tribe and chiefdom and involving reliance on the leadership of key individuals who develop a political following through personal ties and redistributive feasts.

moka a strategy for developing political leadership in highland New Guinea that involves exchanging gifts and favors with individuals and sponsoring large feasts where further gift-giving occurs.

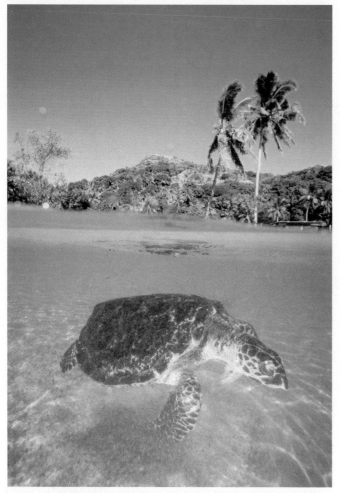

Throughout Melanesia, big-man and big-woman politics has long involved the demonstration of political leaders' generosity. (TOP) Leaders are expected to be able to mobilize resources for impressive feasts such as this one on Tanna Island, one of the many islands of the Republic of Vanuatu in the region of Melanesia. (BOTTOM) A sea turtle off the coast of Fiji, where local people consider them sacred and important as a feasting item.

▶ How does public feasting play a role in politics in a context with which you are familiar?

exchanging favors and gifts, such as pigs, and sponsoring large feasts where further gift-giving occurs. A crucial factor in big-manship in the Mount Hagen area is having at least one wife. An aspiring big-man urges his wife or wives to work harder than ordinary women in order to grow more food to feed more pigs. The number of pigs a man has is an important measure of his status and worth.

Given the importance of a wife or wives in maintaining a large collection of pigs, a man whose parents die when he is young is at an extreme disadvantage because he lacks financial support for the brideprice required for marriage. Without parents, he has no brideprice, no wife, no one to feed and care for pigs, no resource base for moka, and no chance of becoming a big-man. Although big-manship is an achieved position, most big-men (60 percent) in the Mt. Hagen area are the sons of big-men, meaning that ascription (birth-based characteristics) to some extent is involved as well as achievement (Strathern 1971).

A married man relies on his wife's or wives' production as a basis for developing and expanding exchange ties with contacts throughout the region. An aspiring big-man builds moka relationships first with kin and then beyond. By giving goods to people, he gains prestige over them. The recipient is under pressure to make a return gift of equal or greater value. The exchanges go back and forth, over the years. The more the aspiring big-man gives, and the more people he can maintain in his exchange network, the greater prestige he develops.

With few exceptions, the early anthropological literature about tribal politics among indigenous peoples of Melanesia portrays men as dominating public exchange networks and the public political arenas. Women are mentioned as important in providing the material basis for men's political careers, but only in their supportive spousal roles. A study on the island of Vanatinai, however, reveals the existence of big-women and big-men (Lepowsky 1990). In this gender-egalitarian culture, both men and women can gain power and prestige by sponsoring feasts at which valuables are distributed, especially mortuary feasts (feasts for the dead). Although more Vanatinai men than women are involved in political exchange and leadership, some women are extremely active as political leaders. These women lead sailing expeditions to neighboring islands to visit their exchange partners, who are both male and female, and they sponsor lavish feasts attended by many people. Big-women are also powerful sorcerers, famous healers, and successful gardeners.

Chiefdoms

A **chiefdom** is a form of political organization that includes permanently allied tribes and villages under one chief, a leader who possesses power. Compared with most tribes, chiefdoms have large populations, often numbering in the thousands. They are more centralized and socially complex. Hereditary systems of social ranking and economic stratification are a central feature of chiefdoms. Chiefs and their descendants have markedly higher status than commoners, and intermarriage between members of the two strata is forbidden.

The chiefship is an "office" that must be filled at all times. When a chief dies or retires, he or she must be replaced. In contrast, the death of a band leader or of a big-man or big-woman does not require that someone else be chosen as a replacement. A chief has more responsibilities than a band or tribal leader. He or she regulates production and redistribution, solves internal conflicts, and plans and leads raids and warring expeditions. Criteria for becoming a chief include both ascribed and achieved qualities. Ascribed criteria include birth in a chiefly lineage and being the first son or daughter of the chief. Achievement is measured in terms of personal leadership skills, charisma, and accumulated wealth. Chiefdoms have existed throughout the world.

The Iroquois, located mainly in what today is New York State (see Map 4.3, page 90), provide a case of women's indirect political importance (Brown 1975). Men were chiefs, but women and men councilors were the appointing body. Most men were gone for extended periods, waging war as far away

Chief Joseph, or Hin-mah-too-yah-lat-kekt (Thunder Rolling Down the Mountain), of the Nez Perce, was born in northern Oregon in 1840. His father, Joseph the Elder, had been an active supporter of peace with the Whites and signed an agreement establishing the Nez Perce Reservation. In 1863, following the discovery of gold, the government took back 6 million acres of land. After Joseph the Elder died, Joseph the Younger was elected chief. He favored peace, but continued White encroachments on Nez Perce land and U.S. government attempts to forcibly relocate his people prompted him to lead a war of resistance.

▶ Go the Internet and read Chief Joseph's famous speech of surrender delivered in 1877.

The last queen of Hawai'i, Queen Lili'uokalani. Inheriting the throne from her brother, Queen Lili'uokalani reigned for only two years, from 1891 to 1893. She attempted to establish constitutional rights for Hawai'ians and Asians living in the islands. In 1893, she was deposed by a group of European and American businessmen who took political control of the islands. The status of Hawai'i is still contested today by local groups that seek autonomy from the United States.

▶ What did you learn about Hawai'i in your high school history or government classes? Did you learn about Queen Lili'uokalani and her attempt to assert native rights?

as Delaware and Virginia. Women controlled production and distribution of the staple crop, maize. If the women did not want warriors to leave for a particular campaign, they would refuse to provide them with maize, thereby vetoing the plan. Men and women participated equally on the councils.

An expanded version of the chiefdom occurs when several chiefdoms are joined in a confederacy. Such a group is

chiefdom a form of political organization in which permanently allied tribes and villages have one recognized leader who holds an "office."

headed by a chief of chiefs—a "big chief" or paramount chief. Many prominent confederacies have existed, including the Iroquois league of five nations, the Cherokee of Tennessee, the Algonquins of the Chesapeake region in present-day Virginia and Maryland, and confederacies in Hawai'i in the late 1700s. In the Algonquin confederacy, each village had a chief and the regional council was composed of local chiefs and headed by the paramount chief. Powhatan, father of Pocahontas, was paramount chief of the Algonquins when the British arrived in the early 1600s.

States

A **state** is a centralized political unit encompassing many communities, a bureaucratic structure, and leaders who possess coercive power. The state is now the form of political organization in which all people live. Band organizations, tribes, and chiefdoms exist, but they are incorporated to varying degrees within state structures.

STATE POWERS AND ROLES   States have a wide range of powers and responsibilities. Their leaders have more power over people than leaders in bands, tribes, and chiefdoms have. Their leaders have more responsibilities as well:

- States engage in international relations in order to deal with other states about mutual concerns (see Eye on the Environment). The state may use force defensively to maintain its borders and offensively to extend its territory.
- States monopolize the use of force and the maintenance of law and order internally through laws, courts, and the police.
- States maintain standing armies and police (as opposed to part-time forces).
- States define citizenship and its rights and responsibilities. In complex societies, since early times, not all residents have been granted equal rights as citizens.
- States keep track of the number, age, gender, location, and wealth of their citizens through census systems that are regularly updated.
- States have the power to extract resources from citizens through taxation.
- States manipulate information. Information to protect the state and its leaders can be controlled both directly (through censorship, restricting access to certain information by the public, and promotion of favorable images via propaganda) and indirectly (through pressure

on journalists, television networks, and other media to selectively present information or to present information in certain ways).

SYMBOLS OF STATE POWER   Religious beliefs and symbols are often closely tied to the power of state leadership: The ruler may be considered to be a deity or part deity, or may be a high priest of the state religion, or perhaps be closely linked with the high priest, who serves as advisor. Architecture and urban planning remind the populace of the greatness of the state.

In democratic states, where leaders are elected by popular vote, and in socialist states, where political rhetoric emphasizes social equality, expense and elegance are muted by the adoption of more egalitarian ways of dress (even though in private, these leaders may live relatively opulent lives in terms of housing, food, and entertainment). The earlier practice of all Chinese leaders wearing a "Mao jacket," regardless of their rank, was a symbolic statement of their antihierarchical philosophy. A quick glance at a crowd of people, including the Prime Minister of Canada or Britain or the President of the United States, would not reveal who was the leader, because dress differences are avoided. Even members of British royalty wear street clothes on public occasions where regalia are not required.

Beyond clothing, other commodities associated with top leadership positions include the quality of housing, food, and modes of transportation. State leaders live in grand mansions and often have more than one residence. The King of Morocco, for example, has several official palaces around the country, and he travels regularly from one to another. President George W. Bush was considered "one of the people" because he liked to eat hamburgers. State leaders do not travel the way ordinary citizens do. For security reasons, their ground vehicles may have bulletproof windows, and a cavalcade of security vehicles protects the leader's vehicle. In many African countries, the most important new symbol of political power is an expensive imported car (Chalfin 2008).

GENDER AND LEADERSHIP IN STATES   Most contemporary states are hierarchical and patriarchal, excluding members of lower classes and women from equal participation. Some states are less male dominated than others, but none is female dominated. One view of gender inequality in states suggests that increasing male dominance with the evolution of the state is based on men's control of the technology

---

state   a form of political organization in which a centralized political unit encompasses many communities, a bureaucratic structure, and leaders who possess coercive power.

THINKING OUTSIDE THE BOX

What are some prominent symbols of state power in your home country?

Like air, water can move across state boundaries, carrying environmental pollution. Such movements can cause serious international political conflicts and lead to extended negotiations about reparations and planning to prevent future damages. One case is that of mining-related pollution of the Tisza (TEE-suh) River that flows from Romania to Hungary and beyond, within the Danube River basin.

In January 2000, a dam in Romania holding *tailings* (metal-processing by-products) from a gold mine breached and released water containing high levels of cyanide, copper, zinc, and other heavy metals into nearby streams (Harper 2005). Three days later, the *plume*, or water carrying the by-products, had reached Hungary's Tisza River. Within the month, it moved on to Serbia and Bulgaria and eventually reached the Black Sea.

In Hungary, the cyanide killed thousands of tons of fish and waterfowl and raised alarms about people's drinking water. Farmers in the affected region reported the death of cows, and they were unable to sell their farm produce due to negative public perceptions about polluted products. Although cyanide is lethal in the short run, it soon dissipates from the environment, as opposed to the heavy metals, which remain in the river's sediments and continue to affect riverine life for a long time.

In spite of the severity of the disaster, the Hungarian state was slow to file claims against the offending corporation or for compensation from Romania. Although postsocialist Hungarian political leaders took up the cause of environmental activism in their rhetoric, they did not follow through with action. This lack of action may be related to the heritage

MAP 10.3 **The Danube and Tisza Rivers in Eastern Europe.**
The Danube River and its major tributary, the Tisza. Europe's largest remaining natural wetland is in the Danube delta. The core of the delta, which lies mainly in Romania but crosses into Ukraine, was declared a UNESCO World Natural Heritage Site in 1991.

of state socialism, which did not take environmental problems seriously. Another explanatory factor is that a large number of Hungarians live in Romania, and Hungary's leaders may have wished to avoid an international confrontation that would put Hungarians in Romania at risk.

One positive development was that the European Union (EU) offered a wider political framework in which to address the issue of the Tisza River pollution. The Tisza disaster was the first environmental disaster in which the EU took a prominent role. In the end, Hungary decided to sue the mining company for damages in a civil lawsuit, rather than taking on an international lawsuit with its neighbor.

FOOD FOR THOUGHT ▼
The exact reasons for the Hungarian government's inaction are not clear. How can one learn the true reasons behind politicians' actions or inactions?

Rescue workers remove dead fish from the Tisza River in the year 2000 following an accident at a gold mine in northwestern Romania that deposited cyanide and other toxic substances into the Tisza and that also flowed into the Danube River and the Black Sea. The accident caused environmental damage in a vast area involving several countries.

(LEFT) Afghanistan President Hamid Karzai wears a carefully assembled collection of regional political symbols. The striped cape is associated with northern tribes. The Persian-lamb hat is an Uzbek style popular in the capital city, Kabul. He also wears a tunic and loose trousers, which are associated with villagers, and he sometimes adds a Western-style jacket. His clothing implies a statement of unity and diversity about his country. (CENTER) President Barack Obama typically wears a dark suit, white shirt, and necktie for formal occasions. During a Hawai'i themed celebration at the White House, he sports a lei, which signals his close links to the state where he was born and spent much of his youth. (RIGHT) President Ellen Sirleaf-Johnson of Liberia and U.S. Secretary of State Hillary Clinton make contrasting statements through their formal attire with Sirleaf-Johnson clearly signaling a connection to Africa and Clinton conveying a more neutral message in her trademark pantsuit.

of production and warfare (Harris 1993). Women in most cultures have limited access to these areas of power. In more peaceful states, such as Finland, Norway, Sweden, and Denmark, women's political roles are more prominent.

Strongly patriarchal contemporary states preserve male dominance through ideologies that restrict women's political power. In much of the Muslim Middle East, Central Asia, Pakistan, and northern India, the practice of purdah, female seclusion and segregation from the public world, limits women's public roles. In China, scientific beliefs that categorize women as less strong and dependable than men have long been used to rationalize the exclusion of women from politics (Dikötter 1998). Socialist states typically attempt to increase women's political roles, and the proportion of female members in legislative bodies is higher in socialist states than in capitalist democracies. But it is still not equal to that of men. Although women account for roughly half of the world's population, they form only, on average, 16 percent of the world's parliamentary members (Lederer 2006). Regional differences range from an average of 40 percent female parliamentarians in the Nordic states to 8 percent in Arab states.

A few contemporary states have or recently had women as prime ministers or presidents. Powerful women heads of state in recent times include Indira Gandhi in India, Golda Meir in Israel, Margaret Thatcher in the United Kingdom, Benazir Bhutto in Pakistan, Michelle Bachelet in Chile, Angela Merkel in Germany, Ellen Johnson-Sirleaf in Liberia,

Representative Kim Ok-son greets some of her constituents who are members of a local Confucian club in Seoul, Republic of Korea. She is wearing a men's-style suit and has a masculine haircut.

and Tarja Halonen in Finland. Some female heads of state are related by kinship, as wife or daughter, to male heads of state. Indira Gandhi, for example, was the daughter of Jawaharlal Nehru, the popular first prime minister of independent India. It is unclear whether these women inherited the role or achieved it indirectly through socialization as a member of a political family, or both.

◙ ◙ ◙

Social Order and Social Conflict

Many Maasai people of Tanzania and Kenya work in cities and interact with international tourists, and some attend universities. But most rural Maasai, traditionally pastoralists who value their freedom to roam over vast areas, have limited knowledge of global events. Some rural villages lack electricity, so not everyone has access to a television. In 2002, when Kimeli Naiyomeh returned to his village in a remote area of Kenya following his medical studies at Stanford University in California, he told stories that stunned the villagers (Lacey 2002). They had not heard about the attacks on the United States on September 11, 2001. He described how massive fires destroyed buildings so high that they stretched into the clouds. The villagers could not believe that a building could be so tall that people jumping from it would die.

The stories about 9/11 saddened the villagers. They decided they should do something to help the victims. Cows are the most precious objects among the Maasai. As Kimeli Naiyomeh comments, "The cow is almost the center of life for us.... It's sacred. It's more than property. You give it a name. You talk to it. You perform rituals with it" (2002:A7). In June 2002, in a solemn ceremony, the villagers gave 14 cows to the United States. After the cows were blessed, they were transferred to the deputy chief of the U.S. Embassy in Kenya. He expressed his country's gratitude and explained that transporting the cows to the United States would be difficult. The cows were sold and the money went to support Maasai schools. Violence now has global implications more than ever before.

This section discusses social order and peace, including informal arrangements and formal laws and systems of crime prevention and punishment. It begins with the cross-cultural study of social order and then moves to a discussion of conflict and violence.

In anthropology, **social control** is the process by which people maintain orderly life in groups. Social control systems include informal social controls that exist through socialization for proper behavior, education, and peer pressure. They may also include formal systems of codified rules about proper behavior and punishments for deviation. In the United States and Canada, the Amish (review Culturama in Chapter 6, page 136) and Mennonites rely on informal social controls far more than

do most microcultural groups. The Amish and Mennonites have no police force or legal system; the way social order is maintained is through religious teaching and group pressure. If a member veers from correct behavior, punishment such as ostracism ("shunning") may be applied.

Norms and Laws

Cultural anthropologists distinguish two major instruments of social control: norms and laws. A **norm** is an accepted standard for how people should behave that is usually unwritten and learned unconsciously through socialization. All societies have norms. Norms include, for example, the expectation that children should follow their parents' advice, that people standing in line should be orderly, and that an individual should accept an offer of a handshake (in cultures where handshakes are the usual greeting) when meeting someone for the first time. Enforcement of norms is informal. For example, a violation may simply be considered rude and the violator would be avoided in the future. Sometimes, however, direct action may be taken, such as asking someone who disrupts a meeting to leave.

A **law** is a binding rule created through custom or official enactment that defines correct behavior and the punishment for misbehavior. Systems of law are more common and more elaborate in state-level societies, but many nonstate societies have formalized laws. Religion often provides legitimacy for law. Australian Aborigines believe that law came to humans during the *Dreamtime* (also called dreaming), a period in the mythological past when the ancestors created the world. The terms "law" and "religion" are synonymous in contemporary Islamic states. Secular Western states consider their laws to be religiously neutral, although, in fact, much Western law is based on Judeo-Christian beliefs.

Systems of Social Control

The material that follows considers forms of social control in small-scale societies as contrasted with large-scale societies. The former are characterized more by the use of norms. The latter, notably states, rely more on legal sanctions, although local-level groups, such as neighbors, practice social sanctions among themselves. A final topic considers the relationship between the law and social inequality.

---

social control processes that, through both informal and formal mechanisms, maintain orderly social life.

norm a generally agreed-upon standard for how people should behave, usually unwritten and learned unconsciously.

law a binding rule created through enactment or custom that defines right and reasonable behavior and is enforceable by the threat of punishment.

Norms and laws vary cross-culturally. Visitors queue at the site of the World Expo 2010 in Shanghai, China, the site of an expected 70 million visitors over the next six months with an average of 380,000 people expected daily. Queuing makes sense in densely populated situations.

SOCIAL CONTROL IN SMALL-SCALE SOCIETIES

Anthropologists distinguish between small-scale societies and large-scale societies in terms of conflict resolution, social order, and punishment of offenses.

Bands are small, close-knit groups, so disputes tend to be handled at the interpersonal level through discussion or one-on-one fights. Group members may act together to punish an offender through shaming and ridicule. Emphasis is on maintaining social order and restoring social equilibrium, not hurtfully punishing an offender. *Ostracizing* an offending member (forcing the person to leave the group) is a common means of punishment. Capital punishment (execution) is rare.

In some Australian Aboriginal societies, laws restrict access to religious rituals and paraphernalia to men who have gone through a ritual initiation. If an initiated man shared secrets with an uninitiated person, the elders would delegate one of their group to kill the offender. In such instances, the elders act like a court.

In small-scale, nonstate societies, punishment is often legitimized through belief in supernatural forces and their ability to affect people. Among the highland horticulturalists of the Indonesian island of Sumba (see Map 1.1, page 14), one of the greatest offenses is to fail to keep a promise (Kuipers 1990). Breaking a promise will bring on "supernatural assault" by the ancestors of those who have been offended by the person's misbehavior. The punishment may come in the form of damage to crops, illness or death of a relative, destruction of the offender's house, or having one's clothing catch on fire. When such a disaster occurs, the only recourse is to sponsor a ritual that will appease the ancestors.

The overall goal in dealing with conflict in small-scale societies is to return the group to harmony. Village *fission* (breaking up) and ostracism are mechanisms for dealing with more serious conflict.

SOCIAL CONTROL IN STATES

In densely populated societies with more social stratification and more wealth, increased social stress occurs in relation to the distribution of surplus, inheritance, and rights to land. In addition, an increased social scale means that not everyone knows everyone else. Face-to-face accountability exists only in localized groups. Three important factors in state systems of social control are as follows:

- Specialization of roles involved in social control
- Formal trials and courts
- Power-enforced forms of punishment, such as prisons and the death penalty

Informal mechanisms of social control, however, exist alongside these formal systems at the local level.

Specialization The specialization of tasks related to law and order, such as those performed by police, judges, and lawyers, increases with the emergence of state organization. Full-time professionals such as judges and lawyers emerged with the state. These professionals are often members of powerful social groups, a fact that perpetuates elite biases in the justice process itself.

Policing is a form of social control that includes processes of surveillance and the threat of punishment related to maintaining social order (Reiner 1996). Police are the specific

Amish men in a communal barn raising in Pennsylvania. Amish norms support sharing labor and other transfers of goods and services within the group.

▶ *Think of an example of shared work from your microcultural experience.*

organization and personnel who discover, report, and investigate crimes. As a specialized group, police are associated with states.

Japan's low crime rate has attracted the attention of Western law-and-order specialists, who think that it may be the result of the police system there. They ask whether solutions to U.S. crime problems can be found in such Japanese policing practices as neighborhood police boxes, or small, local police offices, staffed by foot patrolmen and volunteer crime-prevention groups organized on a neighborhood basis. Fieldwork among police detectives in the city of Sapporo reveals aspects of Japanese culture and policing that promote low crime rates (Miyazawa 1992). In Japan, the police operate under high expectations that no false arrests will be made and that all arrests should lead to confession. And, in fact, the rate of confession is high. The high rate of confession may be due to the fact that the police do an excellent job of targeting the guilty party, or it may result from the nearly complete control of interrogation by the police. The police are allowed to keep suspects isolated for long periods, a practice that wears down resistance. The suspect's statements are not recorded verbatim or taped; instead, the detectives write them down and the suspect is asked to sign them. Overall, policing culture in Japan gives more power to the police and less to the defendant than in the United States and has the potential to distort the process of justice.

Trials and Courts In societies where spirits and ancestors define wrongdoing and punishment, a person's guilt is proved simply by the fact that misfortune has befallen him or her. If lightning damaged a person's crops, for instance, then that person must have done something wrong. In other cases, guilt may be determined through **trial by ordeal**, a way of judging guilt or innocence in which the accused person is put through a test that is often painful. An accused person may be required to place his or her hand in boiling oil, for example, or to have a part of his or her body touched by a red-hot knife. Being burned is a sign of guilt, whereas not being burned means that the suspect is innocent.

The court system, with lawyers, judge, and jury, is used in many contemporary societies, although variation exists in how cases are presented and juries constituted. The goal of contemporary court trials is to ensure both justice and fairness. Analysis of courtroom dynamics and patterns of decision making in the United States and elsewhere, however, reveals ongoing problems in achieving these goals.

Prisons and the Death Penalty Administering punishment involves doing something unpleasant to someone who has committed an offense. As noted earlier, the most extreme form of punishment in small-scale societies is ostracism and only rarely death. A common form of punishment in the case of theft or murder in pastoralist societies, especially Islamic cultures of the Middle East, is that the guilty party must pay compensation to members of the family that has been harmed.

---

policing the exercise of social control through processes of surveillance and the threat of punishment related to maintaining social order.

trial by ordeal a way of determining innocence or guilt in which the accused person is put to a test that may be painful, stressful, or fatal.

This man, in a military prison in Chechnya, is accused by the Russian government of participating with Chechen rebel forces. Human rights activists have been concerned about the mistreatment of prisoners in Chechnya for several years.

▶ *What human rights do prisoners have in your country?*

The *prison*, as a place where people are forcibly detained as a form of punishment, has a long history but probably emerged only with the state. The dungeons of historic forts and castles are vivid evidence of the power of some people to detain and inflict suffering on others. In Europe, long-term detention of prisoners did not become common until the 1600s (Foucault 1977). The first prison in the United States was built in Philadelphia in the late 1700s (Sharff 1995).

The percentage of imprisoned people varies widely around the world. The United States imprisons more people than any other country in the world, followed by China (Pew Center 2008). In the United States, the prison population of 1.6 million has more than doubled since 1985 (Walmsley 2007). Prison populations have also doubled over that period in Brazil and Mexico.

It is important to look at the rate of imprisonment as well as sheer numbers. The national *incarceration rate* is calculated as the number of people in prison per 100,000 people in a country. Countries vary widely in their incarceration rate. The United States has the highest incarceration rate, 737 per 100,000 people, followed by Russia, 611; Turkmenistan, 489; Cuba, 487; Belarus, 426; South Africa, 335; Iran, 214; and Spain, 145 (Walmsley 2007).

It is also important to look inside national rates. In England and France, a disproportionate number of prisoners are Muslims (Moore 2008). Ethnic and gender differences in incarceration are marked in the United States. One in 15 black men is in prison, and 1 in 9 black men 20 to 34 years of age is in prison. One in 355 white women ages 35 to 39 years is in prison, whereas 1 in 100 black women is behind bars. Among Hispanics, 1 in 36 adult Hispanic men is in prison. The state with the highest incarceration rate is Louisiana, and southern states in general have higher rates than northern states.

Inefficient justice systems may mean that many prisoners are in jail for many years awaiting trial; they have not been convicted of a crime, but they are imprisoned. In Haiti, before the earthquake of January 2010, 9 of every 10 prisoners were awaiting trial (Walmsley 2007). Immediately following the earthquake, unknown numbers of prisoners fled their damaged prisons, while others in at least one location are alleged to have been executed in their cells.

SOCIAL INEQUALITY AND THE LAW   **Critical legal anthropology** is an approach within the cross-cultural study of legal systems that examines the role of law and judicial processes in maintaining the dominance of powerful groups through discriminatory practices rather than protecting members of less powerful groups. Systematic discrimination against ethnic minorities, indigenous peoples, and women, among other categories, has been documented in judicial systems around the world, including those of long-standing democracies. This section presents an example from Australia.

At the invitation of Aboriginal leaders in Australia, Fay Gale and her colleagues conducted research comparing the treatment of Aboriginal youth and White youth in the judicial system (1990). The question posed by the Aboriginal leaders was "Why are our kids always in trouble?" Two directions can be pursued to find the answer. First, structural factors—such as Aboriginal displacement from their homeland, poverty, poor living conditions, and bleak future prospects—can be investigated. Second, the criminal justice system can be examined to see whether it treats Aboriginal and White youth equally. The researchers decided to direct their attention to the judicial system because little work had been done in that area by social scientists.

Findings show that Aboriginal youth are overrepresented at every level of the juvenile justice system, from apprehension (being caught by the police) through pretrial processes, to the ultimate stage of adjudication (the judge's decision) and disposition (the punishment): "A far greater proportion of Aboriginal than other young people follow the harshest route . . . . At each point in the system where discretion operates, young Aborigines are significantly more likely than other young persons to receive the most severe outcomes of those available to the decision-makers" (1990:3). At the time of apprehension (being caught by the police), the suspect can be either formally arrested or informally reported. A formal arrest is made to ensure that the offender will appear in court. Officers ask suspects for a home address and whether they have a job. Aboriginal youth are more likely than White youth to live in an extended family in a poor neighborhood, and they are more likely to be unemployed. Thus, they tend to be placed in the category "undependable," and they are formally arrested more than White youth for the same crime (Figure 10.2). The next step determines whether the suspect will be tried in Children's Court or referred to Children's Aid

	Aboriginal Youth (percent)	White Youth (percent)
Brought into system via arrest rather than police report	43.4	19.7
Referred to Children's Court rather than diverted to Children's Aid Panels	71.3	37.4
Proportion of court appearances resulting in detention	10.2	4.2

Note: Most of these youths are male; data are from 1979 to 1984.

Source: *Aboriginal Youth and the Criminal Justice System: The Injustice of Justice,* by Fay Gale, Rebecca Bailey-Harris, Joy Wundersitz, Copyright © Cambridge University Press 1990. Reprinted by permission of Cambridge University Press.

FIGURE 10.2 Comparison of Outcomes for Aboriginal and White Youth in the Australian Judicial System.

Panels. The Children's Aid Panels in South Australia have gained acclaim worldwide for the opportunities they give to individuals to avoid becoming repeat offenders and take their proper place in society. But most Aboriginal youth offenders are denied access to them and instead have to appear in court, where the vast majority of youthful offenders end up pleading guilty. The clear and disturbing finding from this study is that the mode of arrest tends to determine each subsequent stage.

To counter such unjust systems, many cultural anthropologists and others support and work to promote **social justice**, a concept of fairness based on social equality that seeks to ensure entitlements and opportunities for disadvantaged members of society.

Social Conflict and Violence

All systems of social control have to deal with the fact that public conflict and violence may occur. This section considers several varieties of public conflict and violence.

ETHNIC CONFLICT   Ethnic conflict and grievances may result from an ethnic group's attempt to gain more autonomy or more equitable treatment. It may also be caused by a dominant group's actions to subordinate, oppress, or eliminate an ethnic group by *genocide* (killing large numbers of a distinct ethnic, racial, or religious group) or *ethnocide* (destroying the culture of a distinct group).

In the past few decades, political violence has increasingly been enacted within states rather than between states. It is true that ethnic identity often provides people with an ideological commitment to a cause, but one should look beneath the labels to see whether deeper, structural issues exist. Consider Central Asia (see Map 10.4 on page 250), a vast region populated by many ethnic groups, none of which has a clear claim to the land on the grounds of indigeneity. Yet, in Central Asia, every dispute appears on the surface to have an ethnic basis: "Russians and Ukrainians versus Kazakhs over land rights and

jobs in Kazakhstan, Uzbeks versus Tajiks over the status of Samarkhand and Bukhara, conflict between Kirghiz and Uzbeks in Kyrgyzstan, and riots between Caucasian Turks and Uzbeks in the Fergana Valley of Uzbekistan" (Clay 1990:48). Attributing the causes of all such problems to ethnic differences overlooks competition for resources that is based on regional, not ethnic, differences. Uzbekistan has most of the cities and irrigated farmland, whereas Kyrgyzstan and Tajikistan control most of the water, and Turkmenistan has vast oil and gas riches.

Sectarian Conflict   **Sectarian conflict** is conflict based on perceived differences between divisions or sects within a religion, and often related to rights and resources. For hundreds of years, sectarian conflict has occurred within the British Isles, between Catholics and Protestants, both groups being Christian. Sectarian conflict between Muslims often follows a split between Shias and Sunnis (discussed in Chapter 12). This division is expressed in outright violence such as attacks on each other's sacred sites. It also takes the form of indirect, structural violence, as shown by a study conducted in northern Pakistan during a period of Shia-Sunni conflict (Varley 2010). During the conflict, *exclusionary medical service provision* occurred in which Sunni women experienced second-class treatment at obstetric clinics to the extent that they retreated to using alternative medicine.

WAR   One definition of war says that it is an open and declared conflict between two political units. This definition,

critical legal anthropology   an approach within the cross-cultural study of legal systems that examines the role of law and judicial processes in maintaining the dominance of powerful groups through discriminatory practices rather than protecting less powerful people.

social justice   a concept of fairness based on social equality that seeks to ensure entitlements and opportunities for disadvantaged members of society.

sectarian conflict   conflict based on perceived differences between divisions or sects within a religion.

CRITICAL thinking

Yanomami: The "Fierce People"?

The Yanomami are a horticultural people who live in dispersed villages of between 40 and 250 people in the Amazonian rainforest (Ross 1993). Since the 1960s, biological anthropologist Napoleon Chagnon has studied several Yanomami villages. He has written a widely read and frequently republished ethnography about the Yanomami, with early editions carrying the subtitle *The Fierce People* (1992 [1968]). He also helped produce classic ethnographic films about the Yanomami, including *The Feast* and *The Ax Fight.*

Chagnon's writings and films have promoted a view of the Yanomami as exceptionally violent and prone to lethal warfare. According to Chagnon, about one-third of adult Yanomami males die violently, about two-thirds of all adults lose at least one close relative through violence, and over 50 percent lose two or more close relatives (1992:205). He has reported that one village was raided 25 times during his first 15 months of fieldwork. Although village alliances are sometimes formed, they are fragile and allies may turn against each other unpredictably.

The Yanomami world, as depicted by Chagnon, is one of danger, threats, and counterthreats. Enemies, human and supernatural, are everywhere. Support from one's allies is uncertain. All of this uncertainty leads to what Chagnon describes as the *waiteri* (a Yanomami word) *complex*, a set of behaviors and attitudes that includes a fierce political and personal stance for men and forms of individual and group communication that stress aggression and independence. Fierceness is a dominant theme in socialization, as boys learn how to fight with clubs, participate in chest-pounding duels with other boys, and use a spear. Adult males are aggressive and hostile toward adult females, and boys learn to be aggressive toward girls from an early age.

Chagnon provides a biological, Darwinian explanation for the fierceness shown by the Yanomami. He reports that the Yanomami explain that village raids and warfare are carried out so that men may obtain wives. Although the Yanomami prefer to marry within their village, a shortage of potential brides exists because of the Yanomami practice of female infanticide. Although the Yanomami prefer to marry endogamously, taking a wife from another group is preferable to remaining a bachelor. Men in other groups, however, are unwilling to give up their women—hence the necessity for raids. Other reasons for raids are suspicion of sorcery or theft of food.

Chagnon argues that within this system warfare contributes to reproductive success because successful warriors are able to gain a wife or more than one wife (polygyny is allowed). Thus, successful warriors will have higher reproductive rates than unsuccessful warriors. Successful warriors, Chagnon suggests, have a genetic advantage for fierceness, which they pass on to their sons, leading to a higher growth rate of groups with violent males through genetic selection for fierceness. Male fierceness, in this view, is biologically adaptive.

Marvin Harris, taking the cultural materialist perspective, says that protein scarcity and population dynamics in the area are the underlying causes of warfare (1984). The Yanomami lack plentiful sources of meat, which is highly valued. Harris suggests that when game in an area becomes depleted, pressure rises to expand into the territory of neighboring groups, thus precipitating conflict. Such conflicts in turn result in high rates of adult male mortality. Combined with the effects of female infanticide, this meat-warfare complex keeps population growth rates down to a level that the environment can support.

A third view relies on historical data. Brian Ferguson (1990) argues that the high levels of violence among the Yanomami were caused by the intensified Western presence during the preceding 100 years. Furthermore, diseases introduced from outside, especially measles and malaria, severely depopulated the Yanomami and greatly increased their fears of sorcery (their explanation for disease). The attraction to Western goods such as steel axes and guns would also increase intergroup

---

however, rules out many war-like conflicts, including the American–Vietnam War because it was undeclared. Or, war may be defined simply as organized aggression. But this definition is too broad, because not all organized violence can be considered warfare. Perhaps the best definition is that **war** is organized conflict involving group action directed against another group and involving lethal force (Ferguson 1994, quoted in Reyna 1994:30).

Cultural variation exists in the frequency of war, the objectives of war, how war is waged, and how post-war social relations are rebuilt. Intergroup conflicts among free-ranging foragers

that would fit the definition of war do not exist in the ethnographic record. The informal, nonhierarchical political organization among bands is not conducive to waging armed conflict. Bands do not have specialized military forces or leaders.

Archaeological evidence indicates that warfare emerged during the Neolithic era with settled life. Plant and animal domestication required extensive land use and was accompanied by increased population density. The resulting economic and demographic pressures put more and larger groups in more direct and intense competition with each other.

No evidence of warlike behavior among bands exists, but it does among tribal groups. Tribal leadership patterns, including big-man systems, facilitate the mobilization of warrior

---

war   organized and purposeful group action directed against another group and involving lethal force.

rivalry. Thus, Ferguson suggests that the "fierce people" are a creation of historical forces, especially contact with and pressure from outsiders.

Following Ferguson's position, but with a new angle, journalist Patrick Tierney points the finger of blame at Chagnon himself (2000). Tierney maintains that it was the presence of Chagnon, with his team of coresearchers and many boxes of trade goods, that triggered a series of lethal raids due to increased competition for those very goods. In addition, Tierney argues that Chagnon intentionally prompted the Yanomami to act fiercely in his films and to stage raids that created aggravated intergroup hostility beyond what had originally existed.

In 2001, the American Anthropological Association established a task force to examine five topics related to Tierney's allegations that Chagnon's and others' interactions with and representations of the Yanomami may have had a detrimental impact on them, contributing to "disorganization" among the Yanomami. The report of the El Dorado Task Force appears on the website http://www.aaanet.org of the American Anthropological Association. The task force rejected all charges against Chagnon and instead emphasized the harmfulness of false accusations that might jeopardize future scientific research.

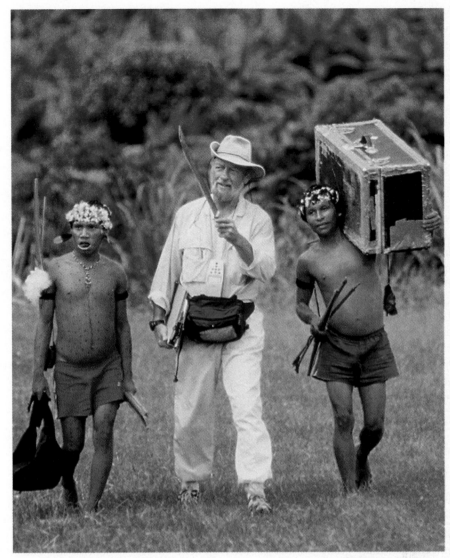

Napoleon Chagnon in the field with two Yanomami men, 1995. Chagnon distributed goods such as steel axes and tobacco to the Yanomami to gain their cooperation in his research.

CRITICAL THINKING QUESTIONS ▼

• Which perspective presented here on Yanomami men's behavior appears most persuasive to you and why?

• What relevance does this case have to the theory that violence is a universal human trait?

• Do you think anthropological research could lead to increased violence among the study population?

groups for raids. Contemporary tribal groups everywhere, though, do not all have the same levels of warfare. At one extreme, with reported high levels of warfare, are the Yanomami of the Amazon (see Map 4.4, page 91 and Critical Thinking).

In states, standing (permanent) armies and complex military hierarchies are supported by increased material resources through taxation and other forms of revenue generation. Greater state power allows for more powerful and effective military structures, which in turn increase the state's power. Thus, a mutually reinforcing relationship emerges between the military and the state. Although most states are highly militarized, not all are, nor are all states equally militarized. Costa Rica (see Map 13.2, page 327) does not maintain an army.

Examining the causes of war between states has occupied scholars in many fields for centuries. Some experts have pointed to common, underlying causes, such as attempts to extend boundaries, secure more resources, ensure markets, support political and economic allies, and resist aggression from other states. Others point to humanitarian concerns that prompt participation in "just wars," to defend values such as freedom or to protect human rights that are defined as such by one country and are being violated in another.

Causes of war in Afghanistan, to take one case, have changed over time (Barfield 1994). Since the seventeenth century, warfare increasingly became a way in which kings justified their power in terms of the necessity to maintain

MAP 10.4 Central Asian States.

The five states of Central Asia are Kazakhstan, Turkmenistan, Uzbekistan, Kyrgyzstan, and Tajikistan. Central Asia is a large, landlocked region that is historically linked with pastoralism and the famous Silk Road, a trade route connecting the Middle East with China. The region's terrain encompasses desert, plateaus, and mountains. Given its strategic location near several major world powers, it has often been a battleground of other states' interests. The predominant religion is Islam, and most Central Asians are Sunnis. Languages are of the Turkic language group. Central Asia has an indigenous form of rap-style music in which lyrical improvisers engage in battles, usually accompanied by a stringed instrument. These musical artists, or *akyns*, are now using their art to campaign for political candidates.

independence from outside forces such as the British and Czarist Russia. The last Afghan king was murdered in a coup in 1978. When the Soviet Union invaded in 1979, no centralized ruling group existed to meet it. The Soviet Union deposed the ruling faction, set up one of its own, and then killed over 1 million people, caused 3 million to flee the country, and left millions of others to be displaced internally. Still, in spite of the lack of a central command, ethnic and sectarian differences, and being outmatched in equipment by Soviet forces, the Afghanis waged a war of resistance that eventually wore down the Soviets, who withdrew in 1989.

The recent history of war in Afghanistan suggests that war was a more effective tool of domination in the premodern period, when it settled matters more definitively (Barfield 1994). In premodern times, fewer troops were needed to maintain dominance after a conquest, because continued internal revolts were less common and the main issue was defense against rivals from outside. Current events show clearly that attacking and taking over a country are only the first stages in a process much more complicated than the term *regime change* implies. Afghanistan is still attempting to recover and rebuild after over four decades of war (Shahrani 2002). Cultural factors influencing the country's recovery include codes of honor that value political autonomy and

require vengeance for harm received, the moral system of Islam, the drug economy, and the effects of intervention from outside powers involving several foreign governments, most notably the United States, and corporations, including Unocal of California, Delta Oil of Saudi Arabia, and Bridas of Argentina. The difficulty of constructing a strong state with loyal citizens in the face of competing internal and external factors is great.

GLOBAL-LOCAL CONFLICT The categories of conflict described above involve units that are roughly parallel: ethnic groups, sectarian groups, or states. Another form of conflict has been taking place around the world since at least the fifteenth century when powerful European countries began to colonize tropical countries. This process, far from being over, is ongoing, though the major actors have shifted over time. The United States, known as the most powerful country in the world, is currently waging two wars: in Iraq and Afghanistan. Although they are termed "wars against terrorism," they could be interpreted as *neocolonial wars*, that is, wars that seek to control strategic world areas for the material and political gain of the dominating country. Such wars are not formally declared, and they often do not conform to accepted international rules of engagement, including the treatment of prisoners.

Some of the many faces of the long war in Afghanistan. (LEFT) A United States soldier in Khost waves "hello" to a village child during a sweep-check of the area. (RIGHT) A burqa-clad Afghan woman walks in a cemetery in Kabul, the capital city. Preventing civilian casualties is a major area of discussion between the leaders of Afghanistan and the United States and others involved in trying to defeat the Taliban.

Another type of conflict involves a *private-sector* (nongovernment) entity such as a multinational corporation versus a local group or groups that typically makes claims against, and often fight physically against, the corporation. Some cultural anthropologists work with multinational corporations to assist them in establishing and maintaining harmonious relations with people affected by their projects such as dams, mines, and oil drilling. The concept of **corporate social responsibility (CSR)** is increasingly adopted by large multinationals, though implemented to varying degrees. The definition of CSR is contested, but most would agree that it boils down to business ethics that seek to generate profits for the corporation while avoiding harm to people and the environment: the goal is to pursue profits in line with protecting people and the planet.

Other anthropologists work as advocates on behalf of the so-called "affected people" to document harm inflicted by businesses and to gain compensation, meager as it typically is, and late-coming due to extended legal processes (see Anthropology Works on page 252). Another role for anthropology is at the beginning of the process of a resource extraction process, documenting the legal steps involved in the Environmental Impact Assessment phase and how, typically, the process is tilted in favor of the companies due to their power networks. In one case, in Peru, the mining company was able to bring in scientific experts to attest on its behalf; the *campesinos* (small farmers), who resisted the mine, lacked the ability to bring in their own counter-experts (Li 2009).

⊡ ⊡ ⊡

Change in Political and Legal Systems

In the early days of political and legal anthropology, researchers examined political organization and social control in the four categories of bands, tribes, chiefdoms, and states.

Political and legal anthropologists are now more interested in global-local political and legal connections and change. This section provides three examples of change.

Emerging Nations and Transnational Nations

Many different definitions exist for a nation, and some of them overlap with definitions given for a state. One definition says that a **nation** is a group of people who share a language, culture, territorial base, political organization, and history (Clay 1990). In this sense, a nation is culturally homogeneous, and the United States would be considered not a nation, but rather a political unit composed of many nations. According to this definition, groups that lack a territorial base cannot be termed nations. A related term is the *nation–state*, which some say refers to a state that comprises only one nation, whereas others think that it refers to a state that comprises many nations. An example of the first view is the Iroquois nation (see Map 4.3, page 90).

Depending on their resources and power, nations and other groups may constitute a political threat to state stability and control. Examples include the Kurds in the Middle East (see Culturama on page 253), the Maya of Mexico and Central America, Tamils in Sri Lanka, Tibetans in China, and Palestinians in the Middle East. In response to local political movements, states seek to create and maintain a sense of unified identity. Political scientist Benedict Anderson, in his book *Imagined Communities* (1991 [1983]), writes about the symbolic efforts that state builders employ to create a sense of belonging—an "imagined community"—among diverse peoples. Strategies include the imposition of one

corporate social responsibility (CSR) business ethics that seek to generate profits for the corporation while avoiding harm to people and the environment.

nation a group of people who share a language, culture, territorial base, political organization, and history.

ANTHROPOLOGY works

Anthropology and Community Activism in Papua New Guinea

A controversial issue in applied anthropology is whether or not an anthropologist should take on the role of community activist on behalf of the people among whom they have conducted research (Kirsch 2002). Some say that anthropologists should maintain a neutral position in a conflict situation and simply offer information that may be used by either side. Others say that it is appropriate and right for anthropologists to take sides and help support less powerful groups against more powerful groups. Those who endorse anthropologists taking an activist role argue that neutrality is never truly neutral: By seemingly taking no position, one indirectly supports the status quo. Information provided to both sides will serve the interests of the more powerful side.

Stuart Kirsch took an activist role after conducting field research for over 15 years in a region of Papua New Guinea that has been negatively affected by a large copper and gold mine called the Ok Tedi mine (see Map 1.2, page 17). The mine releases 80,000 tons of mining wastes into the local river system daily, causing extensive environmental damage that in turn affects people's food and water sources. Kirsch joined the local community in its extended legal and political campaign to limit further pollution and to gain compensation for damages suffered.

He explains his involvement with the community as a form of reciprocal exchange. The community members have provided him with information about their culture for many years. He believes that his knowledge is part of the people's cultural property and that they have a rightful claim to its use. Kirsch's support of the community's goals has taken three forms:

- Providing documentation of the problems of the people living downstream

Yonggom people gather at a meeting in Atkamba village on the Ok Tedi River, Papua New Guinea, to discuss legal proceedings in 1996. At the end of the meeting, leaders signed an agreement to an out-of-court settlement, which was presented to the Victorian Supreme Court in Melbourne, Australia. The current lawsuit concerns the Yonggom people's claim that the 1996 settlement agreement has been breached.

from the mine in terms of their ability to make a living and their health.
- Working with local leaders to help them to convey their views to the public and in the court.
- Serving as a cultural broker, a person familiar with two cultures who can mediate and prevent conflicts, in discussions among community members, politicians, mining executives, lawyers, and representatives of nongovernmental organizations (NGOs) to promote solutions for the problems faced by the Ok Tedi people living downstream from the mine.

In spite of official reports recommending that the mine be closed in 2001, its future remains uncertain. No assessment of past damages to the community has been prepared. As the case goes on, Kirsch continues to support the community's efforts. Indigenous people worldwide are increasingly invoking their rights to anthropological knowledge about themselves.

According to Kirsch, the Ok Tedi case, along with many others, requires cultural anthropologists to rethink their roles and relationships with the people they study. Gone is old-fashioned fieldwork in which community members provide information that the anthropologist records and then keeps for his or her intellectual development alone. The overall goal must be one of collaboration and cooperation and, often, the anthropologist serving as an advocate for the people.

FOOD FOR THOUGHT ▼

Consider the pros and cons of anthropological advocacy in terms of the Ok Tedi case or another issue: should an anthropologist side with the local people with whom they have done research against a powerful outside force? If the anthropologist does not side with the local people, is that equivalent to siding with the outsiders?

Thanks to Stuart Kirsch, University of Michigan, for providing updates.

---

language as the national language; the construction of monuments and museums that emphasize unity; and the use of songs, dress, poetry, and other media messages to promote an image of a unified country. Some states, such as China,

control religious expression in the interest of promoting loyalty to and identity with the state.

Globalization and increased international migration also prompt anthropologists to rethink the concept of the

CULTURAMA

The Kurds of the Middle East

The Kurds are an ethnic group of between 20 and 30 million people, most of whom speak some dialect of the Kurdish language, which is related to Farsi, the language spoken in Iran, among other countries (Major 1996). The majority are Sunni Muslims. Kurdish kinship is strongly patrilineal, and Kurdish family and social relations are male dominated.

Their home region, called Kurdistan ("Place of the Kurds"), extends from Turkey into Iran, Iraq, and Syria. This area is grasslands, interspersed with mountains, with no coastline. Before World War I, many Kurds were full-time pastoralists, herding sheep and goats. Following the war and the creation of Iraq, Syria, and Kuwait, many Kurdish herders were unable to follow their traditional grazing routes because they crossed the new country borders. Herders no longer live in tents year-round, though some do for part of the year. Others are farmers. In towns and cities, Kurds own shops,

are professionals, and are employed in many different occupations.

Reliable population data for the Kurds in the Middle East do not exist, and estimates vary widely. About half of all Kurds—between 10 and 15 million—live in Turkey, where they constitute 20 percent, or perhaps more, of the total population. Approximately 6 million live in Iran, 4 to 5 million in Iraq, and 1.5 million in Syria. Others live in Armenia, Germany, France, and the United States.

The Kurds have attempted to establish an independent state for decades, with no success and often facing harsh treatment from government forces. In Turkey, the state used to refer to them as "Mountain Turks" and in many ways still refuses to recognize them as a legitimate minority group. Use of the Kurdish language is restricted in Turkey. The Kurds have faced similar repression in Iraq, especially following their support of Iran in

the 1980–1988 Iran–Iraq war. Saddam Hussein razed villages and used chemical weapons against the Kurds. After the Persian Gulf War, 2 million Kurds fled to Iran. Many others have emigrated to Europe and the United States. Iraqi Kurds gained political autonomy from Baghdad in 1991 following a successful uprising aided by Western forces.

Many Kurds feel united by the shared goal of statehood, but several strong internal political factions and a guerrilla movement in Turkey also exist among the Kurds. Kurds in Turkey seek the right to have Kurdish-language schooling and television and radio broadcasts, and they would like to have their folklore recognized as well. The Kurds are fond of music and dancing, and Kurdish villages are known for their distinct performance styles.

Thanks to Diane E. King, University of Kentucky, for reviewing this material.

(LEFT) Herding goats and sheep is a major part of the economy throughout Kurdistan.

(CENTER) In Dohuk, Iraq, the Mazi Supermarket and Dream City are a combination shopping center and amusement park. The goods in the market come mainly from Dubai and Turkey.

MAP 10.5 **Kurdish Region in the Middle East.** Kurdistan includes parts of Iran, Iraq, Syria, Turkey, and Armenia. About half of all Kurds live in Turkey.

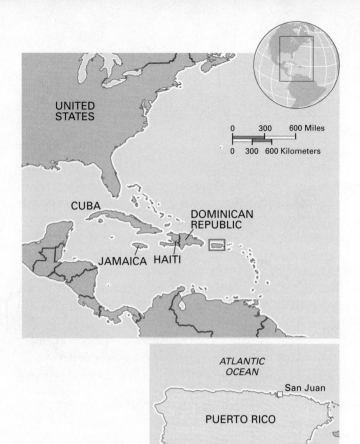

MAP 10.6 Puerto Rico.

The Commonwealth of Puerto Rico is a U.S. territory with commonwealth status. The indigenous population of the island, the Tainos, is extinct. Analysis of DNA of current inhabitants of Puerto Rico reveals a mixed ancestry, including the Taino, Spanish colonialists, and Africans who came to the island as slaves. The economy is based on agriculture, and sugarcane is the main crop. Tourism is also important, as are remittances. Official languages are Spanish and English. Roman Catholicism is the dominant religion, although Protestantism is increasing.

state (Trouillot 2001). The case of Puerto Rico (Map 10.6) is particularly illuminating because of its continuing status as a quasi-colony of the United States (Duany 2000). Puerto Rico is neither fully a state of the United States nor an autonomous political unit with its own national identity. Furthermore, Puerto Rican people do not coexist in a bounded spatial territory. By the late 1990s, nearly as many Puerto Ricans lived in the United States mainland as on the island of Puerto Rico. Migration to Puerto Rico also occurs, creating cultural diversity there. Migrants include returning Puerto Ricans and others from the United States, such as Dominicans and Cubans.

These migration streams—outgoing and incoming—pose a dual complication to the sense of Puerto Rico as constituting a nation. First, half of the "nation" lives outside the home territory. Second, within the home territory, ethnic homogeneity does not exist because of the diversity of people who migrate there. The Puerto Ricans who are return migrants are different from the islanders because many have adopted English as their primary language. All of these processes foster the emergence of a transnational identity, which differs from a national identity centered in either the United States or Puerto Rico. (Chapter 14 provides additional material on transnationalism.)

Democratization

Democratization is the process of transformation from an authoritarian regime to a democratic regime. This process includes several features: the end of torture, the liberation of political prisoners, the lifting of censorship, and the toleration of some opposition (Pasquino 1996). In some cases, what is achieved is more a relaxation of authoritarianism than a true transition to democracy, which would occur when the authoritarian regime is no longer in control. Political parties emerge, some presenting traditional interests and others oppositional.

The transition to democracy appears to be most difficult when the change is from highly authoritarian socialist regimes. This pattern is partly explained by the fact that democratization implies a transition from a planned economy to one based on market capitalism (Lempert 1996). The spotty record of democratization efforts also has to do with the fact that many principles of democracy do not fit in with local political traditions that are based solely on kinship and patronage.

The United Nations and International Peacekeeping

What role might cultural anthropology play in international peacekeeping? Robert Carneiro (1994) has a pessimistic response. Carneiro says that during the long history of human political evolution from bands to states, warfare has been the major means by which political units enlarged their power and domain. Foreseeing no logical end to this process, he predicts that war will follow war until superstates become ever larger and one mega-state is the final result. He considers the United Nations powerless in dealing with the principal obstacle to world peace: state sovereignty interests. Carneiro indicts the United Nations for its lack of coercive power and its

A child soldier named Alfred walks to a UN disarmament camp in the Liberian city of Tubmanburg in 2004. Many countries have programs to help child soldiers adjust to life after war.

▶ *What might be the three most important challenges that child soldiers face in a postconflict situation?*

record of having resolved disputes through military intervention in only a few cases.

If war is inevitable, little hope exists that anthropological knowledge can be applied to peacemaking efforts. Nonetheless, despite Carneiro's views, cultural anthropologists have shown that war is not a cultural universal and that some cultures solve disputes without resorting to war. The cultural anthropological perspective of critical cultural relativism (review this concept in Chapter 1) can provide useful background on issues of conflict and prompt a deeper dialogue between parties.

Two positive points emerge. The United Nations at least affords an arena for airing disputes. International peace organizations may thus play a role in world peace and order by providing a forum for analysis of the interrelationships among world problems and by exposing the causes and consequences of violence. Another positive direction is the role of NGOs and grassroots organizations in promoting local and global peacemaking through initiatives that bridge group interests.

What does political anthropology cover?

Political anthropology is the study of power relationships in the public domain and how they vary and change cross-culturally. Political anthropologists study the concept of power itself and related concepts such as authority and influence. They have discovered differences and similarities between politics and political organization in small-scale and large-scale societies in leadership roles and responsibilities and in the distribution of power.

Foragers have a minimal form of political organization in the band. Band membership is flexible. If a band member has a serious disagreement with another person or spouse, one option is to leave that band and join another. Leadership in bands is informal. The tribe is a more formal type of political organization than the band. A tribe comprises several bands or lineage groups with a headman or headwoman as leader. Big-man and big-woman political systems are an expanded form of the tribe, and leaders have influence over people in several different villages. Chiefdoms may include several thousand people. Rank is inherited, and social divisions exist between members of the chiefly lineage and commoners.

The state is a centralized political unit encompassing many communities and possessing coercive power. States evolved in several locations with the emergence of intensive agriculture. Most states are hierarchical and patriarchal.

What is the scope of legal anthropology?

Legal anthropology encompasses the study of cultural variation in social order and social conflict. The more recent approach of critical legal anthropology points out how legal institutions often support and maintain social inequalities and injustice. Legal anthropologists also study the difference between norms and laws. Systems of social order and social control vary cross-culturally and over time.

Social control in small-scale societies seeks to restore order more than to punish offenders. The presence of a wide variety of legal specialists is more associated with the state than with small-scale societies, in which social shaming and shunning are common methods of punishment. In states, imprisonment and capital punishment may exist, reflecting the greater power of the state. Cross-cultural data on levels and forms of conflict and violence indicate that high levels of lethal violence are more often associated with the state than with earlier forms of political organization. Social conflict ranges from face-to-face conflicts, such as those among neighbors or domestic partners, to larger group conflicts between ethnic groups and states.

Cultural anthropologists are turning their attention to studying global conflict and peace-keeping solutions. Key issues involve the role of cultural knowledge in dispute resolution and how international or local organizations can help achieve or maintain peace.

How are political and legal systems changing?

The anthropological study of change in political and legal systems has documented several trends, many of which are related to the influences of European colonialism and contemporary capitalist globalization. Postcolonial states struggle with internal ethnic divisions and pressures to democratize.

Ethnic politics has emerged within and across states as groups seek to compete for increased rights within the state or for separation from it. The Kurds are an example of an ethnic group fighting for political autonomy.

Cultural anthropologists are increasingly doing research on international topics, including the internal dynamics of international organizations such as the United Nations. Their work demonstrates the relevance of cultural anthropology in global peacekeeping and conflict resolution.

KEY CONCEPTS

authority, p. 235
band, p. 235
big-man or **big-woman system,** p. 237
chiefdom, p. 239
corporate social responsibility (CSR), p. 251
critical legal anthropology, p. 247
influence, p. 235

law, p. 243
moka, p. 237
nation, p. 251
norm, p. 243
policing, p. 245
political organization, p. 235
power, p. 235
sectarian conflict, p. 247

social control, p. 243
social justice, p. 247
state, p. 240
trial by ordeal, p. 245
tribe, p. 237
war, p. 248

SUGGESTED READINGS

Kimberley Coles. *Democratic Designs: International Intervention and Electoral Practices in Postwar Bosnia-Herzegovina.* Ann Arbor: University of Michigan Press, 2008. Coles provides an ethnographic analysis of the interaction between international humanitarian aid workers and the postwar political process by focusing on the electoral process.

Elizabeth F. Drexler. *Aceh, Indonesia: Securing the Insecure State.* Philadelphia: University of Pennsylvania Press, 2008. The author examines corruption, political violence, and the failure of international humanitarian interventions in the Indonesian province of Aceh.

Mona Etienne and Eleanor Leacock, eds. *Women and Colonization: Anthropological Perspectives.* New York: Praeger, 1980. This classic collection examines the impact of Western colonialism and missionary intervention on women of several indigenous groups of North America, South America, Africa, and the Pacific.

Magnus Fiskesjö. *The Thanksgiving Turkey Pardon, The Death of Teddy's Bear, and the Sovereign Exception of Guantánamo.* Chicago: Prickly Paradigm Press, 2003. This interpretation of the U.S. presidential ritual of "pardoning" a turkey every Thanksgiving sheds light on notions of the presidency and its power in the United States.

Thomas Gregor, ed. *A Natural History of Peace.* Nashville: University of Tennessee Press, 1996. This book contains essays on "what is peace?" reconciliation among nonhuman primates, the psychological bases of violent and nonviolent societies, case studies of Amazonia and American Indians, and international relations.

Susan F. Hirsch. *In the Moment of Greatest Calamity: Terrorism, Grief, and a Victim's Quest for Justice.* Princeton: Princeton University Press, 2006. The author's husband was killed in the 1998 bombing of the U.S. embassy in Kenya. In this book, Hirsch describes her experiences in Kenya in the aftermath of the bombing, her grief, and her witnessing of the bombing trials in Manhattan in 2001.

Beatriz Manz. *Paradise in Ashes: A Guatemalan Journey of Courage, Terror, and Hope.* Berkeley: University of California Press, 2004. Manz traces the lives and deaths of some Guatemalan Maya villagers who left their impoverished homeland in the mountains to build a new life in the lowlands. In their new location, they became victims of state-sponsored violence. Many were murdered, and others were forced to flee into the jungle. The survivors have returned to rebuild their homes and lives.

Bruce Miller. *The Problem of Justice: Tradition and Law in the Coast Salish World.* Lincoln: University of Nebraska Press, 2001. The author compares several legal systems operating in the Northwest Coast region from Washington State to British Columbia. The effects of colonialism differ from group to group. Some groups are strong and independent, whereas others are disintegrating.

Carolyn Nordstrom. *Shadows of War: Violence, Power, and International Profiteering in the Twenty-First Century.* Berkeley: University of California Press, 2004. Nordstrom did fieldwork in Sri Lanka and Mozambique to reveal the shadow economy that surrounds and supports war. She focuses on informal trading networks that involve goods ranging from guns to food and the people who profit from this economy.

Jennifer Schirmer. *The Guatemalan Military Project: A Violence Called Democracy.* Philadelphia: University of Pennsylvania Press, 1998. This book is an ethnography of the Guatemalan military, documenting its role in human rights violations through extensive interviews with military officers and trained torturers.

David Sneath. *The Headless State: Aristocratic Orders, Kinship Society, and Misrepresentations of Nomadic Inner Asia.* New York: Columbia University Press, 2008. The author describes how anthropologists since the nineteenth century have misrepresented Inner Asian nomadic political culture. His analysis continues through to the Soviet and post-Soviet periods and then offers a more accurate interpretation.

PEARSON
myanthrolab

For further information about topics covered in this chapter, go to MyAnthroLab at **www.myanthrolab.com** and access the following readings in MyAnthroLibrary:

Roberto J. González. 2009. Anthropologists or "Technicians of Power"? Examining the Human Terrain System. *Practicing Anthropology* 31:34–37. Is participation by cultural anthropologists in the United States' Human Terrain System ethical? Do the ends outweigh the means?

Thomas Lyons. 2010. Recovery Capital, Drug Policy and the Cycle of Incarceration. *Practicing Anthropology* 32:41–44. Estimates are that over half of prison inmates in the United States have a drug or alcohol problem. Interventions overlook the users' families, communities, and poverty and instead focus on the individual and his/her moral failure or brain disease.

Alisa Perkins. 2010. Negotiating Alliances: Muslims, Gay Rights, and the Christian Right in a Polish-American City. *Anthropology Today* 26(2):19–24. Ethnographic research shows how complicated political matters are when they involve religion, sexual identity, immigrants, and public misperceptions of all of these factors.

◉ How do humans communicate?

◉ How does communication relate to cultural diversity and inequality?

◉ How does language change?

COMMUNICATION

◀ Tuareg pastoralists in Niger, West Africa, greeting each other. Tuareg men's greetings involve lengthy handshaking and close body contact.

11

OUTLINE

This chapter is about human communication and language, drawing on work in both linguistic anthropology and cultural anthropology. It looks at communication with a wide-angle lens to include topics from word choice to language extinction. The chapter first discusses how humans communicate and what distinguishes human communication from that of other animals. The second section offers examples of language, microcultures, and inequality. The third section discusses language change from its origins in the distant past to contemporary concerns about language loss.

◉ ◉ ◉

The Varieties of Human Communication

Humans can communicate with words, either spoken or signed, with gestures and other forms of body language such as clothing and hairstyle, and through methods such as telephone calls, postal mail, and e-mail.

Language and Verbal Communication

Most people are in almost constant communication—with other people, with supernaturals, or with pets. We communicate in face-to-face situations or indirectly through mail or email. **Communication** is the process of sending and receiving meaningful messages. Among humans, it involves some form of **language**, a systematic set of symbols and signs with learned and shared meanings. Language may be spoken, hand-signed, written, or conveyed through body movements, body markings and modifications, hairstyle, dress, and accessories.

TWO FEATURES OF HUMAN LANGUAGE Over several centuries, scholars of language have proposed characteristics of human language that distinguish it from commu-

---

communication   the process of sending and receiving meaningful messages.

language   a form of communication that is based on a systematic set of learned symbols and signs shared among a group and passed on from generation to generation.

productivity   a feature of human language whereby people are able to communicate a potentially infinite number of messages efficiently.

call system   a form of oral communication among nonhuman primates with a set repertoire of meaningful sounds generated in response to environmental factors.

displacement   a feature of human language whereby people are able to talk about events in the past and future.

phoneme   a sound that makes a difference for meaning in a spoken language.

Primatologist Sue Savage-Rumbaugh working with Kanzi, an adult male bonobo. Kanzi is involved in a long-term project about ape language. He has learned to use several symbols to communicate with researchers. Some chimpanzees, bonobos, orangutans, and gorillas are also able to communicate in American Sign Language and identify symbols on computer keyboards.

nication among other living beings. The following material describes the two most robust such characteristics.

First, human language has **productivity**, or the ability to create an infinite range of understandable expressions from a finite set of rules. This characteristic is a result of the rich variety of symbols and signs that humans use in their communication. In contrast, nonhuman primates have a more limited set of communicative resources. They rely on a **call system**, or a form of oral communication with a set repertoire of meaningful sounds generated in response to environmental factors. Nonhuman primates do not have the physiological capacity for speech that humans do. In captivity, however, some bonobos and chimpanzees have learned to communicate effectively with humans through sign language and by pointing to symbols on a chart. The world's most famous bonobo is Kanzi, who lives at the Great Ape Trust in Des Moines, Iowa. He can understand much of what humans say to him, and he can respond by combining symbols on a printed board. He can also play simple video games, such as Ms. Pac-Man (http://www.greatapetrust.org).

Second, human language emphasizes the feature of **displacement**, the ability to refer to events and issues beyond the immediate present. The past and the future, in this view, are considered to be *displaced domains*. They include reference to people and events that may never exist at all, as in fantasy and fiction.

With respect to productivity and displacement in human language, the case of language among the Pirahã (pee-duh-hah) of Brazil raises many questions (Everett 2008) (Map 11.1). Their language does not emphasize either productivity or displacement, though both exist to some degree. The Pirahã are a group of about 350 foragers living on a reservation in the

A Pirahã shelter. According to Daniel Everett, who has spent many years learning about their culture and language, the Pirahã do not lead a culturally deprived life. The Pirahã are content with their lifestyle, which includes leisure activities such as playing tag and other games. In spite of their wish to remain living as they are, their reservation is not secure from outside encroachment.

MAP 11.1 Pirahã Reservation in Brazil.
Linguist Daniel Everett helped to define the boundaries of the Pirahã reservation in the 1980s. With support from Cultural Survival and other sources, the demarcation was legally declared in 1994.

Amazonian rainforest near the Maici River. Their language contains only three pronouns, few words associated with time, no past-tense verbs, no color terms, and no numbers other than a word that translates into English roughly as "about one." The grammar is simple, with no subordinate clauses. Kinship terms are simple and few. The Pirahã have no myths or stories and no art other than necklaces and a few rudimentary stick figures. In spite of over 200 years of regular contact with Brazilians and neighboring Indians who speak a different language, the Pirahã remain monolingual.

Since 1977, linguist Daniel Everett has lived with the Pirahã and learned their language, so it is unlikely that he has overlooked major aspects of their language. He insists that their language is in no way "primitive" or inadequate. It has extremely complex verbs and rich and varied uses of stress and intonation, referred to in linguistics as *prosody*. The Pirahã especially enjoy verbal joking and teasing, both among themselves and with researchers.

FORMAL PROPERTIES OF VERBAL LANGUAGE

Human language can be analyzed in terms of its formal properties: sounds, vocabulary, and syntax (sometimes called grammar), which are the formal building blocks of all languages. But languages differ widely in which sounds are important, what words are important in the vocabulary, and how people put words together to form meaningful sentences. Learning a new language often involves learning different sets of sounds. The sounds that make a difference for meaning in a spoken language are called **phonemes**. The study of phonemes is called *phonetics*.

A native English-speaker learning to speak Hindi, the major language of North India, must learn to produce and

recognize several new sounds. Four different "d" sounds exist. None is the same as an English "d," which is usually pronounced with the tongue placed on the ridge behind the upper front teeth (try it). One "d" in Hindi, which linguists refer to as a "dental" sound, is pronounced with the tongue pressed firmly behind the upper front teeth (try it) (Figure 11.1). Next is a dental "d" that is also aspirated (pronounced "with air"); making this sound involves the tongue being in the same position as it is in making the dental "d," but now a puff of air is expelled (try it, and try the regular dental "d" again with no puff of air at all). Next is what is referred to as a "retroflex" sound, made by flipping the tongue back to the central dome of the roof of the mouth (try it, with no puff of air). Finally,

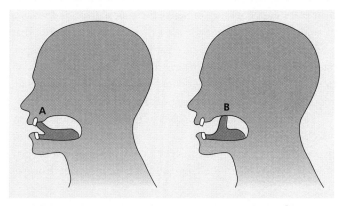

FIGURE 11.1 Dental and Retroflex Tongue Positions. When making a dental sound, the speaker places the tongue against the upper front teeth (position A in the diagram). When making a retroflex sound, the speaker places the tongue up against the roof of the mouth (position B in the diagram).

- Firm, even snow that falls in mild weather
- Thickly packed snow caused by intermittent freezing/thawing and high winds
- Hard-packed snow formed by strong wind
- Dry, large-grained, water-holding snow at the deepest layers, closest to the ground, found in late winter and spring
- Snow that forms a hard layer after rain
- Ice sheet on pastures formed by rain on open ground that freezes
- A layer of frozen snow between other snow layers that acts as an ice sheet

Source: Jernsletten 1997.

FIGURE 11.2 Kinds of "Snow" the Saami Recognize Related to Reindeer Herding.

there is the aspirated retroflex "d" with the tongue in the center of the roof of the mouth and a puff of air. Once you can do this, try the whole series again with a "t," because Hindi follows the same pattern with this letter as with the "d." Several other sounds in Hindi require careful use of aspiration and placement of the tongue for communicating the right word. A puff of air at the wrong time can produce a serious error, such as saying the word for "breast" when you want to say the word for "letter."

Every language has a vocabulary, or *lexicon,* which consists of all of the language's meaningful words. Speakers combine words into phrases and sentences to create meaning. *Semantics* refers to the study of the meaning of words, phrases, and sentences. Anthropologists add the concept of **ethnosemantics,** the study of the meaning of words, phrases, and sentences in particular cultural contexts. They find that languages classify the world in unpredictable ways, categorizing even such seemingly natural things as color and disease differently. (Recall the discussion of Subanun disease categories in Chapter 7.) Ethnosemantic research reveals much about how people define the world and their place in it, how they organize their social lives, and what is of value to them. *Focal vocabularies* are clusters of words that refer to important features of a particular culture. For example, many circumpolar languages have rich focal vocabularies related to snow (Figure 11.2). In mountainous areas of Afghanistan, people use many terms for varieties of rocks.

Syntax, or grammar, consists of the patterns and rules by which words are organized to make sense in a sentence, or string. All languages have rules of syntax, although they vary in form. Even within the languages of contemporary Europe,

syntactical variation exists. In German, for example, the verb often appears at the end of the sentence.

All of the formal aspects of verbal communication allow people to convey, through speech, simple and complex messages about themselves and their experiences. Not all cultures shape their members to be equally "talky" as will be discussed below in the section on the importance of silence. In "talky" cultures, being able to share *narratives* (stories) about one's experiences, especially troubling or traumatic experiences, can be a path to healing (see Anthropology Works).

Nonverbal Language and Embodied Communication

Many forms of language and communication do not rely on verbal speech. Like verbal language, though, they are based on symbols and signs and have rules for their proper combination and meaning.

SIGN LANGUAGE **Sign language** is a form of communication that uses mainly hand movements to convey messages. A sign language provides a fully competent communication system for its users, just as spoken language does (Baker 1999). Around the world, many varieties of sign language exist, including American Sign Language, British Sign Language, Japanese Sign Language, Russian Sign Language, and many varieties of indigenous Australian sign languages. Most sign languages are used by people who are hearing impaired as their main form of communication. But in many indigenous Australian communities, people who are able to communicate verbally often opt to sign (Kendon 1988). They switch to sign language in situations in which verbal speech is forbidden or undesirable, for example, in some sacred contexts, for men during hunting, and for widows during mourning. *Gestures* are movements, usually of the hands, that convey meanings. Some gestures may be universally meaningful, but most are culturally specific and often completely arbitrary. Some cultures have more highly developed gesture systems than others. Black urban youths in the cities of Pretoria and Johannesburg in South Africa use a rich repertoire of gestures (Brookes 2004) (see Map 9.5, page 222). Some of the gestures are widely used and recognized, but many vary by age, gender, and situation (see Figure 11.3 on page 264). Men use more gestures than women do; the reason for this difference is not clear.

Greetings, an important part of communication in every known culture, often involve gestures (Duranti 1997b). They

---

ethnosemantics the study of the meaning of words, phrases, and sentences in particular cultural contexts.

sign language a form of communication that uses mainly hand movements to convey messages.

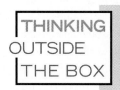

THINKING OUTSIDE THE BOX

Try to compose an English sentence with its main verb at the end.

ANTHROPOLOGY works

Narrating Troubles

Refugee survivors of violence are especially at risk of various mental health problems, including what Western psychiatrists call *post-traumatic stress disorder*, or PTSD. It includes symptoms such as depression, anxiety, sleep disorders, and changes in personality. In treating refugee survivors in North America, several approaches have been used, including *narrative therapy*, in which the sufferer tells about his or her experiences as a way of unloading the pent-up memories. It involves asking the individual to tell in detail, in a safe and caring interpersonal setting, the story of what happened to him or her.

A study of twenty Bosnian refugees who now live in the United States sheds light on the positive effects of having survivors narrate their experiences of terror and suffering (Weine et al. 1995). Ten of the refugees in the study were male and ten were female, ranging in age from 13 to 62 years. All but one were Muslims, and all adults were married and had worked either inside or outside the home. Analysis of their narratives showed that all had experienced many traumatic events, the frequency increasing with a person's age.

Almost all the refugees experienced the destruction of their homes, forced evacuation, food and water deprivation, disappearance of family members, exposure to acts of violence or death, detainment in a refugee camp, and forced emigration: "Nearly all the refugees emphasized the shock that came with the sudden occurrence of human betrayal by neighbors, associates, friends, and relatives" (1995:538).

The testimonies document the genocidal nature of the traumas directed at the entire Muslim Bosnian population. The traumas experienced were "extreme, multiple, repeated, prolonged, and communal" (1995:539). Some of the survivors carry with them constant images of death and atrocity. One man describes them as "films" that play in his head. In contrast, others have lost their memories of the events, and one woman was later unable to remember the trauma story she told three weeks earlier: "All kinds of things come together. Being expelled. Things we lost. Twenty years of work—then suddenly being without anything . . . . All the memories come at the same moment and it's too much" (1995:541).

The massiveness of their suffering, the psychiatrists report, extends beyond the bounds of the psychiatric diagnostic category of PTSD. Yet, in spite of their deep and extensive suffering, many Bosnian refugees in the United States are recovering and rebuilding their lives, perhaps in part due to the success of narrative therapy.

Studies of this therapeutic approach among refugees of other cultures, however, reveal that some people are extremely reluctant to discuss their experiences, even in a supportive setting. Thus, narrative therapy may not be effective in all cultures.

MAP 11.2 Bosnia and Herzegovina.
Formerly part of the Socialist Federal Republic, Bosnia and Herzegovina have a population of around 4 million. Bosnia occupies the northern areas of the country, about four-fifths of the total area, whereas Herzegovina occupies the southern part. The country still faces the challenges of reconstruction following the war of 1992–1995. On a brighter note, it has one of the best income equality rankings in the world, placing eighth among 193 countries. Bosnia and Herzegovina are world champions in Paralympics volleyball, with a team consisting of players who lost their legs in the Yugoslav War.

A forensic expert clears the soil from a skull found in a mass grave in Bosnia. The grave is believed to contain bodies of perhaps 500 Muslim civilians killed by the Bosnian Serb forces during the 1992–1995 war.

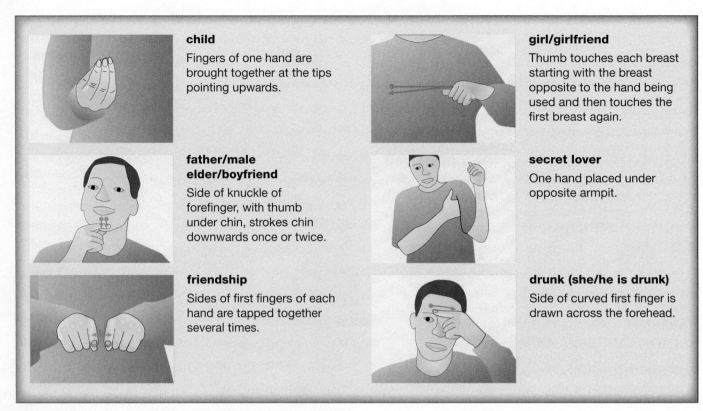

child
Fingers of one hand are brought together at the tips pointing upwards.

girl/girlfriend
Thumb touches each breast starting with the breast opposite to the hand being used and then touches the first breast again.

father/male elder/boyfriend
Side of knuckle of forefinger, with thumb under chin, strokes chin downwards once or twice.

secret lover
One hand placed under opposite armpit.

friendship
Sides of first fingers of each hand are tapped together several times.

drunk (she/he is drunk)
Side of curved first finger is drawn across the forehead.

FIGURE 11.3 Some South African Gestures Used by a Man.

Source: From *A Repertoire of South African Quotable Gestures,* from *The Journal of Linguistic Anthropology,* Copyright © 2004 Blackwell Publishers Ltd. Reproduced with permission of Blackwell Publishers.

are typically among the first communicative routines that children learn, as do tourists and anyone trying to learn a foreign language. Greetings establish a social encounter. They usually involve both verbal and nonverbal language. Depending on the context and the social relationship, many variations exist for both the verbal and the nonverbal component. Contextual factors include the degree of formality or informality. Social factors include gender, ethnicity, class, and age.

SILENCE Silence is another form of nonverbal communication. Its use is often related to social status, but in unpredictable ways. In rural Siberia, an in-marrying daughter-in-law has the lowest status in the household, and she rarely speaks (Humphrey 1978). In other contexts, silence is associated with power. For example, in U.S. courts lawyers speak more than anyone else and the judge speaks rarely but has more power than a lawyer, while the silent jury holds the most power (Lakoff 1990).

Silence is an important component of communication among many American Indian cultures. White outsiders, including social workers, have sometimes misinterpreted this silence as a reflection of dignity or a lack of emotion or intelligence. How ethnocentric such judgments are is revealed by a study of silence among the Western Apache of Arizona (Basso 1972 [1970]) (Map 11.3). The Western Apache use silence in four contexts:

- When meeting a stranger, especially at fairs, rodeos, or other public events. Speaking with a stranger immediately indicates interest in something such as money, work, or transportation, all possibly serving as reasons for exhibiting bad manners.

- In the early stages of courting. Sitting in silence and holding hands for several hours is appropriate. Speaking "too soon" would indicate sexual willingness or interest.

- When a parent and child meet after the child has been away at boarding school. They should be silent for about 15 minutes. It may be two or three days before sustained conversations are initiated.

- When "getting cussed out," especially at drinking parties.

An underlying similarity of all these contexts is the uncertainty, ambiguity, and unpredictability of the social relationships involved.

BODY LANGUAGE Human communication, in one way or another, often involves the body in sending and receiving messages. Beyond the mechanics of speaking, hearing, gesturing, and seeing, the body itself can function as a "text" that conveys messages. The full range of *body language* includes eye movements, posture, walking style, the way one stands and sits, cultural *inscriptions* on the body such as tattoos and hairstyles, and accessories such as dress, shoes, and jewelry. Body language follows patterns and rules just as verbal language

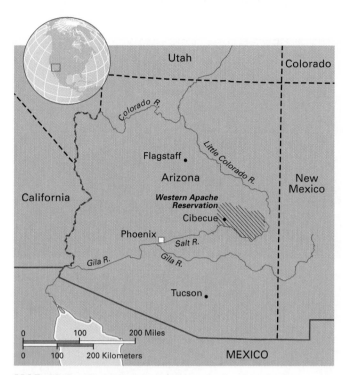

MAP 11.3 Western Apache Reservation in Arizona.
Before European colonialism, the Apache lived in a wide area extending from present-day Arizona to northwestern Texas. Originally foragers, they started planting some food crops in the 1600s. After the arrival of the Spanish, the Apache gained horses from them and became skilled equestrian warriors. In the second half of the nineteenth century, the U.S. government exterminated many Apache groups and forced those who survived to live on reservations in order to make way for White settlements.

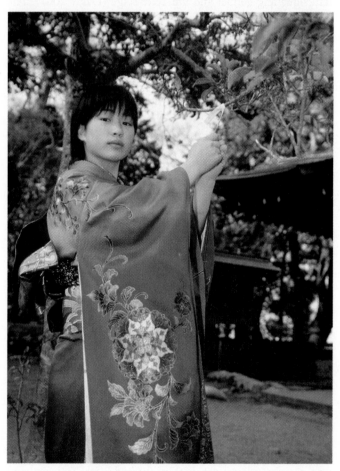

(TOP) Japanese businessmen meet each other, bow, and exchange business cards. Bowing is an important part of nonverbal communication in Japan. (BOTTOM) The *furisode* kimono is distinguished by its fine silk material, long sleeves, and elaborate colors and designs. A girl's 20th birthday gift is typically a furisode, marking her transition to young adulthood. Only unmarried women wear the furisode, so it is a statement of marital availability. Fluttering the long, wide sleeves at a man is a way to express love for him.

▶ *What meanings do the styles and lengths of sleeves convey in your cultural world?*

does. As with verbal language, the rules and meanings are learned, often unconsciously. Without learning the rules and meanings, one will commit communication errors, which are sometimes funny and sometimes serious.

Different cultures emphasize different body language channels more than others. Some are more touch oriented than others, and some use facial expressions more. Eye contact is valued during Euro-American conversations, but in many Asian contexts direct eye contact is considered rude or perhaps a sexual invitation.

Clothing, hairstyles, and modification of or marks on the body convey messages about age, gender, sexual interest or availability, profession, wealth, and emotions. The color of one's clothing can send messages about a person's identity, class, gender, and more. In the United States, gender differentiation begins in the hospital nursery with the color coding of blue for boys and pink for girls. In parts of the Middle East, public dress is black for women and white for men.

Covering or not covering various parts of the body with clothing is another culturally coded matter. Consider the different meanings of women's head or face covering in Egypt and Kuwait (MacLeod 1992). Kuwaiti women's head covering distinguishes them as relatively wealthy, leisured, and honorable, as opposed to the immigrant women workers from Asia, who do not cover their heads. In contrast, head covering in Egypt is done mainly by women from the lower and middle economic levels. For them, it is a way to accommodate conservative Islamic values while preserving their right to work outside the home. In Egypt, the head covering says, "I am a good Muslim and a good wife or daughter," while in Kuwait, the headscarf says, "I am a wealthy Kuwaiti citizen." In many conservative Muslim contexts, it is important for a woman in public to cover more than her head by wearing a full-length loose garment. These rules, along with other patriarchal values, make it difficult for women in some Muslim contexts to participate in sports while in school and in public sporting events such as the international Olympics.

In Japan, the kimono provides an elaborate coding system signalling gender and life-cycle stage (Dalby 2001). The higher one's status, the shorter is the sleeve of one's kimono. Men's kimono sleeves come in one length: short. Unmarried women's sleeve length is nearly to the ground, whereas a married woman's sleeve is nearly as short as that of a man's. An unmarried woman's kimono sleeves reach almost to the ground.

Communicating with Media and Information Technology

Media anthropology is the cross-cultural study of communication through electronic media such as radio, television, film, recorded music, the Internet, and print media, including newspapers, magazines, and popular literature (Spitulnik 1993). Media anthropology is an important emerging area that links linguistic and cultural anthropology (Allen 1994). Media anthropologists study the media process and media content, the audience response, and the social effects of media presentations. **Critical media anthropology** asks to what degree access to media is liberating or controlling and whose interests the media serve. Critical media anthropologists examine journalism, television, advertising, and the Internet, social media, and gaming worlds.

THE POLITICS OF JOURNALISM Mark Pedelty studied war correspondents in El Salvador to learn about journalists and journalistic practices during war (1995) (see Map 14.5, page 349). He found that the lives and identities of war correspondents are highly charged with violence and terror: "War correspondents have a unique relationship to

---

critical media anthropology an approach within the cross-cultural study of media that examines how power interests shape people's access to media and influence the contents of its messages.

digital divide social inequality in access to new and emerging information technology, notably access to up-to-date computers, the Internet, and training related to their use.

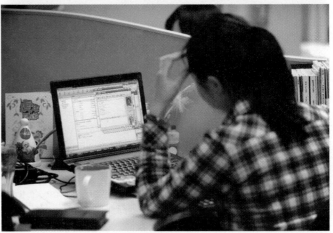

Cultural and linguistic anthropologists study social media to learn about how it can add to human agency as well as how it connects with the global political economy. (TOP) In Cairo, a woman previews a Facebook web page showing the picture of an alleged Egyptian victim of torture who was reportedly brutally tortured to death by the police in the city of Alexandria. (BOTTOM) In China, a woman works online in her cubicle at an office in Beijing. China's media sites like Weibo are booming in the world's largest Internet market.

terror . . . that combines voyeurism and direct participation. . . . They need terror to . . . maintain their cultural identity as 'war correspondents'" (1995:2). The primary job of journalists, including war correspondents, is communication, but communication of a specific sort. They gather information that is time sensitive and often brutal. Their job is to provide brief stories for the public.

A critical media anthropology perspective reveals the important role of the news agency that pays their salary or, if they are freelancers or "stringers," that buys their story. War correspondents in El Salvador write a story about the same event differently, depending on whether they are sending it to a U.S. newspaper or a European newspaper.

GENDER AND JAPANESE TELEVISION PROGRAMMING Most television programming in Japan presents women as housewives, performing traditional domestic roles (Painter 1996). Many Japanese women now reject such shows. In response, producers are experimenting with new sorts of dramas in which women are shown as active workers and aggressive lovers. One such show is a 10-part serial that first aired in 1992 called *Selfish Women*. The story concerns three women: an aggressive single businesswoman who faces discrimination at work, a young mother who is raising her daughter alone while her photographer husband lives with another woman, and an ex-housewife who divorced her husband because she found home life empty and unrewarding. There are several male characters, but, except for one, they are depicted as less interesting than the women.

The show's title is ironic. In Japan, men often label women who assert themselves as "selfish." The lead women in the drama use the term in a positive way to encourage each other: "Let's become even more selfish!" Although dramas like *Selfish Women* may not be revolutionary, they indicate that telerepresentations of gender in Japan are changing, largely through the agency of Japanese women.

ADVERTISING FOR LATINOS IN THE UNITED STATES

Within the U.S. advertising market, one of the most sought-after segments is the Latino population, also called "the Hispanic market" in the advertising industry (Dávila 2002). Interviews with staff of 16 Latino advertising agencies and content analysis of their advertisements reveal their approach of treating Latinos as a unified, culturally specific market. The dominant theme, or *trope*, is that of "the family" as being the most important feature of Latino culture, in contrast to the stereotype of the Anglo population as more individualistic. Recent milk-promotion advertisements for the Anglo

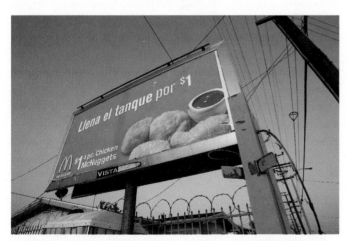

A McDonald's billboard targets an immigrant, Spanish-speaking population in the South Los Angeles area of Los Angeles, California, one of the poorest areas of the city. South LA has the highest concentration of fast-food restaurants in the city and only a few grocery stores. Health problems associated with a fast-food diet, such as obesity and diabetes, plague many of the half-million people living there.

MAP 11.4 Hungary.

The Republic of Hungary has a population of around 10 million. The Roma population, variously estimated at between 450,000, and 600,000, has increased rapidly in recent years. Hungary's landscape is mainly plains with hills and low mountains to the north. One of the newest members of the European Union, Hungary has a growing economy. The main religion is Christianity, with Catholicism accounting for about half of the total; about 30 percent are atheists. Magyar, the Hungarian language, is one of the few European languages that does not belong to the Indo-European language family, but belongs instead to the Finno-Ugric family.

population show a celebrity with a milk moustache. The Latino version shows a grandmother cooking a traditional milk-based dessert, and the caption reads, "Have you given your loved ones enough milk today?" (2002:270). In Spanish-language television and radio networks, a kind of "standard" Spanish is used, a generic form with no hint of regionalism or accent.

Latinos are, however, a highly heterogeneous population. By promoting a monolithic image of Latino culture, media messages may be contributing to identity change toward a more monolithic pattern. At the same time, they are certainly missing opportunities to tap into more specialized markets within the Latino population.

CROSSING THE DIGITAL DIVIDE IN RURAL HUNGARY

The term **digital divide** refers to social inequality in access to new and emerging information technology, especially access to up-to-date computers, the Internet, and training related to their use. Local attempts to overcome the digital divide between Hungary and countries in the European Union involve the development of the Hungarian Telecottage Association (HTA) (Wormald 2005) (Map 11.4). The idea of the telecottage, which started in Sweden and Scotland, involves dedicating some space, such as an unused workshop or part of a house, for public use in which a computer with Internet access is provided.

The HTA, centered in Budapest, promotes village-based Internet access in order to improve the lives of rural people through enhanced communication. Most telecottages in Hungary are located in rural communities of fewer than 5000 people. The HTA website provides announcements about funding opportunities and relevant news. Although these innovations sound highly positive, interpersonal problems related to information hoarding by some managers and to who gets access first to information for posting on the website have emerged.

Like the Hungarian villagers, many marginalized people around the world, including indigenous people, women, and youth, realize the importance of having access to the Internet and to other information and communication technologies (ICTs). These technologies can help people preserve and learn their ancestral languages, record traditional agricultural and medical knowledge, and otherwise protect their culture and improve their lives (Lutz 2005, Turner 2002).

◉ ◉ ◉

Language, Diversity, and Inequality

This section presents material about language, microcultures, and social inequality. It begins by presenting two models of the relationship between language and culture. Examples follow about class, gender and sexuality, "race" and ethnicity, and age.

Language and Culture: Two Theories

During the twentieth century, two theoretical perspectives were influential in the study of the relationship between language and culture. They are presented here as two distinct models, even though they actually overlap in real life and anthropologists tend to draw on both of them (Hill and Mannheim 1992).

The first was formulated by two early founding figures in linguistic anthropology, Edward Sapir and Benjamin Whorf. In the mid-twentieth century, they formulated an influential model called the **Sapir–Whorf hypothesis**, a perspective which says that people's language affects how

they think. If a language has many words for variations of the English word "snow," for example, then someone who speaks that language can "think" about snow in more ways than someone can whose language has fewer "snow" terms. Among the Saami, whose traditional occupation was reindeer herding (see Culturama, page 277), a rich set of terms exists for "snow" (review Figure 11.2, page 262). If a language has no word for "snow," then someone who speaks that language cannot think of "snow." Thus, a language constitutes a *thought world,* and people who speak different languages inhabit different thought worlds. This catchy phrase became the basis for *linguistic determinism,* a theory stating that language determines consciousness of the world and behavior. Extreme linguistic determinism implies that the frames and definitions of a person's primary language are so strong that it is impossible to learn another language fully or, therefore, to understand another culture fully. Most anthropologists see value in the Sapir–Whorf hypothesis, but not in its extreme form.

A second approach to understanding the relationship between language and culture comes from scholars working in the area of **sociolinguistics**, a perspective that emphasizes how people's cultural and social context shapes their language and its meanings. Sociolinguists are, therefore, *cultural constructionists.*

Most anthropologists see some value in both perspectives since language, culture, context, and meaning are highly interactive: Language shapes culture and cultural context shapes language.

Critical Discourse Analysis: Gender and "Race"

Discourse refers to culturally patterned verbal language use including varieties of speech, participation, and meaning. **Critical discourse analysis** is an approach within linguistic anthropology that examines how power and social inequality are reflected in and reproduced through verbal language (Blommaert and Bulcaen 2000). Critical discourse analysis reveals links between language and social inequality, power, and stigma. It also provides insights into agency and resistance through language. The material that follows presents examples of gender and racial power relations as expressed through language.

CLASS AND ACCENT IN NEW YORK CITY

William Labov launched the subfield of sociolinguistics with his classic study of accents among mainly Euro-American people of different socioeconomic classes in New York City (1966). For example, pronunciation of the consonant "r" in words such as car, card, floor, and fourth tends to be associated with upper-class people, whereas its absence ("caw," "cawd," "flaw," "fawth") is associated with lower-class people. Labov used informal observations of sales clerks' speech in three Manhattan

---

Sapir–Whorf hypothesis   a perspective in linguistic anthropology which says that language determines thought.

sociolinguistics   a perspective in linguistic anthropology which says that culture, society, and a person's social position determine language.

discourse   culturally patterned verbal language including varieties of speech, participation, and meaning.

critical discourse analysis   an approach within linguistic anthropology that examines how power and social inequality are reflected and reproduced in communication.

tag question   a question placed at the end of a sentence seeking affirmation.

department stores of different "class" levels: Saks (the highest), Macy's, and S. Klein (the lowest). Labov wanted to find out whether the clerks in the different stores spoke with different class accents. He would approach a clerk and inquire about the location of an item that he knew was on the fourth floor. The clerk would respond, and then Labov would say, "Excuse me?" in order to prompt a more emphatic repeat of the word fourth. He found that the higher-status "r" was pronounced both the first and second times by 44 percent of the employees in Saks, by 16 percent of the employees in Macy's, and by 6 percent of the employees in S. Klein

GENDER IN EURO-AMERICAN CONVERSATIONS

Most languages contain gender differences in word choice, grammar, intonation, content, and style. Early studies of language and gender among white Euro-Americans revealed three general characteristics of female speech (Lakoff 1973):

- Politeness
- Rising intonation at the end of sentences
- Frequent use of **tag questions** (questions seeking affirmation and placed at the end of sentences, such as, "It's a nice day, *isn't it?*")

In English, male speech, in general, is less polite, maintains a flat and assertive tone in a sentence, and does not use tag questions. Related to politeness is the fact that, during cross-gender conversations, men tend to interrupt women more than women interrupt men.

Deborah Tannen's popular book *You Just Don't Understand* (1990) shows how differences in conversational styles between white Euro-American men and women lead to miscommunication. She says that "women speak and hear a language of connection and intimacy, whereas men speak and hear a language of status and independence" (1990:42). Although both men and women use *indirect response* (not really answering the question), their different motivations create different meanings embedded in their speech:

> **Michele:** What time is the concert?
> **Gary:** We have to be ready by seven-thirty. (1990:289)

Gary sees his role as one of protector in using an indirect response to Michele's question. He feels that he is simply "watching out for her" by getting to the real point of her question. Michele feels that Gary is withholding information by not answering her directly and is maintaining a power position. By contrast, a wife's indirect response to a question from her husband is prompted by her goal of being helpful in anticipating her husband's underlying interest:

> **Ned:** Are you just about finished?
> **Valerie:** Do you want to have supper now? (1990:289)

Cross-culturally, women's speech is not universally accommodating, subservient, and polite. In cultural contexts in which women's roles are prominent and valued, their language reflects and reinforces their position.

GENDER AND POLITENESS IN JAPANESE, AND THOSE NAUGHTY TEENAGE GIRLS

Gender registers in spoken Japanese reflect gender differences (Shibamoto 1987). Certain words and sentence structures convey femininity, humbleness, and politeness. One important contrast between male and female speech is the attachment, by female speakers, of the honorific prefix "o-" to nouns, for example, a woman refers to chopsticks as *ohasi*, while a man calls them *hasi* (see Figure 11.4 on page 270). This addition gives women's speech a more refined and polite tone.

A contrasting pattern of gendered language comes from the *kogals*, young Japanese women between 14 and 22 years of age known for their female-centered coolness (Miller 2004). The kogals have distinctive language, clothing, hairstyles, makeup, attitude, and activities, all of which challenge prescriptive norms for young women. Their overall style is flashy and exuberant, combining global and local elements. Heavy users of cell phones, kogals use a complex and ever-changing set of *emoticons*, or "face characters" including icons for "wow,"

A kogal in Tokyo's trendy Shibuyu district displays her cell phone that is covered with stickers. Her facial makeup and dress are characteristic of some, but not all, kogals. Various kogal makeup and dress styles, like their language, exist and keep changing.

	Male	**Female**
Box lunch	bentoo	obentoo
Money	kane	okane
Chopsticks	hasi	ohasi
Book	hon	ohon

Source: *Language, Gender, and Sex in Comparative Perspective*, by Susan U. Philips, Susan Steele, Chrisitne Tanz. Copyright © Cambridge University Press 1987. Reprinted with permission of Cambridge University Press.

FIGURE 11.4 Male-Unmarked and Female-Marked Nouns in Japanese.

"ouch," "applause," and "I can't hear you." They have also invented a unique text message code for their cell phones that uses mixed scripts such as mathematical symbols and Cyrillic (Russian) letters.

The spoken language of the kogals is a rich and quickly changing mixture of slang, some classic but much newly created. They create new words through compounds and by adding the Japanese suffix "-ru," which turns a noun into a verb, such as *maku-ru* ("go to McDonald's"). They intentionally use strongly masculine language forms, openly talk about sex, and rework taboo sexual terms into new meanings. Reactions from mainstream society to kogals are mixed, ranging from horror to fascination. No matter what, they have cultural influence and are shaking up the gender order and language.

"FAT TALK" AMONG EURO-AMERICAN ADOLESCENT GIRLS

In the United States, Euro-American adolescent girls' conversations exhibit a high level of concern with their body weight and image (Nichter 2000). A study of 253 girls in the eighth and ninth grades in two urban high schools of the Southwest reveals the contexts and meanings of fat talk. Fat talk usually starts with a girl commenting, "I'm so fat." The immediate response from her friends is "No, you're not." Girls who use fat talk are typically not overweight and are not dieting. The weight of the girls in the study was within "normal" range, and none suffered from a serious eating disorder. Fat talk occurs frequently throughout a day. Sometimes it appears to function as a call for reinforcement from friends that the initiator is an accepted group member. In other cases, it occurs at the beginning of a meal. In this context, fat talk may function to absolve the girl from guilty feelings and to give her a sense of agency.

GAY LANGUAGE AND BELONGING IN INDONESIA

The national language of Indonesia is referred to as *bahasa Indonesia*. Many homosexual men in Indonesia speak *bahasa gay*, or "gay language" (Boellstorff 2004). Indonesia is the world's fourth-largest country in terms of population, with nearly 250 million citizens living on over 6,000 islands and speaking nearly 700 local languages. In spite of this cultural and linguistic diversity, bahasa gay is highly standardized.

Bahasa gay has a distinct vocabulary that plays humorously on mainstream language and provides a political commentary on mainstream life. Some of the vocabulary changes involve sound-alikes; others add a suffix to a standard word. In terms of the state's strongly heterosexual image, Indonesian gays would seem to be a clearly excluded group. Nonetheless, bahasa gay is moving into mainstream linguistic culture, where it conveys agency and freedom from official control.

CUING AMONG THE AKWESASNE MOHAWKS

Linguistic cues are words or phrases that preface a remark to indicate the speaker's attitude toward what is being said. Standard English cues include *maybe* and *in my opinion* (Woolfson et al. 1995). Three functions of cuing exist in Mohawk English, a version of English spoken by the Akwesasne people of the St. Lawrence River area (see Map 11.5). They are:

- The speaker's unwillingness or inability to verify the certainty of a statement
- Respect for the listener
- The inability to make statements that have to do with matters that are in the domain of religion

Frequent miscommunication occurs between the Akwesasne people and Anglo medical professionals. Analysis of doctor–patient conversations reveals the role that Akwesasne cuing plays and how it is misinterpreted by the professionals. Here is a response to a question posed by an anthropologist about the kinds of diseases Akwesasne people had in the past, with the cues italicized:

> Hmm . . . That [tuberculosis] . . . was mostly, it well . . . they always said cirrhosis. . . . *It seems* like no matter what anybody died from . . . if they drank, it was cirrhosis. *I don't know* if anybody *really* knew a long time ago what anybody really died from. Even if the doctor requested an autopsy, the people would just say no . . . you know . . . it won't be done. So *I don't think* it was . . . you know . . . it was just what the doctor thought that would go down on the death certificate. (1995:506)

The White medical practitioners misinterpret such clues as indications of indecisiveness or noncooperation. The Akwesasne speakers are following linguistic rules about truthfulness, humility, and the sacred.

AFRICAN AMERICAN ENGLISH: PREJUDICE AND PRIDE

The topic of African American English (AAE), or African American Vernacular English (AAVE), is complicated

MAP 11.5 Akwesasne Territory in New York State and Ontario, Canada.

The Akwesasne Territory has an international border running through it with New York State on one side and two provinces of Canada on the other: Ontario and Québec. The Mohawk Council of Akwesasne comprises 12 District Chiefs and a Grand Chief. Since the 1960s, the Akwesasne Territory has been negatively affected by environmental pollution of the water, soil, and food supply from industries along the St. Lawrence River. In 1987, the Akwesasne formed a Task Force to restore and protect the environment and the survival of their culture.

hierarchy in the United States, with AME at the top, speakers of AAE may be both proud of their language and feel stigmatized by those who judge AAE negatively and treat its speakers unfairly (Lanehart 1999).

African American English is a relatively new language, emerging out of slavery to develop a degree of standardization across the United States, along with many local variants. Some of its characteristic grammar results from its African roots. One of the most prominent is the use, or nonuse, of forms of the English verb "to be" (Lanehart 1999:217). In AAE, one says, "She married," which means "She is married" in AME. Viewed incorrectly by outsiders as "bad" English, "She married" follows a grammatical rule in AAE. That AME has its own grammar and usage rules is evident in the fact that when non-AME speakers attempt to speak it or imitate it, they often make mistakes (Jacobs-Huey 1997).

Ethnographic research on African American school-age children in a working-class neighborhood of southwest Philadelphia examined within-gender and cross-gender conversations, including *directives* (getting someone to do something), argument, he-said-she-said accusations, and storytelling (Goodwin 1990). All of these speech activities involve complex verbal strategies that are culturally embedded. In arguments, the children may bring in imaginary events as a "put-on," preceded by the cue term "psych," or use words of a song to create and maintain playfulness within an argument. Much of their arguments involve highly ritualized insults that work quickly to return an insult to the original giver. When a group of girls was practicing some dance steps and singing, a boy said, "You sound terrible." A girl responded, "We sound just like you look" (1990:183). The study revealed the importance of verbal play and art among the children. It also showed that girls often excel at verbal competitions in mixed gender settings.

Children who grow up speaking a version of AAE at home and with peer groups face a challenge in schools, where they are expected to perform in AME. Just like native Spanish speakers or any non–English-speaking new immigrants, African American children are implicitly expected to become bilingual in AAE and AME. More than vocabulary and grammar are involved. Teachers should understand that African American children may have culturally distinct styles of expression that should be recognized and valued. For example, in narrative style, African American children tend to use a spiral pattern, skipping around to different topics before addressing the theme, instead of adopting a linear style. Rather than being considered a deficiency, having AAE speakers in a classroom adds cultural diversity to those whose linguistic worlds are limited to AME.

Inspired by such findings, the Oakland School Board in California approved a resolution in 1996 to recognize *Ebonics*,

by racism of the past and present (Jacobs-Huey 2006). Scholars debate whether AAE/AAVE is a language in its own right or a dialect (nonstandard version) of English. "Linguistic conservatives," who champion standard American Mainstream English (AME), view AAE as an ungrammatical form of English that needs to be "corrected." In the current linguistic

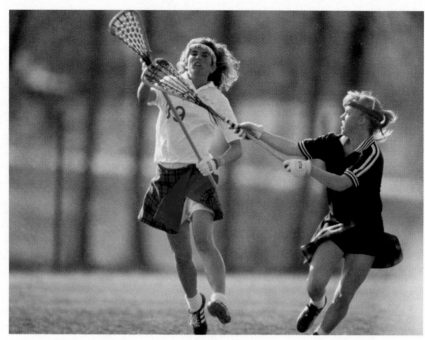

(LEFT) An African bonobo male waves branches in a display of power. (RIGHT) In the United States, women lacrosse players use sticks in a competitive sport invented by American Indians.

▶ *Threat is clearly conveyed by the bonobo's behavior. In lacrosse, can sticks also communicate threats?*

or AAE, as the primary language, or vernacular, of African American students. The school developed a special teaching program, called the Bridge Program, in which AAE speakers were encouraged to learn Standard American English through a process of translation between AAE and SAE (Rickford 1997). After several months, students in the Bridge Program had progressed in their SAE reading ability much faster than African American students who were not in the program. Nevertheless, the program received so much negative publicity and raised such sensitive questions about the best way to enhance minority student learning that it was cancelled within the year.

The underlying issues of the so-called *Ebonics controversy* are still unresolved. One of the thorniest questions debated is whether AAE/AAVE/Ebonics is sufficiently distinct (either as a language separate from SAE or as a dialect) that U.S. schools should address it in their curriculum with special programs.

◉ ◉ ◉

Language Change

Languages, like the cultures of which they are a part, experience both continuity and change, and for similar reasons. Human creativity and contact lead to linguistic innovation and linguistic borrowing. War, imperialism, genocide, and other disasters may destroy languages. This section looks first at what is known about the origins of human language and provides a brief history of writing. Later parts discuss the influence of European colonialism on languages, nationalism and language, world languages, and contemporary language loss and revitalization.

The Origins and History of Language

No one knows how verbal language began. Current evidence of other aspects of human cultural evolution suggests that verbal language began to develop between 100,000 and 50,000 years ago when early modern humans achieved both the physical and mental capacity for symbolic thinking and verbal communication. Facial expressions, gestures, and body postures were likely important features of early human communication, as they are among many nonhuman primate species today.

Early scholars of language were often misled by ethnocentric assumptions that the structure of European languages was normative and that languages with different structures were less developed and deficient. For example, they considered

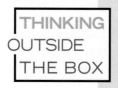

THINKING OUTSIDE THE BOX

Should AAE be suppressed in U.S. public schools in favor of promoting SAE? What are the pros and cons of a mono-language approach in education?

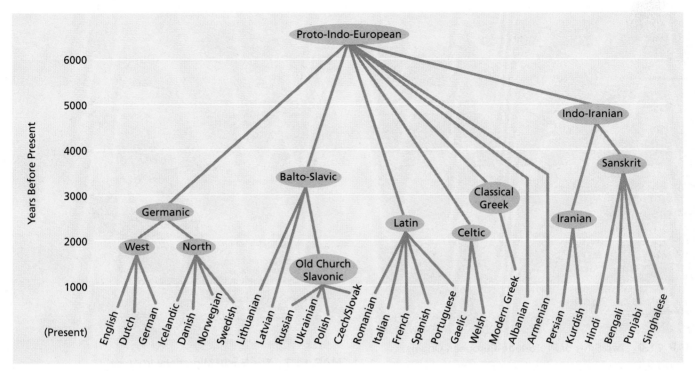

FIGURE 11.5 The Indo-European Language Family.

the Chinese language primitive because it lacks the kinds of verbs that European languages have. As discussed at the beginning of this chapter, the Pirahã language appears simpler in many ways compared with English, as does the Pirahã culture, but both Pirahã and English have to be examined within their cultural contexts. Pirahã is a language that works for a rainforest foraging population. English works for a globalizing, technology-driven, consumerist culture. Languages of foraging cultures today can, with caution, provide insights about what foragers' language may have been like thousands of years ago. But they are not "frozen in time" examples of "Stone Age" language.

Historical Linguistics

Historical linguistics is the study of language change through history. It relies on many specialized methods that compare shifts over time and across space in aspects of language such as phonetics, syntax, and meaning. It originated in the eighteenth century with a discovery made by Sir William Jones, a British colonial administrator working in India. During his spare time, he studied Sanskrit, a classical language of India. He noticed marked similarities among Sanskrit, Greek, and Latin in vocabulary and syntax. For example, the Sanskrit word for "father" is *pitr*; in Greek it is *patéras*, and in Latin it is *pater*. This was an astounding discovery for the time, given the prevailing European mentality that placed its cultural heritage firmly in the classical Graeco–Roman world and depicted the "Orient" as completely separate from "Europe" (Bernal 1987).

Following Jones's discovery, other scholars began comparing lists of words and grammatical forms in different languages: for example, the French *père*, the German *Vater*, the Italian *padre*, the Old English *faeder*, the Old Norse *fadhir*, and the Swedish *far*. These lists allowed scholars to determine degrees of closeness and distance in the relationships among those languages. Later scholars contributed the concept of a **language family**, or groups of languages descended from a parent language (Figure 11.5). Individual languages descended from the same language, such as French and Spanish (both descended from Latin), are referred to as *sister languages*.

Using comparative evidence from historical and contemporary Eurasian languages, historical linguists developed a hypothetical model of the original parent language, or *proto-language*, of most Eurasian languages. It is called *Proto-Indo-European (PIE)*. Linguistic evidence suggests that PIE was located in Eurasia, either north or south of the Black Sea (Map 11.6 on page 274). From its area of origin, between 6000 and 8000 years ago, PIE spread into Europe, then into Central, South, and East Asia, where local versions developed over the centuries.

---

historical linguistics   the study of language change using formal methods that compare shifts over time and across space in aspects of language, such as phonetics, syntax, and semantics.

language family   a group of languages descended from a parent language.

MAP 11.6 Two Sites of Proto-Indo-European Origins.

Two major theories about the location of PIE exist, with the site south of the Black Sea considered to be earlier.

MAP 11.7 The Bantu Migrations in Africa.

Linguistic evidence for the migrations of Bantu-speaking people relies on similarities between languages in parts of eastern, central, and southern Africa and languages of the original Bantu homeland in West Africa. Over 600 African languages are derived from Proto-Bantu.

Similar linguistic methods reveal the existence of the original parent form of the Bantu language family, *Proto-Bantu* (Afolayan 2000). Scholars can trace the *Bantu expansion* in Africa starting around 5000 years ago (Map 11.7). Today, some form of Bantu language is spoken by over 100 million people in Africa, not to mention the number of people in the African diaspora worldwide. Over 600 African languages are derived from Proto-Bantu. According to linguistic analysis, the homeland of Proto-Bantu is the present-day countries of Cameroon and Nigeria, West Africa. It is likely that Proto-Bantu spread through population migration as the farming population expanded and moved, over hundreds of years, into areas occupied by indigenous foragers. Bantu cultural imperialism may have wiped out some local languages, although it is impossible to document any such extinctions. Substantial linguistic evidence, however, suggests some interactions between the farmers and the foragers through which standard Bantu absorbed elements from local languages.

---

logograph   a symbol that conveys meaning through a form or picture resembling that to which it refers.

khipu   cords of knotted strings used during the Inca empire for keeping accounts and recording events.

pidgin   a contact language that blends elements of at least two languages and that emerges when people with different languages need to communicate.

Writing Systems

Evidence of the earliest written languages comes from Mesopotamia, Egypt, and China. The oldest writing system was in use in the fourth millennium BCE in Mesopotamia (Postgate et al. 1995). All early writing systems used **logographs**, signs that indicate a word, syllable, or sound. Over time, some logographs retained their original meaning; others were kept but given more abstract meaning, and non-logographic symbols were added (Figure 11.6).

The emergence of writing is associated with the development of the state. Some scholars take writing as a key diagnostic feature that distinguishes the state from nonstate political forms because recordkeeping was such an essential task of the state. The Inca empire, centered in the Peruvian Andes, is a notable exception to this generalization. It used **khipu** (kee-poo), or cords of knotted strings of different colors, for keeping accounts and recording events. Scholars are not quite sure how khipu worked in the past because the Inca coding system is so complicated. Debates are ongoing as to whether khipu served as an actual language or more simply as an accounting system. Whatever is the answer, the world's largest empire in the fourteenth century relied on khipu.

Two interpretations of the function of early writing systems exist. The first says that early writing was mainly for

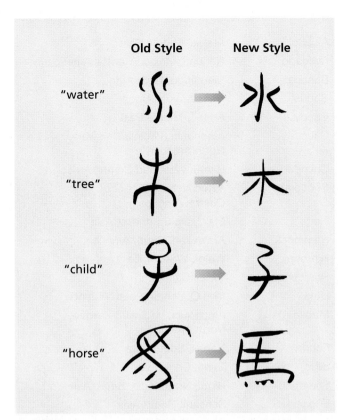

	Old Style	New Style
"water"		
"tree"		
"child"		
"horse"		

FIGURE 11.6 Logographic and Current Writing Styles in China.

ceremonial purposes. Evidence for this position consists of the prevalence of early writing on tombs, bone inscriptions, and temple carvings. The second says that early writing was mainly for secular use in government recordkeeping and trade. The archaeological record is biased toward durable substances, such as stone. Because ceremonial writing was intended to last, it was more likely to be inscribed on stone. Utilitarian writing, in contrast, was more likely to have been

Khipu, or knotted strings, were the basis of state-level accounting in the Incan empire. The knots conveyed substantial information to those who could interpret their meaning.

done on perishable materials because people would be less concerned with permanence. (Consider the way you treat shopping lists.) It is likely, however, that more utilitarian writing, as well as other forms of nonceremonial writing, also existed.

Colonialism, Nationalism, and Globalization

European colonialism was a major force of language change. Not only did colonial powers declare their own language as the language of government, business, and education, but they often took direct steps to suppress indigenous languages and literatures. Widespread *bilingualism*, or competence in a language other than one's birth language, is one prominent effect of colonialism. Also, globalization is having substantial and complex effects on language.

EUROPEAN COLONIALISM AND CONTACT LANGUAGES Beginning in the fifteenth century, European colonialism had dramatic effects on the people with whom it came into contact, as discussed elsewhere in this book. Language change is an important part of the story of colonialism and indigenous cultures. Depending on the type and duration of contact, it resulted in the development of new languages, the decline of others, and the extinction of many, along with the people who spoke them (Silverstein 1997). Two forms of new languages prompted by European colonialism are pidgins and creoles.

A **pidgin** is a language that blends elements of at least two parent languages and that emerges when two different

French colonialism added another cultural layer to Arabic influences in Morocco, resulting in many bilingual and trilingual shop signs.

▶ *Where have you seen multilingualism in public use? What languages were used and why?*

cultures with different languages come in contact and must communicate (Baptista 2005). All speakers of pidgin have their own native language(s) but learn to speak pidgin as a second, rudimentary language. Pidgins are typically limited to specific functional domains, such as trade and basic social interactions. Many pidgins of the Western Hemisphere were the result of the Atlantic slave trade and plantation slavery. Owners needed to communicate with their slaves, and slaves from various parts of Africa needed to communicate with each other. Pidgins are common throughout the South Pacific.

A pidgin often evolves into a **creole**, which is a language descended from a pidgin and which subsequently has its own native speakers, a richer vocabulary than a pidgin has, and a more developed grammar. Throughout the Western Hemisphere, many localized creoles have developed in areas such as Louisiana, the Caribbean, Ecuador, and Suriname. Though a living reminder of the heritage of slavery, Creole languages and associated literature and music are also evidence of resilience and creativity in the African diaspora.

Tok Pisin (the indigenous pronunciation of "talk pidgin"), originally a pidgin language of Papua New Guinea consisting of a mixture of English, Samoan, Chinese, and Malaysian, is now a creole and is recognized as one of the official languages of Papua New Guinea. Two other creoles are also nationally recognized: Seselwa, a blend including French spoken in the Seychelle Islands in the Indian Ocean and Papiamentu, a blend including Dutch spoken in Curaçao (coo-ruh-sao), the Netherland Antilles, in the Caribbean.

NATIONALISM AND LINGUISTIC ASSIMILATION

Nationalist policies of cultural assimilation of minorities have led to the suppression and loss of local dialects and the extinction of many indigenous and minority languages throughout the world. Direct policies of linguistic assimilation include the declaration of a standard language and rules about the language of instruction in public schools. Often, Christian missionaries worked to suppress indigenous languages as part of their attempts to "civilize" "pagan" peoples (see Culturama). Indirect mechanisms include discrimination in hiring on the basis of language and social stigma.

GLOBAL LANGUAGES Ninety-six percent of the world's population speaks 4 percent of the world's languages (Crystal 2000). The eight most-spoken languages are Mandarin, Spanish, English, Bengali, Hindi, Portuguese, Russian, and

Alcohol	Arabic, Middle East
Avocado	Nahuatl, Mexico/Central America
Banana	Mandingo, West Africa
Bogus	Hausa, West Africa
Candy	Arabic, Middle East
Caucus	Algonquin, Virginia/Delaware, North America
Chimpanzee	Bantu, West and Central Africa
Chocolate	Aztec Nahuatl, Mexico/ Central America
Gong	Malaysia, Southeast Asia
Hammock	Arawakan, South America
Hip/hep	Wolof, West Africa
Hurricane	Taino, Caribbean
Lime	Inca Quechua, South America
Moose	Algonquin, Virginia/Delaware, North America
Panda	Nepali, South Asia
Savannah	Taino, Caribbean
Shampoo	Hindi, North India, South Asia
Sugar	Sanskrit, South Asia
Tepee	Sioux, Dakotas, North America
Thug	Hindi, North India, South Asia
Tobacco	Arawak, South America
Tomato	Nahuatl, Mexico/Central America
Tundra	Saami, Lapland, Northern Europe
Typhoon	Mandarin Chinese, East Asia
Zombie	Congo and Angola, Central and West Africa

FIGURE 11.7 Loan Words in North American English.

Japanese, in that order. Languages that are gaining widespread currency are called **global languages**, or *world languages*. Global languages are spoken worldwide in diverse cultural contexts. As they spread to areas and cultures beyond their home area and culture, they take on new, localized identities. At the same time, the "mother language" picks up words and phrases from local languages (Figure 11.7). Global languages may act as both a form of linguistic and economic opportunity and a form of cultural imperialism.

English is the most globalized language in history (Bhatt 2001, Crystal 2003). British English was first transplanted through colonial expansion to the present-day United States, Canada, Australia, New Zealand, South Asia, Africa, Hong Kong, and the Caribbean. English was the dominant language in the colonies, used in government and commerce and taught in schools. Over time, regional and subregional

---

creole a language directly descended from a pidgin but possessing its own native speakers and involving linguistic expansion and elaboration.

global language a language spoken widely throughout the world and in diverse cultural contexts, often replacing indigenous languages.

CULTURAMA

The Saami of Sápmi, or Lapland

The Saami (SAH-mee) are indigenous people who live in the northernmost parts of Norway, Sweden, Finland, and western Russia (Gaski 1993). The area is called Sápmi, the land of the Saami, or Lapland. The total Saami population is around 100,000 people, with the majority in Norway (Magga and Skutnabb-Kangas 2001).

At the time of the earliest written records of 1000 years ago, all Saami hunted wild reindeer, among other land and sea species, and may have kept some tamed reindeer for transport (Paine 2004). Over time, herding domesticated reindeer developed and became the economic mainstay. In the past few hundred years, though, reindeer pastoralism has declined and is now a specialization of about 10 percent of the population. Settled Saami are farmers or work in trade, small-scale industry, handicrafts, services, and the professions.

Traditional Saami reindeer herding has been a family-based system. Men and women cared for the herd, and sons and daughters inherited the rights to the herd equally (Paine 2004). The value of social equality was strong, entailing both rights and privileges.

In their relationships with the modern state, the Saami have experienced discrimination, exclusion, loss of territorial rights, and cultural and linguistic repression. Environmental risks to Saami cultural survival include having been downwind of the prevailing winds after the 1986 Chernobyl disaster, having been near the earlier Soviet atomic testing grounds in Siberia, having had their ancestral territory and sacred spaces lost or damaged by hydroelectric dam construction, and having had grazing lands taken over for use as military training grounds (Anderson 2004).

State policies of cultural assimilation and forced Christianization in the twentieth century marginalized the Saami language and led to language loss (Magga and Skutnabb-Kangas 2001). Several Saami languages and dialects still exist, however, and spatially distant versions are mutually unintelligible (Gaski 1993:116).

Language is of central cultural value to the Saami, and efforts to maintain it have been under way since the 1960s. Besides the Saami language, a traditional song form, the *yoik*, is of particular importance (Anderson 2005). Yoik lyrics allow a subtle system of double meanings that can camouflage political content (Gaski 1997).

Thanks to Myrdene Anderson, Purdue University, for reviewing this material.

(LEFT) The well-known Saami singer–songwriter Marie Boine performs at the Easter Festival in Kautokeino, Sápmi, northern Norway.

(CENTER) A Saami herder with his reindeer in Kautokeino, the northernmost municipality in Norway and the first municipality to be given a Saami name.

MAP 11.8 The Saami of Sápmi, or Lapland. Sápmi extends across Norway, Sweden, Finland, and Russia's Kola Peninsula.

CRITICAL thinking

Should Dying Languages Be Revived?

The Western media often carry articles about endangered biological species, such as certain frogs or birds, and the need to protect them from extinction. The reasons for concern about the loss of biological species are many. One major factor is simply that biological diversity is a good thing to have on the earth. Opponents of taking special measures to protect endangered species find support for their position in a Darwinian view that progress involves competition and the survival of those species which can make it. Economic progress might mean building a new shopping center or airport with a massive parking lot. If that means the extinction of a particular species of nonhuman primate, bird, flower, or worm, so be it, in the name of "progress."

Some parallels exist between the survival of endangered languages and that of endangered biological species (Maffi 2005). Supporters of language preservation and revitalization can point to the sheer fact of diversity on earth as a good thing, a sign of a culturally healthy planet with room for everyone's language. They will argue that a people's language is an intrinsic part of their culture. Without language, the culture, too, will die.

Others take the Darwinian view that languages, like species, live in a world of competition. Language survival means that the strong and fit carry on while the weak and unfit die out. They may point out that preserving linguistic heritage is useless because dying languages are part of a past that no longer exists. They resist spending public funds on language preservation and regard revitalization programs as wasteful.

CRITICAL THINKING QUESTIONS ▼

- Have you read or heard of an endangered biological species in the media recently? What was the species?
- Have you read or heard of an endangered language in the media lately? What was the language?
- Where do you stand on biological species preservation and on language preservation, and why?

---

varieties of English developed, often leading to a "New English" that a native speaker from England cannot understand at all. So many varieties of English now exist that scholars are beginning to talk of the *English language family*, which includes American English, "Spanglish," "Japlish," and "Tex-Mex."

Textese is a new and emerging variant of English and other languages associated with cell phone communications and involving abbreviations and slang. The limited number of characters allowed, so far, in cell phone text message has prompted widespread creativity in shortening words and sentences. In English Textese, vowels are often deleted, numbers may stand in for part of a word or an entire word, and a single letter may convey a word. Many stock phrases exist as acronyms, such as LOL, that are widely recognized by users.

Endangered Languages and Language Revitalization

The emergence of linguistic anthropology, as mentioned in Chapter 1, was prompted by the need to document disappearing indigenous languages in the United States. Today, anthropologists and other scholars, as well as descendant language communities themselves, are still concerned about the rapid loss of languages (Fishman 1991, Maffi 2005). The task of documenting declining languages is urgent.

Textese   an emerging variant of written English and other languages associated with cell phone communication and involving abbreviations and creative slang.

It is often accompanied by applied work aimed at preserving and reviving endangered and dying languages (see Critical Thinking).

Scholars have proposed four phases or degrees of language decline and loss (Walsh 2005):

- *Language shift*, or *language decay*, is a category of language decline when speakers have a limited vocabulary in their native language and more often use a new language in which they may be semifluent or fluent (Hill 2001).

- *Language endangerment* exists when a language has fewer than 10,000 speakers.

- *Near-extinction* is a situation in which only a few elderly speakers are still living.

- *Language extinction* occurs when the language has no competent speakers.

Keeping track of endangered and dying languages is difficult because no one is sure how many languages have existed in the recent past or even how many exist now (Crystal 2000). Estimates of the number of living languages today range between 5000 and 7000. Part of the explanation for the fuzzy numbers is the problem in separating languages from dialects. The largest number of languages of any world region is found on the island of New Guinea, which comprises the country of Papua New Guinea and the Indonesian territory of West Papua, and several neighboring small islands (Foley 2000). Over 1000 languages exist in this area, many from completely separate language families.

Indigenous language dictionaries and usage guides are increasingly available on the Web and help indigenous peoples, such as these Australian boys, preserve their cultures.

▶ *Check out The Internet Guide to Australian Languages.*

Language extinction is especially acute in the Australia–Pacific region, where 99.5 percent of the indigenous languages have fewer than 100,000 speakers (Nettle and Romaine 2000:40). The situation of indigenous languages in the Americas, Siberia, Africa, and South and Southeast Asia is becoming increasingly serious. Over half of the world's languages have fewer than 10,000 speakers, and one-fourth have fewer than 1000 speakers.

Efforts to revive or maintain local languages face many challenges (Fishman 2001). Political opposition may come from governments that fear local identity movements. Governments are often averse to devoting financial resources to supporting minority language programs. Deciding which version of an endangered language to preserve may have political consequences at the local level (Nevins 2004). Notable achievements have been made, however, with perhaps one of the most robust examples of language maintenance occurring in French-speaking Québec.

Approaches to language maintenance and revitalization must respond to local circumstances and to factors such as how serious the degree of loss is, how many living speakers there are, what version of the language should be maintained or revived, and what resources for maintenance and revitalization programs are available. Major strategies include the following (Walsh 2005):

- Formal classroom instruction
- A master–apprentice system in which an elder teaches a nonspeaker in a one-on-one situation
- Web-based tools and services to support language learning

Each method has both promise and pitfalls. One thing is key: It takes living communities to activate and keep alive the knowledge of a language (Maffi 2003).

How do humans communicate?

Human communication is the sending of meaningful messages through language. Language is a systematic set of symbols and signs with learned and shared meanings. It may be spoken, hand-signed, written, or conveyed through body movements, marking, or accessories.

Human language has two characteristics that distinguish it from communicative systems of other living beings: productivity, or the ability to create an infinite number of novel and understandable messages; and displacement, the ability to communicate about the past, the future, and imaginary things.

Language consists of basic sounds, vocabulary, and syntax. Cross-culturally, languages vary substantially in the details of all three features.

Humans use many forms of nonverbal language to communicate with each other. Sign language is a form of communication that uses mainly hand movements to communicate. Silence is a form of nonverbal communication with its own cultural values and meaning. Body language includes body movements and body placement in relation to other people, body modifications such as tattoos and piercing, dress, hairstyles, and odors.

Media anthropology sheds light on how culture shapes media messages and on the social dynamics that play out in media institutions. Critical media anthropology examines the power relations involved in the media.

How does communication relate to cultural diversity and inequality?

The Sapir–Whorf hypothesis emphasizes how language shapes culture. A competing model, called sociolinguistics, emphasizes how one's culture and one's position in it shape language. Each position has merit, and many anthropologists draw on both models.

Critical discourse analysis studies how communication through language can serve the interests of the powerful, maintaining or even increasing social inequality. Although language can reinforce and expand social exclusion, it can also empower oppressed people, depending on the context. In mainstream North America, women's speech is generally more polite and accommodating than that of men. In Japan, gender codes emphasize politeness in women's speech, but some young Japanese women, the kogals, are creating a new linguistic style of resistance. Gay language in Indonesia is entering the mainstream as an expression of freedom from official control. Linguistic cuing among the Akwesasne Mohawks has been frequently misinterpreted by Anglo medical practitioners as a sign of indecisiveness or noncooperation. African American English (AAE), in the view of many experts, has evolved into a standard language with local variants.

How does language change?

The exact origins of human verbal language are not known. Historical linguistics and its discovery of language families provide insights about early human history and settlement patterns. The emergence of writing can be traced to around 6000 years ago, with the emergence of the state in Mesopotamia. The functions of writing vary from context to context. In some situations official recordkeeping predominates, whereas in others writing is important for courtship.

The recent history of language change has been influenced by the colonialism of past centuries and by Western globalization in the current era. Nationalist policies of cultural integration often involve the repression of minority languages and the promotion of a standard language. Colonial contact created the context for the emergence of pidgin languages, many of which evolved into creoles. Western globalization supports the spread of English and the development of localized variants.

In the past 500 years, colonialism and globalization have resulted in the extinction of many indigenous and minority languages. Many others are in danger of dying. Applied linguistic anthropologists seek to preserve the world's linguistic diversity. They document languages and participate in designing programs for teaching dead and dying languages. A key element in language revitalization and survival is having communities use the language.

KEY CONCEPTS

call system, p. 260

communication, p. 260

creole, p. 276

critical discourse
  analysis, p. 268

critical media anthropology,
  p. 266

digital divide, p. 266

discourse, p. 268

displacement, p. 260

ethnosemantics, p. 262

global language, p. 276

historical linguistics, p. 273

khipu, p. 274

language, p. 260

language family, p. 273

logograph, p. 274

phoneme, p. 260

pidgin, p. 274

productivity, p. 260

Sapir–Whorf
  hypothesis, p. 268

sign language, p. 262

sociolinguistics, p. 268

tag question, p. 268

Textese, p. 278

SUGGESTED READINGS

Keith H. Basso, *Wisdom Sits in Places: Landscape and Language among the Western Apache*. Albuquerque: University of New Mexico Press, 1996. Fieldwork on the Fort Apache Indian Reservation, Arizona, reveals the importance of natural places in people's everyday life, thought, and language.

Besnier, Niko. *Gossip and the Everyday Production of Politics*. Honolulu: University of Hawai'i Press, 2009. Besnier examines the political life of gossip on one of the Pacific atolls of Tuvalu.

Thomas F. Carter, *The Quality of Home Runs: The Passion, Politics, and Language of Cuban Baseball*. Durham, NC: Duke University Press, 2009. This ethnography shows how men's talk about baseball in Cuba communicates masculinity, class, and national identity.

David Crystal, *English as a Global Language*, 2nd ed. New York: Cambridge University Press, 2003. This book discusses the history, current status, and future of English as a world language. It covers the role of English in international relations, the media, international travel, education, and "New Englishes."

Joshua A. Fishman, ed. *Can Threatened Languages Be Saved?* Buffalo: Multilingual Matters Ltd., 2001. Seventeen case studies examine language shift, language loss, and the attempts to reverse such changes.

Niloofar Haeri, *Sacred Language, Ordinary People: Dilemmas of Culture and Politics in Egypt*. New York: Palgrave Macmillan, 2003. Classical Arabic is the official language of all Arab states and the language of the Qur'an, but no Arabs speak it as their mother tongue. This book uses research in Cairo to show how the state maintains its identity in people's everyday lives.

Lanita Jacobs-Huey. *From the Kitchen to the Parlor: Language and Becoming in African-American Women's Hair Care*. New York: Oxford University Press, 2006. Jacobs-Huey combines childhood experiences as the daughter of a cosmetologist with multisited fieldwork in the United States and England.

William L. Leap. *Word's Out: Gay Men's English*. Minneapolis: University of Minnesota Press, 1996. Fieldwork among gay men in the Washington, DC, area produced this ethnography. It addresses gay men's speech as a cooperative mode of discourse, examines bathroom graffiti, and looks at discourse about HIV/AIDS.

Julie Lindquist. *A Place to Stand: Politics and Persuasion in a Working-Class Bar*. New York: Oxford University Press, 2002. The author did participant observation while working as a bartender in a White, working-class bar in the U.S. Midwest. The book is an ethnography of speaking in which the bar is a site of cultural performance related to White, working-class identity.

Karen Nakamura. *Deaf in Japan: Signing and the Politics of Identity*. Ithaca, NY: Cornell University Press, 2007. This book combines archival and ethnographic data to help understand ideas about modernity and Westernization.

Lisa Philips Valentine. *Making It Their Own: Ojibwe Communicative Practices*. Toronto: University of Toronto Press, 1995. This ethnography examines speech events in a small Ojibwe community in northern Ontario, Canada. It considers speech variations among speakers and examines code switching, multilingualism, and church music.

PEARSON
myanthrolab

For further information about topics covered in this chapter, go to MyAnthroLab at www.myanthrolab.com and access the following readings in MyAnthroLibrary:

Hillary Haldane. 2010. What Lula Lacks: Grappling with the Discourse of Autism at Home and in the Field. *Anthropology Today* 26:24-26. A anthropologist who is the parent of an autistic child describes how the label "autistic" negatively framed her life as a parent and how the absence of the label in Morocco helped reframe it for the better.

Magnus Marsden. 2009. Talking the Talk: Debating Debate in Afghanistan. *Anthropology Today* 25:20-24. The author describes practices of debate in Chitral, northern Afghanistan. He suggests that outsiders need to pay attention to how Muslims in various contexts debate issues and engage in critical reflection.

Luahìwa Nämähoe and Kaimana Barcarse. 2007. Aha Pünana Leo. *Cultural Survival Quarterly* 31(2):44, ff. The Hawai'ian language program, 'Aha Pünana Leo began in 1983 to recognize the importance of the Hawai'ian language in the lives of indigenous Hawai'ians. Now, several universities offer degrees in Hawai'ian language and culture.

RELIGION

12

◀ An Aboriginal boy in Australia's Northern Territories is painted with his sacred totem and carried to his initiation ceremony. This scene was recorded for the movie *Yolngu Boy.*

While studying the religious life of people of rural Greece, anthropologist Loring Danforth observed rituals in which participants walk across several yards of burning coals (1989). They do not get burned, they say, because their faith in a saint protects them. Back in the United States, Danforth met an American who regularly walks on fire as part of his New Age faith and who organizes training workshops for people who want to learn how to do it. Danforth himself walked on fire in a ceremony in rural Maine.

Not all anthropologists who study religion undertake such challenges, but they all share an interest in questions about humanity's understanding of the supernatural realm and relationships with it: Why do some religions have many gods and others just one? Why do some religions practice sacrifice? Why do some religions have more participation by women? How do religions respond to changing conditions in the political economy?

Religion has been a cornerstone topic in cultural anthropology since the beginnings of the discipline. The early focus, in the nineteenth century, was on religions of indigenous peoples living in places far from Europe. Now anthropologists also study the religions of state-level societies and the effects of globalization on religious change.

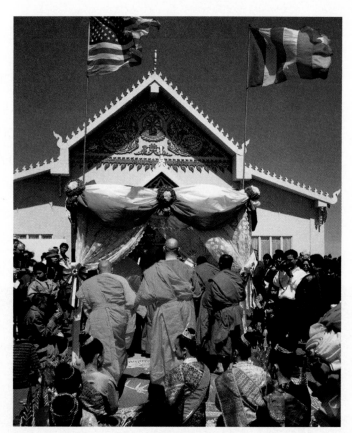

Religion provides an important source of social cohesion and psychological support for many immigrant groups, whose places of worship attract both worshippers and cultural anthropologists interested in learning how religion fits into migrants' adaptation. This is a scene at a Lao Buddhist temple in Virginia.

◎ ◎ ◎

Religion in Comparative Perspective

This section sets the stage for the chapter by discussing basic topics in the anthropology of religion, including how to define religion, theories about the origin of religion, and types of religious beliefs, rituals, and religious specialists.

What is Religion?

Since the earliest days of anthropology, scholars have proposed various definitions of religion. In the late 1800s, British anthropologist Sir Edward Tylor defined religion as the belief in spirits. A more comprehensive, current definition says that **religion** consists of beliefs and behavior related to supernatural beings and forces. This definition specifically avoids linking religion with belief in a supreme deity, because some religions have no concept of a supreme deity, whereas others have multiple deities.

Religion is related to, but not the same as, a people's *worldview*, or way of understanding how the world came to

Christian firewalkers in northern Greece walking on hot coals. They reaffirm God's protection by not getting burned.

▶ *If you have a religious faith, are pain or other physical discomforts involved in any of the rituals?*

---

religion   beliefs and behavior related to supernatural beings and forces.

magic   the attempt to compel supernatural forces and beings to act in certain ways.

myth   a narrative with a plot that involves the supernaturals.

doctrine   direct and formalized statements about religious beliefs.

be, its design, and their place in it. Worldview is a broader concept and does not include the criterion of concern with a supernatural realm. An atheist has a worldview, but does not have a religion.

MAGIC VERSUS RELIGION   Sir Edward Tylor wrote that magic, religion, and science are alike in that they are different ways in which people have tried to explain the physical world and events in it (1871). He considered science to be the superior, most rational of the three. Sir James Frazer, writing not long after Tylor, defined **magic** as people's attempt to compel supernatural forces and beings to act in certain ways (1978 [1890]). He contrasted magic with religion, which he said is the attempt to please supernatural forces or beings. Frazer differentiated two general principles of magic:

- *The law of similarity*, the basis of *imitative magic*, is founded on the assumption that if person or item X is like person or item Y, then actions done to person or item X will affect person or item Y. A familiar example is a voodoo doll. If someone sticks pins into a doll X that represents person Y, then person Y will experience pain or suffering.

- *The law of contagion*, the basis of *contagious magic*, says that persons or things once in contact with a person can still have an effect on that person. Common items for working contagious magic include a person's hair trimmings, nail clippings, teeth, saliva, blood, and fecal matter, as well as the placenta of a baby. In cultures where contagious magic is practiced, people are careful about disposing of their personal wastes so that no one else can get hold of them.

Tylor, Frazer, and other early anthropologists supported an evolutionary model (review Chapter 1), with magic preceding religion. They evaluated magic as being less spiritual and ethical than religion and therefore more "primitive." They assumed that, in time, magic would be completely replaced by the "higher" system of religion, which would eventually be replaced by science as the most rational way of thinking. They would be surprised to see the widespread presence of magical religions in the modern world, such as the so-called Wicca, or Neo-Pagan, religion that centers on respect for the Earth, nature, and the seasonal cycle. The pentacle is an important Wicca symbol (Figure 12.1). As of 2007, the U.S. Department of Veterans Affairs added the pentacle to its list of approved religious symbols that can be placed on the headstones of the graves of deceased veterans and their family members.

Many people turn to magical behavior in situations of uncertainty. Magic, for example, is prominent in sports (Gmelch 1997 [1971]). Some baseball players in the United States repeat actions or use charms, including a special shirt or hat, to help them win. This practice is based on the assumption that if

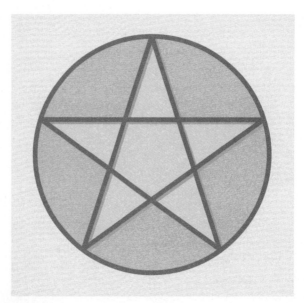

FIGURE 12.1   A Pentacle. Sometimes called a pentagram, it is a five-pointed star surrounded by a circle. An important symbol in Neo-Pagan and Wiccan religions, the pentacle is also a magical tool used for summoning energies and commanding spirits.

it worked before, it may work again. In baseball, pitching and hitting involve more uncertainty than fielding, and pitchers and hitters are more likely to use magic. Magical practices are also common in farming, fishing, the military, and love.

Varieties of Religious Beliefs

Religions comprise beliefs and behavior. Scholars of religion generally address belief systems first because they appear to inform patterns of religious behavior. Religious beliefs are shared by a group, sometimes by millions of people, and are passed on through the generations. Elders teach children through songs and narratives, artists paint the stories on rocks and walls, and sculptors create images in wood and stone that depict aspects of religious belief.

HOW BELIEFS ARE EXPRESSED   Beliefs are expressed and transferred over the generations in two main forms:

- **Myth**, stories about supernatural forces or beings
- **Doctrine**, direct statements about religious beliefs

A myth is a narrative that has a plot with a beginning, middle, and end. The plot may involve recurrent motifs, the

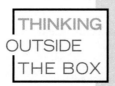

THINKING OUTSIDE THE BOX

Take careful note of your daily activities and events for a week and assess them in terms of how magic, religion, or science are involved. What did you find?

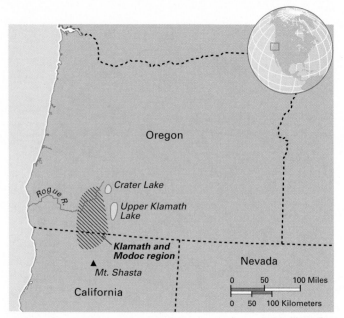

MAP 12.1 Klamath and Modoc Region in Oregon and California.

smallest units of narrative. Myths convey messages about supernatural forces or beings (or, simply, supernaturals) indirectly, through the story itself, rather than by using logic or formal argument. Greek and Roman myths, such as the stories of Zeus, Athena, Orpheus, and Persephone, are world famous. Some people would say that the Bible is a collection of myths; others would object to that categorization as suggesting that the stories are not "real" or "sacred." Myths have long been part of people's oral tradition, and many are still unwritten.

Anthropologists ask why myths exist. Bronislaw Malinowski said that a myth is a *charter* for society in that it expresses core beliefs and teaches morality (1948). The French anthropologist Claude Lévi-Strauss, arguably the most famous mythologist, saw myths as functional in a philosophical and psychological way (1967). In his view, myths help people deal with the deep conceptual contradictions between, for example, life and death or good and evil, by providing stories in which these dualities find a solution in a mediating third factor. These mythological solutions are buried within a variety of surface details in the myth. For example, many myths of the Pueblo Indians of the U.S. Southwest juxtapose grass-eating animals (vegetarians) with predators (carnivores). The mediating third character is the raven, who is a carnivore but unlike other meat eaters does not have to kill to eat meat because it is a scavenger.

A cultural materialist perspective, also functionalist, says that myths store and transmit information related to making a living and managing economic crises (Sobel and Bettles 2000). Analysis of 28 myths of the Klamath and Modoc Indians (Map 12.1) reveals that a consistent theme is

uncertainty about the availability of food. Other prominent themes are how to cope with hunger, food storage, resource diversification, resource conservation, spatial mobility, reciprocity, and supernatural forces. Thus, myths are repositories of knowledge related to economic survival and environmental conservation.

Doctrine, the other major form in which beliefs are expressed, explicitly defines the supernaturals, the world and how it came to be, and people's roles in relation to the supernaturals and to other humans. Doctrine is written and formal. It is close to law because it links incorrect beliefs and behaviors with punishments. Doctrine is associated with institutionalized, large-scale religions rather than small-scale "folk" religions.

Doctrine, however, can and does change (Bowen 1998). Over the centuries, various popes have pronounced new doctrine for the Catholic Church. A papal declaration of 1854, made with the intent of reinvigorating European Catholicism, bestowed authenticity on the concept of the Immaculate Conception, an idea with substantial popular support.

Muslim doctrine is expressed in the Qur'an, the basic holy text of the Islamic faith, which consists of revelations made to the prophet Muhammad in the seventh century and of collections of Muhammad's statements and deeds. In Kuala Lumpur, Malaysia (see Map 8.3, page 190), a small group of highly educated women called the Sisters in Islam regularly debate with members of the local *ulama*, religious authorities who are responsible for interpreting Islamic doctrine, especially concerning families, education, and commercial affairs (Ong 1995). Debates concern such issues as polygamy, divorce, women's work roles, and women's clothing.

BELIEFS ABOUT SUPERNATURAL FORCES AND BEINGS Supernaturals range from impersonal forces to those who look just like humans. Supernaturals can be supreme and all-powerful creators or smaller-scale, annoying spirits that take up residence in people through possession.

The term **animatism** refers to a belief system in which the supernatural is conceived of as an impersonal power. An important example is *mana*, a concept widespread throughout the South Pacific region, including Melanesia, Polynesia, and Micronesia. Mana is a force outside nature that works automatically; it is neither spirit nor deity. It manifests itself in objects and people and is associated with personal status and power, because some people accumulate more of it than others.

Some supernaturals are *zoomorphic*, deities in the shape, or partial shape, of animals. No satisfactory theory has appeared to explain why some religions develop zoomorphic deities and for what purposes, and why others do not. Religions of classical Greece and Rome and ancient and contemporary Hinduism are especially rich in zoomorphic supernaturals. *Anthropomorphic* supernaturals, deities in the form of

---

animatism a belief system in which the supernatural is conceived of as an impersonal power.

humans, are common but not universal. The human tendency to perceive of supernaturals in their own form was noted 2500 years ago by the Greek philosopher Xenophanes (zen-AHF-uh-neez), who lived sometime between 570 and 470 BCE. He said,

> But if horses or oxen, or lions had hands and could draw with their hands and accomplish such works as men, horses would draw the figures of their gods as similar to horses and the oxen as similar to oxen, and they would make the bodies of the sort which each of them had. (Lesher 2001:25)

The question, though, of why some religions have anthropomorphic deities and others do not remains unanswered.

Anthropomorphic supernaturals, like humans, can be moved by praise, flattery, and gifts. They have emotions. They get annoyed if neglected. They can be loving and caring, or they can be distant and nonresponsive. Most anthropomorphic supernaturals are adults, though some are children. Supernaturals tend to have marital and sexual relationships similar to those of the humans who worship them do. Divine marriages are heterosexual, and in some societies male gods have multiple wives. Although many supernaturals have children, grandchildren are not prominent. In *pantheons* (collectivities of deities), a division of labor reflects specializations in human society. There may be deities of forests, rivers, the sky, wind and rain, agriculture, childbirth, disease, warfare, and marital happiness. The supernaturals have political roles and hierarchies. High gods, such as Jupiter and Juno of classical Roman religion, are all-powerful, with a range of less powerful deities and spirits below them.

In some cultures, deceased ancestors can be supernaturals. Many African, Asian, and American Indian religions have a cult of the ancestors in which the living must do certain things to please the dead ancestors and may also ask for their help in time of need (see Eye on the Environment on page 288). In contemporary Japan, ancestor worship is the principal religious activity of many families. Three national holidays recognize the importance of ancestors: the annual summer visit of the dead to their homes and the visits by the living to graves during the two equinoxes.

BELIEFS ABOUT SACRED SPACE Beliefs about sacred space probably exist in all religions, but such beliefs are more prominent in some religions than others. Sacred spaces, such as rock formations or rapids in a river, may or may not be permanently marked (Bradley 2000). Among the Saami (see Culturama in Chapter 11, page 277), traditional religious beliefs were closely tied to sacred natural sites (Mulk 1994). The sites, often unmarked, included rock formations resembling humans, animals, or birds. The Saami sacrificed fish and other animals at these sites until strong pressures from Christian missionaries forced them to repress their practices and beliefs. Many Saami today know

where the sacred sites are, but they will not reveal them to outsiders.

Another important form of sacred space that has no permanent mark occurs in a domestic ritual conducted by Muslim women throughout the world. The ritual is called the *khatam quran* (khuh-tum kuh-rahn), the "sealing" or reading of the holy book of the Qur'an (Werbner 1988). Among Pakistani migrants living in the city of Manchester, northern England (Map 12.2), this ritual involves a gathering of women who read the Qur'an and then share a ritual meal. The reason for gathering is to give thanks or seek divine blessing. During the ritual, the otherwise nonsacred space of the house becomes sacred. A "portable" ritual such as this one is especially helpful in the adaptation of migrants to their new contexts, because it can be conducted without a formally consecrated ritual space. All that is required is a place, a supportive group of kin and friends, and the Qur'an.

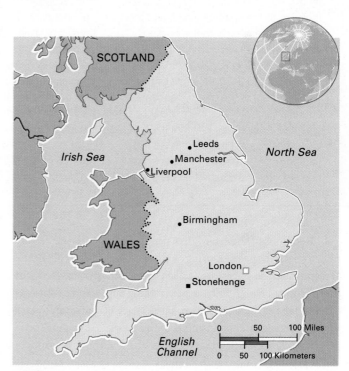

MAP 12.2 England.
England is the largest in area and the most populous of the constituent countries of the United Kingdom. Its population of 50 million accounts for 84 percent of the total. DNA analysis reveals that a majority of the English are of Germanic descent, as is their language. The terrain is mainly rolling hills, with some mountains in the north and east. London is by far the largest city, with Manchester and Birmingham competing for second place. English is the dominant language, with its diverse regional accents. Many other languages brought into the country by immigrant communities are spoken as first languages, including several South Asian languages, Polish, Greek, and Cantonese. An estimated 250,000 people speak British Sign Language. Although the Church of England is the state religion, everyone in England has the right to religious freedom.

eye on the ENVIRONMENT

Eagle Protection, National Parks, and the Preservation of Hopi Culture

For many generations, young men of the Hopi tribe have searched each spring for golden eaglets in the cliffs of Arizona's Wupatki National Park and other parts of northeastern Arizona (Fenstemaker 2007). They bring the young eagles to the reservation and care for them until the summer, when, as mature birds, they are smothered in a ceremony that the Hopi believe frees the spirits of the birds, which convey messages to their ancestors who reside in the spiritual world. This ceremony is the most important Hopi ritual, but the tribe uses golden eagle feathers in all its rituals. For the Hopi, golden eagles are their link to the spiritual world, and their ritual use is essential to the continuity of Hopi culture.

In 1783, the U.S. Continental Congress adopted the bald eagle as the national symbol of the newly independent country. By 1940, numbers of bald eagles had dropped so low that the U.S. Congress passed the Bald Eagle Protection Act to preserve the species that had become established as the symbol of American ideals of freedom. In 1962, Congress amended the act to include golden eagles, because the young of the two species are nearly indistinguishable.

In 1994, President Clinton promoted some official accommodation to Hopi beliefs about golden eagles. His administration established a repository for golden eagle feathers and other remains in Colorado. The demand is, however, greater than the supply.

The Hopi have a permit for an annual take of 40 golden eagles in northeastern Arizona, but they are excluded from Wupatki because of its status as a national park. The United States policy toward national parks follows the *Yellowstone model*, which aims to preserve the physical environment and species but excludes indigenous peoples and their cultures. This model has been applied widely throughout the world to the detriment of peoples who have long successfully lived in regions that are now off limits to them for hunting, fishing, and gathering. In addition, many of these lands are sacred to them, but they are prevented from using them in traditional ways for the sake of "conservation" as defined by the government.

Anthropologists and others support environmental and species preservation, but not to the exclusion of heritage populations and cultures. They suggest that a case-by-case approach should be followed in considering exemptions to national laws. With regard to the golden eagles of Arizona, they point out that golden eagles are abundant and the Hopi requests for the spring take are small and present no threat to the survival of the species.

Environmentalists are concerned, however, that granting exemptions will establish dangerous precedents that will, over time, destroy pristine environments and precious species. Other environmentalists counter that more eagles are killed every year by airplanes or contact with electrical wires, or they die from eating prey that contains lead bullets.

Religions of the Aboriginal people of Australia are closely tied to sacred space. During a mythological past called the Dreamtime, the ancestors walked the earth and marked out the territory belonging to a particular group. People's knowledge of where the ancestors roamed is secret. In several cases that have recently been brought to the courts, Aboriginal peoples have claimed title to land that is being sought by commercial developers. Some anthropologists provide *expert testimony* in court, based on their knowledge of a particular culture, to document the validity of the Aboriginal claims (see Anthropology Works on page 290). In one such case, secret Aboriginal knowledge about a sacred place and its associated beliefs was gender specific: It belonged to women and could not be told to men. The anthropologist who was hired to support the women's claims was a woman, so the women could tell her about the sacred places, but she could not convey that knowledge in court to the male judge, a situation that demanded considerable ingenuity on the part of the anthropological consultant.

Ritual Practices

A **ritual** is patterned, repetitive behavior focused on the supernatural realm. Such *sacred rituals* are the enactment of beliefs expressed in myth and doctrine, for example, the Christian ritual of communion. Sacred rituals are distinct from *secular rituals*, such as sorority or fraternity initiations, that have no connection to the supernatural realm. Some ritual events combine sacred and secular elements. The U.S. holiday of Thanksgiving originated as a Christian sacred meal with the primary purpose of giving thanks to God for the survival of the Pilgrims (Siskind 1992). Its original Christian meaning is not maintained by everyone who celebrates the holiday today. Secular features of the holiday, such as watching football, may be of greater importance than the ritual aspect of thanking God for plentiful food.

Anthropologists categorize sacred rituals in many ways. One division is based on their timing. Regularly performed rituals are called *periodic rituals*. Many periodic rituals are performed annually to mark a seasonal milestone such as

---

ritual   patterned behavior that has to do with the supernatural realm.

life-cycle ritual   a ritual that marks a change in status from one life stage to another.

A Kachina doll. Among the Hopi, the word *Kachina* (kuh-CHEE-nuh) refers to a spirit or "life-bringer." Uncles carve Kachina dolls for their nieces to help them learn about the many spirits that exist in the Hopi religion. Kachina dolls, especially older ones, are highly sought after by non-Indians who collect Indian artifacts.

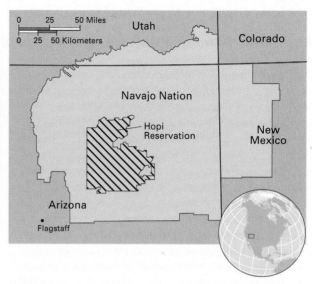

MAP 12.3 Hopi Reservation in Arizona.
The Hopi and Navajo tribes once shared the area known as Big Mountain. U.S. Acts of Congress in 1974 and 1996 divided the area into two reservations, leaving the Hopi completely surrounded by the much larger Navajo reservation. About 7000 people live on the Hopi Reservation.

In contrast to the Yellowstone model, anthropologists advocate for a *parks and people approach,* which builds on community-based conservation that does not exclude heritage populations from continuing to enjoy the economic and religious benefits of their territory while also sharing with the wider population.

FOOD FOR THOUGHT ▼
Consider how you would feel if you were told that you could no longer practice the most important annual ritual in your religion but that other people could have a touristic experience at the place where you would normally practice the ritual. For secular students, consider a secular ritual, for example, watching the Super Bowl.

planting or harvesting or to commemorate an important event. For example, Buddha's Day, an important periodic ritual in Buddhism, commemorates the birth, enlightenment, and death of the Buddha (all on one day). On this day, Buddhists gather at monasteries, hear sermons about the Buddha, and perform rituals such as pouring water over images of the Buddha. Calendrical events, such as the shortest day of the year, the longest day, the new moon, and the full moon, often shape ritual cycles. *Nonperiodic rituals*, in contrast, occur irregularly, at unpredictable times, in response to unscheduled events, such as a drought or flood, or to mark events in a person's life, such as illness, infertility, birth, marriage, or death. The following material presents highlights of various types of ritual.

LIFE-CYCLE RITUALS A **life-cycle ritual**, or rite of passage, marks a change in status from one life stage to another of an individual or group. Victor Turner's (1969) fieldwork among the Ndembu (en-DEM-boo), horticulturalists of northwestern Zambia, provides insights into the phases of life-cycle rituals. Turner found that, among the Ndembu and cross-culturally, life-cycle rituals have three phases: separation, transition, and reintegration.

• In the first phase, the initiate (the person undergoing the ritual) is separated physically, socially, or symbolically from normal life. Special dress may mark the separation. In many cultures of the Amazon and in East and

An Apache girl's puberty ceremony. Cross-cultural research indicates that the celebration of girls' puberty is more likely to occur in cultures in which adult women have valued productive and reproductive roles.

ANTHROPOLOGY works

Aboriginal Women's Culture and Sacred Site Protection

A group of Ngarrindjeri (prounounced NAR-en-jeery) women and their lawyer hired cultural anthropologist Diane Bell to serve as a consultant to them in supporting their claims to a sacred site in southern Australia (Bell 1998). The area on Hindmarsh Island was threatened by the proposed construction of a bridge that would cross sacred waters between Goolwa and the island. The women claimed protection for the area and sought prevention of the bridge building on the basis of their secret knowledge of its sacredness, knowledge passed down in trust from mother to daughter over generations. The High Commission formed by the government to investigate their claim considered it to be a hoax perpetrated to block a project important to the country.

Helping the women prove their case to a White, male-dominated court system was a challenging task for Diane Bell, a White Australian with extensive fieldwork experience among Aboriginal women. Bell conducted research over many months to marshal evidence for the validity of the women's claims. She examined newspaper archives, early recordings of ritual songs, and oral histories of Ngarrindjeri women. She prepared reports for the courtroom about women's sacred knowledge that were general enough to avoid violating the rule of secret, women-only knowledge but detailed enough to convince the High Court judge that the women's knowledge was authentic. In the end, the judge was convinced, and the bridge project was canceled in 1999.

Land developers, however, did not give up, and in 2001, the Federal Court dismissed claims of "secret women's business" as fabricated.

The case is one of the most bitter court conflicts related to "race" in Australia's history—not to mention gender. The senior women who fought for the protection of their sacred places have passed on. Many Ngarrindjeri and those who stood with them during the struggle to stop the construction, will not use the bridge.

In the latest development, in July 2010, high level officials apologized to the Ngarrindjeri women, acknowledging that their claims were genuine when they objected to the construction of the bridge. Following this public apology, some Ngarrindjeri women, in a peace-making move, walked the bridge for the first time. Others say they will never do so.

FOOD FOR THOUGHT ▼

On the Internet, learn more about this case and other disputes in Australia about sacred sites.

MAP 12.4 Hindmarsh Island in Southeast Australia. The Ngarrindjeri name for Hindmarsh Island is Kumarangk.

The pedestrian bridge from Hindmarsh Island to South Australia.

Two religions that seem so far apart actually have much in common. (LEFT) Each year, Muslim pilgrims converge in Mecca and walk around the Kaaba at the Grand Mosque. (RIGHT) At Easter, in Jerusalem, Christians gather in the rotunda of the Church of the Holy Sepulchre.

West Africa, adolescents are secluded for several years in separate huts or areas away from the village.

- The transition, or *liminal*, phase, is when the person is no longer in the previous status but is not yet a member of the next stage. *Liminality* often involves the learning of specialized skills that will equip the person for the new status.

- Reintegration, the last stage, occurs when the initiate emerges and is welcomed by the community as an individual occupying the new status.

Differences in the cross-cultural distribution of puberty rituals for boys and girls reflect the economic value and status of males and females. Most societies have some form of puberty ceremony for boys, but puberty ceremonies for girls are less common. In societies where female labor is important and valued, girls have elaborate, and sometimes painful, puberty rites (Brown 1978). Where their labor is not important, menarche is unmarked and there is no puberty ceremony. Puberty rites function to socialize future members of the labor force, among other things. For example, among the Bemba of northern Zambia, during her initiation a girl learns to distinguish 40 kinds of mushrooms and to know which are edible and which are poisonous.

PILGRIMAGE **Pilgrimage** is round-trip travel to a sacred place or places for purposes of religious devotion or ritual. Prominent pilgrimage places are Varanasi (var-uh-nuh-see) in India (formerly called Banaras or Benares) for Hindus; Mecca in Saudi Arabia for Muslims; Bodh Gaya in India for Buddhists; Jerusalem in Israel for Jews, Christians, and Muslims; and Lourdes in France for Christians. Pilgrimage often involves hardship, with the implication that the more suffering

that is involved, the more merit the pilgrim accumulates. Compared with a weekly trip to church or synagogue, pilgrimage removes a person further from everyday life, is more demanding, and therefore is potentially more transformative.

Victor Turner applied the three sequences of life-cycle rituals to pilgrimage: The pilgrim first separates from everyday life, then enters the liminal stage during the actual pilgrimage, and finally returns to be reintegrated into society in a transformed state (1969). A person who has gone on a pilgrimage often gains enhanced public status as well as spiritual benefits.

RITUALS OF INVERSION In a **ritual of inversion**, normal social roles and relations are temporarily inverted. A functionalist perspective says that these rituals allow for social pressure to be released. They also provide a reminder about the propriety of normal, everyday roles and practices to which people must return once the ritual is over.

Carnival (or *carnaval* in Portuguese) is a ritual of inversion with roots in the northern Mediterranean region. It is celebrated widely throughout southern Europe and the Western Hemisphere. Carnival is a period of riotous celebration before the Christian fast of Lent. It begins at different times in different places, but always ends on Mardi Gras (or Shrove Tuesday), the day before the fasting period of Lent begins. The word *carnival*, from Latin, means "flesh farewell," referring to the fact that believers give up eating meat during Lent.

---

pilgrimage round-trip travel to a sacred place or places for purposes of religious devotion or ritual.

ritual of inversion a ritual in which normal social roles and order are temporarily reversed.

In Bosa, a town in Sardegna (Sardinia), Italy (Map 12.5), carnival involves social-role reversal and the relaxing of usual social norms. Discotheques extend their hours, mothers allow their daughters to stay out late, and men and women flirt with each other in public in ways that are forbidden during the rest of the year (Counihan 1985). Carnival in Bosa has three phases. The first is impromptu street theater and masquerades that take place over several weeks, usually on Sundays. The skits are social critiques of current events and local happenings. In the masquerades, men dress up as exaggerated women:

> Young boys thrust their padded breasts forward with their hands while brassily hiking up their skirts to reveal their thighs. . . . A youth stuffs his shirt front with melons and holds them proudly out. . . . The high school gym teacher dresses as a nun and lifts up his habit to reveal suggestive red underwear. Two men wearing nothing but bikinis, wigs, and high heels feign a stripper's dance on a table top. (1985:15)

The second phase occurs on the morning of Mardi Gras, when hundreds of Bosans, mostly men, dress in black, like widows, and flood the streets. They accost passersby, shaking in their faces dolls and other objects that are maimed in some way or bloodied. They shriek at the top of their lungs as if mourning, and they say, "Give us milk, milk for our babies. . . . They are dying, they are neglected, their mothers have been gallivanting since St. Anthony's Day and have abandoned their poor children" (1985:16).

The third phase, called Giolzi, takes place during the evening. Men and women dress in white, wearing sheets for cloaks and pillowcases for hoods. They blacken their faces. Rushing into the street, they hold hands and chant the word "*Giolzi.*" They storm at people, pretending to search their bodies for Giolzi and then say, "Got it!" It is not clear what Giolzi is, but whatever it is, it represents something that makes everyone happy.

How does a cultural anthropologist interpret these events? Carnival allows people for a short time to act out roles that are normally denied them. It is also a time when everyone has fun. In this way, rituals of inversion may function as a mechanism for maintaining social order. After a few days of revelry, everyone returns to his or her original place for another year.

---

sacrifice   a ritual in which something is offered to the supernaturals.

priest or **priestess**   a male or female full-time religious specialist whose position is based mainly on abilities gained through formal training.

world religion   a term coined in the nineteenth century to refer to a religion that is based on written sources, has many followers, is regionally widespread, and is concerned with salvation.

MAP 12.5   Italy.
Officially the Italian Republic, the country includes the mainland and two large islands. In 2008, Italy had the seventh highest GDP in the world. A mountain system forms the backbone of the peninsula, and the climate varies according to altitude. Its population of nearly 60 million people makes it one of the most densely populated countries in Europe. Roman Catholicism is the dominant religion. Recent waves of immigration, especially from northern Africa, have increased the number of Muslims to perhaps 1 million. The official language is standard Italian, descended from the Tuscan dialect of Firenze (Florence). Many cherished dialects of Italian exist throughout the country, and people in northern border provinces speak dialects of German and French. Italy has the largest number of UNESCO World Heritage Sites of any country.

SACRIFICE   Many rituals involve **sacrifice**, or the offering of something for transfer to the supernaturals. Sacrifice has a long history throughout the world and is probably one of the oldest forms of ritual. It may involve killing and offering animals; making human offerings (of whole people, parts of a person's body, or bloodletting); or offering vegetables, fruits, grains, flowers, or other products. One interpretation of flowers as sacrificial offerings is that they, like vegetables and fruits, are symbolic replacements for former animal sacrifices (Goody 1993).

Spanish documents from the sixteenth century describe the Aztec practice of public sacrifice of humans and other animals to please the gods. The details are gory and involve marching thousands of human victims up to the top of a temple and then cutting out their hearts so that the blood spurts forth. Debate exists among anthropologists as to how many victims were actually sacrificed and why. Cultural materialist Marvin Harris has argued that the numbers were large, up to

100,000 at particular sites, and that the remains of the victims were butchered and eaten by commoners (1977). He maintains that the Aztec state, through such rituals, demonstrated its power and also provided protein to the masses. In opposition to Harris, symbolic anthropologist Peggy Sanday takes an emic perspective and says that the sacrifices were necessary to please the gods and had nothing to do with maintaining the worldly power of leaders (1986).

Religious Specialists

Not all rituals require the presence of a *religious specialist*, or someone with extensive, formal training, but all require some level of knowledge on the part of the performer(s) about how to do them correctly. Even the daily, household veneration of an ancestor requires some knowledge gained through informal learning. At the other extreme, many rituals cannot be done without a highly trained specialist.

SHAMANS AND PRIESTS   General features of the categories of shaman and priest illustrate key differences between these two types of specialists. (Many other specialists fit somewhere in between.) A *shaman* or *shamanka* (defined in Chapter 7) is a religious specialist who has a direct relationship with the supernaturals, often by being "called." A potential shaman may be recognized by special signs, such as the ability to go into a trance. Anyone who demonstrates shamanic abilities can become a shaman; in other words, this is an openly available role. Shamans are more often associated with nonstate societies, yet faith healers and evangelists of the United States could fit into this category. (Review the discussion in Chapter 7 of shamanic specialists as healers.)

In states, the more complex occupational specialization in religion means that there is a wider variety of types of specialists, especially what anthropologists refer to as *priests* (not the same as the specific modern role of the Catholic priest), and promotes the development of religious hierarchies and power structures. The terms **priest** and **priestess** refer to a category of full-time religious specialists whose position is based mainly on abilities gained through formal training. A priest may receive a divine call, but more often the role is hereditary, passed on through priestly lineages. In terms of ritual performance, shamans are more involved with nonperiodic rituals. Priests perform a wider range of rituals, including periodic state rituals. In contrast to shamans, who rarely have secular power, priests and priestly lineages often do.

OTHER SPECIALISTS   Many other specialized religious roles exist cross-culturally. *Diviners* are specialists who are able to discover the will and wishes of the supernaturals through

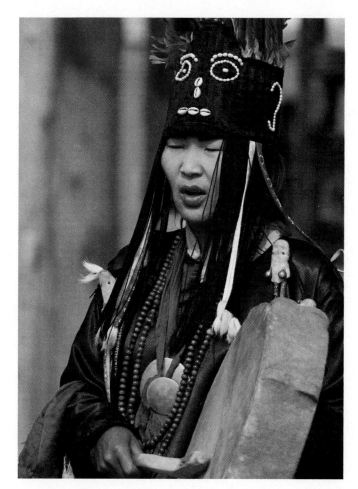

A Mongolian shamanka.

techniques such as reading animal entrails. Palm readers and tarot card readers fit into the category of diviners.

Prophets are specialists who convey divine revelations usually gained through visions or dreams. They often possess charisma, an especially attractive and powerful personality, and may be able to perform miracles. Prophets have founded new religions, some long-lasting and others short-lived.

Witches use psychic powers and affect people through emotion and thought. Mainstream society often condemns witchcraft as negative. Some scholars of ancient and contemporary witchcraft differentiate between positive forms that involve healing and negative forms that seek to harm people.

◉ ◉ ◉

World Religions and Local Variations

The term **world religion** was coined in the nineteenth century to refer to religions that were based on written sources, with many followers that crossed country borders and that had a concern with salvation (the belief that human beings require deliverance from an imperfect world). At that time, the term referred only to Christianity, Islam, and Buddhism. It was later expanded to include Judaism, Hinduism, Confucianism, Taoism, and Shintoism. Because of the global importance of the African diaspora that began with the European colonial slave trade, a sixth category of world religions is included here that describes key elements shared among the diversity of traditional African belief systems even though they are oral, not text-based, traditions.

For many centuries, the world religions have traveled outside their original borders through intentional attempts to expand and gain converts or through the migration of believers to new locales. European colonialism was a major force that led to the expansion of Christianity through the missionary work of Protestant sects. The increased rate of population migration since the twentieth century (Chapter 14) and the expansion of television and the Internet give even greater impetus to religious movement and change. Each world religion comprises many local variants, raising a predicament for centrally organized religions in terms of how to maintain a balance between standardization based on core beliefs and the local differences (Hefner 1998).

The material that follows first discusses five longstanding world religions in terms of their history, distribution, and basic teachings (Figure 12.2). (*Note:* Population statistics for the world religions are rough averages derived from several Internet sources.) They are presented in order by

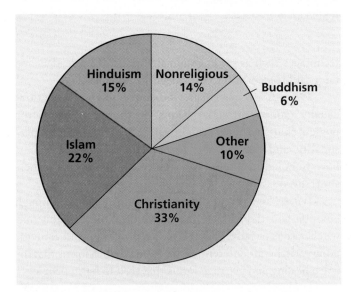

FIGURE 12.2 Population Distribution of Major World Religions. Judaism, due to its relatively small numbers, is classified in "Other."

---

religious pluralism   the condition in which one or more religions coexist either as complementary to each other or as competing systems.

religious syncretism   the blending of features of two or more religions.

An early nineteenth-century painting of the Virgin of Guadalupe by Isidro Escamilla, a Mexican artist. The Virgin of Guadalupe, or Our Lady of Guadalupe, is Mexico's most popular image. Her depiction involves syncretism with the indigenous Aztec goddess Tonantzin, part of a conscious strategy of Christian clergy to convert the Indians. Today, the Virgin of Guadalupe conveys messages of sacrifice and nurturance, as well as strength and hope. She appeals to Mexican mothers, nationalists, and feminists alike.

historical age, based on the dates of written texts. For each religion, an example of a local variation is presented. When a world religion moves into a new cultural region, it encounters local religious traditions. In many cases, the incoming religion and local religions coexist as separate traditions, either as complements or competitors, in what is called **religious pluralism**. In **religious syncretism**, elements of two or more religions blend together. Religious syncretism is most likely to occur when aspects of two religions form a close match with each other. For example, if a local myth involves a hero who has something to do with snakes, there may be a syncretistic link with the Catholic belief in St. Patrick, who is believed to have driven snakes out of Ireland. Many situations of nonfit also exist. For example, Christian missionaries have had difficulty translating the Bible into some indigenous languages because of a lack of matching words or concepts and because of differing kinship and social structures. Some Amazonian groups, such as the Pirahã (review Chapter 11), have no word that corresponds to the Christian concept of "heaven" (Everett 1995, personal communication). In other cases, matrilineal peoples have found it difficult to understand the significance of the Christian construct of "god the father."

The two world religions that emphasize *proselytizing*, or seeking converts, are Christianity and Islam. Their encounters with local religions have sometimes been violent, involving the physical destruction of sacred places and objects (Corbey 2003). Common methods include burning, overturning, dismantling, or cutting up sacred objects, dumping them into rivers, and hiding them in caves. European Christian missionaries in the 1800s often confiscated sacred goods and shipped them to Europe for sale to private owners or museums. Both Christian and Islamic conversion efforts frequently involved the construction of their own places of worship on top of the original sacred site. Conflict between these two religions is, unfortunately, not a matter of the past only.

Hinduism

Over 900 million people, or about 15 percent of the world's population, are Hindus. About 97 percent of all Hindus live in India, where Hinduism accounts for 80 percent of the population. The rest live throughout the world in countries such as Bangladesh, Myanmar, Pakistan, Sri Lanka, the United States, Canada, the United Kingdom, Malaysia, Fiji, Trinidad, Guyana, and Hong Kong.

A Hindu is born a Hindu, and Hinduism does not actively seek converts. The core texts of Hinduism are the four Vedas, which were composed in Sanskrit in northern India between 1200 and 900 BCE . Many other scholarly texts, epics and stories, and oral traditions enrich the Hindu tradition. The two most widely known stories are the *Mahabharata* (muh-huh-bhar-uh-tuh), the story of a war between two patrilineages in which Krishna plays an important role, and the *Ramayana* (ruh-my-uh-nuh), the story of King Rama and his devoted wife, Sita. Throughout India, many local stories also exist, some containing elements from pre-Vedic times.

Hinduism offers a rich polytheism and, at the same time, a philosophical tradition that reduces the multiplicity of deities into oneness. Deities range from a simple stone placed at the foot of a tree to elegantly carved and painted icons of gods such as Shiva and Vishnu and the goddesses Durga and Saraswati. Everyday worship of a deity involves lighting a lamp in front of the god, chanting hymns and mantras (sacred phrases), and taking *darshan* (dar-shun), which means the act of seeing the deity, usually in the form of an icon (Eck 1985). These acts bring blessings to the worshipper. Local variations

Celebration of Holi, a spring festival popular among Hindus worldwide. In this scene in New Delhi, a young woman sprays colored water on a young man as part of the joyous event. The deeper meaning of Holi is tied to a myth about a demon.

▶ *Is the arrival of spring ritually marked in your culture?*

of worship often involve deities and rituals unknown elsewhere. For example, fire walking is an important part of goddess worship in southern and eastern India (Freeman 1981) and among some Hindu groups living outside India, notably in Fiji (Brown 1984).

Caste differences in beliefs and practices are also marked, even within the same village. Lower caste deities prefer offerings of meat sacrifices and alcohol, whereas upper caste deities prefer flowers, rice, and fruit.

A NAYAR FERTILITY RITUAL   The matrilineal Nayars (nye-ers) of Kerala, South India (see Map 15.2, page 364), perform a nonperiodic ritual as a remedy for the curse of the serpent deities who cause infertility in women (Neff 1994). This ritual illustrates the unity of Hinduism in several ritual elements: the use of a camphor flame and incense, the importance of serpent deities, and the offering of flowers to the deity. Locally specific elements are related to the matrilineal cultural context of Kerala.

The all-night ritual includes, first, women painting a sacred design of intertwined serpents on the floor. Several hours of worshipping the deity follow, with the camphor flame, incense, and flowers. Music comes from drumming, playing the cymbals, and singing. The presence of the deity is fully achieved when one of the women goes into a trance. Through her, matrilineal family members may speak to the deity and be blessed.

Among the Nayars, a woman's mother, mother's brothers, and brothers are responsible for ensuring that her desires for motherhood are fulfilled. They share her interest in continuing the matrilineage. What the women say during the trance is important. They typically draw attention to family disharmonies or neglect of the deities. This message diverts blame from the infertile woman for whom the ritual is being held. It reminds family and lineage members of their responsibilities to each other.

HINDU WOMEN AND KARMA IN NORTHERN ENGLAND One of Hinduism's basic concepts is *karma*, translated as "destiny" or "fate." A person's karma is determined at birth on the basis of his or her previous life and how it was conducted. The karma concept has prompted many outsiders to judge Hindus as fatalistic, lacking a sense of agency. But anthropological research on how people actually think about karma in their everyday lives reveals much individual variation, from fatalism to a strong sense of being in charge of one's destiny. One study looked at women's perceptions of karma among Hindus living in the city of Leeds, northern England (Knott 1996) (see Map 12.2, page 287). Some of the women are fatalistic in their attitudes and behavior. One woman who had a strongly fatalistic view of karma said,

> When a baby's born . . . we have a ritual on the sixth day. That's when you name the baby, you know. And on that day, we believe the goddess comes and writes your future . . . we leave a blank white paper and a pen and we just leave it [overnight]. . . . So I believe that my future—whatever happens—is what she has written for me. That tells me [that] I have to do what I can do, and if I have a mishap in between I have to accept that. (1996:24)

Another woman said that her sufferings were caused by the irresponsibility of her father and the "bad husband" to whom she had been married. She challenged her karma and left her husband: "I could not accept the karma of being with Nirmal [her husband]. If I had done so, what would have become of my children?" (1996:25). Because Hindu women's karma dictates being married and having children, leaving one's husband is a major act of resistance.

Options for women seeking support when questioning or changing their karmic roles can be religious, such as praying more and fasting, or secular, such as seeking the advice of a psychological counselor or social worker. Some Hindu women in England have become counselors, working in support of other women's independence and self-confidence. They illustrate how human agency can work against traditional religious rules.

Buddhism

Buddhism originated in a founding figure, Siddhartha Gautama (ca. 566–486 BCE), revered as the Buddha, or Awakened One (Eckel 1995:135). It began in northern India, where the Buddha was born and grew up. From there, it spread throughout the subcontinent, into inner Asia and China, to Sri Lanka, and on to Southeast Asia. Buddhism's popularity declined in India, and Buddhists now constitute less than 1 percent of India's population. Over the past 200 years, Buddhism has spread to Europe and North America.

Buddhism has a great diversity of doctrine and practice, to the extent that it is difficult to point to a single essential feature other than the importance of Gautama Buddha. No one text is accepted as authoritative for all forms of Buddhism. Many Buddhists worship the Buddha as a deity, but others do not. Instead, they honor his teachings and follow the pathway he suggested for reaching *nirvana* (nur-VAH-nuh), or release from worldly life. The total

Buddhism gained an established footing in Japan in the eighth century. The city of Nara was an important early center of Buddhism. An emperor sponsored the casting of this huge bronze statue of the Buddha.

▶ *Is there a Buddhist temple where you live? If so, have you visited it? If not, find out where the nearest one is and visit it if possible.*

number of Buddhists worldwide is around 400 million, or about six percent of the global population.

Buddhism arose as a protest against Hinduism, especially caste inequality, but it retained and revised several Hindu concepts, such as karma. In Buddhism, everyone has the potential through good deeds to achieve a better rebirth with each incarnation, until finally, release from *samsara* (the cycle of birth, reincarnation, death, rebirth, and so on) is achieved. Compassion toward others, including animals, is a key virtue. Branches of Buddhism have different texts that they consider their canon. Buddhism is associated with a strong tradition of monasticism through which monks and nuns renounce the everyday world and spend their lives meditating and doing good works. Buddhists have many annual festivals and rituals. Some events bring pilgrims from around the world to northern India to visit Sarnath, where the Buddha gave his first teaching, and Gaya, where he gained enlightenment.

LOCAL SPIRITS AND BUDDHISM IN SOUTHEAST ASIA Wherever Buddhism exists outside India, it is never the exclusive religion of the devotees, because it arrived to find established local religions already in place (Spiro 1967). In Myanmar (formerly Burma), Buddhism and indigenous traditions coexist without one being dominant. Indigenous beliefs remain strong because they offer a way of dealing with everyday problems. Buddhist beliefs about karma in Myanmar are similar to those in Hinduism: A person's karma is the result of previous births and determines his or her present condition. If something bad happens, the person can do little but suffer through it.

In contrast, indigenous supernaturalism says that the bad things happen because of the actions of capricious spirits called *nats*. Ritual actions, however, can combat the influence of nats. Thus, people can deal with nats but not with karma. The continuity of belief in nats is an example of human agency and creativity. Burmese people kept what was important to them from their traditional beliefs and adopted aspects of the new religion.

Buddhism became an important cultural force and the basis for social integration in Myanmar. A typical village may have one or more Buddhist monasteries and several resident monks. All boys are ordained as temporary members of the monastic order. Almost every villager observes Buddhist holy days. Nonetheless, although Buddhism is held to be the supreme truth, the spirits retain control when it comes to dealing with everyday problems such as a toothache or a monetary loss. In Myanmar, the two traditions exist in a pluralistic situation as two separate options.

Other studies of religion in Southeast Asia provide examples in which there is more thorough blending, or syncretism, of local religions with Buddhism (see Everyday Anthropology on page 298).

Judaism

The first Judaic religious system was defined around 500 BCE, following the destruction of the Temple in Jerusalem by the Babylonians in 586 BCE (Neusner 1995). The early writings, called the Pentateuch (pen-tuh-took), established the theme of exile and return as a paradigm for Judaism that endures today. The Pentateuch is also called the Five Books of Moses, or the Torah. Followers of Judaism share in the belief in the Torah as the revelation of God's truth through Israel, a term for the "holy people." The Torah explains the relationship between the supernatural and human realms and guides people in how to carry out the worldview through appropriate actions. A key feature of all forms of Judaism is the identification of what is wrong with the present and how to escape, overcome, or survive that situation. Jewish life is symbolically interpreted as a tension between exile and return, given its foundational myth in the exile of the Jews from Israel and their period of slavery in Egypt.

Judaism is monotheistic, teaching that God is one, unique, and all powerful. Humans have a moral duty to follow Jewish law, to protect and preserve life and health, and to follow certain duties, such as observing the Sabbath. The high regard for human life is reflected in the general opposition to abortion within Jewish law and in opposition to the death penalty. Words, both spoken and written, are important in Judaism. There is an emphasis on truth telling in life and on the use of established literary formulas at precise times during worship. These formulas are encoded in a *sidur* (sih-door), or prayer book. Dietary patterns distinguish Judaism from other religions; for example, rules of kosher eating forbid the mixing of milk or milk products with meat.

Contemporary varieties of Judaism range from conservative Hasidism to Reform Judaism, which emerged in the early 1800s. One difference between these two perspectives concerns the question of who is Jewish. Jewish law traditionally defined a Jewish person as someone born of a Jewish mother. In contrast, reform Judaism recognizes as Jewish the offspring of a Jewish father and a non-Jewish mother. Currently, the Jewish population numbers about 15 million worldwide, with about half living in North America, a quarter in Israel, and 20 percent in Europe and Russia. Smaller populations are scattered across the globe.

WHO'S WHO AT THE KOTEL The most sacred place to all Jews is the Kotel (ko-TELL), or Western Wall in Jerusalem (see Map 12.6 on page 299). Since the 1967 war, which brought Jerusalem under Israeli rule, the Kotel has been the most important religious shrine and pilgrimage site of Israel. The Kotel is located at one edge of the Temple Mount (also called Haram Sharif), an area sacred to Jews, Muslims, and Christians. According to Jewish scriptures, God asked Abraham to sacrifice his son Isaac on this hill. Later, King Solomon built the First Temple here in the middle of the tenth century BCE. It was destroyed by Nebuchadnezzsar

everyday ANTHROPOLOGY

Tattoos and Sacred Power

Fieldwork with Shan people in northern Thailand reveals the importance of tattooing, a tradition shared with much of Southeast Asia (Tannenbaum 1987). Shan tattooing blends aspects of Buddhism with local spirit beliefs and even elements of Hinduism as practiced by some groups in neighboring Myanmar.

Among the Shan, three types of tattoos exist:

- Tattoos that act on other people, causing them to like or fear the bearer, and that cause the spirits to be kind
- Tattoos that act on the bearer, increasing the bearer's skill
- Tattoos that create a barrier around the person that prevents animals from biting, knives from cutting, and bullets from entering the body

Tattoos are done in two colors—red, and blue-black. The first two types tend to be done in red; the third type tends to be done in blue black. Different designs are associated with each type. For example, the two-tailed lizard is a common tattoo in the first type.

The first type of tattoo is popular among many people, because it brings health to the bearer. It is the main type among women, used to prevent, as well as cure, an illness. A person who falls ill may get a tattoo incorporating a letter of the Shan alphabet in the design, either on the calf, around a body joint, around the mouth, or on the top of the tongue. Some of the most powerful designs in this category are placed on the back or over the heart.

The most powerful tattoo in this category, called the Five Buddha tattoo, is not allowed for women. Men who get this tattoo have to follow five Buddhist precepts at all times: Refrain from killing, stealing, improper sexual behavior, lying, and intoxication. The tattoo is red, but it also includes exfoliated skin from a Buddhist monk. That makes it different from all other tattoos and makes its bearer like a monk. Whereas most tattoos in the first category cause other people to look favorably on the bearer, the Five Buddha tattoo inspires fear and awe.

Tattoos in the second category are related to words. Some increase people's memory and help them on exams. Others strengthen a person's speaking ability. The most powerful tattoos in this group give a person such great verbal skills that he or she can intimidate others. They increase courage as well. One tattoo in the category is the Saraswati tattoo, which depicts, among other things, the head of Saraswati, the Hindu goddess of knowledge, on the bearer's right shoulder. To call on Saraswati for help, the person brushes his or her lips on the tattoo.

The third category of tattoos, those which provide a protective barrier, has one subset that prevents bites from insects, snakes, dogs, cats, tigers, and so on. If the person has the tattoo and gets bitten nonetheless, the tattoo helps reduce the pain. A general antibite tattoo depicts a cat and is on the lower arm. More powerful tattoos in this third category protect people from weapons. They seal off the body. A person should be careful not to get too many of these tattoos, however, because they seal the body off completely and therefore prevent good fortune from entering it.

Over 100 years old, this Shan man of northern Thailand is testimony to positive life forces, whether inscribed on his body as protective tattoos . . . or because of his less-toxic, pre-industrial lifestyle?

Someone with many of these tattoos is likely to be poor or unlucky.

The Shan people do not question why or how their tattoos work. They simply believe that they do. In the case of the Saraswati tattoo, they blend magic with religious beliefs from Buddhism and Hinduism. Sacred power is the key that links all these beliefs together into a coherent system for the Shan.

FOOD FOR THOUGHT ▼
What do people in your microculture do to get people to like them, to succeed on exams, and to protect the body from harmful intrusions?

(neh-boo-kud-NEZZ-er) in 587 BCE, when the Jews were led into captivity in Babylon. Around 500 BCE, the Second Temple was built on the same site. The Kotel is a remnant of the Second Temple. Jews of all varieties, as well as non-Jews, come to the Kotel in vast numbers from around the world. The Kotel plaza is open to everyone, pilgrims and tourists alike. The wall is made of massive rectangular stones weighing between 2 and 8 tons each. At its base is a synagogue area partitioned into men's and women's sections.

This single site brings together a variety of Jewish worshippers and secular visitors. The great diversity among the visitors is evident in the various styles of dress and gesture:

The Hasid . . . with a fur shtreimel on his head may enter the synagogue area alongside a man in shorts who utilizes a cardboard skullcap available for "secular" visitors. American youngsters in jeans may ponder Israeli soldiers of their own age, dressed in uniform, and wonder what their lot might have been if they [had been] born in another country. Women from

The Kotel, or Western Wall, in Jerusalem is a sacred place of pilgrimage, especially for Jews. Men pray in a section marked off on the left, women in the area on the right. Both men and women should cover their heads, and when leaving the wall area, women should take care to keep their faces toward it and avoid turning their backs to it.

▶ *Think of some behavioral rules at another sacred place you have visited.*

MAP 12.6 Sacred Sites in the Old City of Jerusalem, Israel. Jerusalem is the holiest city of Judaism, the third holiest city of Islam, and holy to Christians. The section called the Old City is surrounded by walls that have been built, razed, relocated, and rebuilt over several hundred years. The Old City contains four quarters—Armenian, Christian, Jewish, and Muslim—and many sacred sites, such as the Kotel and the Via Dolorosa.

Yemen, wearing embroidered trousers under their dresses, edge close to the Wall as do women accoutred in contemporary styles whose religiosity may have been filtered through a modern education.... (Storper-Perez and Goldberg 1994:321)

In spite of plaques that state the prohibition against begging, beggars offer to "sell a blessing" to visitors. They may remind visitors that it was the poor who built the wall in the first place. Another category of people is young Jewish men who, in search of prospective "born again" Jews, "hang around" looking for a "hit" (in their words). Most of the hits are young Americans, who are urged to take their Jewishness

more seriously and, if male, to be sure to marry a Jewish woman. Other regulars are Hebrew-speaking men who are available to organize a prayer service. One of the most frequent forms of religious expression at the Kotel is the insertion of written prayers into the crevices of the wall.

The social heterogeneity of the Jewish people is thus transcended in a single space, creating some sense of what Victor Turner (1969) called *communitas*, a sense of collective unity that bridges individual differences.

PASSOVER IN KERALA The Jews of the Kochi (kochee) area of Kerala, South India, have lived there for about 1000 years (Katz and Goldberg 1989) (see Map 15.2, page 364). The Maharaja of Kochi had respect for the Jewish people, who were mainly merchants. He relied on them for external trade and contacts. In recognition of this relationship, he allowed a synagogue, which is still standing, to be built next to his palace. Syncretism is apparent in Kochi Jewish lifestyle, social structure, and rituals. Basic aspects of Judaism are retained, along with many aspects of Hindu practices.

Three aspects of syncretism with Hinduism are apparent in Passover, one of the most important annual rituals of the Jewish faith. First, the Western/European Passover celebration is typically joyous and a time of feasting. In contrast, the Kochi version has adopted a tone of austerity and is called "the fasting feast." Second, Kochi Passover allows no role for children, whereas, at a traditional Western/European ritual meal, or *seder* (say-der), children usually ask four questions as a starting point of the narrative. The adult Kochi Jews chant the questions in unison. (In Hinduism, children do not have solo roles in rituals.) Third, a Kochi seder stresses purity even more than standard Jewish requirements do. Standard rules about maintaining the purity of kosher wine usually mean that no gentile (non-Jew) should touch it. But Kochi Jews expand the rule to say that if the shelf or table on which the wine sits is touched by a gentile, the wine is impure. This extra level of "contagion" is influenced by Hindu concepts of pollution.

Christianity

Christianity has many ties with Judaism, from which it sprang. One of the strongest ties is the biblical teaching of a coming savior, or *messiah* (anointed one). Christianity began in the eastern Mediterranean in the second quarter of the first century (Cunningham 1995). Most of the early believers were Jews who took up the belief in Jesus Christ as the messiah who came to earth in fulfillment of prophesies contained in the Hebrew scriptures.

Today, Christianity is the largest of the world religions, with about 2 billion adherents, roughly one-third of the world's population. It is the majority religion of Australia, New Zealand, the Philippines, Papua New Guinea, most countries of Europe and of North and South America, and about a dozen southern African countries. Christianity is a minority religion throughout Asia, but Asian Christians constitute 16 percent of the world's Christians and are thus a significant population.

Christians accept the Bible (Old and New Testaments) as containing the basic teachings of their faith, believe that a supreme God sent His son to earth as a sacrifice for the welfare of humanity, and look to Jesus as the model to follow for moral guidance. The three largest branches of Christianity are Roman Catholic, Protestant, and Eastern Orthodox. Within each of these branches, various denominations exist. The greatest growth in Christianity is occurring in sub-Saharan Africa, India, Indonesia, and Eastern Europe.

PROTESTANTISM AMONG WHITE APPALACHIANS

Studies of Protestantism in Appalachia describe local traditions that outsiders who are accustomed to standard, urban versions may view as "deviant." For example, some churches in rural West Virginia and North Carolina, called Old Regulars, practice three obligatory rituals: footwashing, communion (a ritual commemorating the Last Supper that Jesus had with his disciples), and baptism (Dorgan 1989). The footwashing ceremony occurs once a year in conjunction with communion, usually as an extension of the Sunday service. An elder is called to the front of the church, and he preaches for 10 to 20 minutes. A round of handshaking and embracing follows. Two deaconesses then come forward to "prepare the table" by uncovering the sacramental elements placed there earlier under a white tablecloth. The elements are unleavened bread, serving plates for the bread, cups for the wine, and a decanter or quart jar or two of wine. The deacons break the bread into pieces and the moderator pours the wine into the cups. Men and women form separate groups as the deacons serve the bread and wine. The deacons serve each other, and then it is time for the footwashing.

The moderator begins by quoting from the New Testament (John 13:4): "He riseth from supper, and laid aside his garments; and he took a towel and girded himself." The moderator takes a towel and basin from the communion table, puts water in it, and selects a senior elder and removes his shoes and socks. The moderator washes his feet slowly and attentively. Other members come forward and take towels and basins and take turns washing others' feet and having their feet washed. Soon "the church is filled with crying, shouting, and praising as these highly poignant exchanges unleash a flood of emotions" (Dorgan 1989:106). A functional interpretation of the ritual of footwashing is that it helps maintain social cohesion.

Another feature of worship in some small Protestant churches in Appalachia, especially remote areas of rural West Virginia, involves the handling of poisonous snakes. This

(LEFT) The Vatican in Rome. The Vatican attracts more pilgrims/visitors each year than any religious site in the world. (RIGHT) In the nearby neighborhood, shops cater to pilgrims and tourists by offering a variety of religious and secular goods.

practice finds legitimation in the New Testament (Daugherty 1997 [1976]). According to a passage in Mark (16:15–18), "In my name shall they cast out devils; they shall speak with new tongues; they shall take up serpents; and if they drink any deadly thing, it shall not hurt them; they shall lay hands on the sick, and they shall recover." Members of "Holiness-type" churches believe that the handling of poisonous snakes is the supreme act of devotion to God. Biblical literalists, these people choose serpent handling as their way of celebrating life, death, and resurrection and of proving that only Jesus has the power to deliver them from death. Most serpent handlers have been bitten many times, but few have died.

One interpretation says that the risks of handling poisonous snakes mirror the risks of the environment. In Appalachia, unemployment rates are high and many people are economically poor. The structurist view (review Chapter 1) points to the fact that serpent handling increased when local people lost their land rights to big mining and forestry companies (Tidball and Toumey 2003:4). As their lives became more economically insecure, they turned to a way of increasing their sense of stability through a dramatic religious ritual. Outsiders might ask whether such dangerous ritual practices indicate that the people are disturbed. In fact, psychological tests indicate that members of Holiness churches are more emotionally healthy, on average, than members of mainline Protestant churches.

THE LAST SUPPER IN FIJI Among Christians in Fiji (Map 12.7), the image of the Last Supper is a dominant motif (Toren 1988). This scene, depicted on tapestry hangings, adorns most churches and many houses. People say, "Christ is the head of this household, he eats with us and

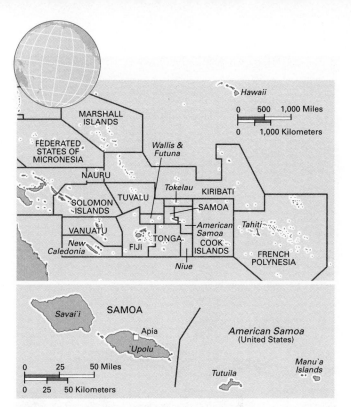

MAP 12.7 Samoa and American Samoa.
Samoa, or the Independent State of Samoa, was known as German Samoa (1900–1919) and Western Samoa (1914–1997) until recognized by the United Nations as a sovereign country. Its population is around 177,000. American Samoa, or Amerika Samoa in Samoan English, is a territory of the United States with a population of about 57,000. During World War II, U.S. Marines in American Samoa outnumbered the local population and had a strong cultural influence. Unemployment rates are high and the U.S. military is the largest employer.

A celebration of the Christian holy day of Palm Sunday in Port-au-Prince, Haiti. European colonialism brought African slaves to the New World and Christianity through missionary efforts. Many forms of Christianity are now firmly established in the Caribbean region.

▶ *Discover through a website or other source what the major Christian denominations in Haiti are.*

overhears us" (1988:697). The image's popularity is the result of its fit with Fijian notions of communal eating and kava drinking. Seating rules at such events place the people of highest status, such as the chief and others close to him, at the "above" side of the room, away from the entrance. Others sit at the "lower" end, facing the highly ranked people. Intermediate positions are located on either side of the person of honor, in ranked order.

Leonardo Da Vinci's fifteenth-century painting of the Last Supper places Jesus Christ in the position of a Fijian chief, with the disciples in an ordered arrangement around him. The disciples and the viewers "face" the chief and eat and drink together, as is appropriate in Fijian society. The positioning parallels the orderly placement of Fijian people around the kava as encountered "virtually every day in the village" (1988:706). This kind of cultural fit is a clear example of religious syncretism.

Islam

Islam is based on the teachings of the prophet Muhammad (570–632 CE) and is thus the youngest of the world religions

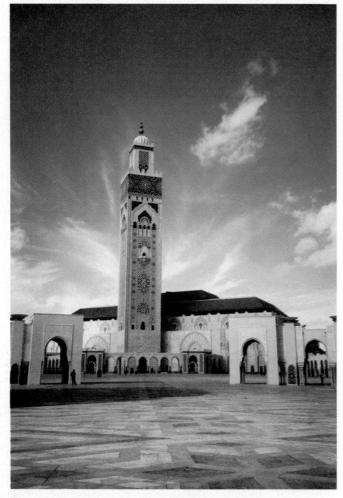

The Hassan II Mosque was built for the sixtieth birthday of Morocco's previous king, Hassan II. It is the second largest religious monument in the world, after Mecca, with space for 25,000 worshippers inside and another 80,000 outside. The minaret, 210 meters in height, is the tallest in the world.

(Martin 1995:498–513). The Arabic word *Islam* means "submission" to the will of the one god, Allah, through which peace will be achieved. Followers of Islam, known as Muslims, believe that Muhammad was God's final prophet. Islam has several denominations with essentially similar beliefs but also distinct theological and legal approaches. The two major schools of thought are Sunni and Shi'a. About 85 percent of the total Muslim population worldwide is Sunni, and about 15 percent is Shi'a. Sufism is a more mystical variant of Islam, with much smaller numbers of adherents. Many other subgroups exist. The Five Pillars of Islam are profession of faith in Allah, daily prayer, fasting, contributing alms for the poor, and the *Hajj* (pilgrimage to Mecca). The five pillars are central to Sunni Islam but less so to other branches of Islam, such as the Shi'as and the Sufis.

The total number of Muslims worldwide is about 1.4 billion, making it the second-largest religion with 22 percent of the world's population. Muslim-majority nations are located in northern Africa; the Middle East, including Afghanistan, Pakistan, and Bangladesh in South Asia; and several nations in Central Asia and Southeast Asia. Most of the world's Muslims (60 percent) live in South Asia or Southeast Asia. Muslims are minorities in many other countries, including China, where they seek to maintain their religious practices (see Culturama). Although Islam originally flourished among pastoralists, only 2 percent of its adherents are now in that category.

A common and inaccurate stereotype of Islam prevalent among many non-Muslims is that it is the same no matter where it exists. This erroneously monolithic model tends to be based on an image of conservative Wahhabist Islam as practiced in Saudi Arabia. But Wahhabist Islam is only one of many varieties of Islam.

A comparison of Islam in highland Sumatra (part of Indonesia in Southeast Asia) and Morocco (in North Africa) reveals differences that are the result of local cultural adaptations (Bowen 1992). Eid-ul-Adha (eed-ull-ah-dah), or the Feast of Sacrifice, is celebrated annually by Muslims around the world. It commemorates Ibrahim's willingness to sacrifice his son Ishmael (Isaac in the Christian tradition, Yitzhak in the Jewish) to Allah. It occurs on the tenth of the last month of the year, called Pilgrimage Month, and marks the end of the Hajj. The ritual reminds Muslims of their global unity within the Islamic faith. An important aspect of this ritual in Morocco (see Map 6.2, page 139) involves the king publicly plunging a dagger into a ram's throat, a reenactment of Muhammad's performance of the sacrifice on the same day in the seventh century. Each male head of household follows the pattern and sacrifices a ram. The size and virility of the ram are a measure of the man's power and virility. Other men of the household stand to witness the sacrifice, while women and children are absent or in the background. After the ram is killed, the men come forward and dab its blood on their faces. In some villages, women play a more prominent role before the sacrifice by daubing the ram with henna (red dye), thus sanctifying it, and using its blood afterward in rituals to protect the household. These state and household rituals are symbolic of male power in the public and private domains—the power of the monarchy and the power of patriarchy.

In Isak (ee-suk), Sumatra (see Map 8.3, page 190), the cultural context is less patriarchal and the political structure does not emphasize monarchy. Isak is a traditionalist Muslim village where people have been Muslims since the seventeenth century. They sacrifice many kinds of animals: chickens, ducks, sheep, goats, and water buffalo. The people believe that so long as the animal's throat is cut and the meat is eaten, the sacrifice satisfies God. Most sacrifices are family affairs and receive little public notice. They are done in the back of the house. Both women and men of the household refer to it as "their" sacrifice, and there are no signs of male dominance. Women may sponsor a sacrifice, as did one wealthy woman trader who sacrificed a buffalo. (The cutting was done by a man.)

CULTURAMA

Hui Muslims of Xi'an, China

The Hui (hway), one of China's largest designated minorities, number around 10 million people. Most live in the northwestern part of the country. The state classifies the Hui as "backward" and "feudal" in comparison to China's majority Han population. Hui residents of Xi'an (shee-ahn), however, reject the official characterization of them as less civilized and less modern than the Han majority (Gillette 2000).

About 60,000 Hui live in Xi'an, mainly in the so-called Old Muslim Quarter, which is dominated by small shops, restaurants, and mosques. The quality of housing and public services is inferior to that found elsewhere in the city. Parents worry that their children are not getting the best education and feel that the state is not providing adequate schooling in their neighborhood. Many Hui have taken steps to improve their houses themselves and to send their children to schools outside the district.

The Hui of Xi'an construct what they consider to be a modern and civilized lifestyle by choosing aspects of Muslim culture and Western culture.

Their form of "progress" is visible in many aspects of their daily life, such as eating habits, dress styles, housing, religious practices, education, and family organization.

Being Muslim in China poses several challenges in relation to the dominant Han culture. Diet is one prominent example. The Qur'an forbids four types of food to Muslims: animals that have not been consecrated to God and properly slaughtered, blood, pork, and alcohol (Gillette 2000:116). Three of the four rules apply to meat, and meat is the central part of a proper meal for Muslims. The Hui say that pork is especially impure. This belief differentiates the Hui clearly from other Chinese people, for whom pork is a major food item. Given the Hui belief that the kinds of food one eats affect a person's essence and behavior, they view pork eaters with disdain.

Hui residents consider alcohol even more impure than pork (Gillette 2000:167). Hui of Xi'an do not drink alcohol. They avoid using utensils that have touched alcohol and people who

are drinking it. Many Hui of Xi'an, however, make a living in the restaurant business, which caters to Chinese Han and foreign tourists. Although selling alcohol boosts business, many Hui object to it. Some community members say that restricting alcohol has improved the quality of life by making the neighborhood more peaceful and orderly.

In 2003, an urban development project in the Old Muslim Quarter was launched with financial support from the Norwegian government (*People's Daily* 2003). The project will widen the main street, replace "shabby" housing and infrastructure, and restore crumbling buildings of historic interest. A commercial area will be dedicated to restaurants serving Hui food in recognition of the touristic appeal of traditional Hui specialties such as baked beef and mutton, buns with beef, mutton pancake, and mutton soup. It is unclear where alcohol consumption will fit into this plan.

Thanks to Maris Boyd Gillette, Haverford College, for reviewing this material.

MAP 12.8 **The City of Xi'an in China.** Xi'an, the capital of Shaanxi province, is one of the most economically developed cities in

(LEFT) At a street stand in Xi'an, Hui men prepare a noodle dish. Like Muslim men in many parts of the world, they wear a white cap.

(CENTER) Hui women in Xi'an participate in a ritual that commemorates Hui people who died in a conflict that spread across northwestern China from 1862 to 1874.

The Moroccan ritual emphasizes fathers and sons, whereas the Isak ritual includes attention to a wider range of kin on both the husband's and wife's side, daughters as well as sons, and even dead relatives. In Isak, the ritual carries no centralized political meanings. The differences are not due to the fact that Moroccans know the scriptures better than Sumatrans do. The Isak area has many Islamic scholars who are familiar with the scriptures and regularly discuss them with each other. Rather, the two cultural contexts, including kinship and politics, shape the ritual to local realities.

African Religions

Many African religions are now global. In earlier centuries, they spread outside Africa through the coerced movement of people as slaves. African diaspora religions are especially prominent in the United States, the Caribbean region, and Central and South America. This section summarizes some key features of African religions and then offers two examples of African religions in the Western Hemisphere.

FEATURES OF AFRICAN RELIGIONS   With its diverse geography, cultural variation, and long history, Africa encompasses a wide range of religious affiliations, including many Muslims, Christians, Jews, Hindus, practitioners of indigenous religions, and people who follow some combination of these.

Indigenous African religions are difficult to typify, but some of their shared features are as follows:

- Myths about a rupture that once occurred between the creator deity and humans
- A pantheon that includes a high god and many secondary supernaturals ranging from powerful gods to lesser spirits
- Elaborate initiation rituals
- Rituals involving animal sacrifices and other offerings, meals, and dances
- Altars within shrines as focal places where humans and deities meet
- Close links with healing

Although these features are fairly constant, African religions are rethought and reshaped locally and over time, with complex and variable results (Gable 1995). In their home locations, they have been influenced by foreign religions, notably Islam and various types of Christianity. The outmigration of African peoples has brought African religions to new locations, where they have been localized and revitalized in their new contexts (Clarke 2004). Kamari Clarke's research on the Yorùbá (YOR-uh-buh) revivalist religion in the United States took her from New York City to South Carolina and Nigeria. The focal point of her fieldwork was in Óyótúnji Village near Beaufort, South Carolina (see Map 13.3, page 328). African American Yorùbá revivalists have created a place that

A sacred altar in a local African religion in Togo, West Africa.

▶ *Can you distinguish some of the ritual elements displayed here? Are some incomprehensible to you? How would an anthropologist begin to learn about the beliefs involved in this religion?*

reconstructs royal Yorùbá spiritual leadership and worship that helps some African Americans reconnect with their lost identity. In the words of Kamari Clarke, "Ritual initiations and rhythmic drumming echo in the endless hours of the night as residents remake their ancestral homeland outside the territory of Africa" (2004:51). The place, the rituals, and the music tie the people to Africa. Many Yorùbá-descent Americans, like other African Americans, go even further in their attempt to reconnect with their heritage. "Roots tourism" is a growing industry that provides culturally informed travel for African Americans to their places of ancestral origin in Africa.

Religious syncretisms in North and South America often combine aspects of Christianity with African traditions and elements of indigenous Indian beliefs and practices. Widely popular in Brazil are blended religions such as *umbanda*, *santería*, and *condomblé* that appeal to people of all social classes, urban and rural, especially for providing social support and alleviation of stress (Burdick 2004).

RAS TAFARI   Also called Rastafarianism, Ras Tafari is an Afro-Caribbean religion with its original roots in Jamaica. It is not known how many Rastafarians there are, because they refuse to be counted (Smith 1995:23). Ras Tafari is a protest religion that shares only a few of the features of the African religions just mentioned. It traces its history to several preachers of the early twentieth century who taught that Ras ("Prince") Tafari, then the Ethiopian emperor Haile Selassie,

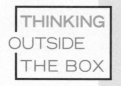

THINKING OUTSIDE THE BOX

Learn about Óyótúnji Village from the web. What goes on there? Do people live there? If you went to visit, where would you stay, what would you eat, and what would you do?

Bob Marley, legendary reggae artist and Rastafarian, performing at the Roxy Theater in Hollywood, California, in 1979. Marley died in 1981 at the age of 36, but he is still the most revered reggae musician. He launched the global spread of Jamaican music. Reggae is a genre of Jamaican music associated with Rastafarianism. Its songs address poverty, social injustice, love, and sexuality.

was the "Lion of Judah" who would lead Blacks to the African promised land.

Rastafarianism does not have an organized set of doctrines or written texts. Shared beliefs of the many diffuse groups in the Caribbean, the United States, and Europe include the belief that Ethiopia is heaven on earth, that Haile Selassie is a living god, and that all Blacks will be able to return to the homeland through his help. Since the death of Haile Selassie in 1975, more emphasis has been placed on pan-African unity and Black power, and less on Ethiopia.

Rastafarianism is particularly strong in Jamaica, where it is associated with reggae music, dreadlocks, and *ganja* (marijuana) smoking. Variations within the Rastafarian movement in Jamaica range from the belief that one must fight oppression to the position that living a peaceful life brings victory against evil.

◉ ◉ ◉

Directions of Religious Change

All religions have mythologies and doctrines that provide for continuity in their beliefs and practices. Yet no religion is frozen and unchanging. Cultural anthropologists have traced the resurgence of religions that seemed to be headed toward extinction through colonial forces, and they have documented the emergence of new religions. Likewise, they are observing the contemporary struggle of once-suppressed religions in socialist states to find a new position in the postsocialist world. Religious *icons* (images, pictures, or other forms of representation), once a prominent feature in Russian Orthodox churches, had been removed and placed in museums. The churches want them back.

Indigenous people's beliefs about the sacredness of their land are an important part of their attempts to protect their territory from encroachment and development by outside commercial interests. The world of religious change offers these examples, and far more, as windows into wider cultural change.

Revitalization Movements

Revitalization movements are religious movements that seek to bring about positive change through reestablishing a religion that has been threatened by outside forces or through adopting new practices and beliefs. These movements often arise in the context of rapid cultural change and appear to represent a way for people to try to make sense of their changing world and their place in it. One such movement that emerged as a response of Native Americans to the invasion of their land by Europeans and Euro-Americans was the Ghost Dance movement (Kehoe 1989). In the early 1870s, a shaman named Wodziwob of the Paiute (pie-yoot) tribe in California declared that the world would soon be destroyed and then renewed: Native Americans, plants, and animals would come back to life. He instructed people to perform a circle dance, known as the Ghost Dance, at night.

The movement spread to other tribes in California, Oregon, and Idaho but ended when the prophet died and his prophecy was unfulfilled. A similar movement emerged in 1890, led by another Paiute prophet, Wovoka, who had a

---

revitalization movement a socioreligious movement, usually organized by a prophetic leader, that seeks to construct a more satisfying situation by reviving all or parts of a religion that has been threatened by outside forces or by adopting new practices and beliefs.

A Ghost Dance shirt of the Arapaho Indians of the U.S. Plains region, with painted designs of birds, turtle, and stars. These specially decorated garments were believed to protect the wearer from the White man's bullets.

vision during a total eclipse. His message was the same: destruction, renewal, and the need to perform circle dances in anticipation of the impending event. The dance spread widely and had various effects. Among the Pawnee, it provided the basis for a cultural revival of old ceremonies that had fallen into disuse. The Sioux altered Wovoka's message and adopted a more overtly hostile stance toward the government and White people. Newspapers began to carry stories about the "messiah craze," referring to Wovoka. Ultimately, the government took action against the Sioux, killing Chief Sitting Bull and Chief Big Foot and about 300 Sioux at Wounded Knee. In the 1970s, the Ghost Dance was revived again by the American Indian Movement, an activist organization that seeks to advance Native American rights.

Cargo cults are a type of revitalization movement that emerged throughout Melanesia in response to Western influences. Most prominent in the first half of the nineteenth century, cargo cult behavior emphasized the acquisition of Western trade goods, or *cargo* in local terms. Typically, a prophetic leader emerged with a vision of how the cargo will

---

cargo cult   a form of revitalization movement that emerged in Melanesia in response to Western and Japanese influences.

arrive. In one instance, the leader predicted that a ship would come, bringing not only cargo but also the people's dead ancestors. Followers set up tables for the expected guests, complete with flower arrangements.

Later, after World War II and the islanders' experiences of aircraft arrivals bringing cargo, the mode of anticipated arrival changed to planes. Once again, people would wait expectantly for the arrival of the plane. Cargo cults emerged as a response to the disruptive effects of new goods being suddenly introduced into indigenous settings. The outsiders imposed a new form of exchange system that emphasized the importance of Western goods and suppressed the importance of indigenous valuables such as shells and pigs. This transformation undermined traditional patterns of gaining status through the exchange of indigenous goods. Cargo cult leaders sought help, in the only way they knew, in obtaining Western goods so that they could acquire social status in the new system.

Contested Sacred Sites

Religious conflict often becomes focused on sacred sites. One place of recurrent conflict is Jerusalem, where many religions and sects within religions compete for control of sacred terrain. Three major religions claim that they have primary rights: Islam, Judaism, and Christianity. Among the Christians, several different sects vie for control of the Church of the Holy Sepulchre (see Map 12.6, page 299). In India, frequent conflicts over sacred sites occur between Hindus and Muslims. Hindus claim that Muslim mosques have been built on sites sacred to Hindus. On some occasions, the Hindus have destroyed the mosques. Many conflicts that involve secular issues surrounding sacred sites also exist worldwide. In the United States, White racists

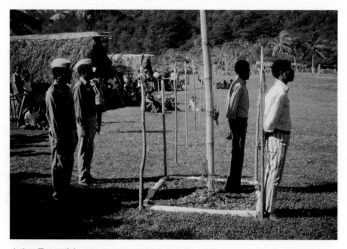

John Frum Movement supporters stand guard around one of the cult's flagpoles at Sulphur Bay village, on Tanna Island, Vanuatu, in the region of Melanesia. The movement is an example of a cargo cult.

▶ *Do Internet research on John Frum.*

After the Chinese takeover of Tibet, many Tibetans became refugees, including the revered head of Tibetan Buddhism, the Dalai Lama. Buddhism, founded in India as a protest against Hinduism, is a minority religion in its homeland. It has millions of followers elsewhere, from Scotland to San Francisco.

have burned African American churches. In Israel, some Jewish leaders object to archaeological research because they believe that the ancient Jewish burial places should remain undisturbed.

A similar situation exists among indigenous populations in the Western Hemisphere. Their sacred sites and burial grounds have often been destroyed for the sake of urban growth, petroleum and mineral extraction, and recreational sports. Resistance to such destruction is growing, with indigenous people finding creative ways to protect, restore, and manage their heritage.

Religious Freedom as a Human Right

According to a United Nations Declaration, freedom from religious persecution is a universal human right. Yet violations of this right by countries and by competing religions are common. Sometimes people who are persecuted on religious grounds can seek and obtain sanctuary in other places or nations. Thousands of Tibetan Buddhist refugees, including their leader, the Dalai Lama, fled Tibet after it was taken over by the Chinese. Many Tibetan communities have been established in exile in India, the United States, and Canada, where the Tibetan people attempt to keep their religion, language, and heritage alive.

The post-9/11 policy enactments in the United States related to its campaign against terrorism are seen by many as dangerous steps against constitutional principles of personal liberty—specifically, as infringements on the religious rights of practicing Muslims. The prevalent mentality in the U.S. government, and in much of the general populace, links the whole of Islam with terrorism and thereby stigmatizes all Muslims as potential terrorists. Several anthropologists (for example, Mamdani 2002) have spoken out against the inaccuracy and indecency of labeling an entire religion dangerous and putting all its members under the shadow of suspicion.

Religions are often the focal point of conflict and dissension and sometimes a source of conflict resolution. As an integral part of the heritage of humanity, religions are best understood within a cross-cultural and contextualized perspective. Such an understanding is essential for building a more peaceful future.

What is religion and what are the basic features of religions?

Early cultural anthropologists defined religion in contrast to magic and suggested that religion was a more evolved form of thinking about the supernatural realm. They collected information on religions of non-Western cultures and constructed theories about the origin and functions of religion. Since then, ethnographers have described many religious systems and documented a rich variety of beliefs, forms of ritual behavior, and types of religious specialists. Beliefs are expressed in either myth or doctrine and often are concerned with defining the roles and characteristics of supernatural beings and how humans should relate to them.

Religious beliefs are enacted in rituals that are periodic or nonperiodic. Some common rituals worldwide are life-cycle rites, pilgrimage, rituals of inversion, and sacrifice. Rituals are transformative for the participants.

Many rituals require the involvement of a trained religious specialist, such as a shaman/shamanka or priest/priestess. Compared with the situation in states, religious specialist roles in nonstate contexts are fewer, less than full time, and less formalized, and they carry less secular power. In states, religious specialists are often organized into hierarchies, and many specialists gain substantial secular power.

How do world religions illustrate globalization and localization?

The so-called world religions are based on texts and generally agreed-on teachings and beliefs shared by many people around the world. In order of historic age, the five longstanding world religions are Hinduism, Buddhism, Judaism, Christianity, and Islam. Christianity has the largest number of adherents, with Islam second and Hinduism third. Due to accelerated global population migration in the past few centuries, many formerly local religions now have a worldwide membership. Because of Western colonialism and slavery, African religions are prominent in the Western Hemisphere, with a variety of syncretistic religions attracting many adherents.

As members of the world religions have moved around the globe, religious beliefs and practices have become contextualized into localized variants. When a new religion moves into a culture, it may be blended with local systems (syncretism), may coexist with indigenous religions in a pluralistic fashion, or may take over and obliterate the original beliefs.

What are some important aspects of religious change in contemporary times?

Religious movements of the past two centuries have often been prompted by colonialism and other forms of social contact. In some instances, indigenous religious leaders and cults have arisen in an attempt to resist unwanted outside forces of change. In other cases, they evolve as ways of incorporating selected outside elements. Revitalization movements, such as the Ghost Dance movement in the U.S. Plains region, look to the past and attempt to recover lost and suppressed religious beliefs and practices.

Issues of contemporary importance include the increasing amount of conflict surrounding sacred sites, hostilities related to the effects of secular power interests on religious institutions and spaces, and religious freedom as a human right.

KEY CONCEPTS

animatism, p. 286
cargo cult, p. 306
doctrine, p. 284
life-cycle ritual, p. 288
magic, p. 284
myth, p. 284

pilgrimage, p. 291
priest or **priestess,** p. 292
religion, p. 284
religious pluralism, p. 294
religious syncretism, p. 294
revitalization movement, p. 305

ritual, p. 288
ritual of inversion, p. 291
sacrifice, p. 292
world religion, p. 292

SUGGESTED READINGS

Paulo Apolito. *The Internet and the Madonna: Religious Visionary Experience on the Web*. Antony Shugaar, trans. Chicago: University of Chicago Press, 2003. This book traces the Christian cult of Mary as it has developed and grown through the medium of the World Wide Web.

Janet Bennion. *Desert Patriarchy: Mormon and Mennonite Communities in the Chihuahua Valley*. Tucson: University of Arizona Press, 2004. The ethnographer, raised in a Mormon family, reports on her fieldwork among Mormons in a desert region in Mexico.

John Bowen. *Can Islam Be French? Pluralism and Pragmatism in a Secular State*. Princeton: Princeton University Press, 2009. Bowen provides an ethnographic perspective on the French approach to Islam among French Muslims.

Karen McCarthy Brown. *Mama Lola: A Vodou Priestess in Brooklyn*. Berkeley: University of California Press, 1991. This life story of Mama Lola, a voodoo practitioner, is set within an ethnographic study of a Haitian community of New York City.

Timothy Daniels. *Islamic Spectrum in Java*. Burlington, VT: Ashgate Publishing Company, 2010. Fieldwork in Yogyakarta, the capital city of Java, Indonesia, reveals the wide variety of Islamic practices and movements there.

Sondra L. Hausner. *Wandering with Sadhus: Ascetics in the Hindu Himalayas*. Bloomington: Indiana University Press, 2008. This ethnographic study explores the interactions of Hindu ascetics in northern India with ordinary households and considers how these believers are part of the public community.

Klara Bonsack Kelley and Harris Francis. *Navajo Sacred Places*. Bloomington: Indiana University Press, 1994. The authors report on the results of a research project undertaken to learn about Navajo cultural resources, especially sacred sites, and the stories associated with them in order to help protect these places.

Melvin Konner. *Unsettled: An Anthropology of the Jews*. New York: Penguin Compass, 2003. A biological anthropologist is the author of this cultural history of the Jewish people and their religion. It extends from the origins of Judaism among pastoralists in the Middle East through enslavement in the Roman Empire, to the Holocaust and the creation of Israel.

J. David Lewis-Williams and D. G. Pearce. *San Spirituality: Roots, Expression, and Social Consequences*. New York: AltaMira Press, 2004. This book examines the interplay of cosmology, myth, ritual, and art among the San people of southern Africa.

Charlene Makley. *The Violence of Liberation: Gender and Tibetan Buddhist Revival in Post-Mao China*. Berkeley: University of California Press, 2007. Makley combines archival research with fieldwork in a Buddhist monastery in Tibet. She describes the incorporation of the region of Labrang into China.

Todd Sanders. *Beyond Bodies: Rainmaking and Sense Making in Tanzania*. Toronto: University of Toronto Press, 2008. This study of rainmaking rituals among the Inhanzu of central Tanzania reveals ideas about gender roles and relations.

Maureen Trudelle Schwarz. *Blood and Voice: Navajo Women Ceremonial Practitioners*. Tucson: University of Arizona Press, 2003. Contemporary Navajo women are increasingly taking on the ritual role of ceremonial Singer, formerly the domain of men. This book describes how women gain sacred knowledge.

Stephen Selka. *Religion and the Politics of Ethnic Identity in Bahia, Brazil*. Gainesville: University Press of Florida, 2008. This study shows how Catholicism, evangelical Protestantism, and the traditional Brazilian religion of Candomblé shape the discourse of race and identity in northeastern Brazil.

Katharine L. Wiegele. *Investing in Miracles: El Shaddai and the Transformation of Popular Catholicism in the Philippines*. Honolulu: University of Hawai'i Press, 2005. This book examines the widespread popularity in the Philippines of Brother Mike, a charismatic businessman who became a Catholic preacher using mass media to spread his message of economic prosperity.

PEARSON
myanthrolab

For further information about topics covered in this chapter, go to MyAnthroLab at **www.myanthrolab.com** and access the following readings in MyAnthroLibrary:

Julie Adkins. 2010. Helping the Homeless in Dallas: Lessons and Challenges from a Faith-Based Nonprofit. *Practicing Anthropology* 32:11–16. This article considers the role of a Presbyterian church in advocating for the homeless poor.

David Geary. 2008. Destination Enlightenment: Branding Buddhism and Spiritual Tourism in Bodhgaya, India. *Anthropology Today* 24(3):11–14. In 2002, the Mahabodhi Temple in northern India, where Buddha attained enlightenment, was declared a World Heritage Site. Since then, commercialization has brought new complexities in terms of managing and conserving a living place of worship in the face of increasing numbers of tourists.

Holly Wissler. 2009. Grief-Singing and the Camera: The Challenges and Ethics of Documentary Production in an Indigenous Andean Community. *Ethnomusicology Forum* 18(1):37–53. This article discusses the ethical challenges of making a documentary about Quechua musical rituals.

Soutar, Louise. 2010. British Female Converts to Islam: Choosing Islam as a Rejection of Individualism. *Language and Intercultural Communication* 10:3–16. The author, though not a cultural anthropologist, uses three in-depth interviews to reveal motivations of White British women who convert to Islam.

◉ How is culture
expressed
through art?

◉ What do play and
leisure activities reveal
about culture?

◉ How is expressive
culture changing in
contemporary times?

EXPRESSIVE CULTURE

◀ Colombia's singer Shakira holds
the football that will be used for
the final game of the 2010 World
Cup tournament in South Africa.
She stands next to the official
2010 mascot, Zakumi. This was
the first World Cup tournament
held in Africa. In the end, two
European teams vied for
the prize.

13

This chapter considers a vast area of human behavior and thought called **expressive culture**, or behavior and beliefs related to art, leisure, and play. (Definitions of these terms are provided later.) It begins with a discussion of theoretical perspectives on cross-cultural art and how anthropologists study art and expressive culture. The second section considers the topics of play and leisure cross-culturally. The last section provides examples of change in expressive culture.

◎ ◎ ◎

Art and Culture

Compared with the definition of art and how to study the subject as presented in art history classes you may have taken, the approach of cultural anthropologists is rather different. Their findings, here as in other cultural domains, stretch and subvert Western concepts and categories and prompt us to look at art within its context. Thus, anthropologists consider many kinds of products, practices, and processes to be art. They also study the artist and the artist's place in society. In addition, they ask questions about how art, and expressive culture more generally, is related to microcultural variation, inequality, and power. They question how cross-cultural art is to be selected and put on display in museums.

What Is Art?

Are ancient rock carvings art? Is subway graffiti art? An embroidered robe? A painting of a can of Campbell's soup? Philosophers, art critics, anthropologists, and art lovers have all struggled with the question *What is art?* The issue of how to define art involves more than mere word games. The way art is defined affects the manner in which a person values and treats artistic creations and those who create art (see Critical Thinking).

Anthropologists propose broad definitions of art to take into account emic definitions cross-culturally. One definition says that **art** is the application of imagination, skill, and style to matter, movement, and sound that goes beyond the purely practical (Nanda 1994:383). Such imagination, skill, and style can be applied to many substances and activities, and the product can be considered art—for example, a beautifully presented meal, a well-told story, or a perfectly formed basket. In this sense, art is a human universal, and no culture can be said to lack artistic activity completely. The Pirahã of the Brazilian Amazon, however, appear to have very little visual art, but they do have verbal art (review Chapter 11).

In addition to studying the art product itself, anthropologists pay attention to the process of making art, variations in art and its preferred forms cross-culturally, and the way culture constructs and changes artistic traditions. They also consider various categories of art. Within the general category of art, subcategories exist, sometimes denoting eras, such as Paleolithic or modern art. Other subcategories are based on the medium of expression, such as graphic or plastic arts (painting, drawing, sculpture, weaving, basketry, and architecture); decorative arts (interior design, landscaping, gardens, costume design, and body adornment such as hairstyles, tattooing, and painting); performance arts (music, dance, and theater); and verbal arts (poetry, writing, rhetoric, and telling stories and jokes). A long-standing distinction in the Western view exists between *fine art* and *folk art*. This distinction is based on a Western-centric judgment that defines fine art as rare, expensive art produced by artists usually trained in the Western classical tradition. This is the kind of art that is included in college courses called "Fine Arts." The implication is that all other art is less than fine and is more appropriately called folk art, ethnic art, primitive art, or crafts. Characteristics of Western fine art are as follows: The product is created by a formally schooled artist, it is made for sale on the market, it is clearly associated with a particular artist, its uniqueness is valued, and it is not primarily utilitarian but is rather "art for art's sake." In contrast, all the rest of the world's art that is non-Western and nonclassical is supposedly characterized by the opposite features:

Painting walls has a long heritage, going back at least to prehistoric cave paintings discovered in Europe and Australia. (LEFT) Graffiti in New York City in the 1980s. (CENTER) A mural in west Belfast, Northern Ireland, where the Irish Republican Army and its opponents frequently expressed their views in large wall paintings. (RIGHT) Albetina Mahalangu paints a wall with Ndebele designs in South Africa.

Probably every reader of this book, at one time or another, has looked at an object in an art museum or in an art book or magazine and exclaimed, "But that's not art!" As a critical thinking research project on "What is art?" visit two museums, either in person or on the Internet. One of these should be a museum of either fine art or modern art. The other should be a museum of natural history. In the former, examine at least five items on display. In the latter, examine several items on display that have to do with human cultures (that is, skip the bugs and rocks).

Take notes on all the items that you are examining. Then answer the following questions.

CRITICAL THINKING QUESTIONS ▼
• What is the object?

• What contextual explanation does the museum provide about the object?
• Was the object intended as a work of art or as something else?
• In your opinion, is it art or not, and why or why not?
• Compare your notes on the objects in the two types of museums. What do your notes tell you about categories of art?

• It is created by an artist who has not received formal training.
• It is not produced for the market.
• The artist is anonymous and does not sign or individually claim the product.
• It is made primarily for everyday use, such as food procurement, processing, or storage; in ritual; or in war.

A closer examination of these two categories is in order. All cultures have art, and all cultures have a sense of what makes something art versus non-art. The term *esthetics* refers to socially accepted notions of quality (Thompson 1971). Before anthropologists proved otherwise, Western art experts believed that esthetics either did not exist or was poorly developed in non-Western cultures. We now know that esthetic principles, or established criteria for artistic quality, exist everywhere, whether or not they are written down and formalized. **Ethno-esthetics** refers to culturally specific definitions of what art is.

The standards for wood carving in West Africa illustrate the importance of considering cross-cultural variation in the criteria for art (Thompson 1971). Among the Yorúbà (YOR-uh-buh) of Nigeria, esthetic guidelines for wood carving include these:

• Figures should be depicted midway between complete abstraction and complete realism so that they resemble "somebody," but no one in particular. Portraiture in the Western sense is considered dangerous.
• Humans should be depicted at their optimal physical peak, not in infancy or old age.
• Line and form should have clarity.
• The sculpture should have the quality of luminosity achieved through a polished surface and the play of incisions and shadows.
• The piece should exhibit symmetry.

Yorúbà wood carving follows esthetic principles that require clarity of line and form, a polished surface that creates a play of light and shadows, symmetry, and the depiction of human figures that are neither completely abstract nor completely realistic.

▶ Have you seen African sculptures that follow these principles? Visit an African art museum on the Web for further exploration.

Some anthropological studies have documented intracultural differences in esthetic standards, as well as cross-cultural variation. For example, an anthropologist showed

---

expressive culture   behaviors and beliefs related to art, leisure, and play.

art   the application of imagination, skill, and style to matter, movement, and sound that goes beyond what is purely practical.

ethno-esthetics   culturally specific definitions of what art is.

computer-generated graphics to the Shipibo (shih-PEE-bo) Indians of the Peruvian Amazon and learned that the men liked the abstract designs whereas the women thought they were ugly (Roe, cited in Anderson and Field 1993). If you are wondering why this difference would exist, consider the interpretation of the anthropologist: Shipibo men are the shamans and take hallucinogenic drugs that may give them familiarity with more "psychedelic"/abstract images.

Studying Art in Society

The anthropological study of art seeks to understand not only the products of art but also who makes it and why, the role of art in society, and its wider social meanings. Franz Boas was the first anthropologist to emphasize the importance of studying the artist in society. Functionalism (review Chapter 1) was the most important theory informing anthropological research on art in the first half of the twentieth century. Anthropologists wrote about how paintings, dance, theater, and songs serve to socialize children into the culture, provide a sense of social identity and group boundaries, and promote healing. Art may legitimize political leaders and enhance efforts in war through body painting, adornment, and magical decorations on shields and weapons. Art may also serve as a form of social control, as in African masks worn by dancers who represent deities visiting humans to remind them of the moral order. Art, like language, can be a catalyst for political resistance or a rallying point for ethnic solidarity in the face of oppression.

The anthropology of art relies on a range of methods in data gathering and analysis. The basic method is participant observation, supplemented by collecting and analyzing oral or written material such as video and tape recordings. Thus, strong ties often exist between cultural and linguistic anthropologists in the study of art.

Many anthropologists have become apprentices in an artistic tradition. For John Chernoff, learning to play African drums was an important part of building rapport during his fieldwork in Ghana and an essential aspect of his ability to gain an understanding of the importance of music in Ghanaian society (1979). His book, *African Rhythm and African Sensibility*, takes into account the position and role of the ethnographer and how it shapes what the ethnographer learns. Reading the book's introduction will convince you that fieldwork in cultural anthropology is far more than simply gathering the data you think you need for the project you have in mind, especially if your project concerns processes of creativity and expression.

Chernoff argues that only by relinquishing a scientific approach can a researcher learn about creativity and how it is related to society. As one of his drumming teachers said, "The heart sees before the eyes." Chernoff had to do more than practice participant observation. His heart had to participate,

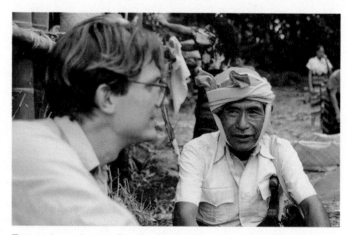

Expressive culture in Sumba, Indonesia. (TOP) A woman weaves ikat (ih-kut) cloth on a bamboo loom. Ikat is a style of weaving that uses a tie-dye process on either the warp or weft before the threads are woven. The process will create a design in the final product. Double ikat is when both warp and weft threads are tie-dyed before weaving. The motif on this piece of ikat is the Tree of Life flanked by roosters. (BOTTOM) Linguistic anthropologist Joel Kuipers interviews a ritual speaker who is adept at verbal arts performance.

▶ What is a form of verbal art in your culture?

too. During his early months in the field, Chernoff often found himself wondering why he was there. To write a book? To tell people back in the United States about Ghana? No doubt, many of the Ghanaians he met wondered the same thing, especially given that his early efforts at drumming were pretty bad, although he did not realize it because he always drank copious amounts of gin before playing. Eventually, he became the student of a master drummer and went through a formal initiation ceremony. For the ceremony, he had to kill two chickens himself and eat parts of them in a form that most North Americans will never see in a grocery store. Still he was not playing well enough. He went through another ritual to make his wrist "smart" so that it would turn faster, like a cat chasing a mouse. For that ritual, he had to go into the bush, 10 miles outside town, and collect ingredients. The ritual worked. Having a cat's hand was a good thing, but anthropologically it was more important to Chernoff that he had begun to gain an understanding of drumming in its social and ritual contexts.

Chernoff learned about Ghanaian family life and how it is connected to individual performers and to rituals that have to do with music. He also grew to see where his performance fell short and what he needed to do to improve. He gained great respect for the artists who taught him and admiration for their striving for respect. Chernoff's personality was an important ingredient of the learning process. He comments, "I assumed that I did not know what to do in most situations. I accepted what people told me about myself and what I should be doing. . . . I waited to see what people would make of me. . . . By staying cool I learned the meaning of character" (1979:170).

FOCUS ON THE ARTIST In the early twentieth century, Franz Boas urged his students to go beyond the study of the products of art and study the artists. One goal of the anthropologist, he said, is to study art from the artist's perspective. Ruth Bunzel's (1972 [1929]) research with Native American potters in the U.S. Southwest is a classic example of this focus. While undergoing training as an apprentice potter, she asked individual potters about their choices for pot designs. One Zuni (zoo-nee) potter commented, "I always know the whole design before I start to paint" (1972:49). A Laguna potter said, "I learned this design from my mother. I learned most of my designs from my mother" (1972:52). Bunzel discovered the importance of both individual agency and following tradition.

The social status of artists is another aspect of the focus on the artist. Artists may be revered and wealthy as individuals or as a group, or they may be stigmatized and economically marginal. In ancient Mexico, goldworkers were highly respected. In American Indian groups of the Pacific Northwest coast, male carvers and painters had to be initiated into a secret society, and they had higher status than other men. Often a gender division exists. Among the Navajo of Arizona, women weave and men do silversmithing. In the Caribbean, women of African descent are noted for their carvings of calabashes (large gourds). In the contemporary United States, most famous and successful graphic artists are men, although the profession includes many women. Depending on the genre, "race"/ethnicity/indigeneity is another factor shaping success as an artist.

As with other occupations, the performing arts are more specialized in state-level societies. Generally, among free-ranging foragers, little specialization exists. Artistic activity is

Rap star LL Cool J hosts and performs at Wet Republic Ultra Pool grand opening day at MGM Grand Resort in Las Vegas, Nevada.

▶ *Do your parents or grandparents know who LL Cool J is?*

open to all, and artistic products are shared equally by all. Some people may be especially appreciated as singers, storytellers, or carvers. With increasing social complexity and a market for art, specialized training is required to produce certain kinds of art, and the products are sought after by those who can afford them. Class differences in artistic styles and preferences emerge along with the increasingly complex division of labor.

MICROCULTURES, ART, AND POWER Art forms and styles, like language, are often associated with microcultural groups' identity and sense of pride. For example, the Berbers of highland Morocco are associated with woolen carpets, Maya Indians with woven and embroidered blouses, and the Inuit of Alaska with stone carvings of figurines. Cultural anthropologists provide many examples of linkages between various microcultural dimensions and power issues. In some instances, more powerful groups appropriate the art forms of less powerful groups. In others, forms of art are said to be expressive of resistance. One study reveals how nationalist interests in Israel result in co-opting Arab art and handicrafts (see Everyday Anthropology).

An example of how gender relations play out in expressive culture comes from a study of male strip dancing in Florida (Margolis and Arnold 1993). Advertisements in the media tell women that seeing a male strip dancer is "their chance," "their night out." Going to a male strip show is marketed as a time of reversal of traditional gender roles in which men are dominant and women submissive. Are gender roles actually reversed in a male stripper bar? The short answer is no. Women customers are treated like juveniles. As they stand in line waiting for the show to open, the manager instructs them on how to tip. They are symbolically dominated by the dancers, who take on various roles such as lion tamers. The *dive-bomb* is further evidence of women's subordinate position. The dive-bomb is a form of tipping the dancer in which the woman customer gets on her hands and knees and tucks a bill held between her teeth into the dancer's g-string. The interpretation of all this behavior is that, rather than reversing the gender hierarchy, it reinforces it.

Not all forms of popular art and performance are mechanisms of social control and maintenance of hierarchies. In the United States, for example, hip-hop and urban Black youths' verbal arts and rap music can be seen as a form of protest through performance (Smitherman 1997). Their lyrics report on their experience of economic oppression, the danger of drugs, and men's disrespect for women. The global spread of hip-hop and related music is another example of social resistance through song and performance.

Performance Arts

The performance arts include music, dance, theater, rhetoric (speechmaking), and narrative (storytelling). One important

If you were doing an ethnographic study of gender roles in musical performance, the following questions would be useful in starting the inquiry. But they would not exhaust the topic. Can you think of questions that should be added to the list?

1. Are men and women equally encouraged to use certain instruments and repertoires?
2. Is musical training available to all?
3. Do male and female repertoires overlap? If so, how, when, and for what reasons?
4. Are the performances of men and women public, private, or both? Are women and men allowed to perform together? In what circumstances?
5. Do members of the culture give equal value to the performances of men and women? On what criteria are these evaluations based, and are they the same for men and women performers?

Source: From "Power and Gender in the Musical Experiences of Women" by Carol E. Robertson, pp. 224–225 in *Women and Music in Cross-Cultural Perspective*, ed. by Ellen Koskoff. Copyright © 1987. Reprinted by permission of the Greenwood Publishing Group, Inc. Westport, CT.

FIGURE 13.1 Five Ethnographic Questions about Gender and Music.

area has developed its own name: **ethnomusicology**, the cross-cultural study of music. Ethnomusicologists study a range of topics, including the form of the music itself, the social position of musicians, how music interacts with other domains of culture such as religion or healing, and change in musical traditions. This section provides examples about music and gender in Malaysia, music and globalization in Brazil, and theater and society in India.

MUSIC AND GENDER AMONG THE TEMIAR OF MALAYSIA An important topic for ethnomusicologists is gender differences in access to performance roles in music. (For ideas about research on this topic, see Figure 13.1.) A cultural materialist perspective would predict that in cultures where gender roles are quite egalitarian, access to and meanings in music will also be egalitarian for males and females. This is the case among the Temiar (tem-ee-yar), foragers of the highlands of peninsular Malaysia (see Map 8.3, page 190). Their musical traditions emphasize balance and complementarity between males and females (Roseman 1987).

Among the Temiar, kinship and marriage rules are flexible and open. Marriages are based on the mutual desires of the partners. Descent is bilineal (review Chapter 8), and marital residence follows no particular rule after a period of bride service. Marriages often end in separation, and serial monogamy is common. Men, however, do have a slight edge over women in political and ritual spheres. They are typically the village leaders, and they are the spirit mediums who sing the songs that energize the spirits.

---

ethnomusicology the cross-cultural study of music.

everyday ANTHROPOLOGY

The Invisible Hands That Craft Souvenirs

Tourists who buy arts and crafts souvenirs rarely learn much about the people who actually made the items. Yet they probably have some mental image of, for example, a village potter sitting at the wheel or a silversmith hammering at a piece of metal in a quaint workshop.

Souvenir shops come in different varieties, from street stalls that sell a few items such as embroidered clothing or "ethnic" jewelry to national emporiums that offer a wide range of arts and crafts.

An upscale store of the latter category in Israel, called Maskit, caters mainly to tourists (Shenhav-Keller 1993:183). Ethnographic study shows how the sellers "put Israeli society on display via its souvenirs." It also reveals how certain artists and craftspeople are selectively rendered invisible.

The tourist artifact, or souvenir, can be analyzed like a "text" that contains social messages. In the Maskit stores, three central themes in Israeli society are expressed in the choice and presentation of souvenirs: Israel's attitudes toward its ancient and recent past, its view of its religion and culture, and its approach to Arab Israelis and Palestinians.

Shelly Shenhav-Keller (1993) conducted participant observation in the original Maskit store in Tel Aviv and interviewed Jewish Israeli, Arab Israeli, and Palestinian artists and artisans whose products were sold there.

Maskit was founded by Ruth Dayan (then the wife of Moshe Dayan) as a Ministry of Labor project in 1954. Its purpose was "to encourage artisans to continue their native crafts in the new surrounding . . . to retain and safeguard the ancient crafts" (Shenhav-Keller 1983:183). Maskit was a success, and a chain of shops was eventually opened. As its status increased, Maskit came to be perceived as an "ambassador of Israel." Dignitaries who traveled from Israel abroad

An embroidered Palestinian dress.

were loaded with gifts from the shop. Official visitors to Israel were given Maskit gifts.

The shop had two floors. The top floor, where the entrance was located, had five sections: fashion (women's clothing, wedding gowns, and dresses with three different styles of Arab embroidery); jewelry; ritual articles (candlesticks, goblets, incense burners); decorative items; and books. The larger lower floor had five thematic sections: the Bar-Mitzvah Corner with prayer books and other ritual items; the children's corner (clothing, games, toys, and T-shirts); the embroidery section (tablecloths, linens, pillow covers, wallets, eyeglass cases); the carpet section; and a large area for ceramics, glassware, and copperware.

Over the years, changes have occurred in who produces the art sold in Maskit. The amount of Jewish ethnic art has declined as older artists have aged and their children have not taken up the craft. Many of the original Jewish Israeli artists gained eminence and opened their own shops. Those who continue to supply Maskit specialize in ceramics, jewelry, carpet design, and

ritual articles. These pieces are considered to have the status of art and may be displayed as an "individual collection" within the store. To make up for the decline in objects made by Jewish Israelis, Maskit has turned to Arab artists and craftsmakers.

After the 1967 Six-Day War, Arab Israeli and Palestinian craftsmanship became increasingly available with the incorporation of new areas within Israel, including the Occupied Territories. Most of the Arabs absorbed into the souvenir industry became hired laborers in factories and workshops owned by Maskit or by Israeli artisans who sold their works to Maskit as "Israeli." Maskit provides no information about the artistic role of Israeli Arabs or Palestinians in creating its products. The carpets, for example, are presented simply as hand-woven "Israeli" carpets, even though Arab Israelis wove them.

FOOD FOR THOUGHT ▼

Do you know of another example in which something attributed to one ethnic group or culture is actually produced by people of a different group?

Although the spirits enter the community through male singers, the male spirit-medium role is not of greater importance or status than a woman's performance role in singing choruses. The singing of the male spirit medium and the female chorus is blurred through overlap between phrases and repetition. The performance is one of general community participation, with integrated male and female roles, as in Temiar society in general.

COUNTRY MUSIC AND GLOBALIZATION IN BRAZIL

Linguistic anthropologist Alexander Dent studies the growing popularity of *música sertaneja* (MOO-see-kah ser-tah-NAY-shah), Brazilian country music (2005). Música sertaneja draws heavily on U.S. country music, but it is significantly localized within Brazilian contexts. Brazilian performers creatively use North American country music songs, such as "Achy Breaky Heart," to convey messages about gender relationships, intimacy, the family, the past, and the importance of the countryside that make sense in the Brazilian context. In their performances and recordings, they use an American genre to critique American-driven processes such as extreme capitalism and globalization and to critique the Brazilian adoption of such Western ways.

A prominent feature of Brazilian country music is performance by a *dupla* (doo-plah), or two "brothers," who may or may not be biological brothers. They emphasize their similarity by cutting their hair the same way and wearing similar clothes. Musically, they blend their voices, with neither voice dominating the other. When performing, they sing part of a song with their arms over each other's shoulders and gaze at each other affectionately. The *dupla* and their music emphasize kinship and caring as important aspects of Brazilian tradition that should be preserved.

THEATER AND MYTH IN SOUTH INDIA

Theater is a type of enactment that seeks to entertain through movement and through words related to dance, music, parades, competitive games and sports, and verbal art (Beeman 1993). Cross-culturally, strong connections exist among myth, ritual, and performance.

One theatrical tradition that offers a blend of mythology, acting, and music is the Kathakali (kuh-tuh-kal-lee) ritual dance-drama of southern India (Zarrilli 1990). Stylized hand gestures, elaborate makeup, and costumes contribute to the attraction of these performances, which dramatize India's great Hindu epics, especially the *Mahabharata* (review Chapter 12) and the *Ramayana*. Costumes and makeup transform the actor into one of several well-known characters from Indian mythology. The audience easily recognizes the basic character types at their first entrance by the performers'

(LEFT) Many forms of theater combine the use of facial makeup, masks, and costumes to transform an actor into someone (or something) else. This Kathakali dancer is applying makeup before a performance in Kerala, South India. (RIGHT) A new use for classical dance-drama in India is for raising social awareness about problems such as excessive dowries and female infanticide. Street theater groups go into neighborhoods and act out skits, drawing members of the audience into dialogue with them.

costumes and makeup. Six types of makeup exist to depict characters ranging from the most refined to the most vulgar. Kings and heroes have green facial makeup, reflecting their refinement and moral uprightness. Vulgar characters are associated with black facial makeup and occasionally black beards. With their black faces dotted with red and white, they are the most frightening of the Kathakali characters.

Architecture and Decorative Arts

Like all art forms, architecture is interwoven with other aspects of culture. Architecture may reflect and protect social rank and class differences, as well as gender, age, and ethnic differences (Guidoni 1987). Decorative arts—including interior decoration of homes and buildings, and external design features such as gardens—likewise reflect people's social position and "taste." Local cultures have long defined preferred standards in these areas of expression, but global influences from the West and elsewhere, such as Japan and other non-Western cultures, have been adopted and adapted by other traditions.

ARCHITECTURE AND INTERIOR DESIGN Foragers, being highly mobile, build dwellings as needed and then abandon them. (Refer to Photo of Ju/'hoansi shelter on page 85.) Having few personal possessions and no surplus goods, they need no permanent storage structures. The construction of dwellings does not require the efforts of groups larger than the family unit. Foragers' dwellings are an image of the family and not of the wider society. The dwellings' positioning in relation to each other reflects the relations among families.

More elaborate shelters and greater social cohesiveness in planning occur as foraging is combined with horticulture, as in the semipermanent settlements of the Amazon rainforest. People live in the settlement part of the year but break into smaller groups that spread out into a larger area for foraging. Important decisions concern how the site will fare with respect to the weather, the availability of drinking water, and defensibility. The central plaza must be elevated for drainage and drainage channels dug around the hearths. The overall plan is circular. In some groups, separate shelters are built for extended family groups; in others, they are joined into a continuous circle with connected roofs. In some cases, the headman has a separate and larger shelter.

Pastoralists have designed ingenious portable structures, such as the North American teepee and the Mongolian *ger*, or yert. The teepee is a conical tent made with a framework of four wooden poles tied at the top with thongs, to which are joined other poles to complete the cone. This frame is then covered with buffalo hide. A ger is also a circular, portable dwelling, but its roof is flatter. The covering is made of cloth. This lightweight structure is easy to set up, take down, and transport, and it is adaptable to all weather conditions. Encampments are often arranged around the teepees or gers in several concentric circles. Social status was the structuring principle, and the council of chiefs and the head chief were located in the center.

With the development of the state, urban areas grew and showed the effects of centralized planning and power, for example, in grid-style planning of streets rather than haphazard placement. The symbolic demonstration of the power, grandeur, and identity of states was and is expressed architecturally through the construction of impressive urban monuments: temples, administrative buildings, memorials, and museums.

Interior decoration of domestic dwellings also became more elaborate. In settled agricultural communities and urban centers, where permanent housing is the norm, decoration is more likely to be found in homes. Wall paintings, sculptures, and other features distinguish the homes of wealthier individuals. Research on interior decoration in contemporary Japan involved studying the contents of home-decorating magazines and doing participant observation within homes (Rosenberger 1992). Findings reveal how people incorporate and localize selected aspects of Western decorating styles.

Home-decorating magazines target middle- and upper-class Japanese housewives who seek to express their status through new consumption styles. A trend is the abandonment of three features of traditional Japanese design: *tatami*, *shoji*, and *fusuma*. Tatami are 2-inch-thick mats that are about 3 feet wide and 6 feet long. A room's size is measured in terms of the number of tatami it holds. Shoji are the sliding screen doors of tatami rooms; one door is covered with glass and the other with translucent rice paper often printed with a design of leaves or waves. Fusuma are sliding wall panels made of thick paper; they are removable so that rooms can be enlarged for gatherings. The tatami room usually contains a low table in the center, with pillows for seating on the floor. A special alcove may contain a flower arrangement, ancestors' pictures, and a Buddhist altar. Futons are stored in closets around the edges and brought out at night for sleeping.

In distancing themselves from the old style, "modern" Japanese housewives make several changes. The kitchen has a central rather than marginal location and is merged with a space called the DK (dining-kitchen) or LDK (living-dining-kitchen), with wood, tile, or carpeting on the floor. Western products such as carpeting and curtains (instead of the fusuma, the tatami, and shoji) are used to cover surfaces and to separate rooms. The LDK has a couch, a dining set, a VCR, a stereo, and an array of small items on display, such as Western-style teapots, cuckoo clocks, and knickknacks.

---

theater   a form of enactment, related to other forms such as dance, music, parades, competitive games and sports, and verbal art, that seeks to entertain through acting, movement, and sound.

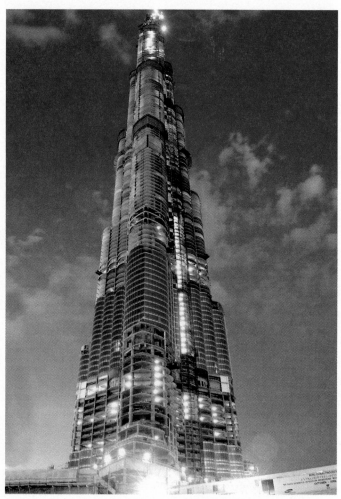

In the politics of architecture, size often matters. (LEFT) The Duomo in Florence, Italy. The Duomo, or Cathedral of Santa Maria del Fiore, was begun in 1296. Its massive dome, designed by architect and sculptor Filippo Brunelleschi, was not completed until 1436. The goal was to surpass all other edifices in height and beauty. The Duomo still physically dominates the city of Florence and also attracts many tourists from around the world. (RIGHT) Burj Dubai, or Dubai Tower, in Dubai, United Arab Emirates, is currently the tallest building in the world. Its immense height signals the importance of Dubai in the modern world and, more generally, the success and prosperity of the Middle East.

These design choices accompany deeper social changes that involve new aspirations about marriage and family relationships. Home-decorating magazines promote the idea that the modern style brings with it happier children who earn better grades and closer husband–wife ties. Tensions exist, however, between these ideals and the realities of middle- and upper-class life in Japan. Women feel compelled to work either part time or full time to be able to contribute income for satisfying their new consumer needs in spite of societal pressure against careers and for devoting more time to domestic pursuits. Children are in the conflicting position of being indulged as new consumer targets even as the traditional

value of self-discipline still holds. Husbands are in the conflicting position of needing to be more attentive to wife and home, whereas the corporate world calls them for a "7–11" working day. Last, the Western image of the happy nuclear family contains no plan for the aged. Only the wealthiest Japanese families manage to satisfy both individualistic desires and filial duties because they can afford a large house in which they dedicate a separate floor for the husband's parents, complete with tatami mats. Less wealthy people have a more difficult time caring for their aged parents.

GARDENS AND FLOWERS   Gardens for use, especially for food production, are differentiated from gardens for decorative purposes. The concept of the decorative garden is not a cultural universal. Circumpolar peoples cannot construct gardens in the snow, and highly mobile pastoralists have no gardens because they are on the move. The decorative garden is a product of state-level societies, especially in the Middle East,

heterotopia   something formed from elements drawn from multiple and diverse contexts.

museum   an institution that collects, preserves, interprets, and displays objects on a regular basis.

Europe, and Asia (Goody 1993). Within these contexts, variation exists in what are considered to be the appropriate contents and designs for gardens. A Japanese garden may contain no blooming flowers, focusing instead on the shape and placement of trees, shrubs, stones, and bodies of water.

Elite Muslim culture, with its core in the Middle East, has long been associated with formal decorative gardens. The Islamic garden pattern involves a square design with a symmetrical layout, fountains, waterways, and straight pathways, all enclosed within walls. A garden, enclosed with four walls, is symbolically equivalent to the concept of paradise. Islamic gardens often surround the tombs of prominent people. India's Taj Mahal, built by a Muslim emperor, follows this pattern, with one modification: The tomb is placed at one edge of the garden rather than in the center. The result is a dramatic stretch of fountains and flowers leading from the main gate to the monument.

The contents of a personal garden, like a dinner menu with all its special ingredients or a collection of souvenirs from around the world with all their memories and meanings, make a statement about its owner's identity and status. For example, in Europe during the height of colonialism, imperial gardens contained specimens from remote corners of the globe, collected through scientific expeditions. Such gardens were created through the collection and placement of plants from many parts of the world and are thus examples of what the French cultural theorist Michel Foucault refers to as a **heterotopia**, or something formed from elements drawn from multiple and diverse contexts (Foucault 1970). Heterotopias can be constructed in architecture, cuisine, dress, and more. In the case of the colonial European gardens, the heterotopic message conveyed the owner's worldliness and intellectual status.

Cut flowers are now important economic products. They provide income for gardeners throughout the world, and they are also exchange items. In France, women receive flowers from men more than any other kind of gift (Goody 1993:316). In much of the world, special occasions require gifts of flowers: In the West, as well as in East Asia, funerals are times for displays of flowers. Ritual offerings to the deities in Hinduism are often flowers such as marigolds woven into a chain or necklace.

Flowers are prominent motifs in Western and Asian secular and sacred art, but less so in African art (Goody 1993). Some possible reasons for this variation include ecological and economic factors. Eurasia's more temperate environment possesses a greater variety of blooming plants than Africa's does. Also, sheer economic necessity in developing countries of Africa limits the amount of space that can be used for decorative purposes. In wealthy African kingdoms, prominent luxury goods include fabrics, gold ornaments, and wooden carvings rather than flowers. This pattern of production is changing with globalization, and many African countries now grow flowers for export to the world market.

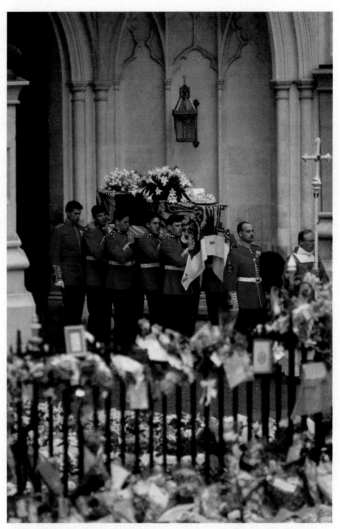

Say it with flowers. Guardsmen of the Prince of Wales Company of the Welsh Guards carry the casket out of Westminster Abbey following the funeral of Diana, Princess of Wales.

Museums and Culture

This section considers the concept of the museum and the debates about the role of museums in exhibiting and representing culture. Museum studies, in anthropology, includes anthropologists who work in museums helping to prepare exhibits and anthropologists who study museums—what they choose to display and how they display it—as important sites of culture itself.

WHAT IS A MUSEUM?   A **museum** is an institution that collects, preserves, interprets, and displays objects on a regular basis (Kahn 1995:324). Its purpose may be esthetic or

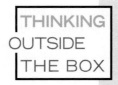

THINKING OUTSIDE THE BOX

Think of some occasions in your cultural world in which cut flowers are important. What role do they play?

(LEFT) A display of African artifacts collected by British colonial-era explorers and early anthropologists, shown with minimal labels, at the Powell-Cotton Museum in Kent, southeast England. This museum is moving toward exhibits that provide more context while preserving some of its "colonialist" exhibits as examples of their time. (RIGHT) In Port Blair, the Andaman Islands, the Anthropological Museum is a small building containing some artifacts, but mainly photographs of the indigenous people. The so-called Jarawa, shown here, are the most well-known and feared group for their false reputation as being cannibals. The Jarawa photographs are the museum's main attraction.

educational. The idea of gathering and displaying objects goes back at least to the babylonian kings of the sixth century BCE who ruled in what is now Iraq (Maybury-Lewis 1997a). The word comes from a Greek word referring to a place where the *muses* (spirits who inspire thought and creativity) congregate, or a place to have philosophical discussions or see artistic performances. In Europe, it came to denote a place where art objects were housed and displayed. Ethnographic and science museums came later, inspired by Europe's emerging interests in exploration in the 1500s and the accompanying scientific urge to gather specimens from around the world and classify them into an evolutionary history.

The Western concept of the museum and its several forms diffused throughout the world through colonialism. Many museums in developing countries still bear a strong colonial imprint and fail to connect with local people's interests (Fogelman 2008). In spite of these problems, such museums play an important role in preserving aspects of culture that would otherwise have been lost forever. A recent program through the European Economic Community (EEC) supports the remodeling and expansion of national museums throughout Africa. In 2008, the revamped Kenya National Museum, funded by the EEC, opened with great fanfare. Its prominent attractions include original fossils of early hominins and a garden displaying healing plants found in the country, organized by species and providing information on their uses.

THE POLITICS OF EXHIBITS Within anthropology, the subfield of *museum anthropology* is concerned with studying how and why museums choose to collect and display particular objects (Ames 1992, Jones 1993). Museum anthropologists are at the forefront of debates about who gets to represent whom, the ownership of particular objects, and the public-service role of museums versus possible elitism. One issue is whether objects from non-Western cultures should be exhibited, like western art objects, with little or no ethnographic context (Clifford 1988, Watson 1997).

Most anthropologists support the need for context, and not just for non-Western objects but for all objects on display. For example, a museum label of Andy Warhol's hyperrealistic painting of a can of Campbell's soup should include information on the social context in which such art was produced and some background on the artist. The anthropological view that all forms of expressive culture are context bound and are better understood and appreciated within their social context is, however, still rare among Western art historians and critics (Best 1986).

Another contentious issue concerns who should have control of objects in museums that were acquired through colonialism and neocolonialism. The issue of **repatriation**, or returning objects to their original peoples, is a matter of international and intranational concern. In the United States and Canada, many Native American groups have lobbied successfully for the return of ancestral bones, grave goods, and potlatch goods. In 1990, the United States passed the *Native American Graves Protection and Repatriation Act* (*NAGRPA*) after two decades of lobbying by Native American groups (Bray 1996; Rose, Green, and Green 1996). This act requires universities, museums, and federal agencies in the United States to inventory their archaeological holdings in preparation for repatriating skeletons to their Native American descendant communities. Estimates of the number of Native American skeletons in museums in the United States (not

---

repatriation   returning art or other objects from museums to the people with whom they originated.

MAP 13.1 Ukraine.

Ukraine became independent after the collapse of the Soviet Union in 1991. It is mostly fertile plains, or steppes, crossed by rivers. Since independence and privatization, the economy has been unstable, with high inflation rates. Related to the economic crisis, sex trafficking of women became a major problem, infant mortality rates rose, and the birth rate fell. The total population is around 50 million and declining. Ukrainian is the official language, though many people speak Russian, especially in the south and east. Many people speak a mixture of both languages. Government policy promotes the increased use of the Ukrainian language. The dominant religion is Eastern Orthodox Christianity. The tradition of coloring Easter eggs began in Ukraine in pre-Christian times.

including Hawai'i) range from 14,000 to 600,000. Unknown numbers of other items are being inventoried for possible repatriation, a process that is stretching slender museum budgets (Watson 1997).

The breakup of the former Soviet Union prompted claims from several newly independent states seeking to retrieve artistic property that originated in their locale and had been taken to Soviet national museums in Moscow and St. Petersburg. Ukraine, for example (Map 13.1), has asked for the return of about 2 million art objects from Russia (Akinsha 1992a).

Another disputed area about art in Russia concerns the state and the church. The Soviet state put many icons (images of the Christian deities, Mary, and Jesus) and other religious objects in museums and turned churches into museums. The Russian Orthodox Church has campaigned for the return of church property. Churches ask that all sacred objects of the church, church buildings, and masterpieces of church art confiscated by the state after 1917 be returned to the ownership of the Russian Orthodox Church (Akinsha 1992b). Art historians and museum officials worry that the churches lack the resources and the experience to care for these treasures. Another complication comes from occasional threats of theft and violence to museums by those who seek the return of icons to churches and monasteries. In response, some museums have removed certain pieces from display.

◙ ◙ ◙

Play, Leisure, and Culture

This section turns to the area of expressive culture related to what people do for "fun." It is impossible to draw a clear line between the concepts of *play* or *leisure* and art or performance, however, because they often overlap. For example, a person could paint watercolors in her leisure time, yet simultaneously be creating a work of art. In most cases, though, play and leisure can be distinguished from other activities (Huizinga, as summarized in Hutter 1996). In the case of play:

- it is an unnecessary activity
- it serves no direct utilitarian purpose for the participants
- it is limited in terms of time
- it has rules
- it may contain chance and tension

Leisure activities often overlap with play, but many leisure activities, such as reading or lying on a beach, would not be considered play because they lack rules, chance, and tension. Within the broad category of play and leisure activities, several subcategories exist, including varieties of games, hobbies, and recreational travel. Although play and leisure, as well as their subcategories, may be pursued from a nonutilitarian perspective, they are often situated in a wider context of commercial and political interests. Major international competitions are examples of such complexities. South Africa's hosting of the 2010 World Cup soccer games was an opportunity for it to demonstrate its position as a world leader. At the same time, the major advertising sponsors for the events were big-name American companies such as McDonald's, Coco-Cola, and Budweiser.

Cultural anthropologists study play and leisure within their cultural contexts as part of social systems. They ask, for example, why some leisure activities involve teams

South Africa hosts the 2010 World Cup. (TOP) The South African tradition of blowing the vuvuzela (voo-voo-zell-uh) prompted heated debate during the 2010 World Cup games. The French team said the noise distracted them, causing them to lose. No matter what, the vuvuzela gained instant global fame. (BOTTOM) The influences of global capitalism are apparent at the Cape Town Stadium.

rather than individuals; what the social roles and statuses of people involved in particular activities are; what the goals of the games are and how those goals are achieved; how much

wa a Japanese word meaning discipline and self-sacrifice for the good of the group.

blood sport a competition that explicitly seeks to bring about a flow of blood from, or even the death of, human–human contestants, human–animal contestants, or animal–animal contestants.

danger or violence is involved; how certain activities are related to group identity; and how such activities link or separate different groups within or between societies or countries.

Games and Sports as a Cultural Microcosm

Games and sports, like religious rituals and festivals, can be interpreted as reflections of social relationships and cultural ideals. In Clifford Geertz's terms, they are both *models of a culture*, depicting basic ideals, and *models for a culture*, socializing people into certain values and ideals (1996). American football can be seen as a model for corporate culture in its clear hierarchy with leadership vested in one person (the quarterback) and its goal of territorial expansion by taking over areas from the competition.

A comparison of baseball as played in the United States and in Japan reveals core values about social relationships in each country (Whiting 1979). The differences emerge clearly when U.S. players are hired by Japanese teams. The U.S. players bring with them an intense sense of individualism, which promotes the value of "doing your own thing." This pattern conflicts with a primary value that influences the playing style in Japan: **wa**, meaning discipline and self-sacrifice for the good of the group. In Japanese baseball, players must seek to achieve and maintain team harmony. Japanese baseball players have a negative view of extremely individualistic, egotistical plays and strategies.

SPORTS AND SPIRITUALITY: MALE WRESTLING IN INDIA In many contexts, sports are closely tied to religion and spirituality. Asian martial arts, for example, require

Wrestlers in a village in northern India. They follow a rigorous regimen of dietary restrictions and exercise in order to keep their bodies and minds under control.

▶ *Think of another sport that emphasizes dietary restrictions.*

forms of concentration much like meditation, leading to spiritual self-control. Male wrestling in India, a popular form of entertainment at rural fairs and other public events, involves a strong link with spiritual development and asceticism (Alter 1992).

In some ways, these wrestlers are just like other members of Indian society. They go to work, and they marry and have families, but their dedication to wrestling involves important differences. A wrestler's daily routine is one of self-discipline. Every act—defecation, bathing, comportment, devotion—is integrated into a daily regimen of discipline. Wrestlers come to the *akhara* (AKH-uh-ruh), equivalent to a gymnasium, early in the morning for practice under the supervision of a guru or other senior akhara member. They practice moves with different partners for two to three hours. In the early evening, they return for more exercise. In all, a strong young wrestler will do around 2000 push-ups and 1000 deep-knee bends a day in sets of 50 to 100.

The wrestler's diet is strictly defined. Most wrestlers are mainly vegetarian. Although they avoid alcohol and tobacco, they do consume *bhang*, a beverage made of blended milk, spices, almonds, and concentrated marijuana. In addition to regular meals, wrestlers consume large quantities of milk, ghee (clarified butter), and almonds. These substances are sources of strength because, according to traditional dietary principles, they help to build up the body's semen.

Several aspects of the wrestler's life are similar to those of a Hindu *sannyasi* (sun-YAH-see) or holy man, who renounces life in the normal world. The aspiring sannyasi studies under a guru and learns to follow a strict routine of discipline and meditation called yoga, and he adheres to a restricted diet to achieve control of the body and its life force. Both wrestler and sannyasi roles focus on discipline to achieve a controlled self. Therefore, in India, wrestling does not involve the "dumb jock" stereotype that it sometimes does in North America. Rather, wrestlers have respect because their sport requires perfected physical, spiritual, and moral health.

PLAY, PLEASURE, AND PAIN Many leisure activities combine pleasure and pain. Serious injuries can result from mountain climbing, horseback riding, or playing touch football in the backyard. A more intentionally dangerous category of sports is **blood sports**, competitions that explicitly seek to bring about a flow of blood or even death. Blood sports may involve human contestants, humans contesting against animal competitors, or animals or birds fighting other animals or birds (Donlon 1990). In the United States and Europe, professional boxing is an example of a popular blood sport that few, if any, anthropologists have studied so far. Cultural anthropologists have looked at the use of animals in blood sports such as cockfights and bullfights.

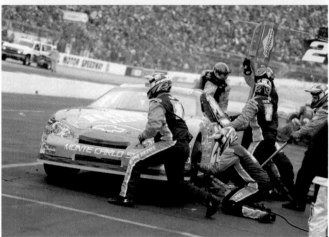

Two of the many male-dominated sports worldwide. (TOP) Laotians attend a cockfight on the outskirts of Vientiane, capital of the Lao People's Democratic Republic. Officials of the World Health Organization are concerned that this sport may be one cause of the spread of avian or bird flu in Southeast Asia. (BOTTOM) Tony Stewart, driver of the No. 20 Home Depot Chevrolet, makes a pit stop during the NASCAR NEXTEL Cup Series at Bristol Motor Speedway in Tennessee.

These sports are variously interpreted as providing sadistic pleasure, as offering vicarious self-validation (usually of males) through the triumph of their representative pit bulls or fighting cocks, and as the triumph of culture over nature in the symbolism of bullfighting.

Even the seemingly pleasurable leisure experience of a Turkish bath can involve discomfort and pain. One phase involves scrubbing the skin vigorously several times with a rough natural sponge, a pumice stone, or a piece of corkwood wrapped in cloth (Staats 1994). The scrubbing removes layers

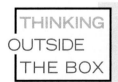

THINKING OUTSIDE THE BOX

In your cultural world, what are some examples of leisure activities that combine pleasure and pain?

of dead skin and opens the pores so that the skin will be beautiful. In Turkey, an option for men is a massage that can be quite violent, involving deep probes of leg muscles, cracking of the back, and being walked on by the often weighty masseur. In Ukraine, being struck repeatedly on one's bare skin with birch branches is the final stage of the bath. Violent scrubbing, scraping, and beating of the skin, along with radical temperature changes in the water, are combined with valued social interaction at the bathhouse.

Leisure Travel

Anthropologists who study leisure travel, or tourism, often comment that their research is dismissed as trivial and based on "hanging out" at beautiful beaches or at five-star hotels. Research on tourism, however, is just as challenging as the anthropological study of any other topic.

Tourism is one of the major economic forces in the world, and it has dramatic effects on people and places in tourist destination areas. A large percentage of worldwide tourism involves individuals from Europe, North America, and Japan traveling to less industrialized countries. Ethnic tourism, cultural tourism, and ecotourism are attracting increasing numbers of travelers. They are often marketed as providing a view of "authentic" cultures. Images of indigenous people figure prominently in travel brochures and advertisements (Bruner 2005).

Tourist promotional literature often presents a "myth" of other peoples and places and offers travel as a form of escape

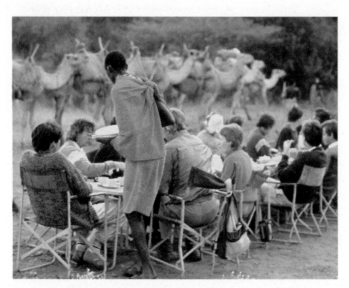

Many international tourists seek "cultural tourism" so that they can participate in what is presented to them as "authentic." Safari tour groups in Africa, as in this visit to Maasailand, combine sightings of exotic wildlife and contact with Maasai people.

▶ Go to the Web to learn about cultural tourism opportunities among the Maasai.

to a mythical land of wonder. Research on Western travel literature shows that, from the time of the earliest explorers to the present, it has been full of *primitivist* images about indigenous peoples who are portrayed as having static or "stone age" traditions, largely unchanged by the forces of Western colonialism, nationalism, economic development, and even tourism. Tourists often seek to find the culture that the tourist industry defines rather than gaining a genuine, more complicated, and perhaps less photogenic view of it. For the tourist, obtaining these desired cultural images through mass tourism involves packaging the "primitive" with the "modern" because most tourists want comfort and convenience along with their "authentic" experience. Thus, advertisements minimize the foreignness of the host country, noting, for example, that English is spoken and that the destination is remote, yet accessible, while simultaneously promoting primitivist and racist imagery.

The tensions involved in accurately presenting a cultural experience, sensationalism, and social stigma emerge clearly in research on tourism in the coal-mining region of Appalachia in Virginia (LaLone 2003). Mary LaLone pinpoints some of the challenges that arise in representing Appalachian culture with accuracy and dignity while at the same time responding to marketing demands of tourists. For example, in portraying people's everyday lives, accuracy says that it is right to show people wearing shoes and using indoor plumbing, whereas tourists may expect and want to see displays of "hillbilly life" that emphasize poverty, shoelessness, outhouses, feuding, and "moonshining" (producing and consuming illicit alcohol). LaLone suggests that cultural anthropologists can help find a way toward the interpretation and presentation of a region's heritage that provides a more complex view so that hosts retain their dignity, accuracy is maintained, and tourists learn more than they expected.

The anthropology of tourism has focused on the impact of global and local tourism on indigenous peoples and places. Such studies are important in exposing the degree to which tourism helps or harms local people and local ecosystems. For example, the formation of Amboseli National Park in Kenya prevented Maasai herders from accessing traditional water resources (Drake 1991). The project staff promised benefits (such as shares of the revenues from the park) to the Maasai if they stayed off the reserve, but most of the benefits never materialized. In contrast, in Costa Rica, local people were included in the early planning stages of the Guanacaste National Park (Map 13.2), and now they play a greater role in the park management system and share in some of the benefits.

Local people with long-standing rights to land, water, and other resources often attempt to exercise agency and take an active role in transforming the effects of tourism to their advantage, designing and managing tourist projects

High-end tourism in Costa Rica.

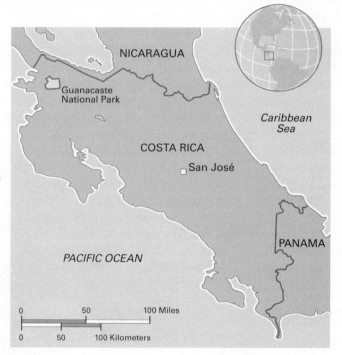

MAP 13.2 Costa Rica.

The Republic of Costa Rica was the first country in the world to constitutionally abolish its army, and it has largely escaped the violence that its neighbors have endured. Agriculture is the basis of the economy, with tourism—especially ecotourism—playing an increasing role. Most of the 4 million inhabitants of Costa Rica are descended from Spanish colonialists. Less than 3 percent are Afro-Costa Ricans, and less than 2 percent, or around 50,000, are indigenous people. Seventy-five percent of the people are Roman Catholic and 14 percent Protestant. The official language is Spanish.

(Natcher, Davis, and Hickey 2005; Miller 2009). The Gullah people of South Carolina are one such example (see Culturama on page 328). The last section of this chapter provides others.

Change in Expressive Culture

Nowhere are forms and patterns of expressive culture frozen in time. Much change is influenced by Western culture through globalization, but influence does not occur in only one direction. African musical styles have transformed the U.S. musical scene since the days of slavery. Japan has exerted a strong influence on upper-class garden styles in the United States. Cultures in which tradition and conformity have been valued in pottery making, dress, or theater find themselves having to make choices about whether to innovate and, if so, how. Many contemporary artists (including musicians and playwrights) from Latin America to China are fusing ancient and "traditional" motifs and styles with more contemporary themes and messages.

Changes occur through the use of new materials and technology and through the incorporation of new ideas, tastes, and meanings. These changes often accompany other aspects of social change, such as colonialism, global tourism, or political transitions.

Colonialism and Syncretism

Western colonialism had dramatic effects on the expressive culture of indigenous peoples. In some instances, colonial disapproval of particular art forms and activities resulted in their extinction. For example, when colonialists banned headhunting in various cultures, the change also meant that body decoration, weapon decoration, and other related expressive activities were abandoned. This section provides an example of how colonial repression of indigenous forms succeeded, but only temporarily.

In the Trobriand Islands of Papua New Guinea (see Culturama, Chapter 3, page 59), British administrators and missionaries sought to eradicate the frequent tribal warfare as part of a pacification process. One strategy was to replace it with intertribal competitive sports (Leach 1975). In 1903, a British missionary introduced the British game of cricket in the Trobriands as a way of promoting a new morality, separate from the warring traditions. As played in England, cricket involves particular rules of play and a proper look of pure white uniforms. In the early stages of the adoption of cricket in the Trobriands, the game followed the British pattern closely. As time passed and the game spread into more parts of the islands, it developed localized and syncretized versions.

Throughout the Trobriands, the islanders merged cricket into indigenous political competition between bigmen (Foster 2006). Big-men leaders urged their followers to increase production in anticipation of a cricket match because matches were followed by a redistributive feast. (Review the discussion of moka in Chapter 10.) The British

CULTURAMA

The Gullah of South Carolina

The Gullah (goo-luh) culture in South Carolina stretches along the coast, going inland about 30 miles (National Park Service 2005). The Gullah are descended from African slaves originating in West and Central Africa. In the early eighteenth century, Charleston, South Carolina, was the location of the largest slave market in British North America.

The enslaved people brought with them many forms of knowledge and practice. Rice was a central part of their African heritage and identity. They knew how to plant it in swamps, harvest it, and prepare it. Gullah ancestors in colonial South Carolina were influential in developing tidal irrigation methods of rice growing, using irrigation and management of the tides to increase yields compared with yields from rainfall-dependent plantings.

Experts at net fishing, the Gullah made handwoven nets that are masterpieces of folk art. Their textile arts include a form of quilting, or sewing strips of cloth together into a larger piece. Gullah women combined their African quilting styles with those of Europeans to form new styles and patterns. Many quilts tell a story in their several panels.

Gullah cuisine combines African elements such as rice, yams, peas, okra, hot peppers, peanuts, watermelon, and sesame seeds with European ingredients and with American Indian foods such as corn, squash, tomatoes, and berries (National Park Service 2005). Popular dishes are stews of seafood and vegetables served over rice. Rice is the cornerstone of the meal, and the family rice pot is a treasured possession passed down over the generations.

Gullah culture in South Carolina has become a major tourist attraction, including music, crafts, and cuisine. If there is a single item that tourists identify with the Gullah, it is sweetgrass baskets. Basketmaking, once common among all Gullah people in South Carolina, is now a specialized activity. In South Carolina, it is thriving in the Charleston area largely through a combination of tourist demand and the creativity of local artists. Both men and women "sew" the baskets. They sell them in shops in Charleston's historic center and along Highway 17.

As the success of the basketmakers has grown and the popularity of the baskets increased, so too, has the need for sweetgrass. Sweetgrass baskets thus are a focal point of conflict between Gullah cultural producers and local economic developers who are destroying the land on which the sweetgrass grows. Because tourism in low-country South Carolina is increasingly dependent on cultural tourism, some planners are trying to find ways to devote land to growing sweetgrass.

The story of the Gullah of South Carolina begins with their rich African cultural heritage, through their suffering as slaves, to racism and social exclusion, and to their current situation in which their expressive culture is a key factor in the state economy.

(LEFT) The hands of Charleston artist Mary Jackson are shown making a sweetgrass basket.

(CENTER) Drummers at the Gullah Festival in Beaufort (BO-fert). The Festival celebrates the culture and accomplishments of the Gullah people.

MAP 13.3 **The Gullah Region of South Carolina.** The heartland of Gullah culture is in the low-country areas of South Carolina, Georgia, and Florida, and on the Sea Islands.

In the Trobriand Islands, British missionaries tried in the late nineteenth century to substitute their game of cricket for intertribal rivalries and warfare. It did not take long, however, for the Trobriand people to transform British rules and style to Trobriand ways.

▶ *If you wanted to watch a cricket match, what would be the closest place for you to go?*

missionaries discouraged traditional magic in favor of Christian beliefs, but the Trobriand Islanders brought war-related magic into cricket. For example, they used spells against opposing teams, and they decorated bats like war weapons. Weather magic was important, too. If things were not going well, a ritual specialist might use a spell to bring rain and force cancellation of the game.

Over time, the Trobrianders stopped wearing the crisp white uniforms and instead painted their bodies and adorned themselves with feathers and shells. The teams announced their entry into the host village with songs and dances, praising their team in contrast to the opposition. Syncretism is notable in team songs and dances, which draw on Western elements. An example is the famous entry song of the "P-K" team. (P-K is the name of a Western chewing gum.) The P-K team chose its name because the stickiness of gum is like the ability of their bat to hit the ball. Other teams incorporated sounds and motions of airplanes, objects that they first saw during World War II. The songs and dances were explicitly sexual and enjoyed by all, in spite of Christian missionary attempts to suppress the "immoral" aspects of Trobriand culture, which included sexual metaphors in songs about large yams and thrusting hip movements of the dancers among other things.

The Trobrianders also changed some of the rules of play. The home team should always win, but not by too many runs. In this way, guests show respect to the hosts. Winning is not the major goal. The feast after the match is the climax, in which hosts demonstrate their generosity to their guests, establishing the requirement for the next match and feast.

Tourism's Complex Effects

Global tourism has had varied effects on indigenous arts. Often, tourist demand for ethnic arts and souvenirs has led to the mass production of sculpture, woven goods, or jewelry of a lesser quality than was created before the demand. Tourists' interest in seeing an abbreviated form of traditionally long dance or theater performances has led to the presentation of "cuts" rather than an entire piece. As a result, some scholars say that tourism leads to the decline in quality and authenticity of indigenous arts.

Tourist support for indigenous arts, however, is often the sole force maintaining them because local people in a particular culture may themselves be more interested in foreign music, art, or sports. Vietnamese water puppetry is an ancient performance mode, dating back at least to the Ly Dynasty of 1121 (Contreras 1995). Traditionally, water puppet shows took place in the spring during a lull in the farm work, or at special festival times. The stage for this performance art is either a small natural pond or an artificial water tank with a backdrop that hides the puppeteers from the audience. The puppeteers operate carved and painted wooden figures with bamboo poles, wires, and strings, making them appear to glide over the water on their own. Since the 1980s, water puppetry has grown in popularity among Vietnamese people and international tourists (Foley 2001). It has spread from its core area in the Red River Delta in the northern part of the country to being nationwide and from being a seasonal performance to being year-round.

An even more complicated situation exists in the growth of belly dancing as an essential touristic performance in Istanbul, Turkey (Potuoğlu-Cook 2006). International and Turkish tourists associate belly dancing with the Ottoman

MAP 13.4 Turkey.

Turkey straddles two continents, with most of its territory being in Asia. Its largest city, Istanbul, is located in the European part. The capital city, Ankara, is located in the Asian part, called Anatolia. Turkey's culture is a blend between East and West. Its population is over 70 million. Under the leadership of Mustafa Kamal Atatürk, a constitutional, representative political system was established in 1923, following the breakup of the Ottoman Empire after World War I. Turkish is the only official language of the country. It is also widely spoken in countries that were once part of the Ottoman Empire, including Albania, Bosnia-Herzegovina, the Republic of Macedonia, Greece, Romania, and Serbia. Over 2 million Turkish-speaking immigrants live in Germany. Islam is the overwhelmingly predominant religion of Turkey, with 99 percent of the people Muslim. Of these, 75 percent are Sunni, 20 percent Shia, and 5 percent Sufi. According to the constitution, Turkey is a secular state, so there is no official state religion. The most popular sport is football (soccer). The most serious internal security issue is the Kurdish quest for greater cultural autonomy and rights.

A belly dancer performing in Istanbul, Turkey. Belly dancing may have originated in Egypt. In Turkey, it is influenced by Egyptian styles and also by Roma traditions, because many prominent contemporary Turkish belly dancers are Roma. Turkish belly dancing is distinguished by its highly energetic and athletic style and the adept use of *zils*, or finger cymbals.

past, and it is increasingly available in various venues, including classical concerts, restaurants, and nightclubs in Istanbul and other major cities (Map 13.4). In spite of Muslim values about female modesty, commercial interests are promoting this performance mode. Even middle-class housewives are taking belly-dancing lessons, a sign that a formerly stigmatized and lower-class activity is gentrifying. The rising popularity of belly dancing is evidence of Turkey's growing cosmopolitanism.

---

material cultural heritage   the sites, monuments, buildings, and movable objects considered to have outstanding value to humanity.

intangible cultural heritage   UNESCO's view of culture as manifested in oral traditions, languages, performing arts, rituals and festive events, knowledge and practices about nature and the universe, and craftmaking.

One positive result of global tourism is the growing international and local support for the preservation of **material cultural heritage**, which includes sites, monuments and buildings, and movable objects considered of outstanding world value in terms of history, art, and science (Cernea 2001). UNESCO proposed the basic definition of material cultural heritage in 1972. Since then, several hundred locations worldwide have been placed on its World Heritage List and receive some financial support for preservation. Many other invaluable sites are lost, and will be lost in the future, through destructive engineering projects, urbanization, war, looting, private collecting, and climate change.

Applied anthropologists are involved in promoting improved stewardship of material cultural heritage. Some are motivated by a desire to preserve the record of humanity for future generations or for science. Some know that studying how people interact with and perceive the value of a particular site reveals much about culture, identity, and belonging. For example, an ethnographic study of local Korean tourists who visit Changdoek Palace, a World Heritage Site in Seoul, South Korea, offers insights into its role in reinforcing Korean nationalism (Park 2010). Many tourists mention how visiting the site reinforced their sense of being Korean through bringing forth sentiments and feelings about their heritage, even among visitors who said they are not very nationalistic: "It makes my stomach churn to feel that I am naturally connected with this place. I am part of it and it is part of me" (page 126). Cultural heritage sites, both material and intangible (discussed next) are also sources of local economic development, if managed correctly (see Anthropology Works).

In 2003, UNESCO ratified a new policy aimed at protecting **intangible cultural heritage**, or living heritage, manifested

ANTHROPOLOGY works

A Strategy on Cultural Heritage for the World Bank

With headquarters in Washington, DC, and offices throughout the world, the World Bank is an international organization funded by member nations that works to promote and finance economic development in poor countries. Even though most of its permanent professional staff members are economists, the Bank has begun to pay more attention to noneconomic factors that affect development projects.

A major move in that direction occurred in 1972 when the Bank hired its first anthropologist, Michael Cernea (CHAIR-nyuh). For three decades, Cernea has drawn attention to the cultural dimensions of development, especially in terms of the importance of local participation in development projects and people-centered approaches to resettlement (when, for example, large dams are being planned). He has worked to convince top officials at the World Bank that the Bank should become involved in supporting cultural heritage projects as potential pathways to development.

The World Bank already has in place a "do no harm" rule when it approves projects such as roads, dams, and mines. Cernea agrees that a "do no harm" rule is basic to preventing the outright destruction of cultural heritage, but he points out that it is a passive rule and does nothing to provide resources to preserve sites. Cernea wants the Bank to move beyond its "do no harm" rule. He has written a strategy that is

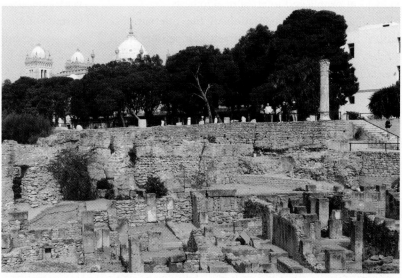

The UNESCO world Heritage Site of Carthage in Tunisia. Carthage was once the heart of a powerful Phoenician empire that extended throughout the Mediterranean region. The Romans destroyed it in 146 BCE. It later revived to become an important early Christian center until Islamic invaders sacked it in the 7th century.

active, not passive. It has two objectives:

- The World Bank should support cultural heritage projects that help to reduce local poverty by creating employment and generating capital from tourism.
- Projects should emphasize the educational value of preserving cultural heritage to local people and international visitors on the grounds that cultural understanding promotes goodwill and good relations at all levels—local, state, and international.

Cernea offers two suggestions for better management of cultural heritage projects: selectivity in site selection on the basis of the impact of the project on reducing poverty; and building partnerships for project planning and implementation among local, national, and international institutions.

FOOD FOR THOUGHT ▼
On the Internet, find the UNESCO World Heritage Site that is nearest to where you live. What does the site contain, and what can you learn about its potential role in generating income for the local people?

---

in oral traditions, languages, performing arts, rituals and festive events, knowledge and practices about nature and the universe, and craftmaking. Support for this policy is based on the understanding that intangible culture provides people with a sense of identity and continuity, promotes respect for cultural diversity and human creativity, is compatible with the promotion of human rights, and supports sustainable development. Through this initiative, member countries of the United Nations are asked to make lists of valuable forms of intangible culture and take steps to preserve them. This policy has stimulated discussion and debate among cultural anthropologists, who see culture as more than a list of traits—highly contextualized, always

changing, and not amenable to being managed or preserved through policy mandates (Handler 2003).

Cultural anthropologists point to the fact that the preservation of expressive culture sometimes occurs as a form of resistance to outside development forces. One example of this phenomenon is the resurgence of the hula, a traditional Hawai'ian dance (Stillman 1996). Beginning in the early 1970s, the *Hawai'ian Renaissance* grew out of political protest, mainly against American colonialism. Hawai'ian youth began speaking out against encroaching development that was displacing indigenous people from their land and destroying their natural resources. They launched a concerted effort to revive the Hawai'ian language, the hula, and canoe paddling, among other things. Since then, hula schools have proliferated, and hula competitions among the islands are widely attended by local people and international tourists.

The 1990s saw the inauguration of the International Hula Festival in Honolulu, which attracts competitors from around the world. Although the hula competitions have helped ensure the survival of this ancient art form, some Hawai'ians voice concerns. First, they feel that allowing non-Hawai'ians to compete is compromising the quality of the dancing. Second, the format of the competition violates traditional rules of style and presentation, which require more time than is allowed, so important dances have to be cut. Third, for Hawai'ians, hula has close ties to religious beliefs and stories about the deities (Silva 2004). Performing hula in a mainly secular format is offensive to the gods and violates the true Hawai'ian way.

Another approach to preserving cultural heritage that is not top-down is "people-first" cultural heritage projects (Miller 2009). These are projects designed by the people whose culture is to be preserved—designed for their benefit and managed by them. A growing number of examples worldwide demonstrate the value of *people-first cultural heritage preservation* as having strong positive, measurable effects. One major area of impact is on the very survival of a culture through territorial entitlements, community security, poverty reduction, improved mental health, and the education of youth in traditional knowledge. Other important domains where people-first cultural heritage preservation has demonstrable positive effects include minority rights, conflict prevention and resolution, and environmental conservation and sustainability.

An example of people-first heritage preservation with implications for territorial entitlements and cultural survival is the Waanyi Women's History Project in Northern Queensland, Australia (Smith, Morgan, and van der Meer 2003). This is a case of a community-driven project devoted to archiving cultural heritage and to establishing local community management. The "community" is a group of Waanyi (waan-yee) women who value their family history as heritage. The traditional way of maintaining this heritage has been to pass it on verbally from mother to daughter. The women wanted to have a written record of their history and documentation of sites and places of significance to them. They hired an anthropologist consultant to collect and record their narratives. An interesting feature of the case, which contrasts with traditional academic research, is that the knowledge generated cannot be published. The role of the researcher is limited to supporting the aspirations of the Waanyi women. The project generated new sources of cash income for some Waanyi women through their employment in the National Park as "cultural rangers" responsible for the conservation of women's sites. It thus helped reduce material deprivation and entitlement insecurity and offers a clear case of a locally initiated and locally

A young woman crowd surfs at a nightclub in Beijing, China.

controlled heritage project with financial benefits going to local people and not to outsiders.

Postcommunist Transitions

Major changes have occurred in the arts in the states of the former Soviet Union for two reasons: loss of state financial support and removal of state controls over subject matter and creativity. A new generation of talented young artists has appeared (Akinsha 1992c). They are looking for something new and different. Art for art's sake, independent from the socialist project, is now possible. Many of the new artists find inspiration in nostalgia for the popular culture of the 1950s and 1960s, such as a pack of Yugoslav chewing gum, or the cover of a Western magazine. Commercial galleries are springing up, and a museum of modern art in Moscow opened in 1999. Classical music is thriving, and Russian opera and ballet groups are performing worldwide.

Theater in China is passing through a transition period with the recent development of some features of capitalism. Since the beginning of the People's Republic in 1949, the arts have gone through different phases, from being suppressed as part of the old feudal tradition to being revived under state control. China's theater companies have experienced financial crises in recent times (Jiang 1994). Steep inflation means that actors can no longer live on their pay. Theater companies are urging their workers to find jobs elsewhere, such as making movies or videos, but this is not an option for provincial troupes. As of the 1990s, local audience preferences changed: "People are fed up with shows that 'educate,' have too strong a political flavor, or convey 'artistic values.' They no longer seem to enjoy love stories, old Chinese legends, or Euro-American theater. Most of the young people prefer nightclubs, discos, or karaokes. Others stay at home watching TV" (1994:73). The new materialism in China means that young people want to spend their leisure time having fun. For the theater, too, money now comes first. One trend is toward the production of Western plays.

For example, Harold Pinter's *The Lover* was an immediate success when it was performed in Shanghai in 1992 (Jiang 1994). In explaining its success, sex is a big part of the answer. The topic of sex was taboo in China for a long time and censored in theater and films. The producers of the play warned parents not to bring children with them, fueling speculation about a possible sex scene. Although *The Lover* contains only hints of sexuality, by traditional Chinese standards it was bold. The actress's alluring style of dress had seldom, if ever, been seen by Chinese theatergoers in the early 1990s. There was also bold language: talk about female breasts, for example. Another feature was the play's focus on private life, interiority, and individual thoughts and feelings. This emphasis corresponds with a new focus on and cultivation of private lives in China. Change in the performing arts in China thus is being shaped both by changes in the local political economy and by globalization. As of the first decade of the twenty-first century, China's new (mainly urban) cultural revolution is moving in directions that no one would have predicted even a decade ago.

How is culture expressed through art?

Cultural anthropologists choose a broad definition of art that takes into account cross-cultural variations. From the anthropological perspective, all cultures have some form of art and a concept of what is good art.

Anthropologists who study art examine it within its cultural context. To do this, anthropologists often become apprentices, learning how to make pots or play drums and, in that way, gaining both artistic skills and valuable insights into the culture of art, artists, the meanings of art, the role of the artist in society, and how art changes. A current trend is to examine how art and other forms of expressive culture are related to power issues and social inequality.

Various categories of art exist cross-culturally, and different cultures emphasize different forms. These categories include performance arts, architecture and decorative arts, graphic arts, and more.

Anthropologists study museum displays as a reflection of cultural values as well as sites where perceptions and values are formed. Many indigenous and formerly colonized people are reclaiming objects from museums as part of their cultural heritage.

What do play and leisure activities reveal about culture?

Anthropological studies of play and leisure examine these activities within their cultural contexts. Cultural anthropologists view games as cultural microcosms, both reflecting and reinforcing dominant social values. Sports and leisure activities, although engaged in for nonutilitarian purposes, are often tied to economic and political interests. In some contexts, sports are related to religion and spirituality.

Tourism is a rapidly growing part of the world economy with vast implications for culture. Anthropologists who study tourism examine both its impact on local cultures and questions of authenticity in the touristic experience. Tourism companies often market "other" cultures to appeal to consumers, a phenomenon that perpetuates stereotypes and denigrates the "host" culture. Some cultural anthropologists work with the tourism industry and local people to find better ways of representing culture that are more accurate, less stigmatizing to the host culture, and more informative for tourists. Local groups are actively seeking ways to share in the benefits of large-scale tourism and conservation projects and to contribute to cultural and environmental sustainability.

How is expressive culture changing in contemporary times?

Major forces of change in expressive culture include Western colonialism, contemporary tourism, and globalization in general. As with other kinds of cultural change through contact, expressive culture may reject, adopt, or adapt new elements. Cultural resistance and syncretism are increasingly frequent, as exemplified in the Trobriand Islanders' co-optation and re-creation of cricket.

In some cases, outside forces have led to the extinction of local forms of expressive culture. In others, outside forces have promoted continuity or the recovery of practices that had been lost. The rising popularity of belly dancing among the middle and upper classes of Istanbul is partly inspired by the demand for its performance by international tourists. Resistance to colonialism and neocolonialism has often inspired cultural revitalization, as in the Hawai'ian Renaissance and community-designed projects in Australia. In postcommunist contexts, Western-style forms of leisure and relaxation frequently involve relaxed rules about nonmarital sexual interaction.

UNESCO's policies about the preservation of material cultural heritage and intangible cultural heritage are increasing worldwide attention to, and protection of, many sites and cultural practices. At the same time, tourism may have detrimental effects on the sustainability of a site and the vitality of a cultural practice. In contrast to international policies, many local indigenous groups are taking cultural rights into their own hands and trying to preserve and protect their heritage for themselves and their descendants, rather than for tourists.

KEY CONCEPTS

art, p. 313

blood sport, p. 324

ethno-esthetics, p. 313

ethnomusicology, p. 316

expressive culture, p. 313

heterotopia, p. 320

intangible cultural heritage, p. 330

material cultural heritage, p. 330

museum, p. 320

repatriation, p. 322

theater, p. 319

wa, p. 324

SUGGESTED READINGS

Adams, Kathleen M. *Art as Politics: Re-Crafting Identities, Tourism, and Power in Tana Toraja, Indonesia*, 2006. Adams explores the intersection of art, Christian-Muslim politics, and tourism in Sulawesi, Indonesia using her ethnographic research that began in the 1980s.

Eduardo Archetti. *Masculinities: Football, Polo, and the Tango in Argentina*. New York: Berg, 1999. An Argentinean anthropologist examines expressive culture in Buenos Aires and how it is related to elite tastes, gender, and international competitiveness.

Edna G. Bay, ed. *Asen, Ancestors, and Vodun: Tracing Change in African Art*. Champaign-Urbana: University of Illinois Press, 2008. This book documents the rise and decline in Benin, West Africa, of the production of *asen*, metal art objects created to honor the spirits of ancestors and vodun deities.

Jennifer Loureide Biddle. *Breasts, Bodies, Canvas: Central Desert Art as Experience*. Seattle: University of Washington Press, 2008. This study of artists in Australia's Central Desert draws on fieldwork among the Walpiri people.

Kevin K. Birth. *Bacchanalian Sentiments: Musical Experiences and Political Counterpoints in Trinidad*. Durham, NC: Duke University Press, 2008. The author explores links among several Trinidadian musical styles and political consciousness on the island.

Tara Browner. *Heartbeat of the People: Music and Dance of the Northern Pow-Wow*. Urbana: University of Illinois Press, 2002. An ethnomusicologist of Choctaw heritage uses archival research on the pow-wow and participant observation to show how elements of the pow-wow in North America have changed.

Shirley F. Campbell. *The Art of Kula*. New York: Berg, 2002. The author focuses on designs painted on *kula* canoes and finds that kula art and its associated male ideology linked to the sea competes with female ideology and symbolism linked to the earth.

Michael Chibnik. *Carving Tradition: The Making and Marketing of Oaxacan Wood Carvings*. Austin: University of Texas Press, 2003. Chibnik examines the production of, and international trade in, Oaxacan wood carvings, an art form developed for tourists.

Alaina Lemon. *Between Two Fires: Gypsy Performance and Romani Memory from Pushkin to Post-Socialism*. Durham, NC: Duke University Press, 2000. This book examines how theater in Moscow both liberates Roma in Russia and reinforces their status as stigmatized outsiders.

Beverly B. Mack. *Muslim Women Sing: Hausa Popular Song*. CD included. Bloomington: Indiana University Press, 2004. This ethnography provides an intimate portrait of the life and art of Hausa women singers in northern Nigeria. It shows how Hausa women exercise agency and creativity through music and dance.

Roger Magazine. *Golden and Blue Like My Heart: Masculinity, Youth, and Power among Soccer Fans in Mexico City*. Tucson: University of Arizona Press, 2007. This book is an ethnography of fan clubs devoted to the Pumas, one of the most popular soccer teams in Mexico City.

Laura Miller. *Beauty Up: Selling and Consuming Body Aesthetics in Japan*. Berkeley: University of California Press, 2006. The author, a linguistic anthropologist, examines the diversity of Japanese personal beauty practices of both males and females. She links eyelid surgery, body hair removal, and beauty products to a wider context of body esthetics.

Ntarangwi, Mwenda. *East African Hip-Hop: Youth Culture and Globalization*. Champaign-Urbana: University of Illinois Press, 2009. Cross-cultural exchange of hip-hop music among Kenya, Uganda, and Tanzania is creating a rich blend of music shaped by youth culture.

PEARSON
myanthrolab

For further information about topics covered in this chapter, go to MyAnthroLab at www.myanthrolab.com and access the following readings in MyAnthroLibrary:

Allan Abramson and Robert Fletcher. 2007. Recreating the Vertical: Rock-Climbing as Epic and Deep Eco-Play. *Anthropology Today* 23(6):3–7. The authors explore why vertical rock-climbing is so compelling to those who do it and how risky rock-climbing practices interact with pleasure.

David Hume. 2008. The Development of Tourist Art and Souvenirs— The Arc of the Boomerang: From Hunting, Fighting and Ceremony to Tourist Souvenir. *International Journal of Tourism Research* 11(1):55–70. How does the boomerang, a functional tool, become a highly sought-after tourist item? The author examines this and other questions about how everyday things become souvenirs.

Carolyn Jones, Felicity Baker, and Toni Day. 2004. From Healing Rituals to Music Therapy: Bridging the Cultural Divide between Sudanese Refugees. *The Arts in Psychotherapy* 31(2):89–100. This article examines how a school in the United States encourages non-English speaking immigrant students to explore and express their feelings through music and talking about song lyrics.

◉ What are the
major categories
of migration?

◉ What are examples
of the new
immigrants in the
United States and
Canada?

◉ How do
anthropologists
contribute to
migration policies
and programs?

PEOPLE ON THE MOVE

◀ The Marsh Arab people suffered
under the rule of Saddam
Hussein from political repression
and government projects that
drained the marshes. Many who
fled the country as refugees have
returned and some of the
marshes have been restored.

14

The current generation of North American youth will move more times during their lives than previous generations did. College graduates are likely to change jobs an average of eight times during their careers, and these changes are likely to require relocation.

Environmental, economic, familial, and political factors are causing population movements worldwide at seemingly all-time high levels. Research in anthropology shows, however, that frequent moves during a person's life and mass movements have occurred throughout human evolution. Foragers, horticulturalists, and pastoralists relocate frequently as a normal part of their lives.

Migration is the movement of a person or people from one place to another. Its causes are linked to basic aspects of life, such as providing for one's food or for marriage. It often has profound effects on a person's economic and social status, for better or worse, as well as on health, language, religious identity, and education.

Thus, migration is of great interest to many academics and many professions. Historians, economists, political scientists, sociologists, and scholars of religion, literature, art, and music have studied migration. The professions of law, medicine, education, business, architecture, urban planning, public administration, and social work have specialties that focus on the process of migration and the period of adaptation following a move. Experts working in these areas share with anthropologists an interest in such issues as the kinds of people who

migrate, causes of migration, processes of migration, health and psychosocial adaptation to new locations, and implications for planning and policy.

Cultural anthropologists do research on many issues related to migration. They study how migration is related to economic and reproductive systems, health and human development over the life cycle, marriage and household formation, politics and social order, and religion and expressive culture. Because migration affects all areas of human life, it pulls together the material in preceding chapters of this book.

Three tendencies characterize research on migration in cultural anthropology:

- Fieldwork experience in more than one location in order to understand the places of origin and destination.

- The combination of macro- and microperspectives. Studying migration challenges the traditional fieldwork focus on one village or neighborhood, creating the need to take into account national and global economic, political, and social forces.

- Involvement in applied work. Many opportunities exist for anthropologists to contribute their knowledge and insights toward improving government policies and programs related to migration. Anthropologists assist efforts to address the situation of people forced to move by war, environmental destruction, and development projects such as dams.

Two scenes of the Chinese diaspora. (LEFT) The Chinatown Cultural Plaza in Honolulu, Hawai'i. Ninety-five percent of Chinese Americans in Hawai'i live in Honolulu. (RIGHT) Chinese Canadians also live mainly in urban areas such as Vancouver and Toronto. In Vancouver, they constitute about 16 percent of the population. Vancouver's Chinatown is a vibrant tourist site and a place where Chinese Canadians reaffirm their cultural heritage, as in the celebration, shown here, of Chinese New Year.

▶ *When does Chinese New Year take place, and how is the date determined?*

This chapter first presents information on the most important categories of migrants and the opportunities and challenges they face. The second section provides descriptions of several examples of immigrants to the United States and Canada. The last section considers urgent issues related to migration, such as human rights and risk prevention programs.

◎ ◎ ◎

Categories of Migration

Migration and its effects on people come in many forms. Both vary in terms of the distance involved, the purpose of the move, whether the move was forced or a matter of choice, and the migrant's status in the new destination. Microcultures play an important role in migration and its consequences for the migrant, as the rest of this chapter will document.

Categories Based on Spatial Boundaries

This section reviews the basic features of three categories of population movement defined in terms of the spatial boundaries crossed:

- **Internal migration**, movement within country boundaries
- **International migration**, movement across country boundaries
- **Transnational migration**, movement in which a person regularly moves back and forth between two or more countries and forms a new cultural identity transcending a single geopolitical unit

INTERNAL MIGRATION   Rural-to-urban migration was the dominant form of internal population movements in most countries during the twentieth century. A major reason that people migrate to urban areas is the availability of work. According to the **push–pull theory** of labor migration, rural areas are unable to support population growth and rising expectations about the quality of life (*the push factor*). Cities (*the pull factor*), in contrast, attract people, especially youths, for employment and lifestyle reasons. According to this theory, rural people weigh the costs and benefits of rural versus urban life and then decide to go or stay. The theory is related to the approach in anthropology that emphasizes human agency, or choice (review Chapter 1). Many instances of urban migration, however, are shaped by structural forces that are beyond the control of the individual, such as war or poverty.

INTERNATIONAL MIGRATION International migration has grown in volume and significance since 1945 and especially since the mid-1980s. Around 100 million people, or nearly 2 percent of the world's population, including legal and

An Iraqi girl carries her sister at a camp for internally displaced persons (IDPs) near Falluja in 2004. Iraq has the most IDPs of any country in the world. Some IDPs live in the same city but in a different neighborhood because they fear their former neighbors.

undocumented immigrants, live outside of their home countries. Migrants who move for work-related reasons constitute most of the people in this category. The driving forces behind the trend are economic and political changes that affect labor demands and human welfare (see Critical Thinking on page 340).

The major destination countries of early international immigration were the United States, Canada, Australia, New Zealand, and Argentina. The immigration policies that these countries applied in the early twentieth century are labeled "White immigration" because they explicitly limited non-White immigration (Ongley 1995). In the 1960s, Canada made its immigration policies less racially discriminatory and more focused on skills and experience. The "White Australia" policy formally ended in 1973. In both the Canadian and Australian cases, a combination of changing labor needs and interest in improving those countries' international image prompted the reforms.

---

migration   movement from one place to another.

internal migration   movement within country boundaries.

international migration   movement across country boundaries.

transnational migration   regular movement of a person between two or more countries resulting in a new cultural identity.

push–pull theory   an explanation for rural-to-urban migration that emphasizes people's incentives to move because of a lack of opportunity in rural areas (the "push") compared with urban areas (the "pull").

CRITICAL thinking

Haitian Cane Cutters in the Dominican Republic: Structure or Agency?

The circulation of male labor from villages in Haiti (see Map 15.3, page 367) to work on sugar estates in the neighboring Dominican Republic is the oldest and perhaps largest continuing population movement within the Caribbean region (Martínez 1996). Beginning in the early twentieth century, Dominican sugarcane growers began to recruit Haitian workers, called **braceros** (bruh-SARE-ohs) in Spanish—agricultural laborers permitted entry to a country to work for a limited time. Between 1852 and 1986, an agreement between the two countries' governments regulated and organized the labor recruitment. Since then, recruitment has become a private matter, with men crossing the border on their own or with recruiters working in Haiti without official approval.

Many studies and reports have addressed this system of labor migration. Two competing perspectives exist:

- View 1, the structurist position: The bracero system is neo-slavery and a clear violation of human rights.
- View 2, the human agency position: Braceros are not slaves because they migrate voluntarily.

View 1

Supporters of this position point to interviews with Haitian braceros in the Dominican Republic that indicate, they say, a consistent pattern of labor rights abuses. Haitian recruiters approach poor men, and boys as young as seven years old, and promise them easy, well-paid employment in the Dominican Republic. Those who agree to go are taken to the frontier on foot and then either transported directly to a sugar estate in the Dominican Republic or turned over to Dominican soldiers for a fee for each recruit and then passed on to the sugar estate. Once there, the workers are given only one option for survival: cutting sugarcane, for which even the most experienced workers can earn only a few U.S. dollars a day. Working and living conditions on the estates are bad. The cane cutters are coerced into working even if they are ill, and working hours start before dawn and extend into the night. Many estate owners prevent Haitian laborers from leaving by having armed guards patrol the estate grounds at night. Many of the workers say that they cannot save enough from their meager wages to return home.

View 2

According to this view, reports of coercion are greatly exaggerated and miss the point that most Haitian labor migrants cross the border of their own volition. On the basis of his fieldwork in Haiti, cultural anthropologist Samuel

---

During the 1980s and 1990s, the United States, Canada, and Australia experienced large-scale immigration from new sources, especially from Asia, and—to the United States—from Latin America and the Caribbean. These trends continue in the twenty-first century.

The earlier classic areas of outmigration—northern, western, and southern Europe—are now, instead, receiving many immigrants, including refugees from Africa and the Middle East. International migration flows in the Middle East are complex, with some countries, such as Turkey, experiencing substantial movements both in and out. Millions of Turkish people immigrated to Germany in the later decades of the twentieth century. Turkey, in turn, has received many Iraqi and Iranian Kurdish refugees (review Culturama, Chapter 10, page 253). Over 2 million Palestinian refugees and their descendants live in Jordan and Lebanon. Israel has attracted Jewish immigrants from Europe, northern Africa, the United States, and Russia.

TRANSNATIONAL MIGRATION Transnational migration is increasing along with other aspects of globalization. It is important to recall, however, that rising rates of transnational migration are related to the creation of state boundaries in recent centuries. Pastoralists with extensive seasonal herding routes were "transnational" migrants long before state boundaries cut across their pathways.

Much contemporary transnational migration is motivated by economic factors. The spread of the global corporate economy is the basis for the growth of one category of transnational migrants nicknamed "astronauts": businesspeople (mainly men) who spend most of their time flying among different cities as investment bankers or corporate executives. At the lower end of the income scale are transnational migrant laborers, who spend substantial amounts of time working in different places and whose movements depend on the demand for their labor.

An important feature of transnational migration is how it affects a migrant's identity, sense of citizenship, and entitlements. Constant movement weakens the sense of having one home and promotes instead a sense of belonging to a community of similar transnational migrants whose lives "in between" take on a new cultural reality.

As a response to the increased rate of transnational migration and the growth of overseas diaspora populations (review the definition in Chapter 9), many "sending" countries (countries that are the source of emigrants, or people who leave) are redefining themselves as *transnational countries*. A transnational country is a country with a substantial

A Haitian migrant laborer. It is a matter of debate how much choice such a laborer has regarding whether he will migrate to the neighboring Dominican Republic for short-term work cutting cane, given the fact that he cannot find paid work in Haiti.

Martínez comments that "Recruitment by force in Haiti seems virtually unheard of. On the contrary, if this is a system of slavery, it may be the first in history to turn away potential recruits" (1996:20). Some recruits have even paid bribes to recruiters in order to be hired. Most people, even young people, are aware of the terrible working conditions in the Dominican Republic, so they are making an informed choice when they decide to migrate. Repeat migration is common and is further evidence of free choice. The major means of maintaining labor discipline and productivity on the sugar estates is not force but wage incentives, especially piecework. The life histories of braceros show that many of them move from one estate to another, thus discrediting the view that the estates are "concentration camps."

Martínez does, however, raise the issue of how free the "choice" to migrate to the Dominican Republic really is, given the extreme poverty in which many Haitians live. In Haiti, few work opportunities exist, and the prevailing wage for rural workers is very low. Thus,

the poor are not truly free to choose to work in their home country: Labor migration to the Dominican Republic becomes a necessity.

In this view, what looks like a free choice to participate in the bracero system is actually *structured choice*. It is based on the unavailability of the option to work for a decent wage in Haiti.

CRITICAL THINKING QUESTIONS ▼

- What are the comparative strengths of View 1 and View 2?
- What does each perspective support in terms of policy recommendations?
- How does the concept of structured choice change these policy recommendations?

---

proportion of its population living outside the country's boundaries (Glick Schiller and Fouron 1999). Examples are Haiti, Colombia, Mexico, Brazil, the Dominican Republic, Portugal, Greece, and the Philippines. These countries grant continuing citizenship to emigrants and their descendants in order to foster a sense of belonging and willingness to continue to send **remittances**, or transfers of money or goods from a migrant to his or her family back home. Remittances are an increasingly large, though difficult to quantify, proportion of the global economy and often a large part of a country's economy. For example, at least 60 percent of the gross domestic product of the small Pacific island country of Tonga comes from remittances from members of the Tongan diaspora (Lee 2003:32) (see Map 14.1 on page 342). India is the country that receives the largest total amount of money through remittances.

A debate that crosses the social sciences is about the effects of remittances on the welfare of the people and the development of the countries to which they are sent (Binford 2003). The major issue is whether remittances go into long-term investments that raise people's quality of life or are used for short-term consumption purposes. The term "investment," though, is difficult to define. Is taking a child to a clinic for a vaccination a short-term expenditure or an investment?

Semantic quibbles aside, most experts agree that, overall, remittances are important in helping families maintain their health and welfare and in promoting local development through donations to build schools, roads, and clinics.

Categories Based on Reason for Moving

Migrants are also categorized on the basis of their reason for relocating. The spatial categories just discussed overlap with the categories based on reason. An international migrant, for example, may also be a person who moved for employment reasons. Migrants experience different kinds of spatial change and, at the same time, have various reasons for moving.

LABOR MIGRANTS   Many thousands of people migrate each year to work for a specific length of time. They do not intend to establish permanent residence and are often

---

bracero   an agricultural laborer in Latin America and the Caribbean who is permitted entry to a country to work for a limited time.

remittance   the transfer of money or goods by a migrant to his or her family in the country of origin.

MAP 14.1 Tonga.

The Kingdom of Tonga is an archipelago of 169 islands, nicknamed by Captain Cook as the Friendly Islands on the basis of his reception there. A constitutional monarchy, Tonga has great reverence for its king, stemming from a tradition of the sacred paramount chief. The current king, who has reigned since 1965, is Taufa'ahau Tupou IV. Before him, Queen Salote Tupou II reigned from 1918 to 1965. The population is around 113,000, with two-thirds living on the main island, Tongatapu. Rural Tongans are small-scale farmers. Most Tongans are ethnically Polynesian, and Christianity is by far the dominant religion. Languages are Tongan and English. Many Tongans have emigrated, and remittances are a major part of the economy.

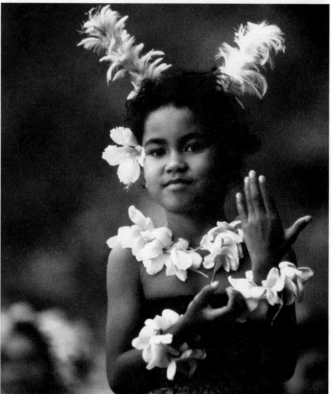

Two faces of Tonga. (TOP) Haloti Ngata, born in California of Tongan ancestry, was drafted in 2006 to play for the Baltimore Ravens, a U.S. football team. (BOTTOM) A Tongan girl in traditional dress.

explicitly barred from doing so. This form of migration, when legally contracted, is called *wage labor migration*. The period of work may be brief, or it may last several years.

Asian women are the fastest-growing category among the world's more than 35 million migrant workers (http://www.ilo.org). More than 1.5 million Asian women are working abroad. Most are in domestic service jobs, and some work as nurses and teachers. Major sending countries are Indonesia, the Philippines, Sri Lanka, and Thailand. Main receiving countries are Saudi Arabia and Kuwait, and, to a lesser degree, Hong Kong, Japan, Taiwan, Singapore, Malaysia, and Brunei. Such women are usually alone and typically are not allowed to marry or have children in the countries where they are temporary workers. They are sometimes illegally recruited and have no legal protection against unjust working conditions.

Circular migration is a regular pattern of population movement between two or more places. It may occur within or between countries. Internal circular migrants include, for example, female domestic workers throughout Latin America and the Caribbean. These women have their permanent residences in rural areas, but they work for long periods for better-off people in the cities. They may leave their children in the care of grandparents in the country, sending remittances for the children's support.

DISPLACED PERSONS **Displaced persons** are people who are evicted from their homes, communities, or countries and forced to move elsewhere (Guggenheim and Cernea 1993). Colonialism, slavery, war, persecution, natural disasters, and large-scale mining and dam building are major causes of population displacement.

Refugees are internationally displaced persons. Many refugees are forced to relocate because they are victims or potential victims of persecution on the basis of their race, religion, nationality, ethnicity, gender, or political views (Camino and Krulfeld 1994). Refugees constitute a large and growing category of displaced persons. An accurate count of all refugees globally is unavailable, but it is about 16 million people, meaning that about 1 of every 500 people is a refugee (UNHCR 2008). Around one-fourth of the world's refugees are Palestinians.

Women and children, who form the bulk of refugees, are vulnerable to abuse in refugee camps, including rape and trading sex for food (Martin 2005). Some case studies, however, shed a more positive light on the refugee experience. Many refugee women from El Salvador, for example, learned to read and write in the camps and found positive role models in the humanitarian aid workers and their vision of social equality (Burton 2004).

Internally displaced persons (IDPs) are people who are forced to leave their homes and communities but who remain within their country. They are the fastest-growing category of displaced people, with an estimated number of total IDPs worldwide of 51 million people (UNHCR 2008), or about one of every 250 people displaced worldwide. Africa is the continent with the most IDPs. Within Africa, Sudan (see Map 15.6, page 374) has the highest number, estimated at 2.7 million people. Iraq has an estimated 2.8 million IDPs, making it the country with the largest number of IDPs. As of January 2010, following the devastating earthquake, Haiti now has around 1.5 million IDPs out of a total population of around 10 million. Thus 15 percent of its population is displaced, or one of every seven Haitians.

Many IDPs, like refugees, live for extended periods in makeshift housing or refugee camps with limited access to basic amenities such as latrines, health care, and schools. Because IDPs do not cross country boundaries, they are not under the purview of the United Nations or other international bodies, which have no authority over problems within countries. Several social activists have taken up the cause of IDPs and worked to raise international awareness of the immensity of the problem including the formal definition of IDPs.

Political violence and conflicts over access to critical resources are major causes of people becoming IDPs. But other factors come into play as well, including natural disasters and large-scale development projects (discussed in Chapter 15). Dam construction, mining, and other projects have displaced millions in the past several decades. Dam construction alone is estimated to have displaced around 80 million people since 1950 (Worldwatch Institute 2003). Forced migration due to development projects is called **development-induced displacement**. Depending on a country's policy, people displaced by development may or may not be compensated financially for the loss of their homes and homeland. Even with monetary compensation, it is rarely possible to replace the life one had and the local knowledge that made life livable.

Mega-dam projects, or dam construction projects that involve costs in the billions of dollars and affect massive areas of land and huge numbers of people, are now attracting the attention of concerned people worldwide who support local resistance to massive population displacement. One of the most notorious cases is India's construction of a series of high dams in its Narmada River Valley, which cuts across the middle of the country from the west coast. This project involves relocating hundreds of thousands of people. The relocation is against the residents' wishes, and government compensation to the "oustees" for the loss of their homes, land, and livelihood is inadequate. Thousands of people in the Narmada Valley have organized protests over the many years of construction, and international environmental organizations have lent support. Celebrated Indian novelist Arundhati Roy joined the cause by learning everything she could about the 20 years of government planning for the Narmada dam projects, interviewing people who have been relocated, and writing a passionate statement called *The Cost of Living* (1999) in opposition to the project. In her book, a man who was displaced and living in a barren resettlement area tells how he used to pick 48 kinds of fruit in the forest. In the resettlement area, he and his family have to purchase all their food, and they cannot afford to eat any fruit at all (1999:54–55).

circular migration   repeated movement between two or more places, either within or between countries.

displaced person   someone who is forced to leave his or her home, community, or country.

refugee   someone who is forced to leave his or her home, community, or country.

internally displaced person (IDP)   someone who is forced to leave his or her home or community but who remains in the same country.

development-induced displacement   the forced migration of a population due to development.

During construction of the massive Three Gorges Dam project in China, residents of a village to be flooded by the dam collect their belongings from their homes as the bulldozers arrive.

▶ *Do research so that you can present a five-minute briefing on the social and environmental implications of the Three Gorges Dam to the people in the "affected" areas.*

MAP 14.2 Site of Three Gorges Dam in China.
The Three Gorges Dam, the world's biggest dam, is one of several projects that are transforming China's environment. The dam has created a vast reservoir upstream to Chongqing. Engineers believe that the dam will solve the problem of annual flooding of the Yangtze River, the world's third-largest river, and generate immense amounts of power. Environmentalists point to the downsides, which include the decline of many important fish species, destabilizing slopes, and eroding islands in the Yangtze River delta. Cultural anthropologists are concerned about the forced migration of over 1 million people from 13 major cities and 140 villages, and the loss of rural farming livelihoods as land is flooded. Archaeologists decry the loss of unknown numbers of prehistoric and historic sites now buried under water. Others mourn the loss of one of the most beautiful places in the world, with its "gumdrop" mountains and breathtaking vistas that have inspired artists for centuries.

Governments promote mega-dam projects as important to the general welfare of the country. The uncalculated costs, however, are high for the local people who are displaced (Map 14.2). In fact, the benefits are skewed toward corporate profits, energy for industrial plants, and energy and water for urban consumers who can pay.

The manner in which displaced persons are relocated affects how well they will adjust to their new life. Displaced persons in general have little choice about when and where they move, and refugees typically have the least choice of all. The Maya people of Guatemala suffered horribly during years of state violence and genocide. Many became refugees, relocating to Mexico and the United States. Others fit into the category of internally displaced persons (see Culturama).

Cultural anthropologists have done substantial research on refugee populations, especially those affected by war and other forms of violence and terror (Camino and Krulfeld 1994, Hirschon 1989, Manz 2004). They have discovered some key factors that ease or increase relocation stresses. One critical factor is the extent to which the new location resembles or differs from the home place in features such as climate, language, and food (Muecke 1987). Generally, the more different the places of origin and destination are, the greater are the adaptational demands and stress. Other key factors are the refugee's ability to get a job commensurate with his or her training and experience, the presence of family members, and whether people in the new location are welcoming or hostile to the refugees.

INSTITUTIONAL MIGRANTS **Institutional migrants** are people who move into a social institution, either voluntarily or involuntarily. They include monks and nuns, the elderly, prisoners, boarding school or college students, and soldiers. The following examples address students and soldiers.

Boarding school/college adjustment challenges often parallel those of other forms of migration, including possible mental distress depending on the culture shock involved and the living situation in the school (see Everyday Anthropology on page 346). International students face serious challenges of spatial and cultural relocation. They are at greater risk of adjustment stress than are local students. Many international students report mental health problems, depending on age, marital status, and other factors. Spouses who accompany international students also suffer the strains of dislocation.

Soldiers are often sent on long-distance assignments for lengthy periods. Their destination may have detrimental physical and mental health effects on them, in addition to the fact that they may face combat. During the British and French colonial expansion, thousands of soldiers were assigned to tropical countries (Curtin 1989). Colonial soldiers faced new diseases in their destination areas. Their death rates from disease were twice as high as those of soldiers who stayed home,

institutional migrant   someone who moves into a social institution either voluntarily or involuntarily.

CULTURAMA

The Maya of Guatemala

The term *Maya* refers to a diverse range of indigenous people who share elements of a common culture and speak varieties of the Mayan language. (*Note:* The adjective includes a final *n* only when referring to the language.) Most Maya people live in Mexico and Guatemala, with smaller populations in Belize and the western parts of Honduras and El Salvador. Their total population in Mexico and Central America is about 6 million.

In Guatemala, the Maya live mainly in the western highlands. The Spanish treated the Maya as subservient, exploited their labor, and took their land. Descendants of a formerly rich and powerful civilization, most Maya now live in poverty and lack basic human rights.

The Maya in Guatemala suffered years of genocide during the country's 36-year civil war, when about 200,000 Maya "disappeared" and were brutally murdered by government military

forces (Manz 2004). Many more were forcibly displaced from their homeland, and today around 250,000 Maya live as IDPs (Fitigu 2005). Thousands left the country as refugees, fleeing to Mexico and the United States.

Beatriz Manz tells a chilling story of one group of K'iche' Maya and their struggle to survive during the war (2004). Manz began her fieldwork in 1973 among the Maya living in the rural areas near the highland town of Santa Cruz del Quiché in the province of El Quiché. The Maya farmed small plots, growing maize and other food items, but found it increasingly difficult to grow enough food for their families. An American Catholic priest came to them with an idea for a new settlement, over the mountains to the east, in Santa María Tzeá.

Several Maya from the highlands decided to establish a new village. They divided land into equal-size plots so that everyone had enough

to support their families. Over time, more settlers came from the highland village. They cleared land for houses, farms, workshops, and a school.

In the late 1970s, their lives were increasingly under surveillance by the Guatemalan military, who suspected the village of harboring insurgents. In the early 1980s, the military began taking village men away. These men were never seen alive again. In 1982, a brutal attack left the village in flames and survivors fleeing into the jungle. Some went to Mexico, where they lived in exile for years, and others migrated as refugees to the United States. The peace accords of 1996 officially ended the bloodshed. Many of the villagers returned and began to rebuild.

Thanks to Beatriz Manz, University of California at Berkeley, for reviewing this material.

(LEFT) Maya women pray in a church 55 miles southeast of Guatemala City in 2003. The coffins contain the remains of the victims of a 1982 massacre inside the church.

(CENTER) Maya women are active in market trade.

MAP 14.3 **Guatemala.** Within the Republic of Guatemala, the Maya constitute about 40 percent of the country's population of 14.6 million.

everyday ANTHROPOLOGY

Stress among Boarding School Girls in Madagascar

Ethnographic research conducted among adolescent boarding school children in Ambanja, a town in Madagascar, showed that girls experience more adjustment strains than boys (Sharp 1990). Ambanja is a booming migrant town characterized by **anomie**, an individual's feeling of alienation and isolation due to the breakdown of traditional values about identity and social relationships, often due to rapid social change. Boarding school children in this town constitute a vulnerable group because they have left their families and come alone to the school.

Many of the boarding school girls, between the ages of 13 and 17, experienced bouts of spirit possession. Local people say that the prettiest girls are the ones who become possessed.

The data on possession patterns showed, instead, that possession is correlated with a girl's being unmarried and pregnant. Many of these schoolgirls become the mistress of an older man (a "sugar daddy"), who showers them with expensive gifts such as perfume and gold jewelry. Such girls attract the envy of both other girls and schoolboys, who are being passed over in favor of adult men.

Thus, the girls have little peer support among their schoolmates. If a girl becomes pregnant, school policy requires that she is expelled. If the baby's father refuses to help her, she faces severe hardship. Her return home will be a great disappointment to her parents.

Within this context, a girl's spirit possession may be understood as an expression of distress. Through the spirits, girls act out their difficult position between country and city and between girlhood and womanhood.

FOOD FOR THOUGHT ▼

Consider the patterns of psychological stress among college students and their possible gender dimensions. How do these patterns of stress differ from or resemble the situation described here?

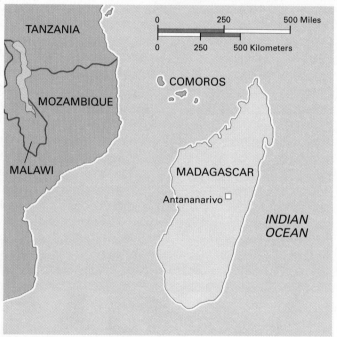

MAP 14.4 Madagascar.

The Republic of Madagascar includes the main island of Madagascar and several much smaller islands off its coast. It is the home of 5 percent of the world's plant and animal species, of which 80 percent are unique to Madagascar. The terrain varies from highlands to lowlands, rainforests, and deserts. The economy is reliant on tourism, especially ecotourism, and mining is increasing. The total population is 18 million. DNA analysis reveals that the population is a mixture of Malay and East African heritage. The primary language is Malagasy, which shares about 90 percent of its vocabulary with a language in southern Borneo. About half the people practice traditional religions related to ancestors, and most others are Catholics or Protestants.

A new platoon of U.S. Army troops are briefed on arrival at Jaghatu Combat Outpost, Afghanistan. They are entering a life and death situation in the combat zone from which they will never fully exit psychologically.

with two exceptions—in Tahiti and Hawai'i—where soldiers experienced better health than soldiers at home.

Anthropologists have published little about the effects of military migration on people in the military and on local people. During wartime, soldiers are trained primarily to seek out and destroy the enemy, not to engage in cross-cultural communication. As mentioned in Chapter 10, winning a war in contemporary times often hinges on what the conquerors do after the outright conflict is over, and that often means keeping troops stationed on foreign soil for a long time. Such extended assignments take a heavy toll on military personnel's mental health and appear to be linked to high rates of suicide, interpersonal violence, stress-based acts of violence against people in the occupied country, and readjustment problems after returning home. Journalist Sebastian Junger, who has a B.A. in cultural anthropology, spent extended time with an American platoon at a remote and dangerous outpost in the mountains of Afghanistan between 2007 and 2008. His book, *War* (2010) and the film he co-directed, *Restrepo* (2010), are anthropologically informed documentaries of everyday life in a war zone. More than that, Junger's work documents the difficulty for combat soldiers in returning home to their wives and families and the high likelihood that they will opt to return to combat and recreate the strong male bonding of the platoon. Many combat soldiers become circular migrants, moving in and out of combat, never completely comfortable in one place or the other.

◉ ◉ ◉

The New Immigrants to the United States and Canada

The term **new immigrant** refers to a person who moved internationally since the 1960s. The category of new immigrants worldwide includes rapidly increasing proportions of refugees, most of whom are destitute and desperate for asylum. Three trends characterize the new international migration in the twenty-first century:

- *Globalization*: More countries are involved in international migration, leading to increased cultural diversity in both sending and receiving countries.
- *Acceleration*: Growth in numbers of migrants has occurred worldwide.
- *Feminization*: Women are a growing percentage of international migrants to and from all regions and in all types of migration; some types exhibit a majority of women.

In the United States, the category of new immigrants refers to people who arrived after the 1965 amendments to the Immigration and Naturalization Act. This change made it possible for far more people from developing countries to enter, especially if they were professionals or trained in some desired skill. Later, the *family reunification* provision allowed permanent residents and naturalized citizens to bring in close family members. Most of the new immigrants in the United States are from Asia, Latin America, and the Caribbean, although increasing numbers are from Eastern Europe, especially Russia.

The United States offers two kinds of visas for foreigners: immigrant visas (also called residence visas) and nonimmigrant visas for tourists and students (Pessar 1995:6). An immigration visa is usually valid indefinitely and allows its holder to be employed and to apply for citizenship. A nonimmigrant visa is issued for a limited period and usually bars its holder from paid employment. Some immigrants are granted visas because of their special skills in relation to labor market needs, but most are admitted under the family unification provision.

The New Immigrants from Latin America and the Caribbean

Since the 1960s, substantial movements of the *Latino* or *Hispano* population (people who share roots in former Spanish colonies in the Western Hemisphere) have occurred, mainly to the United States. Latinos are about 10 percent of the U.S. population, excluding the population of Puerto Rico.

In the United States as a whole, and in some cities, such as Los Angeles, Miami, San Antonio, and New York, Latinos are the largest minority group. Within Latino new immigrants, the three largest subgroups are Mexicans, Puerto Ricans, and Cubans. Large numbers also come from the Dominican Republic, Colombia, Ecuador, El Salvador, Nicaragua, and Peru.

anomie   breakdown of traditional values associated with rapid social change.

new immigrant   an international migrant who has moved since the 1960s.

New immigrant scenes in the United States. (LEFT) Latino immigrants studying English in a program in Virginia. (RIGHT) A Dominican Day parade in New York City.

▶ *Learn about an ethnic festival or event that is being held in the near future. Attend it and observe what signs and symbols of ethnicity are displayed, who attends, and what messages about identity are conveyed.*

MEXICAN IMMIGRANTS: NEITHER HERE NOR THERE Mexico is by far the major source of foreign-born immigrants to the United States, generating roughly one-third all United States immigrants (http://www.migrationinformation. org). Nearly 12 million foreign-born Mexicans live in the United States, a number that doubled from 1995 to 2008. Most live in the traditional destination states of California, Texas, and Illinois, but since the 1990s, more are settling in states such as Georgia, Arkansas, North Carolina, Nebraska, and Ohio. Mexico is also the major source of unauthorized immigration into the United States. Due to the large number of out-migrants, many rural areas in Mexico are left with mainly elderly people and their grandchildren until the Christmas holidays, when migrant workers return to join their families for a week or two.

While it is impossible to generalize about the vast numbers of migrants to the United States from Mexico, a theme of "neither here nor there" seems currently applicable for many adult immigrants (Striffler 2007). Through the 1980s, many Mexican men were seasonal labor migrants to the traditional destination areas, working in the United States for several months of the year but always returning home for at least a few months. Due to changing legal and economic conditions in the United States starting in the late 1980s, job opportunities declined in the traditional areas of migration, especially California, and opened up in "heartland" states. A study of poultry processing workers in Arkansas reveals how Mexican immigrants shifted from seasonal work in California to year-around work in a Tyson Foods processing plant (Striffler 2007). This shift made it possible for the men to bring their wives and children to live with them, and the women also started working at the plant.

As seasonal migrants, the men considered "home" to be in Mexico. In Arkansas, as families have been able to reunite, "home" for adults is both here and there, or neither here nor there. For their children, however, the United States is home. For them, travelling to Mexico is a "vacation" to a foreign place where they complain about the food and experience stomach problems.

CHAIN MIGRATION OF DOMINICANS The Dominican Republic has ranked among the top 10 source countries of immigrants to the united states since the 1960s (Pessar 1995) (see Map 15.3, page 367), and Dominicans are one of the fastest-growing immigrant groups in the united states. They live in clusters in a few states, with their highest concentration in New York State.

Patricia Pessar conducted fieldwork in the Dominican Republic and with Dominican immigrants living in New York City. She studied aspects of the departure process, such as getting a visa, arrival, and adaptation. Like many anthropologists who study immigrants, she became involved in helping some of her participants: "Along the way I also endeavored to repay people's help by brokering for them with institutions such as the Immigration and Naturalization Service, social service agencies, schools, and hospitals" (1995:xv).

For Dominican immigrants, as for many other immigrant groups, the *cadena*, or chain, links one immigrant to another. **Chain migration** is a form of population movement in which a first wave of migrants comes and then attracts relatives and friends to join them in the destination place. Most Dominicans who are legal immigrants have sponsored other family members. Thus, many Dominicans have entered the United States through the family unification provision. The policy, however, defines a family as a nuclear unit (review Chapter 8) and excludes important members of Dominican extended families, such as cousins and ritual kin (*compadres*).

---

chain migration a form of population movement in which a first wave of migrants comes and then attracts relatives and friends to join them in the destination.

To overcome this barrier, some Dominicans use a technique called the *business marriage*. In a business marriage, an individual seeking to migrate pays a legal immigrant or citizen a fee, perhaps $2,000, to contract a "marriage" with that person. The migrant then acquires a visa through the family unification provision. A business marriage does not involve cohabitation or sexual relations; it is meant to be broken.

In New York City, most Dominicans work in manufacturing industries, including the garment industry. They are more concentrated in these industries than is any other ethnic group. Recent declines in manufacturing jobs in New York City, and the redefining of better positions into less desirable ones, have therefore disproportionately affected Dominicans. Many Dominicans have established their own retail businesses, or *bodegas*. Bodegas are often located in unsafe areas, and some owners have been assaulted or killed. Economic challenges are aggravated by the arrival of even newer immigrants, especially from Mexico and Central America, who are willing to accept lower wages than Dominicans do and worse working conditions.

Although many middle-class and upper-class Dominican migrants secured fairly solid employment in the United States on their arrival, they have generally not prospered since then. Dominicans have the highest poverty rate in New York City, 37 percent, compared with a city average of 17 percent. Wages are higher for men than women. Poverty is concentrated among women-headed households with young children, and women are more likely than men to be on public assistance.

Still, Dominican women in the United States are more often regularly employed than they would be in the Dominican Republic. This pattern upsets a patriarchal norm in which the nuclear household depends on male earnings and female domestic responsibilities. A woman's earning power means that husband–wife decision making is more egalitarian. A working Dominican woman is likely to obtain more assistance from the man in doing household chores. All of these changes help explain why more Dominican men are eager to return to the Dominican Republic than women are. As one man said, "Your country is a country for women; mine is for men" (Pessar 1995:81). Although most Dominicans left their homeland in search of a better life, many hope to return to the Dominican Republic. A common saying is that in the United States, "there is work but there is no life."

SALVADORANS: ESCAPING WAR TO STRUGGLE WITH POVERTY Salvadorans make up the fourth largest Latino population in the United States, numbering around 1,200,000 in 2008 (http://www.migrationinformation.org). The civil war in El Salvador, which began in 1979 and continued for over a decade, was the major stimulus for Salvadoran emigration (Mahler 1995) (Map 14.5). By 1984, one-fourth of the country's population consisted of either refugees or IDPs (Burton 2004). Most of the refugees came

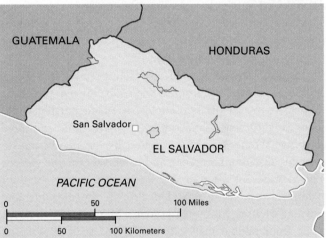

MAP 14.5 El Salvador.

In recent times, the Republic of El Salvador has tended to emphasize one or two major export crops, with coffee being dominant. Coffee growing requires high-altitude land, and therefore coffee production has displaced many indigenous people. The country's total population is nearly 7 million. About 90 percent are mestizo, 9 percent of European descent (mostly Spanish), and 1 percent indigenous. The dominant language is Spanish, although some indigenous people speak Nahuat. Eighty-three percent of the people are Roman Catholic, and Protestants are 15 percent and growing in number.

to the United States. About half of all Salvadorans in the United States live in California, especially Los Angeles (Baker-Christales 2004), with another large cluster in the Washington, DC, area. Many also settled around New York City, including some 60,000 who moved to suburban areas of Long Island.

THINKING OUTSIDE THE BOX

Find a detailed map that shows the geography of the United States, Mexico, and Central America, including El Salvador. Trace a possible overland migration route from El Salvador to the U.S., and find the three rivers that Salvadoran refugees had to cross.

Middle-class and upper-class Salvadorans obtained tourist or even immigration visas relatively easily. The poor, however, were less successful, and many entered the United States illegally as a *mojado* (mo-HAH-do), derogatory slang meaning a "wetback." Like Mexican illegal immigrants, Salvadorans use the term *mojado* to describe their journey. The Salvadorans, though, had to cross three rivers instead of one. These three crossings are a prominent theme of their escape stories, which are full of physical and psychological hardships, including hunger, arrests, and women being beaten and raped along the way. Once they arrived, things were still not easy, especially in the search for work and housing. Lack of education and marketable skills limit the job search. For undocumented immigrants, getting a decent job is even harder. These factors make it more likely that Salvadorans work in the informal sector (review Chapter 4), where they are easy targets for economic exploitation.

Salvadorans living on Long Island receive low wages and labor in poor conditions. Their jobs involve providing services to better-off households. Men do outside work, such as gardening, landscaping, construction, and pool cleaning. Women work as nannies, live-in maids, house-cleaners, restaurant workers, and caregivers for the elderly. The Salvadorans often hold down more than one job—for example, working at a McDonald's in the morning and cleaning houses in the afternoon. Men's pride prevents them from taking lowly ("female") jobs such as washing dishes. Women are more flexible and hence are more likely than men to find work. For the poorest Salvadoran refugees, even exploitative jobs may be an economic improvement compared with conditions back home, where they could not support their families at all.

The Salvadorans were attracted to Long Island by its thriving informal economy, a sector where checking for visas was less likely to occur. Unfortunately, the cost of living on Long Island is higher than in many other places. The combination of low wages and high cost of living has kept most Salvadorans in the category of the working poor, with few prospects for improvement. They attempt to cope with high housing costs by crowding many people into units meant for small families. Compared with El Salvador, where most people, except for the urban poor, owned their own homes, only a few Salvadorans on Long Island own homes. Residential space and expenses are shared among extended kin and nonkin who pay rent. This situation causes intrahousehold tension and stress. In spite of all these difficulties, most Salvadorans evaluate their experience in the United States positively.

The New Immigrants from Asia

Research on how international migrants change their behavior in the new destination have addressed, among other things, the question of whether different consumption patterns emerge and, if so, how, why, and what effects such changes have on other aspects of their culture.

CHANGING PATTERNS OF CONSUMPTION AMONG HONG KONG CHINESE A Canadian study examined consumption patterns among four groups: Anglo-Canadians, Hong Kong Immigrants who had arrived within the previous seven years, long-time Hong Kong immigrants, and Hong Kong residents (Lee and Tse 1994). Since 1987, Hong Kong has been the single largest source of migrants to Canada. The new immigrant settlement pattern in Canada is one of urban clustering. The Hong Kong Chinese have developed their own shopping centers, television and radio stations, newspapers, and country clubs. Because of generally high incomes, Hong Kong immigrants have greatly boosted Canadian buying power.

For most of the poor Hong Kong migrants, however, the move brought a lowered economic situation, reflected in consumption patterns. New immigrants may have to reduce spending on entertainment and expensive items. Primary needs of the new immigrants in the 1990s included items that only about half of all households owned: TVs, a car, a house, a VCR, carpets, and a microwave oven. Items in the second-needs category were a dining room set, a barbecue, a deep freezer, and a dehumidifier. Long-time immigrants owned more secondary products.

At the same time, businesses in Canada have responded to Hong Kong immigrant tastes by providing Hong Kong–style restaurants, Chinese branch banks, and China-oriented travel agencies. Supermarkets offer specialized Asian sections. Thus, traditional patterns and ties are maintained to some extent. Two characteristics of Hong Kong immigrants distinguish them from other groups discussed in this section: their relatively secure economic status and their high level of education. Still, in Canada, they often have a difficult time finding suitable employment. Some have named Canada "Kan Lan Tai," meaning a difficult place to prosper, a fact that leads many to become "astronauts," or transnational migrants.

THREE PATTERNS OF ADAPTATION AMONG VIETNAMESE-AMERICANS More than 125 million refugees left Vietnam during and after the wartime 1970s. Most relocated to the United States, but many others went to Canada, Australia, France, Germany, and Britain (Gold 1992). Vietnamese immigrants in the United States constitute the nation's fourth-largest Asian American minority group. Three distinct subgroups are the 1975-era elite, the "boat people," and the ethnic Chinese. Although they interact frequently, they have retained distinct patterns of adaptation.

The first group, the 1975-era elite, avoided many of the traumatic elements of flight. They were U.S. employees and members of the South Vietnamese government and military. They left before having to live under the communists, and they spent little time in refugee camps. Most came with intact

Nearly half of overseas Vietnamese live in the United States, with California having the most, followed by Texas. Many also settled in New Orleans and the Gulf Coast where they play a prominent role in fishing and vegetable growing. They suffered severe economic losses from the hurricanes of 2005 and the oil spill of 2010. (LEFT) A Vietnamese American maid working in the Hilton Hotel in Washington, DC. (RIGHT) Vietnamese American college students have fun in a Hollywood nightclub.

families and received generous financial assistance from the United States. Using their education and English language skills, most found good jobs quickly and adjusted rapidly.

The boat people began to enter the United States after the outbreak of the Vietnam–China conflict of 1978. Mainly of rural origin, they had lived for three years or more under communism. Their exit, either by overcrowded and leaky boats or on foot through Cambodia, was dangerous and difficult. More than 50 percent died on the way. Those who survived faced many months in refugee camps in Thailand, Malaysia, the Philippines, or Hong Kong before being admitted to the United States. Because many more men than women escaped as boat people, these refugees are less likely to have arrived with intact families. They were less well educated than the earlier wave, with half lacking competence in English. They faced the depressed U.S. economy of the 1980s. By the time of their arrival, the U.S. government had severely reduced refugee cash assistance and had canceled other benefits. These refugees had a much more difficult time adjusting to life in the United States than the 1975-era elite did.

The ethnic Chinese, a distinct and socially marginalized class of entrepreneurs in Vietnam, arrived in the United States mainly as boat people. Following the 1987 outbreak of hostilities between Vietnam and China, the ethnic Chinese were allowed to leave Vietnam. Some, using contacts in the overseas Chinese community, were able to reestablish their roles as entrepreneurs. Most have had a difficult time in the United States because they lacked a Western-style education. They were also sometimes subject to discrimination from other Vietnamese in the United States.

The general picture of first-generation Vietnamese adjustment in the United States shows high rates of unemployment, welfare dependency, and poverty. Interviews with Vietnamese refugees in southern California reveal generational change and fading traditions among youths. Vietnamese teenagers in southern California, for example, have adopted the lifestyle of low-income U.S. teenagers. Their Euro-American friends are more important to them than their Vietnamese heritage is. Given social variations and regional differences in adaptation throughout the United States, however, generalizations about Vietnamese Americans must be made with extreme caution.

HINDUS OF NEW YORK CITY MAINTAIN THEIR CULTURE With the 1965 change in legislation in the United States, a first wave of South Asian immigrants dominated by male professionals from India arrived (Bhardwaj and Rao 1990). Members of this first wave settled primarily in eastern and western cities. Subsequent immigrants from India, who were less well educated and less wealthy, tend to be concentrated in New York and New Jersey. New York City has the largest population of South Asian Indians in the United States, with about one-eighth of the total number (Mogelonsky 1995).

In Flushing, New York, a major Hindu temple holds a ceremony with a priest from India (wearing orange) offering prayers.

Members of the highly educated first wave are concentrated in professional fields such as medicine, engineering, and management (Helweg and Helweg 1990). One of the major immigrant groups in Silicon Valley, California, is South Asian Indians. Members of the less educated, later wave find work in family-run businesses or service industries. Indians dominate some trades, such as convenience stores. They have penetrated the ownership of budget hotels and motels and operate nearly half of the total number of establishments in this niche. More than 40 percent of New York City's licensed cab drivers are Indians, Pakistanis, or Bangladeshis (Mogelonsky 1995).

The South Asian Indian population in the United States is one of the better-off immigrant groups and is considered an immigrant success story. South Asian Indians place high value on their children's education and urge them to pursue higher education in fields such as medicine and engineering. They tend to have few children and invest heavily in their schooling and social advancement.

A continuing concern of many members of the first wave is the maintenance of Hindu cultural values in the face of patterns prevalent in mainstream U.S. culture, such as dating, premarital sex, drinking, and drugs (Lessinger 1995). The Hindu population supports the construction of Hindu temples that offer Sunday school classes for young people and cultural events as a way of passing on the Hindu heritage to the next generation. South Asian Hindus attempt to appeal to their youths by accommodating to their lifestyles and preferences in terms of things such as the kind of food served after rituals. Vegetarian pizza is now a common temple menu item for the young people.

Another challenge for Hinduism in the United States and Canada is to establish temples that offer ritual diversity that speaks to Hindus of many varieties. In New York City, the growth of one temple shows how its ritual flexibility helped it to expand. The Ganesha (guh-NAY-shuh) Temple was founded in 1997 under leadership from Hindus from southern India. Temple rituals at first were the same as those conducted in southern Indian temples. Over the years, though, in order to widen its reach, the temple expanded its rituals to include those that would appeal to Hindus from other regions of India. The congregation has grown, and the physical structure has expanded to provide for this growth. The daily and yearly cycle has become more elaborate and more varied than what one would find at a typical Hindu temple in southern India.

The New Immigrants from the Former Soviet Union

The breakup of the Soviet Union into 15 separate countries spurred the movement of over 9 million people throughout Eastern Europe and Central Asia. Many, of Slavic descent,

lived in Central Asia during the existence of the Soviet Union and seek to return to their homelands. Another large category includes people who were forcibly relocated to Siberia or Central Asia. Since 1988, refugees from the former Soviet Union have been one of the largest refugee nationalities to enter the United States (Gold 1995).

SOVIET JEWS FLEE PERSECUTION Many of the refugees from the former Soviet Union are Soviet Jews. Although most soviet Jews live in Israel, since the mid-1960s more than 300,000 have settled in the United States, especially in California (Gold 1995). Several features characterize the experience of Soviet Jewish refugees in the United States. First, their origins in the Soviet Union accustomed them to the fact that the government controlled most aspects of life and provided many public services, including jobs, housing, day care, and health care. In their new locations, they had to find ways of meeting these needs in a market economy. Second, Soviet Jews, as "White Europeans," become members of the "racial" majority group. Their high level of education places them in the elite of new immigrant groups. Third, they have access to established and prosperous communities of American Jews, which provides them with sponsors when they arrive. Most other new immigrant groups do not have these advantages.

Soviet Jewish immigrants, however, face several challenges. Many have a difficult time finding a job commensurate with their education and previous work in the Soviet Union. Throughout the United States, many Soviet Jewish immigrants remain unemployed or work at menial jobs far beneath their qualifications. This pattern is especially true for women. They were employed professionals in the Soviet

In 2004, more than 50,000 Russian immigrants to Israel returned to Russia. Motivations for the move back include the difficult living conditions for many Russian immigrants in Israel, violence, and the improving economic situation in Russia. Nonetheless, people from Russia continue to migrate to Israel, and they now number over 1 million people, about 13 percent of the population.

▶ Learn how many people left Russia after the breakup of the Soviet Union in 1989 and where they went.

---

lifeboat mentality a view that seeks to limit growth of a particular group because of perceived resource constraints.

Union but can find no work in the United States other than housecleaning or babysitting. Another major challenge involves marriage options. Cultural norms promote intraethnic marriage, but the number in the U.S. marriage pool is small.

◉ ◉ ◉
Migration Policies and Programs in a Globalizing World

The major questions related to migration policies and programs concern state and international policies of inclusion and exclusion of particular categories of people. The human rights of various categories of migrants vary dramatically. Migrants of all sorts, including long-standing migratory groups such as pastoralists and horticulturalists, seek ways of protecting their lifestyles, maintaining their health, and creating security for the future.

Protecting Migrants' Health

Health risks to migrants are many and varied, depending on the wide variety of migrant types and destinations. One group of migrants of special concern consists of those whose livelihoods depend on long-standing economic systems requiring spatial mobility, such as foragers, horticulturalists, and pastoralists. The frequency of drought and food shortages in the Sahel region of Africa (Map 14.6) in recent decades is prompting research by cultural anthropologists to learn how to prevent such situations through better monitoring and enhanced service provision (see Anthropology Works on page 354).

Inclusion and Exclusion

National policies that set quotas on the quantity and types of immigrants who are welcome and that determine how they are treated are dictated largely by political and economic interests. Even in cases of seemingly humanitarian quotas, governments undertake a cost–benefit analysis of how much will be gained and how much will be lost. Governments show their political support or disapproval of other governments through their immigration policies. One of the most obvious economic factors affecting policy is labor flow. Cheap, including illegal, immigrant labor is used around the world to maintain profits for businesses and services for the better off. Flows of such labor undermine labor unions and the status of established workers.

State immigration policies are played out in local communities. In some instances, local resentments are associated with a so-called **lifeboat mentality**, a view that seeks to limit enlarging a particular group because of perceived constraints on resources. This perspective may be part of the explanation for many recent outbreaks of hostility throughout the world in which host populations, instead of being gracious and sharing what they have, seek to drive out the immigrants to protect their own entitlements.

Labor immigrants are not always the subject of resentment, as a study of Palermo, Italy, shows (Cole 1996). The number of immigrants has grown substantially in southern Italy since the early 1980s. The city of Palermo, on the island of Sicilia, or Sicily (see Map 12.5, page 292), has a total population of 1 million people, of which nearly 30,000 are immigrants from Africa, Asia, and elsewhere. Does working-class racism exist among the working class in Palermo? Two conditions seem to predict that it would: large numbers of

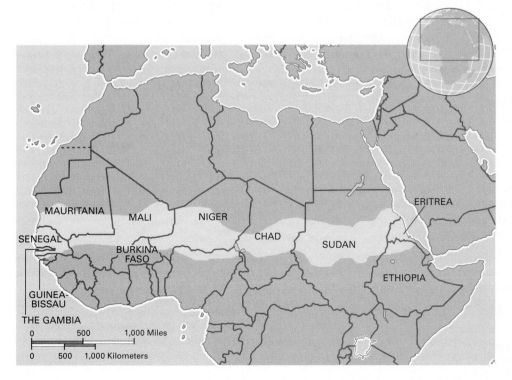

MAP 14.6 Sahel Region.

The word *sahel* comes from the Arabic for "shore" or "border," referring in this case to the area between the Sahara desert and the more fertile regions to the south. Primarily savanna, the region has been the home to many rich kingdoms that controlled Saharan trade routes. Most people make their living from pastoralism and semisedentary cattle raising. The region has recently experienced several major droughts, leading to the widespread death of herd animals, widespread human starvation and malnutrition, and forced population displacement.

ANTHROPOLOGY works

Mapping African Pastoralists' Movements for Risk Assessment and Service Delivery

Pastoralists are often vulnerable to malnutrition as a consequence of climate changes, fluctuations in food supply, war, and political upheaval. Because of their spatial mobility, they are difficult to reach with relief aid during a crisis.

Cultural anthropologists are devising ways to gather and manage basic information about pastoralists' movements in the Sahel region in order to prevent crises and improve basic service delivery (Watkins and Fleisher 2002). The data required for such proactive planning include the following:

- Information about the number of migrants and the size of their herds in a particular location at a particular time. Such data can inform planners about the level of services required for public health programs, educational programs, and veterinary services. This information can be used to assess the demand on particular grazing areas and water sources and is therefore important in predicting possible future crises.
- Information about patterns of migratory movements. This information can enable planners to move services to where the people are, rather than expecting people to move to the services. Some nongovernmental organizations, for example, are providing mobile banking services and mobile veterinary services. Information about pastoralist movements can be used as an early warning to prevent social conflicts that might result if

A Tuareg herdsman fights his way through a sandstorm in Mali.

several groups arrived in the same place at the same time.

The data collection involves interviews with pastoralists, often with one or two key participants, whom the anthropologists select for their specialized knowledge. Interviews cover topics such as the migratory paths followed (both typical and atypical), population levels, the size of herds, and the nutritional and water requirements of people and animals. Given the complex social systems of pastoralists, the data gathering must also include information on group leadership, decision-making practices, and concepts about land and water rights.

The anthropologists organize this information into a computerized database, linking the ethnographic data

with other data collected and managed through what is called a *geographic information system* (GIS). It includes data on the environment and climate information from satellites. The anthropologists then construct various scenarios and assess the relative risks to the people's health. Impending crises can be foreseen, and warnings can be issued to governments and international aid agencies.

FOOD FOR THOUGHT ▼
The tracking system described here remains outside the control of the pastoralists themselves. How might it be managed so that they can participate more meaningfully and gain greater autonomy?

---

foreign immigrants and a high rate of unemployment. So far, however, instead of expressing racist condemnation of the immigrants, working-class residents of Palermo accept the immigrants as fellow poor people. One critical factor may be the lack of competition for jobs because Palmeritans and immigrants occupy different economic niches. African immigrant men work in less desirable jobs in bars and restaurants,

as building cleaners, or as street vendors. African and Asian women work as domestic servants in the better-off neighborhoods. Sicilians do refer to immigrants by certain racial or ethnic names, but these seem to be used interchangeably and imprecisely. For example, a common term for all immigrants, Asian or African, is *turchi*, which means "Turks," but it can also be applied teasingly to a Sicilian. In a questionnaire given to schoolchildren, the great majority agreed with the statement that "a person's race is not important." Although the tolerance among Palermo's working class

---

right of return the United Nations' guaranteed right of a refugee to return to his or her home country to live.

may be only temporary and may change to resentment if economic conditions worsen or the number of immigrants increases, it nonetheless suggests that working-class racism against immigrants is not inevitable.

Recent politically conservative trends in the United States have succeeded in reversing earlier, more progressive immigration policies. Police raids in areas thought to have many undocumented migrants have brought mass expulsions. This lifeboat mentality of exclusiveness is held mainly by the dominant White majority and others who have achieved the "American dream" and resent competition from outsiders.

Migration and Human Rights

Several questions arise about migration and human rights. One of the most basic is whether migration is forced or voluntary (review Critical Thinking, this chapter). Forced migration itself may be considered a violation of a person's human rights. Another issue is whether members of a displaced group have a guaranteed **right of return**, or a refugee's entitlement to return to and live in his or her homeland. The right of return has been considered a basic human right in the West since the time of the signing of the Magna Carta. It is included in United Nations General Assembly Resolution 194, passed in 1948, and was elevated by the United Nations to an "inalienable right" in 1974.

The right of return is a pressing issue for the hundreds of thousands of Palestinians who fled or were driven from their homes during the 1948 war. They went mainly to Jordan, the West Bank/East Jerusalem, Gaza, Lebanon, Syria, and other Arab states. Jordan and Syria have granted Palestinian refugees rights equal to those of their citizens. In Lebanon, where estimates of the number of Palestinian refugees range between 200,000 and 600,000, the government refuses them such rights (Salam 1994). Israel favors the lower number because it makes the problem seem less severe. The Palestinians favor the higher number to highlight the seriousness of their plight. The Lebanese government also favors the higher number to emphasize its burden in hosting so many refugees. Palestinians know that they are not welcome in Lebanon, but they cannot return to Israel because Israel denies them the right of return. Israel responds to the Palestinians' claims by saying that its acceptance of Jewish immigrants from Arab countries constitutes an equal exchange.

The right of return can be considered, just as validly, within states, even though most have no policy close to that of the United Nations. A stark instance of internal displacement and loss of rights to return home comes from the 2005 hurricanes in New Orleans and the coastal counties of Mississippi and Louisiana. The "racial" lines of displacement are nowhere clearer than in the statistics for the city of New Orleans (Lyman 2006). Before Hurricane Katrina, the population of New Orleans was 54 percent White, 36 percent Black, and 6 percent Latino. In 2006, the population was 68 percent White and 21 percent Black, with no change in the Latino percentage. The causes of the differential displacement of the Black population are one problem. The fact that many Black people, all these many years later, have little chance of returning to their homes—*differential resettlement*—is another.

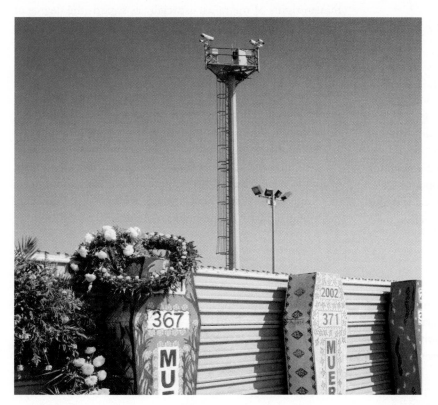

Memorials to illegal border crossers on the Mexico side of a fence at the U.S.–Mexico border. U.S.-built barriers along the border with Mexico have existed for decades. Recent increases in illegal crossings and a closed-border policy prompted President George W. Bush to push for the Secure Fence Act of 2007, which authorized the construction of 700 additional miles of fencing. Human rights supporters say that the fences simply push immigrants to attempt to cross into the United States in more desolate and dangerous areas, adding to the mortality rate of illegal immigrants.

▶ *The World Trade Organization supports the free trade of goods between countries. Where does it stand, if at all, on the free movement of labor between countries?*

What are the major categories of migration?

Migrants are classified as internal, international, or transnational. Another category is based on the migrants' reason for moving. On this dimension, migrants are classified as labor migrants, institutional migrants, or displaced persons. People's adjustment to their new situation depends on the degree of voluntarism involved in the move, the degree of cultural and environmental difference between the place of origin and the destination, and how well expectations about the new location are met, especially in terms of making a living and establishing social ties.

Displaced persons are one of the fastest-growing categories of migrants. Refugees fleeing from political persecution or warfare face serious adjustment challenges because they often leave their home countries with few material resources and frequently have experienced much psychological suffering. The number of internally displaced persons is growing even faster than the number of refugees. Mega-dams and other large-scale development projects result in thousands of people becoming IDPs, and these individuals do not fall under the purview of international organizations such as the United Nations.

What are examples of the new immigrants in the United States and Canada?

Worldwide, the "new immigrants" are contributing to growing transnational connections and to the formation of increasingly multicultural populations within countries. In the United States, the new immigrants from Latin America, especially Mexico, are the largest and fastest-growing category.

In the United States, members of most refugee immigrant groups tend to have jobs at the lower end of the economic scale. Jewish refugees from the Soviet Union experience a major gap in what their employment was like in Russia versus their limited options in the United States. Immigrants from East and South Asia, who are more likely than others to have immigrated to the United States voluntarily, have achieved greater levels of economic success than most other new immigrant groups.

Immigrant groups throughout the world may face discrimination in their new destinations, although the degree to which it occurs among those already residing in those locales varies with the level of perceived competition for resources. Gender can affect immigrant experiences.

How do anthropologists contribute to migration policies and programs?

Anthropologists have studied national and international migration policies and programs in terms of social inclusion and exclusion. Fieldwork in particular contexts reveals a range of patterns between local residents and immigrants. Working-class resentment among local people against immigrants is not universal and varies with the overall amount and type of employment available.

Anthropologists examine possible infringements of the human rights of migrants, especially as regards the degree of voluntarism in their move and the conditions they face in the destination area. Another human rights issue related to migration is the right of return. The United Nations proclaimed the right of return for internationally displaced populations. Most countries, however, have no such policy. Internally displaced persons, including the evacuees from the 2005 hurricanes in the Gulf region of the United States, have no guarantee that they can return to their home area.

Cultural anthropologists find many roles in applied work related to migration. Gathering data on migratory movements of traditionally mobile people, such as pastoralists, can help make humanitarian aid programs more timely and effective.

KEY CONCEPTS

anomie, p. 347
bracero, p. 341
chain migration, p. 348
circular migration, p. 343
development-induced
  displacement, p. 343

displaced person, p. 343
institutional migrant, p. 344
internal migration, p. 339
internally displaced person
  (IDP), p. 343

international migration,
  p. 339
lifeboat mentality, p. 352
migration, p. 339
new immigrant, p. 347
push–pull theory, p. 339

refugee, p. 343
remittance, p. 341
right of return, p. 354
transnational migration,
  p. 339

SUGGESTED READINGS

Rogaia Mustafa Abusharaf. *Wanderings: Sudanese Migrants and Exiles in North America*. Ithaca, NY: Cornell University Press, 2002. Abusharaf provides historical background on the first wave of Sudanese migration to the United States and Canada, information on various Sudanese groups that have migrated, and an interpretation of Sudanese identity in North America.

Beth Baker-Cristales. *Salvadoran Migration to Southern California: Redefining El Hermano Lejano*. Gainesville: University of Florida Press, 2004. This book provides a history of Salvadoran migration to the United States and a detailed description of the lives of Salvadoran migrants in Los Angeles.

Jeffrey H. Cohen. *The Culture of Migration in Southern Mexico*. Austin: University of Texas Press, 2004. Migration is a way of life for many individuals and entire families in the Mexican state of Oaxaca. Cohen discusses outmigration in 12 communities and its effects on those who remain.

Kesha Fikes. *Managing African Portugal: The Citizen-Migrant Distinction*. Durham, NC: Duke University Press, 2010. Portugal's entry into the European Union affected perceptions of the suitability of domestic employment for working-class Portuguese women compared to immigrant Black women from Cape Verde.

Alyshia Gálvez. *Guadalupé in New York: Devotion and the Struggle for Citizenship Rights among Mexican Immigrants*. New York: New York University Press, 2010. This ethnography shows the importance of devotion to the Virgin of Guadalupe in the lives of undocumented Mexican immigrants in New York City.

Julianne Hammer. *Palestinians Born in Exile: Diaspora and the Search for a Homeland*. Austin: University of Texas Press, 2004. In the decade following the 1993 Oslo Peace Accords, 100,000 diasporic Palestinians moved to the West Bank and Gaza. This ethnography documents the experiences of young adults and their adjustment to the move.

Josiah McC. Heyman. *Finding a Moral Heart for U.S. Immigration Policy: An Anthropological Perspective*. Washington, DC: American Ethnological Society, Monograph Series, Number 7, 1998. This critique finds that U.S. immigration policy is basically anti-immigrationist. The author suggests steps toward a more inclusive policy.

Helen Morton Lee. *Tongans Overseas: Between Two Shores*. Honolulu: University of Hawai'i Press, 2003. This book about Tongan migrants in Melbourne uses participant observation and analysis of messages on a Tongan Internet forum called Kava Bowl.

Ann Aurelia López. *The Farmworkers' Journey*. Berkeley: University of California Press, 2007. Interviews conducted over a 10-year period document the lives of farm workers who migrate from west-central Mexico to central California.

Martin F. Manalansan, IV. *Global Divas: Filipino Gay Men in the Diaspora*. Durham, NC: Duke University Press, 2004. This book is based on the life narratives of 50 Filipino gay men in New York City and participant observation in homes, bars, hospitals, restaurants, and the Gay Pride Parade.

Karen Richman. *Migration and Vodou*. Gainesville: University of Florida Press, 2005. This book and its accompanying CD reveal the innovative ways that Haitian migrants in South Florida maintain their religious traditions and familial connections.

Archana B. Verma. *The Making of Little Punjab in Canada: Patterns of Immigration*. Thousand Oaks, CA: Sage Publications, 2002. Verma describes the historical connections between Hindu migrants from a village in India's northern state of Punjab to Vancouver Island, British Columbia.

PEARSON
myanthrolab

For further information about topics covered in this chapter, go to MyAnthroLab at www.myanthrolab.com and access the following readings in MyAnthroLibrary:

Mary Beth Chrostowsky. 2010. The Role of Asylum Location on Refugee Adjustment Strategies: The Case of Sudanese in San Diego, California. *Practicing Anthropology* 32(1):38–42. Sudanese refugees in the United States experience a large gap between their home culture and their destination, a fact that puts them at risk for greater stress. In addition, most refugees had already spent several years in refugee camps in Egypt of Kenya, further adding to their adjustment challenges.

Judith Friedenberg and Gail Thakur. 2009. Immigrant Life Histories as a Heritage Resource for Civic Engagement. *Practicing Anthropology* 31(3):30–35. This article considers factors that play into either immigrants having "historical amnesia" or valuing their past and memorializing it.

Deborah James and Evan Killick. 2010. Ethical Dilemmas? UK Immigration, Legal Aid Funding Reform and Caseworkers. *Anthropology Today* 26(1):13–15. A study of caseworkers and clients in South London sheds light on the legal process of asylum-seeking in the United Kingdom and the role of cultural anthropologists as expert witnesses.

◉ What is development, and what are the approaches to achieving it?

◉ How has development affected indigenous people and women?

◉ What are urgent issues in development?

PEOPLE DEFINING DEVELOPMENT

◀ A herding boy and his goats in southern Sudan near an oil pumping station. Many animals in the region have died after drinking polluted water.

15

We have had many visitors to Walpole Island since the French "discovered us" in the seventeenth century in our territory, Bkejwanong. In many cases, these visitors failed to recognize who we were and to appreciate our traditions. They tried to place us in their European framework of knowledge, denying that we possessed our indigenous knowledge. They attempted to steal our lands, water, and knowledge. We resisted. They left and never came back. We continued to share our knowledge with the next visitors to our place. . . . It was a long-term strategy that has lasted more than three hundred years. (Dr. Dean Jacobs, Executive Director of Walpole Island First Nation, from his foreword in VanWynsberghe 2002:ix)

These are the words of a leader of the Walpole Island First Nation, located in southern Ontario, Canada (Map 15.1). They, along with many other indigenous groups worldwide, have taken strong action in recent decades to protect their culture and natural environment. The Walpole Island First Nation organized itself and successfully fought to control industrial waste that was polluting its water and land. In the process, the people have regained their pride and cultural integrity.

The subfield of development anthropology looks at how culture and "development" interact to improve people's lives and reduce poverty. Thus, it has a strong applied component, as well as a critical component that asks hard questions about the causes of poverty. This chapter's first section considers concepts related to change and development and various approaches to development. The second section focuses on development in relation to indigenous peoples and women. The third section looks at urgent issues in development and what cultural anthropology can contribute to them.

MAP 15.1 Walpole Island Reservation in Southern Ontario, Canada.

◉ ◉ ◉

Defining Development and Approaches to It

This chapter focuses on the topic of contemporary cultural change as shaped by **development**, or directed change aimed at improving human welfare. A major focus of development

---

development   change directed toward improving human welfare.

poverty   the lack of tangible and intangible assets that contribute to life and the quality of life.

invention   the discovery of something new.

diffusion   the spread of culture through contact.

acculturation   a form of cultural change in which a minority culture becomes more like the dominant culture.

assimilation   a form of cultural change in which a culture is thoroughly acculturated, or decultured, and is no longer distinguishable as having a separate identity.

---

efforts is preventing or reducing poverty. Poverty is extremely difficult to define, but one workable definition says that **poverty** is the lack of tangible and intangible assets that contribute to life and the quality of life. Some approaches to reducing poverty focus on *basic needs* such as access to decent food, water, housing, and clothing, factors without which a person may die or certainly fail to thrive. More expanded definitions include access to things such as education and *personal security* (freedom from fear). Development experts in Paris, Rome, and Washington, DC, spend much time discussing how to measure poverty rates, how to assess whether poverty is increasing or decreasing and why, and what kinds of policies and programs are best to reduce poverty. More locally, real people in real places experience poverty and attempt to deal with it.

Two Processes of Cultural Change

Two basic processes underlie all cultural change. The first is **invention**, the discovery of something new. The second is **diffusion**, the spread of culture through contact.

INVENTION Most inventions evolve gradually through experimentation and the accumulation of knowledge, but some appear suddenly. Examples of technological inventions that have created cultural change include the printing press, gunpowder, the polio vaccine, and satellite communication. Conceptual innovations, such as Jeffersonian democracy, are also inventions. Many inventions bring about positive cultural change, but not all inventions have positive social outcomes. Inventions inspired by a socially positive goal may have mixed or unintended negative consequences.

DIFFUSION Diffusion is logically related to invention because new discoveries are likely to spread. Diffusion can occur in several ways. First, in mutual borrowing, two societies that are roughly equal in power exchange aspects of their culture. Second, diffusion sometimes involves a transfer from a dominant culture to a less powerful culture. This

Canadian Prime Minister Stephen Harper, center (standing), officially apologizes for more than a century of abuse and culture loss related to Indian boarding schools at a ceremony in the House of Commons on Parliament Hill in Ottawa, Canada, in June 2008. From the 19th century to the 1970s, more than 150,000 aboriginal children were required to attend state-funded Christian schools as part of a program to assimilate them into the Canadian state.

process may occur through force or, more subtly, through education or marketing processes that promote the adoption of new practices and beliefs. Third, a more powerful culture may appropriate aspects of a less powerful culture, through *cultural imperialism*. Last, a less powerful and even oppressed cultural group often provides sources of cultural change in a dominant culture.

Changes in a minority culture that make it more like the dominant culture are referred to as **acculturation**. In extreme cases, a culture becomes so thoroughly acculturated that it is **assimilated**, or *decultured*—that is, it is no longer distinguishable as having a separate identity. In the most extreme cases, the impact on the minority culture is that it becomes extinct. These processes parallel degrees of language change resulting from contact with dominating cultures and languages. Such changes have occurred among many indigenous people as the result of globalization and the introduction of new technology (see Anthropology Works on page 362). Other responses to acculturative influences include the partial acceptance of something new with localization and syncretism, as in the case of the game of cricket in the Trobriand Islands (Chapter 13), or rejection and resistance.

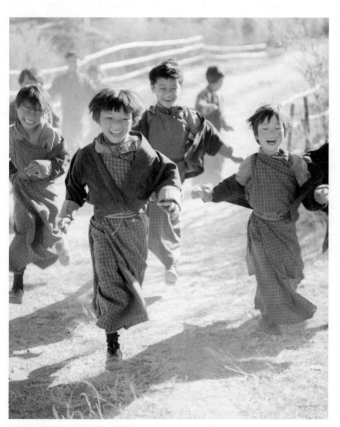

Schoolgirls in Bhutan. The government of Bhutan rejects the Western concept of the gross domestic product (GDP) as the best measure of a country's success and instead uses a measure called gross domestic happiness (GDH).

▶ *Go to the Internet to learn more about Bhutan and the government's aspirations for its people.*

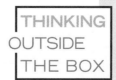

THINKING OUTSIDE THE BOX

Choose two inventions made in your lifetime and assess how they affect your everyday activities, social interactions, and way of thinking.

ANTHROPOLOGY works

The Saami, Snowmobiles, and Social Impact Analysis

How might the adoption of a new belief or practice benefit or harm a particular culture and its various members? Although often difficult to answer, this question must always be asked. A classic study of the snowmobile disaster among a Saami group in Finland offers a careful response to the question in a context of rapid technological diffusion (Pelto 1973).

In the 1950s, the Saami of Finland (review Culturama, Chapter 11, page 277) had an economy based on reindeer herding, which provided most of their diet. Besides supplying meat, reindeer had other important economic and social functions. They were used as draft animals, especially for hauling wood for fuel. Their hides were made into clothing and their sinews used for sewing. Reindeer were key items of exchange, in both external trade and internal gift-giving. Parents gave a child a reindeer to mark the appearance of the child's first tooth. When a couple became engaged, they exchanged a reindeer with each other to mark the commitment.

By the 1960s, all this had changed because of the introduction of the snowmobile. Previously, people herded the reindeer herds on skis. The use of snowmobiles for herd management had several unintended and interrelated consequences, all of which were detrimental to the herding way of life.

First, the herds were no longer kept domesticated for part of the year, a practice during which they became tame. Instead, they were allowed to roam freely all year and thus became wilder. Second, snowmobiles allowed herders to cover larger amounts of territory at roundup time and to do more than one roundup. As the number of snowmobiles increased, herd sizes declined dramatically. The reasons for the decline included the stress inflicted on the reindeer by the extra distance traveled during roundups, the multiple

A Saami herder riding a skidoo in northern Norway leads his herd.

roundups instead of a single one, and the fear aroused by the noisy snowmobiles. Furthermore, roundups were held at a time when the females were near the end of their pregnancies, a factor that induced reproductive stress.

Negative economic changes occurred, including a new dependence on the outside through the cash economy. Cash is needed in order to purchase a snowmobile, buy gasoline, and pay for parts and repairs. This delocalization of the economy created social inequality, which had not existed before. Other economic and related repercussions ensued as well:

- The cash cost of effective participation in herding exceeded the resources of some families, which then had to drop out of participation in herding.
- The snowmobile pushed many Saami into debt.
- Dependence on cash and indebtedness forced many Saami to migrate to cities for work.

Snowmobiles also changed Saami gender relations by increasing the prominence of young men in herding (Larsson 2005). Before the snowmobiles, reindeer herding was a family operation. Although men did more of the long-distance herd-

ing, women also worked closely with the herd. After snowmobiles were adopted, parents began steering their sons toward herding and their daughters toward education and professional careers. Two rationales for such gender tracking are that driving a snowmobile is difficult because the vehicle is heavy and that the driver may get stuck somewhere. The use of snowmobiles also changed the age pattern of reindeer herding in favor of youth over age; thus, older herders were squeezed out.

Pertti Pelto, the anthropologist who first documented this case, calls these transformations a disaster for Saami culture (1973). He offers a recommendation for the future: Communities confronting the adoption of new technology should have a chance to weigh evidence on the pros and cons and make an informed judgment. Pelto's work is one of the early warnings from anthropology about the need for a **social impact assessment**—a study that attempts to predict the potential social costs and benefits of particular innovations before change is undertaken.

FOOD FOR THOUGHT ▼
If you were a Saami herder, what would you have done if you had been able to consider a social impact assessment of the effects of snowmobiles?

(LEFT) A doctor administering polio vaccine in Ecuador. In 1985, the Pan American Health Organization (PAHO) established a plan for eradicating the polio virus from the Americas by 1990. (RIGHT) A patient rests with acupuncture needles on her face during a "face lift" treatment (to remove wrinkles and make the individual look younger) in New York City. This acupuncture procedure, based in traditional Chinese medicine, follows the theory that the face is where the essence of yin and the energy of yang meet. The procedure seeks to adjust imbalances in yin and yang through the insertion of needles at particular places.

▶ *Do research to find out whether traditional Chinese acupuncture had a specialization in "face lifting." If not, can you learn when and where this specialization emerged?*

Theories and Models of Development

This subsection reviews theories and models of development and the various kinds of institutions involved in development. It then examines development projects and how anthropologists work with, or sometimes against, those projects.

No single view of development or how to achieve it exists. Debates about these issues are heated and involve experts from many disciplines, governments, and local people worldwide. Five theories or models of development are presented here. They differ in terms of the following characteristics:

- The definition of development
- The goal of development
- Measures of development
- Attention to environmental and financial sustainability

MODERNIZATION **Modernization** is a form of change marked by economic growth through industrialization and market expansion, political consolidation through the state, technological innovation, literacy, and options for social mobility. It originated in Western Europe in the beginning of the seventeenth century with the emerging emphasis on secular rationality and scientific thinking as the pathways to progress (Norgaard 1994). Given the insights of rationality and science, modernization is thought to spread inevitably throughout the world and lead to improvement in people's lives everywhere. The major goals of modernization are material progress and individual betterment.

Supporters and critics of modernization are found in both rich and poor countries. Supporters claim that the benefits of

modernization (improved transportation, electricity, biomedical health care, and telecommunications) are worth the costs to the environment and society.

Others take a critical view and regard modernization as problematic because of its focus on ever-increasing consumption levels and heavy use of nonrenewable resources. Many cultural anthropologists are critical of Westernization and modernization because their research shows how modernization often brings environmental ruin, increases social inequality, destroys indigenous cultures, and reduces global cultural and biological diversity. In spite of strong cautionary critiques from anthropologists, environmentalists, and others about the detrimental effects of modernization, most countries worldwide have not slowed their attempts to achieve it. Some governments and citizen groups, however, are promoting lifestyles that rely less on nonrenewable resources and include a concern for protecting the environment.

GROWTH-ORIENTED DEVELOPMENT Development as "induced" change, brought about through applying modernization theory in so-called developing countries, emerged after World War II. At that time, the United States began to expand its role as a world leader, and aid for development was part of

---

social impact assessment a study conducted to predict the potential social costs and benefits of particular innovations before change is undertaken.

modernization a model of change based on belief in the inevitable advance of science and Western secularism and processes, including industrial growth, consolidation of the state, bureaucratization, a market economy, technological innovation, literacy, and options for social mobility.

its international policy agenda. International development, as defined by major Western development institutions, is similar to modernization in terms of its goals. The process emphasizes economic growth as the most crucial element. According to growth-oriented development theory, investments in economic growth will lead to improved human welfare through the *trickle-down effect*: the gradual increase in wealth among the less well off as it filters down from the more well off.

Promoting economic growth in developing countries includes two strategies:

- Increasing economic productivity and trade through modernized agriculture and manufacturing and through participation in world markets.
- Reducing government expenditures on public services such as schools and health in order to reduce debt and reallocate resources to increase productivity. This strategy, called *structural adjustment*, has been promoted by the World Bank since the 1980s.

One measure for assessing the achievement of development through this model is the rate of growth of the economy, especially the *gross domestic product*, or *GDP*.

DISTRIBUTIONAL DEVELOPMENT *Distributional development* contrasts with growth-oriented development in its emphasis on social equity in benefits, especially in terms of increased income, literacy, and health. It rejects the trickle-down process as ineffective in reaching poor people. Its position is based on evidence that growth-oriented strategies, applied without concern for distribution, actually increase social inequality. In this view, the growth model ensures that "the rich get richer and the poor get poorer."

The distributional approach opposes structural adjustment policies because they further undermine the welfare of the poor by removing the few entitlements they had in the form of services. Advocates of the distributional model see the need for benevolent governments to ensure equitable access to crucial resources in order to enhance the ability of the poor to provide for their own needs (Gardner and Lewis 1996).

Although conservative, "neoliberal" economists argue that redistribution is neither realistic nor feasible, supporters of the distributive approach point to cases that have worked. As an example, anthropological research in a village in central Kerala (KARE-uh-luh), a state in southern India (Map 15.2), assessed whether redistribution was an effective development strategy (Franke 1993). The findings showed the answer to be affirmative. Even though Kerala's per capita income is the lowest of any state in India, it has the highest social indicators in the country in health and literacy.

Government attention to distribution in Kerala came about through democratic channels, including demonstrations and pressure on the government by popular movements and

MAP 15.2 Kerala, South India.

With a population of 30 million, Kerala has living standards, literacy rates, and health indicators that are high compared with the rest of India. Kerala comprises 14 districts and three historical regions: Travancore in the south, Kochi in the central part, and Malabar in the north. Long a socialist democracy, Kerala now allows the free market and foreign direct investment to play larger roles. A major tourist destination because of its tropical ecology and cultural features such as dramatic martial arts and theater, Kerala also hosts a growing Ayurvedic health tourism industry along its coast.

labor unions. These groups forced the state to reallocate land ownership, thereby alleviating social inequality somewhat. In other instances, people pressured government leaders to improve village conditions by providing school lunches for poor children, increasing school attendance by dalit children (review Chapter 9), and investing in school facilities. Through public action, Nadur village became a better place to live for many people.

HUMAN DEVELOPMENT Another alternative to the growth-first model is called *human development*, the strategy that emphasizes investing in human welfare. The United Nations adopted the phrase "human development" to emphasize the need for improvements in human welfare in terms of health, education, and personal security and safety. In this model, investments in improving human welfare will lead to economic development. The reverse is not invariably true: The level of economic growth of a country (or region within a country) is not necessarily correlated with its level of human development, as is clear from the case of Kerala. Thus, in this view, economic growth is neither an end in itself nor even a necessary component of development as measured by human welfare. Economic resources, combined with distributive policies, are a strong basis for attaining high levels of human development.

Scenes of Kerala. (LEFT) Children attending school via boat in the interior of the state. (RIGHT) Fishing nets on the coast.

▶ *Learn more about Kerala and prepare a briefing memo on it for the class with attention to how Kerala differs socially from northern India.*

SUSTAINABLE DEVELOPMENT *Sustainable development* refers to forms of improvement that do not destroy non-renewable resources and are financially supportable over time. Advocates of sustainable development argue that the economic growth of wealthy countries has been, and still is, costly in terms of the natural environment and people whose lives depend on fragile ecosystems. They say that such growth cannot be sustained at even its present level, not to mention projected demands as more countries become industrialized.

Institutional Approaches to Development

Cultural anthropologists are increasingly aware of the importance of examining the institutions, organizations, and specialists involved in development policy making, programs, and projects. With this knowledge, cultural anthropologists have a better chance of shaping development policies and programs. Institutional research includes studying the management systems of both large-scale institutions such as the World Bank and small-scale organizations in diverse settings. Topics include behavior within the institutions, social interactions with the "client population," and institutional discourse. This section describes first some large development institutions and then some smaller organizations.

LARGE-SCALE DEVELOPMENT INSTITUTIONS
Two major types of large-scale development institutions exist. First are the *multilateral institutions*—those that include several countries as "donor" members. Second are the *bilateral institutions*—those that involve only two countries: a "donor" and a "recipient."

The largest multilaterals are the United Nations and the World Bank. Each is a vast and complex social system. The United Nations, established in 1945, includes more than 160 member states. Each country contributes money according to its ability, and each has one vote in the General Assembly. Several United Nations agencies exist, fulfilling a range of functions, such as the United Nations Development Programme (UNDP), the Food and Agriculture Organization (FAO), the World Health Organization (WHO), the United Nations Children's Fund (UNICEF), the United Nations Educational, Scientific, and Cultural Organization (UNESCO), and the United Nations High Commissioner for Refugees (UNHCR).

The World Bank is supported by contributions from over 150 member countries. Founded in 1944, the Bank is dedicated to promoting the concept of economic growth worldwide. Its main strategy is to promote international investment through loans. The World Bank is guided by a board of governors made up of the finance ministers of member countries. The World Bank system assigns each country a number of votes based on the size of its financial commitment. The economic superpowers, therefore, dominate.

The World Bank system includes the International Bank for Reconstruction and Development (IBRD) and the International Development Association (IDA). Both are administered at the World Bank headquarters in Washington, DC. They lend for similar types of projects and often in the same country, but their loan conditions differ. The IBRD provides loans to poor countries that are generally regarded as "bad risks" on the world commercial market. Thus, the IBRD is a source of interest-bearing loans to countries that otherwise would not be able to borrow. Most of its loans support large infrastructure projects such as roads and dams.

Prominent bilateral institutions include the Japan International Cooperation Agency (JICA), the United States Agency for International Development (USAID), the Canadian International Development Agency (CIDA), Britain's

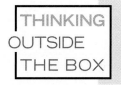

THINKING OUTSIDE THE BOX

Visit the website of one multilateral development organization and one bilateral organization to learn about their goals, programs, and internship opportunities.

World Bank headquarters in Washington, DC. The World Bank employs more than 10,000 people from over 160 countries. Two-thirds of its employees are based in Washington.

Department for International Development (DfID), the Swedish Agency for International Development (SIDA), and the Danish Organization for International Development (DANIDA). These agencies vary in terms of the total size of their aid programs, the types of programs they support, and the proportion of aid disbursed as loans that have to be repaid with interest as opposed to aid disbursed as grants that do not require repayment. Compared to other bilaterals, USAID tends to give more loans (which must be repaid, with interest) than grants (which are more like gifts).

Loans and grants also differ in terms of whether they are *tied* or *untied*. Tied loans and grants require that a certain percentage of project expenditures go for goods, expertise, and services originating in the donor country. For example, a tied loan to a certain country for road construction would require allocating a designated percentage of the funds to donor country construction companies, to airfare for donor country road experts, and to in-country expenses, such as hotels, food, and local transportation, for donor country experts. When loans or grants are untied, the recipient country may decide freely how to use the funds. USAID offers more tied than untied aid, whereas countries such as Sweden, the Netherlands, and Norway tend to give untied aid.

Another difference among the bilaterals is the proportion of their total aid that goes to the poorest countries. The United Kingdom's DfID sends more than 80 percent of its aid to the poorest countries, whereas most of U.S. foreign aid dollars go to Egypt and Israel. Emphasis on certain types of aid also varies from one bilateral institution to another. Cuba has long played a unique role in bilateral aid, concentrating on aid for training health-care providers and for promoting preventive health care (Feinsilver 1993). Its

development assistance goes to like-minded socialist countries, including many in Africa and in Latin America. Within Latin America, Brazil and Venezuela are taking on a visible role in development aid to neighboring countries, and they were among the earliest responders to the Haiti earthquake of January 2010.

GRASSROOTS APPROACHES   Many countries have experimented with *grassroots approaches* to development, or locally initiated small-scale projects. This alternative to the top-down development pursued by the large-scale agencies described in the previous section is more likely to be culturally appropriate, supported through local participation, and successful.

The term **social capital** refers to the intangible resources that exist through social ties, trust, and cooperation. Many local grassroots organizations around the world use social capital to provide basic social needs, and they are successful even in the poorest countries (see Culturama).

Religious organizations sponsor a wide variety of grassroots development projects. In the Philippines, the Basic Ecclesiastical Community (BEC) movement is based on Christian teachings and follows the model of Jesus as a supporter of the poor and oppressed (Nadeau 2002) (see Map 7.2, page 160). BECs seek to follow the general principles of liberation theology, which blends Christian principles of compassion and social justice, political consciousness raising among the oppressed, and communal activism. In the rural areas, several BECs have successfully built trust among group members and leaders and developed people's awareness of the excesses of global capitalism and the dangers of private greed and accumulation. Part of their success is due to the fact that members were able to pursue new economic strategies outside the constraints of capitalism and that require little capital input, such as organic farming.

A young boy embroiders a sari in India. Child labor is a human rights issue in much of the world. In the absence of being able to eradicate child labor, many programs exist to provide education and health care for child workers.

---

social capital   the intangible resources existing in social ties, trust, and cooperation.

Peyizan Yo of Haiti

Haiti and the Dominican Republic share the island of Hispaniola. Following the island's discovery by Columbus in 1492, Spanish colonialists exterminated the island's indigenous Arawak Indians. In 1697, the French took control of what is now Haiti and instituted an exceptionally cruel system of African plantation slavery. In the late 1700s, the half million slaves revolted. In what is the only successful slave revolution in history, they ousted the French and established the first Black republic in the Western Hemisphere.

Haiti's population of around 10 million people occupies a territory somewhat smaller than the state of Maryland in the United States. The land is rugged, hilly, or mountainous. More than 90 percent of the forests have been cleared. In economic terms, Haiti is the poorest country in the Western Hemisphere. Extreme income inequality exists between the urban elite, who work and live in and near the capital city of Port-au-Prince, and everyone else. The people in the countryside are called *peyizan yo* (the plural form of *peyizan*), a Creole term for small farmers who produce for their own use and for the market (Smith 2001). Many also participate in small-scale marketing. Most peyizan yo in Haiti own their land. They grow vegetables, fruits (especially mangoes), sugarcane, rice, and corn.

Haiti has the highest prevalence of HIV/AIDS of any country in the Caribbean region. Medical anthropologist Paul Farmer emphasizes the role of colonialism in the past and global structural inequalities now in causing these high rates (1992). In the nineteenth century, colonial plantation owners grew fabulously rich from this island. Haiti produced more wealth for France than all of France's other colonies combined and more than the thirteen colonies in North America produced for Britain.

After the revolution, in 1804, Haiti became the first free country in Latin America and the first in the Western Hemisphere to abolish slavery. Yet, the heritage of colonialism left an imprint of rule by a few and the sheer act of abolishing slavery brought economic and political isolation from slave-holding countries including the United States which did not recognize Haiti until after the Civil War. Now, neocolonialism and globalization leave new scars. For decades, the United States has played a major role in supporting conservative political regimes. Powerful drug traffickers use Haiti's coastline as a haven for moving drugs from South America to markets in North America and Europe.

Although the United States and other rich countries pledged billions of dollars to help Haiti "build back better" after the 2010 earthquake, very little of the money pledged has found its way to Haiti, and of that, far less to the people in need. Yet, the Haitian people find hope and resilience in their families, their faith, and their cultural pride, even the many thousands living in camps for displaced people.

Thanks to Jennie Smith-Pariola, Berry College, for reviewing this material.

MAP 15.3 **Haiti.** The Republic of Haiti occupies one-third of the Caribbean island of Hispaniola.

(LEFT) A woman repays her loan at a small-scale savings and loan business in rural Haiti. Many of the credit union members use their loans to set up small businesses.

(CENTER) A child injured in the January 2010 earthquake sits in a makeshift hospital tent. The 7.0 magnitude earthquake devastated the capital city of Port au Prince, killed an estimated 200,000 people, and displaced around 1.5 million people.

See more at PEARSON **myanthrolab**

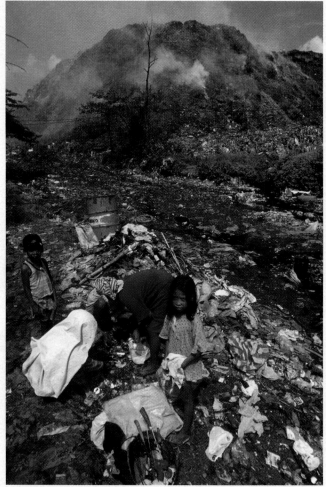

Scavenging for a livelihood in an urban dump in the Philippines.

▶ *What kind of an entitlement is this?*

A BEC in Cebu City, on the Island of Cebu (suh-BOO), the Philippines, however, was unsuccessful. It faced the challenge of organizing people who make a living scavenging in a nearby city dump. Both adults and children scavenge for materials that are then sorted and sold for recycling, such as plastic. They work for fourteen hours a day, seven days a week. It is an organized operation, with district officials monitoring the dump. Customary arrangements among the scavengers regulate their work areas. Scavenging requires no formal education and few tools—just a basket and a steel hook, and a kerosene lantern for nighttime work. Scavengers earn more than other nonskilled laborers in the city. In the BEC meetings, the scavengers found little on which to build solidarity. Instead, they bickered with each other and complained about each other to the leaders. The sheer poverty of the people was so great that communal values could not compete against their daily economic struggle. In cases of extreme poverty with limited or no options for alternative forms of income generation, government programs may be required to complement faith-based, grassroots initiatives.

The Development Project

Development institutions, whether they are large multilaterals or local nongovernmental organizations (NGOs), implement their goals through the **development project**, a set of activities designed to put development policies into action. For example, suppose a government sets a policy of increased agricultural production by a certain percent within a designated period. A development project to achieve the policy goal might be the construction of irrigation canals that would supply water to a targeted number of farmers.

THE DEVELOPMENT PROJECT CYCLE Although details vary among organizations, all development projects have a **project cycle**, or the full process of a project from initial planning to completion (Cernea 1985). The project cycle includes five basic steps from beginning to end (Figure 15.1).

Since the 1970s, applied anthropologists have been involved in development projects. Early on, they were hired primarily to do project evaluations, to determine whether the project had achieved its goals. Their research shows that projects were often dismal failures (Cochrane 1979). Three major reasons for these failures are as follows:

- The project did not fit the cultural and environmental context.
- The project benefits did not reach the target group, such as the poor or women; instead, project benefits went to elites or some other less needy group.
- The intended beneficiaries were worse off after the project than before it.

One factor underlying these three problems is poor project design. The projects were designed by bureaucrats, usually Western economists, who lived in cities far from the project site with no firsthand experience of the lives of the target population. These experts applied a universal formula ("one size fits all") to all situations (Cochrane 2009). The cultural anthropologists who evaluated the projects, in contrast, knew the local people and context and were therefore shocked by the degree of nonfit between the projects and the people.

Project identification	Selecting a project to fit a particular purpose
Project design	Preparing the details of the project
Project appraisal	Assessing the project's budgetary aspects
Project implementation	Putting the project in place
Project evaluation	Assessing whether the project goals were fulfilled

FIGURE 15.1 The Development Project Cycle.

Applied anthropologists gained a reputation in development circles as troublemakers—people to be avoided by those who favored a move-ahead approach to getting projects funded and implemented. Applied anthropologists are still considered a nuisance by many development policy makers and planners, but sometimes, at least, a necessary nuisance. On a more positive note, through persistent efforts they have made progress in gaining a role earlier in the project cycle, at the stages of project identification and design.

CULTURAL FIT A review of many development projects over the past few decades reveals the importance of **cultural fit**, or taking the local culture into account in project design (Kottak 1985). A glaring case of nonfit between a project and its target population is a project intended to improve nutrition and health in some South Pacific islands by promoting increased milk consumption (Cochrane 1974). The project involved the transfer of large quantities of powdered milk from the United States to an island community. The local people, however, were lactose intolerant (unable to digest raw milk), and they all soon had diarrhea. They stopped drinking the milk and used the powder to whitewash their houses. Beyond wasting resources, inappropriately designed projects result in the exclusion of the intended beneficiaries. Two examples are when a person's signature is required but the people do not know how to write and when photo identification cards are requested from Muslim women, whose faces may not be shown in public.

Applied anthropologists can provide insights into how to achieve cultural fit in order to enhance the success of a project. Anthropologist Gerald Murray played a positive role in redesigning a costly and unsuccessful reforestation project supported by USAID in Haiti (1987). Since the colonial era in Haiti (see Map 15.3, page 367), deforestation has been dramatic, with an estimated 50 million trees cut annually. Some of the deforestation is driven by the market demand for wood for construction and for charcoal in the capital city of Port-au-Prince. Another reason is that peyizan yo, or small farmers, need cleared land for growing crops and grazing their goats. The ecological consequences of so much clearing, however, are extensive erosion of the soil and declining fertility of the land.

In the 1980s, USAID sent millions of tree seedlings to Haiti and the Haitian government urged rural people to plant them. Peyizan yo, however, refused to plant the seedlings on their land and instead fed them to their goats. Murray, who had done his doctoral dissertation on rural Haitian land tenure practices, was called on by USAID to diagnose the problem and suggest an alternative approach. He advised that the kind of seedling promoted be changed from that of fruit trees, in which peyizan yo saw little benefit because they are not to be cut, to that of fast-growing trees, such as eucalyptus, which could be cut as early as four years after planting and

sold in Port-au-Prince. Peyizan yo quickly accepted this plan because it would yield profits in the foreseeable future. The cultural nonfit was that USAID wanted trees to stay in place for many years, but peyizan yo viewed trees as things that were meant to be cut in the short term.

THE ANTHROPOLOGICAL CRITIQUE OF DEVELOPMENT PROJECTS The early decades of development anthropology were dominated by what I call **traditional development anthropology**. In traditional development anthropology, the anthropologist takes on a role of helping to make development policies and programs work better. It is the "add an anthropologist and stir" approach to development. Like good applied anthropology in any domain, traditional developmental anthropology does work. For example, an anthropologist familiar with a local culture can provide information about what kinds of consumer goods would be desired by the people or what might persuade people to relocate with less resistance. The anthropologist may act as a cultural broker, someone who uses knowledge of both the *donor culture* and the *recipient culture* to devise a workable plan.

Concern exists among many anthropologists about development projects that have negative effects on local people and their environments. For example, a comparison of the welfare of local inhabitants of the middle Senegal River Valley (see Map 15.4 on page 370) before and after the construction of a large dam shows that people's level of food insecurity increased after the dam was built (Horowitz and Salem-Murdock 1993). Before the dam, periodic flooding of the plain provided for a dense population supporting itself with agriculture, fishing, forestry, and herding. After the dam was constructed, water was released less often. The people downstream lacked sufficient water for their crops, and fishing was no longer a dependable source of food. At other times, dam managers released a large flood of water, damaging farmers' crops. Many downstream residents have had to leave the area because of the effects of the dam; they are victims of development-induced displacement (review Chapter 14). Downstream people now have high rates of schistosomiasis, a severely debilitating disease caused by parasites, because the disease spreads quickly in the slow-moving water below the dam.

---

development project a set of activities designed to put development policies into action.

project cycle the steps of a development project from initial planning to completion: project identification, project design, project appraisal, project implementation, and project evaluation.

cultural fit a characteristic of informed and effective project design in which planners take local culture into account.

traditional development anthropology an approach to international development in which the anthropologist accepts the role of helping to make development work better by providing cultural information to planners.

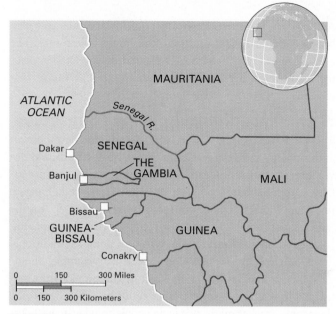

MAP 15.4 Senegal.

The Republic of Senegal is mainly rolling sandy plains of the western Sahel. Senegal's economy is mainly agricultural, with peanuts being the main crop. Social inequality is extreme, and urban unemployment is high. The population of Senegal is over 11 million, of which 70 percent live in rural areas. Of the many ethnic groups, the Wolof are the largest. Sufi Islam is the major religion, practiced by 94 percent of the population, with Christians making up 4 percent.

Other "dam stories" document the negative effects of dam construction on local people, including the destruction of their economy, social organization, sacred space, sense of home, and environment (Loker 2004). Such mega-projects force thousands, even millions, of people in the affected area to cope with the changes in one way or another. Many leave; others stay and try to replace what they have lost by clearing new land and rebuilding. Most end up in situations far worse than the one in which they lived originally.

The growing awareness of the detrimental effects of many supposedly positive development projects has led to the emergence of what I call **critical development anthropology**. In this approach, the anthropologist takes on a critical-thinking role. The question is not *What can I do to make this project successful?* Instead, the anthropologist asks, *Is this a good project from the perspective of the local people and their environment?* If the answer is yes, then an applied anthropologist can take a supportive role. If the answer is no, then the anthropologist can intervene with relevant information, taking on the role of either a whistle-blower to stop the project or an advocate promoting ideas about how to change the project in order to

---

critical development anthropology an approach to international development in which the anthropologist takes a critical-thinking role and asks why and to whose benefit particular development policies and programs are pursued.

mitigate harm. In the case of the Senegal River dam project, applied anthropologists worked in collaboration with engineers and local people to devise an alternative management plan for the water flow in which regular and controlled amounts of water were released. In many other cases, the process has a less positive outcome, with planners ignoring the anthropologist's advice (Loker 2000).

◉ ◉ ◉

Development, Indigenous People, and Women

This section considers two categories of people who are increasingly taking an active role in redefining development in their own terms: indigenous people and women. Although they are overlapping categories, the section presents material about them separately for purposes of illustration.

Indigenous People and Development

Indigenous peoples have been victimized by many aspects of growth-oriented development, as they were by colonialism before it. But now many indigenous groups are redefining development and taking it into their own hands.

As noted in Chapter 1, indigenous people are usually a numerical minority in the states that control their territory. The United Nations distinguishes between indigenous peoples and other minority groups such as African Americans, the Roma, and the Tamils of Sri Lanka. It is more useful to view all "minority" groups as forming a continuum, from

In the southern part of Madagascar, there is pressure to grow more rice, which means irrigating more land. The expansion of intensive rice cultivation will bring the death of many baobab trees and threaten the habitats of wild animal species, including lemurs.

▶ *Assume that you have just been appointed as Madagascar's minister of people, nature, and development. What do you want your research staff to brief you about during your first month of service?*

purely indigenous groups to minority/ethnic groups that are not geographically original to a place but that share many problems with indigenous peoples as a result of displacement and living within a more powerful majority culture (Maybury-Lewis 1997b).

Indigenous peoples differ from most minorities in that they tend to occupy remote areas and, often, areas rich in natural resources. Remoteness has, to some extent, protected them from outsiders. Now, however, governments, international business, conservationists, and tourists increasingly recognize that the lands of these people contain valuable natural resources, such as gas in the circumpolar region, gold in Papua New Guinea and the Amazon, sapphires in Madagascar, hydroelectric potential in large rivers throughout the world, and cultural attractions.

Accurate statistics on indigenous populations do not exist. Several reasons account for this lack of information (Kennedy and Perz 2000). First, no one agrees about whom to count as indigenous. Second, some governments do not bother to conduct a census of indigenous people, or if they do, they may undercount indigenous people in order to downplay recognition of their existence. Third, it is often physically difficult, if not impossible, to carry out census operations in indigenous areas. The indigenous people of North Sentinel Island in India's Andaman Islands remain uncounted because Indian officials cannot land on the island without being shot at with arrows (Singh 1994).

Rough estimates of the total population of indigenous people worldwide range between 300 million and 350 million people, or about 5 percent of the world's population (Hughes 2003). The greatest numbers are in Asia, including Central Asia, South Asia, East Asia, and Southeast Asia. Canada's First Nation population is under 2 million. The American Indian population in the United States numbers around 1 million.

INDIGENOUS PEOPLE AS VICTIMS OF COLONIALISM AND DEVELOPMENT Like colonialism, contemporary global and state political and economic interests often involve the takeover and control of indigenous people's territory. Over the past several hundred years, many indigenous groups and their cultures have been exterminated as a result of contact with outsiders. Death and population decline have resulted from contagious diseases, slavery, warfare, and other forms of violence. With colonialism, indigenous people experienced wholesale attacks as outsiders sought to take their land by force, prevented them from practicing their traditional lifestyles, and integrated them into the colonial state as marginalized subjects. The loss of economic, political, and expressive autonomy have had devastating physical and psychological effects on indigenous peoples. Reduction in the biodiversity of their natural environments is directly linked to impoverishment, despair, and overall cultural decline (Maffi 2005, Arambiza and Painter 2006). These processes are common

worldwide, creating unforeseen new risks for indigenous people's welfare.

In Southeast Asia, states use policies of "planned resettlement" that displace indigenous people, or "hill tribes," in the name of progress (Evrard and Goudineau 2004). Development programs for the hill tribes in Thailand, for example, reveal the links among international interests, state goals, and the well-being of the tribes (Kesmanee 1994). The hill tribes include groups such as the Karen, Hmong, Mian, Lahu, Lisu, and Akha. They total about half a million people. International pressures are applied to have the hill tribes replace the cultivation of opium with other cash crops. International aid agencies therefore sponsor alternative agricultural projects and tourism. The Thai government, however, is more concerned with political stability and security in the area, given its strategic location, and therefore promotes development projects such as roads and markets to establish links between the highlands and the lowlands. Either way, the hill tribes are the target of outsiders' interests; thus, they face a challenge to the promotion of their own agendas.

Efforts to find viable substitute crops for opium have been unsuccessful, especially among the Hmong, who are most dependent on opium as a cash crop. Alternative crops require the heavy use of fertilizers and pesticides, which are costly to the farmers and greatly increase environmental pollution; moreover, such crops are less lucrative for the farmers. Logging companies have gained access to the hills and have done far more damage to the forests than the highlanders' horticultural practices have. Increased penetration of the hill areas by lowlanders and international tourists have promoted rising HIV/AIDS rates, illegal trafficking of girls and boys for sex, and opium addiction among the highlanders.

The Thai government, like the government of neighboring Laos, has attempted to relocate highland horticulturalists to the plains through various resettlement schemes. Highlanders who opt for relocation find the lowland plots to be unproductive because of poor soil quality. Relocated highlanders find that their quality of life and economic status decline in the lowlands. Yet another new risk for the resettlers in Thailand and Laos is that they are now heavy consumers of methamphetamines, an addictive, euphoria-inducing compound with serious negative side effects, such as rapid weight loss, tooth decay, diarrhea, nausea, and agitation (Lyttleton 2004). Overall, 50 years of so-called development have been disastrous for Southeast Asia's hill peoples.

INDIGENOUS PEOPLE AND TERRITORIAL ENTITLEMENTS Throughout their history of contact with the outside world, indigenous peoples have actively sought to resist the deleterious effects of "civilization." Since the 1980s, more effective and highly organized forms of protest have become prominent. Indigenous groups now hire lawyers and other experts as consultants in order to reclaim and defend their territorial rights, gain self-determination, and secure protection from outside risks. Many indigenous people have themselves become trained as lawyers, researchers, and advocates. Conflicts range from lawsuits to attempts at secession (Stidsen 2006).

This section provides an overview on the status of indigenous people's territorial rights claims. Within each large world region, country-by-country variation exists in legal codes and in the adherence to any such codes that may exist.

Latin America Few Latin American countries provide legal protection against encroachment on the land of indigenous groups. Nicaragua, Peru, Colombia, Ecuador, Bolivia, and Brazil have taken the lead in enacting policies that legitimize indigenous rights to land and in demarcating and titling indigenous territories (Stocks 2005). A wide gap often exists, however, between policy and actual protection. Despite these efforts, increasing numbers of Indians throughout the entire region of Latin America have been forced off their land in the past few decades through poverty, violence, and environmental degradation due to encroachment by logging companies, mining operations, ranch developers, and others. In response, many migrate to cities and seek wage labor. Those who

remain face extreme poverty, malnutrition, and personal and group insecurity.

A surge of political activism by indigenous people has occurred since the 1990s, sometimes involving physical resistance. Violence continues to erupt between indigenous groups and state-supported power structures, especially in the southern Mexican state of Chiapas (see Map 6.3, page 140). In 2005, participants at the First Symposium on Isolated Indigenous Peoples of the Amazon created a group called the International Alliance for the Protection of Isolated Indigenous Peoples. The group seeks to make the relevant state governments aware of the current endangered situation of many indigenous people. These people demand their right to isolation, if that is their choice, and to protection from unwelcome outside contact and encroachment. In 2008, the International Alliance of Forest Peoples formed to push for indigenous people's participation in global climate change talks and to devise a plan whereby wealthy countries would compensate developing countries for conserving tropical forests (Barrionuevo 2008).

Canada In Canada, the law distinguishes between two different types of Native Peoples and their land claims (Plant 1994). *Specific claims* concern problems arising from previous

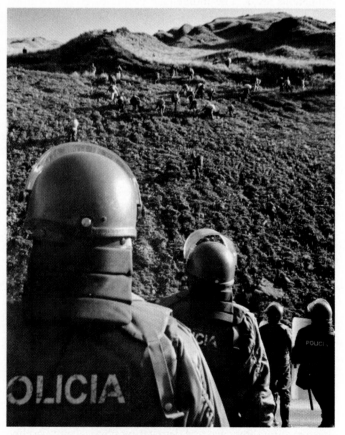

The costs of cocaine. (LEFT) In Colombia, a 5-year-old boy has blisters on his face caused by the herbicide sprayed on coca farms from planes working for Plan Colombia, financed by the U.S. war on cocaine. (RIGHT) Bolivian security forces confront coca farmers during a protest march to the capital city of La Paz, and the farmers scatter to avoid arrest. The farmers were protesting the U.S.-backed coca eradication plan that affects their livelihoods. This photograph was taken before President Evo Morales was elected. His policy allows coca farmers to grow a small amount of coca for traditional consumption.

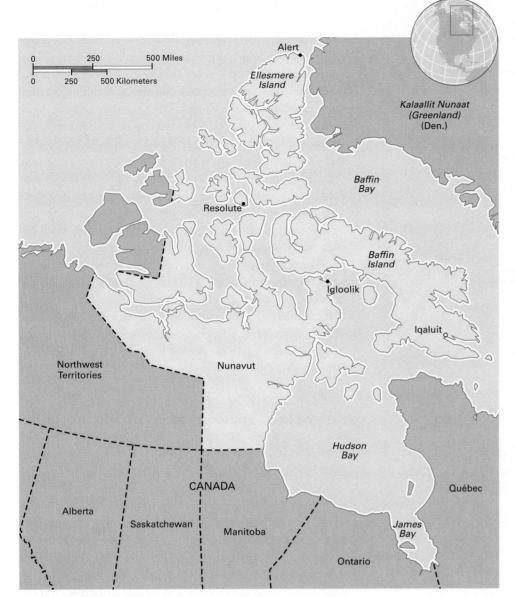

MAP 15.5 Nunavut Province, Canada.

Created in 1999, Nunavut is the newest and largest of Canada's provinces. It is also the least populated, with 30,000 people. About 85 percent of the people are First Nations peoples, mainly Inuit. Official languages are Inuktitut, Inuinnagtun, English, and French. The landscape is mainly Arctic tundra. The award-winning movie *Atanarjuat* (*The Fast Runner*) was produced by Inuit filmmakers and filmed in Nunavut.

agreements or treaties, and *comprehensive claims* are those made by Native Peoples who have not been displaced and have made no treaties or agreements. Most of the former claims have led to monetary compensation. In the latter category, interest in oil and mineral exploration has prompted governments to negotiate with indigenous people in an effort to have the latter's native claims either relinquished or redefined. In some provinces, especially British Columbia, claims affect most of the province. The Nunavut land claim was settled, granting about 25,000 Inuit access to a vast tract of land, including subsurface rights (Jensen 2004) (Map 15.5).

Asia   In Asia, most countries have been reluctant to recognize the territorial rights of indigenous people (Plant 1994). In Bangladesh, the Chittagong Hill Tracts area in the southeast is being massively encroached upon by settlers from the crowded plains region (see Map 9.1, page 210). Encroachers from the lowlands now occupy the most fertile land, and the indigenous people and their culture are endangered in many

ways, including suffering loss of land and livelihood as well as new health threats. In Thailand, no legal recognition of hill tribes' land rights exists, whereas in Laos and Vietnam, some land has been allocated to indigenous communities (Jensen 2004:5). Indigenous people actively contesting the state's hold over land and resources in the Asia–Pacific region include the Moros of the southern Philippines (see Map 7.2, page 160) and the people of Western Papua, the western part of the island of New Guinea controlled by Indonesia (see Map 1.2, page 17). In some cases, indigenous people's fight for secession from the state continues to cost many lives, mainly their own.

Africa   In Africa, political interests of state governments in establishing and enforcing territorial boundaries have created difficulties for indigenous peoples, especially mobile populations such as foragers and pastoralists. Many formerly autonomous pastoralists of the Sahel region (see Map 14.6, page 353) have been transformed into refugees living in terrible conditions. The Tuareg (TWAH-reg), for example, have

MAP 15.6 Sudan.

The Republic of Sudan gained its independence from Britain in 1956 but, unlike other former British colonies, did not join the Commonwealth. The year before independence, a civil war began between the north and south. In 2003, conflict erupted in the Darfur region. In 2005, a treaty granted southern Sudan the status of an autonomous region for six years, to be followed by a referendum. Most of the economy depends on agriculture, although oil production and trade have increased. The population of 37 million includes two ethnic groups: Arabs with Nubian roots and non-Arab Black Africans. Arabic is the dominant language of the north. Most Sudanese also speak local tribal languages. Sunni Islam is the dominant religion (70 percent) in the north, with indigenous religions also important (25 percent). Christianity (5 percent) is practiced mainly in the south.

traditionally lived and herded in a territory that now crosses five different countries: Mali, Niger, Algeria, Burkina Faso, and Libya (Childs and Chelala 1994).

Because of political conflict in the region, thousands of Tuareg people live in exile in Mauritania, and their situation is grim. Resistance movements spring up, but states act to suppress them. The people of southern Sudan and Darfur have been living in violence for many years (Map 15.6). They have been subject to genocide and violent displacement for global and local political and economic reasons, not the least of which involves the rich deposits of oil in the southern part of the country (Warren 2001). As mentioned in the Culturama in Chapter 1 (page 21), South Africa has established more protective legislation for San peoples than have Namibia or Botswana.

Australia and New Zealand The picture is also mixed in Australia and New Zealand, with more progress in Australia in terms of legal recognition of Aboriginal territorial rights.

Urban development, expansion of the non-Aboriginal population, road building, mineral extraction, and international tourism are some of the major threats to both livelihoods and the protection of sacred space. Aboriginal activism has seen some notable successes in achieving what is referred to as *native title* (Colley 2002). A key turning point in Australia occurred through the efforts of Eddie Koiko Mabo (koy-ko mah-bo), from the Torres Strait Islands. He and his group, the Miriam people, took their claim of rights to their traditional land and water to the High Court, contesting the principle of *terra nullius*, or "empty land." Colonialists and neocolonialist developers use *terra nullius* to justify territorial take-overs, claiming that no one lives in a particular place because there is no evidence of property ownership, agriculture, or permanent structures. This claim justified the colonial takeover of large parts of the world occupied by foragers, horticulturalists, and pastoralists. In this landmark case, Mabo convinced the High Court of the legitimacy of the Miriams' claim in 1992 and set a precedent for a series of future land claims by indigenous peoples of Australia.

ORGANIZING FOR CHANGE Many indigenous peoples have formed organizations for change in order to promote *development from within*. In Ethiopia, for example, several NGOs organized by local people have sprung up since the 1990s (Kassam 2002). One organization in the southern region, Hundee, seeks to provide a model of development based on the oral folk traditions of the Oromo people. It combines elements of Western-defined development with Oromo values and traditional laws, thus offering an approach that recasts external notions of development in terms of Oromo lifeways. Hundee's long-term goal is to empower Oromo communities to be self-sufficient. It takes the view that the Oromo culture is a positive force for, rather than a barrier to, social and economic change. Hundee members use a participatory approach in all their endeavors. They consult with traditional legal assemblies to identify needs and then to shape projects that address those needs. Activities include the establishment of a credit association and a grain bank to help combat price fluctuations and food shortages. The Oromo feel that these are elements of *good development*, as distinguished from the outsiders' *bad development*, which has inflicted hunger and dependency on the Oromo people.

In many cases, indigenous people's development organizations join forces in response to external threats (Perry 1996:245–246). In Australia, several indigenous groups have formed regional coalitions and pan-Australian organizations that have been successful in land-claim cases. In Canada, the Grand Council of the Cree collaborates with other northern groups over land issues and opposition to a major hydroelectric dam project (Coon Come 2004, Craik 2004). In southern Africa, several San groups joined together to claim a share in the profits from commercial marketing of hoodia as a diet pill (review Culturama, Chapter 1, page 21). Indigenous groups are taking advantage of new technology and media to build and maintain links with each other over large areas.

Although it is tempting to see hope in the newly emerging forms of resistance, self-determination, and organization among indigenous peoples, such hope cannot be generalized to all indigenous groups. Many are making progress in asserting their claims, and their economic status is improving, but many others are suffering extreme political and economic repression and possible extinction.

Women and Development

The category of women contrasts with that of indigenous peoples because women, as a group, do not have a recognized territory associated with them. But the effects of colonialism, and now development, on women are similar to their effects on indigenous people: Women have often lost economic entitlements and political power in their communities. Matrilineal kinship, for example, which keeps property in the female line (review Chapter 8), is in decline throughout the world. Westernization and modernization are frequently the cause of this change. Another factor that has had a pervasive negative effect on women's status is the **male bias in development**, or the design and implementation of development projects with men as beneficiaries and without regard to their impact on women's roles and status.

THE MALE BIAS IN DEVELOPMENT In the 1970s, researchers began to notice and write about the fact that development projects were male biased (Boserup 1970, Tinker 1976). Many projects completely bypassed women as beneficiaries, targeting men for such initiatives as growing cash crops and learning about new technology. This male bias in development contributed to increased gender inequality by giving men greater access to new sources of income and by depriving women of their traditional economic roles. The development experts' image of a farmer, for example, was male, not female.

Women's projects were typically focused on the domestic domain—for example, infant feeding practices, child care, and family planning. This emphasis led to the *domestication of women* worldwide, meaning that their lives became more focused on the domestic domain and more removed from the public domain (Rogers 1979). For example, agricultural projects bypassed female horticulturalists, who were taught to spend more time in the house bathing their babies, and political leadership projects focused on men and left women out even in contexts where women traditionally had public political roles.

The male bias in development also contributed to the failure of some projects. In the West African country of Burkina Faso (see Map 14.6, page 353), a reforestation project

included men as the sole participants, whose tasks would include planting and caring for the trees. Cultural patterns there, however, dictate that men do not water plants; women do. The men planted the seedlings and left them. Excluding women from the project ensured its failure. The exclusion of women from development continues to be a problem, in spite of many years of attempting to keep women's roles on the development agenda.

The inclusion of women's knowledge, concerns, and voices in research has brought new and important issues to the fore, redefining development to fits women's needs (Figure 15.2). One such issue is gender-based violence. This issue has gained attention even among large multilateral organizations, whose experts now realize that women cannot participate in a credit program, for example, if they fear that their husbands will beat them for leaving the house. The United Nations Commission on the Status of Women drafted a declaration in opposition of violence against women that was adopted by the General Assembly in 1993 (Heise, Pitanguy, and Germain 1994). Article 1 of the declaration states that violence against women includes "any act of gender-based violence that results in, or is likely to result in, physical, sexual or psychological harm or suffering to women, including threats of such acts, coercion or arbitrary deprivations of liberty, whether occurring in public or private life" (Economic and Social Council 1992). This definition cites women as the focus of concern but also includes girls.

Prebirth	Sex-selective abortion, battering during pregnancy, coerced pregnancy
Infancy	Infanticide, emotional and physical abuse, deprivation of food and medical care
Girlhood	Child marriage, genital mutilation, sexual abuse by family members and strangers, rape, deprivation of food and medical care, child prostitution
Adolescence	Dating and courtship violence, forced prostitution, rape, sexual abuse in the workplace, sexual harassment
Adulthood	Rape and partner abuse, partner homicide, sexual abuse in the workplace, sexual harassment
Old Age	Abuse and neglect of widows, elder abuse

Source: Adapted from Heise, Pitanguy, and Germain 1994:5.

FIGURE 15.2 Violence against Girls and Women throughout the Life Cycle.

male bias in development the design and implementation of development projects with men as beneficiaries and without regard to the impact of the projects on women's roles and status.

In the town of San Cristóbal de las Casas, the capital city of Chiapas state in Mexico, a Maya vendor sells her goods. The city is located near the Tzotzil Maya community of Zinacantán.

Programs that target violence against girls and women tend to deal with their effects rather than the causes, often with disastrous results. For example, programs may seek to increase personal security of women and girls in refugee camps by augmenting the number of guards at the camp when, in fact, the guards are often guilty of abusing refugee women and girls (Martin 2005).

WOMEN'S ORGANIZATIONS FOR CHANGE In many countries, women have improved their status and welfare through forming organizations, which are sometimes part of their traditional culture and sometimes a response to outside inspiration. These organizations range from mothers' clubs that help provide for communal child care to credit organizations that give women opportunities to start their own businesses. Some are local and small scale; others are global, such as Women's World Banking, an international organization that started in India and Bangladesh and grew out of credit programs for poor working women.

In another case, an informal system of social networks emerged to help support poor Maya women vendors in San Cristóbal, Chiapas, Mexico (Sullivan 1992) (see Map 6.3, page 140). Many of the vendors who work in the city square have fled from the highlands because of long-term political conflict there. They manufacture and sell goods to tourists, earning an important portion of household income. In the city, they find social support in an expanded network that helps compensate for the loss of support from the extensive godparenthood system (review Chapter 8) of the highlands. The vendors' new networks include relatives, neighbors, church members, and other vendors, regardless of their religious, political, economic, or social background.

The networks first developed in response to a series of rapes and robberies that began in 1987. Because the offenders were persons of power and influence, the women did not dare to press charges. Mostly single mothers and widows, they adopted a strategy of self-protection. First, they began to gather during the slow period each afternoon. Second, they always travel in groups. Third, they carry sharpened corset bones and prongs: "If a man insults one of them, the group surrounds him and jabs him in the groin" (Sullivan 1992:39–40). Fourth, if a woman is robbed, the other women surround her, comfort her, and help contribute something toward compensating her for her loss. The mid-afternoon gatherings developed into support groups that provide financial assistance, child care, medical advice, and training in job skills. The groups have publicly demonstrated against city officials' attempts to prevent them from continuing their vending. Through their collective efforts, they have succeeded in bringing greater security into their lives.

A last example of women's empowerment and personal risk reduction through organized efforts comes from Kazakhstan, Central Asia (see Map 10.4, page 250). In response to the widespread domestic violence of husbands against wives, an NGO called the Society of Muslim Women (SMW) defines domestic violence as a problem that the Islamic faith should address at the grassroots level (Snajdr 2005). The organization declines to work with the police and civic activists, who provide secular responses that involve criminalization of the offense, arrest of offenders, and other public procedures. Instead, SMW views domestic violence as

---

development aggression the imposition of development projects and policies without the free, prior, and informed consent of the affected people.

life project local people's definition of the direction they want to take in life, informed by their knowledge, history, and context.

a private matter that should be dealt with by using Islamic and Kazakh values. Its three approaches are counseling and shelter for abused women and couples' mediation. SMW's guiding principle is to find a way, if possible, to rebuild the family, something that may sound conservative, and even dangerous, in a situation where wife abuse is reported to occur in four out of five marriages. Yet, without funding or professional training, SMW members have provided support for countless women. They help the women overcome isolation by offering shelter, which conforms to the Kazakh custom of hospitality and the Muslim virtue of patience. SMW support gives the spouses time to think about their relationship and shifts blame from the victims by invoking Islamic values of familial commitment and gender equality. Nationalist rhetoric shifts blame for men's alcoholism from the individual to the Russian occupation. Thus, SMW works within the bounds of Kazakh culture and uses that culture for positive outcomes within those bounds.

Grameen Bank, a development project in Bangladesh that provides small loans to poor people, is one of the most successful examples of improving human welfare through microcredit. Muhammad Yunus (right) founded Grameen Bank. He is a Bangladeshi economist and recipient of the Nobel Peace Prize.

▶ *How does the success of Grameen Bank cause you to question your previous image of Bangladesh?*

◉ ◉ ◉

Urgent Issues in Development

This chapter opened with a quotation about the people of Walpole Island Reservation in Canada and their ongoing attempt to recover from the damage that colonialism and neo-colonialism have wreaked on their culture and natural environment. In spite of much progress of local people and women in redefining development to improve their lives, rather than the lives of external groups such as international businesses and neocolonial states, the bulk of "development" money still goes for mega-projects that do more for people who already have resources than for the poor.

As discussed earlier in the chapter, development projects are the main mechanism through which development institutions implement their goals. These projects are typically designed by outsiders, often with little local knowledge, and they follow a universal, one-size-fits-all pattern. They range from mega-projects such as massive dams to small projects, with the former being much more damaging to local people than the latter. The so-called beneficiaries or target population are often not consulted at all about projects that will affect their community. Critics of such externally imposed and often damaging initiatives refer to them as **development aggression**, the imposition of development projects and policies without the free, prior, and informed consent of the affected people (Tauli-Corpuz 2005). Such development violates the human rights of local people, including their right to pursue a livelihood in their homeland and to prevent environmental destruction of their territory. It also contributes nothing to prevent or alleviate poverty.

Life Projects and Human Rights

Moving beyond critique, indigenous people, women, and others who are victimized by development aggression are redefining what should be done to improve their lives or protect them from further decline. They propose the concept of the life project rather than the development project. A **life project** is local people's vision of the direction they want to take in life, informed by their knowledge, history, and context, and how to achieve that vision.

Life projects can be considered a human right and thus in accord with the United Nations's Declaration of Human Rights that was ratified in 1948. Development that leads to environmental degradation, including loss of biological diversity, air and water pollution, deforestation, and soil erosion, is a human rights abuse. Many examples exist worldwide of how rich natural resources are improperly exploited to the gain of a few and the detriment of many, turning what could be a blessing into a curse (see Eye on the Environment on page 378).

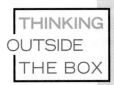

THINKING OUTSIDE THE BOX

What lessons might SMW be able to share with programs that seek to prevent wife abuse in other countries? See pages 376–377 for information about the Society of Muslim Women (SMW). (Recall the case of wife abuse in Kentucky presented in Chapter 8, page 201.)

eye on the ENVIRONMENT

Oil, Environmental Degradation, and Human Rights in the Niger Delta

During the British colonial era, Nigeria provided wealth for the Crown through the export of palm oil (Osha 2006). In the postcolonial era of globalization, a different kind of oil dominates the country's economy: petroleum. Starting in the 1950s, with the discovery of vast petroleum reserves in Nigeria's Delta region, several European and American companies have explored for, drilled for, and exported crude oil to the extent that Nigeria occupies an important position in the world economy.

Most local people in the delta, however, have gained few economic benefits from the oil industry and instead have reaped major losses in their agricultural and fishing livelihoods due to environmental pollution. They are poorer now than they were in the 1960s. In

© 2010 Tim Lambon Greenpeace

(LEFT) A farmer walks through an oil-soaked field. About 500,000 Ogoni people live in Ogoniland, a deltaic region in southern Nigeria. The fertility of the Niger delta has supported farming and fishing populations at high density for many years. Since Shell discovered oil there in 1958, 100 oil wells were constructed in Ogoniland and countless oil spills have occurred. (RIGHT) Ogoni author and Nobel prizewinner Ken Saro-Wiwa founded the Movement for Survival of Ogoni People (MOSOP) in 1992 to protest Shell's actions in Ogoniland and the Nigerian government's indifference. In 1995, he was arrested, tried for murder under suspicious circumstances, and executed by hanging. Shell has denied any role in his death.

The major extractive industries of mining, oil, and gas are driven by the profit motive to the extent that they are disinclined to take local people's interests and environmental concerns seriously. An **extractive industry** is a business that explores for, removes, processes, and sells minerals, oil, and gas that are found on or beneath the earth's surface and are nonrenewable. The many tragic cases of local violence around the world where local people seek to prevent or remove an extractive industry project from their land, however, have been a wake-up call to some companies. Rio Tinto, one of the largest mining companies in the world, seeks to use cultural anthropology expertise to find ways to treat "affected peoples" more fairly and to do a better job of ensuring that environmental "mitigation" will occur once a mine is closed (Cochrane 2008).

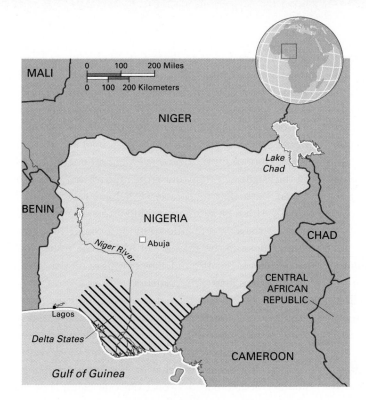

MAP 15.7 Nigeria and the Niger Delta.

Nigeria is the most populous country in Africa, with over 140 million people. It has more than 250 ethnic groups, with the largest being the Fulani, Hausa, Yorùbá, and Igbo. Nigerians speak over 500 languages; English is the official language. Nigeria is Africa's biggest petroleum producer, with an average of 2 million barrels a day extracted in the Niger Delta. The delta makes up 7.5 percent of Nigeria's landmass, but its population of 31 million accounts for 22 percent of the population. The Niger Delta's petroleum industry supports a high economic growth rate for the country, making it one of the fastest growing economies in the world. Yet little of this wealth filters back to the local people of the delta, who bear the brunt of the environmental and cultural damage caused by the petroleum industry. Oil spills are a frequent problem. One of the world's richest wetlands and richest areas of cultural diversity, with over 40 ethnic groups, is endangered by large-scale petroleum mining that benefits people in the capital city and in other countries.

for Survival of the Ogoni People (MOSOP) in 1992 to protest Shell's actions in Ogoniland and the Nigerian government's militarized repression in the region. In 1995, he and eight other Ogoni activists were arrested, tried under suspicious circumstances, and executed by hanging.

In a 1992 speech to the United Nations Working Group on Indigenous Populations, Saro-Wiwa eloquently points to the connections among resource extraction, the environment, and Ogoni human rights and social justice:

> Environmental degradation has been a lethal weapon in the war against the indigenous Ogoni people. . . . Oil exploration has turned Ogoni into a wasteland: lands, streams, and creeks are totally and continually polluted; the atmosphere has been poisoned, charged as it is with hydrocarbon vapors, methane, carbon monoxide, carbon dioxide, and soot emitted by gas which has been flared 24 hours a day for 33 years in close proximity to human habitation. . . . All one sees and feels around is death. (quoted in Sachs 1996:13–16)

Many social scientists agree with Saro-Wiwa that such forms of development violate human and cultural rights because they undermine a people's way of life and threaten its continued existence (Johnston 1994).

FOOD FOR THOUGHT ▼

Use the Internet to explore the concept of corporate social responsibility, and be prepared to discuss its relationship to the Ogoni situation.

addition to economic suffering, they have lost personal security. Many have become victims of the violence that has increased in the region since the 1990s through state and corporate repression of a local resistance movement. Many others have become IDPs (review Chapter 14), leaving the delta region to escape the pervasive violence.

The Ogoni, who live in the southeastern portion of the delta, are one of the most negatively affected groups. Ogoni author and Nobel prizewinner Ken Saro-Wiwa founded the Movement

What drives extractive industries to continue to explore for gold, drill for oil, and cut down trees? What drives countries to build mega-dams and mega-highways? The demand lies with all of us, in our consumerist lifestyle that requires diamonds for engagement rings, gold and platinum for computers and gold and copper for cell phones, electrical power for air conditioning, and fuel to transport us, our food and water,

and everything else we buy. Entire mountains in West Virginia are being leveled to provide coal to power the air conditioning used in Washington, DC. Forests in Brazil and

---

extractive industry a business that explores for, removes, processes, and sells minerals, oil, and gas that are found on or beneath the earth's surface and are nonrenewable.

New Guinea are taken down so that we can read the newspaper. Corn is being harvested to move vehicles rather than to feed people, and millions of gallons of water are being used to process minerals such as aluminum, rather than being available for human drinking, bathing, and swimming, or for fish and water fowl. It will take a lot to turn this pattern around from destructive projects to life projects.

Cultural Heritage and Development: Linking the Past and Present to the Future

Chapter 13 discussed the potential of cultural heritage, both tangible and nontangible, in creating employment opportunities for local people through cultural tourism. This section goes more deeply into the complicated connections between cultural heritage and improving people's welfare from a life project perspective.

The connection of cultural heritage tourism to development is a double-edged sword, with both benefits and costs (Bauer 2006). Promoting cultural heritage through tourism requires an expansion of supportive infrastructure such as roads and hotels and electricity, the provision of food and other supplies for tourists, and labor to provide services for tourists. Thus, at the same time that it generates revenue, such tourism can preserve and protect cultural heritage, but the presence of the tourism industry and the tourists themselves may damage and even destroy it. Such famous World Heritage Sites as Angkor Wat in Cambodia and Machu Picchu in Peru are physically suffering the strains of huge numbers of tourists. Venice, the world's most touristed city, is also a World Heritage Site. Given its particular attraction as a city of canals, it is at particular risk of overload and environmental degradation from the ever-increasing number of tourist boats in the canals, not to mention the massive amount of solid and liquid trash that tourists leave behind (David and Marvin 2004). Although promotional literature advertising Venice to tourists shows a romantic scene of a couple in a gondola or sitting alone in the Piazza San Marco, the reality is that the couple would be surrounded by crowds of tourists and heckled by ambitious local entrepreneurs.

A growing area related to cultural heritage preservation is intellectual property rights law, or cultural property rights law. Lawyers worldwide are increasingly involved in providing legal definitions and protections of rights to various forms of cultural knowledge and behavior. The legalization of culture is another double-edged sword: On one hand, laws may help people, such as the San of southern Africa, to gain a share of the profits from the hoodia plant. On the other hand, the legalization of culture can transform much of everyday life into a legal battle requiring expensive legal specialists. For thousands of years, the San had full and unquestioned entitlement to hoodia and its benefits. They did not need to hire international lawyers.

  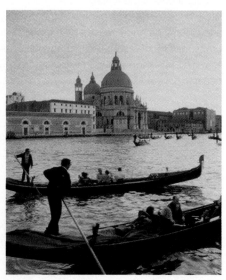

These World Heritage Sites both benefit and suffer from the designation because of the many tourists drawn to them. (LEFT) Located high in the Peruvian Andes, the fifteenth-century palace complex at Machu Picchu (mah-choo pee-choo) was designated a World Heritage Site in 1983. (CENTER) Angkor Wat, which means "The Temple City," was designated a World Heritage Site in 1983. It was built in the twelfth century as a Hindu temple, but later additions to it were Buddhist. Current tourist numbers are harming the site due to trash, pedestrian traffic, and hotel development. In 1983, fewer than 8000 tourists visited the site. Projections starting with 2010 are 3 million and more per year. (RIGHT) Gondolas on the Grand Canal, Venice, Italy. Venice, or Venezia in Italian, is considered to be one of the world's most beautiful cities. It was designated a World Heritage site in 1987.

▶ *Plan a trip to one of these sites and learn whether "green" options exist for accommodations, or if the sites otherwise promote ways to reduce damage from tourists.*

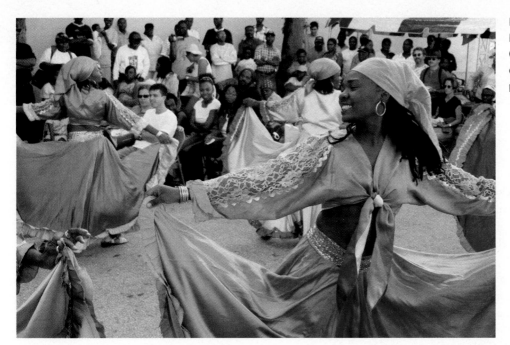

Haitian dancers perform on Discover Miami Day at Miami's Little Haiti Caribbean Marketplace. Haitian culture in Miami is an increasingly popular tourist attraction.

Everything from website addresses that may use tribal names to the designation of what is or is not champagne can now become grounds for litigation. And money, you can be sure, is involved from the start to the finish, as is the more difficult to quantify sense of identity of people who define themselves in relation to a place, a product, or a taste.

Cultural Anthropology and the Future

Over the next several years, culture will be a major factor in international, regional, and local development and change.

Determining how knowledge in cultural anthropology can contribute more effectively to a better future for humanity is a challenge for a field with its intellectual roots in studying *what is* rather than *what might be*. But just as local people everywhere are redefining development and reclaiming their culture, so are they also helping to redefine the theory, practice, and application of cultural anthropology. Although we live in a time of war, it is also a time of hope, in which insights and strength often come from those with the least in terms of material wealth but with cultural wealth beyond measure.

15 the BIG questions REVISITED

What is development, and what are the approaches to achieving it?

Several theories or models of development exist, including modernization, growth-oriented development, distributional development, human development, and sustainable development. They differ in terms of how they define development and how to achieve it.

Institutional approaches to development, whether pursued by large-scale or grassroots organizations, tend to rely on the development project as a vehicle of local change. Cultural anthropologists have been hired as consultants on development projects, typically at the end of the project cycle to provide evaluations. Anthropologists have pushed for involvement earlier in the project so that their cultural knowledge can be used in project planning to avoid common errors. A one-size-fits-all project design often results in failed projects.

In traditional development anthropology, anthropological knowledge contributes to a development project by adding insights that will make the project work. In critical development anthropology, anthropological knowledge may suggest that the most socially beneficial path is either to stop the project or to redesign it.

How has development affected indigenous people and women?

Indigenous people and women have been affected by international development in various ways, often negatively. They are taking an increasingly active role in redefining development to better suit their vision of the future.

Colonialism, neocolonialism, and globalization have eroded the entitlements of indigenous peoples and women worldwide. Often, such losses are tied to environmental degradation and violence. Indigenous peoples throughout the world suffer because they lack a secure claim to their ancestral territories. They seek social recognition of territorial claims from state governments and protection from encroachment. Some governments are responding to their claims; others are not. Establishing activist organizations has been a major source of strength for promoting indigenous people's rights.

Western development planning and projects have long suffered from a male bias in project design. Excluding women from projects serves to domesticate women and often results in failed projects. Women are stating their needs and visions for the future, thus redefining development in ways that are helpful to them. They have added the issue of violence against women and girls to the policy agendas of development institutions worldwide, including the large multilateral organizations.

What are urgent issues in development?

Three urgent issues, as informed by cultural anthropology and the views and voices of people themselves, are the redefinition of development projects as life projects, or people-centered projects; the relationship between human rights and development; and the role of cultural heritage in development. Indigenous people, women, and others adversely affected by certain forms of development are promoting these new kinds of development in order to enhance their prospects for the future.

The concept of the life project is a human right and a right to live in one's cultural world without encroachment, threat, or discrimination. Cultural anthropologists contribute insights from different cultures about perceptions of basic human and cultural rights, and this knowledge, linked to advocacy, may be able to help prevent human/cultural rights abuses in the future.

People's cultural heritage can be a path toward improved welfare, but it is a double-edged sword. Promoting cultural tourism can protect culture but also lead to damage and destruction. An emerging area is the legalization of cultural heritage through intellectual property rights law, another double-edged sword.

Culture is a central issue of our time, and local people are working with cultural anthropologists to address the challenges of an increasingly globalized and insecure, but exciting, world.

KEY CONCEPTS

SUGGESTED READINGS

Mario Blaser, Harvey A. Feit, and Glenn McRae, eds. *In the Way of Development: Indigenous Peoples, Life Projects and Globalization*. New York: Zed Books, 2004. The authors are indigenous leaders, social activists, and anthropologists. Topics include the environment, women's status, social justice, participation, and dealing with mega-development projects.

Glynn Cochrane. *Festival Elephants and the Myth of Global Poverty*. Boston: Pearson, 2009. More than 40 years of experience in international development inform this memoir and critique. Cochrane argues that no single form of global poverty exists but that poverty is local and must be addressed with local solutions.

Ann Frechette. *Tibetans in Nepal: The Dynamics of International Assistance among a Community in Exile*. New York: Bergahn Books, 2002. Frechette shows how aid complicates exiled Tibetans' attempts to define and maintain a sense of community.

Dorothy L. Hodgson. *Once Intrepid Warriors: Gender, Ethnicity, and the Cultural Politics of Maasai Development*. Bloomington: Indiana University Press, 2004. This ethnography shows how Maasai identity and gender connect with development and globalization to shape Maasai life today.

Gideon M. Kressel. *Let Shepherding Endure: Applied Anthropology and the Preservation of a Cultural Tradition in Israel and the Middle East*. Albany: SUNY Press, 2003. Kressel presents a case study of the Bedu of the Negev, southern Israel, showing how globalization is encroaching on herders to their great detriment and laying out an applied anthropology program for reconstituting and promoting pastoralism.

Goodale, Mark. *Surrendering to Utopia: An Anthropology of Human Rights*. Stanford: Stanford University Press, 2009. Goodale examines the influence of cultural anthropology on human rights doctrine following World War II.

William Loker. *Changing Places: Environment, Development, and Social Change in Rural Honduras*. Durham, NC: Carolina Academic Press, 2004. Loker uses qualitative and quantitative data to assess the social and environmental effects of a large dam in the El Cajón region of Honduras.

Mathews, Gordon and Carolina Izquierdo, eds. *Pursuits of Happiness: Well-Being in Anthropological Perspective*, 2009. Case studies provide varied notions about individual and social well-being in different contexts.

Richard J. Perry. *From Time Immemorial: Indigenous Peoples and State Systems*. Austin: University of Texas Press, 1996. Perry provides a comparative review of the history and status of indigenous peoples of Mexico, the United States, Canada, and Australia. Topics covered are state policies, state violence, resistance of the indigenous people, and efforts at self-determination.

Joanne Rappaport. *Intercultural Utopias: Public Intellectuals, Cultural Experimentation, and Ethnography*. Durham, NC: Duke University Press, 2005. Drawing on collaborative research with indigenous activists in Colombia, the author documents the country's complex indigenous political movement with a focus on the southwestern Cauca region.

John Sherry. *Land, Wind and Hard Words: A Story of Navajo Activism*. Albuquerque: University of New Mexico Press, 2002. This book presents the story of the community-based activists of a Navajo environmental organization called Diné CARE, which seeks to protect Navajo forests from logging.

Jennie M. Smith. *When the Hands Are Many: Community Organization and Social Change in Rural Haiti*. Ithaca, NY: Cornell University Press, 2001. Fieldwork in southwest Haiti reveals how poor rural people use social organizing and expressive culture to unite in resistance to the larger forces that impoverish them.

For further information about topics covered in this chapter, go to MyAnthroLab at **www.myanthrolab.com** and access the following readings in MyAnthroLibrary:

Ben J. Wallace. Doing Development One Chicken at a Time: Happy Hollow Egg Production as an Unlikely Spin-Off from an Agro-forestry Development Project. *Practicing Anthropology* 31(1):9–10, 2010. Wallace describes how community members came up with an idea that worked for them, but it was not about trees.

Cheryl White. Saramaka Maroon Community Environmental Heritage. *Practicing Anthropology* 31(3):45–49, 2009. The Sara maka Maroons of Suriname, South America, have been asserting their human rights in the face of government-supported logging on and destruction of their ancestral land.

Text Credits

Fig. 6.2, Page 135: Model of the Demographic Transition Source: Nebel, Bernard J.; Wright, Richard T. *Environmental Science: The Way the World Works*, 7/e. © 2000. Reproduced by permission of Pearson Education. [for ebook: Electronically reproduced by permission of Pearson Education]; **Fig. 6.3, Page 137:** Source: Statistics Bureau, MIC, Ministry of Health, Labor and Welfare. Reproduced with permission.; **Fig. 10.2, Page 247:** From *Aboriginal Youth and the Criminal Justice System: The Injustice of Justice?* by Fay Gale, Rebecca Bailey-Harris and Joy Wundersitz. Copyright © 1990 by Cambridge University Press. Reprinted with permission.; **Fig. 11.3, Page 264:** Redrawing of photos from "A Repertoire of South African Quotable Gestures," by Heather Brookes from *The Journal of Linguistic Anthropology*. Vol. 14, # 2, Dec. 2004, published by the American Anthropological Association. Used by permission of the author.; **Fig. 11.4, Page 270:** Male-Unmarked and Female-Marked Nouns in Japanese Source: *Language, Gender, and Sex in Comparative Perspective* by Susan U. Philips, Susan Steele, Christine Tanz. Copyright © 1987 Cambridge University Press. Reprinted with permission of Cambridge University Press; **Fig. 13.1, Page 316:** From "Power and Gender in the Musical Experiences of Women" pp. 224–225 by Carol E. Robertson in *Women and Music in Cross-Cultural Perspective*, ed. by Ellen Kostoff. Copyright © 1987. Reprinted by permission of ABC-CLIO, LLC.

Photo Credits

Chapter 1: Page 2: Keren Su/Getty Images, Inc.—Lonely Planet Images; **Page 4:** © Lindsay Hebberd/CORBIS All Rights Reserved; **Page 4:** J.A. English-Lueck, Cofounder Silicon Valley Cultures Project; **Page 6:** Scott Sady\AP Wide World Photos; **Page 6:** © Photo by Richard Gould; **Page 7:** Barbara D. Miller; **Page 8:** © David Fernandez/CORBIS All Rights Reserved; **Page 11:** © Bettmann/CORBIS All Rights Reserved; **Page 11:** Courtesy of the Library of Congress; **Page 12:** Dr. Patricia Tovar; **Page 13:** © Viviane Moos/CORBIS All Rights Reserved; **Page 13:** © Peter Dench/CORBIS All Rights Reserved; **Page 14:** Michael Newman\PhotoEdit Inc.; **Page 15:** © Philip Gould/CORBIS All Rights Reserved; **Page 16:** © Soeren Stache/CORBIS All Rights Reserved; **Page 16:** © Mariana Bazor/CORBIS All Rights Reserved; **Page 17:** Barbara D. Miller; **Page 19:** Barbara D. Miller; **Page 21:** © Stan Washburn/Anthro-Photo; **Page 21:** © Leslie Gubb/CORBIS All Rights Reserved; **Page 20:** © Bob Krist/CORBIS All Rights Reserved; **Page 23:** Mike Perry\Alamy Images; **Page 24:** © Jack Fields/CORBIS All Rights Reserved; **Page 24:** AP Wide World Photos

Chapter 2: Page 31: Newscom; **Page 33:** © Theo Allofs/Zefa/CORBIS All Rights Reserved; **Page 34:** AP Photo/Al Behrman\AP Wide World Photos; **Page 34:** Karl & Kay Amman\A.G.E. FotoStock; **Page 34:** Connie Bransilver\Photo Researchers, Inc.; **Page 36:** Spooner/Redmond-Callow\ZUMA Press—Gamma; **Page 37:** © Heather Angel/Natural Visions; **Page 38:** © Patrick Robert/CORBIS All Rights Reserved; **Page 37:** © 2009 Frans Lanting/www.lanting.com; **Page 39:** Donald Johanson/Institute of Human Origins, Arizona State University; **Page 40:** © Lowell Georgia/CORBIS All Rights Reserved; **Page 41:** Werner Forman\Art Resource, N.Y.; **Page 42:** © Mick Tsikas/epa/CORBIS All Rights Reserved; **Page 45:** Sally McBrearty; **Page 46:** Courtesy Dept. of Library Services, American Museum of Natural History.; **Page 47:** Réunion des Musées Nationaux\Art Resource, N.Y.; **Page 47:** Naturhistorisches Museum, Vienna, Austria. © Photography by Erich Lessing/Art Resource, NY; **Page 47:** Head of the "Woman of Brassempouy". Paleolithic sculpture, mammoth ivory. Musee des Antiquites Nationales, Saint-Germain-en-Laye, France. Reunion des Musees Nationaux. J.G. Berizzi/Art Resource, NY; **Page 47:** Courtesy Arizona State Museum © Jerry Jacka Photography; **Page 49:** © Yann Arthus-Bertrand; **Page 50:** © Adam Woolfitt/CORBIS All Rights Reserved; **Page 51:** © Nik Wheeler/Bettmann/CORBIS All Rights Reserved; **Page 51:** The Granger Collection, New York; **Page 52:** Dave Rudkin © Dorling Kindersley, Courtesy of the Birmingham Museum and Art Galleries; **Page 52:** Cahokia

Mounds State Historic Site - painting by Michael Hampshire; **Page 28:** Luis Escobar

Chapter 03: Page 56: © Ed Tronick/Anthro-Photo; **Page 58:** Helena Malinowski Wayne\Pearson Education/PH College; **Page 58:** A.R. Radcliffe-Brown, "The Andaman Islanders". Cambridge: Cambridge University Press, 1964 [1922]; **Page 59:** © Irven Devore/Anthro-Photo; **Page 59:** © Albrecht G. Schaefer/CORBIS All Rights Reserved; **Page 60:** Lanita Jacobs-Huey; **Page 61:** © Left Lane Productions/CORBIS All Rights Reserved; **Page 62:** © Philippe Issac/Godong/ CORBIS All Rights Reserved; **Page 62:** © Wolfgang Kumm/epa/CORBIS All Rights Reserved; **Page 62:** © Kazuyoshi Nomachi/CORBIS All Rights Reserved; **Page 64:** Jennifer Robertson; **Page 66:** Liza Dalby; **Page 67:** Isabel Balseiro; **Page 70:** © Mel Konner/Anthro-Photo; **Page 70:** Gananath Obeyesekere; **Page 71:** © Michael M. Horowitz; **Page 73:** © Atlantide Phototravel/CORBIS All Rights Reserved; **Page 74:** © Catherine Karnow/CORBIS All Rights Reserved; **Page 76:** Danny Gawlowski; **Page 77:** Danny Hoffman

Chapter 4: Page 80: Atul Loke/PANOS; **Page 82:** Joel Savishinsky\Dr. Joel Savishinsky; **Page 84:** Barbara D. Miller; **Page 84:** Sven Torfinn\Panos Pictures; **Page 85:** © Irven DeVore/Anthro-Photo; **Page 87:** Dr. Joel Savishinsky; **Page 88:** Pankaj Sekhsaria; **Page 88:** Pankaj Sekhsaria; **Page 89:** © Charles O. Cecil; **Page 90:** Stock Montage, Inc./Historical Pictures Collection; **Page 92:** Barbara D. Miller; **Page 92:** Elliot Fratkin; **Page 93:** KENNETH GARRETT\National Geographic Image Collection; **Page 95:** © Jeremy Horner/CORBIS All Rights Reserved; **Page 95:** Tim Flach/Stone/Getty Images; **Page 97:** Barbara D. Miller; **Page 98:** Sven Torfinn\Panos Pictures; **Page 100:** Samanti de Silva\Samanti De Silva; **Page 100:** Art Directors & TRIP\Alamy Images; **Page 101:** © Adrian Arbib/CORBIS All Rights Reserved

Chapter 5: Page 110: Barbara D. Miller; **Page 111:** Michelangelo Gratton\Getty Images/Digital Vision; **Page 111:** Getty Images, Inc.; **Page 112:** Borderlands\Alamy Images; **Page 112:** Edward Keller, Photographer; **Page 113:** © Stephanie Kuykendal/CORBIS All Rights Reserved; **Page 114:** © Shannon Stapleton/Reuters/CORBIS All Rights Reserved; **Page 116:** Peter Hendrie\Lonely Planet Images/Photo 20-20; **Page 118:** Charles O. Cecil\Cecil Images; **Page 119:** Charles O. Cecil\Cecil Images; **Page 120:** J Marshall\Alamy Images; **Page 123:** Barbara D. Miller; **Page 123:** © Bob Krist/CORBIS All Rights Reserved; **Page 124:** © Miguel Gandert/CORBIS All Rights Reserved; **Page 126:** © Wilson Melo/CORBIS All Rights Reserved; **Page 129:** Barbara D. Miller; **Page 128:** Vickie Jensen; **Page 128:** Vickie Jensen; **Page 106:** Caroline Penn\Panos Pictures

Chapter 6: Page 133: adam eastland\Alamy Images; **Page 136:** © David and Peter Turnley/Bettmann/CORBIS All Rights Reserved; **Page 136:** Barbara D. Miller; **Page 138:** Lee Page/ Stone/Getty Images; **Page 139:** Stephanie Dinkins\Photo Researchers, Inc.; **Page 141:** Barry Iverson\Woodfin Camp & Associates, Inc.; **Page 141:** © Reza; Webistan/CORBIS All Rights Reserved; **Page 142:** © Bettmann/CORBIS All Rights Reserved; **Page 143:** Nancy Scheper-Hughes; **Page 146:** © Napoleon A. Chagnon/Anthro-Photo; **Page 146:** © Bill Varie/CORBIS All Rights Reserved; **Page 147:** Bill Varie/Corbis; **Page 148:** Abigail E. Adams; **Page 150:** unknown\National Museum of American History/Smithsonian Institution, Photographic Collection; **Page 151:** © Kim Kyung-Hoon/ Reuters/CORBIS All Rights Reserved; **Page 152:** Dr. Barry S. Hewlett

Chapter 7: Page 156: © Kevin Fleming/CORBIS All Rights Reserved; **Page 158:** © Janet Jarman/CORBIS All Rights Reserved; **Page 164:** Barbara D. Miller; **Page 164:** Mary Beth Mills; **Page 164:** © Irven DeVore/Anthro-Photo; **Page 165:** © Ricardo Azoury/CORBIS All Rights Reserved; **Page 166:** © Ed Kashi/CORBIS All Rights Reserved; **Page 168:** © kcna/epa/CORBIS All Rights Reserved; **Page 169:** Lynn Johnson/National Geographic-\Getty-National Geographic Society; **Page 172:** Bloomberg via Getty Images\Getty Images, Inc—Bloomberg News; **Page 173:** Getty Images, Inc.; **Page 174:** © Str/Reuters/CORBIS All Rights Reserved; **Page 174:** Barbara D. Miller; **Page 175:** Holly Farrell/ABC/Getty Images,

acculturation a form of cultural change in which a minority culture becomes more like the dominant culture.

Acheulian tradition the tool kit of *H. erectus*, used from 1.7 million years ago to 300,000 years ago and characterized by handaxes.

achieved position a person's standing in society based on qualities that the person has gained through action.

adolescence a culturally defined period of maturation from the time of puberty until adulthood that is recognized in some, but not all, cultures.

age set a group of people close in age who go through certain rituals, such as circumcision, at the same time.

agency the ability of humans to make choices and exercise free will even within dominating structures.

agriculture a mode of livelihood that involves growing crops with the use of plowing, irrigation, and fertilizer.

amazon a person who is biologically female but takes on a male gender role.

Anatomically Modern Humans (AMH) or *Homo sapiens* or **modern humans** the species to which modern humans belong and also referred to by that term; first emerged in Africa between 300,000–160,000 years ago and then spread throughout the Old and New Worlds.

animatism a belief system in which the supernatural is conceived of as an impersonal power.

anomie breakdown of traditional values associated with rapid social change.

anthropogenic caused by humans.

anthropology the study of humanity, including its prehistoric origins and contemporary human diversity.

applied anthropology the use of anthropological knowledge to prevent or solve problems or to shape and achieve policy goals.

applied medical anthropology the application of anthropological knowledge to furthering the goals of health-care providers.

archaeology the study of past human cultures through their material remains.

archaic *Homo* a category of several extinct hominin species that lived from 2.4 million years to 19,000 years ago and is characterized by different stone tool traditions, depending on the species.

art the application of imagination, skill, and style to matter, movement, and sound that goes beyond what is purely practical.

artifact a portable object made or modified by humans.

ascribed position a person's standing in society based on qualities that the person has gained through birth.

asexuality lack of sexual attraction or interest in sexual activity.

assimilation a form of cultural change in which a culture is thoroughly acculturated, or decultured, and is no longer distinguishable as having a separate identity.

australopithecines a category of several extinct hominin species found in East and Central Africa that lived between 4.5 and 3 million years ago.

authority the ability to take action based on a person's achieved or ascribed status or moral reputation.

balanced exchange a system of transfers in which the goal is either immediate or eventual equality in value.

band the form of political organization of foraging groups, with flexible membership and minimal leadership.

berdache a blurred gender category, usually referring to a person who is biologically male but who takes on a female gender role.

big-man system or **big-woman system** a form of political organization midway between tribe and chiefdom and involving reliance on the leadership of key individuals who develop a political following through personal ties and redistributive feasts.

bilineal descent the tracing of descent through both parents.

biological anthropology the study of humans as biological organisms, including evolution and contemporary variation.

biological determinism a theory that explains human behavior and ideas as shaped mainly by biological features such as genes and hormones.

bipedalism upright locomotion on two feet.

blood sport a competition that explicitly seeks to bring about a flow of blood from, or even the death of, human–human contestants, human–animal contestants, or animal–animal contestants.

bracero an agricultural laborer in Latin America and the Caribbean who is permitted entry to a country to work for a limited time.

brachiation arboreal travel, using the forelimbs to swing from branch to branch, that is distinct to apes.

brideprice the transfer of cash and goods from the groom's family to the bride's family and to the bride.

brideservice a form of marriage exchange in which the groom works for his father-in-law for a certain length of time before returning home with the bride.

call system a form of oral communication among nonhuman primates with a set repertoire of meaningful sounds generated in response to environmental factors.

cargo cult a form of revitalization movement that emerged in Melanesia in response to Western and Japanese influences.

cash crop a plant grown primarily for sale rather than for one's own use.

caste system a form of social stratification linked with Hinduism and based on a person's birth into a particular group.

chain migration a form of population movement in which a first wave of migrants comes and then attracts relatives and friends to join them in the destination.

chiefdom a form of political organization in which permanently allied tribes and villages have one recognized leader who holds an "office."

circular migration repeated movement between two or more places, either within or between countries.

civil society the collection of interest groups that function outside the government to organize economic and other aspects of life.

class a way of categorizing people on the basis of their economic position in society, usually measured in terms of income or wealth.

Clovis culture New World population characterized by the Clovis point with the earliest site dated to 11,000 years ago in the Southwest United States.

collaborative research an approach to learning about culture that involves anthropologists working with members of the study population as partners and participants rather than as "subjects."

communication the process of sending and receiving meaningful messages.

community healing healing that emphasizes the social context as a key component and that is carried out within the public domain.

consumerism a mode of consumption in which people's demands are many and infinite and the means of satisfying them are insufficient and become depleted in the effort to satisfy these demands.

consumption fund a category of a personal or household budget used to provide for consumption needs and desires.

corporate social responsibility (CSR) business ethics that seek to generate profits for the corporation while avoiding harm to people and the environment.

couvade customs applying to the behavior of fathers during and shortly after the birth of their children.

creole a language directly descended from a pidgin but possessing its own native speakers and involving linguistic expansion and elaboration.

critical development anthropology an approach to international development in which the anthropologist takes a critical-thinking role and asks why and to whose benefit particular development policies and programs are pursued.

critical discourse analysis an approach within linguistic anthropology that examines how power and social inequality are reflected and reproduced in communication.

critical legal anthropology an approach within the cross-cultural study of legal systems that examines the role of law and judicial processes in maintaining the dominance of powerful groups through discriminatory practices rather than protecting less powerful people.

critical media anthropology an approach within the cross-cultural study of media that examines how power interests shape people's access to media and influence the contents of its messages.

critical medical anthropology an approach within medical anthropology involving the analysis of how economic and political structures shape people's health status, their access to health care, and the prevailing medical systems that exist in relation to them.

Cro-Magnons the first modern humans in Europe, dating from 40,000 years ago.

cross-cousin offspring of either one's father's sister or one's mother's brother.

cultural anthropology the study of living peoples and their cultures, including variation and change.

cultural broker someone who is familiar with two cultures and can promote communication and understanding across them.

cultural constructionism a theory that explains human behavior and ideas as shaped mainly by learning.

cultural fit a characteristic of informed and effective project design in which planners take local culture into account.

cultural materialism a theory that takes material features of life, such as the environment, natural resources, and mode of livelihood, as the bases for explaining social organization and ideology.

cultural relativism the perspective that each culture must be understood in terms of the values and ideas of that culture and not judged by the standards of another culture.

culture shock persistent feelings of uneasiness, loneliness, and anxiety that often occur when a person has shifted from one culture to a different one.

culture people's learned and shared behaviors and beliefs.

culture-specific syndrome a collection of signs and symptoms that is restricted to a particular culture or a limited number of cultures.

dalit the preferred name for the socially defined lowest groups in the Indian caste system; the name means "oppressed" or "ground down."

deductive approach (to research) a research method that involves posing a research question or hypothesis, gathering data related to the question, and then assessing the findings in relation to the original hypothesis.

demographic transition the change from the agricultural pattern of high fertility and high mortality to the industrial pattern of low fertility and low mortality.

descent the tracing of kinship relationships through parentage.

development change directed toward improving human welfare.

development aggression the imposition of development projects and policies without the free, prior, and informed consent of the affected people.

development-induced displacement the forced migration of a population due to development.

development project a set of activities designed to put development policies into action.

diaspora population a dispersed group of people living outside their original homeland.

diffusion the spread of culture through contact.

digital divide social inequality in access to new and emerging information technology, notably access to up-to-date computers, the Internet, and training related to their use.

discourse culturally patterned verbal language including varieties of speech, participation, and meaning.

disease in the disease–illness dichotomy, a biological health problem that is objective and universal.

disease of development a health problem caused or increased by economic development activities that have detrimental effects on the environment and people's relationship with it.

displaced person someone who is forced to leave his or her home, community, or country.

displacement a feature of human language whereby people are able to talk about events in the past and future.

doctrine direct and formalized statements about religious beliefs.

domestication a process by which human selection causes changes in the genetic material of plants and animals.

dowry the transfer of cash and goods from the bride's family to the newly married couple.

ecological/epidemiological approach an approach within medical anthropology that considers how aspects of the natural environment and social environment interact to cause illness.

economic system the linked processes of livelihood, consumption, and exchange.

emic insiders' perceptions and categories, and their explanations for why they do what they do.

endogamy marriage within a particular group or locality.

entitlement a culturally defined right to life-sustaining resources.

ethnicity a shared sense of identity among members of a group based on heritage, language, or culture.

ethnocentrism judging another culture by the standards of one's own culture rather than by the standards of that particular culture.

ethno-esthetics culturally specific definitions of what art is.

ethno-etiology a culturally specific causal explanation for health problems and suffering.

ethnography a firsthand, detailed description of a living culture, based on personal observation.

ethnomedicine the study of cross-cultural health systems.

ethnomusicology the cross-cultural study of music.

ethnosemantics the study of the meaning of words, phrases, and sentences in particular cultural contexts.

etic an analytical framework used by outside analysts in studying culture.

evolution inherited and cumulative change in the characteristics of a species, population, or culture.

exogamy marriage outside a particular group or locality.

expected reciprocity an exchange of approximately equally valued goods or services, usually between people roughly equal in social status.

expressive culture behaviors and beliefs related to art, leisure, and play.

extended household a coresidential group that comprises more than one parent–child unit.

extensive strategy   a form of livelihood involving temporary use of large areas of land and a high degree of spatial mobility.

extractive industry   a business that explores for, removes, processes, and sells minerals, oil, and gas that are found on or beneath the earth's surface and are nonrenewable.

family   a group of people who consider themselves related through a form of kinship, such as descent, marriage, or sharing.

family farming   a form of agriculture in which farmers produce mainly to support themselves but also produce goods for sale in the market system.

female genital cutting (FGC)   a range of practices involving partial or total removal of the clitoris and labia.

fertility   the rate of births in a population or the rate of population increase in general.

fieldwork   research in the field, which is any place where people and culture are found.

food security   the ability of an individual, household, group, or country to obtain an adequate diet over time in order to sustain health.

foraging   obtaining food available in nature through gathering, hunting, or scavenging.

formal sector   salaried or wage-based work registered in official statistics.

fossil   the preserved remains of a plant or animal of the past.

functionalism   the theory that a culture is similar to a biological organism, in which parts work to support the operation and maintenance of the whole.

gender   culturally constructed and learned behaviors and ideas attributed to males, females, or blended genders.

gender pluralism   the existence within a culture of multiple categories of femininity, masculinity, and blurred genders that are tolerated and legitimate.

generalized reciprocity   exchange involving the least conscious sense of interest in material gain or thought of what might be received in return.

global language   a language spoken widely throughout the world and in diverse cultural contexts, often replacing indigenous languages.

globalization   increased and intensified international ties related to the spread of Western, especially U.S., capitalism that affects all world cultures.

great apes   a category of large and tail-less primates that includes orangutans, gorillas, chimpanzees, bonobos, and humans.

heterotopia   something formed from elements drawn from multiple and diverse contexts.

hijra   in India, a blurred gender role in which a person, usually biologically male, takes on female dress and behavior.

historical linguistics   the study of language change using formal methods that compare shifts over time and across space in aspects of language, such as phonetics, syntax, and semantics.

historical trauma   the intergenerational transfer of the detrimental effects of colonialism from parents to children.

holism   the perspective in anthropology that cultures are complex systems that cannot be fully understood without paying attention to their different components, including economics, social organization, and ideology.

hominins   a category of primates that includes modern humans and extinct species of early human ancestors that are more closely related to humans than to living chimpanzees and bonobos.

horticulture   a mode of livelihood based on growing domesticated crops in gardens, using simple hand tools.

household   either one person living alone or a group of people who may or may not be related by kinship and who share living space.

humoral healing   healing that emphasizes balance among natural elements within the body.

illness   in the disease–illness dichotomy, culturally shaped perceptions and experiences of a health problem.

incest taboo   a strongly held prohibition against marrying or having sex with particular kin.

indigenous knowledge   local understanding of the environment, climate, plants, animals, and making a living.

indigenous people   groups of people who have a long-standing connection with their home territories that predates colonial or outside societies.

inductive approach (to research)   a research approach that avoids hypothesis formation in advance of the research and instead takes its lead from the culture being studied.

industrial capital agriculture   a form of agriculture that is capital-intensive, substituting machinery and purchased inputs for human and animal labor.

industrialism/informatics   a mode of livelihood in which goods are produced through mass employment in business and commercial operations and through the creation and movement of information through electronic media.

infanticide   the killing of an infant or child.

influence   the ability to achieve a desired end by exerting social or moral pressure on someone or some group.

informal sector   work that is not officially registered and sometimes illegal.

informed consent   an aspect of fieldwork ethics requiring that the researcher inform the research participants of the intent, scope, and possible effects of the proposed study and seek their consent to be in the study.

institutional migrant   someone who moves into a social institution either voluntarily or involuntarily.

intangible cultural heritage   UNESCO's view of culture as manifested in oral traditions, languages, performing arts, rituals and festive events, knowledge and practices about nature and the universe, and craftmaking.

intensive strategy   a form of livelihood that involves continuous use of the same land and resources.

internal migration   movement within country boundaries.

internally displaced person (IDP)   someone who is forced to leave his or her home or community but who remains in the same country.

international migration   movement across country boundaries.

interpretive anthropology   the view that cultures are best understood by studying what people think about, their ideas, and the meanings that are important to them.

interview   a research technique that involves gathering verbal data through questions or guided conversation between at least two people.

invention   the discovery of something new.

khipu   cords of knotted strings used during the Inca empire for keeping accounts and recording events.

kinship system   the predominant form of kin relationships in a culture and the kinds of behavior involved.

knuckle-walking   a form of terrestrial travel that involves walking flat-footed while supporting the upper body on the front of fingers bent beyond the knuckle.

kula   a trading network, linking many of the Trobriand Islands, in which men have long-standing partnerships for the exchange of everyday goods, such as food, as well as highly valued necklaces and armlets.

language   a form of communication that is based on a systematic set of learned symbols and signs shared among a group and passed on from generation to generation.

language family   a group of languages descended from a parent language.

law a binding rule created through enactment or custom that defines right and reasonable behavior and is enforceable by the threat of punishment.

leveling mechanism an unwritten, culturally embedded rule that prevents an individual from becoming wealthier or more powerful than anyone else.

lifeboat mentality a view that seeks to limit growth of a particular group because of perceived resource constraints.

life-cycle ritual a ritual that marks a change in status from one life stage to another.

life project local people's definition of the direction they want to take in life, informed by their knowledge, history, and context.

linguistic anthropology the study of human communication, including its origins, history, and contemporary variation and change.

localization the transformation of global culture by local cultures into something new.

logograph a symbol that conveys meaning through a form or picture resembling that to which it refers.

magic the attempt to compel supernatural forces and beings to act in certain ways.

male bias in development the design and implementation of development projects with men as beneficiaries and without regard to the impact of the projects on women's roles and status.

market exchange the buying and selling of commodities under competitive conditions, in which the forces of supply and demand determine value.

marriage a union, usually between two people who are likely to be, but are not necessarily, coresident, sexually involved with each other, and procreative.

material cultural heritage the sites, monuments, buildings, and movable objects considered to have outstanding value to humanity.

matrescence motherhood, or the cultural process of becoming a mother.

matriarchy the dominance of women in economic, political, social, and ideological domains.

matrifocality a household pattern in which a female (or females) is the central figure around whom other members cluster.

matrilineal descent a descent system that highlights the importance of women by tracing descent through the female line, favoring marital residence with or near the bride's family, and providing for property to be inherited through the female line.

medical pluralism the existence of more than one health system in a culture; also, a government policy to promote the integration of local healing systems into biomedical practice.

medicalization the labeling of a particular issue or problem as medical and requiring medical treatment when, in fact, that issue or problem is economic or political.

menarche the onset of menstruation.

menopause the cessation of menstruation.

mestizaje literally, a racial mixture; in Central and South America, indigenous people who are cut off from their Indian roots, or literate and successful indigenous people who retain some traditional cultural practices.

microculture a distinct pattern of learned and shared behavior and thinking found within a larger culture.

migration movement from one place to another.

minimalism a mode of consumption that emphasizes simplicity, is characterized by few and finite consumer demands, and involves an adequate and sustainable means to achieve them.

mode of consumption the dominant pattern, in a culture, of using things up or spending resources in order to satisfy demands.

mode of exchange the dominant pattern, in a culture, of transferring goods, services, and other items between and among people and groups.

mode of livelihood the dominant way of making a living in a culture.

mode of reproduction the predominant pattern, in a culture, of population change through the combined effect of fertility (birth rate) and mortality (death rate).

modernization a model of change based on belief in the inevitable advance of science and Western secularism and processes, including industrial growth, consolidation of the state, bureaucratization, a market economy, technological innovation, literacy, and options for social mobility.

moka a strategy for developing political leadership in highland New Guinea that involves exchanging gifts and favors with individuals and sponsoring large feasts where further gift-giving occurs.

money a medium of exchange that can be used for a variety of goods.

monogamy marriage between two people.

Mousterian tradition the tool kit of the Neanderthals, characterized by small, light, and more specialized flake tools, such as points, scrapers, and awls.

multisited research fieldwork conducted in more than one location in order to understand the culture of dispersed members of the culture or relationships among different levels of culture.

museum an institution that collects, preserves, interprets, and displays objects on a regular basis.

myth a narrative with a plot that involves the supernaturals.

nation a group of people who share a language, culture, territorial base, political organization, and history.

natural selection the process by which organisms better adapted to the environment reproduce more effectively compared with less well-adapted forms.

Neolithic Revolution a time of rapid transformation in technology, related to plant and animal domestication, which includes tools such as sickle blades and grinding stones.

new immigrant an international migrant who has moved since the 1960s.

norm a generally agreed-upon standard for how people should behave, usually unwritten and learned unconsciously.

nuclear household a domestic unit containing one adult couple (married or partners) with or without children.

Oldowan tradition the oldest hominin tool kit, characterized by core tools and flake tools.

parallel cousin offspring of either one's father's brother or one's mother's sister.

participant observation basic fieldwork method in cultural anthropology that involves living in a culture for a long time while gathering data.

pastoralism a mode of livelihood based on keeping domesticated animals and using their products, such as meat and milk, for most of the diet.

patrescence fatherhood, or the cultural process of becoming a father.

patriarchy the dominance of men in economic, political, social, and ideological domains.

patrilineal descent a descent system that highlights the importance of men in tracing descent, determining marital residence with or near the groom's family, and providing for inheritance of property through the male line.

personality an individual's patterned and characteristic way of behaving, thinking, and feeling.

phoneme a sound that makes a difference for meaning in a spoken language.

phytotherapy healing through the use of plants.

pidgin a contact language that blends elements of at least two languages and that emerges when people with different languages need to communicate.

pilgrimage round-trip travel to a sacred place or places for purposes of religious devotion or ritual.

placebo effect a positive result from a healing method due to a symbolic or otherwise nonmaterial factor.

policing the exercise of social control through processes of surveillance and the threat of punishment related to maintaining social order.

political organization groups within a culture that are responsible for public decision making and leadership, maintaining social cohesion and order, protecting group rights, and ensuring safety from external threats.

polyandry marriage of one wife with more than one husband.

polygamy marriage involving multiple spouses.

polygyny marriage of one husband with more than one wife.

potlatch a grand feast in which guests are invited to eat and to receive gifts from the hosts.

poverty the lack of tangible and intangible assets that contribute to life and the quality of life.

power the ability to take action in the face of resistance, through force if necessary.

priest or **priestess** a male or female full-time religious specialist whose position is based mainly on abilities gained through formal training.

primary group a social group in which members meet on a face-to-face basis.

primates an order of mammals that includes modern humans.

productivity a feature of human language whereby people are able to communicate a potentially infinite number of messages efficiently.

project cycle the steps of a development project from initial planning to completion: project identification, project design, project appraisal, project implementation, and project evaluation.

pronatalism an attitude or policy that encourages childbearing.

puberty a time in the human life cycle that occurs universally and involves a set of biological markers and sexual maturation.

pure gift something given with no expectation or thought of a return.

push–pull theory an explanation for rural-to-urban migration that emphasizes people's incentives to move because of a lack of opportunity in rural areas (the "push") compared with urban areas (the "pull").

qualitative data non-numeric information.

quantitative data numeric information.

questionnaire a formal research instrument containing a preset series of questions that the anthropologist asks in a face-to-face setting, by mail, or by e-mail.

"race" a classification of people into groups on the basis of supposedly homogeneous and largely superficial biological traits such as skin color or hair characteristics.

rapport a trusting relationship between the researcher and the study population.

redistribution a form of exchange that involves one person collecting goods or money from many members of a group, who then, at a later time and at a public event, "returns" the pooled goods to everyone who contributed.

refugee someone who is forced to leave his or her home, community, or country.

religion beliefs and behavior related to supernatural beings and forces.

religious pluralism the condition in which one or more religions coexist either as complementary to each other or as competing systems.

religious syncretism the blending of features of two or more religions.

remittance the transfer of money or goods by a migrant to his or her family in the country of origin.

repatriation returning art or other objects from museums to the people with whom they originated.

revitalization movement a socioreligious movement, usually organized by a prophetic leader, that seeks to construct a more satisfying situation by reviving all or parts of a religion that has been threatened by outside forces or by adopting new practices and beliefs.

right of return the United Nations' guaranteed right of a refugee to return to his or her home country to live.

ritual of inversion a ritual in which normal social roles and order are temporarily reversed.

ritual patterned behavior that has to do with the supernatural realm.

sacrifice a ritual in which something is offered to the supernaturals.

Sapir–Whorf hypothesis a perspective in linguistic anthropology which says that language determines thought.

savanna an environment that consists of open plains with tall grasses and patches of trees.

secondary group a group of people who identify with one another on some basis but may never meet with one another personally.

sectarian conflict conflict based on perceived differences between divisions or sects within a religion.

sedentism residence in permanent settlements such as villages, towns, and cities, which began with plant and animal domestication and intensified during the Neolithic era and the emergence of farming.

shaman or **shamanka** a male and female healer, respectively.

sign language a form of communication that uses mainly hand movements to convey messages.

social capital the intangible resources existing in social ties, trust, and cooperation.

social control processes that, through both informal and formal mechanisms, maintain orderly social life.

social group a cluster of people beyond the domestic unit who are usually related on grounds other than kinship.

social impact assessment a study conducted to predict the potential social costs and benefits of particular innovations before change is undertaken.

social justice a concept of fairness based on social equality that seeks to ensure entitlements and opportunities for disadvantaged members of society.

social stratification a set of hierarchical relationships among different groups as though they were arranged in layers, or "strata."

sociality the preference for living in groups and interacting regularly with members of the same species.

sociolinguistics a perspective in linguistic anthropology which says that culture, society, and a person's social position determine language.

somatization the process through which the body absorbs social stress and manifests symptoms of suffering.

state a form of political organization in which a centralized political unit encompasses many communities, a bureaucratic structure, and leaders who possess coercive power.

status a person's position, or standing, in society.

stem household a coresidential group that comprises only two married couples related through males, commonly found in East Asian cultures.

structural suffering human health problems caused by such economic and political factors as war, famine, terrorism, forced migration, and poverty.

structurism a theoretical position concerning human behavior and ideas that says large forces such as the economy, social and political organization, and the media shape what people do and think.

susto fright/shock disease, a culture-specific illness found in Spain and Portugal and among Latino people wherever they live; symptoms include back pain, fatigue, weakness, and lack of appetite.

symbol   an object, word, or action with culturally defined meaning that stands for something else; most symbols are arbitrary.

tag question   a question placed at the end of a sentence seeking affirmation.

tell   a human-made mound resulting from the accumulation of successive generations of house construction, reconstruction, and trash.

Textese   an emerging variant of written English and other languages associated with cell phone communication and involving abbreviations and creative slang.

theater   a form of enactment, related to other forms such as dance, music, parades, competitive games and sports, and verbal art, that seeks to entertain through acting, movement, and sound.

toponymy   the naming of places.

trade   the formalized exchange of one thing for another according to set standards of value.

traditional development anthropology   an approach to international development in which the anthropologist accepts the role of helping to make development work better by providing cultural information to planners.

transnational migration   regular movement of a person between two or more countries resulting in a new cultural identity.

trial by ordeal   a way of determining innocence or guilt in which the accused person is put to a test that may be painful, stressful, or fatal.

tribe   a form of political organization that comprises several bands or lineage groups, each with a similar language and lifestyle and occupying a distinct territory.

unbalanced exchange   a system of transfers in which one party seeks to make a profit.

unilineal descent   the tracing of descent through only one parent.

Upper Paleolithic   the period of modern human occupation in Europe and Eurasia (including the Middle East) from 45,000–40,000 years ago to 12,000 years ago, characterized by microlithic tools and prolific cave art and portable art.

use rights   a system of property relations in which a person or group has socially recognized priority in access to particular resources such as gathering, hunting, and fishing areas and water holes.

wa   a Japanese word meaning discipline and self-sacrifice for the good of the group.

war   organized and purposeful group action directed against another group and involving lethal force.

Western biomedicine (WBM)   a healing approach based on modern Western science that emphasizes technology for diagnosing and treating health problems related to the human body.

world religion   a term coined in the nineteenth century to refer to a religion that is based on written sources, has many followers, is regionally widespread, and is concerned with salvation.

youth gang   a group of young people, found mainly in urban areas, who are often considered a social problem by adults and law enforcement officials.

Abu-Lughod, Lila. 1993. *Writing Women's Worlds: Bedouin Stories.* Berkeley: University of California Press.

Adams, Abigail E. 2002. Dyke to Dyke: Ritual Reproduction at a U.S. Men's Military College. In *The Best of Anthropology Today* (pp. 34–42). Jonathan Benthall, ed. New York: Routledge.

Adams, Vincanne. 1988. Modes of Production and Medicine: An Examination of the Theory in Light of Sherpa Traditional Medicine. *Social Science and Medicine* 27:505–513.

Afolayan, E. 2000. Bantu Expansion and Its Consequences. In *African History before 1885* (pp. 113–136). T. Falola, ed. Durham, NC: Carolina Academic Press.

Agar, Michael and Heather Schacht Reisinger. 2003. Going for the Global: The Case of Ecstasy. *Human Organization* 62(1):1–11.

Ahmadu, Fuambai. 2000. Rites and Wrongs: An Insider/Outside Reflects on Power and Excision. In *Female "Circumcision" in Africa: Culture, Controversy, and Change* (pp. 283–312). Bettina Shell-Duncan and Ylva Hernlund, eds. Boulder, CO: Lynne Reiner Publishers.

Albro, Robert and Joanne Bauer. 2005. Introduction. Human Rights Dialogue: An International Forum for Debating Human Rights. Special issue on Cultural Rights: What They Are, Why They Matter, How They Can Be Realized. *Carnegie Journal* 2(12):2–3.

Allen, Catherine J. 2002. *The Hold Life Has: Coca and Cultural Identity in an Andean Community.* Washington, DC: Smithsonian Institution Press.

Allen, Susan. 1994. What Is Media Anthropology? A Personal View and a Suggested Structure. In *Media Anthropology: Informing Global Citizens* (pp. 15–32). Susan L. Allen, ed. Westport, CT: Bergin & Garvey.

Alter, Joseph S. 1992. The Sannyasi and the Indian Wrestler: Anatomy of a Relationship. *American Ethnologist* 19(2):317–336.

Amster, Matthew H. 2000. It Takes a Village to Dismantle a Longhouse. *Thresholds* 20:65–71.

Ancrenaz, Marc, Olivier Gimenez, Laurentius Ambu, Karine Ancrenaz, Patrick Andau, Benoît Goossens, John Payne, Arzi Sawang, Augustine Tuuga, and Isabelle Lackmann-Ancrenaz. 2005. Aerial Surveys Give New Estimates for Orangutans in Sabah, Malaysia. *PloS Biology* 3(1):e3. www.plosbiology.org.

Anderson, Benedict. 1991 [1983]. *Imagined Communities: Reflections on the Origin and Spread of Nationalism.* New York: Verso.

Anderson, Myrdene. 2004. Reflections on the Saami at Loose Ends. In *Cultural Shaping of Violence: Victimization, Escalation, Response* (pp. 285–291). Myrdene Anderson, ed. West Lafayette, IN: Purdue University Press.

———. 2005. The Saami Yoik: Translating Hum, Chant and/or Song. In *Song and Significance: Virtues and Vices of Vocal Translation* (pp. 213–233). Dinda Gorlée, ed. Amsterdam: Rodopi.

Anderson, Richard L. and Karen L. Field. 1993. Chapter Introduction. In *Art in Small-Scale Societies: Contemporary Readings* (p. 247). Richard L. Anderson and Karen L. Fields, eds. Englewood Cliffs, NJ: Prentice-Hall.

Applbaum, Kalman D. 1995. Marriage with the Proper Stranger: Arranged Marriage in Metropolitan Japan. *Ethnology* 34(1): 37–51.

Arambiza, Evelio and Michael Painter. 2006. Biodiversity Conservation and the Quality of Life of Indigenous People in the Bolivian Chaco. *Human Organization* 65:20–34.

Ariès, Philippe. 1962. *Centuries of Childhood: A Social History of Family Life.* Trans. Robert Baldick. New York: Vintage Books.

Baker, Colin. 1999. Sign Language and the Deaf Community. In *Handbook of Language and Ethnic Identity* (pp. 122–139). Joshua A. Fishman, ed. New York: Oxford University Press.

Baker-Christales, Beth. 2004. *Salvadoran Migration to Southern California: Redefining El Hermano Lejano.* Gainesville: University of Florida Press.

Baptista, Marlyse. 2005. New Directions in Pidgin and Creole Studies. *Annual Review of Anthropology* 34:34–42.

Barfield, Thomas J. 1994. Prospects for Plural Societies in Central Asia. *Cultural Survival Quarterly* 18(2&3):48–51.

———. 2001. Pastoral Nomads or Nomadic Pastoralists. In *The Dictionary of Anthropology* (pp. 348–350). Thomas Barfield, ed. Malden, MA: Blackwell Publishers.

Barkey, Nanette, Benjamin C. Campbell, and Paul W. Leslie. 2001. A Comparison of Health Complaints of Settled and Nomadic Turkana Men. *Medical Anthropology Quarterly* 15:391–408.

Barnard, Alan and Anthony Good. 1984. *Research Practices in the Study of Kinship.* New York: Academic Press.

Barrionuevo, Alexei. Amazon's "Forest People" Seek a Role in Striking Global Climate Agreements. *New York Times.* April 5:6.

Bartlett, Peggy F. 1989. Industrial Agriculture. In *Economic Anthropology* (pp. 253–292). Stuart Plattner, ed. Stanford, CA: Stanford University Press.

Barth, Frederik. 1993. *Balinese Worlds.* Chicago: University of Chicago Press.

Basch, Linda, Nina Glick Schiller, and Christina Szanton Blanc. 1994. *Nations Unbound: Transnational Projects, Postcolonial Predicaments, and Deterritorialized Nation–States.* Langhorne, PA: Gordon and Breach Science Publishers.

Basso, Keith. H. 1972 [1970]. "To Give Up on Words": Silence in Apache Culture. In *Language and Social Context* (pp. 67–86). Pier Paolo Giglioni, ed. Baltimore: Penguin Books.

Bauer, Alexander A. 2006. Heritage Preservation in Law and Policy: Handling the Double-Edged Sword of Development. Paper presented at the International Conference on Cultural Heritage and Development, Bibliothèca Alexandrina, Alexandria, Egypt, January.

Beals, Alan R. 1980. *Gopalpur: A South Indian Village. Fieldwork Edition.* New York: Holt, Rinehart and Winston.

Beeman, William O. 1993. The Anthropology of Theater and Spectacle. *Annual Review of Anthropology* 22:363–393.

Belikov, Vladimir. 1994. Language Death in Siberia. *UNESCO Courier* 1994(2):32–36.

Bell, Diane. 1998. *Ngarrindjeri Wurruwarrin: A World That Is, Was, and Will Be.* North Melbourne, Australia: Spinifex.

Bernal, Martin. 1987. *Black Athena: The Afroasiatic Roots of Classical Civilization.* New Brunswick, NJ: Rutgers University Press.

Berreman, Gerald D. 1979 [1975]. Race, Caste, and Other Invidious Distinctions in Social Stratification. In *Caste and Other Inequities: Essays on Inequality* (pp. 178–222). Gerald D. Berreman, ed. New Delhi: Manohar.

Bestor, Theodore C. 2004. *Tsukiji: The Fish Market at the Center of the World.* Berkeley: University of California Press.

Beyene, Yewoubdar. 1989. *From Menarche to Menopause: Reproductive Lives of Peasant Women in Two Cultures.* Albany: State University of New York Press.

Bhardwaj, Surinder M. and N. Madhusudana Rao. 1990. Asian Indians in the United States: A Geographic Appraisal. In *South Asians Overseas: Migration and Ethnicity* (pp. 197–218). Colin

Clarke, Ceri Peach, and Steven Vertovec, eds. New York: Cambridge University Press.

Bhatt, Rakesh M. 2001. World Englishes. *Annual Review of Anthropology* 30:527–550.

Bilharz, Joy. 1995. First among Equals? The Changing Status of Seneca Women. In *Women and Power in Native North America* (pp. 101–112). Laura F. Klein and Lillian A. Ackerman, eds. Norman: University of Oklahoma Press.

Billig, Michael S. 1992. The Marriage Squeeze and the Rise of Groomprice in India's Kerala State. *Journal of Comparative Family Studies* 23:197–216.

Blackwood, Evelyn. 1995. Senior Women, Model Mothers, and Dutiful Wives: Managing Gender Contradictions in a Minangkabau Village. In *Bewitching Women, Pious Men: Gender and Body Politics in Southeast Asia* (pp. 124–158). Aihwa Ong and Michael Peletz, eds. Berkeley: University of California Press.

Bledsoe, Caroline H. 1983. Stealing Food as a Problem in Demography and Nutrition. Paper presented at the annual meeting of the American Anthropological Association.

Blommaert, Jan and Chris Bulcaen. 2000. Critical Discourse Analysis. *Annual Review of Anthropology* 29:447–466.

Blood, Robert O. 1967. *Love Match and Arranged Marriage.* New York: Free Press.

Bodenhorn, Barbara. 2000. "He Used to Be My Relative." Exploring the Bases of Relatedness among the Inupiat of Northern Alaska. In *Cultures of Relatedness: New Approaches to the Study of Kinship* (pp. 128–148). Janet Carsten, ed. New York: Cambridge University Press.

Bodley, John H. 1990. *Victims of Progress,* 3rd ed. Mountain View, CA: Mayfield Publishing.

Boellstorff, Tom. 2004. Gay Language and Indonesia: Registering Belonging. *Journal of Linguistic Anthropology* 14:248–268.

Boserup, Ester. 1970. *Woman's Role in Economic Development.* New York: St. Martin's Press.

Bourdieu, Pierre. 1984. *Distinction: A Social Critique of the Judgement of Taste.* Trans. Richard Nice. Cambridge, MA: Harvard University Press.

Bourgois, Philippe I. 1995. *In Search of Respect: Selling Crack in El Barrio.* New York: Cambridge University Press.

Bourgois, Philippe and Jeff Schonberg. 2009. *Righteous Dopefiend.* Berkeley: University of California Press.

Bowen, John R. 1992. On Scriptural Essentialism and Ritual Variation: Muslim Sacrifice in Sumatra. *American Ethnologist* 19(4):656–671.

———. 1998. *Religions in Practice: An Approach to the Anthropology of Religion.* Boston: Allyn and Bacon.

Bradley, Richard. 2000. *An Archaeology of Natural Places.* New York: Routledge.

Brana-Shute, Rosemary. 1976. Women, Clubs, and Politics: The Case of a Lower-Class Neighborhood in Paramaribo, Suriname. *Urban Anthropology* 5(2):157–185.

Brandes, Stanley H. 1985. *Forty: The Age and the Symbol.* Knoxville: University of Tennessee Press.

———. 2002. *Staying Sober in Mexico City.* Austin: University of Texas Press.

Brave Heart, Mary Yellow Horse. 2004. The Historical Trauma Response among Natives and Its Relationship to Substance Abuse. In *Healing and Mental Health for Native Americans: Speaking in Red* (pp. 7–18). Ethan Nebelkopf and Mary Phillips, eds. Walnut Creek, CA: AltaMira Press.

Brink, Judy H. 1991. The Effect of Emigration of Husbands on the Status of Their Wives: An Egyptian Case. *International Journal of Middle East Studies* 23:201–211.

Brookes, Heather. 2004. A Repertoire of South African Quotable Gestures. *Journal of Linguistic Anthropology* 14:186–224.

Brooks, Alison S. and Patricia Draper. 1998 [1991]. Anthropological Perspectives on Aging. In *Anthropology Explored: The Best of AnthroNotes* (pp. 286–297). Ruth Osterweis Selig and Marilyn R. London, eds. Washington, DC: Smithsonian Press.

Broude, Gwen J. 1988. Rethinking the Couvade: Cross-Cultural Evidence. *American Anthropologist* 90(4):902–911.

Brown, Carolyn Henning. 1984. Tourism and Ethnic Competition in a Ritual Form: The Firewalkers of Fiji. *Oceania* 54:223–244.

Brown, Judith K. 1970. A Note on the Division of Labor by Sex. *American Anthropologist* 72(5):1073–1078.

———. 1975. Iroquois Women: An Ethnohistoric Note. In *Toward an Anthropology of Women* (pp. 235–251). Rayna R. Reiter, ed. New York: Monthly Review Press.

———. 1978. The Recruitment of a Female Labor Force. *Anthropos* 73(1/2):41–48.

———. 1999. Introduction: Definitions, Assumptions, Themes, and Issues. In *To Have and To Hit: Cultural Perspectives on Wife Beating,* 2nd ed. (pp. 3–26). Dorothy Ayers Counts, Judith K. Brown, and Jacquelyn C. Campbell, eds. Urbana: University of Illinois Press.

Browner, Carole H. 1986. The Politics of Reproduction in a Mexican Village. *Signs: Journal of Women in Culture and Society* 11(4):710–724.

Browner, Carole H. and Nancy Ann Press. 1995. The Normalization of Prenatal Diagnostic Screening. In *Conceiving the New World Order: The Global Politics of Reproduction* (pp. 307–322). Faye D. Ginsberg and Rayna Rapp, eds. Berkeley: University of California Press.

———. 1996. The Production of Authoritative Knowledge in American Prenatal Care. *Medical Anthropology Quarterly* 10(2):141–156.

Bruner, Edward M. 2005. *Culture on Tour: Ethnographies of Travel.* Chicago: University of Chicago Press.

Bunzel, Ruth. 1972 [1929]. *The Pueblo Potter: A Study of Creative Imagination in Primitive Art.* New York: Dover Publications.

Burdick, John. 2004. *Legacies of Liberation: The Progressive Catholic Church in Brazil at the Turn of a New Century.* Burlington, VT: Ashgate Publishers.

Burton, Barbara. 2004. The Transmigration of Rights: Women, Movement and the Grassroots in Latin American and Caribbean Communities. *Development and Change* 35:773–798.

Call, Vaughn, Susan Sprecher, and Pepper Schwartz. 1995. The Incidence and Frequency of Marital Sex in a National Sample. *Journal of Marriage and the Family* 57:639–652.

Camino, Linda A. and Ruth M. Krulfeld, eds. 1994. *Reconstructing Lives, Recapturing Meaning: Refugee Identity, Gender and Culture Change.* Basel: Gordon and Breach Publishers.

Caplan, Pat. 2000. "Eating British Beef with Confidence": A Consideration of Consumers' Responses to BSE in Britain. In *Risk Revisited* (pp. 184–203). Pat Caplan, ed. Sterling, VA: Pluto Press.

Carneiro, Robert L. 1994. War and Peace: Alternating Realities in Human History. In *Studying War: Anthropological Perspectives* (pp. 3–27). S. P. Reyna and R. E. Downs, eds. Langhorne, PA: Gordon and Breach Science Publishers.

Carstairs, G. Morris. 1967. *The Twice Born.* Bloomington: Indiana University Press.

Carsten, Janet. 1995. Children in Between: Fostering and the Process of Kinship on Pulau Langkawi, Malaysia. *Man* (n.s.) 26:425–443.

Carsten, Janet, ed. 2000. *Cultures of Relatedness: New Approaches to the Study of Kinship.* New York: Cambridge University Press.

Carter, William E., José V. Morales, and Mauricio P. Mamani. 1981. Medicinal Uses of Coca in Bolivia. In *Health in the Andes* (pp. 119–149). Joseph W. Bastien and John M. Donahue, eds. Washington, DC: American Anthropological Association.

Cassell, Joan. 1991. *Expected Miracles: Surgeons at Work.* Philadelphia: Temple University Press.

Cátedra, María. 1992. *This World, Other Worlds: Sickness, Suicide, Death, and the Afterlife among the Vaqueiros de Alzada of Spain.* Chicago: University of Chicago Press.

Cernea, Michael M. 1985. Sociological Knowledge for Development Projects. In *Putting People First: Sociological Variables and Rural Development* (pp. 3–22). Michael M. Cernea, ed. New York: Oxford University Press.

———. 2001. *Cultural Heritage and Development: A Framework for Action in the Middle East and North Africa.* Washington, DC: The World Bank.

Chagnon, Napoleon. 1968. *Yanomamö, The Fierce People.* New York: Holt, Rinehart and Winston.

———. 1992. *Yanomamö,* 4th ed. New York: Harcourt Brace Jovanovich.

Chalfin, Brenda. 2004. *Shea Butter Republic: State Power, Global Markets, and the Making of an Indigenous Commodity.* New York: Routledge.

———. 2008. Cars, the Customs Service, and Sumptuary Rule in Neoliberal Ghana. *Comparative Studies in Society and History* 50:424–453.

Chavez, Leo R. 1992. *Shadowed Lives: Undocumented Immigrants in American Society.* New York: Harcourt Brace Jovanovich.

Checker, Melissa. 2005. Polluted Promises: *Environmental Racism and the Search for Justice in a Southern Town.* New York: New York University Press.

———. 2007. "But I Know It's True": Environmental Risk Assessment, Justice, and Anthropology. *Human Organization* 66:112–124.

Chernoff, John Miller. 1979. *African Rhythm and African Sensibility: Aesthetics and African Musical Idioms.* Chicago: University of Chicago Press.

Childs, Larry and Celina Chelala. 1994. Drought, Rebellion and Social Change in Northern Mali: The Challenges Facing Tamacheq Herders. *Cultural Survival Quarterly* 18(4):16–19.

Chin, Elizabeth. 2001. *Purchasing Power: Black Kids and American Consumer Culture.* Minneapolis: University of Minnesota Press.

Chiñas, Beverly Newbold. 1992. *The Isthmus Zapotecs: A Matrifocal Culture of Mexico.* New York: Harcourt Brace Jovanovich.

Chowdhury, A. N. 1996. The Definition and Classification of Koro. *Culture, Medicine and Psychiatry* 20(1):41–65.

Clarke, Maxine Kumari. 2004. *Mapping Yorùbá Networks: Power and Agency in the Making of Transnational Communities.* Durham, NC: Duke University Press.

Clay, Jason W. 1990. What's a Nation: Latest Thinking. *Mother Jones* 15(7):28–30.

Cochrane, D. Glynn. 1974. Barbara Miller's class lecture notes in Applied Anthropology, Syracuse University.

———. 1979. *The Cultural Appraisal of Development Projects.* New York: Praeger Publishers.

———. 2009. *Festival of Elephants and the Myth of Global Poverty.* Boston: Pearson.

Cohen, Mark Nathan. 1989. *Health and the Rise of Civilization.* New Haven, CT: Yale University Press.

Cohen, Roberta. 2002. Nowhere to Run, No Place to Hide. *Bulletin of the Atomic Scientists,* November/December:36–45.

Cohn, Bernard S. 1971. *India: The Social Anthropology of a Civilization.* New York: Prentice-Hall.

Cole, Douglas. 1991. *Chifly Feasts: The Enduring Kwakiutl Potlatch. Aldona Jonatis, ed.* Seattle: University of Washington Press/New York: American Museum of Natural History.

Cole, Jeffrey. 1996. Working-Class Reactions to the New Immigration in Palermo (Italy). *Critique of Anthropology* 16(2):199–220.

Colley, Sarah. 2002. *Uncovering Australia: Archaeology, Indigenous People and the Public.* Washington, DC: Smithsonian Institution Press.

Comaroff, John L. 1987. Of Totemism and Ethnicity: Consciousness, Practice and Signs of Inequality. *Ethnos* 52(3–4):301–323.

Contreras, Gloria. 1995. Teaching about Vietnamese Culture: Water Puppetry as the Soul of the Rice Fields. *The Social Studies* 86(1):25–28.

Coon Come, Matthew. 2004. Survival in the Context of Mega-Resource Development: Experiences of the James Bay Crees and the First Nations of Canada. In *In the Way of Development: Indigenous Peoples, Life Projects, and Globalization* (pp. 153–165). Mario Blaser, Harvey A. Feit, and Glenn McRae, eds. New York: Zed Books in Association with the International Development Research Centre.

Corbey, Raymond. 2003. Destroying the Graven Image: Religious Iconoclasm on the Christian Frontier. *Anthropology Today* 19:10–14.

Cornia, Giovanni Andrea. 1994. Poverty, Food Consumption, and Nutrition During the Transition to the Market Economy in Eastern Europe. *American Economic Review* 84(2):297–302.

Counihan, Carole M. 1985. Transvestism and Gender in a Sardinian Carnival. *Anthropology* 9(1&2):11–24.

Coward, E. Walter, Jr. 1976. Indigenous Organisation, Bureaucracy and Development: The Case of Irrigation. *The Journal of Development Studies* 13(1):92–105.

———. 1979. Principles of Social Organization in an Indigenous Irrigation System. *Human Organization* 38(1):28–36.

Craik, Brian. 2004. The Importance of Working Together: Exclusions, Conflicts and Participation in James Bay, Quebec. In *In the Way of Development: Indigenous Peoples, Life Projects, and Globalization* (pp. 166–186). Mario Blaser, Harvey A. Feit, and Glenn McRae, eds. Zed Books in Association with the International Development Research Centre.

Crowe, D. 1996. *A History of the Gypsies of Eastern Europe and Russia.* New York: St. Martin's Press.

Crystal, David. 2000. *Language Death.* New York: Cambridge University Press.

———. 2003. *English as a Global Language,* 2nd ed. New York: Cambridge University Press.

Cunningham, Lawrence S. 1995. Christianity. In *The HarperCollins Dictionary of Religion* (pp. 240–253). Jonathan Z. Smith, ed. New York: HarperCollins.

Curtin, Philip D. 1989. *Death by Migration: Europe's Encounter with the Tropical World in the Nineteenth Century.* New York: Cambridge University Press.

Dalby, Liza Crihfield. 1998. *Geisha,* 2nd ed. New York: Vintage Books.

———. 2001. *Kimono: Fashioning Culture.* Seattle: University of Washington Press.

Dalton, Rex. 2010. Hobbit Origins Pushed Back. *Nature* 464(7287):335.

Daly, Martin and Margo Wilson. 1984. A Sociobiological Analysis of Human Infanticide. In *Infanticide: Comparative and Evolutionary Perspectives* (pp. 487–582). Glen Hausfater and Sarah Blaffer Hrdy, eds. New York: Aldine.

Danforth, Loring M. 1989. *Firewalking and Religious Healing: The Anestenaria of Greece and the American Firewalking Movement.* Princeton, NJ: Princeton University Press.

Dannhaeuser, Norbert. 1989. Marketing in Developing Urban Areas. In *Economic Anthropology* (pp. 222–252). Stuart Plattner, ed. Stanford, CA: Stanford University Press.

Daugherty, Mary Lee. 1997 [1976]. Serpent-Handling as Sacrament. In *Magic, Witchcraft, and Religion* (pp. 347–352). Arthur C.

Lehmann and James E. Myers, eds. Mountain View, CA: Mayfield Publishing.

Dávila, Arlene. 2002. Culture in the Ad World: Producing the Latin Look. In *Media Worlds: Anthropology on New Terrain* (pp. 264–280). Faye D. Ginsburg, Lila Abu-Lughod, and Brian Larkin, eds. Berkeley: University of California Press.

David, Robert C. and Garry R. Marvin. 2004. *Venice, the Tourist Maze: A Cultural Critique of the World's Most Touristed City.* Berkeley: University of California Press.

Davis, Susan Schaefer and Douglas A. Davis. 1987. *Adolescence in a Moroccan Town: Making Social Sense.* New Brunswick: Rutgers University Press.

Davis-Floyd, Robbie E. 1987. Obstetric Training as a Rite of Passage. *Medical Anthropology Quarterly* 1:288–318.

———. 1992. *Birth as an American Rite of Passage.* Berkeley: University of California Press.

de la Cadena, Marisol. 2001. Reconstructing Race: Racism, Culture and Mestizaje in Latin America. *NACLA Report on the Americas* 34:16–23.

de la Pradelle, Michelle. Amy Jacobs, trans. 2006. *Market Day in Provence.* Chicago: University of Chicago Press.

Deitrick, Lynn. 2002. Commentary: Cultural Brokerage in the Newborn Nursery. *Practicing Anthropology* 24:53–54.

Dent, Alexander Sebastian. 2005. Cross-Culture "Countries": Covers, Conjuncture, and the Whiff of Nashville in *Música Sertaneja* (Brazilian Commercial Country Music). *Popular Music and Society* 28:207–227.

Devereaux, George. 1976. *A Typological Study of Abortion in Primitive Societies: A Typological, Distributional, and Dynamic Analysis of the Prevention of Birth in 400 Preindustrial Societies.* New York: International Universities Press.

Diamond, Jared. 1994 [1987]. The Worst Mistake in the History of the Human Race. In *Applying Cultural Anthropology: A Reader* (pp. 105–108). Aaron Podolefsky and Peter J. Brown, eds. Mountain View, CA: Mayfield Publishing.

Dickemann, Mildred. 1975. Demographic Consequences of Infanticide in Man. *Annual Review of Ecology and Systematics* 6:107–137.

DiFerdinando, George. 1999. Emerging Infectious Diseases: Biology and Behavior in the Inner City. In *Urbanism, Health, and Human Biology in Industrialised Countries* (pp. 87–110). Lawrence M. Schell and Stanley J. Ulijaszek, eds. New York: Cambridge University Press.

digim'Rina, Linus S. 2005. Food Security through Traditions: Replanting Trees and Wise Practices." *People and Culture in Oceania* 20:13–36.

———. 2006. Personal communication.

Dikötter, Frank. 1998. Hairy Barbarians, Furry Primates and Wild Men: Medical Science and Cultural Representations of Hair in China. In *Hair: Its Power and Meaning in Asian Cultures* (pp. 51–74). Alf Hiltebeitel and Barbara D. Miller, eds. Albany: State University of New York Press.

Divale, William T. 1974. Migration, External Warfare, and Matrilocal Residence. *Behavior Science Research* 9:75–133.

Divale, William T. and Marvin Harris. 1976. Population, Warfare and the Male Supremacist Complex. *American Anthropologist* 78:521–538.

Doi, Yaruko and Masami Minowa. 2003. Gender Differences in Excessive Daytime Sleepiness among Japanese Workers. *Social Science and Medicine* 56:883–894.

Donlon, Jon. 1990. Fighting Cocks, Feathered Warriors, and Little Heroes. *Play & Culture* 3:273–285.

Dorgan, Howard. 1989. *The Old Regular Baptists of Central Appalachia: Brothers and Sisters in Hope.* Knoxville: University of Tennessee Press.

Drake, Susan P. 1991. Local Participation in Ecotourism Projects. In *Nature Tourism: Managing for the Environment* (pp. 132–155). Tensie Whelan, ed. Washington, DC: Island Press.

Dreifus, Claudia. 2000. Saving the Orangutan, Preserving Paradise. *New York Times,* March 21:D3.

Drucker, Charles. 1988. Dam the Chico: Hydropower Development and Tribal Resistance. In *Tribal Peoples and Development Issues: A Global Overview* (pp. 151–165). John H. Bodley, ed. Mountain View, CA: Mayfield Publishing.

Duany, Jorge. 2000. Nation on the Move: The Construction of Cultural Identities in Puerto Rico and the Diaspora. *American Ethnologist* 27:5–30.

Duranti, Alessandro. 1994. *From Grammar to Politics: Linguistic Anthropology in a Western Samoan Village.* Berkeley: University of California Press.

———. 1997a. *Linguistic Anthropology.* New York: Cambridge University Press.

———. 1997b. Universal and Culture-Specific Properties of Greetings. *Journal of Linguistic Anthropology* 7:63–97.

Durkheim, Emile. 1965 [1915]. *The Elementary Forms of the Religious Life.* New York: Free Press.

Durrenberger, E. Paul. 2001. Explorations of Class and Class Consciousness in the U.S. *Journal of Anthropological Research* 57:41–60.

Eck, Diana L. 1985. *Darsán: Seeing the Divine Image in India,* 2nd ed. Chambersburg, PA: Anima Books.

Eckel, Malcolm David. 1995. Buddhism. In *The HarperCollins Dictionary of Religion* (pp. 135–150). Jonathan Z. Smith, ed. New York: HarperCollins.

Economic and Social Council. 1992. *Report of the Working Group on Violence against Women.* Vienna: United Nations. E/CN.6/WG.2/1992/L.3.

The Economist. 2010. On Your Tractor, If You Can. May:50.

Eisler, Kim Isaac. 2001. *Revenge of the Pequots: How a Small Native American Tribe Created the World's Most Profitable Casino.* New York: Simon and Schuster.

Ember, Carol R. 1983. The Relative Decline in Women's Contribution to Agriculture with Intensification. *American Anthropologist* 85(2):285–304.

Englund, Harri. 1998. Death, Trauma and Ritual: Mozambican Refugees in Malawi. *Social Science and Medicine* 46(9): 1165–1174.

Ennis-McMillan, Michael C. 2001. Suffering from Water: Social Origins of Bodily Distress in a Mexican Community. *Medical Anthropology Quarterly* 15(3):368–390.

Erickson, Barbra E. 2007. Toxin or Medicine? Explanatory Models of Radon in Montana Health Mines. *Medical Anthropology Quarterly* 21:1–21.

Ervin, Alexander M., Antonet T. Kaye, Giselle M. Marcotte, and Randy D. Belon. 1991. *Community Needs, Saskatoon—The 1990's: The Saskatoon Needs Assessment Project.* Saskatoon, Canada: University of Saskatchewan, Department of Anthropology.

Escobar, Arturo. 2002. Gender, Place, and Networks: A Political Ecology of Cyberculture. In *Development: A Cultural Studies Reader* (pp. 239–256). Susan Schech and Jane Haggis, eds. Malden, MA: Blackwell Publishers.

Esman, Milton. 1996. Ethnic Politics. In *The Social Science Encyclopedia* (pp. 259–260). Adam Kuper and Jessica Kuper, eds. New York: Routledge.

Estrin, Saul. 1996. Co-operatives. In *The Social Science Encyclopedia* (pp. 138–139). Adam Kuper and Jessica Kuper, eds. New York: Routledge.

Etienne, Mona and Eleanor Leacock, eds. 1980. *Women and Colonization: Anthropological Perspectives.* New York: Praeger.

Evans-Pritchard, E. E. 1951. *Kinship and Marriage among the Nuer.* Oxford: Clarendon.

Everett, Daniel L. 1995. Personal communication.

———. 2005. Cultural Constraints on Grammar and Cognition in Pirahã: Another Look at Design Features in Human Language. *Current Anthropology* 46:621–634, 641–646.

———. 2008. *Don't Sleep, There Are Snakes: Life and Language in the Amazonian Jungle.* New York: Knopf Publishing Group.

Evrard, Olivier and Yves Goudineau. 2004. Planned Resettlement, Unexpected Migrations and Cultural Trauma in Laos. *Development and Change* 35:937–962.

Fabian, Johannes. 1995. Ethnographic Misunderstanding and the Perils of Context. *American Anthropologist* 97(1):41–50.

Fabrega, Horacio, Jr. and Barbara D. Miller. 1995. Adolescent Psychiatry as a Product of Contemporary Anglo-American Society. *Social Science and Medicine* 40(7):881–894.

Fadiman, Anne. 1997. *The Spirit Catches You and You Fall Down: A Hmong Child, Her American Doctors, and the Collision of Two Cultures.* New York: Farrar, Straus and Giroux.

Faiola, Anthony. 2005. Sick of Their Husbands in Graying Japan: Stress Disorder Diagnosed in Many Women after Spouses Retire. *Washington Post,* October 10: A1, A16.

Farmer, Paul. 1992. *AIDS and Accusation: Haiti and the Geography of Blame.* Berkeley: University of California Press.

———. 2005. *Pathologies of Power: Health, Human Rights, and the New War on the Poor.* Berkeley: University of California Press.

Fasulo, Linda. 2003. *An Insider's Guide to the UN.* New Haven, CT: Yale University Press.

Feinsilver, Julie M. 1993. *Healing the Masses: Cuban Health Politics at Home and Abroad.* Berkeley: University of California Press.

Fenstemaker, Sarah. 2007. Conservation Clash and the Case for Exemptions: How Eagle Protection Conflicts with Hopi Cultural Preservation. *International Journal of Cultural Property* 14:315–328.

Ferguson, R. Brian. 1990. Blood of the Leviathan: Western Contact and Amazonian Warfare. *American Ethnologist* 17(1):237–257.

Ferguson, James. 1994. *The Anti-Politics Machine: "Development," Depoliticization, and Bureaucratic Power in Lesotho.* Minneapolis: University of Minnesota Press.

Fields, Jason and Lynne M. Casper. 2000. *America's Families and Living Arrangements: Population Characteristics.* Washington, DC: United States Census Bureau. Current Population Reports P20-537.

Fisher, James. 1990. *Sherpas: Reflections on Change in Himalayan Nepal.* Berkeley: University of California Press.

Fishman, Joshua A. 1991. *Reversing Language Shift: Theoretical and Empirical Foundations of Assistance to Threatened Languages.* Clevedon, UK: Multilingual Matters Ltd.

Fishman, Joshua A., ed. 2001. *Can Threatened Languages Be Saved? Reversing Language Shift, Revisited: A 21st Century Perspective.* Buffalo, NY: Multilingual Matters Ltd.

Fitigu, Yodit. 2005. Forgotten People: Internally Displaced Persons in Guatemala. www.refugeesinternational.org/content/article/detail/6344.

Foley, Kathy. 2001. The Metonymy of Art: Vietnamese Water Puppetry as Representation of Modern Vietnam. *The Drama Review* 45(4):129–141.

Foley, William A. 2000. The Languages of New Guinea. *Annual Review of Anthropology* 29:357–404.

Foster, Helen Bradley and Donald Clay Johnson, eds. 2003. *Wedding Dress across Cultures.* New York: Berg.

Foster, Robert J. 2002. *Materializing the Nation: Commodities, Consumption, and Media in Papua New Guinea.* Bloomington: Indiana University Press.

———. 2006. From Trobriand Cricket to Rugby Nation: The Mission of Sport in Papua New Guinea. *The International Journal of the History of Sport* 23(5):739–758.

Foucault, Michel. 1970. *The Order of Things: An Archaeology of the Human Sciences.* New York: Random House.

———. 1977. *Discipline and Punish: The Birth of the Prison.* New York: Pantheon Books.

Fox, Robin. 1995 [1978]. *The Tory Islanders: A People of the Celtic Fringe.* Notre Dame: University of Notre Dame Press.

Frake, Charles O. 1961. The Diagnosis of Disease among the Subanun of Mindanao. *American Anthropologist* 63:113–132.

Franke, Richard W. 1993. *Life is a Little Better: Redistribution as a Development Strategy in Nadur Village, Kerala.* Boulder, CO: Westview Press.

Frankel, Francine R. 1971. *India's Green Revolution: Economic Gains and Political Costs.* Princeton, NJ: Princeton University Press.

Fratkin, Elliot. 1998. *Ariaal Pastoralists of Kenya: Surviving Drought and Development in Africa's Arid Lands.* Boston: Allyn and Bacon.

Frazer, Sir James. 1978 [1890]. *The Golden Bough: A Study in Magic and Religion.* New York: Macmillan.

Freeman, Derek. 1983. *Margaret Mead and Samoa: The Making and Unmaking of an Anthropological Myth.* Cambridge, MA: Harvard University Press.

Freeman, James A. 1981. A Firewalking Ceremony that Failed. In *Social and Cultural Context of Medicine in India* (pp. 308–336). Giri Raj Gupta, ed. New Delhi: Vikas Publishing.

———. 1989. *Hearts of Sorrow: Vietnamese-American Lives.* Stanford, CA: Stanford University Press.

Frieze, Irene, Jacquelynne E. Parsons, Paula B. Johnson, Diane N. Ruble, Gail L. Zellman, Esther Sales, Jeanne Marecek, Gwendolyn Lewis, Joan Hertzberg, and Deborah Lee. 1978. *Women and Sex Roles: A Social Psychological Perspective.* New York: W. W. Norton.

Furst, Peter T. 1989. The Water of Life: Symbolism and Natural History on the Northwest Coast. *Dialectical Anthropology* 14:95–115.

Gable, Eric. 1995. The Decolonization of Consciousness: Local Skeptics and the "Will to Be Modern" in a West African Village. *American Ethnologist* 22(2):242–257.

Galdikas, Biruté. 1995. *Reflections of Eden: My Years with the Orangutans of Borneo.* Boston: Little, Brown.

Gale, Faye, Rebecca Bailey-Harris, and Joy Wundersitz. 1990. *Aboriginal Youth and the Criminal Justice System: The Injustice of Justice?* New York: Cambridge University Press.

Galvin, Kathleen A. 2009. Transitions: Pastoralists Living with Change. *Annual Review of Anthropology* 38:185–198.

Gardner, Katy and David Lewis. 1996. *Anthropology, Development and the Post-Modern Challenge.* Sterling, VA: Pluto Press.

Garland, David. 1996. Social Control. In *The Social Science Encyclopedia* (pp. 780–783). Adam Kuper and Jessica Kuper, eds. Routledge: New York.

Gaski, Harald. 1993. The Sami People: The "White Indians" of Scandinavia. *American Indian Culture and Research Journal* 17:115–128.

———. 1997. Introduction: Sami Culture in a New Era. In *Sami Culture in a New Era: The Norwegian Sami Experience* (pp. 9–28). Harald Gaski, ed. Seattle: University of Washington Press.

Geertz, Clifford. 1966. Religion as a Cultural System. In *Anthropological Approaches to the Study of Religion* (pp. 1–46). Michael Banton, ed. London: Tavistock.

Gegiow vs. Uhl. 1915. No. 340. Supreme Court of the United States.

Giles, Jim. 2004. Guatemalan Work Brings Award and Death Threats. *Nature* 427:664.

Gillette, Maris Boyd. 2000. *Between Mecca and Beijing: Modernization and Consumption among Urban Chinese Families.* Stanford: Stanford University Press.

Ginsberg, Faye D. and Rayna Rapp. 1991. The Politics of Reproduction. *Annual Review of Anthropology* 20:311–343.

Glick Schiller, Nina and Georges E. Fouron. 1999. Terrains of Blood and Nation: Haitian Transnational Social Fields. *Ethnic and Racial Studies* 22:340–365.

Global Times. 2010. China: 24 Million Men to be Mateless by End of Decade. January 11.

Gmelch, George. 1997 [1971]. Baseball Magic. In *Magic, Witchcraft, and Religion* (pp. 276–282). Arthur C. Lehmann and James E. Myers, eds. Mountain View, CA: Mayfield Publishing.

Gold, Stevan J. 1992. *Refugee Communities: A Comparative Field Study.* Newbury Park: Sage Publications.

———. 1995. *From the Workers' State to the Golden State: Jews from the Former Soviet Union in California.* Boston: Allyn and Bacon.

Goldstein-Gidoni, Ofra. 2003. Producers of "Japan" in Israel: Cultural Appropriation in a Non-Colonial Context. *Ethnos* 68(3): 365–390.

Goodwin, Marjorie H. 1990. *He-Said-She-Said: Talk as Social Organization among Black Children.* Bloomington: Indiana University Press.

Goody, Jack. 1976. *Production and Reproduction: A Comparative Study of the Domestic Domain.* New York: Cambridge University Press.

———. 1993. *The Culture of Flowers.* New York: Cambridge University Press.

Goossens, Benoît, Lounès Chikhi, Marc Ancrenaz, Isabelle Lackman-Ancrenaz, Patrick Andau, and Michael W. Bruford. 2006. Genetic Signature of Anthropogenic Population Collapse in Orangutans. PloS Biology 4(2):e25. www.plosbiology.org.

González, Roberto A. 2009. *American Counterinsurgency: Human Science and the Human Terrain.* Chicago: University of Chicago Press.

Green, Richard et al. 2010. A Draft Sequence of the Neandertal Genome. *Science* 328:710–722.

Greenhalgh, Susan. 2003. Science, Modernity, and the Making of China's One-Child Policy. *Population and Development Review* 29:163–196.

———. 2008. *Just One Child: Science and Policy in Deng's China.* Berkeley: University of California Press.

Gregg, Jessica L. 2003. *Virtually Virgins: Sexual Strategies and Cervical Cancer in Recife, Brazil.* Stanford: Stanford University Press.

Gremillion, Helen. 1992. Psychiatry as Social Ordering: Anorexia Nervosa, a Paradigm. *Social Science and Medicine* 35(1):57–71.

Grinker, Roy Richard. 1994. *Houses in the Rainforest: Ethnicity and Inequality among Farmers and Foragers in Central Africa.* Berkeley: University of California Press.

Gross, Daniel R. 1984. Time Allocation: A Tool for the Study of Cultural Behavior. *Annual Review of Anthropology* 13:519–558.

Gruenbaum, Ellen. 2001. *The Female Circumcision Controversy: An Anthropological Perspective.* Philadelphia: University of Pennsylvania Press.

Guggenheim, Scott E. and Michael M. Cernea. 1993. Anthropological Approaches to Involuntary Resettlement: Policy, Practice, and Theory. In *Anthropological Approaches to Resettlement: Policy, Practice, and Theory* (pp. 1–12). Michael M. Cernea and Scott E. Guggenheim, eds. Boulder, CO: Westview Press.

Guidoni, Enrico. 1987. *Primitive Architecture.* Trans. Robert Erich Wolf. New York: Rizzoli.

Günes-Ayata, Ayse. 1995. Women's Participation in Politics in Turkey. In *Women in Modern Turkish Society: A Reader* (pp. 235–249). Sirin Tekeli, ed. London: Zed Books.

Hackenberg, Robert A., B. H. Hackenberg, H. F. Magalit, and El Cabral. 1983. Migration, Modernization and Hypertension: Blood Pressure Levels in Four Philippine Communities. *Medical Anthropology* 7(1):45–71.

Hacker, Andrew. 1992. *Two Nations: Black and White, Separate, Hostile, Unequal.* New York: Ballantine Books.

Haddix McCay, Kimber. 2001. Leaving Your Wife and Your Brothers: When Polyandrous Marriages Fall Apart. *Evolution and Human Behavior* 22:47–60.

Hamabata, Matthews Masayuki. 1990. *Crested Kimono: Power and Love in the Japanese Business Family.* Ithaca, NY: Cornell University Press.

Hammond, Peter B. 1966. *Yatenga: Technology in the Culture of a West African Kingdom.* New York: Free Press.

Hancock, Graham. 1989. *Lords of Poverty: The Power, Prestige, and Corruption of the International Aid Business.* New York: Atlantic Monthly Press.

Handler, Richard. 2003. Cultural Property and Cultural Theory. *Journal of Social Archaeology* 3:353–365.

Harner, Michael. 1977. The Ecological Basis of Aztec Sacrifice. *American Ethnologist* 4:117–135.

Harper, Krista. 2005. "Wild Capitalism" and "Ecocolonialism": A Tale of Two Rivers. *American Ethnologist* 107:221–233.

Harris, Marvin. 1974. *Cows, Pigs, Wars and Witches: The Riddles of Culture.* New York: Random House.

———. 1975. *Culture, People, Nature: An Introduction to General Anthropology,* 2nd ed. New York: Thomas Y. Crowell.

———. 1977. *Cannibals and Kings: The Origins of Culture.* New York: Random House.

———. 1984. Animal Capture and Yanomamo Warfare: Retrospect and New Evidence. *Journal of Anthropological Research* 40(10):183–201.

———. 1989. *Our Kind: The Evolution of Human Life and Culture.* New York: Harper & Row Publishers.

———. 1992. Distinguished Lecture: Anthropology and the Theoretical and Paradigmatic Significance of the Collapse of Soviet and East European Communism. *American Anthropologist* 94:295–305.

———. 1993. The Evolution of Human Gender Hierarchies. In *Sex and Gender Hierarchies* (pp. 57–80). Barbara D. Miller, ed. New York: Cambridge University Press.

Hawn, Carleen. 2002. Please Feedback the Animals. *Forbes* 170(9):168–169.

Hefner, Robert W. 1998. Multiple Modernities: Christianity, Islam, and Hinduism in a Globalizing Age. *Annual Review of Anthropology* 27:83–104.

Heise, Lori L., Jacqueline Pitanguy, and Adrienne Germain. 1994. Violence against Women: The Hidden Health Burden. *World Bank Discussion Papers No. 255.* Washington, DC: The World Bank.

Helweg, Arthur W. and Usha M. Helweg. 1990. *An Immigrant Success Story: East Indians in America.* Philadelphia: University of Pennsylvania Press.

Henshaw, Anne. 2006. Pausing along the Journey: Learning Landscapes, Environmental Change, and Toponymy amongst the Sikusilarmiut. Arctic Anthropology 43:52–66.

Herdt, Gilbert. 1987. *The Sambia: Ritual and Gender in New Guinea.* New York: Holt, Rinehart and Winston.

Hewlett, Barry S. 1991. *Intimate Fathers: The Nature and Context of Aka Pygmy Paternal Care.* Ann Arbor: University of Michigan Press.

Hill, Jane H. 2001. Dimensions of Attrition in Language Death. In *On Biocultural Diversity: Linking Language, Knowledge, and the Environment* (pp. 175–189). Luisa Maffi, ed. Washington, DC: Smithsonian Institution Press.

Hill, Jane H. and Bruce Mannheim. 1992. Language and World View. *Annual Review of Anthropology* 21:381–406.

Hiltebeitel, Alf. 1988. *The Cult of Draupadi: Mythologies from Gingee to Kuruksetra.* Chicago: University of Chicago Press.

Hirschon, Renee. 1989. *Heirs of the Catastrophe: The Social Life of Asia Minor Refugees in Piraeus.* New York: Oxford University Press.

Hodge, Robert W. and Naohiro Ogawa. 1991. *Fertility Change in Contemporary Japan.* Chicago: University of Chicago Press.

Hoffman, Danny. 2003. Frontline Anthropology: Research in a Time of War. *Anthropology Today* 19:9–12.

Hoffman, Danny and Stephen Lubkemann. 2005. Warscape Ethnography in West Africa and the Anthropology of "Events." *Anthropological Quarterly* 78:315–327.

Holland, Dorothy C. and Margaret A. Eisenhart. 1990. *Educated in Romance: Women, Achievement, and College Culture.* Chicago: University of Chicago Press.

Hopkins, Nicholas S. and Sohair R. Mehanna. 2000. Social Action against Everyday Pollution in Egypt. *Human Organization* 59:245–254.

Hornbein, George and Marie Hornbein. 1992. *Salamanders: A Night at the Phi Delt House.* Video. College Park: Documentary Resource Center.

Horowitz, Irving L. 1967. *The Rise and Fall of Project Camelot: Studies in the Relationship between Social Science and Practical Politics.* Boston: MIT Press.

Horowitz, Michael M. and Muneera Salem-Murdock. 1993. Development-Induced Food Insecurity in the Middle Senegal Valley. *GeoJournal* 30(2):179–184.

Horst, Heather and Daniel Miller. 2005. From Kinship to Link-up: Cell Phones and Social Networking in Jamaica. *Current Anthropology* 46:755–764, 773–778.

Howell, Nancy. 1979. *Demography of the Dobe !Kung.* New York: Academic Press.

———. 1990. *Surviving Fieldwork: A Report of the Advisory Panel on Health and Safety in Fieldwork.* Washington, DC: American Anthropological Association.

Huang, Shu-Min. 1993. A Cross-Cultural Experience: A Chinese Anthropologist in the United States. In *Distance Mirrors: America as a Foreign Culture* (pp. 39–45). Philip R. DeVita and James D. Armstrong, eds. Belmont, CA: Wadsworth.

Hughes, Charles C. and John M. Hunter. 1970. Disease and "Development" in Africa. *Social Science and Medicine* 3:443–493.

Hughes, Lotte. 2003. *The No-Nonsense Guide to Indigenous Peoples.* London: Verso.

Humphrey, Caroline. 1978. Women, Taboo and the Suppression of Attention. In *Defining Females: The Nature of Women in Society* (pp. 89–108). Shirley Ardener, ed. New York: John Wiley and Sons.

Hunte, Pamela A. 1985. Indigenous Methods of Fertility Regulation in Afghanistan. In *Women's Medicine: A Cross-Cultural Study of Indigenous Fertility Regulation* (pp. 44–75). Lucile F. Newman, ed. New Brunswick, NJ: Rutgers University Press.

Hutter, Michael. 1996. The Value of Play. In *The Value of Culture: On the Relationship between Economics and the Arts* (pp. 122–137). Arjo Klamer, ed. Amsterdam: Amsterdam University Press.

Ingham, John M. 1996. *Psychological Anthropology Reconsidered.* New York: Cambridge University Press.

Inhorn, Marcia C. 2003. Global Infertility and the Globalization of New Reproductive Technologies: Illustrations from Egypt. *Social Science and Medicine* 56:1837–1851.

———. 2004. Middle Eastern Masculinities in the Age of New Reproductive Technologies: Male Infertility and Stigma in Egypt and Lebanon. *Medical Anthropology Quarterly* 18(2):162–182.

International Alliance for the Protection of Isolated Indigenous Peoples. 2005. *Belém Declaration on Isolated Indigenous Peoples.* Adopted at the First International Symposium on Isolated Indigenous Peoples of the Amazon, Belém, Brazil, November.

IUCN/SSC Conservation Breeding Specialist Group. 2004. *Orangutan: Population and Habitat Viability Assessment: Final Report.* Apple Valley, MN: IUCN/SSC Conservation Breeding Specialist Group. www.cbsg.org.

Jacobs-Huey, Lanita. 1997. Is There an Authentic African American Speech Community: Carla Revisited. *University of Pennsylvania Working Papers in Linguistics* 4(1):331–370.

———. 2002. The Natives Are Gazing and Talking Back: Reviewing the Problematics of Positionality, Voice, and Accountability among "Native" Anthropologists. *American Anthropologist* 104:791–804.

———. 2006. *From the Kitchen to the Parlor: Language and Becoming in African American Women's Hair Care.* New York: Oxford University Press.

Janes, Craig R. 1990. *Migration, Social Change, and Health: A Samoan Community in Urban California.* Stanford, CA: Stanford University Press.

———. 1995. The Transformations of Tibetan Medicine. *Medical Anthropology Quarterly* 9(1):6–39.

Jankowski, Martín Sánchez. 1991. *Islands in the Street: Gangs and American Urban Society.* Berkeley: University of California Press.

Jenkins, Gwynne. 2003. Burning Bridges: Policy, Practice, and the Destruction of Midwifery in Rural Costa Rica. *Social Science and Medicine* 56:1893–1909.

Jenkins, Gwynne L. and Marcia C. Inhorn. 2003. Reproduction Gone Awry: Medical Anthropology Perspectives. *Social Science and Medicine* 56:1831–1836.

Jensen, Marianne Wiben, ed. Elaine Bolton, trans. 2004. Land Rights: A Key Issue. *Indigenous Affairs* 4.

Jernsletten, Nils. 1997. Sami Traditional Terminology: Professional Terms Concerning Salmon, Reindeer and Snow. In *Sami Culture in a New Era: The Norwegian Sami Experience* (pp. 86–106). Harald Gaski, ed. Seattle: University of Washington Press.

Jinadu, L. Adele. 1994. The Dialectics of Theory and Research on Race and Ethnicity in Nigeria. In *"Race," Ethnicity and Nation: International Perspectives on Social Conflict* (pp. 163–178). Peter Ratcliffe, ed. London: University College of London Press.

Johnson, Walter R. 1994. *Dismantling Apartheid: A South African Town in Transition.* Ithaca, NY: Cornell University Press.

Johnson-Hanks, Jennifer. 2002. On the Limits of Life Stages in Ethnography: Toward a Theory of Vital Conjectures. *American Anthropologist* 104:865–880.

Johnston, Barbara Rose. 1994. Environmental Degradation and Human Rights Abuse. In *Who Pays the Price? The Sociocultural Context of Environmental Crisis* (pp. 7–16). Barbara Rose Johnston, ed. Washington, DC: Island Press.

Jonaitis, Aldona. 1995. *A Wealth of Thought: Franz Boas on Native American Art.* Seattle: University of Washington Press.

Joralemon, Donald. 1982. New World Depopulation and the Case of Disease. *Journal of Anthropological Research* 38:108–127.

Jordan, Brigitte. 1983. *Birth in Four Cultures,* 3rd ed. Montreal: Eden Press.

Joseph, Suad. 1994. Brother/Sister Relationships: Connectivity, Love, and Power in the Reproduction of Patriarchy in Lebanon. *American Ethnologist* 21:50–73.

Jourdan, Christine. 1995. Masta Liu. In *Youth Cultures: A Cross-Cultural Perspective* (pp. 202–222). Vered Amit-Talai and Helena Wulff, eds. New York: Routledge.

Judah G., P. Donachie, E. Cobb, W. Schmidt, M. Holland, and V. Curtis. 2010. Dirty Hands: Bacteria of Faecal Origin on Commuters' Hands. *Epidemiology and Infections* 138(3):409–414.

Judd, Ellen. 2002. *The Chinese Women's Movement: Between State and Market.* Stanford, CA: Stanford University Press.

Junger, Sebastian. 2010. *War.* New York: Twelve.

Kaberry, Phyllis. 1952. *Women of the Grassfields: A Study of the Economic Position of Women in Bamenda, British Cameroons.* London: Her Majesty's Stationery Office.

Kapchan, Deborah A. 1994. Moroccan Female Performers Defining the Social Body. *Journal of American Folklore* 107(423):82–105.

Karan, P. P. and Cotton Mather. 1985. Tourism and Environment in the Mount Everest Region. *Geographical Review* 75(1):93–95.

Kassam, Aneesa. 2002. Ethnodevelopment in the Oromia Regional State of Ethiopia. In *Participating in Development: Approaches to Indigenous Knowledge* (pp. 65–81). Paul Sillitoe, Alan Bicker, and Johan Pottier, eds. ASA Monographs No. 39. New York: Routledge.

Kata, Anna. 2010. A Postmodern Pandora's Box: Anti-Vaccination Information on the Internet. *Vaccine* 28:1709–1716.

Katz, Nathan and Ellen S. Goldberg. 1989. Asceticism and Caste in the Passover Observances of the Cochin Jews. *Journal of the American Academy of Religion* 57(1):53–81.

Katz, Richard. 1982. *Boiling Energy: Community Healing among the Kalahari Kung.* Cambridge, MA: Harvard University Press.

Katz, Richard, Megan Biesele, and Verna St. Denis. 1997. *Healing Makes Our Hearts Happy: Spirituality and Cultural Transformation among the Kalahari Jul'hoansi.* Rochester, VT: Inner Traditions.

Kaul, Adam. 2004. The Anthropologist as Barman and Tour-guide: Reflections on Fieldwork in a Touristed Destination. *Durham Anthropology Journal* 12:22–36.

Kawanishi, Y. 2004. Japanese Youth: The Other Half of the Crisis? *Asian Affairs* 35:22–32.

Kehoe, Alice Beck. 1989. *The Ghost Dance: History and Revitalization.* Philadelphia: Holt.

Kendon, A. 1988. Parallels and Divergences between Warlpiri Sign Language and Spoken Warlpiri: Analyses of Spoken and Signed Discourse. *Oceania* 58:239–254.

Kennedy, David P. and Stephen G. Perz. 2000. Who Are Brazil's Indígenas? Contributions of Census Data Analysis to Anthropological Demography of Indigenous Populations. *Human Organization* 59:311–324.

Kerns, Virginia. 1999. Preventing Violence against Women: A Central American Case. In *To Have and To Hit: Cultural Perspectives on Wife Beating,* 2nd ed. (pp. 153–168). Dorothy Ayers Counts, Judith K. Brown, and Jacquelyn C. Campbell, eds. Urbana: University of Illinois Press.

Keskitalo, Jan Henry. 1997. Sami Post-Secondary Education: Ideals and Realities. In *Sami Culture in a New Era: The Norwegian Sami Experience* (pp. 155–171). Harald Gaski, ed. Seattle: University of Washington Press.

Kesmanee, Chupinit. 1994. Dubious Development Concepts in the Thai Highlands: The Chao Khao in Transition. *Law & Society Review* 28:673–683.

Kidder, Tracy. *Mountains beyond Mountains: The Quest of Paul Farmer, the Man Who Would Cure the World.* New York: Random House, 2003.

Kirsch, Stuart. 2002. Anthropology and Advocacy: A Case Study of the Campaign against the Ok Tedi Mine. *Critique of Anthropology* 22:175–200.

Kleinman, Arthur. 1995. *Writing at the Margin: Discourse between Anthropology and Medicine.* Berkeley: University of California Press.

Klima, Alan. 2002. *The Funeral Casino: Meditation, Massacre, and Exchange with the Dead in Thailand.* Princeton: Princeton University Press.

Knott, Kim. 1996. Hindu Women, Destiny and Stridharma. *Religion* 26:15–35.

Kolenda, Pauline M. 1978. *Caste in Contemporary India: Beyond Organic Solidarity.* Prospect Heights, IL: Waveland Press.

Kolling, Marie, Kirsty Winkley, and Mette von Deden. 2010. "For Someone Who's Rich, It's Not a Problem": Insights from Tanzania on Diabetes Health-Seeking and Medical Pluralism among Dar es Salaam's Urban Poor. *Globalization and Health* 6.

Kondo, Dorinne. 1997. *About Face: Performing "Race" in Fashion and Theater.* New York: Routledge.

Konner, Melvin. 1989. Homosexuality: Who and Why? *New York Times Magazine.* April 2:60–61.

Kottak, Conrad Phillip. 1985. When People Don't Come First: Some Sociological Lessons from Completed Projects. In *Putting People First: Sociological Variables and Rural Development* (pp. 325–356). Michael M. Cernea, ed. New York: Oxford University Press.

———. 1992. *Assault on Paradise: Social Change in a Brazilian Village.* New York: McGraw-Hill.

Kovats-Bernat, J. Christopher. 2002. Negotiating Dangerous Fields: Pragmatic Strategies for Fieldwork amid Violence and Terror. *American Anthropologist* 104:1–15.

Kramer, Jennifer. 2005. Personal communication.

Krantzler, Nora J. 1987. Traditional Medicine as "Medical Neglect": Dilemmas in the Case Management of a Samoan Teenager with Diabetes. In *Child Survival: Cultural Perspectives on the Treatment and Maltreatment of Children* (pp. 325–337). Nancy Scheper-Hughes, ed. Boston: D. Reidel.

Kraybill, Donald B. and Steven M. Nolt. 2004. *Amish Enterprise: From Plows to Profits,* 2nd ed. Baltimore: Johns Hopkins University Press.

Kroeber, A. L. and Clyde Kluckhohn. 1952. *Culture: A Critical Review of Concepts and Definitions.* New York: Vintage Books.

Kuipers, Joel C. 1990. *Power in Performance: The Creation of Textual Authority in Weyéwa Ritual Speech.* Philadelphia: University of Pennsylvania Press.

———. 1991. Matters of Taste in Weyéwa. In *The Varieties of Sensory Experience: A Sourcebook in the Anthropology of the Senses* (pp. 111–127). David Howes, ed. Toronto: University of Toronto Press.

———. 2004. Ethnography of Language in the Age of Video: "Voices" in Context of Religious and Clinical Authority. In *Discourse and Technology: Multimodal Discourse Analysis* (pp. 167–183). Philip LeVine and Ron Scollon, eds. Washington, DC: Georgetown University Press.

Kuipers, Joel C. and Ray McDermott. 1996. Insular Southeast Asian Scripts. In *The World's Writing Systems* (pp. 474–484). Peter T. Daniels and William Bright, eds. New York: Oxford University Press.

Kumar, Krishna. 1996. Civil Society. In *The Social Science Encyclopedia* (pp. 88–90). Adam Kuper and Jessica Kuper, eds. New York: Routledge.

Kurin, Richard. 1980. Doctor, Lawyer, Indian Chief. *Natural History* 89(11):6–24.

Kurkiala, Mikael. 2003. Interpreting Honor Killings: The Story of Fadime Sahindal (1975–2002) in the Swedish Press. *Anthropology Today* 19:6–7.

Kuwayama, Takami. 2004. *Native Anthropology: The Japanese Challenge to Western Academic Hegemony.* Melbourne, Australia: Trans Pacific Press.

Kwiatkowski, Lynn M. 1998. *Struggling with Development: The Politics of Hunger and Gender in the Philippines.* Boulder, CO: Westview Press.

Labov, William. 1966. *The Social Stratification of English in New York City.* Washington, DC: Center for Applied Linguistics.

Lacey, Marc. 2002. Where 9/11 News Is Late, But Aid Is Swift. *New York Times,* June 3:A1, A7.

Ladányi, János. 1993. Patterns of Residential Segregation and the Gypsy Minority in Budapest. *International Journal of Urban and Regional Research* 17(1):30–41.

Laderman, Carol. 1988. A Welcoming Soil: Islamic Humoralism on the Malay Peninsula. In *Paths to Asian Medical Knowledge* (pp. 272–288). Charles Leslie and Allan Young, eds. Berkeley: University of California Press.

LaFleur, William. 1992. *Liquid Life: Abortion and Buddhism in Japan.* Princeton, NJ: Princeton University Press.

Lakoff, Robin. 1973. Language and Woman's Place. *Language in Society* 2:45–79.

———. 1990. *Talking Power: The Politics of Language in Our Lives.* New York: Basic Books.

LaLone, Mary B. 2003. Walking the Line between Alternative Interpretations in Heritage Education and Tourism: A Demonstration of the Complexities with an Appalachian Coal Mining Example. In *Signifying Serpents and Mardi Gras Runners: Representing Identity in Selected Souths* (pp. 72–92). Southern Anthropological Proceedings, No. 36. Celeste Ray and Luke Eric Lassiter, eds. Athens: University of Georgia Press.

Lamphere, Louise. 1992. Introduction: The Shaping of Diversity. In *Structuring Diversity: Ethnographic Perspectives on the New Immigration* (pp. 1–34). Louise Lamphere, ed. Chicago: University of Chicago Press.

Lane, Sandra D., Robert H. Keefe, Robert A. Rubenstein, Brooke A. Levandowski, Michael Freedman, Alan Rosenthal, Donald A. Cibula, and Maria Czerwinski. 2004. Marriage Promotion and Missing Men: African American Women in a Demographic Double Bind. *Medical Anthropology Quarterly* 18:405–428.

Lanehart, Sonja L. 1999. African American Vernacular English. In *Handbook of Language and Ethnic Identity* (pp. 211–225). Joshua A. Fishman, ed. New York: Oxford University Press.

Larsen, Ulla and Marida Hollos. 2003. Women's Empowerment and Fertility Decline among the Pare of Kilimanjaro Region, Northern Tanzania. *Social Science and Medicine* 57:1099–1115.

Larsen, Ulla and Sharon Yan. 2000. Does Female Circumcision Affect Infertility and Fertility? A Study of the Central African Republic, Côte d'Ivoire, and Tanzania. *Demography* 37:313–321.

Larsson, Sara. 2005. Legislating Gender Equality: In Saami Land, Women Are Encouraged to Become Lawyers—But Many Would Rather Be Reindeer Herders. *Cultural Survival Quarterly* 28(4):28–29.

Lassiter, Luke Eric, Hurley Goodall, Elizabeth Campbell, and Michelle Natasya Johnson. 2004. *The Other Side of Middletown: Exploring Muncie's African American Community.* Walnut Creek, CA: AltaMira Press.

Leach, Jerry W. 1975. *Trobriand Cricket: An Ingenious Response to Colonialism.* Video.

Lederer, Edith. 2006. Record Number of Women in Politics. *Guardian Weekly,* March 10–15:9.

Lee, Gary R. and Mindy Kezis. 1979. Family Structure and the Status of the Elderly. *Journal of Comparative Family Studies* 10:429–443.

Lee, Helen Morton. 2003. *Tongans Overseas: Between Two Shores.* Honolulu: University of Hawai'i Press.

Lee, Richard B. 1969. Eating Christmas in the Kalahari. *Natural History,* December 14–22, 60–63.

———. 1979. *The !Kung San: Men, Women, and Work in a Foraging Society.* New York: Cambridge University Press.

Lee, Wai-Na and David K. Tse. 1994. Becoming Canadian: Understanding How Hong Kong Immigrants Change Their Consumption. *Pacific Affairs* 67(1):70–95.

Lempert, David. 1996. *Daily Life in a Crumbling Empire.* 2 volumes. New York: Columbia University Press.

Lepowsky, Maria. 1990. Big Men, Big Women, and Cultural Autonomy. *Ethnology* 29(10):35–50.

———. 1993. *Fruit of the Motherland: Gender in an Egalitarian Society.* New York: Columbia University Press.

Lesher, James H., trans. 2001. *Xenophanes of Colophon: Fragments.* Toronto: University of Toronto Press.

Lessinger, Johanna. 1995. *From the Ganges to the Hudson: Indian Immigrants in New York City.* Boston: Allyn and Bacon.

Levine, Robert, Suguru Sato, Tsukasa Hashimoto, and Jyoti Verma. 1995. Love and Marriage in Eleven Cultures. *Journal of Cross-Cultural Psychology* 26:554–571.

Levinson, David. 1989. *Family Violence in Cross-Cultural Perspective.* Newbury Park, CA: Sage Publications.

Lévi-Strauss, Claude. 1967. *Structural Anthropology.* New York: Anchor Books.

———. 1968. *Tristes Tropiques: An Anthropological Study of Primitive Societies in Brazil.* New York: Atheneum.

———. 1969 [1949]. *The Elementary Structures of Kinship.* Boston: Beacon Press.

Levy, Jerrold E., Eric B. Henderson, and Tracy J. Andrews. 1989. The Effects of Regional Variation and Temporal Change in Matrilineal Elements of Navajo Social Organization. *Journal of Anthropological Research* 45(4):351–377.

Lew, Irvina. 1994. Bathing as Science: Ancient Sea Cures Gain Support from New Research. *Condé Nast Traveler* 29(12):86–90.

Lewis, Oscar. 1966. The Culture of Poverty. *Scientific American* 215:19–25.

Leynaud, Emile. 1961. Fraternités d'âge et sociétés de culture dans la Haute-Vallée du Niger. *Cahiers d'Etudes Africaines* 6:41–68.

Li, Fabiana. 2009. Documenting Accountability: Environmental Impact Assessment in a Peruvian Mining Project. *Political and Legal Anthropology Review* 32:218–236.

Lightfoot, David. 2006. *How New Languages Emerge.* New York: Cambridge University Press.

Lincoln, Kenneth. 1993. *Indi'n Humor: Bicultural Play in Native America.* New York: Oxford University Press.

Lindenbaum, Shirley. 1979. *Kuru Sorcery: Disease and Danger in the New Guinea Highlands.* Mountain View, CA: Mayfield Publishing.

Lipka, Jerry, Maureen P. Hogan, Joan Parker Webster, Evelyn Yanez, Barbara Adams, Stacy Clark, and Doreen Lacy. 2005. Math in a Cultural Context: Two Case Studies of a Successful Culturally Based Math Project. *Anthropology and Education Quarterly* 36(4):367–385.

Lock, Margaret. 1993. *Encounters with Aging: Mythologies of Menopause in Japan and North America.* Berkeley: University of California Press.

Loker, William. 2000. Sowing Discord, Planting Doubts: Rhetoric and Reality in an Environment and Development Project in Honduras. *Human Organization* 59:300–310.

———. 2003. Dam Impacts in a Time of Globalization: Using Multiple Methods to Document Social and Environmental Change in Rural Honduras. *Current Anthropology* 44(supplement): S112–S121.

———. 2004. *Changing Places: Environment, Development, and Social Change in Rural Honduras.* Durham, NC: Carolina Academic Press.

Long, Susan Orpett. 2005. *Final Days: Japanese Culture and Choice at the End of Life.* Honolulu: University of Hawai'i Press.

Lorch, Donatella. 2003. Do Read This for War. *Newsweek* 141(11):13.

Low, Setha M. 1995. Indigenous Architecture and the Spanish American Plaza in Mesoamerica and the Caribbean. *American Anthropologist* 97(4):748–762.

Lubkemann, Stephen C. 2002. Refugees. In *World at Risk: A Global Issues Sourcebook* (pp. 522–544). Washington, DC: CQ Press.

———. 2005. Migratory Coping in Wartime Mozambique: An Anthropology of Violence and Displacement in "Fragmented Wars." *Journal of Peace Research* 42:493–508.

Lutz, Ellen L. 2005. The Many Meanings of Technology: A Message from our Executive Editor. *Cultural Survival Quarterly* 29(2):5.

Lyman, Rick. 2006. Reports Reveal Hurricanes' Impact on Human Landscape. *New York Times,* May 6, p. A16.

Lyttleton, Chris. 2004. Relative Pleasures: Drugs, Development and Modern Dependencies in Asia's Golden Triangle. *Development and Change* 35:909–935.

MacLeod, Arlene Elowe. 1992. Hegemonic Relations and Gender Resistance: The New Veiling as Accommodating Protest in Cairo. *Signs: The Journal of Women in Culture and Society* 17(3):533–557.

Macnair, Peter. 1995. From Kwakiutl to Kwakwaka'wakw. In *Native Peoples: The Canadian Experience*, 2nd ed. (pp. 586–605). R. Bruce Morrison and C. Roderick Wilson, eds. Toronto: McClelland & Stewart.

Maffi, Luisa. 2003. The "Business" of Language Endangerment: Saving Languages or Helping People Keep Them Alive? In *Language in the Twenty-First Century: Selected Papers of the Millennial Conference of the Center for Research and Documentation on World Language Problems* (pp. 67–86). H. Tonkin and T. Reagan, eds. Amsterdam: John Benjamins.

———. 2005. Linguistic, Cultural, and Biological Diversity. *Annual Review of Anthropology* 34:599–617.

Magga, Ole Henrik and Tove Skutnabb-Kangas. 2001. The Saami Languages: The Present and the Future. *Cultural Survival Quarterly* 25(2):26–31.

Mahler, Sarah J. 1995. *Salvadorans in Suburbia: Symbiosis and Conflict*. Boston: Allyn and Bacon.

Major, Marc R. 1996. No Friends but the Mountains: A Simulation on Kurdistan. *Social Education* 60(3):C1–C8.

Malinowski, Bronislaw. 1929. *The Sexual Life of Savages*. New York: Harcourt, Brace & World.

———. 1948. *Magic, Science and Religion, and Other Essays*. Boston: Beacon Press.

———. 1961 [1922]. *Argonauts of the Western Pacific*. New York: E. P. Dutton & Co.

Mamdani, Mahmoud. 1972. *The Myth of Population Control: Family, Caste, and Class in an Indian Village*. New York: Monthly Review Press.

———. 2002. Good Muslim, Bad Muslim: A Political Perspective on Culture and Terrorism. *American Anthropologist* 104:766–775.

Manz, Beatriz. 2004. *Paradise in Ashes: A Guatemalan Journey of Courage, Terror, and Hope*. Berkeley: University of California Press.

Marcus, George. 1995. Ethnography in/of the World System: The Emergence of Multi-Sited Ethnography. *Annual Review of Anthropology* 24:95–117.

Margolis, Maxine. 1994. *Little Brazil: An Ethnography of Brazilian Immigrants in New York City*. Princeton, NJ: Princeton University Press.

Margolis, Maxine L. and Marigene Arnold. 1993. Turning the Tables? Male Strippers and the Gender Hierarchy in America. In *Sex and Gender Hierarchies* (pp. 334–350). Barbara D. Miller, ed. New York: Cambridge University Press.

Martin, Richard C. 1995. Islam. In *The HarperCollins Dictionary of Religion* (pp. 498–513). Jonathan Z. Smith, ed. New York: HarperCollins.

Martin, Sarah. 2005. *Must Boys Be Boys? Ending Sexual Exploitation and Abuse in UN Peacekeeping Missions*. Washington, DC: Refugees International.

Martínez, Samuel. 1996. Indifference with Indignation: Anthropology, Human Rights, and the Haitian Bracero. *American Anthropologist* 98(1):17–25.

Masquelier, Adeline. 2005. The Scorpion's Sting: Youth, Marriage and the Struggle for Social Maturity in Niger. *Journal of the Royal Anthropological Institute* 11:59–83.

Maybury-Lewis, David. 1997a. Museums and Indigenous Cultures. *Cultural Survival Quarterly* 21(1):3.

———. 1997b. *Indigenous Peoples, Ethnic Groups, and the State*. Boston: Allyn and Bacon.

McCallum, Cecilia. 2005. Explaining Caesarean Section in Salvador da Bahia, Brazil. *Sociology of Health and Illness* 27(2):215–242.

McCallum, Cecilia and Ana Paula dos Reis. 2005. Childbirth as Ritual in Brazil: Young Mothers' Experiences. *Ethnos* 70(3):335–360.

McCully, Patrick. 2003. Big Dams, Big Trouble. *New Internationalist* 354:14–15.

McDade, T. W., V. Reyes-Garcia, P. Blackinton, S. Tanner, T. Huanca, and W. R. Leonard. 2007. Ethnobotanical Knowledge is Associated with Indices of Child Health in the Bolivian Amazon. *Proceedings of the National Academy of Sciences* 104: 6134–6139.

McElroy, Ann and Patricia K. Townsend. 1996. *Medical Anthropology in Ecological Perspective*, 3rd ed. Boulder, CO: Westview Press.

McMahon, April M. S. 1994. *Understanding Language Change*. New York: Cambridge University Press.

Mead, Margaret. 1961 [1928]. *Coming of Age in Samoa: A Psychological Study of Primitive Youth for Western Civilization*. New York: Dell Publishing.

———. 1986. Field Work in the Pacific Islands, 1925–1967. In *Women in the Field: Anthropological Experiences* (pp. 293–331). Peggy Golde, ed. Berkeley: University of California Press.

Meador, Elizabeth. 2005. The Making of Marginality: Schooling for Mexican Immigrants in the Rural Southwest. *Anthropology and Education Quarterly* 36(2):149–164.

Meigs, Anna S. 1984. *Food, Sex, and Pollution: A New Guinea Religion*. New Brunswick, NJ: Rutgers University Press.

Mencher, Joan P. 1974. The Caste System Upside Down, or The Not-So-Mysterious East. *Current Anthropology* 15(4):469–493.

Mendenhall, Emily, Rebecca A. Seligman, Alicia Fernandez, and Elizabeth A. Jacobs. 2010. Speaking through Diabetes: Rethinking the Lay Discourses on Diabetes. *Medical Anthropology Quarterly* 24:220–239.

Mernissi, Fatima. 1987. *Beyond the Veil: Male–Female Dynamics in Modern Muslim Society*. Revised edition. Bloomington: Indiana University Press.

Merry, Sally Engle. 2006. *Human Rights and Gender Violence: Translating International Law into Local Justice*. Chicago: University of Chicago Press.

Messer, Ellen. 1993. Anthropology and Human Rights. *Annual Review of Anthropology* 22:221–249.

Michaelson, Evelyn Jacobson and Walter Goldschmidt. 1971. Female Roles and Male Dominance among Peasants. *Southwestern Journal of Anthropology* 27:330–352.

Michaud, Catherine M., W. Scott Gordon, and Michael R. Reich. 2005. *The Global Burden of Disease Due to Schistosomiasis*. Cambridge, MA: Harvard School of Public Health, Harvard Center for Population and Development Studies, Schistosomiasis Research Program Working Paper Series. Volume 14, Number 1.

Miller, Barbara D. 1987. Social Patterns of Food Expenditure Among Low-Income Jamaicans. In *Papers and Recommendations of the Workshop on Food and Nutrition Security in Jamaica in the 1980s and Beyond*. Kenneth A. Leslie and Lloyd B. Rankine, eds. Kingston, Jamaica: The Caribbean Food and Nutrition Institute.

———. 1993. Surveying the Anthropology of Sex and Gender Hierarchies. In *Sex and Gender Hierarchies* (pp. 3–31). Barbara D. Miller, ed. New York: Cambridge University Press.

———. 2009. Heritage Management Inside Out and Upside Down: Questioning Top-Down and Outside Approaches. *Heritage Management* 2:5–9.

Miller, Barbara D. and Showkat Hayat Khan. 1986. Incorporating Voluntarism into Rural Development in Bangladesh. *Third World Planning Review* 8(2):139–152.

Miller, Bruce G. 1994. Contemporary Native Women: Role Flexibility and Politics. *Anthropologica* 36:57–72.

Miller, Daniel, ed. 2001. *Car Cultures*. New York: Berg.

Miller, Laura. 2004. Those Naughty Teenage Girls: Japanese Kogals, Slang, and Media Assessments. *Journal of Linguistic Anthropology* 14:225–247.

Milton, Katherine. 1992. Civilization and Its Discontents. *Natural History* 3(92):37–92.

Miner, Horace. 1965 [1956]. Body Ritual among the Nacirema. In *Reader in Comparative Religion: An Anthropological Approach* (pp. 414–418). William A. Lessa and Evon Z. Vogt, eds. New York: Harper & Row.

Mines, Mattison. 1994. *Public Faces, Private Voices: Community and Individuality in South India.* Berkeley: University of California Press.

Mintz, Sidney. 1985. *Sweetness and Power: The Place of Sugar in Modern History.* New York: Viking.

Miyazawa, Setsuo. 1992. *Policing in Japan: A Study on Making Crime.* Frank G. Bennett, Jr. with John O. Haley, trans. Albany: State University of New York Press.

Modell, Judith S. 1994. *Kinship with Strangers: Adoption and Interpretations of Kinship in American Culture.* Berkeley: University of California Press.

Moerman, Daniel. 2002. *Meaning, Medicine and the "Placebo" Effect.* New York: Cambridge University Press.

Moffat, Tina. 2010. The "Childhood Obesity Epidemic": Health Crisis or Social Construction? *Medical Anthropology Quarterly* 24:1–21.

Mogelonsky, Marcia. 1995. Asian-Indian Americans. *American Demographics* 17(8):32–39.

Montesquieu, Charles. 1949 [1748]. *The Spirit of the Laws.* Trans. T. Nugent. New York: Hafner.

Moore, Molly. 2008. In France, Prisons Filled with Muslims. *Washington Post* April 29:A1, A4.

Morgan, Lewis Henry. 1851. *The League of the [Ho-de-nesau, or] Iroquois.* New York: Russell Sage.

Morris, Brian. 1998. *The Power of Animals: An Ethnography.* New York: Berg.

Morris, Rosalind. 1994. Three Sexes and Four Sexualities: Redressing the Discourses on Gender and Sexuality in Contemporary Thailand. *Positions* 2:15–43.

Muecke, Marjorie A. 1987. Resettled Refugees: Reconstruction of Identity of Lao in Seattle. *Urban Anthropology* 16(3–4): 273–289.

Mulk, Inga-Maria. 1994. Sacrificial Places and Their Meaning in Saami Society. In *Sacred Sites, Sacred Places* (pp. 121–131). David L. Carmichael, Jane Hubert, Brian Reeves, and Audhild Schanche, eds. New York: Routledge.

Mullings, Leith. 2005. Towards an Anti-Racist Anthropology: Interrogating Racism. *Annual Review of Anthropology* 34:667–693.

Murdock, George Peter. 1965 [1949]. *Social Structure.* New York: Free Press.

Murray, Gerald F. 1987. The Domestication of Wood in Haiti: A Case Study of Applied Evolution. In *Anthropological Praxis: Translating Knowledge into Action* (pp. 233–240). Robert M. Wulff and Shirley J. Fiske, eds. Boulder, CO: Westview Press.

Myerhoff, Barbara. 1978. *Number Our Days.* New York: Simon and Schuster.

Myers, James. 1992. Nonmainstream Body Modification: Genital Piercing, Branding, Burning, and Cutting. *Journal of Contemporary Ethnography* 21(3):267–306.

Myers, Norman. 2000. Sustainable Consumption. *Science* 287 (March 31):2419.

Myrskylä, Mikko, Hans-Peter Kohler, and Francesco C. Billari. 2009. Advances in Development Reverse Fertility Trends. *Nature* 460(6):741–743.

Nadeau, Kathleen M. 2002. *Liberation Theology in the Philippines: Faith in a Revolution.* Westport: Praeger.

Nader, Laura. 1972. Up the Anthropologist—Perspectives Gained from Studying Up. In *Reinventing Anthropology* (pp. 284–311). Dell Hymes, ed. New York: Vintage Books.

Nag, Moni. 1972. Sex, Culture and Human Fertility: India and the United States. *Current Anthropology* 13:231–238.

———. 1983. Modernization Affects Fertility. *Populi* 10:56–77.

Nag, Moni, Benjamin N. F. White, and R. Creighton Peet. 1978. An Anthropological Approach to the Study of the Economic Value of Children in Java and Nepal. *Current Anthropology* 19(2):293–301.

Nanda, Serena. 1990. *Neither Man nor Woman: The Hijras of India.* Belmont, CA: Wadsworth.

———. 1994. *Cultural Anthropology.* Wadsworth, CA: Wadsworth.

Natcher, David C., Susan Davis, and Clifford G. Hickey. 2005. Co-Management: Managing Relationships, Not Resources. *Human Organization* 64:240–250.

National Park Service. 2005. *Low Country Gullah Culture: Special Resource Study and Final Environmental Impact Statement.* Atlanta: NPS Southeast Regional Office. www.nps.gov.

Neff, Deborah L. 1994. The Social Construction of Infertility: The Case of the Matrilineal Nayars in South India. *Social Science and Medicine* 39(4):475–485.

Nettle, Daniel and Suzanne Romaine. 2000. *Vanishing Voices: The Extinction of the World's Languages.* New York: Oxford University Press.

Neusner, Jacob. 1995. Judaism. In *The HarperCollins Dictionary of Religion* (pp. 598–607). Jonathan Z. Smith, ed. New York: HarperCollins.

Nevins, M. Eleanor. 2004. Learning to Listen: Confronting Two Meanings of Language Loss in the Contemporary White Mountain Apache Speech Community. *Journal of Linguistic Anthropology* 14:269–288.

Newman, Lucile. 1972. *Birth Control: An Anthropological View.* Module No. 27. Reading, MA: Addison-Wesley.

Newman, Lucile, ed. 1985. *Women's Medicine: A Cross-Cultural Study of Indigenous Fertility Regulation.* New Brunswick: Rutgers University Pres.

Ngokwey, Ndolamb. 1988. Pluralistic Etiological Systems in Their Social Context: A Brazilian Case Study. *Social Science and Medicine* 26:793–802.

Nichter, Mark. 1992. Of Ticks, Kings, Spirits and the Promise of Vaccines. In *Paths to Asian Medical Knowledge* (pp. 224–253). Charles Leslie and Allan Young, eds. Berkeley: University of California Press.

———. 1996. Vaccinations in the Third World: A Consideration of Community Demand. In *Anthropology and International Health: Asian Case Studies* (pp. 329–365). Mark Nichter and Mimi Nichter, eds. Amsterdam: Gordon and Breach Publishers.

Nodwell, Evelyn and Neil Guppy. 1992. The Effects of Publicly Displayed Ethnicity on Interpersonal Discrimination: Indo-Canadians in Vancouver. *The Canadian Review of Sociology and Anthropology* 29(1):87–99.

Nordstrom, Carolyn. 1997. *A Different Kind of War Story.* Philadelphia: University of Pennsylvania Press.

Norgaard, Richard B. 1994. *Development Betrayed: The End of Progress and the Coevolutionary Revisioning of the Future.* New York: Routledge.

Obeyesekere, Gananath. 1981. *Medusa's Hair: An Essay on Personal Symbols and Religious Experience.* Chicago: University of Chicago Press.

Ohnuki-Tierney, Emiko. 1980. Shamans and Imu: Among Two Ainu Groups. In *The Culture-Bound Syndromes* (pp. 91–110). Ronald C. Simons and Charles C. Hughes, eds. Dordrecht: D. Reidel Publishing.

...elix J. 1993. Couvade in Estonia. *Slavic & East European Journal* 37(3):339–345.

...ng, Aihwa. 1995. State versus Islam: Malay Families, Women's Bodies, and the Body Politic in Malaysia. In *Bewitching Women, Pious Men: Gender and Body Politics in Southeast Asia* (pp. 159–194). Aihwa Ong and Michael G. Peletz, eds. Berkeley: University of California Press.

Ongley, Patrick. 1995. Post–1945 International Migration: New Zealand, Australia and Canada Compared. *International Migration Review* 29(3):765–793.

Ortner, Sherry. 1999. *Life and Death on Mt. Everest: Sherpas and Himalayan Mountaineering.* Princeton, NJ: Princeton University Press.

Osha, Sanya. 2006. Birth of the Ogoni Protest Movement. *Journal of Asian and African Studies* 41:13–38.

Paine, Robert. 2004. Saami Reindeer Pastoralism: Quo Vadis? *Ethnos* 69:23–42.

Paley, Julia. 2002. Toward an Anthropology of Democracy. *Annual Review of Anthropology* 31:469–496.

Park, Hynug yu. 2010. Heritage Tourism: Emotional Journeys into Nationhood. *Annals of Tourism Research* 37(1):116–135.

Parker, Richard G. 1991. *Bodies, Pleasures, and Passions: Sexual Culture in Contemporary Brazil.* Boston: Beacon Press.

Parrillo, Vincent N. 1997. *Strangers to These Shores: Race and Ethnic Relations in the United States.* Boston: Allyn and Bacon.

Parry, Jonathan P. 1996. Caste. In *The Social Science Encyclopedia* (pp. 76–77). Adam Kuper and Jessica Kuper, eds. New York: Routledge.

Pasquino, Gianfranco. 1996. Democratization. In *The Social Science Encyclopedia* (pp. 173–174). Adam Kuper and Jessica Kuper, eds. New York: Routledge.

Patterson, Thomas C. 2001. *A Social History of Anthropology in the United States.* New York: Berg.

Paxson, Heather. 2003. With or Against Nature: IVF, Gender and Reproductive Agency in Athens, Greece. *Social Science and Medicine* 56:1853–1866.

Peacock, James L. and Dorothy C. Holland. 1993. The Narrated Self: Life Stories in Process. *Ethos* 21(4):367–383.

Pedelty, Mark. 1995. *War Stories: The Culture of Foreign Correspondents.* New York: Routledge.

Peletz, Michael. 2006. Transgenderism and Gender Pluralism in Southeast Asia since Early Modern Times. *Current Anthropology* 47(2):309–325, 333–340.

Pelto, Pertti. 1973. *The Snowmobile Revolution: Technology and Social Change in the Arctic.* Menlo Park, CA: Cummings.

People's Daily. 2003. Xi'an Protects Oldest Residential Area. April 9.

Perry, Richard J. 1996. *From Time Immemorial: Indigenous Peoples and State Systems.* Austin: University of Texas Press.

Pessar, Patricia R. 1995. *A Visa for a Dream: Dominicans in the United States.* Boston: Allyn and Bacon.

Petryna, Adriana, Andrew Lakoff, and Arthur Kleinman, eds. 2007. *Global Pharmaceuticals: Ethics, Markets, Practices.* Durham, NC: Duke University Press.

Pew Center. 2008. One in 100: Behind Bars in America. www.pewcenteronthestates.org.

———. 2010. *The Return of the Multi-Generational Family Household.* Washington, DC: Pew Research Center.

Pieterse, Jan Nederveen. 2004. *Globalization and Culture.* Global Mélange. New York: Rowman and Littlefield.

Plant, Roger. 1994. *Land Rights and Minorities.* London: Minority Rights Group.

———. 1998. *Issues in Indigenous Poverty.* Washington, DC: Interamerican Development Bank. No. IND-105.

Plattner, Stuart. 1989. Markets and Marketplaces. In *Economic Anthropology* (pp. 171–208). Stuart Plattner, ed. Stanford, CA: Stanford University Press.

Population Reference Bureau. 2005. *2005 World Population Data Sheet.* Washington, DC: Population Reference Bureau.

Posey, Darrell Addison. 1990. Intellectual Property Rights: What Is the Position of Ethnobiology? *Journal of Ethnobiology* 10:93–98.

Postgate, Nicholas, Tao Wang, and Toby Wilkinson. 1995. The Evidence for Early Writing: Utilitarian or Ceremonial? *Antiquity* 69:459–480.

Potter, Jack M. 1976. *Thai Peasant Social Structure.* Chicago: University of Chicago Press.

Potter, Sulamith Heins. 1977. *Family Life in a Northern Thai Village: A Study in the Structural Significance of Women.* Berkeley: University of California Press.

Pratt, Jeff. 2007. Food Values: The Local and the Authentic. *Critique of Anthropology* 27:285–300.

Price, David H. 1995. Water Theft in Egypt's Fayoum Oasis: Emics, Etics, and the Illegal. In *Science, Materialism, and the Study of Culture* (pp. 96–110). Martin F. Murphy and Maxine L. Margolis, eds. Gainesville: University of Florida Press.

Pruetz, Jill D. and Thomas C. LaDuke. 2009. Brief Communication: Reaction to Fire by Savanna Chimpanzees (*Pan troglodytes verus*) at Fongoli, Senegal: Conceptualization of "Fire Behavior" and the Case for a Chimpanzee Model. *American Journal of Physical Anthropology* 141:646–650.

Psychology Today. 1995. Child Support. 28:16.

Purdum, Elizabeth D. and J. Anthony Paredes. 1989. *Facing the Death Penalty: Essays on Cruel and Unusual Punishment.* Philadelphia: Temple University Press.

Potuoğlu-Cook, Öykü. 2006. Beyond the Glitter: Belly Dance and Neoliberal Gentrification in Istanbul. *Cultural Anthropology* 21:633–660.

Radcliffe-Brown, A. R. 1964 [1922]. *The Andaman Islanders.* Cambridge, UK: Cambridge University Press.

Raheja, Gloria Goodwin. 1988. *The Poison in the Gift: Ritual, Presentation, and the Dominant Caste in a North Indian Village.* Chicago: University of Chicago Press.

Ramesh, A., C. R. Srikumari, and S. Sukumar. 1989. Parallel Cousin Marriages in Madras, Tamil Nadu: New Trends in Dravidian Kinship. *Social Biology* 36(3/4):248–254.

Ramphele, Mamphela. 1996. Political Widowhood in South Africa: The Embodiment of Ambiguity. *Daedalus* 125(1):99–17.

Raphael, Dana. 1975. Matrescence: Becoming a Mother: A "New/Old" *Rite de Passage.* In *Being Female: Reproduction, Power, and Change* (pp. 65–72). Dana Raphael, ed. The Hague: Mouton Publishers.

Rathje, William and Cullen Murphy. 1992. *Rubbish! The Archaeology of Garbage.* New York: Harper & Row.

Rehbun, L. A. 1994. Swallowing Frogs: Anger and Illness in Northeast Brazil. *Medical Anthropology Quarterly* 8:360–382.

Reid, Russell M. 1992. Cultural and Medical Perspectives on Geophagia. *Medical Anthropology* 13:337–351.

Reiner, R. 1996. Police. In *The Social Science Encyclopedia* (pp. 619–621). Adam Kuper and Jessica Kuper, eds. New York: Routledge.

Restrepo [film]. 2009. Co-directed by Tim Hetherington and Sebastian Junger. Washington, DC: National Geographic Channel.

Reyna, Stephen P. 1994. A Mode of Domination Approach to Organized Violence. In *Studying War: Anthropological Perspectives* (pp. 29–65). S. P. Reyna and R. E. Downs, eds. Langhorne, PA: Gordon and Breach Science Publishers.

Rhodes, Lorna A. 2001. Toward an Anthropology of Prisons. *Annual Review of Anthropology* 30:65–83.

Rich, Bruce. 1994. *Mortgaging the Earth: The World Bank, Environmental Impoverishment, and the Crisis of Development.* Boston: Beacon Press.

Rickford, John. 1997. Unequal Partnership: Sociolinguistics and the African American Speech Community. *Language in Society* 26:161–198.

Robson, Colin. 1993. *Real World Research: A Resource for Social Scientists and Practitioner–Researchers.* Cambridge, MA: Blackwell Publishers.

Rogers, Barbara. 1979. *The Domestication of Women: Discrimination in Developing Societies.* New York: St. Martin's Press.

Roscoe, Will. 1991. *The Zuni Man–Woman.* Albuquerque: University of New Mexico Press.

Roseman, Marina. 1987. Inversion and Conjuncture: Male and Female Performance among the Temiar of Peninsular Malaysia. In *Women and Music in Cross-Cultural Perspective* (pp. 131–149). Ellen Koskoff, ed. New York: Greenwood Press.

Rosenberger, Nancy. 1992. Images of the West: Home Style in Japanese Magazines. In *Re-made in Japan: Everyday Life and Consumer Taste in a Changing Society* (pp. 106–125). James J. Tobin, ed. New Haven, CT: Yale University Press.

Rosenblatt, Paul C., Patricia R. Walsh, and Douglas A. Jackson. 1976. *Grief and Mourning in Cross-Cultural Perspective.* New Haven, CT: HRAF Press.

Ross, Marc Howard. 1993. *The Culture of Conflict: Interpretations and Interests in Comparative Perspective.* New Haven, CT: Yale University Press.

Roy, Arundhati. 1999. *The Cost of Living.* New York: Modern Library.

Rubel, Arthur J., Carl W. O'Nell, and Rolando Collado-Ardon. 1984. *Susto: A Folk Illness.* Berkeley: University of California Press.

Rylko-Bauer, Barbara, Merrill Singer, and John van Willigen. 2006. Reclaiming Applied Anthropology: Its Past, Present, and Future. *American Anthropologist* 108:178–190.

Sachs, Aaron. 1996. Dying for Oil. *WorldWatch*, June:10–21.

Sahlins, Marshall. 1963. Poor Man, Rich Man, Big Man, Chief. *Comparative Studies in Society and History* 5:285–303.

Saitoti, Tepilit Ole. 1986. *The Worlds of a Maasai Warrior.* New York: Random House.

Salam, Nawaf A. 1994. Between Repatriation and Resettlement: Palestinian Refugees in Lebanon. *Journal of Palestine Studies* 24:18–27.

Salamandra, Christa. 2004. *A New Old Damascus: Authenticity and Distinction in Urban Syria.* Bloomington: Indiana University Press.

Salih, M. A. Mohamed. 1999. Land Alienation and Genocide in the Nuba Mountains, Sudan. *Cultural Survival Quarterly* 22(4): 36–38.

Sanday, Peggy Reeves. 1973. Toward a Theory of the Status of Women. *American Anthropologist* 75:1682–1700.

———. 1986. *Divine Hunger: Cannibalism as a Cultural System.* New York: Cambridge University Press.

———. 1990. *Fraternity Gang Rape: Sex, Brotherhood, and Privilege on Campus.* New York: New York University Press.

———. 2002. *Women at the Center: Life in a Modern Matriarchy.* Ithaca, NY: Cornell University Press.

Sanders, Douglas E. 1999. Indigenous Peoples: Issues of Definition. *International Journal of Cultural Property* 8:4–13.

Sanders, William B. 1994. *Gangbangs and Drive-Bys: Grounded Culture and Juvenile Gang Violence.* New York: Aldine de Gruyter.

Sanjek, Roger. 1990. A Vocabulary for Fieldnotes. In *Fieldnotes: The Making of Anthropology* (pp. 92–138). Roger Sanjek, ed. Ithaca, NY: Cornell University Press.

———. 1994. The Enduring Inequalities of Race. In *Race* (pp. 1–17). Steven Gregory and Roger Sanjek, eds. New Brunswick, NJ: Rutgers University Press.

———. 2000. Keeping Ethnography Alive in an Urbanizing World. *Human Organization* 53:280–288.

Sargent, Carolyn F. 2005. Counselling Contraception for Malian Migrants in Paris: Global, State and Personal Politics. *Human Organization* 64:147–156.

Saugestad, Sidsel. 2001. *The Inconvenient Indigenous: Remote Area Development in Botswana, Donor Assistance, and the First People of the Kalahari.* Uppsala, Sweden: The Nordic Afrika Institute.

Sault, Nicole L. 1985. Baptismal Sponsorship as a Source of Power for Zapotec Women of Oaxaca, Mexico. *Journal of Latin American Lore* 11(2):225–243.

———. 1994. How the Body Shapes Parenthood: "Surrogate" Mothers in the United States and Godmothers in Mexico. In *Many Mirrors: Body Image and Social Relations* (pp. 292–318). Nicole Sault, ed. Brunswick, NJ: Rutgers University Press.

Savishinsky, Joel S. 1974. *The Trail of the Hare: Life and Stress in an Arctic Community.* New York: Gordon and Breach.

———. 1991. *The Ends of Time: Life and Work in a Nursing Home.* New York: Bergin & Garvey.

Schaft, Kai and David L. Brown. 2000. Social Capital and Grassroots Development: The Case of Roma Self-Governance in Hungary. *Social Problems* 47(2):201–219.

Scheffel, David Z. 2004. Slovak Roma on the Threshold of Europe. *Anthropology Today* 20(1):6–12.

Scheper-Hughes, Nancy. 1992. *Death without Weeping: The Violence of Everyday Life in Brazil.* Berkeley: University of California Press.

Scherrer, Kristin S. 2008. Coming to an Asexual Identity: Negotiating Identity, Negotiating Desire. *Sexualities* 11:621–641.

Schlegel, Alice. 1995. A Cross-Cultural Approach to Adolescence. *Ethos* 23(1):15–32.

Schlegel, Alice and Herbert Barry, III. 1991. *Adolescence: An Anthropological Inquiry.* New York: Free Press.

Schneider, David M. 1968. *American Kinship: A Cultural Account.* Englewood Cliffs, NJ: Prentice-Hall.

Scott, James C. 1998. *Seeing Like a State: How Certain Schemes to Improve the Human Condition Have Failed.* New Haven, CT: Yale University Press.

Scrimshaw, Susan. 1984. Infanticide in Human Populations: Societal and Individual Concerns. In *Infanticide: Comparative and Evolutionary Perspectives* (pp. 463–486). Glenn Hausfater and Sarah Blaffer Hrdy, eds. New York: Aldine.

Scudder, Thayer. 1973. The Human Ecology of Big Dam Projects: River Basin Development and Resettlement. *Annual Review of Anthropology* 2:45–55.

Senghas, Richard J. and Leila Monaghan. 2002. Signs of Their Times: Deaf Communities and the Culture of Language. *Annual Review of Anthropology* 31:69–97.

Shachtman, Tom. 2006. *Rumspringa: To Be or Not to Be Amish.* New York: North Point Press.

Shahrani, Nazif M. 2002. War, Factionalism, and the State in Afghanistan. *American Anthropologist* 104:715–722.

Shanklin, Eugenia. 2000. Representations of Race and Racism in American Anthropology. *Current Anthropology* 41(1):99–103.

Shapiro, Thomas M. 2004. *The Hidden Cost of Being African American.* New York: Oxford University Press.

Sharff, Jagna Wojcicka. 1995. "We Are All Chickens for the Colonel": A Cultural Materialist View of Prisons. In *Science, Materialism, and the Study of Culture* (pp. 132–158). Martin F. Murphy and Maxine L. Margolis, eds. Gainesville: University of Florida Press.

Sheriff, Robin E. 2000. Exposing Silence as Cultural Censorship: A Brazilian Case. *American Anthropologist* 102:114–132.

Shibamoto, Janet. 1987. The Womanly Woman: Manipulation of Stereotypical and Nonstereotypical Features of Japanese Female Speech. In *Language, Gender, and Sex in Comparative Perspective* (pp. 26–49). Susan U. Philips, Susan Steel, and Christine Tanz, eds. New York: Cambridge University Press.

Shore, Bradd. 1998. Status Reversal: The Coming of Age in Samoa. In *Welcome to Middle Age! (And Other Cultural Fictions)* (pp. 101–138). Richard A. Shweder, ed. Chicago: University of Chicago Press.

Short, James F. 1996. Gangs. In *The Social Science Encyclopedia* (pp. 325–326). Adam Kuper and Jessica Kuper, eds. New York: Routledge.

Shostak, Marjorie. 1981. *Nisa: The Life and Times of a !Kung Woman.* Cambridge, MA: Harvard University Press.

Shweder, Richard A. 1998. Preface. In *Welcome to Middle Age! (And Other Cultural Fictions)* (pp. vii–viii). Chicago: University of Chicago Press.

———. 2003. *Why Do Men Barbecue? Recipes for Cultural Psychology.* Cambridge, MA: Harvard University Press.

Sidnell, Jack. 2000. *Primus inter pares:* Storytelling and Male Peer Groups in an Indo-Guyanese Rumshop. *American Ethnologist* 27:72–99.

Silva, Noenoe K. 2004. *Aloha Betrayed: Native Hawaiian Resistance to American Colonialism.* Durham, NC: Duke University Press.

Silver, Ira. 1993. Marketing Authenticity in Third World Countries. *Annals of Tourism Research* 20:302–318.

Silverstein, Michael. 1997. Encountering Language and Languages of Encounter in North American Ethnohistory. *Journal of Linguistic Anthropology* 6:126–144.

Singh, K. S. 1994. *The Scheduled Tribes. Anthropological Survey of India, People of India, National Series Volume III.* Delhi: Oxford University Press.

Siskind, Janet. 1992. The Invention of Thanksgiving: A Ritual of American Nationality. *Critique of Anthropology* 12(2):167–191.

Skocpol, Theda. 1979. *States and Social Revolutions: A Comparative Analysis of France, Russia, and China.* New York: Cambridge University Press.

Smith, Jennie M. 2001. *When the Hands Are Many: Community Organization and Change in Rural Haiti.* Ithaca, NY: Cornell University Press.

Smith, Jonathan Z., ed. 1995. *The HarperCollins Dictionary of Religion.* New York: HarperCollins.

Smith, Laurajane, Anna Morgan, and Anita van der Meer. 2003. Community-driven Research in Cultural Heritage Management: The Waanyi Women's History Project. *International Journal of Heritage Studies* 9(1):65–80.

Smitherman, Geneva. 1997. "The Chain Remain the Same": Communicative Practices in the Hip Hop Nation. *Black Studies* 28(1):3–25.

Snajdr, Edward. 2005. Gender, Power, and the Performance of Justice: Muslim Women's Responses to Domestic Violence in Kazakhstan. *American Ethnologist* 32:294–311.

Sobel, Elizabeth and Gordon Bettles. 2000. Winter Hunger, Winter Myths: Subsistence Risk and Mythology among the Klamath and Modoc. *Journal of Anthropological Archaeology* 19:276–316.

Sperber, Dan. 1985. *On Anthropological Knowledge: Three Essays.* New York: Cambridge University Press.

Spilde Contreras, Kate. 2006. Indian Gaming in California Brings Jobs and Income to Areas that Need It Most. Indian Gaming. www.indiangaming.com/regulatory/view/?id=35.

Spiro, Melford. 1967. *Burmese Supernaturalism: A Study in the Explanation and Reduction of Suffering.* Englewood Cliffs, NJ: Prentice-Hall.

———. 1990. On the Strange and the Familiar in Recent Anthropological Thought. In *Cultural Psychology: Essays on Comparative Human Development* (pp. 47–61). James W. Stigler, Richard A. Shweder, and Gilbert Herdt, eds. Chicago: University of Chicago Press.

Spitulnik, Deborah. 1993. Anthropology and Mass Media. *Annual Review of Anthropology* 22:293–315.

Squires, Susan. 2002. Doing the Work: Customer Research in the Product Development and Design Industry. In Susan Squires and Bryan Byrne, eds. *Creating Breakthrough Ideas: The Collaboration of Anthropologists and Designers in the Product Development Industry.* Pp. 102–124. Westport, CT: Bergin and Garvey.

Srinivas, M. N. 1959. The Dominant Caste in Rampura. *American Anthropologist* 1:1–16.

Staats, Valerie. 1994. Ritual, Strategy or Convention: Social Meaning in Traditional Women's Baths in Morocco. *Frontiers: A Journal of Women's Studies* 14(3):1–18.

Stack, Carol. 1974. *All Our Kin: Strategies for Survival in a Black Community.* New York: Harper & Row.

Stephen, Lynn. 1995. Women's Rights Are Human Rights: The Merging of Feminine and Feminist Interests among El Salvador's Mothers of the Disappeared (CO-MADRES). *American Ethnologist* 22(4):807–827.

Stidsen, Sille, comp. and ed. Elaine Bolton, trans. 2006. *The Indigenous World 2006.* Rutger, NJ: Transaction Books.

Stillman, Amy Ku'uleialoha. 1996. Hawaiian Hula Competitions: Event, Repertoire, Perfor-mance and Tradition. *Journal of American Folklore* 109(434):357–380.

Stivens, Maila, Cecelia Ng, and Jomo K. S., with Jahara Bee. 1994. *Malay Peasant Women and the Land.* Atlantic Highlands, NJ: Zed Books.

Striffler, Steve. 2007. Neither Here nor There: Mexican Immigrant Workers and the Search for Home. *American Ethnologist* 34(4):674–688.

Stocks, Anthony. 2005. Too Much for Too Few: Problems of Indigenous Land Rights in Latin America. *Annual Review of Anthropology* 34:85–104.

Stoler, Ann Laura. 1985. *Capitalism and Confrontation in Sumatra's Plantation Belt, 1870–1979.* New Haven, CT: Yale University Press.

Storper-Perez, Danielle and Harvey E. Goldberg. 1994. The Kotel: Toward an Ethnographic Portrait. *Religion* 24:309–332.

Strathern, Andrew. 1971. *The Rope of Moka: Big-Men and Ceremonial Exchange in Mount Hagen, New Guinea.* London: Cambridge University Press.

Stringer, Martin D. 1999. Rethinking Animism: Thoughts from the Infancy of Our Discipline. *Journal of the Royal Anthropological Institute* 5:541–556.

Stronza, Amanda. 2001. Anthropology of Tourism: Forging New Ground for Ecotourism and Other Alternatives. *Annual Review of Anthropology* 30:261–283.

Sullivan, Kathleen. 1992. Protagonists of Change: Indigenous Street Vendors in San Cristobal, Mexico, Are Adapting Tradition and Customs to Fit New Life Styles. *Cultural Survival Quarterly* 16:38–40.

Suttles, Wayne. 1991. The Traditional Kwakiutl Potlatch. In *Chiefly Feasts: The Enduring Kwakiutl Potlatch* (pp. 71–134). Aldona Jonaitis, ed. Washington, DC: American Museum of Natural History.

Tabac, Lara. 2003. Slate. http://slate.msn.com/id/2088748/entry/2088987/.

Tannen, Deborah. 1990. *You Just Don't Understand: Women and Men in Conversation.* New York: Morrow.

Tannenbaum, Nicola B. 1987. Tattoos: Invulnerability and Power in Shan Cosmology. *American Ethnologist* 14:693–711.

Tauli-Corpuz, Victoria. 2005. Indigenous Peoples and the Millennium Development Goals. Paper submitted to the Fourth Session of the UN Permanent Forum on Indigenous Issues, New York City, May 16–27. www.tebtebba.org.

Taussig, Michael. 1978. Nutrition, Development, and Foreign Aid: A Case Study of U.S.-Directed Health Care in a Colombian Plantation Zone. *International Journal of Health Services* 8:101–121.

———. 2004. *My Cocaine Museum.* Chicago: University of Chicago Press.

Thomas, Frédéric, François Renaud, Eric Benefice, Thierry de Meeüs, and Jean-François Guégan. 2001. International Variability of Ages at Menarche and Menopause: Patterns and Main Determinants. *Human Biology* 73(2):271–290.

Thompson, Nile R. and C. Dale Sloat. 2004. The Use of Oral Literature to Provide Community Health Education on the Southern Northwest Coast. *American Indian Culture and Research Journal* 28(3):1–28.

Thompson, Robert Farris. 1971. Aesthetics in Traditional Africa. In *Art and Aesthetics in Primitive Societies* (pp. 374–381). Carol F. Jopling, ed. New York: E. P. Dutton.

Tice, Karin E. 1995. *Kuna Crafts, Gender, and the Global Economy.* Austin: University of Texas Press.

Tidball, Keith G. and Christopher P. Toumey. 2003. Signifying Serpents: Hermeneutic Change in Appalachian Pentecostal Serpent Handling. In *Signifying Serpents and Mardi Gras Runners: Representing Identity in Selected Souths* (pp. 1–18). Southern Anthropological Society Proceedings, No. 36. Celeste Ray and Luke Eric Lassiter, eds. Athens: University of Georgia Press.

Tierney, Patrick. 2000. *Darkness in El Dorado: How Scientists and Journalists Devastated the Amazon.* New York: W. W. Norton.

Tiffany, Walter W. 1979. New Directions in Political Anthropology: The Use of Corporate Models for the Analysis of Political Organizations. In *Political Anthropology: The State of the Art* (pp. 63–75). S. Lee Seaton and Henri J. M. Claessen, eds. New York: Mouton.

Tinker, Irene. 1976. The Adverse Impact of Development on Women. In *Women and World Development* (pp. 22–34). Irene Tinker and Michele Bo Bramsen, eds. Washington, DC: Overseas Development Council.

Tooker, Elisabeth. 1992. Lewis H. Morgan and His Contemporaries. *American Anthropologist* 94(2):357–375.

Toren, Christina. 1988. Making the Present, Revealing the Past: The Mutability and Continuity of Tradition as Process. *Man* (n.s.) 23:696–717.

Trelease, Murray L. 1975. Dying among Alaskan Indians: A Matter of Choice. In *Death: The Final Stage of Growth* (pp. 33–37). Elisabeth Kübler-Ross, ed. Englewood Cliffs, NJ: Prentice-Hall.

Trotter, Robert T. II. 1987. A Case of Lead Poisoning from Folk Remedies in Mexican American Communities. In *Anthropological Praxis: Translating Knowledge into Action* (pp. 146–159). Robert M. Wulff and Shirley J. Fiske, eds. Boulder, CO: Westview Press.

Trouillot, Michel-Rolph. 1994. *Haiti: State against Nation: The Origins and Legacy of Duvalierism.* New York: Monthly Review Press.

———. 2001. The Anthropology of the State in the Age of Globalization. *Current Anthropology* 42:125–133, 135–138.

Turner, Terrence. 2002. Representation, Politics, and Cultural Imagination in Indigenous Video: General Points and Kayapo Examples. In *Media Worlds: Anthropology on New Terrain* (pp. 75–89). Faye D. Ginsburg and Lila Abu-Lughod, eds. Berkeley: University of California Press.

Turner, Victor W. 1969. *The Ritual Process: Structure and Anti-Structure.* Chicago: Aldine.

Tylor, Edward Burnett. 1871. *Primitive Culture: Researches into the Development of Mythology, Philosophy, Religion, Art, and Custom.* 2 volumes. London: J. Murray.

Uhl, Sarah. 1991. Forbidden Friends: Cultural Veils of Female Friendship in Andalusia. *American Ethnologist* 18(1):90–105.

UNFPA. Accessed June 15, 2006. www.unfpa.org.

UNHCR. 2008. 2007 Global Trends: Refugees, Asylum-seekers, Returnees, Internally Displaced Persons, and Stateless Persons. New York: The United Nations, United Nations High Commission for Refugees.

United Nations Development Programme. 1995. *Human Development Report 1994.* New York: Oxford University Press.

United Nations Environment Programme. 2002. *Impact of Global Warming on Mountain Areas Confirmed by UNEP-Backed Mountaineers.* News Release.

Uphoff, Norman T. and Milton J. Esman. 1984. *Local Organizations: Intermediaries in Rural Development.* Ithaca, NY: Cornell University Press.

van der Geest, Sjaak, Susan Reynolds Whyte, and Anita Hardon. 1996. The Anthropology of Pharmaceuticals: A Biographical Approach. *Annual Review of Anthropology* 25:153–178.

Van Gennep, Arnold. 1960 [1908]. *The Rites of Passage.* Chicago: University of Chicago Press.

Van Wynsberghe, Robert M. 2002. *AlterNatives: Community, Identity, and Environmental Justice on Walpole Island.* Boston: Allyn and Bacon.

Varley, Emma. 2010. Targeted Doctors, Missing Patients: Obstetric Health Services and Sectarian Conflict in Northern Pakistan. *Social Science and Medicine* 70:61–70.

Vellinga, Marcel. 2004. *Constituting Unity and Difference: Vernacular Architecture in a Minangkabau Village.* Leiden: KITLV Press.

Walmsley, Roy. 2007. Prison Planet. *Foreign Policy* May/June: 30–31.

Walsh, Michael. 2005. Will Indigenous Languages Survive? *Annual Review of Anthropology* 34:293–315.

Ward, Martha C. 1989. Once Upon a Time. In *Nest in the Wind: Adventures in Anthropology on a Tropical Island* (pp. 1–22). Martha C. Ward, ed. Prospect Heights, IL: Waveland Press.

Warren, Carol A. B. 1988. *Gender Issues in Field Research. Qualitative Research Methods, Volume 9.* Newbury Park, CA: Sage Publications.

Warren, Seth. 2001. Oil and Human Rights in Sudan. *Cultural Survival Quarterly* 25(3):20.

Watkins, Ben and Michael L. Fleisher. 2002. Tracking Pastoralist Migration: Lessons from the Ethiopian Somali National Regional State. *Human Organization* 61:328–338.

Watson, James, L., ed. 1997. *Golden Arches East: McDonald's in East Asia.* Stanford, CA: Stanford University Press.

Watson, Rubie S. 1986. The Named and the Nameless: Gender and Person in Chinese Society. *American Ethnologist* 13(4): 619–631.

Weatherford, J. 1981. *Tribes on the Hill.* New York: Random House.

Weber, Linda R., Andrew Miracle, and Tom Skehan. 1994. Interviewing Early Adolescents: Some Methodological Considerations. *Human Organization* 53(1):42–47.

Websdale, Neil. 1995. An Ethnographic Assessment of the Policing of Domestic Violence in Rural Eastern Kentucky. *Social Justice* 22(1):102–122.

Webster, Gloria Cranmer. 1991. The Contemporary Potlatch. In *Chiefly Feasts: The Enduring Kwakiutl Potlatch* (pp. 227–250). Aldona Jonaitis, ed. Washington, DC: American Museum of Natural History.

Weiner, Annette B. 1976. *Women of Value, Men of Renown: New Perspectives in Trobriand Exchange.* Austin: University of Texas Press.

———. 1988. *The Trobrianders of Papua New Guinea.* New York: Holt, Rinehart and Winston.

Werbner, Pnina. 1988. "Sealing the Koran": Offering and Sacrifice among Pakistani Labour Migrants. *Cultural Dynamics* 1:77–97.

Whitehead, Tony Larry. 1986. Breakdown, Resolution, and Coherence: The Fieldwork Experience of a Big, Brown, Pretty-talking Man in a West Indian Community. In *Self, Sex, and Gender in Cross-Cultural Fieldwork* (pp. 213–239). Tony Larry Whitehead and Mary Ellen Conway, eds. Chicago: University of Illinois Press.

Whiting, Beatrice B. and John W. M. Whiting. 1975. *Children of Six Cultures: A Psycho-Cultural Analysis.* Cambridge, MA: Harvard University Press.

Whiting, Robert, 1979. You've Gotta Have "Wa." *Sports Illustrated,* September 24:60–71.

Whyte, Martin King. 1993. Wedding Behavior and Family Strategies in Chengdu. In *Chinese Families in the Post-Mao Era* (pp. 189– 216). Deborah Davis and Stevan Harrell, eds. Berkeley: University of California Press.

Wikan, Unni. 1977. Man Becomes Woman: Transsexualism in Oman as a Key to Gender Roles. *Man* 12(2):304–319.

———. 2000. Citizenship on Trial: Nadia's Case. *Daedalus* 129:55–76.

Williams, Brett. 1984. Why Migrant Women Feed Their Husbands Tamales: Foodways as a Basis for a Revisionist View of Tejano Family Life. In *Ethnic and Regional Foodways in the United States: The Performance of Group Identity* (pp. 113–126). Linda Keller Brown and Kay Mussell, eds. Knoxville: University of Tennessee Press.

Williams, Brett. 1994. Babies and Banks: The "Reproductive Underclass" and the Raced, Gendered Masking of Debt. In *Race* (pp. 348–365). Steven Gregory and Roger Sanjek, eds. Ithaca, NY: Cornell University Press.

Williams, Walter. 1992. *The Spirit and the Flesh: Sexual Diversity in American Indian Cultures,* 2nd ed. Boston: Beacon Press.

Williamson, Nancy. 1976. *Sons or Daughters: A Cross-Cultural Study of Parental Preferences.* Beverly Hills, CA: Sage Publications.

Wolf, Charlotte. 1996. Status. In *The Social Science Encyclopedia* (pp. 842–843). Adam Kuper and Jessica Kuper, eds. New York: Routledge.

Wolf, Margery. 1968. *The House of Lim: A Study of a Chinese Farm Family.* New York: Appleton-Century-Crofts.

World Bank. 2003. *Roma Poverty Remains Key Hurdle to Shared Prosperity in Central and Eastern Europe.* Washington, DC: The World Bank. www.worldbank.org/roma.

Worldwatch Institute. 2003. *Vital Signs 2003: The Trends That Are Shaping Our Future.* Washington, DC: Worldwatch Institute/ W.W. Norton.

Wormald, Tom. 2005. Visions of the Future: Technology and the Imagination in Hungarian Civil Society. *Anthropology Matters* 7(1):1–10. http://www.anthropologymatters.com.

Wu, David Y. H. 1990. Chinese Minority Policy and the Meaning of Minority Culture: The Example of Bai in Yunnan, China. *Human Organization* 49(1):1–13.

www.greatapetrust.org/bonobo/meet/kanzi.php.

www.migrationinformation.org.

www.ilo.org.

www.npr.org.

Xizhe, Peng. 1991. *Demographic Transition in China: Fertility Trends since the 1980s.* New York: Oxford University Press.

Zaidi, S. Akbar. 1988. Poverty and Disease: Need for Structural Change. *Social Science and Medicine* 27:119–127.

Zarrilli, Phillip B. 1990. Kathakali. In *Indian Theatre: Traditions of Performance* (pp. 315–357). Farley P. Richmond, Darius L. Swann, and Phillip B. Zarrilli, eds. Honolulu: University of Hawaii Press.

Zureik, Elia. 1994. Palestinian Refugees and Peace. *Journal of Palestine Studies* 24(1):5–17.

INDEX

Italicized page numbers indicate photos, figures, or maps.

AA. *See* Alcoholics Anonymous (AA)
AAA. *See* American Anthropological Association (AAA)
AAE. *See* African American English (AAE)
AAVE. *See* African American Vernacular English (AAVE)
Aboriginal people of Australia
    the Dreamtime, 243
    indigenous land rights, 374
    initiation ceremony for young boy, *283*
    racism in the youth judicial system, 246–247, *247*
    religions of, 288
    social control among, 244
    women's culture and sacred site protection, 290
Abortion, induced, 141–142
Absolute cultural relativism, 22, *22*
Abstract art, 114
Abu Hureyra, (Syria), 48–49
Abu-Lughod, Lila, 75
Acceleration, of international migration, 347
Acculturation, 361
Acheulian tradition, 41, *41*
Achieved position, 218
Activist groups, 227–229
Acupuncture, 172, 174, *363*
Adams, Abigail, 148–149
Adolescence, 145–151
    coming-of-age rituals, 146, 147–149
    debate about whether is universal life-cycle stage, 145–151
    defined, 145
    gender identity and, 147–149
    sexual identity and, 149–151
Adolescent females. *See also* Gender; Girls; Women
    "fat talk" among Euro-American, 270
    female genital cutting and, 147–149
    initiation practices, 147–148
    kogals in Japan, *269*, 269–270
    menarche, 138
    politeness in Japanese, 269–270
    sororities, 214
    stress among boarding school girls, 346
    violence against, *375*
Adolescent males. *See also* Boys; Gender; Men
    circumcision of, 147
    fraternities, 213–214, *214*
    initiation practices, 147, 148–149
    Maasai warriors, 146, *147*
    youth gangs, 214–215
Adoption, 189
Adulthood, 151–153
    becoming a parent, 151–152
    middle age, 152–153
    senior years, 1543
Advertising, for Latinos in U.S., 267
Advocacy in anthropology
    for orangutan conservation, 36
    in support of Yonggom claims, 252
Adze, stone, *4*
Afghanistan
    focal vocabularies in, 262
    indigenous fertility control in, 141
    induced abortion in, 141
    violence and warfare in, 249–250, *251*
    women's clinic, *141*
Africa. *See also specific regions, countries, and peoples*
    Bantu migrations, *274*
    child fostering in, 189
    early hominins and archaic *Homo* in, *38*

indigenous people's defense of territorial entitlement in, 373–374
    internally displaced persons in, 343
    mapping pastoralists' movements in, 354
    migration of archaic *Homo* out of, 41–42
    migration of modern humans out of, 45
    modern human origins in, 44–45, *45*
African American English (AAE), 270–272
African Americans
    burning of churches of, 307
    friendship among the urban poor, 212
    incarceration rate among, 246
    as minority ethnic group, 20, 370
    Muncie (Indiana) community, 76
    romantic love and, 195
    step dancing, *214*
    women, hair styles, 60, *60*
    Yorùbá revivalist religion and, 304
African American Vernacular English (AAVE), 270–271
African diaspora, religion, *165*, 294, 304
African religions, 304–305
    features, 304
    Ras Tafari (Rastafarianism), 304–305
African Rhythm and African Sensibility (Chernoff), 314
Age, 20
    40 syndrome among American men, 152
    child's age and maternal bonding, 144
    division of labor among farmers, 95
    division of labor among foragers and, 86
    division of labor among horticulturalists and, 89
    division of labor among pastoralists and, 91–92
    effect on fieldwork, 67
    at first marriage, 202
    at menarche, 138
    senior years, 153
    sexual intercourse and, 138
    status and, 218
Age hypergyny, 194
Age hypogyny, 194
Agency, *See* Individual agency
Age set, 210
Aging, of population, 137
    in Japan, *137*
Agriculture, 49, *83*, 92–96. *See also* Family farming
    as an intensive strategy, 92
    cash crops and, 94–95
    consumption and exchange and, *109*
    defined, 92
    division of labor, *94*, 94–95
    family farming, 94–95
    indigenous knowledge and, 93
    industrial, 95–96, *96*
    kinship, *185*
    Maya of Chiapas and, 102
    mode of reproduction, *134*, 134–135
    modes of political organization, conflict and social control, *235*
    occupational specialization and, 94
    Old Order Amish of the U.S. and Canada, 136
    property relations and, 96
    raised field, 51, 93
    social groups and, *211*
    sustainability of, 96
Ahmadu, Fuambai, 148–149
AIDS and Accusation (Farmer), 8
Aka of Central African Republic
    paternal child care among, 152, *152*
    overview and map, *152*
Akhara, 325
Akwesasne Mohawks (U.S. and Canada)
    linguistic cuing among, 270
    overview and map, *271*

Alaska. *See* Inuit of Alaska
Alcoholic beverages
    beer-drinking rituals, 14
    exchange of, 118–119
    gender and, 13
    Islamic prohibition against, 303
Alcoholics Anonymous (AA) in Mexico, 217
Algonquin confederation, 240
Alpacas, 50, 52
Alternative food movements, 127
Alternative medicine, 172
Amazon region. *See also specific countries and peoples*
    consumption patterns in Brazilian, 126
    indigenous resistance to mega development projects, 236
    men's houses in, 214
Amazon (woman), 150
Amboseli National Park (Kenya), 326
Amchis, 175
AME. *See* American Mainstream English (AME)
American Anthropological Association (AAA)
    code of ethics, 76
    El Dorado Task Force, 249
    on fieldwork safety, 77
American Indian Movement, 306
American Indians. *See also individual groups*
    berdache, 150
    collection of texts, 70–71
    confederacies among, 240
    cult of ancestors and, 287
    dancer, *23*
    ethnomedical knowledge and, 159–160
    gaming and, 124
    historical trauma and, 171–172
    pastoralism, 91
    potters, 315
    precolonial distribution of tribes, *170*
    repatriation of museum objects and, 322–323
    reservations, *171, 172*
    revitalization movements, 305–306
    ritual use of urine by, 16
    sharing among, 109
    use of silence by, 264
American Mainstream English (AME), 271
American Samoa, overview and map, *177, 301*
American Sign Language, 260, 262
AMH. *See* Anatomically modern humans (AMH)
Amish of U.S. and Canada
    labor sharing, 119, *245*
    birth rate, 135, 136
    farm families, 95
    Old Order, overview and map, 136, *136*
    social control among, 243
Anatomically modern humans (AMH), 44–47
    art, in Europe, *47*
    blades in Africa, *45*
    Clovis culture, 45–46, *47*
    European artifacts, *46*
    evolution of, 44–47
    interbreeding with Neanderthals, 43
    migration to New World, 45–46
    morphological change in, 44
    origins in Africa, 44–45
    during Upper Paleolithic in Europe, 45, *46*
Ancestor worship, *189*, 287
Andalucia (Spain), 212
Andaman Islanders of India
    Andaman girl, *58*
    Anthropological Museum, *322*
    overview and map, 88, *88*
    population, 371
    property relations in, 86
Andean region of South America, 91 *See also* countries and peoples

Bosnia and Herzegovina
mass grave, *263*
narrative therapy and refugees from, 263
overview and map, *263*
Botanical knowledge, mothers', 167
Bourdieu, Pierre, 114
Bourgois, Philippe, 75, 77, 200
Bowing, *265*
Bows and arrows, 84
Boxing, 325
Boys. *See also* Adolescent males; Gender; Men
crying and, 144
preference for sons, 135, 140, 151
relationships with sisters in Lebanon, 199–200
work patterns, 86, 90, 92, 95
BPO. *See* Business-processing outsourcing (BPO)
Braceros, 340–341
Brachiation, 32, *32*
Brahmans, 224, *224, 225,* 226
Brazil. *See also specific peoples*
abortion in, 142
Bom Jesus, 143, *143,* 172
caesarian births in, 158–159
carnival parade, *221*
consumption patterns in the Amazon region, 126
country music in, 318
ethno-etiologies in, 162
HIV positive girl, *158*
household head in, 198
indigenous land rights in, 372
infanticide in, 143
Kayapo region, *236*
medicalization of poverty in, 172
mother-child bonding in, 144
overview and map, *159*
playing dominoes in, *213*
prison population, 246
religious syncretism in, 304
stratified reproduction in, 137
as transnational country, 341
umbanda in, *165*
Breaking Out ritual, *148,* 149
Breastfeeding, birth intervals and, 134
Bride
and groom, Japanese, *203*
Moroccan, *139*
Brideprice (bridewealth), 195, *195*
Brideservice, 195, *195*
Brother-sister marriage, 193
Buddha's Day, 289
Buddhism
abortion and, 142
Buddha's Day, 289
Hinduism and, 297
Japanese, *296*
karma and, 297
local spirits in southeast Asia and, 297
overview, 296–297
pilgrimage, 291
population distribution of, *294,* 296–297
tattoos and, 298, *298*
Theravada, *151*
Tibetan, 176, 307
in the United States, *284*
Buffett, Warren, *219*
Bulgaria, 127, 223
Bulimia, 161
Bullfighting, 325
Bullying, 212
Bunzel, Ruth, 315
Bureaucracy, 51
Burial, 153
Burial grounds, 307
Cohokia, 52–53
Neanderthal, 42–43
Burkina Faso
male bias in development in, 375
marital sexual activity, 199
Bush, George W., *114,* 240, *355*
Business marriage, 349
Business-processing outsourcing (BPO), *160*

Caesarian births, 158–159
Cahokia, 52, *52*
California
ebonic controversy in, 271–272
effect of Indian gaming on, 124
efforts to control consumerism in, 110
green jobs program in, *220*
homeless heroin addicts in, 200
Indian immigrants in Silicon Valley, 352
Klamath and Modoc region, *286*
sadomasochist community in, 215–216
Call system (nonhuman primate), 260
Cambodia
Angkor Wat, 380, *380*
hip hop dancing, *216*
overview and map, *151*
Camels, 91, *92,* 101
Campesinos, 251
Canada. *See also specific regions and peoples*
below-replacement fertility in, 135
as destination country for migrants, 339–340
discrimination against migrants in, 224
Hong Kong Chinese immigrants in, 350
Indian boarding schools in, *361*
indigenous people's defense of territorial entitlement in, 372–373
indigenous people's development organizations in, 374
infanticide among circumpolar foragers, 143
Kwakwaka'wakw, 128, *128,* 129
new immigrants to, 347–353
Nunavat land claim, 373
Old Order Amish in, 136
Canadian International Development Agency (CIDA), 365
Cancian, Frank, 102
Capitalism, *See also* Industrialism/Informatics, Market exchange, Globalization; effects of spread of, 99
Capitalization, industrial agriculture and, 96
Careers, in cultural anthropology, 25
Cargo cults, 306, *306*
Caribbean countries. *See also countries and peoples.*
new immigrants from, 347–350
overview and map, *213*
Carneiro, Robert, 254
Carnival (or carnaval), 291–292
Cars, *24,* 62
Cash crops, 112
Cassava, *89,* 90
Caste system
dalits and, 225–226
defined, 224
features of, 224–227
Hinduism and, 224–227
in India, 224–227, *225*
in Nepal, 224, 226
varna categories, *224*
Catalhöyük (Turkey), 49
Cátedra, María, 73
Cattle, *See* Cows
Causality, levels of, 162
CCNN. *See* Center for California Native Nations (CCNN)
Cedar, Kwakwaka'wakw and, 128
Cell phones
friendship and use of, 211–212
Textese and, 278
Center for California Native Nations (CCNN), 124
Central African Republic, Aka region, *153*
Central America, overview and map, *163. See also countries and peoples*
Central Asia. *See also countries and peoples*
overview and map, *250*
political conflict in, 247
Ceremonial fund, 111
Cernea, Michael, 331
Chagnon, Napoleon, 248–249, *249*
Chain migration, 348–349

Changdoek Palace (South Korea), 330
Charms, 163, 285
Chavez, Leo, 96
Chechnya, military prison, *246*
Chernobyl disaster, effect on Saami, 277
Chernoff, John, 314–315
Cherokee of Tennessee, 240
Cheyenne, sharing among, 109
Chiapas (Mexico)
Maya women vendors, 376, *376*
violence between state and indigenous people, 372
Chiefdoms, 52, 238–240
Cahokia, 52–53
war and, 248–249
Chief Joseph, *239*
Childcare, 152
Childhood malnutrition, 172
Child labor
in Guatemala, *112*
in India, *366*
on sugarcane plantation, *62*
Child-rearing. *See also* Birth and infancy; Boys;
Children; Girls; Son preference
Mead on, 10
men's role in, 152
women's role in, 144, 145, 152
Children. *See also* Adolescence; Adolescent
females; Adolescent males; Boys; Girls
adoption of, 189
in agricultural societies, 95
class and birthday parties, 114, 116
factors affecting desire for, 140
fostering, 189–191
in herding societies, 92
in horticultural societies, 90
lead poisoning among Mexican American, 178
marriage and legitimacy of, 191
modes of livelihood and value of, *134*
naming, 188–189
obesity epidemic among, 174, *175*
in poverty, *112*
race and shopping preferences of, 115–116
as refugees, 343
as sex workers, 98–99
socialization of, 145
theft of food in West Africa and, 125
Chile, birth rate in, 135
Chimpanzees, 31–32, 33–35, *34, 35*
tool use among, 34, 36
Chin, Elizabeth, 115–116
China. *See also specific regions and peoples*
access to abortion in, 142
consumerism in, 109
control of religious expression in, 252
dominoes in, *213*
dowry in, 195
ethnic minorities in, 222
food preferences in, 13
hookworm in rural, 168, *169*
logographic and current writing styles in, *275*
marriage crisis in, 203
Muslims in, 302, *303*
nightclub in, *332*
occupation of Tibet and, 307
police in, *234*
preference for sons, 140
prison population, 246
"race" in, 19
research restrictions in, 63, 227
restriction of women in politics in, 242
social media in, 266
stem household in, *198*
theater in, 333
Three Gorges Dam project, *344*
treatment of Uyghurs, *209*
women's movement in, 227
Zhuang people of, *3*
Chinatowns, *338*
Chinese diaspora, *338*
Chinese language, 273
Chittagong Hill Tracts area (Bangladesh), 373

Human rights *(Cont.)*
    migration and, 355
    religious freedom as, 307
Humans (*See* Anatomically modern humans (AMH))
    common ancestor, 32
    interbreeding with Neanderthals, 43
Human sacrifice, 292–293
Human subjects (in research), 63, 76
Human Terrain System (HTS), 76
Humoral healing, 165
Hundee, 374
Hungarian Telecottage Association (HTA), 267
Hungary
    digital divide in, 267–268
    overview and map, *267*
    Roma in, 223
    Tisza River pollution and, 241
Hunt, George, 128
Hunting, *See also* Foraging
Huntington (West Virginia), childhood obesity in, *175*
Hurricane Katrina, 113, *114*
    displaced persons and, 355
Hurricanes of 2005, 113, *114*
Hurston, Zora Neale, *10*
Hussein, Saddam, 253, *337*
Hutterites, 135
Hybridization, 18
Hypergyny, 194
Hypogyny, 194
Hypothesis, 68
Hyssop, *166*

IBRD. *See* International Bank for Reconstruction and Development (IBRD)
ICD. *See International Classification of Diseases (ICD)*
Ice-free corridor, 45
Iceland
    overview and map, *74*
    ram exhibition, 73–74, *74*
Icons, 305
ICTs. *See* Information and communication technologies (ICTs)
IDA. *See* International Development Association (IDA)
IDPs. *See* Internally displaced persons (IDPs)
Ikat weaving, *314*
Illegal immigration, *355*
Illegal trafficking, people and goods, 98–99
Illness, 159. *See also* Disease
Imagined Communities (Anderson), 251–252
Imitative magic, 285
Immediate cause, 162
Immigrants. *See also* Migration; New immigrants; Refugees
    from Caribbean countries, 347–350
    Dominican, 348–349
    from former Soviet Union, 352–353
    Hindu, 351–352
    Hong Kong Chinese, 350
    Indian, in California, 352
    labor, 353–355
    from Latin America, 347–350
    Latino, 347, *348*
    Mexican, 20, 22, 348, *348*, *355*
    Salvadoran, 349–350
    Vietnamese, 350–351, *351*
Immigrant visas, 347
Inca empire, 51–52, 274, *275*
Incarceration rate, 246
Incest taboo, 121, 192–193
Inclusion policies, 353–355
India. *See also* Hinduism; Islam; *specific countries, regions, and peoples*
    abortion in, 142
    caste system in, *224*, 224–227, *225*
    child labor in, *366*
    cross-cousin marriage in, 193
    dam projects in, 343
    Dharavi, *81*
    dining rules, 13

eliminating in, 16
endogamy in, 193
fertility ritual in, 295–296
hijra, 159
Hindu immigrants from, 351–352
hypergyny in, 194
intercourse frequency among Hindus in, 139–140
Passover in, 299–300
pilgrimage to Varanasi, 291
preference for sons, 140, 151
pronatalism in, 135
remittances and, 341
research restrictions in, 63
sacred strings, 163, *164*
sleeping habits, 15
South India overview and map of, *193*
Taj Mahal, *194*, 321
vaccination programs in, 178
widowhood in, *17*
Women's World Banking in, 376
wrestling in, *324*, 324–325
Indigenous knowledge, 72
Indigenous languages
    dictionaries, *279*
    extinction of, 7
Indigenous methods of fertility control, 141
Indigenous peoples, 20
    development and, 370–375
    effect of tourism on, 326–327
    health problems of, 169–170
    infectious disease and, 169–170
    minority groups *vs.*, 370–371
    natural resources of, 371
    organizing for change, 374–375
    population statistics on, 371
    territorial entitlements and, 371–374
    as victims of colonialism and development, 371
Indirect entitlement, 112
Indirect infanticide, 142
Individual agency, structurism *vs.*, 24–25
Indo-Canadians, 224
Indo-European language family, *273*
Indonesia
    gay language in, 270
    hominin sites on islands of, *42*
    Weyéwa people and region, *14*
Induced abortion, 141–142
Inductive approach, 68, *68*
Industrial archaeology, 6, *7*
Industrial capital agriculture, 95–96
    social effects, *96*
Industrial capitalism, 97
Industrialism/informatics, *83*, 96–99
    consumption and exchange and, *109*
    consumption budgets, 111
    defined, 96–97
    entitlements and, 112
    fertility rates in, 140
    formal sector, 97
    informal sector, 97–99
    kinship, *185*
    mode of reproduction, *134*, 135–137
    mode of political organization, conflict and social control, *235*
    social groups and, *211*
    Taiwanese industrialists, 102–103
Industrial spy, anthropologist labeled as, 65, 226
Inequality. *See* Social inequality
Infancy. *See* Birth and infancy
Infanticide, 142–143
Infant mortality rate, 143
Infectious diseases
    European colonialism and, 169–170
    new, 174
Infibulation, 147, 148
Influence, 234
Informal sector, 97
    street vendors, drugs, and sex workers, *97*, 97–99
Informants, 76

Information and communication technologies (ICTs), 268
Information processing, 97
Information technology, study of, 7
Informed consent, 63
Infrastructure, 23–24
Inheritance practices, 92, 95, 113. *See also* descent
Initiation practices, 148–149, 304 *See also* life-cycle ceremonies
In Search of Respect (Bourgois), 75
Insectivores, 31
Institutional isolation, domestic violence and, 201
Institutional migrants, 344–347
Institutional review boards (IRBs), 63
Institutions, 20, 22
    ascribed status and, 220
    international development, 365
Intangible cultural heritage, 330–331
Intellectual property rights, 380–381
Intensive strategy, 92
Interior design, 319–320
Intermediate cause, 162
Internally displaced persons (IDPs), *339*, 343, 349, 379
Internal migration, 339
International Alliance for the Protection of Isolated Indigenous Peoples, 372
International Alliance of Forest Peoples, 372
International Bank for Reconstruction and Development (IBRD), 365
International Classification of Diseases (ICD), 160
International development, 363–364
International Development Association (IDA), 365
International level, family planning policies, 141
International migration, 339. *See* countries and peoples
    changes in households and, 204–205
    changes in marriage and, 202
International peacekeeping, UN and, 254–255
International students, 344
Internet
    analysis of social meaning of websites, 71
    indigenous language dictionaries on, 279
    new social movements and, 229
    religious movement and change and, 294
    self-help groups and, 217
    village-based access to, 267–268
Interpretive anthropology (interpretivism)
    as approach to medical anthropology, 170–171
    cultural materialism *vs.*, 23–24
    defined, 11
    definition of culture within, 12
    emic data and, 68
    Geertz and, *10*, 12
    on human sacrifice among the Aztecs, 293
Interviews, 69, 72
Intrahousehold entitlements, 113
Inuit people
    of Alaska, 153, 184, 316
    of Baffin Island, 10
    of Nunavut, 10, *373*
    place names and landscape knowledge of, 72
Invention
    among nonhuman primates, 37
    cultural change and, 361
In vitro fertilization (IVF), 142
Iran
    incarceration rate, 246
    Kurds in, 253
    overview and map, *91*
Iraq
    playing dominoes in, *213*
    internally displaced persons in, *339*
    Kurds in, 253
    museums in, 322
    refugees, 343
    U.S. in, 250
IRBs. *See* Institutional review boards (IRBs)
Ireland
    overview and map, *184*
    Tory Islanders, 184
Iron Bridge (England), 7

language, 276
    Russian Orthodox Church, 305, 323
    social inequality in, 126–127
Russian immigrants, to Israel, *352*, 352–353
Rye, 48

Saami people of Lapland
    impact of snowmobiles on culture, 362
    language, 268, 277
    overview and map, 277, *277*
    reindeer herding and, 91, 92, 277, 362
    sacred space beliefs, 287
Sacred space, 287–288
    Aboriginal women and protection of, 290
    contested, 306–307
    indigenous people and, 305
    in Judaism, 297–299, *299*
Sacred strings, 163, *164*
Sacrifice, 292–293, 302, 304
Sadomasochist community, in San Francisco,
        215–216
Safety, in the field, 77
Sahelanthropus tchadensis, *38*, 38–39
Sahel region of Africa
    domesticates in, 49
    environmental conditions in, 353–354, *353*
    female genital cutting in, 147
    indigenous land rights in, 373–374
    mapping pastoralists' movements in, 354
    overview and map, *353*
    protecting migrants' health in, 353
Salamandra, Christa, 65
Salvadoran immigrants in U.S., 349–350
Sambia of Papua New Guinea, 146, 149
Same-gender marriage, 191, *191*
Samoa
    health risk and immigration, 175–177
    overview and map, *177*, *301*
Sanday, Peggy, 213–214, 293
San Francisco (California)
    efforts to control consumerism in, 110
    homeless heroin addicts in, 200
    sadomasochist community in, 215–216
San Juan fiesta of Ecuador, 118–119
Sannyasi, 325
San of southern Africa, 20
    development organizations of, 374–375
    hoodia and, 21, 375, 380
    overview and map, 21, *21*
    protective legislation for, 374
    San hunters, *236*
Sanskrit, 273
Santería, 304
Sapir, Edward, 268
Sapir-Whorf hypothesis, 268
Sápmi, 277
Sapphires, 371
Sardinia (Italy), carnival in, 292
Sarnath (India), 297
Saro-Wiwa, Ken, *378*, 379
SARS. *See* Severe acute respiratory syndrome (SARS)
Satellite dishes, *102*
Savage-Rumbaugh, Sue, *260*
Savanna, *37*, 40
Savishinsky, Joel, *82*, 86
Scavenging, in Philippines, 368, *368*
Scheper-Hughes, Nancy, *10*, 143, 144, 172
Schistosomiasis, 174, 369
Scrapers, 40, 43
Sculpture,
    Neanderthal, *44*
    Upper Paleolithic, 47, *47*
    West Africa, 313, *313*
Secondary group, 210
Sectarian conflict, 247
Secular rituals, 288
Sedentism, sedentarization, 48, 92
Selassie, Haile, 304–305
Selection, of healers, *166*
Self-help groups, 216–217
Semantics, 262
Sen, Amartya, 112

Senegal, overview and map, *370*
Senegal River Valley, dam project on, 369, 370
Senior years, 153
Sentinelese of the Andaman Islands (India), 88
Separation phase, of life-cycle ritual, 289–290
September 11, 2001 attacks
    classifying cause of death of victims of, 160
    gift of Maasai people following, 243
    religious rights of Muslims and aftermath of, 307
Service sector, 97
Sesame, 95
Severe acute respiratory syndrome (SARS), 173, 174
Sex, 20
    gender *vs.*, 144
Sexism, 224
Sexual behavior
    among bonobos, 35
    among gay men, 138
    intercourse, 137–140
    intercourse frequency and fertility, 139–140
    in marriage, 199
    sexually transmitted diseases, 137
Sexual dimorphism, 194
    among great apes, 32, 33
Sexual identity, 149–151
Sexually transmitted diseases, 137
Sexual orientation, 149
Sex work, 98–99
Seychelle Islands, 276
Shakira, *311*
Shaman Gray Squirrel, *157*
Shamankas, 165, 293, *293*
Shamans, 165, 175, 293
    childbirth song, 170
Shan of Thailand, tattoos and, 298, *298*
Sharing, 109, 116; *See also* Levelling mechanisms
Shea butter, 62
Sheep, 48, 91, 101
    ram exhibition in Iceland, 73–74, *74*
Shell Oil, 378–379
Shell wealth, 117
Shenhav-Keller, Shelly, 317
Sherpa of Nepal, 175
    overview and map, 176, *176*
Shi'a Muslims, 247, 302, *330*
Shifting cultivation, 89
Shipibo Indians of Peru, 314
Shoji, 319
Shopping
    African American children's, in New Haven
        (Connecticut), 115–116
    at the fish market in Tokyo, 123, *123*
    for candy in Valencia (Spain), *110*
    at farmers' markets, 110
    for locally produced food, 127, *129*
    marketplaces as sites for, 122–123, *123*
Shostak, Marjorie, *70*
Shudras, 224, *224*
Siberia, 42, 264
Sibling relationships, 199–200
Sickle blades, 48
SIDA. *See* Swedish Agency for International
        Development (SIDA)
Siddhartha Gautama, 296
Sidur, 297
Sierra Leone, 125
    female genital cutting in, 148
    food-ration queue, 77
    overview and map, *149*
Sign language, human, 262–264
    bonobo use of, 260
Sikhs, 224
Silence, 264
Silicon Valley (California), 4, 352
Simple clothing, 43
Sioux of the United States, 306
Sirleaf-Johnson, Ellen, 242, *242*
Sister languages, 273
Sisters in Islam, 286
Site, defined, 63
Site selection, 63–64
Six Cultures Study, 90, 95, 145

Slash-and-burn cultivation, *89*
Slavery, 90, 121
    African American English and, 271
    as a form of exploitation, 125
Sleeping, *13*, 14–16
Sleeping nests of nonhuman primates, 37
Slovakia, Roma in, 223
Slow Food Movement, 127
Slums, *81*, 159
Smallpox, *178*
    European colonialism and, 169–170
Small-scale societies, social control in, 244
SMW. *See* Society of Muslim Women (SMW)
Snake handling in Appalachian Christian
        churches, 300–301
Snow, in Saami language, *262*, 268
Snowmobiles, impact on Saami culture, 362
Sobil, Tuy (Kay Kay), *216*
Social capital, 366
Social conflict, 247–251. *See also* Violence; War
    ethnic conflict, 247
    global-local conflict, 250–251
    modes of livelihood and, *235*
    research on, 62
    sectarian conflict, 247
    war, 247–250
Social control
    art and, 314
    defined, 243
    modes of livelihood and, *235*
    norms and laws, 243
    in small-scale societies, 244
    social inequality and the law, 246–247
    in states, 244–246
    systems of, 243–247
Social groups, 31, 210–217
    body modification groups, 215–216, *217*
    clubs and fraternities/sororities, 212–216
    cooperatives, 216
    countercultural, 214
    defined, 210
    friendship, 211–212
    mode of livelihood and, 210, *211*
    self-help groups, 216–217
    youth gangs, 214–215
Social impact assessment, ,362
Social inequality. *See also* Social stratification
    agriculture and, 96
    at Cohokia (United States), 52–53
    consumption and, 112–116
    delocalization of economy and, 362
    law and, 246–247
    poverty and, 171–172
    in Russia and Eastern Europe, 126–127
    stratified reproduction and, 137
Social isolation, domestic violence and, 201
Socialist states
    symbols of, 240
    transition to democracy, 254
    women in leadership roles and, 242
Sociality, 30
Socialization, 143
Social justice, 247
Social media, *266*
    new social movements and, 229
Social mobility, within caste system, 226
Social networking, for women vendors, 376
Social organization, consumption and, 109
Social race, 220
Social-role reversal, at carnival, 292
Social stratification, 217–227
    achieved position, 218
    ascribed position, 218, 219–227
    caste and casteism, *224*, 224–227
    civil society, 227–229
    class: achieved status, 219
    defined, 217
    ethnicity, 221–224
    gender and sexism, 224
    race, 220–221
    status, 218–219
Society of Muslim Women (SMW), 376–377